Human *and climate change*

Human choice and climate change

EDITED BY
Steve Rayner & Elizabeth L. Malone

VOLUME ONE
The societal framework

VOLUME TWO
Resources and technology

VOLUME THREE
The tools for policy analysis

VOLUME FOUR
"What have we learned?"

Human choice and climate change

VOLUME ONE
The societal framework

EDITED BY

Steve Rayner
Elizabeth L. Malone

Pacific Northwest National Laboratory

Battelle Press

PACIFIC NORTHWEST NATIONAL LABORATORY
Operated by
BATTELLE MEMORIAL INSTITUTE for the
UNITED STATES DEPARTMENT OF ENERGY
Under contract DE-AC06-76RLO 1830

Library of Congress Cataloging-in-Publication Data
Human choice and climate change / edited by Steve Rayner and Elizabeth L. Malone.
    p. cm.
Includes bibliographical references and index.
Contents: v. 1. The societal framework – v. 2. Resources and technology – v. 3. The tools for policy analysis – v. 4. What have we learned?
    ISBN 1-57477-045-4 (hc: alk. paper). ISBN 1-57477-040-3 (softcover: alk. paper)
        1. Climatic changes—Social aspects. 2. Human ecology.
    3. Environmental policy. I. Rayner, Steve, 1953–. II. Malone, Elizabeth L., 1947–
    QC981.8.C5H83   1998
    363.738'74—dc21   97-49711
                                                                                  CIP

	Hardover	Softcover
Four Volume Set	1-57477-045-4	1-57477-040-3
Volume 1: The Societal Framework	1-57477-049-7	1-57477-044-6
Volume 2: Resources and Technology	1-57477-046-2	1-57477-041-1
Volume 3: The Tools for Policy Analysis	1-57477-047-0	1-57477-042-X
Volume 4: What Have We Learned?	1-57477-048-9	1-57477-043-8

Printed in the United States of America.

Battelle Press
505 King Avenue
Columbus, Ohio 43201-2693
614-424-6393 or 1-800-451-3543
FAX: 614-424-3819
E-Mail: press@battelle.org
Home page: www.battelle.org/bookstore

These volumes are dedicated to Chester L. Cooper and to the memory of William R. Wiley, mentors and friends whose vision and support made this work possible.

Contents

CONTENTS

Foreword

The International Advisory Board

In contrast to other state-of-the-art reviews of climate change research, this project sees the world through a social science lens. This focus is reflected not only in the subject matter, but also in the authors' approach. It is a fundamental assumption of the project that the social sciences have ways of defining and analyzing the issues grouped under the term *global climate change* that are distinct from, yet potentially complementary to, those used in the natural sciences, and that social science analyses can generate findings of relevance to the policymaking community. The unique contributions that a social science story of global climate change can make include the awareness of human agency and value-based assumptions; a willingness to grapple with uncertainty, indeterminacy, and complexity; the consideration of social limits to growth; and the distinctiveness of an interdisciplinary social science approach.

We have been involved with this project from its early stages and have met to consider various aspects of the product on several occasions. The importance of social science research in formulating policies that are realistic and implementable can hardly be overstated. Thus, we have insisted that *Human choice and climate change* be policy-relevant. We hope that it will stimulate new scientific approaches to the processes involved in reaching and adhering to environmental agreements. Climate change impacts will be felt regionally and locally, and responses to these changes will be effected at these levels as well. Therefore, widespread understanding of the issues and potential choices is extremely important; focusing on the social dimension is critical for understanding them.

A social science framing of global climate change will help to make both natural and social science more relevant and more effective contributors to the policymaking process. Reflexive interdisciplinary research that recognizes the rich array of human motivations, actions, and perspectives can supply information that will better support the challenges of decisionmaking under sustained conditions of indeterminacy such as those surrounding global climate change.

We are pleased to have been associated with this project and hope its products promote the same level of thoughtful consideration that they did during our meetings and discussions of these challenging and significant issues.

The International Advisory Board

Dr Francisco Barnes
The Honorable Richard Benedick
Professor Harvey Brooks
Dr Jiro Kondo
Professor the Lord Desai
  of St Clement Danes
Professor George Golitsyn

Pragya Dipak Gyawali
The Honorable Thomas Hughes
Dr Hoesung Lee
Professor Tom Malone
The Honorable Robert McNamara
Professor Richard Odingo
Professor Thomas Schelling

Preface

When the Pacific Northwest National Laboratory (PNNL) established the Global Studies Program in 1989, I initiated an agenda to develop an integrated understanding of the important new linkages between human and natural systems, linkages that are affecting the evolution of both systems. To this end, the program encompassed the full range of the climate issue, focusing particularly on a sensible coupling between an understanding of the climate system itself and the human decisions that might affect it. This led a decision to assess the state of the art of the social sciences, in terms of their contribution to research on, and understanding of, the climate change issue. Thus, in the winter of 1993, as part of the Global Studies Program effort, the program launched the enterprise that, in due course, became *Human choice and climate change.*

This effort focused on what the social sciences have contributed to the climate change debate and on their potential to contribute more. My hope was that, at a minimum, the work would contribute to the development of a social science research agenda based on more than a call for funding parity with the physical sciences. I was also concerned that the finished document be directed not only to the academic community but also to the policy community.

From the very outset, the object was not to seek the creation of a consensus document of the kind developed by the Intergovernmental Panel on Climate Change, but rather the individual points of view on the climate issue from our 120 authors and contributors, representing a score of countries. Through their direct participation and from a host of peer reviewers, we now have a snapshot of the social sciences in the mid-1990s commenting not only on climate change but also on many aspects of sustainable development.

It is clear from these volumes that economics is by no means the only social science discipline that has relevant things to say about the issue of climate change. Despite the academic language and perspective, the pages of this document have put a human face on the climate change issue.

Some of the authors address social science itself as an issue, rather than social science contributions to climate change research. Indeed, a superficial reading of this material might cause some to question the credibility of social science in addressing climate change issues. For example, rather than speaking directly to the question of human behavior and climate change, the social sciences seem to have a penchant for placing climate change within a larger context, to consider climate change together with many other issues on the social agenda.

Human choice and climate change also reveals the social sciences to be a heterogeneous set of research programs, in which climate change research varies from being a peripheral issue to a highly refined subdiscipline with strong interdisciplinary connections to the natural sciences.

While the physical and natural sciences have been pursuing the questions of how much humans might affect climate, how fast these changes might take place and what the regional effects of these changes might be, our authors have added another question: even if we knew how climate were to change, what could we do about it and how would we decide to do it? Our assessment is that this question, among others, reveals a lack of fundamental knowledge of how society operates, and merits addition to the climate change research agenda.

The enterprise has borne fruit in ways that could not have been foreseen. It addressed the state of the art of the social sciences with regard to the climate change issue, but it also brought together social scientists in the pursuit of a collective goal; it has spotlighted strengths and weaknesses in social science research programs dealing with climate change; and it has laid the foundation for a substantive program of future climate change research.

The editors have conscientiously attempted to reflect the views of the many authors without endorsement or censure. PNNL is pleased to have provided a forum for the expression of a wide range of views and diverse, sometimes even contradictory, conclusions. We thank the International Advisory Board for its wise guidance. The editors, authors, contributors, and peer reviewers deserve substantial credit for striving to bridge and link fields of inquiry that have grown up in isolated traditions.

Gerald M. Stokes
Associate Director
Pacific Northwest National Laboratory

Why study human choice and climate change?

Steve Rayner & Elizabeth Malone

Why the concern with climate change?

Time and again over the course of the past decade, climate change has been described by scientists, environmentalists, and politicians as a threat unprecedented in human experience. Tolba's (1991: 3) statement is representative of such concerns: "We all know that the world faces a threat potentially more catastrophic than any other threat in human history: climate change and global warming." Many reasons and combinations of reasons are advanced for this claim, especially the potential rapidity of temperature rise, the irreversibility of change once the forces are set in motion, the geographical scale of the threat, the complexity and nonlinearity of the natural systems involved, the ubiquity and strength of human commitment to combustion technologies, and the political challenges of global cooperation that climate change seems to demand. The real danger, say many, lies in the potential for catastrophic surprise.

Similarly, several candidate causes have been identified. Emissions of greenhouse-related gases from human activities constitute the proximate cause, of course. In the background lurk possible underlying causes: population growth, overconsumption, humans' inability to control the technologies they have created, their inability to implement environmentally benign technologies, their unwillingness to spend current wealth to benefit future generations, their powerlessness to forge effective international agreements and abide by them. Whatever the cause, climate change is framed as a problem, which admits the possibility of solution.

Solutions come in many forms and approach the problem from different angles. Solutions to scientific problems take the form of improved knowledge, understanding, and predictability of natural systems. Solutions to technological problems require innovation and commitment of resources. Solutions to problems of societal cooperation and coordination are offered in the form of international treaties and policy instruments such as taxes or emissions controls. However, all solutions imply choices that must be made, consciously or unconsciously, enthusiastically or reluctantly, and with levels of information that may be satisfactory or unsatisfactory to the choosers.

Why the concern with human choice?

The possibility of human choice, albeit constrained, underlies all of these discussions; that is, humans can choose to respond to the prospect of climate change and can decide, with undetermined and perhaps undeterminable degrees of freedom, what steps to take. However, choice does not merely underlie any possible solution to climate change; it also underlies the problem itself. Increasing global greenhouse gas concentrations are the result of myriad choices that compose the history and contemporary operation of industrial society. Any attempt to change the course upon which human society appears to be embarked requires not only new choices about future actions, but also understanding of past choices—the existing social commitments that have set the world on its present course. The possibility, indeed the inevitability, of choice lies at the core of the climate change issue.

Everyone makes choices about accepting participation in any sort of society (even rebelling against it). Much of human life is devoted to negotiating within families, laboratories, firms, communities, nations, and other institutions the particular balance of independence and interdependence that each person is willing to accept. This tension, characteristic of all forms of social existence, is thrown into stark relief by the controversies that rage and the choices that must be made about the potential for climate change. Questions of choice, therefore, lie at the heart of not only the climate change issue but also the social sciences.

Possible choices with reference to climate change can be grouped into three broad categories, which can be combined in various ways:

- Do nothing. Some say that concern about climate change is unwarranted; the science is unproven, based on speculation bolstered by models so inaccurate they cannot reproduce historical shifts in climate. Others believe that impacts will be gradual, easily accommodated through technology, or insignificant on a global scale. If climate change does occur, then piecemeal adaptation will suffice. Even some who do believe that climate change is likely and may be disruptive suggest that the aggregate benefits of allowing climate change to run its course would outweigh the costs.
- Mitigate, that is, lessen emissions to reduce the magnitude of climate change. If one is convinced that anthropogenic emissions are giving rise to climate change, the obvious direct solution to the problem is to reduce

net emissions. Motivations for preferring this option include not only its directness but also, perhaps more importantly, that it can be conjoined with favored solutions to other perceived problems, such as population growth or the income disparities between industrialized and less industrialized nations.

- Anticipate and adapt; that is, change crops and growing regions, retreat from or defend coastal areas, prepare for population shifts and health impacts. Advocates of anticipatory adaptation also regard it as an opportunity to develop policies and technologies that would be beneficial in any event, such as infrastructure that is more resilient to extreme weather events.

For all three strategies, or any combination of them, it makes sense to invest in new knowledge. Improving the accuracy of climate forecasting may confirm that humans need not take any concerted action. Mitigation may require developing new technologies that will allow economic development while reducing the anthropogenic contributions to climate change. Society could invest in geoengineering techniques or large-scale removal of carbon dioxide from the atmosphere. Anticipatory adaptation will require foresight about impacts and new technological and social developments to respond to them.

But who should choose among the possible responses and combinations of responses to climate change? Since it is a global issue, the obvious decision-makers are the governments of nation states who have enjoyed legitimacy as the arbiters of high policy throughout the modern era. People habitually turn to their governments to choose goals (such as emissions reductions) and policy instruments (e.g., a carbon tax). Often climate change research among the social sciences focuses on the macro level of national and international political choice. Certainly the knowledge of how choice processes and mechanisms operate at these levels is valuable in framing issues and conducting negotiations.

However, research at the macro level may reduce important dimensions of social choice to simple instrumental issues. For example, the fundamental concept of fairness, as the glue holding societies together, may be reduced to an instrumental factor affecting the efficient implementation of the goal of emissions reduction. Furthermore, who chooses when the nation state or the market fails to produce a solution? The slogan, "Think globally—act locally" expresses the widespread recognition that choices are made at the micro level, by individuals and groups in particular places. Even in the context of national or international regulations, firms, families, communities, and citizens choose how to respond to incentives and sanctions. Moreover, other institutions, such as environmental organizations, can choose to respond in more robust ways and to try persuasive strategies so others will act voluntarily to comply with or even exceed statutory requirements.

Behind all such questions about choices associated with climate change lurk general questions about how societies and institutions choose the choosers and confer legitimacy upon their decisions. These are problems of collective choice. Choices are embedded and intertwined in social institutions of all kinds, including interest groups, pressure groups, lobbies, elected officials, citizens, and so on. Choices are often so deeply entrenched in societal norms that people will resist persuasion and coercion aimed at changing their behavior.

In part, the role of the social sciences is to probe these background choices by providing the capability to continually examine and re-examine our assumptions, that is, to provide what social scientists call "reflexivity" about societal choice. In the case of climate change, the social sciences remind us to question assumptions and propositions that those who are already committed to a course of action may take for granted. For instance, the conscious choice of responses arises only after we have chosen which issues to take seriously. How do people choose from among a large set of possible problems to work on as scientists, activists, entrepreneurs, homemakers, or politicians? How do individual choices influence what happens at a societal level? What roles do cultural and institutional processes play? How did the choice set of possible or potential issues come to be framed? How did other issues get to be excluded or incorporated into others? With regard specifically to climate change, various questions about choice are intertwined, for example:

- How do scientists choose to study climate change? How do they form a scientific consensus?
- How do people decide that climate change is worthy of attention?
- How do people attribute blame for climate change and choose solutions?
- How do people choose whom to believe about climate change and at what level of risk do they or should they choose to act?
- How do people and institutions mobilize support for (or against) policy action on climate change?
- What is the relationship between resource management choices and climate change?
- How do governments establish where climate change stands in relation to other political priorities?
- How are climate change policy instruments chosen?
- Why and how did the international community choose to address climate change?
- How do societies select technologies that cause, mitigate, or assist adaptation to climate change?
- How can research on social or collective action be useful to the global climate change debate?

Understandably, those who are unshakably convinced, either that climate change is an urgent and impending catastrophe or that talk of climate change is merely, to quote one US Congressman, "liberal claptrap," are likely to be impatient with such questions. For almost everyone else concerned about the issue, such questions may be the starting point from which society can work to make wise decisions about its future.

Different disciplines approach the kinds of questions that we pose from different perspectives, frequently simply modifying or fine-tuning the tools already in hand to account for choice. Issues of human needs and wants, the social bases for cultural or institutional choices, uncertainty, imperfect knowledge, and irrationality are often elided because they are too difficult to represent in equations and computer models.

As we venture among the social sciences, we run into rival prescriptions about how such choices ought to be made (e.g., by experts, by majority vote, by consensus, by preferences revealed in the marketplace) as well as the criteria to be used (e.g., the greatest happiness of the greatest number, or safeguarding individual or majority rights). In this sense, the social sciences reflect the diversity and the unity of human societies, institutions, and individuals on the issues of human choice facing the prospect of climate change.

The problem of collective choice has usually been framed as one of aggregation or of coercion:

- how to aggregate individual preferences into a collective preference, or
- how to persuade individuals to conform with normative requirements of corporations and governments, as implemented by the decisionmakers who are their officials.

Arrow (1951) has famously demonstrated the impossibility of aggregating individual preferences into a collective one in a way that satisfies certain minimal conditions of rationality and transitivity. For Arrow, the dictatorial social welfare function is the only one possible. However, dictatorship is incompatible with democracy. We seem to be caught in a bind. But Arrow's analysis assumes that preferences are inherently individual. If we use another set of assumptions—for example, that preferences are inherently relational (that is, expressions of social solidarity)—we change the nature of the problem from being one of aggregating individuals to discerning the structure and dynamics of social solidarity, which in turn may open up a new solution space for the problem of collective action.

Social science has long been confronted with the central issues of choice and constraint, and, thus, climate change is far from being a unique problem for the social sciences. Moreover, the individual–society tension within the social sciences often reflects a theoretical and methodological gap between the mindsets and methods of various social science disciplines. Even within disciplines, social science paradigms differ in their views of collective action. The problem of understanding and choosing a course of action with respect to climate change is that of articulating choices and consequences across the local and global levels.

For some analysts, social choice is an issue of aggregating individual preferences (from citizens to nations), whereas for others it is rather a problem of decomposing national or communal preferences into appropriate units of social solidarity, such as the household, the village, or the firm. It is pointless to ask which approach is right and which is wrong. Like wave and particle explanations of light, each offers insights that the other cannot reproduce. The characteristics of light's wave and particle properties cannot be simultaneously measured, yet both sets of properties are essential to understanding the behavior of light. Similarly, it is important to understand the sources and consequences of the divergent social science approaches to explaining human behavior so that climate change researchers and practitioners can capitalize on the strengths of that diversity.

The conceptual architecture of this assessment

Human choice and climate change is a climate-oriented assessment firmly rooted in the social sciences. That is, it takes as its starting point human social conditions around the world. Instead of examining the physical and chemical processes of climate change, this assessment looks at climate change in the broader context of global social change. Analysis of climate change needs to be conducted in the context of mainstream social science concerns with human choice and global (not just environmental) change. A global developmental and environmental perspective can be helpful to policymakers and scholars for at least two reasons:

- Social systems intersect and interact with several natural systems simultaneously and interdependently. Human activity therefore represents a crosscutting system constituting major linkages among natural cycles and systems. Hence, changes in human activity stimulated by interaction with one such system tend to influence others in potentially significant ways.
- The scale and rate of change in social systems may well outpace the scale and rate of climate change for the foreseeable future. For example, even vulnerable populations and vulnerable natural resources may plausibly be more directly affected by general economic conditions than by climate change over the course of the next hundred years.

The entry point of a global social science perspective allows us to set our bounds very widely. For instance, in the social sciences, the topic of "climate change" encompasses people's perceptions and behavior based on the threat (or, in a few cases, the promise) of such change, as well as the causes, processes, and prospective impacts of the change itself. In *Human choice and climate change*, we broaden our scope beyond that of the Intergovernmental Panel on Climate Change (IPCC) Working Group on the Economic and Social Dimensions of Climate Change (Bruce et al. 1996) to include research that, although relevant, is not focused specifically on climate change itself. At the same time, we have retained the orientation of climate change as an important policy issue that can act as a touchstone or reference point for theories and research.

Just as the same physical object confronted from different angles may present very different appearances to an observer, so can the same problem be very differently defined when viewed from different paradigms. One strategy for our assessment would have been to accept the conventional framing of the human dimensions of climate change in terms of proximate causes and impacts. Most extant texts concerned with the human dimensions of climate change or, more broadly, of global environmental change begin with a summary of the way that the natural sciences describe the changes that are occurring on the land and in the atmosphere and oceans (e.g., Jacobsen & Price 1991, Stern et al. 1992). These assessments draw directly on the natural sciences to frame the issues for social science inquiry. However, the authors and contributors to this project opted for a riskier approach of attempting to define climate change and, by extension, global environmental change from a thoroughgoing social science perspective.

We seek to learn from approaching the natural sciences from a social science viewpoint rather than through what has been the more orthodox approach of wading into the social science waters from the conventional terra firma of the natural sciences. In so doing, we do not seek to subvert the findings of the natural sciences or discover some social pretext to dismiss societal concern about climate. Rather, we seek to provide an additional footing from which the intellectual landscape of the climate change issue can be viewed. We have tried to complement the natural science perspective, not to replace it with another single vantage point.

Human choice and climate change is presented in four volumes. In the first three volumes, our goal is twofold: to create a text that could serve as an overview of social science relevant to global climate change for researchers with backgrounds in the natural sciences or in the social sciences but not as those backgrounds relate to global climate change; and to provide a reference work for both scholars and practitioners as they perform research, conduct negotiations, or plan and implement policies. To accomplish this goal, the assessment seeks to:

- Represent the range of social science research applicable to global climate change
- Provide insights into the world as viewed through the lens of social

science topics, tools, and data
- Review what is currently known, uncertain, and unknown within the social sciences in relation to global climate change
- Assemble and summarize findings from the international research communities of industrialized, less industrialized, and newly democratic nations
- Report these findings within diverse interdisciplinary frameworks
- Relate research results to policy issues and problems.

The fourth volume provides an editorial overview of the first three, reflexively focusing on the challenges that climate change issues present to the intellectual organization of social science, the lessons that the social sciences can bring to understanding climate change issues, and the implications of all of this for policymakers.

In each volume, we have sought to present the subject at a level of detail and theoretical sophistication to make the assessment useful as a reference work for scholars. We have also attempted to tie the material to practical issues useful to decisionmakers and their advisors. We are acutely aware that in aiming the assessment at two audiences we run the risk of pleasing neither. To the first audience we may seem simplistic, even instrumental in our approach. We may strike the second audience as excessively abstract and academic. However, it is our hope that the dual focus of this assessment can be fruitful in pointing to convergence between scholarship and action.

Human choice and climate change, volume 1: the societal framework

Volume 1 of *Human choice and climate change* begins our inquiry into social science perspectives and climate change with an assessment of the state of the Earth's social, cultural, political, and economic systems, which provide the context that supports and consists of the activities that contribute to the emissions of greenhouse gases and within which:
- climate change is perceived and debated
- the impacts of change will be experienced
- human beings will make the critical choices about their future, including choices about how to confront the prospect of changing climate in a changing world.

Climate change is occurring in a complex and rapidly changing framework of human choices that shapes people's perception of it and the opportunities for human response. The social context of climate change and knowledge about it are usually taken for granted. Subjecting it to social science analysis reveals the extent to which our understanding of the science, diagnoses of underlying causes, and views of appropriate action are not merely technical judgments, but embody deep-seated social commitments that provide the context for response options.

"Science and decisionmaking," the first chapter, examines the social processes by which technical knowledge about climate change (and other science-based issues) is created by scientists and communicated to policymakers. The authors begin with four interlocking questions that remained unasked, even unacknowledged, in earlier assessments of social science and climate change:

- How do scientists and their societies identify and delimit distinct problems related to climate change that are considered amenable to scientific resolution?
- How do scientists come to know particular facts and causal relationships regarding climate change and to persuade others that their knowledge is credible?
- How do conflicts over risk arise, and how are responses to them handled in a world of conflicting and plural political interests?
- How do human societies and their designated policy actors draw upon scientific knowledge to justify collective action on a worldwide scale?

The authors describe the role that the production and dissemination of scientific knowledge have played in the elevation of climate change to a topic of worldwide interest and political concern. Their analysis reveals how the normal model of the relationship between science and policy, which has been termed "speaking truth to power," assumes that the two domains are and should be largely distinct. However, social science analysis indicates a level of interdependence between science and politics so strong as to constitute a process of co-production of relevant knowledge, which most often occurs unrecognized by either scientists or policymakers.

Science and technology studies demonstrate how scientists build on local experiments and knowledges in laboratories and field studies to formulate generally accepted methods, facts, and theories. Through a process of standardization and network building, scientific knowledge can attain a universal validity, as climate change science has through the deliberations of the IPCC. Applying insights from studies of the social processes of scientific inquiry, the chapter examines the implicit assumptions embedded in theories and models used to study interactions between the biogeophysical and social systems. Making these assumptions explicit provides an opportunity to question them and to examine their validity in the specific situations to which the theories and models are being applied. This reflexivity is important because scientific research that fails to engage in such self-examination risks becoming irrelevant to the world beyond the laboratory or academy walls. Perhaps worse, it leaves science susceptible to political backlash against scientific consensus on climate change—just as has happened in the US Congress. Policymakers who rely on data from unreflexive research risk errors in their decisionmaking that may cost them (and the societies in whose name they act) dearly, whether financially, politically, or socially.

 The interdependence between scientists and policy-makers constitutes a process of co-production of knowledge seldom recognized by either.

"Population and health" and "Human needs and wants," the next two chapters, demonstrate that neither of the standard diagnoses of the underlying causes of climate change—overpopulation and overconsumption—can be justified by social science research. Chapter 2, "Population and health," lays out the world's changing sociodemographic profile, the social science controversies about the role of population in climate and other environmental change, and the micro-scale factors that shape peoples' preferences about family size and spacing of children. Although the authors find that rapid population growth has a negative effect on the development of many, albeit not all, less industrialized countries, the extent of this effect is difficult to quantify, or even to demonstrate on a global scale because of the complexity and multiplicity of relationships involved and the variability of local circumstances. The authors conclude that population policy has too often been based on the easy, specious logic "You would be happier if you had fewer children," which cannot be justified by rigorous social science evidence. The real underlying logic is often "I would be happier if you had fewer children."

 The real logic underlying population policy is often "I would be happier if you had fewer children."

Population, as such, is not the issue shaping climate change or other environmental degradation. The appropriate question is how are population factors mediated through institutional and social structures to affect natural resources and the environment? In some areas population makes a big difference to environmental impacts; in others it does not. Where it does make a difference, the costs and benefits of intervening directly to affect population must be weighed against the costs and benefits of policies designed to loosen institutional rigidities that prevent families from responding flexibly to the pressures of population growth. The people most vulnerable to impacts of climate change tend to be members of impoverished populations living in environmentally fragile zones of less industrialized countries. These populations already adapt very flexibly to the impacts of extreme climatic fluctuations, such as storms and droughts, albeit at considerable cost of human life and suffering. But climate change may overstretch their coping capacity. Although it is quite unlikely to change the big picture of world population size, rate of growth, and age structure, climate change will have an impact on mortality, fertility, and migration at regional and local levels.

If the impact of population is less than straightforward, what can be said about consumption? What justification is there for distinguishing consumption for survival from luxury consumption? Chapter 3, "Human needs and wants," evaluates the attempts of various disciplines to establish human needs as the basis for climate policies compatible with individual fulfillment and societal development. The authors show that the concept of basic human needs has universal rhetorical appeal, but it cannot made operational coherently in a way that helps policymakers to define climate policy goals. Everyone may agree that clean air, access to potable water, a minimum ration of calories and protein— even entitlements to atmospheric carbon sinks—are all somehow basic human needs, but in practice it is impossible to devise universally standardized measures for their operationalization. How clean is clean? How pure is potable? What constitutes access? What is the age and level of activity of the individual to be fed?

 Only by understanding the essentially social character of needs, wants, and their satisfaction through consumption can analysts and policymakers lay the basis for behavioral change.

Furthermore, needs and wants cannot be usefully distinguished. Needs turn out to be wants that someone is unwilling to give up. So long as social scientists and policymakers continue to treat wants as private appetites, they cannot understand how wants come to be standardized in society and how those standards change. The issue of how societal preferences change is a critical one for long-term modeling and for policy interventions that seek to alter either the scale of consumer demands (including demands for small or large families) or the technologies by which demands are satisfied. If consumption choices are recast—not as private preferences but as public statements establishing or confirming community identity, group membership, or social solidarity— then fundamental changes in consumption patterns are likely to require very basic changes in the kinds of society people live in. Only by understanding the essentially social character of needs, wants, and their satisfaction through consumption can analysts and policymakers lay the basis for behavioral change.

The authors of Chapter 3 focus attention on the emergence of new models of wealth, based on the notion of social capital, that includes the levels of social support that people can expect from the communities and institutions to which they belong (rather than focusing on dollars per individual). Criteria for measuring social capital are being explored; however, they have not yet reached the level of development or received the recognition already being given to the valuation of natural capital and so-called green accounting.

> ... debate about climate change is often a surrogate for a broader, so-far intractable political discourse about population, lifestyles, and international development.

The broader "Cultural discourses" about climate are the subject of the fourth chapter, which probes deeper into societal controversy over diagnoses and prescriptions and exposes the social commitments that underlie the range of opinions and political positions. In the course of debating climate change at home, at work, in the media, or in the halls of power, experts and lay people alike diagnose the underlying human causes of climate change as lying in population growth, profligate consumption, or incorrect pricing and property rights allocations. In response to these diagnoses, participants in these cultural discourses seek prescriptions to remedy climate change while protecting competing principles for procedural fairness as well as distributional and intergenerational equity. Disagreements about the underlying human causes of climate change and proposed solutions to it are deeply rooted in competing institutional narratives about nature as well as rival principles of fairness. The chapter illustrates that debate about climate change is often a surrogate for a broader, so-far intractable political discourse about population, lifestyles, and international development.

In elucidating the various voices of experts and lay people in the climate change debate, the chapter demonstrates that the basis for such discourses is essentially institutional. The authors make a strong claim that social relationships, rather than individual preferences, stabilize the public expression of values about what is natural and what is right. How people bind themselves to each other simultaneously shapes the way they bind themselves to nature. Social and cultural variables of network density, interconnectedness, and rule sharing account more effectively for variations in environmental perceptions and behavior than do standard demographic variables such as age and sex. To guide the reader through this novel landscape, the authors present a conceptual map of human values to help social scientists identify and track the strength of support for alternative positions and to help policymakers identify opportunities for effective intervention in the debates.

Public information campaigns that assume that discrepancies between lay and experts accounts of climate change are simply attributable to knowledge deficiencies are bound to fail.

The social science perspective represented in this chapter suggests that public information and education campaigns to change people's energy use or other environmentally relevant behavior fail because changing behavior is not simply a problem of removing exogenous barriers to the natural flow of knowledge. The social science perspective redirects efforts at communication from simply overcoming ignorance to creating shared frames of reference and opportunities for shared action. Public information campaigns that assume that discrepancies between lay and experts accounts of climate change are attributable simply to knowledge deficiencies are bound to fail.

Climate discourses are complex and turbulent. Many voices join in, and they are often inconsistent, even self-contradictory, but not randomly so, nor in a way that can simply be ascribed to naked self-interest. By labeling the present state of affairs as disorderly, each voice seeks to legitimate the reordering of society along its own preferred institutional principles. How these institutional arrangements are structured and operate in the climate change arena is the topic of Chapter 5, "Institutions for political action," which ties the value commitments of climate discourses to the institutional arrangements that human beings use for making collective choices about society and the environment.

The growing prominence of global environmental issues as matters of high politics is itself a sign that the nation state retains an important and powerful position. However, the character and the role of the state are changing rapidly in fundamental aspects of its international and domestic roles. Political influence and real power is diffusing to international and domestic policy networks in which governments and their agencies interact directly with social movements, firms, and communities. The notion of unitary national interest is increasingly difficult to sustain. The rising importance of nonstate actors and the emergence of aspects of a global civil society, in the light of global climate change, are now garnering much attention from sociologists and international relations scholars alike.

 The real business of responding to climate concerns may well be through smaller, often less formal, agreements among states; states and firms; and firms, nongovernmental organizations, and communities.

The new landscape of world politics—and global environmental politics in particular—has given voice to those formerly marginalized or excluded from political dialogue. The authors conclude that, although the Framework

Convention on Climate Change represents an important expression of world-wide concern about climate and the persistent issues of global development that are inextricably bound up with it, the real business of responding to climate concerns may well be through smaller, often less formal, agreements among states; states and firms; and firms, nongovernmental organizations, and communities.

However, this response process is likely to be messy and contested—not that messiness or contestation are to be disparaged. Patterns of interest-group mobilization and representation help to sustain a bias in favor of activities that lead to increasing greenhouse gas emissions. The status quo is insulated from fundamental change by the influence of routines, established procedures, and traditional and close ties among economic and political elites. Climate policies as such are bound to be hard to implement. Simply incorporating climate change into existing political agendas is unlikely to produce the desired outcomes. Similarly, presenting climate change measures as ways of achieving higher taxation or welfare expenditure is also likely to meet significant opposition. True win–win solutions prove to be elusive. Effective actions designed to mitigate or respond opportunistically or adaptively to climate change are likely to be those most integrated into general policy strategies for economic and social development.

Volume 1 places climate change in the dynamic context of a changing societal landscape that shapes changes in the atmosphere. Here the responses of political and social institutions are crucial, and human choice must be taken into account. Sometimes the separation of the biogeophysical systems from the social systems has led global climate change researchers to focus on climate change as if it were the most important issue facing the sustainable development of human society. Yet sustained consideration of one issue can be maintained only at the cost of excluding others. Decisionmakers need to consider the opportunity costs as well as the benefits of directing their present attention to climate change. Furthermore, for most of humankind, climate change is not life's most pressing issue, certainly not on a day-to-day basis. A social science framing of the problem introduces a more complex view by asking what else is going on in the development of human society and how climate change will affect and be affected by these societal changes. Volume 2 looks at climate change in relation to human resource use, and opportunities to reduce human impacts on the climate and climate impacts on humans, particularly through a broadly defined conception of technological change.

Human choice and climate change, volume 2: resources and technology

Volume 2 of *Human choice and climate change* anchors both the climate change issue and social science approaches to it in the context of the Earth's resources: climate, land, water, energy sources, and materials used in technologies. Climate change is the result of fundamental human choices about the conversion of energy and human occupation of the Earth's surface. These activities have been identified as both the proximate causes of greenhouse-related emissions and the sites of primary impacts on human activity.

Chapter 1, "The natural science of climate change" summarizes the present state of the international scientific consensus about climate change, drawing on the findings of the Second Assessment Report of the IPCC, as well as on other research. The social processes that go into producing and standardizing this kind of scientific consensus are described in the first chapter of Volume 1. Current scientific claims about climate change and its impacts introduce Volume 2 because it focuses on the major resource systems, or human support systems, that enable people to live as they do on the Earth: that is, land use, occupation of coastal zones, energy production and use, and the processes of technological change. As human systems, these are no less institutional systems than the ones examined in Volume 1. However, each is perhaps more directly dependent on constraints and opportunities presented by natural systems than (with the possible exception of population) the frameworks presented in Volume 1. Thus, it is appropriate at this point to introduce material from the natural sciences that social scientists should be aware of in analyzing and understanding the human dimensions of climate change.

This chapter explains the greenhouse effect, the results of greenhouse gas emissions on radiative forcing, and the mechanisms by which forcing translates into climate change. The complexities of these processes are further compounded by emissions of aerosols, the role of clouds, and interactions of gases in the atmosphere. Furthermore, the natural variability of climate is an undisputed fact, so the possible human contributions must be analyzed in the context of natural changes.

The current scientific consensus is that the global mean surface temperature has increased by 0.3–0.6° Kelvin (K) over the past century. The global temperatures in recent years have been among the warmest in historical records and probably one of the warmest periods in the past six hundred years. However, the warming is not uniform over the globe, with some areas even experiencing a cooling. The understanding of this climatic change is a high priority in the natural science community. Although the signal is still emerging from the noise of natural variability, recent studies suggest that the current changes in climate are indeed related to human activities, including the emissions of carbon dioxide and other radiatively important gases and aerosols.

The chapter goes on to outline the potential effects of changes in various climatic factors, specifically sea level rise, human health, agriculture and food supplies, water resources, and nonagricultural ecosystems. Although knowledge is improving in these areas, many aspects of climate change remain highly uncertain. In particular, the regional changes in climate expected from global climate change are poorly understood, as are the impacts on humanity and the biosphere.

 Although the signal is still emerging from the noise of natural variability, recent studies suggest that the current changes in climate are indeed related to human activities.

The next four chapters trace the origins of climate change in human behavior at aggregated and disaggregated levels and focus on the potential impacts of climate change on fundamental human systems of productivity.

Chapter 2, "Land and water use," examines human activities that increase greenhouse gas emissions from the use of land and water resources. It also assesses the potential impacts of climate change and climate change policies on land and water use for the production of food, energy, fiber, and construction material, as well as for recreation, aesthetic and spiritual satisfaction, and creation of a sense of identity.

The intensification of land and water use has been a global trend during the five centuries of the colonial, industrial, and postindustrial periods. Today, every accessible hectare and waterway are managed (or deliberately not managed) for human ends. The most remote tundra in the Arctic North and the most forbidding reaches of the Sahara Desert are subject to human management decisions of one sort or another.

Land use and water use are important to global climate change in at least three ways. First, land use affects the exchange of carbon dioxide, methane, and other greenhouse-related gases between the Earth and its atmosphere. Second, agriculture, forestry, and other land-based productive activities depend crucially on surface energy and water balance, which are closely linked to climate. Hence, they are more likely than other human activities to be affected by climate change. Third, projected growth in both population and resource-demands presents important challenges to land and water use in coming decades, whether climate changes or not. Discussions of global environmental change have tended to subjugate the issues of sustainable development of land and water resources to the globally systemic changes of ozone depletion and climate change. Analysts seek to identify no-regrets strategies that would enhance sustainability and at the same time help to prevent or adapt to climate change. Many opportunities exist for sequestering carbon or limiting emissions, although they require a searching analysis of their full social and environmental repercussions.

The chapter concludes that climate change is by no means necessarily the most important challenge to the sustainability of land and water resources. The connections between land use and climate change are important, but should not be allowed to set the land-use research agenda. There is room for serious concern about the adequacy of land and water resources to meet current and likely future demands locally and globally, whether climate changes or not. Around the world, increasing misuse of land and water resources already threatens human welfare in the near to medium term. The apparent failure in these regions of management to forestall such threats underlines the need to study land-use and water-use adaptation strategies, regardless of any efforts toward reducing greenhouse-related emissions. Responses that can address these issues while addressing the challenges of climate change should be a priority for research.

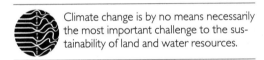

Climate change is by no means necessarily the most important challenge to the sustainability of land and water resources.

Measures encouraging adaptation to climate change may likewise offer collateral gains in other areas, improved agricultural research being an important case in point, and institutional strengthening to facilitate adaptive shifts in land and water use another. The key lesson of social science analysis is that the constraints on and opportunities for successful response are not only technical, and that influencing land and water use in desired ways requires a sound understanding of how and why these resources are used.

Similar themes emerge from Chapter 3, "Coastal zones and oceans." Coastal regions are particularly important because of high concentrations of human population living close to the sea and their particular vulnerability to potential climate impacts.

Coastal zones have historically generated economic activities that allowed societies to flourish. Many coastal problems now being encountered worldwide result from many people's use of the terrestrial and aquatic resources over a long period of mostly unrestricted development of coastal areas. These problems include the accumulation of contaminants in coastal areas, shoreline erosion, and the rapidly accelerating decline of habitats and natural resources. Population growth and migration associated with economic development places additional demands on coastal areas and resources, posing another threat to the sustainability of these areas. The impacts of unsustainable and often uncoordinated coastal development are likely ultimately to result in the degradation of natural systems that provide protection against the sea, habitat for many species, and food for many people. These impacts could pose significant risks to public health and welfare.

With or without climate change, coastal zones will see further growth in urban areas and increased tourism. The growing population density along the coasts will put further pressure on the resource base, including ocean fishing, wetlands-dependent products, and unique ecosystems and species. This pressure will probably result in deteriorating living conditions for many inhabitants, especially in less industrialized countries. Hence, there are strong imperatives to adopt integrated coastal zone management strategies that will combine responses to growing demands on coastal and ocean resources and the threat of climate change. Local knowledge will be essential to the success of these strategies. The adaptive coping abilities of coastal, often rural, and often nonliterate people have enabled their survival under stress. They have detailed knowledge of local conditions and past responses, as well as the complex and varied patterns of ownership and use of marine and coastal resources. In the policy hierarchy they seldom get their due recognition. Consultative and participatory approaches that include local stakeholders offer challenges and opportunities for both analysis and decisionmaking.

 The adaptive coping abilities of coastal, often rural, and often nonliterate people have enabled their survival under stress. In the policy hierarchy they seldom get their due recognition.

The fourth chapter in Volume 2, "Energy and industry," examines global and regional patterns of greenhouse-related emissions arising from the production of goods and services. Over the twentieth century, energy use has become the most important human-generated source of greenhouse gases, especially carbon dioxide produced by fossil-fueled energy generation. Most analyses predict steady increases in worldwide energy consumption over the next several decades. Thus, any attempt to limit greenhouse gas concentrations in the atmosphere must focus on energy supply and demand and the costs associated with reducing greenhouse-related emissions from fossil fuel combustion. There is considerable uncertainty about what the levels of energy use and associated carbon dioxide emissions will be over the next century. Worldwide emissions of carbon from fossil fuel combustion are currently about 6 billion tonnes per year. In the absence of new policy initiatives, emissions projections range from a modest decrease to an increase by a factor of 15 over the next century.

Three complementary methods have been used to forecast the evolution of these changes:

- a top-down economic approach, relating aggregate energy use to fuel prices, labor and capital prices, and various measures of economic activity
- a bottom-up approach, employing engineering calculations on a technology-by-technology basis
- a social-psychological approach, focusing on how and why decisions regarding energy use are made at a more micro level than the top-down approach and embodying a more human-behavioral approach than the bottom-up approach.

 In the absence of new policy initiatives, emissions projections range from a modest decrease to an increase by a factor of 15 over the next century.

A decade ago top-down and bottom-up approaches produced dramatically different projections. Since then it has become evident that each approach has its strengths and weaknesses, and various hybrid approaches have been proposed. Assumptions regarding the characteristics and likely rate of penetration of new technologies have been developed, and researchers have started sorting through the various explanations for slower than expected adoption of new technologies. There is still some debate about whether some of these explanations describe market failures or simply reflect indirect costs not typically included in the engineering estimates of using a new technology, but that debate has shifted from one about the analytic method to one about the fundamental assumptions employed.

All analyses point towards a much greater rate of growth in greenhouse gas emissions in the less industrialized countries than in the highly industrialized countries for at least three reasons:

- much higher rates of population growth
- higher rates of economic growth driven by technology transfer from the industrialized countries
- a propensity to pursue development through very rapid increases in the output of the heavy industries required to construct the facilities and infrastructure required to modernize economies.

Despite the greater importance of the presently less industrialized countries in shaping the greenhouse-related gas emissions and concentrations of the next century, analysis of these countries has been seriously undertaken only recently.

Two major research directions would greatly improve the usefulness of the analysis to policymakers:

- more intensive study of the less industrialized countries, where most of the growth in emissions is expected to occur
- improved integration between the economic, engineering, and social-psychological approaches.

The second of these is the topic of Chapter 5.

Whereas Chapter 4 concentrates on modeling energy production and use at the macro level, Chapter 5, "Energy and social systems," scrutinizes energy-related institutional decisionmaking about production and consumption at the level of the firm and household behavior. The chapter highlights the meaning and evolution of energy-consuming practice in everyday life. The authors advocate moving beyond conventional policy-oriented research, focused on the beliefs and behaviors of individual end users, to a focus on people as social actors operating within households, offices, government departments, or other institutions. Such a shift entails viewing energy-related decisions as processes of social negotiation rather than as the result of personal attitudes or enthusiasms. Rather than focusing on energy in isolation, or on the services that energy provides, energy-related practices are instead addressed as forms of consumption, much like any other.

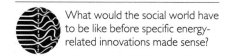

What would the social world have to be like before specific energy-related innovations made sense?

Instead of taking the social goals and purposes of energy consumption for granted, the approaches explored in this chapter call those ends into question. The rationalistic notion that technologies are neutral problem-solving devices gives way to the view that problem and solution are, as it were, joined at the hip. The authors challenge researchers and policymakers to rethink the relationship between policy and energy demand and the way in which energy analysts and policymakers conceptualize the future. Instead of trying to predict the future, the authors advocate efforts to specify the sociotechnical preconditions for a range of possible futures. Rather than seeking to model people's impact on future energy demand, the question would be, what would the social world have to be like before specific energy-related innovations made sense?

Much of the research reviewed in this chapter emphasizes the extent to which the future is already inscribed in existing practices, infrastructures, and cultural arrangements that limit the scope for doing things differently. Together these suggest that, even in the most favorable of circumstances, policy levers that focus on end-users are unlikely to modify the web of interests and histories that surround their choices and habits. But conventional tools and forms of policy analysis configure the conceptual landscape and the perception of possible courses of action, just as the tools and technologies of energy consumption configure their users. Discussion of the human dimensions of energy and global environmental change is currently embedded in a policy paradigm that contains within it a somewhat limited and restricting theory of social and technological change.

The dynamics of technological change have important implications for the expectation of many researchers and policymakers that such change will be important to resolving the issues of climate change. The final chapter in Volume 2, "Technological change," brings these issues into the foreground, illustrating how individuals, institutions, and societies select and reject technological opportunities. The chapter focuses on the important issues surrounding the dynamics of technical change and their outcomes, particularly in relation to attempts to orient technological developments.

"Technological change" begins with the fundamental question, "What is technology?" The answer is that the social sciences conceptualize technology in different ways, ranging from concrete artifacts and skills to more abstract, less nuts-and-bolts notions of technology as material culture or as sociotechnical landscapes.

Artifacts are black boxes that work; they are black boxes because users cannot see beyond their functions to their inner workings or their energy sources. Technological regimes, such as the hydrocarbon-based energy regime, consist of many commitments, sunk investments, and institutionalized practices that evolve in their own terms and are hard to change. Sociotechnical landscapes are the patterns of physical infrastructures, artifacts, institutions, values, and consumption patterns—the material culture of our societies—and the backdrop against which specific technological changes are played out. It is important to include all three levels of understanding technology, because its implication in climate change is as much through sociotechnical landscapes and technological regimes as through particular artifacts such as steam generators or internal combustion engines.

Thus, the conventional technology policy model of technology describes artifacts emerging from research and development establishments and subsequently transferred to the marketplace. However, this model tells only part of the story of technology in society. Other aspects include the processes and conditions of novelty creation, the messiness of implementation and introduction, and the aggregation of myriads of little decisions that underlie the development and embedding of technology in society. All of these elements are part of successful technological transformations that involve growing irreversibility and interdependence among social, economic, and material components of the sociotechnical landscape and that make it very difficult (but not impossible) to consciously direct technological change to meet climate policy ends.

There is no simple technical fix.

In exposing the societal embeddedness of technical systems and highlighting the opportunities and constraints for changing the ways in which humans use energy and the Earth's surface, the final chapter of this volume drives home the fact that there is no simple technical fix. What tools do we have? This question is the topic of the chapters assembled in Volume 3.

Human choice and climate change, volume 3: the tools for policy analysis

Public policy and private decisionmakers often look to the simplifying frameworks of formal tools of analysis to guide their decisions. The third volume of *Human choice and climate change* evaluates the adequacy of the conventional tools of policy analysis for supporting or making prudent human choices in the face of climate change.

Chapter 1, "Economic analysis," describes the strengths and limitations of the most widely applied toolkit of contemporary industrialized society and a substantial contributor to the current state of understanding climate change. "Economic analysis" seeks to explain how the wants of a population interact with the technical means for their satisfaction to produce demand for goods and services; what the scale of that demand, expressed as economic growth, implies for the global environment; and what constraints on growth might result from climate change policies. Proposed policies may be evaluated from a variety of perspectives; a mainstream approach usually includes growth-oriented economic analyses of the costs and benefits. Costs of mitigation in the near and medium term are weighed against often diffuse and uncertain benefits in the very long term, and must account for countries whose economic development may depend upon emissions-generating activities and who may thus be unwilling to trade off growth for emissions reductions. The result of most studies employing cost–benefit analysis is that relatively modest near-term actions are required, although the degree of intervention grows over time.

Global climate change is part of a class of problems that tend to exacerbate the shortcomings of the mainstream approaches to economics,

Other issues for economic analysis include valuing nonmarket (environmental) goods and nonmonetary transactions and assets; global efficiency, trade, and the implications of inequities in the global distribution of income; handling surprises; and the choice of time-cost discount rates, which must be based on social criteria that lie outside of the framework of economic analysis. Global climate change is part of a class of problems that tend to exacerbate the shortcomings of the mainstream approaches to economics, although economic analysis remains a powerful tool to evaluate candidate policy options.

Policymakers have readily adopted the economics approach to analyze future prospects for growth in greenhouse-related emissions and the consequences of attempts at intervention. This useful, if somewhat narrow, focus has been criticized from within and without the economics paradigm for ignoring shortcomings in the assumptions and methodology of economic growth, as well as the insights available from other fields of social science. Confronted with environmental degradation and resource exhaustion, growth practitioners have added depreciation of these resources to the depreciation of capital stock depicted in their models, thus reducing sustainability to a constraint in the optimizing problem of maximizing per capita income. Other practitioners have devised means of valuation for nonmarket effects and nonuse values. These values can be included in the conventional calculus of cost–benefit analysis, where they lose their visibility and are often discounted if they grow too large for comfort.

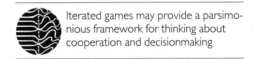

Iterated games may provide a parsimonious framework for thinking about cooperation and decisionmaking

Even in its expanded forms, the economic paradigm is essentially based on the concept of the rational individual decisionmaker—the rational actor paradigm. Chapter 2, "Games and simulations," describes frameworks for explicitly exploring the interactions among multiple decisionmakers, in this case nation states, each acting out of self-interest. The authors argue that, although one-shot games are recognized as having very limited application to continuing relations among states, iterated games may provide a parsimonious framework for thinking about cooperation and decisionmaking in situations that fall between the levels of a single benevolent dictator and an anonymous market populated by many well-behaved individuals.

Game theoretic approaches preserve the idea of uniform or universal rationality. Often they do not take account of tensions among rival viewpoints and values within a state that can cause it to change course during negotiations in ways that cannot be predicted. Where two-level games have been developed (nesting intrastate games within interstate games), internal differences within states are still framed using the same assumptions about the universality of individual rationality. Simulations, involving human actors representing diverse experiences as well as interests within teams of players representing national actors, are one way of confronting this limitation. Simulation games, particularly when formal models are used within the simulation, can support focused communication among analysts and decisionmakers. Although significant risks accompany these benefits, principally bias and overgeneralization from small samples, simulation-gaming methods have potential value as devices for policy assessment, as supplements to conventional forms of analysis or sober critical reflection.

Both game-theoretic and simulation-gaming approaches move beyond atomistic rationality, but continue to rely on two core assumptions:
- Parties rationally perceive and act on self-interest.
- All of the participants share the same standards of rationality.

Generations of researchers have elaborated this universalistic notion of individual rationality to high levels of sophistication. One of its most prominent features is the rigid separation of reason and values. Chapter 3, "Decision analysis" explores the implications of this separation for global climate policymaking.

The separation of reason and values is deeply entrenched, not only in social science research but actually in the fabric of contemporary culture. Indeed, it has been suggested that the pervasiveness of behavioral sciences based on individualistic rationality derives from their role as *folk sciences*, providing security and guidance to their clientele, largely independent of their effectiveness in practice.

Beginning with the problem of climate risks from the viewpoint of a single decisionmaker who is able to control global greenhouse-related emissions, the authors of this chapter delve into the problems of multiple actors and multiple rationalities. The chapter surveys various social science approaches to the perception, communication, and management of technological and environmental risks, and assesses the potential role of risk assessments and decision rules in formulating climate change policy. In place of individual rationality, many of these approaches emphasize an analytic framework of social rationality in which collective or societal preferences are not merely aggregated from pre-existing individual preferences, but are collectively formulated in daily life and stabilized by institutional arrangements of social solidarity, rather than by the atomized choices of individual human agents.

Embedding the expertise of risk professionals in a broader social discourse requires appropriate forms of public participation

The authors argue that the basic problem of risk management, global and local, could be tackled in the emerging field of integrated assessment. For this purpose, advanced tools for integrated assessment need to combine the knowledge of experts, decisionmakers, stakeholders, and citizens. Such tools would reintegrate the faculty of reason with the intuition and emotional intelligence rooted in life experience and craft skills. Taking advantage of a broader range of human experiences in the integrated assessment of global climate change requires a critical appraisal of the historical process by which the rational actor paradigm has established an exclusive professional claim for objective knowledge in risk management. Embedding the expertise of risk professionals in a broader social discourse requires appropriate forms of public participation. This would profoundly move the role of science in society toward what is variously described as vernacular, civic, or postnormal science.

 Predicting the degree of climate change, even quite accurately, is inadequate for deciding how important its consequences will be for human societies and what, if anything, should be done about it.

New forms of scientific collaboration engaging universal specialists (scientists) with local specialists (citizens) will require more than a broader decision-making framework. Such collaboration will also require more inclusive ideas of evidence and information. For example, Volume 1, Chapter 1 describes how climate change scientists tend to base much of their argument on mathematical modeling. On the other hand, citizens and politicians tend to draw more heavily on a holistic approach of reasoning by analogy (see for example, Gore 1992). This set of decisionmaking tools is explored in Chapter 4, "Reasoning by analogy." Past experience is a natural, inevitable source of human management strategies. All decisionmakers tend to compare present situations with past experience and adopt similar strategies for seemingly similar situations. Drawing on information about the past relationships between climate and society, researchers attempt to construct guidelines about possible future states, impacts, and coping strategies. The authors find that past climate and society interactions repay the attention of those seeking to understand the human dimensions of global climate change. Historically, the impact of climate as a hazard and a resource has been directly dependent on the adaptive capability of the society affected. It follows that predicting the degree of climate change, even quite accurately, is inadequate for deciding how important its consequences will be for human societies and what, if anything, should be done about it. It also suggests that changes in the characteristics of societies over time will alter the consequences of climate changes, and researchers should be very cautious about projecting potential long-term climate impacts onto the world as it is known today.

These useful insights notwithstanding, significant methodological difficulties arise in drawing rigorous analogies from past human experience of adaptation to climate. Although it is an enormously suggestive resource, the holistic philosophy of reasoning by analogy, almost by definition, makes it very difficult to draw valid comparisons across cases. Valid comparisons of future scenarios require greater formality than is provided by the analogue approach alone. Such formality turns inquiry back in the direction of simplifying models, although not necessarily so simple as the economic models discussed in the first chapter of the volume.

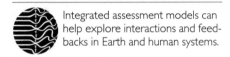

Integrated assessment models can help explore interactions and feedbacks in Earth and human systems.

The final chapter of Volume 3, "Integrated assessment," examines the current state of the various modeling tools that contribute to our understanding of the human dimensions of climate change and the operation of climate change policies. Integrated assessment is an issue-oriented approach to research that knits together diverse knowledge from many disciplines to focus holistically on climate change processes. Integrated assessment includes model-based systems, simulation gaming, scenario analysis, and qualitative studies. At present, the dominant integrated assessment activity is computer-based modeling, which draws on multiple disciplines to focus on climate change processes. In that sense, integrated assessment models attempt to emulate the holism of analogies within the more formalized frameworks of (predominantly economic) modeling. Integrated assessment models can help explore interactions and feedbacks in Earth and human systems, function as flexible and rapid simulation tools, foster insights (sometimes counterintuitive) that would not be available from a single disciplinary approach, and provide tools for mutual learning and communication among researchers and policymakers.

Integrated assessment has contributed to the climate change debate by exploring impacts of climate change, mitigation and abatement strategies, issues in cooperative implementation, the likely equity effects of candidate policies, and complicating factors such as aerosols. Models have also provided information on balancing the carbon budget and on various integrated aspects of land use.

However, existing models leave considerable room for improvement. In particular, more satisfactory and representative models of social dynamics and ecological systems, as well as improved treatments of uncertainty, are needed before integrated assessment models can be made more realistic. There is also a need to focus on the factors that shape policymakers' decisions and to include policymakers and other stakeholders in the design and exercise of the models as advocated in Chapter 3.

As scientists develop modeling tools that are more open and flexible, policymakers will be able to use the model results and other insights from different integrated assessment approaches to inform decisions that bear on global climate change and on the social context in which climate change issues are to be considered.

 A broad-based approach to integrated assessment embedded in a pluralistic and participatory decision process promises to be the best available guide to policymaking

As a whole, Volume 3 describes the existing toolkit of rational analysis and planning techniques available to scientific researchers and political elites. In so doing, the volume reveals a series of important shortcomings of the toolkit in the face of large complex problems facing multiple stakeholders over intergenerational timeframes. Under such conditions, the mainstream social science tools are presently incapable of providing a reliable basis for rational goal setting and policy implementation. They are overly dependent on a narrow concept of rationality and an approach to policy as the means for making the real world conform to a rational model. The dominant rational-actor approach is in many respects a normative framework masquerading as an analytic one. Social scientists have yet to develop any clearly superior alternatives, but a broad-based approach to integrated assessment embedded in a pluralistic and participatory decision process promises to be the best available guide to policymaking.

Human choice and climate change, volume 4: what have we learned?

The task of preparing *Human choice and climate change* has confirmed the conviction with which we started out, that a variety of social science theories, tools, and techniques, along with different ways of combining them, are essential to move climate change analysis and decisionmaking onto a robust foundation. In this fourth volume, we move into the realm of editorial commentary. We stress that responsibility for these interpretations belongs with the editors alone, although we are confident that all of our authors and contributors endorse most of our selections and emphases.

Our editorial chapters address three questions:

- How does climate change challenge the ability of social science to produce useful knowledge?
- What does social science have to say about global climate change and the debates that surround it?
- What might decisionmakers do differently in the light of our present knowledge of social science and climate change?

"The challenge of climate change for social science" sets out to explore how the intellectual organization of social science and its location in the larger framework of human intellectual inquiry may be constraining the ability of social scientists to realize the full potential of their contribution to climate change research and policy debate. The reasons may lie in the division of intellectual labor that has dominated Western science since the Enlightenment. In the social sciences, this division of labor has resulted in the emergence of two distinctive approaches to subject matter, research methods, and explanatory frameworks. We label these the descriptive and interpretive approaches. Although each potentially adds essential ingredients to humanity's understanding of climate change and related issues, the descriptive and interpretive practitioners of social science seldom communicate with each other, let alone integrate their insights.

Of the two approaches, the descriptive approach is usually considered to be more appealing to policymakers because of its apparent technical neutrality and its ability to generate a numerical bottom line. For example, quantitative analyses of responsiveness to tax rates or the effectiveness of regulation can, in principle, be directly translated into a set of policy choices about whether to implement a carbon tax or appliance efficiency standards and even at what level taxes or standards should be set. Interpretive social science tends to be less readily embraced by policymakers as lacking this potential to provide practical guidance.

But, in fact, the bottom-line solution provided by descriptive research is seldom adopted by policymakers, who actually use such studies to provide background or understanding to their own interpretations and decisionmaking inclinations. Hence, neither kind of social science has any real practical advantage. They merely provide different insights from different standpoints. Making space for both descriptive and interpretive social science in the process of reforming the relationship between scientific research and policymaking offers many advantages.

In "Social science insights into climate change," we draw on the whole of *Human choice and climate change* to elucidate some significant crosscutting themes in social science research related to global climate change. The research and analysis that underpins these themes is developed in detail in the earlier chapters—sometimes in several chapters, as they cover the same issues from different standpoints.

In the grand scheme of things, climate change is probably not the deciding factor in whether humanity as a whole flourishes or declines. The resilience of human institutions and their ability to monitor and adapt to changing conditions seems to be more important. However, changes in regional patterns of habitability are likely to harm poor populations in environmentally fragile areas. Although aggregated global effects may be negligible, regional effects may be severe, including violent storms, inundation caused by sea level rise, and formerly fertile land becoming unsuitable for agriculture.

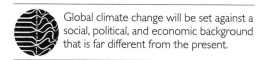

Global climate change will be set against a social, political, and economic background that is far different from the present.

Global climate change will be inexorable, but also incremental, and will be set against a social, political, and economic background that is far different from the present. In fact, social and political structures and processes will probably change faster than the IPCC projects for climate. This difference in rates of change may lead policymakers to delay taking action to mitigate or adapt to climate change until disaster overtakes them. However, the same difference also offers the potential to allow societies to stay ahead of climate change, that is, to build in the capability to monitor, anticipate, and respond effectively to changes in many Earth systems resulting from climate change.

Whether or not humanity realizes the potential to get ahead and stay ahead of climate change impacts depends on what happens at the level of decision-making in households, firms, and communities. Diversity, complexity, and uncertainty will frustrate the search for top-down global policymaking and implementation. Social science research in all disciplines indicates that policymakers should attempt to reach agreement on high-level environmental and associated social goals, then look for local and regional opportunities to use policy in various ways appropriate to the institutional arrangements, cultural values, economic and political conditions, and environmental changes.

Overall we find that social scientists have contributed to climate change research by identifying human activities that cause climate change, highlighting environmental changes that affect human welfare, and examining the research process itself and its relationship to policymaking.

Finally, we conclude *Human choice and climate change* with 10 suggestions of ways in which decisionmakers concerned with climate change might modify their goals and approaches to climate policy.

1. View the issue of climate change holistically, not just as the problem of emissions reductions.
2. Recognize that institutional limits to global sustainability are at least as important for climate policymaking as environmental limits.

3. Prepare for the likelihood that social, economic, and technological change will be more rapid and have greater direct impacts on human populations than climate change.
4. Recognize the limits of rational planning.
5. Employ the full range of analytic perspectives and decision aids from the natural and social sciences and the humanities in climate change policy-making.
6. Design policy instruments for real world conditions rather than try to make the world conform to a particular policy model.
7. Integrate climate change concerns with other, more immediate policies such as employment, defense, economic development, and public health.
8. Take a regional and local approach to climate policymaking and implementation.
9. Direct resources into identifying vulnerability and promoting resilience, especially where the impacts will be largest.
10. Use a pluralistic approach to decisionmaking.

Human choice and climate change thus begins with describing the human landscape of the Earth and centers on the role of human choice in the development of climate change as an issue, the definition of causes and likely effects, and the analysis of possible responses. Along with natural science assessments and other related assessments, this social science assessment brings together a wealth of information—but *Human choice and climate change* is not just a report on the state of the social sciences as they have been applied to climate change. Performing an assessment broadens the research focus and generates new insights by the multifaceted analyses and approaches presented here. Theoretical and practical insights that have grown out of the process of producing this assessment can also enlarge the potential application of social science insights and methods to global change—for social scientists, policymakers, and natural scientists.

References

Arrow, K. 1951. *Social choice and individual values*. New York: John Wiley.
Bruce, J. P., H. Lee, E. F. Haites (eds) 1996. *Economic and social issues of climate change*. Cambridge: Cambridge University Press.
Gore, A. 1992. *Earth in the balance: ecology and the human spirit*. New York: Houghton Mifflin.
Jacobsen, H. & M. Price 1991. *A framework for research on the human dimensions of global environmental change*. Paris: International Social Science Council.
Stern, P. O. Young, D. Druckman 1992. *Global environmental change: understanding the human dimensions*. Washington DC: National Academy Press.
Tolba, M. K. 1991. Opening address. In *Climate change: science, impacts and policy*, J. Jaeger & H. L. Ferguson (eds). Cambridge: Cambridge University Press.

CHAPTER 1

Science and decisionmaking

Sheila Jasanoff & Brian Wynne

Contributors
Frederick H. Buttel, Florian Charvolin, Paul N. Edwards,
Aant Elzinga, Peter M. Haas, Chunglin Kwa,
W. Henry Lambright, Michael Lynch, Clark A. Miller

Climate change emerged in the 1980s as a public policy issue posing apparently intractable challenges to science and politics (Gore 1992). The possible dangers of inaction seemed compelling, and policymakers around the world agreed on the need for more reliable data and assessments from the natural and social sciences. The move to constitute the Intergovernmental Panel on Climate Change (IPCC) and to ask for periodic state-of-the-art assessments followed a familiar conceptual model for linking science to politics or knowledge to action. It presupposed that scientific research could be targeted, in linear fashion, to fill gaps in the existing knowledge base. Once the gaps were filled, and uncertainties either reduced or eliminated, policymakers could rationally apply the products of science to formulating policy responses.

Confidence in the power of strategic or mission-oriented research to influence policy led to the commitment of substantial public funds to new climate change programs. Scientists and policymakers generally accepted that planetary changes could best be understood, and mastered, by identifying a collection of causal forces, both natural and social; by objectively mapping, measuring, and analyzing them; by predicting their effects; by aggregating them through large-scale quantitative techniques of modeling and assessment; and, finally, by using the assessments as inputs to policy. US global change research programs reflected the orientation toward studying objectively accessible large-scale patterns, with inquiry centered in the natural sciences. Whereas natural scientists studied interactions among the Earth's biogeophysical systems, social science research focused primarily on the aggregate social forces thought to produce environmental impacts on a global scale. (Table 1.1 presents funding for research in the social sciences in the US Global Change Research Program, including support from 11 federal agencies.)

Table 1.1   US federal funding for global change research (in millions of US$).

Fiscal year	1989	1990	1991	1992	1993	1994
Total Global Change Program, all agencies	133.9	659.3	953.7	1109.8	1326.0	1475.1
Total human interactions, all agencies	22.7	4.8	28.3	16.8	22.2	23.6
Percentage of total program, all agencies	16.4	0.7	3.0	1.5	1.7	1.7

Source: *Human Dimensions Quarterly* 1(1), 12.

Almost immediately, however, it became clear that traditional policy-analytic approaches would not contain a problem of this dimension. The scale, complexity, and interconnectedness of the causes of climate change—and the fundamental links between climate change and other global processes—tested science's incremental and discipline-based approaches to investigating nature. Concurrently, the contested, open-ended, and geographically dispersed character of climate-linked phenomena strained the power of established policy institutions, both national and international, to build scientific consensus or formulate adequate policy responses (Skolnikoff 1990, Mann 1991, Messner et al. 1992). Controversies about the IPCC's conclusions intensified, constituting a backlash not only against particular scientific findings and assessments but, more profoundly, against the politics of globalization (e.g., Seitz et al. 1989, Balling 1992, Michaels 1992, Bailey 1993).

This chapter draws on several decades of social science research on scientific knowledge and policymaking to show why initial assumptions about how to study and respond to climate change have proved inadequate and to present a richer accounting to guide future responses to this complex issue. The discussion draws upon and reinterprets several science–policy initiatives that have been extensively studied and that have instructive parallels to the science–policy relationship in climate change. These include the protection of stratospheric ozone, the Green Revolution, the International Biological Program, the International Geosphere–Biosphere Program, and environmental models such as general circulation models.

The relationship between natural and social science research on climate was initially conceived as a matter of mutual agenda setting: "Natural scientists help set the research agenda for social scientists by identifying human activities that are major, proximate causes of environmental change. . . . Social scientists help set the research agenda for natural scientists by highlighting environmental changes that would severely affect human welfare" (Young & Stern 1992: 2). This characterization validly represents one part of the social science research program, indeed the dominant part from the standpoint of state support.

However, social scientists also have complex stories to tell about the framing of problems for research, the production and validation of scientific knowledge, and its uptake into policy decisions. In addition, a considerable body of social science research has illuminated the origins of controversy and uncertainty in public policy. Given the prominence of backlash critiques of climate change, this line of work will grow in importance as policymakers confront the challenge of international cooperation on so indeterminate and potentially catastrophic a problem as climate change.

The early framing and funding of climate change research generally overlooked the contribution made by the qualitative social sciences to understanding the processes by which societies recognize new threats to their security or well-being, formulate responses, and collectively act upon them. Yet, knowledge about these issues has accumulated rapidly in the past two decades. A growing body of work—much of it located in social studies of science and technology (hereafter referred to as science and technology studies)—has challenged the notion that allegedly global problems such as climate change exist in a world that can be unproblematically accessed through direct observation of nature. Contemporary science and technology studies suggest instead that environmental issues of global scale (or indeed of *any* scale) emerge from an interplay of scientific discovery and description with other political, economic, and social forces. Persuasive accounts of environmental phenomena are constructed, according to this view, by myriad social interactions, encompassing not only the diverse activities and practices of scientific communities, but also the work of nonscientific actors and institutions in defining problems and endorsing solutions.

Following Kuhn's (1962) seminal work on scientific revolutions, social scientists have questioned traditional assumptions about the relationship of knowledge accumulation to political, and even scientific, progress. This is evident in a challenging of themes commonly grouped together under the label of *modernity* and carrying significant implications for environmental policy: for example, that technological development is the prime marker of progress and enlightenment; that nonscientific belief systems are based on popular ignorance and superstition; that advances in scientific knowledge inevitably reduce uncertainty; and that increased absorption of science leads to convergence in social understanding and public policy. An account of climate change (or any other perceived environmental problem) grounded in contemporary social science research would reject as too linear and reductionist the modernist narrative in which science first finds evidence of new environmental phenomena, and further discoveries and inventions inevitably lead to informed social responses via avenues of prediction, rational choice, and control.

The more interpretive orientation of the social sciences, informed by the humanities, does not take issue with the enterprise of managerial policymaking but insists that the various contingencies inherent in such endeavors be recognized and taken seriously. Social science research has therefore attempted to illuminate the diversity of investigative, argumentative, institutional, and material resources that human beings bring to bear in creating the universal truths of science and applying them to technical problem solving. Work in this genre can be broadly characterized as *interpretive*, because it emphasizes the significance of meanings, texts, and local frames of reference in knowledge creation (Geertz 1973, 1983); *reflective*, because it focuses on the role of human reflection and ideas in building institutions (Keohane 1988, Beck et al. 1994); and *constructivist*, because it examines the practices by which accounts of the natural world are put together and achieve the status of reality (Fleck 1935, Bloor 1976, Latour & Woolgar 1979). For consistency, we use the term *constructivist* throughout the chapter to designate the array of qualitative social science approaches—grounded in such fields as cultural anthropology, sociology, comparative politics, policy studies, and international relations—that shed light on the social and cultural elements involved in producing environmental knowl-

4

edge. Our aim in this is not to understate the role of nature in shaping scientific knowledge but to foster a deeper understanding of how scientific knowledge assumes authority in the public domain.

The shift toward constructivist studies in the social sciences has encouraged a parallel shift in science policy studies toward an increased concern with the dynamics of problem framing and consensus building in the face of widespread uncertainty. This impetus arises from a recognition that problems and solutions in the policy realm are seldom clear-cut: in practice, there are no neat boundaries separating knowledge from ignorance, fact from value, scientific knowledge from other forms of knowledge about the world, and, indeed, policy questions from knowledge-based answers. To question how *science* acquires meaning and stability, by exploring its social commitments, is to question *policy* in the same way. Political institutions and structures, the issues they pose for solution, as well as their techniques of management and control, are all seen as more fluid, and more open to interpretation and manipulation by divergent actors, than was assumed in earlier approaches to policy analysis. At the same time, the institutionalization of social norms and practices into stable patterns of political culture is increasingly seen as influencing the direction of research strategies, the production of knowledge, and the application of knowledge to action.

Constructivist policy analysis recognizes not only that issue framings do not flow deterministically from problems fixed by nature, but also that particular framings of environmental problems build upon specific models of agency, causality, and responsibility. These frames in turn are intellectually constraining in that they delimit the universe of further scientific inquiry, political discourse, and possible policy options. Constructivist policy analysis, therefore, begins with the assumption that questions about how problems are defined and framed must be addressed to have a basis for evaluating the efficacy, merits or legitimacy of competing social policies. Why do some issues come to be expressed as matters of policy concern in particular ways, at particular times, in particular locations, and through the efforts of particular groups or cultures? What makes problem formulations change over time or, alternatively, cohere across different historical periods and political systems? How do issues come to be perceived as natural or technical rather than social, as public rather than private, or as global or universal rather than local? And what roles do science and scientists play in these processes of definition and change?

In the context of climate change, these new directions in policy research point to the centrality of several interlocking questions that remained unasked and virtually unacknowledged in earlier frameworks of analysis:

- *How do scientists and their societies identify and delimit distinct problems related to climate change that are considered amenable to scientific resolution?* What makes problems look mainly scientific or mainly social and political, and in what ways do the institutions and processes of science and politics steer public perceptions on this issue? How are conflicts over alternative framings negotiated and resolved, both domestically and in international arenas?

- *How do scientists come to know particular facts and causal relationships regarding climate change and to persuade others that their knowledge is credible?* In particular, how does scientific knowledge generated in different disciplines, within specialized or localized research communities, and under varying conditions of epistemological and political uncertainty, come to be accepted as authoritative by wider scientific and social constellations? In what ways do scientific accounts of phenomena interact with competing or overlapping beliefs about the way the world works?

- *How do conflicts over risk arise, and how are responses to them handled in a world of conflicting and plural political interests?* With respect to the vigorous backlash on climate change, what procedures and mechanisms can best make room for open debate while also supporting closure around reasonable conclusions and commitments? On a global level, how can productive identification with such processes be secured from far-flung local actors and interests?

- *How do human societies and their designated policy actors draw upon scientific knowledge to justify collective action on a worldwide scale?* For example, how do environmental problems come to be construed as global and universal rather than private, particularistic, local, or national; and how, in turn, do they come to be defined as environmental—and therefore requiring a unique form of collaboration between scientists and policymakers—rather than economic, political, or cultural? How are conflicts about the scale or means of intervention understood, managed or resolved? To what extent is science itself counted upon to address these problems, and what distinctive issues of science policy and politics are raised by such characterizations?

This chapter reviews several bodies of social science literature that shed significant light on the foregoing questions. It begins with a critical examination of the place accorded to scientific knowledge in several current models of public policymaking, all of which view the production and validation of knowledge as largely independent of the use of knowledge in policy decisions. These approaches are contrasted with a theoretical framing of the science–policy linkage that appears more consistent with findings from constructivist studies of science, technology, and the environment. According to this latter view, scientific knowledge and political order are *co-produced* at multiple stages in their joint evolution, from the stabilization of specialized factual findings in laboratories and field studies to the national and international acceptance of causal explanations offered by science and their use in decisionmaking.

The central sections of the chapter review the evidence for the model of co-production, grouping it under the following specific topics:

- the production and validation of scientific knowledge and its integration across disciplines
- the standardization of science and technology, their movement outside their original locations of production, and the interplay of technical standardization with ideology and social belief systems
- the formation of closure or agreement around credible, public accounts of scientific phenomena or, alternatively, the deconstruction of such accounts in skeptical environments
- the management of uncertainty in policy processes and the uptake of science into both national and international decisionmaking.

Illustrative materials include, where possible, examples of environmental science, controversy, and policy closure, including the ongoing debates about the reality and implications of climate change (see Seitz et al. 1989, Lindzen 1990, Kellogg 1991, Balling 1992, Michaels 1992, Bailey 1993).

The final sections of the chapter discuss, in the light of theoretical issues raised earlier, the efforts of international science and science policymakers to model the human and physical determinants of climate change. Ambiguities in the design of models are associated with issues about their use in policymaking. The concluding section returns to the conflicts that have emerged in trying to build a policy-relevant consensus on climate change science and briefly outlines the institutional and political implications of bringing about substantial changes in the dynamics of international policymaking.

Scientific knowledge and public policy

Vannevar Bush, in his famous report to President Roosevelt, *Science, the endless frontier* (1945), laid out a distinction between basic and applied science that continues to underpin the discussion of science related to policy. Bush distinguished between a science that was grounded in research alone (the R of R&D) and a science applied to product development (the D of R&D). Other formulations have since been found to express Bush's binary vision. Thus, in today's language, *pure* science is often contrasted with *strategic* or *mission-oriented* science, and *opportunity-driven* research is distinguished from *needs-driven* research. What endures, however, is the view that scientific activity, to be truly disinterested and impartial, must be conducted in a space removed from its possible political applications (Merton 1973). The role of scientists, according

Speaking truth to power

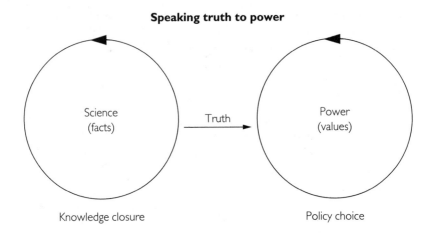

Science and trans-science

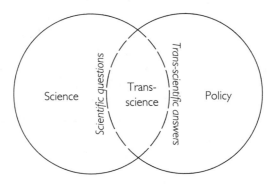

Figure 1.1   Views of the relationship between scientific knowledge and public policy.

to this view, is to stand apart from politics while proffering impartial knowledge to formal policy institutions, a role memorably captured in the phrase "speaking truth to power" (Price 1965) (Fig. 1.1). The perception that scientists have failed to maintain the distance presupposed by this model offers grounds for energetic, though frequently misguided, assaults on their credibility (see, for example, Maduro & Schauerhammer 1992, Michaels 1992).

Continued efforts by both scientists and policy analysts to preserve the distinctness of their spheres of action underscores the dominance of the Bush paradigm, even though the participants sometimes admit that the separation, if any, is more honored in the breach than the observance. Weinberg addressed this difficulty in an enormously influential essay entitled "Science and trans-science" (Weinberg 1972). His solution was to locate between the zones of pure science and pure politics a region of *trans-science*, consisting of those issues that could be asked of science but to which science could not give answers (Fig. 1.1). Weinberg's formulation performed a careful balancing act: it preserved the authority of pure science as a source of credible policy advice while conceding that something more was needed—specifically, trans-science—in order to provide useful answers to contemporary policy questions (Jasanoff 1987, 1990).

Weinberg's essay can be seen as defining a historical moment when the hybrid character of science done for policy became briefly apparent within the US scientific community. Trans-science, for Weinberg, comprised in effect a domain of co-production, where policy criteria (e.g., protection of public health) dictated the choice of seemingly scientific decision rules and models (e.g., extrapolation methods from animals to humans in health risk assessment and prediction of rare accidents in engineering contexts such as nuclear power plants), which in turn were invoked to legitimate public policy. However, as Latour (1993) argued some two decades later, such hybrid domains are continually threatened in modern societies, where, as part of the process of legitimation, much social energy is devoted to purifying the hybrids into clearly separate domains of nature and culture, or science and society. A prime objective of recent critical social theory has been to resurrect the complexity of the hybrid domain of nature–culture (Geertz 1973, Merchant 1980, Douglas & Wildavsky 1982, Haraway 1991, Redclift & Benton 1994).

In the environmental sciences, formal computer modeling supplies an exceptionally powerful tool for reestablishing an authoritative space for science, even in areas of cognitive uncertainty, that is, the very domain of trans-science. Models in effect recast trans-science as a problem area subject to systematic investigation, analysis, and control. Science can, after all, provide answers to political questions, downplaying any problems in the nature–culture relationship that lie beyond the predictive and meliorative capabilities of modern science. Efforts in the United States over the past 20 years to carry out quantitative risk assessments of environmental pollutants, and to separate risk assessment from risk management, exemplify the widespread use of modeling to define and manage uncertainty in national environmental policy (see also Vol. 3, Ch. 3). Vigorous debate about the validity and feasibility of these efforts provides evidence that such decisionmaking can be highly controversial despite attempts to separate truth from power (US NRC 1983, 1994, Jasanoff 1991a).

As described later in this chapter, modelers of global systems must make even more controversial choices of scientific parameters (e.g., end-points and surrogate markers) that are underdetermined by science. Policy directives, or scientists' beliefs about these, provide one set of influences on model-builders' choices, thereby shaping the structure of scientific inquiry relevant to policy (Houghton et al. 1990). Global models also contain embedded philosophical and ideological biases, as explored in detail in Meadows et al. (1982), Ashley (1983), Cartwright (1983), Bloomfield (1986), Oreskes et al. (1994), and Edwards (1996). Equally, these complex discursive productions promise—in their legitimating role—that uncertainty can be continually reduced and contained within manageable bounds. By representing modeling of the future as a form of problem solving, models imply that uncertainties that are not yet so contained will be in future, so long as policymakers remain committed to investigate relevant scientific parameters.

Attempts to replace the linear schema of speaking truth to power with something more descriptively accurate have achieved varying coherence and comprehensiveness. At least five major alternative conceptual frameworks exist:
- agenda setting as the confluence of problems, policies, and politics
- agenda setting as a product of power relationships and initial framing choices
- knowledge change as dependent on systems uncertainties and decision stakes
- policy cultures as the locus of divergent science–policy formulations
- policy interests and competing discourses as struggling to interpret or shape scientific knowledge in ways that will serve these interests.

Although no framework fully accounts for all the interrelations in the production of scientific knowledge, each contributes insights and strengthens the view of the policy–science relationship as complex and nonlinear.

In one well-known model of agenda setting by a US political scientist (Kingdon 1984), policy emerges from the temporary confluence of three streams: problems, policies, and politics (Fig. 1.2). These three streams have lives of their own, except at moments when they flow together under the influence of triggering events (e.g., natural or manmade disasters) or through the actions of policy entrepreneurs, such as James Hanson of the US National Aeronautics and Space Administration (NASA), testifying before Congress on global warming, or the later efforts by skeptical scientists to persuade the Bush administration that climate change did not merit serious political concern (Seitz et al. 1989). Knowledge, in Kingdon's model, gains public prominence largely by accident, through chance occurrences or strategic decisions by exceptional individuals. Historical and structural influences on agenda setting are largely ignored in this formulation, as they are in some other widely accepted pictures of public decisionmaking. Thus, the policy cycle (Fig. 1.2) makes no explicit mention of how knowledge enters the cycle and either shapes or is shaped by its various components. The metaphor of the cycle also suggests that legitimation is internal to the process of policymaking, both institutionally and temporally, and that implementation and evaluation lead straightforwardly back to policy reformulation.

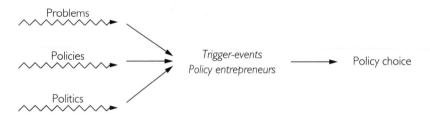

Policy stream: agenda setting

Problems

Policies

Trigger-events
Policy entrepreneurs

Policy choice

Politics

Policy cycle

Policy formulation

Policy change

Policy legitimation

Policy evaluation

Policy implementation

Figure 1.2 Agenda setting as the confluence of problems, policies (Kingdon 1984), and politics, and the policy cycle.

Cobb & Elder (1972) presented a picture of agenda setting that is more sensitive to power relationships and to the impact of initial framing choices on subsequent policies and decisions. They called attention to four well-known, but often unacknowledged, constraints on the form in which issues are placed on the policy agenda:

- unequal distribution of, and access to, influence
- consequent systematic biases in the range of issues a society considers
- inertia in changing the prevailing bias
- significance of pre-political and pre-decisional forces in shaping policy.

Although usefully recognizing the role of power and equity, however, their account of agenda setting, like Kingdon's, accorded no special status to scientific knowledge. In particular, their analysis left unclear what role, if any, science plays in either cementing or else overcoming societal biases in the selection of issues for the policy agenda.

Funtowicz & Ravetz (1992) proposed a model that is both more centrally

11

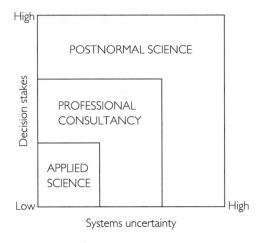

Figure 1.3   Three kinds of science (based on Funtowicz & Ravetz 1985, 1992).

focused on the internal dynamics of scientific inquiry and somewhat more nuanced in its understanding of knowledge change. Policy options, or problem-solving strategies, arise as functions of *systems uncertainties* on the one hand and *decision stakes* on the other (Fig. 1.3). When both variables are low, the puzzle-solving approaches of Kuhnian normal science are adequate to produce consensus. If either variable rises to the medium level, unresolved methodological debates come to the fore, and new actors and skills must be brought into play to forge solutions to policy problems. Funtowicz & Ravetz characterized this middle region of scientific activity as professional consultancy. Finally, when both variables are high, they saw a region of *postnormal science*, where scientific experts share the field of knowledge production with amateurs, such as stakeholders, media professionals, and even theologians or philosophers. The wide-open democratized debates of postnormal science lead, in their view, to new research and new facts that eventually drive issues back toward the more manageable domain of professional consultancy or even normal science.

The modification of the conventional linear model of science policy given by Funtowicz & Ravetz reflects important developments in knowledge and policy relationships which others have noted (Gibbons et al. 1994, Ziman et al. 1994). However, this particular model is problematic under either of two assumptions: either it assumes that the uncertainty and decision stakes axes are independent of each other, conflicting with findings that show uncertainty rising with the increase in stakes and attendant political scrutiny of competing claims (Wynne 1980, Collingridge & Reeve 1986, Jasanoff 1991a); or else it presupposes that reducing the uncertainty dimension of postnormal science simultaneously reduces decision stakes. The latter presupposition is questionable in the light of MacKenzie's (1990) discussion of the *certainty trough* and similar observations showing that reductions in uncertainty occur only if decision stakes are lowered for other exogenous reasons (see Fig. 1.4).

The implicitly forward-looking storyline of the Funtowicz & Ravetz model echoes the idea of knowledge acquisition as perpetual progress. But accounts that stress the growth of knowledge and the reduction of scientific uncertainty are belied by other strands of scholarship that point toward altogether more complex and unpredictable linkages between the worlds of scientific knowledge production and of politics. Work on science and the state, much of it by European social theorists reaching back to Marx, Mannheim, Horkheimer, and Adorno, adds a powerful counterweight to internalist and uncritically progressivist views of the policy process. For instance, Foucault (1970, 1978, 1979, 1980) suggested that human science fields such as demography and economics received their impetus from the disciplinary interests of the state and its programs of normalizing its citizens. Other accounts link the organization and pursuits of science more directly to the economic and political organization of the post-Enlightenment state (Noble 1977, Shapin & Schaffer 1985, Ezrahi 1990, Solingen 1993) or to the state's demands for material and ideological support (Mukerji 1989, Porter 1995). Critical theorists have also pointed to the driving force of instrumental rationality in the modern world, which penetrates ever more deeply into the social and cultural *life worlds* and makes competing beliefs and practices appear irrational (Habermas 1970, 1971, 1975, Ezrahi 1990, Beck 1992). The existence of multiple, competing forms of rationality, sustained by different forms of social cohesion and ideology, is the focus of yet another body of writing on science, politics, and culture (Douglas 1970, Douglas & Wildavsky 1982, Ezrahi 1984, Rayner 1984, Thompson et al. 1986).

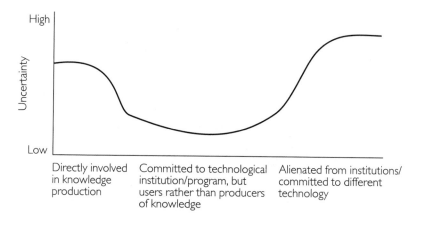

Figure 1.4 The certainty trough (from MacKenzie 1990).

13

Some of these ideas are reflected in an analysis of policymaking that locates the interaction between science and politics in four main *policy cultures*—bureaucratic, economic, academic, and civic—which coexist in industrial countries, compete for influence and resources, and seek to steer science and technology in different directions (Elzinga & Jamison 1995). Each policy culture has its own doctrinal assumptions, its images and ideals of science, and its own political constituencies. In this model, a policy framework is the outcome of mutual conflict and accommodation among policy cultures (Fig. 1.5). Thus, the civic culture's interest in democratizing science by allowing more diverse inputs or by making it more socially accountable (Almond & Verba 1965, Jamison et al. 1990, Yearley 1991) resists and partially overcomes the bureaucratic culture's insistence on making policy more monolithically rational, scientific, or rule bound (Breyer 1993).

A deficiency of the policy cultures model is that it understates the historical and institutional interconnections among the four cultures. For example, Porter (1986, 1995) persuasively linked the demand for objectivity in the social sciences to the needs of the modern administrative state, thereby tying together the values and goals of the academic and bureaucratic cultures. Nevertheless, if the cultures are conceived of as ideal types, struggles among them may explain why heterogeneous framings of environmental problems are produced and placed before policymakers: as questions of pollution control rather than pollution prevention, of economic efficiency rather than environmental justice, of scarcity rather than maldistribution. Such framing choices, together with their causes and limitations, are especially important to understand with regard to climate change, which has proved amenable to many different framings across scientific, political, and policy cultures (Zheng-Kang 1990, Agarwal & Narain 1991,

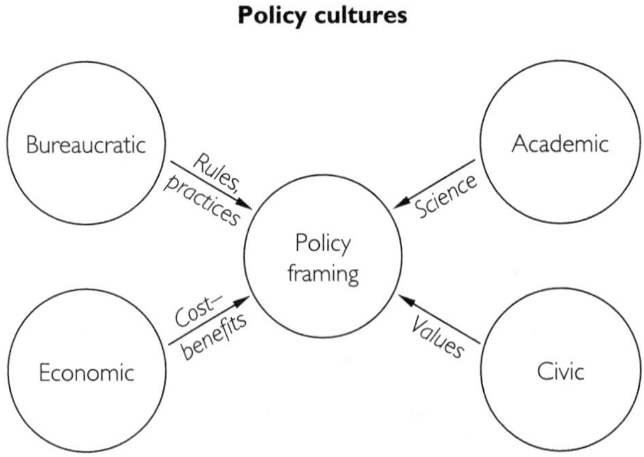

Policy cultures

Figure 1.5   Policy cultures as the locus of science and policy interactions.

14

Kellogg 1991). As Lipschutz (1991: 40) related, for example, technological efforts to control air pollution in the United States fell short because they "focused almost entirely on the `hardware'—the car—rather than on the entire web of material, structural, and ethical relations that constitute the `Automobile.'"

The policy cultures model also leaves inexplicit how authoritative scientific knowledge is formed around contested policy issues such as climate change. In this respect, it most resembles the interest model familiar from many studies of scientific controversies in the policy domain (Dennis 1985, Rushefsky 1986, Nelkin 1992). According to interest analysts, scientific uncertainty creates a domain of interpretive flexibility where competing social actors are free to appropriate and promote readings consistent with their policy interests. Collingridge & Reeve (1986) have argued that in high-stakes policy proceedings, where interests by definition are always divided, the expected result will be endless technical debate, with no prospect of policy closure. Ezrahi (1984), by contrast, discerned a more pervasive fragmentation of science to meet the demands of many microsocial groupings—environmentalists, disease coalitions, the aging, and others—for facts that validate their identity and legitimate their claims on state services or resources.

Another influential perspective that recognizes the intertwined relationship of knowledge and policy is discourse analysis (e.g., Dryzek 1990). Hajer's (1995) use of the concept of discourse coalitions to account for the development and implementation of acid rain policies in the United Kingdom and the Netherlands offers a good example. Unlike conventional interest analysts (e.g. Nelkin 1992), who would see political and scientific language being constructed and deployed to further hidden interests and to legitimate commitments made on less impartial grounds, Hajer recognized that actors and institutions are shaped by their own discourses, which delimit their moral identity, and their cognitive horizons, shaping in effect what they care to know. Hajer showed how different combinations of contingent local commitments, knowledges, practices, and discourses led to very different dominant constructions of the "acid rain problem" in the United Kingdom and the Netherlands. Although, on a superficial reading, the same scientific knowledge was available to policymakers in each country, differences in their epistemic commitments influenced what was recognized in each setting as evidence, fact, and good science.

The theoretical insights that emerge from much of the social science literature, especially in the domain of environmental policy and politics, thus cast doubt on the adequacy of decisionmaking models that employ wholly different explanatory resources to explain the production of scientific knowledge (or of scientific uncertainty) on the one hand and the production of political order (including policy choices) on the other. This literature calls for a more interactive accounting, in which natural knowledge and political order are co-produced through a common social project that shores up the legitimacy of each. Key to such an account is the recognition that knowledge, including knowledge about nature, is not the exclusive preserve of any particular domain of society. Each ideal type of culture—the civic–social, bureaucratic–political, economic, and scientific—may more fruitfully be regarded as a distinctive form of life that engages in the production of its own knowledge, ideas, beliefs and meanings, and sustains these activities in turn through characteristic practices and discourses. At the same time, as participants in a shared sociocultural space, these cultural ideal-types are highly interdependent, linked together both by hybrid cultural forms (e.g., corporations, epistemic communities, international organizations—see Ch. 5) and by shared social projects. For example, the economic and civic cultures participate in a common project of consumption; the scientific and economic cultures engage together in technology development; and the bureaucratic and scientific cultures cooperate in the domain of policy-relevant research. Figure 1.6 presents a highly schematic rendition of these ideas.

Evidence for the model of co-production derives from many disparate sources: ethnographic and sociological investigations of laboratory science; historical studies of scientific change; work on indigenous knowledge systems and their replacement with allegedly universal models of science; cultural and social studies of scientific controversies; inquiries into public perceptions and understanding of science; empirical studies of science policy. Together, this body of work calls attention to the fact that social and cultural commitments are built into every phase of knowledge production and consequent social action, even though enormously effective steps are often taken to eliminate the traces of the social from the scientific world. The forms in which environmental knowledge and environmental policy issues are publicly expressed have to be seen against this background as historically and socially contingent, even though they are equally constrained by nature. The remainder of this chapter reviews and critically evaluates the multiple scholarly foundations of the model of co-production, as well as the model's implications for understanding and responding to climate change.

Knowledge production:
contingency to stabilization within the scientific community

Scientific findings about the environment are not simply reflections of nature, produced within a self-contained matrix of scientific discovery. Knowledge and the technologies it sustains are produced through complex forms of communal work by scientists and technical experts who engage with nature in

16

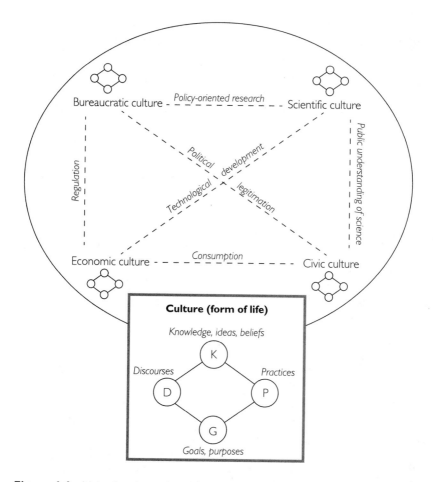

Figure 1.6 Natural order and social order. Hybrid cultures: social movements, non-governmental organizations, multinational corporations, international organizations, epistemic communities.

interaction with their multiple audiences of sponsors, specialist peers, other scientists, consumers, interpreters, and users. Shared beliefs, discourses, practices, and goals (as depicted in the inset to Fig. 1.6) are all part of the context in which knowledge is formulated and technologies are developed. The general name for this theoretical approach to knowledge production is *social construction*.

A constructivist account of science and technology seeks to understand the role of human agency and cognition, cultural discourses and practices, and social goals and norms in the making of scientific knowledge and technological products. Researchers acknowledge nature's part in controlling the production of scientific knowledge, but that part is considered less determinative and more complex than in other models of science. The constructivist framework for studying science, together with its extensions into the social studies of technology, has proved useful in explaining both why controversies about policy-relevant science arise and what brings such controversies to a close. Understanding these processes can be of great practical value to those who find themselves in the midst of controversy about climate change and who wish to chart a course to resolve the disputes about scientific knowledge and its implications.

Science and practice: the construction of facts and artifacts

Bloor's (1976) enunciation of a *strong programme* for social studies of science provides a convenient starting point for examining the contributions made by this field of inquiry. Bloor called for a sociology of scientific knowledge that would subscribe to four methodological tenets:

- causality (i.e., concerned with the conditions that bring about beliefs or states of knowledge)
- impartiality with respect to truth and falsity
- symmetry (i.e., the same types of cause would be invoked to explain true and false beliefs)
- reflexivity (i.e., its patterns of explanation would be applicable to sociology of science as well as to science).

Studies building on Bloor's proposed research strategy over the past 20 years have shown that many scientific knowledge claims can be productively explained as statements about the natural world that are mediated through social relations. Pioneering work in the history (Forman 1971, Rudwick 1972, Shapin & Schaffer 1985), philosophy (Hesse 1974, Hacking 1983), and sociology of science (Barnes & Bloor 1982, Collins 1985, Latour 1987) shows to what extent scientific knowledge, even in the physical sciences and mathematics, develops through significant processes of social negotiation and consensus building. To explore the social conditions of knowledge production in this fashion does not weaken or debunk science's claim to truth finding. Rather, an important consequence of this research has been to expand our understanding of the sources of certainty in science and the basis for the relative credibility of scientific claims and their robustness under social challenge (Shapin 1995, Jasanoff 1996a).

The social work of knowledge production begins at the level of observation and experiment within a laboratory or other research environment. Even at this level, the scientific community plays a crucial role in what becomes accepted as knowledge. For example, Collins (1985) demonstrated that disputes over scientific replication, one of the mainstays of the scientific enterprise, cannot be settled through direct appeals to nature but are worked out in micronegotiations among scientists about what counts as proper replication. These standards include purely local assessments of the credibility and competence of researchers, as well as more general practical agreements about good technique or analysis. Accordingly, no experimental practice can ever be said to replicate a previous one in accordance with fixed or absolute standards. What counts as replication is partly settled by whether the results are thought to agree with previous ones, so that an inevitable confusion comes about between the correctness of observation on the one hand and the rightness of the observer's practices and prior cognitive commitments on the other. Agreement among scientists, according to this analysis, is the ultimate means of closure. By the same token, inability to agree forces scientists into a potentially never-ending search for tests of tests of tests, which Collins termed *experimenters' regress*. In more diffuse and complex research outside the laboratory (such as research about climate change), researchers find increasing difficulty in establishing knowledge claims that will be generally accepted.

In a related vein, Latour & Woolgar (1979) showed that the everyday practices of scientists at work in the laboratory resulted in the construction of facts from perceived laboratory phenomena through a paper trail of "inscriptions"—texts such as tables, graphs, and charts that represent scientific observations. Such constructs become progressively more difficult to refute as they are codified and as the systems through which they were produced are partly consolidated into hardened artifacts—standardized scientific instruments such as the spectrophotometer, test organisms such as the *Drosophila* fruit fly (Kohler 1994), protocols such as good laboratory practices, or commonly used models. Scientific claims and techniques which, for all practical purposes, can no longer be unmade or deconstructed, are said to be black-boxed (Latour 1987). That is, their internal nature is taken to be objectively established, immutable, and beyond the power of human reconstruction or reinterpretation. The complexities and caveats that originally attended black-boxed claims or techniques are lost.

A parallel process goes on in technological change. Building on ideas of social construction in science studies and on the systems approach in the history of technology (Hughes 1983), actor network theory provides an account of the way in which durable technological systems are built and held together (see Vol. 2, Ch. 6). Functioning technological systems require the participation of a series of actors, both local and trans-local, who eventually constitute a stable network (Callon 1987, Law 1987, Law & Callon 1988). Technological networks are sometimes regarded as products of heterogeneous engineering (Law 1986), because they include varied technical and nontechnical practices offered by people and their ideas and skills, social institutions, even nonhuman species (e.g., scallops in Callon 1986), and artifacts. Case histories of network stabilization emphasize the active work that must be done to hold elements of the network in place. Disciplining and vigilant monitoring (Law 1986) emerge as crucial elements in standardization. The actors enrolled and incorporated into the network may need to have their properties renegotiated and redefined in ways that reinforce the governing network; in the case of social actors, this includes renegotiation of their interests, capabilities, and identities. A key insight of the actor network approach is that the identities of natural and human actors in the network are (re-)aligned so as to constitute stable, robust, and efficient media of circulation and replication of standardized methods, facts, and practices. These points are developed more fully below.

Standardization of science and technology

Although scientific knowledge is locally produced, and is always contingent on local circumstances, it can attain a kind of pragmatic universality. This universality is a complex and fragile social production, and sometimes a very expensive one. It requires the construction of an infrastructure (e.g., an actor network) that enables knowledge to be stabilized, transported, and reproduced in different times and places. Consequently, when science and technology are disseminated globally, success owes less to the intrinsic properties of facts and artifacts than to the standardized regimes that support their reproduction and stabilization. Although standardization of science is an important topic in science and technology studies, it is grounded, like many of the field's more central theoretical concerns, in social theories of modernity, where standardization is linked to a family of related concepts—industrialization, globalization, rationalization, mechanization, automation, and discipline. The IPCC, an organization explicitly formed to pursue a global science agenda, has done much to standardize the climate change science agenda and the scientific approaches to address that agenda (Box 1.1).

Many familiar discussions of standardization (especially, but not only, those in the Marxist tradition) center on the relations between rationalization, mechanization, automation, and the labor process. Partly inspired by the Marxist tradition, and partly also by existential philosophy and other European intellectual traditions, Foucault (1970, 1978, 1979, 1980) concentrated on standardization in areas of civil society besides the economy: social services, medicine, psychiatry, demography, and the human sciences. He tried to show that many of the themes associated with the rationalization of production (discipline, hierarchical control over labor processes, standardization) have become rooted in the most intimate areas of life (sex, education, personal identity, conceptions of language and meaning).

Box 1.1   The Intergovernmental Panel on Climate Change (IPCC)

The IPCC operates at two overlapping but distinct, levels: as a formal intergovernmental body and as a scientific and technical assessment body. Government representatives meet in formal plenary sessions to approve the options for assessment and the overall workplans for preparation of the scientific reports. They also review and accept the detailed scientific and technical reports as well as approve on a line-by-line basis the Panel's Summaries for Policymakers. It is through this intergovernmental review and approval mechanism that the work of the IPCC is connected to international and national policy concerns.

The detailed scientific and technical reports themselves are prepared through the cooperation of scientists and technical experts from around the world. Hundreds of experts are involved in preparing the different chapters of the reports; hundreds more are involved in providing expert peer review. These experts come from many countries and are trained in disciplines ranging from atmospheric chemistry to economics. They include university professors, researchers working in private industry and at national laboratories, and scientific experts affiliated with nongovernmental organizations.

Since its inception in 1988, the IPCC has prepared a series of reports and methodologies, including the 1990 comprehensive, three-volume assessment of climate change, which evaluated anthropogenic alteration of the climate system, potential impacts, and available response measures. This report became a standard reference, widely used by policymakers, scientists, and other experts. It was followed in 1996 by the Second Assessment Report, also in three volumes, which focused on the functioning of the climate system and potential changes to it resulting from human activities; potential impacts of climate change, adaptation strategies, and measures that could be adopted to reduce greenhouse gas emissions; and evaluating the economic implications of climate change, a task that involves assessing potential economic damages and the applicability of cost–benefit analysis to decisionmaking.

An important institutional innovation in the second IPCC review process was the inclusion of nongovernmental organizations (NGOs) and governmental policy advisers in both the formal reviewing procedures and, more importantly, in preparing the policymakers' summaries. These summaries provided a politically self-aware interpretation of the scientific and social scientific analysis. The meetings that led to the final drafting were, to some extent, tug-of-war affairs between the two sides of science: the analytical and the judgmental. This new procedure not only met the need for the politics of inclusion but also gave an air of legitimacy to the crucial interpretations of the findings. Thus, the IPCC came to be regarded as an active participant in the science/policy interface, and not just an adviser.

This bleak vision of disciplined social cohesion—like Weber's (1922) iron cage of rational efficiency, Ellul's (1964) society dominated by technique, Baudrillard's (1983) fanciful account of an epoch of simulations, and even Beck's (1992) risk society—calls attention to the dilemmas and compromises attendant upon the standardizing and rationalizing impulses of the modern condition. But movements toward defining social problems as rational problems to be solved by scientific knowledge do not necessarily exclude the possibility of local initiative or autonomy. The closely focused social histories that constitute an important part of the literature of science and technology studies present globalizing discourses as constructs that embody social commitments;

hence, standardizing processes are susceptible to social modification.

Latour (1987, 1990) provided an influential summary of the case study literature. He used the evocative metaphor of the *immutable mobile* to refer to the historical products of print and other media through which practices and perceptions are standardized, thus helping to shape stable networks on a wide scale and to transact actions-at-a-distance. The same metaphor describes standardization in both science and in technology (see Vol. 2, Ch. 6). Maps, measures, and other stable and mobile representations enable the operations at a center of calculation to be extended in space and time. Over time, more and more practices that once were locally diverse, reflecting contextual practices and traditions, become realigned as elements of a singular global discourse. Scientific observations and experiments, and technological innovations, can thus be reproduced at many independent points, linked together by the dissemination of documents, graphic representations, computer codes, and so forth; the identities of both nature and humans are redefined through this network-building process.

New social meanings and forms of life can arise through standardization. Anderson (1991) has argued in his influential work on *imagined communities* that phenomena of standardization play an important part in forming national identities, permitting geographically dispersed inhabitants to re-envision themselves as citizens of a common nation state with clearly demarcated, physical boundaries, and nationalized symbols.

Latour sometimes comes close to endowing specific forms of inscriptive technology with a life (or agency) of their own, contrary to the more relativistic lines of science and technology studies. As has often been noted (Collins 1985, Suchman 1987, Knorr Cetina & Amann 1991), written accounts of experiments, plans, blueprints, and maps by themselves do not assure compliance with an original project. They require local interpretation and extrapolation, often guided by hands-on instruction; as in the context of experimental replication, lingering questions often remain about whether the end result is the same as the original (as illustrated, for example, by patent disputes, Cambrosio et al. 1990). Shapin's (1984) notion of *virtual witnessing* also stressed the work that must be done by knowledge producers to secure the assent of distant observers. He argued that Boyle's experimental accounts in the seventeenth century were not primarily means for enabling the reproduction of experiments, but instead were descriptions that convincingly exhibited the actuality of the experiment to communities of readers who were in no position to see them directly or to replicate them.

These observations are compatible with Latour's point that network building requires the extension of an elaborate infrastructure supporting a prescribed standard use of an artifact or scientific program while maintaining the authority of the center. Pasteur, for instance, did not just send results out from his lab; he engaged in a prolonged program to convince farmers, vintners, hygienists, hospitals, and so forth, that he was acting in their interests, and that they ought to incorporate elements of his laboratory regime into their ways of life (Latour 1988). Woven into the practices Pasteur wished to disseminate was an embodied way of interpreting the world—an intensely political vision. Social histories of the development of electrical standards in the nineteenth and early twentieth centuries tell a similar story (Smith & Wise 1989, Schaffer 1992, O'Connell 1993). Latour's account suggests that the achieved fact of stable, standardized methods, techniques, and measurements cannot be explained as a simple function of inscription devices or other technologies but must be seen as a product of persuasion, negotiation, assent, and institution building.

As is implied in the above work, the reproduction of standards requires coordinating and co-producing global (i.e., centrally administered, context free) and local (i.e., regionally specific, context particular) activities (Porter 1992). The effective use of a standard need not imply a totalizing construction of the various orders of activity linked together by the standard. Standardization thus differs somewhat from Foucault's idea of discipline as a strict regimentation of the means through which actions are enacted and coordinated in detail. Indeed, as seen below, the use of allegedly universal, context-free policy tools, such as risk assessment or cost–benefit analysis, often leaves intact an underlying social plasticity and diversity that resists the imposition of centrally imposed controls. A further key point is that local skill, extending Foucault's (1980) notion of micropolitics, is crucial in relating global standards and knowledge to particular contexts (Bowker 1994), thus preserving an active space for local agency. Indeed, this local skill is widely seen as an important condition for the effective working of global systems of science and technology. This point is crucially important to evaluating whether or not policy tools can be implemented in different social contexts.

The production of standard measures, objects, techniques, and beliefs often requires the formation of relationships between initially unrelated activities. Friedman's (1989) historical study of Bjerknes' invention of the Polar front— a fundamental twentieth-century concept that helped give rise to modern meteorology—provides a parallel to climate change. Bjerknes exploited the wartime emplacement of ship and submarine monitoring stations in the North Sea by persuading military authorities to order the taking of windspeed and direction, water current, and temperature measurements at each station. These measurements, plotted on an organizational grid designed for other purposes, were used by Bjerknes as the basis for envisioning large-scale movements of air masses from the polar regions to northern Europe. Rudwick (1976) presented the similar case of protogeologists using mine shafts for arrays of probes into the distributions of underlying geological strata.

Establishing a standard geometry or metric is relatively simple when considered purely as a matter of calculation, but, when taken together with the project of building the necessary infrastructure, metrology begins to seem like moving mountains. Latour (1987) observed that the cost of building and maintaining the metric system greatly overshadowed that of more glamorous scientific projects. The abstract rationality proposed at an administrative center was but a tiny part of the overall story. To borrow an expression Sacks (1984) once used in a different context, the task was one of constructing an order at all points: countless road signs, tables, scales, records, forms, and so forth, all of which constituted the fabric of the network that eventually enabled a knowledge or practice that could meaningfully be seen as universal.

Finally, standardization involves a commonality of approaches and outlook on the world that can promote regimentation at the ideological as well as the material and social level. Shapin (1994) showed in detail how pre-existing social ties (in his case, seventeenth-century gentlemanly codes) facilitated the acceptance of scientific representations. Pyenson (1985) discussed the standardizing role of science in the broader context of cultural imperialism; metropolitan strategies of spreading science in a national mold contributed to implanting institutions and social order, as well as introducing a language of comparison whereby events in the colonies could be classified to fit the ruling categories of the home countries. As noted earlier, Marxist scholars have also linked automation and standardization to the spread of particular ideologies of production and control (Chandler 1977, Noble 1977, 1984). Others have noted how the appearance of climate change on the formal policy agenda has reinforced institutional integration agendas in the politics of particular regions such as the European Union (e.g., see O'Riordan & Jäger 1996).

Scientific discourses of policy and production

Public policy increasingly relies on technical knowledge, with the result that researchers have developed neutral, policy-relevant, scientific discourses. These discourses provide another pathway by which science overcomes spatial, temporal, and cultural barriers and achieves a practical universality. A similar discursive process emerges when science is harnessed to economic production through technological development (see Fig. 1.6). In interactions with the worlds of policy and production, the specialized knowledges, discourses, and practices of science are harmonized with those of bureaucratic and economic cultures. Competing claims of knowledge arising in the social–cultural realm are construed by contrast as local or particular as opposed to universal.

Although research on these topics is in tune with wider critiques of modernity in the social sciences, the fine-grained specificity of many science and technology studies explores more deeply the processes by which the global or universal vision comes to prevail over regionally or locally articulated ways of understanding nature. If an impersonal, technocratic imperative of science wrenches knowledge out of locally embedded, interactively constructed systems of experience (Habermas 1970, 1975, Beck 1992), empirical studies of science-based technologies and policy-relevant science make transparent the mechanics of this translation process. In Latour's (1993) formulation, such studies help to explain how the hybrid sociotechnical networks created by modern societies are artificially purified in both scientific and everyday discourses and are partitioned into either a nonhuman (natural) or a human (cultural) world.

The adoption of universal concepts and vocabulary—the globalization of scientific discourse—occurs plainly in the development of biomedical and agricultural technologies of worldwide application. Oudshoorn (1994) recounted how the concept of a universal woman was created as a part of the testing program for the birth control pill. When the makers of the pill could not discipline users in Puerto Rican clinical trials to behave uniformly, as generic women, they invented impersonal scientific units—the menstrual cycle and the woman-year—to convert women's disparate experiences to a common unit of measurement. Martin (1987) has shown the power of such expert languages to subordinate lay experiences of reproduction.

In the policy realm, the language of chemical risk assessment provides another example. Bioassays with animals often involve the flattening of observable differences in order to produce results that can be compared across species boundaries. The interpretive conventions of chemical testing programs may require that cancers at different sites be aggregated, that both benign and malignant tumors be counted for purposes of risk assessment, and that mathematical models be used to extrapolate from observed high-dose effects in animals to nonobservable low-dose effects in humans. These techniques downplay differences in test conditions and in response among species so as to furnish a seemingly rational and ethical basis for regulation (although, as discussed below, these conventions may be deconstructed by dissatisfied policy adversaries; for case studies, see Jasanoff 1986, 1990).

The universalism of technical discourses is often maintained through scientists' unstated naturalization of their own assumptions concerning social behavior; that is, scientists come to accept their own assumptions as natural and not open to question. Wynne has argued that such strategies are invariably at play when expert bodies establish and implement safety standards for hazardous technologies. In deciding upon suitable exposure levels for pesticide chemicals, regulatory agencies necessarily, although often inadvertently, make normative judgments about the way workers should behave (Wynne 1989a).

Standards for operating and maintaining technical systems contain built-in, although often untested and possibly erroneous, assumptions about contingent social factors, ranging from consumer or worker behavior to the remedial capacity of the law (Wynne 1988, Jasanoff 1994). The naïve sociology of the expert community, as well as the prescriptive social standards implied in institutional logics of policy and production, remains hidden behind safety standards seemingly dictated by nature and revealed by science. More generally, discrepancies between scientific cultures and traditional, indigenous, or lay cultures of knowledge are often represented in expert discourse as matters of scientific uncertainty, and hence as potentially amenable to reduction by science.

Failure to accept lay knowledge as relevant to science may give rise to a false sense of certainty and universality, as in Wynne's (1989b) study of British public health policies after Chernobyl. Here, experts omitted the critical variable of soil acidity from their calculations of radiation uptake by plants; sensitivity to local sheepfarmers' experiences with the variability of the terrain might have alerted the experts to how bounded, indeed localized, their own knowledge was. In Balogh's (1991) account of US nuclear power policy, by contrast, different systems of expert knowledge helped to deconstruct each other's hidden assumptions; in the process, expert and lay beliefs became enmeshed, achieved scientific status, and created a nation of nuclear experts everywhere.

The attempts of policymakers to reconstruct the causes of environmental degradation, especially in nonindustrialized parts of the world, offer additional examples of scientific expert discourses edging out competing causal narratives. Thompson et al. (1986) found that vast discrepancies in experts' estimates of per capita fuelwood consumption to explain Himalayan deforestation were attributable to their different cultural perspectives. Such politicoscientific narratives regularly combine accounts of nature with accounts of human actors, either assigning or removing human responsibility for perceived environmental harms. In India, this dynamic can be observed in disputes over the sources of flooding in the Indo-Gangetic plain. The mountains hypothesis favored by some experts holds that flooding below is a result of deforestation caused by the poor forest management practices of the hill dwellers. By contrast, the plains hypothesis favored by the tribals and their political allies holds that deforestation is not to blame for a problem that is occasioned in part by natural seismic forces and in part by the irrigation practices of lowland dwellers who have blocked and silted India's great river basins.

Similar examples have emerged from the field of environmental and development studies. Fairhead & Leach (1994) argued that colonial scientists and policymakers have for a century held to the notion that forest patches in Guinea's Kissidougou prefecture are relics of an earlier, more forested era. Although scientists disagreed about the precise origins of the supposed deforestation that led to the present mosaic of forest and savanna in the region, none sought to question the premise that inhabitants' fire-setting practices were responsible for creation of savanna in the region and its projected degeneration into desert. Fairhead & Leach combined data from modern satellite imaging, evidence from old maps and documents, and sophisticated oral histories, to construct a different longitudinal tale, integrating observations of nature and society. In their version the forest islands surrounding present-day villages— far from being relics—were formed through human settlement and management. Yet, the expert discourse of policymakers even today remains dominated by the modernist image of primitive, unscientific practices leading to desertification.

The Green Revolution is widely regarded as one of the foremost success stories of mobilizing science for policy in the twentieth century. It is, in this respect, a durable testament to the universality of modern science and technology. It also may well be the most thoroughly studied instance of technological modernization in the social science literature (Box 1.2). As such, it offers an extraordinarily rich site for observing the universalizing momentum of scientific knowledge, practices, and discourse, and the backlash against these—in turn prompting critical questions about the development and application of a global science of climate change.

Controversy and consensus

When science is produced explicitly to serve social needs, scientific discourses, however powerful, provide insufficient protection against the skepticism of receiving audiences. The degree to which scientists' simplifying assumptions are questioned or exposed to public criticism depends on the mediating role of communicative institutions, such as courts, regulatory agencies, expert advisory bodies, and the news media. In cases where science does become publicly controversial, as with climate change, experimental methods, instruments, analytic strategies, and even personal integrity, may all be intensively scrutinized by fellow scientists, the media, and the lay public—sometimes to the point where the scientific claim in question can no longer be sustained as credible fact (e.g., the cold fusion claims of the University of Utah scientists B. Stanley Pons and Martin Fleischmann).

Richards & Martin (1995) identified four major social science approaches to studying scientific controversies (Table 1.2): *positivist, group politics, sociology of scientific knowledge* (SSK), and *social structural*. These approaches differ along several dimensions, including whether the focus of study is inside or outside the scientific community, and the variables used to explain closure. Except for

---

Box 1.2   Science and universalism in the Green Revolution

There have been sharp disagreements over whether or not the Green Revolution led to unequal social impacts (landlessness, dispossession of tenants and landless laborers, unequal access to and benefits from technology, regional concentration of benefits), to intolerable levels of environmental degradation (soil erosion, land degradation, loss of crop genetic diversity), or to adverse health impacts from excessive use of pesticides. Even today, there is active debate on whether the Green Revolution was on balance "poor friendly," because it led to expanded food output and therefore to lower food prices, or whether the additional output either required additional price supports or found its way disproportionately to the export market and thus canceled much of the benefit to poor consumers. Most recently, debate has centered on whether the Green Revolution of the 1960s and 1970s was sustainable (Anderson et al. 1989, Shiva 1989, Hazell & Ramasamy 1991). Both the success and the failure stories hold important keys to understanding the phenomenon of co-production in global science policy.

The Green Revolution involved an internationalized arena of research that displaced the existing diversity of scientific approaches and agrarian practices, entailing manifold social struggles among indigenous groups, nongovernmental organizations (NGOs), development agencies, and development banks. The template for the Green Revolution in the decades preceding the Second World War was the US experience with hybrid corn, which rescued American agricultural science from its weak and pre-paradigmatic (to use Kuhn's term) status at the turn of the century. The Mexican Agricultural Program, established by the Rockefeller Foundation in Mexico in 1941, provided the globalizing pattern of upstream technology development and the subordination of indigenous agricultural science that would characterize the Consultative Group for International Agricultural Research (CGIAR) and other similar institutes.

The architects of the Green Revolution saw it both as a program to disseminate modern methods to the developing world's agricultural research communities and as a project to expand food production and feed hungry people. The Green Revolution reflected a socio-political ideology that may be called Productionist Malthusianism; this is the notion that the purpose of agricultural research is to expand output in order to head off famine caused by rapid population growth. Productionist Malthusianism became the core ideology in identifying and justifying research priorities: for example, a focus on research that could lead to new big-hit technologies that would expand output over large areas in preference to research on many different kinds of crops tailored to different growing environments; a preference for research on output-augmenting technologies rather than technologies that would reduce risk or increase the stability of production systems; and an emphasis on foreign-aid funding of international agricultural research.

---

the positivist school, which sees controversy over scientific claims largely as a struggle between superior and inferior knowledge, these approaches have offered a variety of social factors—scientific networks, government policy, social movements, class struggle—to explain both the origin and ending of disputes.

An important implication of the nonpositivist literature is that societies and groups within them construct what they elect not to know (whether explicitly or tacitly) just as much as what they claim they do know about nature and the environment. Studies in political science suggest, for instance, that the degree

Table 1.2   Four major social science approaches to studying controversies.

Approach	Focus of analysis	Main reason for closure of debate
Positivist	Inside the scientific community (on which outside events impinge)	Superior knowledge (for closing the scientific controversy)
Group politics	Outside the scientific community	Superior political/economic/social resources
Sociology of scientific knowledge	Inside the scientific community	Superior persuasiveness or networking ability in the micropolitics of the scientific community; superior knowledge/politics
Social structural	Outside the scientific community	Hegemony of dominant social structure

Source: Jasanoff et al. (1995).

of audience skepticism toward science correlates strongly with features of political organization, interests and culture, such as the distribution of power within government, the formal channels for public participation, and the traditions of governmental accountability to the public (Gillespie et al. 1979, Jasanoff 1986). Perspectives from cultural anthropology have persuasively linked skepticism toward experts to features of social organization that encourage blaming (Douglas & Wildavsky 1982, Douglas 1985, Thompson 1986).

Social arrangements promote not only skepticism and disbelief, but also credibility, by hiding from view—through varying institutional knowledge claims, practices, and discourses—the limiting assumptions that scientists make in order to produce relevant knowledge. Claims of (or attributions of) expertise, for example, may shield the constructions of scientific bodies from critical scrutiny except by their explicitly acknowledged peers (Merton 1973, Chubin & Hackett 1990, Gieryn 1995). Science is perhaps nowhere more exposed to skeptical review than in the intensely contested corridors of litigation and governmental regulation in North America (Brickman et al. 1985, Jasanoff 1986, Salter 1988). Here, deconstruction of scientific claims into their constituent components is routinely the order of the day, and technical debate takes the place of political consensus building and policy closure (Collingridge & Reeve 1986, Jasanoff 1989). But even in this environment, institutionalized stopping points, such as legal judgments or expert advice, can put an end to technoscientific conflict (Jasanoff 1990, 1995).

Legal proceedings and legal discourse are especially influential in producing facts from uncertainty, in part through techniques of boundary work that demarcate regions of profound social and cognitive indeterminacy—and even cognitive dissonance—into domains of evidence and fact finding. Because the legal process attempts to purify facts and holds them distinct from the means by which they were produced or evaluated for policy, criticism of scientific claims conducted through the legal process seldom engenders a reflexive self-awareness about the process of construction. Wynne (1982) showed how this supremacist tendency of the law aligned itself with the interests of the technoscientific community in the British inquiry on the Windscale nuclear fuels reprocessing plant. As in many US regulatory proceedings, the legal discourse of fact finding imposed a layer of objectivity on the underlying reality of different factual claims about safety, risks, and costs, reflecting different framings of the decision problem and opposing judgments about the trustworthiness of controlling institutions. In the guise of discovering the facts about nuclear safety, the inquiry served for all practical purposes as an instrument for making the facts, and thereby reinforced prevailing judgments about the integrity and authority of dominant social institutions.

Scientific advisory committees employed in policymaking offer a more covert, although equally powerful, form of legitimation for knowledge claims. Members' moral and epistemological commitments, ranging from a shared predilection for a high standard of proof to untested presumptions concerning how the world works, enter into assessments of the evidence. As in adjudicatory proceedings, expert bodies use the rhetorical strategy of boundary work to distinguish what counts as science from the surrounding matrix of nonscience, but this work remains for the most part unnoticed and unremarked by the agents themselves (Jasanoff 1990, Gieryn 1995). Engaged in the construction of knowledge, scientists return to the rhetorical repertoires of empiricism (Gilbert & Mulkay 1984) or essentialism (Gieryn 1995) to designate their shared viewpoints as science. Accounts authenticating particular sides in scientific controversies can then be reinforced by judges or other agents of institutionalized public authority.

Uncertainties generated by the interplay of social and political interests around science and technology seem to vary with distance from the point of knowledge production. MacKenzie's (1990: 371–2) notion of a "certainty trough" (Fig. 1.4) suggested that the perception of uncertainty may be highest among those "very close to the knowledge-producing technical heart of programs" and those most alienated from them, with a dip toward greater certainty in between. This schema suggests that technical consensus may increase if the distance between program proponents and opponents is reduced through policy change, as apparently happened in the case of US weapons policy under President Reagan (Box 1.3). In this respect, MacKenzie's reading of what underlies the formation of a technoscientific consensus around policy (i.e., the development of consensual values leading to consensual knowledge) was virtually the inverse of the account provided by Funtowicz & Ravetz (1990) of the progression from postnormal science, through more research, to the less contentious territories of professional consultancy and normal science.

Box 1.3   Inventing accuracy

MacKenzie's (1990) study tells the story of "inventing accuracy" in US and Soviet intercontinental ballistic missiles (ICBMs). For the reasons elaborated by sociologists of science and technology (Collins 1985, Bijker et al. 1987, Pinch 1993), the accuracy of ICBMs could not be subjected to definitive tests. The conditions under which tests were carried out were, always and inevitably, only an approximation to real conditions in times of war. The two superpowers were particularly at a disadvantage when seeking to interpret the results of each other's testing (based on highly imperfect knowledge), but controversies arose even within the United States about the reliability of national guidance systems. Again, as in the context of experimental replication, success or validity, in terms of the technology working, was a matter for open-ended negotiation.

The ozone case—science, policy, backlash

The foregoing account of scientific practices and discourse, and of standardization and controversy, allows us to reevaluate two radically different stories concerning international efforts to protect the Earth's stratospheric ozone layer—the case that many take as the paradigmatic example of successful global environmental policy. In one version, scientists discovered a potentially catastrophic environmental threat and persuaded policymakers to take timely preventive action, ratifying their commitment through landmark environmental accords, including the 1987 Montreal Protocol and its Helsinki, London and Copenhagen revisions (Benedick 1991, Parson 1994). In the second version, scientists eagerly told doomsday stories so as to secure more public funds for research, twisted and fabricated data, used unwarranted assumptions, and shamelessly manipulated the news media to win support for their project (Maduro & Schauerhammer 1992, Taubes 1993). Both stories enjoyed wide currency well into 1995, years after the signing of the Montreal accord. The scientist heroes of the first version—Paul Crutzen, Mario Molina, and F. Sherwood Rowland—won the 1995 Nobel prize for chemistry, at the very time that a conservative Republican-led Congress was considering legislation to repeal the US ban on chlorofluorocarbons. How could two such diametrically opposed interpretations of a major scientific result persist in rational, enlightened societies?

The constructivist framework of analysis provides some useful entry points for addressing this question. Like Rome, the scientific and policy agreements on ozone were not built in a day; they engaged the energies of many actors, with partially converging agendas, and never won the assent of all. The facts of the case may be set down, as is done in the following paragraphs, but the interpretations of the facts may vary widely. Indeed, the selection of the facts and their circumstances may be disputed. Yet elements of standardization, scientific consensus building, and eventual universalism are evident.

The US ozone research program began in response to the Congressional pressure triggered when two University of California scientists, Molina &

Rowland (1974), published their theory that chlorofluorocarbons used in such mundane sources as refrigerators and air conditioners could pose a threat to the stratospheric ozone layer. A US Congress broadly sympathetic to environmental concerns, and particularly sensitive to threats of cancer, authorized the National Aeronautics and Space Administration (NASA) in 1975 to mount an upper atmosphere research program. Over the next ten years, NASA developed a two-pronged effort geared to satellite development and to basic research in atmospheric science. Policymaking, too, moved haphazardly onward. In 1977 the US Congress banned nonessential uses of chlorofluorocarbons in aerosols, and an international meeting in Washington resulted in an agreement to cooperate on ozone research; and in 1985, 20 nations and the European Community signed the framework Vienna Convention (Parson 1994).

In May 1985 a British scientific group reported significant drops in stratospheric ozone levels beginning around 1980 (Farman et al. 1985). The British Antarctic Survey, which had been monitoring ozone from a Dobson spectrophotometer station in Halley Bay as part of a program begun in 1957, found a 40 percent ozone loss over Antarctica. NASA satellites, programmed to isolate extremely anomalous measurements for possible later rechecking (or *flagging*), had not yet recorded the hole. Ironically, Farman's group had delayed reporting their results because they had assumed that, if the low ozone levels were real, they would have been picked up by NASA's satellite equipment (Zehr 1994).

When the skeptical NASA scientists looked at their flagged data, they not only confirmed what Farman had seen but discovered a hole the size of the continental United States. The images of a "swirling dark hole surrounded by bands of color" provided an awesome, eerie spectacle on television and in the print media. These dramatic immutable mobiles (Latour 1987) "shook many policymakers into action by early 1986" (Roan 1989: 142).

The ozone hole provided further impetus to science and policy, but progress was neither smooth nor linear. NASA's Robert Watson saw an opportunity to orient his agency's science program more closely to international policy needs and he emerged as an effective entrepreneur and scientific network builder. An international scientific assessment, launched by NASA in 1984, reported in January 1986 that conclusions once based on theoretical projections were now being confirmed by observations. Although Farman had referred to the Rowland–Molina hypothesis in his paper, most scientists still stressed the need for caution about the causes of the ozone hole. Nevertheless, they wondered whether the hole could be an early warning sign of more severe changes to come. If chlorofluorocarbon emissions continued at 1980 rates, the NASA report said, the average amount of ozone loss would increase from 4.9 percent to 9.4 percent by the middle of the twenty-first century (Roan 1989). There were also disagreements over whether the ozone loss would be homogeneous or whether such average figures might conceal more extreme depletions in different parts of the globe, as Farman had found in the case of Antarctica.

Watson continued to strengthen the knowledge networks internally within NASA, nationally, and internationally. Working closely with the National Oceanic and Atmospheric Administration (NOAA), the National Science Foundation (NSF), and the Chemical Manufacturers Association, NASA organized the 13-person National Ozone Expedition to Antarctica in August and September, when ozone loss was at its height. NASA provided most of the money, but Watson worked in partnership with other actors, especially Dan Albritton (Director of NOAA's Aeronomics Laboratory), and his assistant Susan Solomon, who headed the expedition. At the end of the expedition, Solomon publicly reported, "We suspect a chemical process is fundamentally responsible for the formation of the hole" (quoted in Roan 1989: 172). But other scientists immediately contested the finding, reflecting a continuing disciplinary or paradigmatic split between atmospheric chemists and physical modelers such as those in the UK Meteorological Office and, especially, the Goddard Institute for Space Studies in the United States.

As debate and dissent persisted, Watson organized another large international body to assess global effects, the Ozone Trends Panel, comprising 100 scientists from around the world. He also commissioned and funded yet another Antarctic expedition, called the Airborne Antarctic Ozone Experiment. With more time to prepare and better awareness of what was needed, it was possible to deploy far more sophisticated equipment. This included the ER-2, a converted U-2 spy plane in NASA's possession, that was fitted out with new measuring devices to take readings at the core of the ozone hole. In addition, Watson was able to enroll 60 scientists into the new effort, as contrasted with the 13 participants in the first Antarctic expedition. Many of the new scientists were chosen from non-US countries in a deliberate move to internationalize the quest for answers.

Movement was occurring on other fronts as well. The chemical industry and several of the larger European countries had at first actively opposed the emerging heterogeneous network that was investigating the ozone–chlorofluorocarbon link. But by 1986 DuPont, the major US producer, acknowledged that substitutes for chlorofluorocarbons could be available and endorsed international controls. Breaks in the industry ranks, aggressive campaigning by international NGOs, and political leadership from the United States, several European countries, and the United Nations Environment Programme (UNEP) propelled the diplomatic process toward its most dramatic point of closure, the 1987 Montreal Protocol, calling for a 50 percent cut in chlorofluorocarbon production by the summer of 1999 and incorporating an explicit commitment to modifying these goals in the light of evolving scientific knowledge. A striking feature of this politicoscientific closure was that the international agreement pre-dated the resolution of controversy between the chemical and physical theorists about the causes of the ozone hole at a 1988 UNEP meeting of experts in Würzburg, Germany (Benedick 1991).

Thus, a monumental feat of globalization was the result of incremental, jerky, loosely coordinated, and mutually reinforcing initiatives at multiple, localized, centers of action (NASA, NOAA, UNEP, US Congress, Nordic countries, environmental NGOs, among others), with the constructivist dynamics of science, policy, economics, and civic activism more transparently in view than in more closely focused stories of scientific controversy.

Far from imposing a strict discipline, such a tale virtually invites different interpretations. Not surprisingly, both skeptics and celebrants of international environmentalism pulled from the tapestry of the ozone accords the threads and patterns that satisfied their need for less ambiguous narratives. At the same time, both sides remained wedded to an idealized and socially decontextualized picture of scientific discovery—the skeptics decrying what they saw as a perversion of true science, and the celebrants finding another confirmation of science's capacity for deliverance. Yet, in Geertz's (1973) terms, a *thick description* of the ozone depletion hypothesis would stress its multiply tested and embedded character, thus providing a potentially more robust framework for public affirmation of its credibility.

We turn below to some of the factors that prompt modern societies to seek disparate meanings in particular productions of science, without relinquishing their commitment to science's cognitive autonomy.

Climate change science as global knowledge

Science that seeks to understand global phenomena requires the integration of many fields of research, accompanied by an extraordinary invention and interconnection of measures, measuring devices, and cultures of measurement, as well as a process that one might call heterogeneous archaeology. Like other projects in environmental science, the science of climate change involves an investigation and integration of diverse domains containing records of past human activities and natural events. Unlike heterogeneous engineering in the construction of technology (Law 1986), the establishment of climate change as a scientific phenomenon is at once retrospective and prospective, reconstructive as well as constructive. Moreover, climate change science requires a resolution of local, regional, and global data to determine global signals and trends.

The sources of data used in measuring the Earth's past are wide-ranging: standard temperature records taken by government agencies; centuries-old descriptions, ships' logs, paintings of Alpine glaciers and outdoor scenes (used as observations, although often not intended as such); historical records of climate change found by drilling into ice cores, and reading the record of radio-carbon locked up in tree rings (Broecker 1992); temperature measurements around cities that must now be adjusted to compensate for the slight upward skew around such heat islands (see Vol. 3, Ch. 4). Patently social productions, such as parish records from previous centuries, may have to be related to obser-vations of nature, such as the chemical analysis of fossilized pollen. Many prob-lems of incompatibility, unevenness, and lack of standardization are associated with such aggregation of records. Means of interlinkage, of common identity, between such diverse entities are often attempted—sometimes successfully.

Even within a more homogeneous field, similar difficulties remain unre-solved. Temperature records are available only from sites that had the means of producing them. The strata in one regional ice core or the record of alpine glacier movements in one region may not generalize to another. Arctic ice caps do not necessarily record the same story that is read from Antarctic cores, and cores from various Greenland sites also vary among themselves. With respect to glacial movements, the Alps, the Peruvian Andes, and Chinese mountains all tell different tales. The complexities are compounded when one tries to factor out natural cycles and fluctuations from anthropogenic ones, a task that requires scientists to account for such divergent phenomena as large volcanic eruptions, changes in the ocean–atmosphere system, sunspot activity, solar wind, and so on, and to distinguish each of these from the effects of industrial or agricultural activity.

Instructive parallels to these problems can be found in the examples of acid rain and ozone depletion, both of which required the establishment and main-tenance of national and transnational monitoring networks. As described by Zehr (1994), the formation of the US National Acid Deposition Program (NADP), which by the mid-1980s included about 200 sites, became possible only when scientists agreed not to insist on measuring dry as well as wet deposition. Tech-nology for dry collection proved harder to design and standardize than for wet collection. Once established, the NADP flexibly permitted the problem of acid rain (its causes and its impacts) to be constructed differently at local, regional, and national scales. By contrast, ozone measurements were initially coordi-nated through a network of ground-based Dobson spectrophotometers. Efforts to calibrate these instruments in relation to the World Dobson Spectrophotom-eter Central Laboratory in Boulder, Colorado, were undercut by local variations in equipment upkeep, variant analytic practices, and the uneven global dis-tribution of instruments. These weaknesses in the local network prompted greater reliance on satellite techniques, which led in turn to an emphasis on global ozone depletion (as reflected in the satellite system's initial bracketing of extremely low readings), with consequent downgrading of the important regional and local variations picked up by the Dobson network.

Boehmer-Christiansen's (1994) analysis of the international bodies set up to advise governments on climate change during the 1980s provided one of the earliest case studies of scientific advice systematically produced to inform policymaking on a global scale. In her account, an early, somewhat politically independent, network of climate change scientists forged a successful alliance with environmentalists and clean-energy interests to promote widespread political response to their research agendas. This coalition was weakened when falling energy prices, privatization, and deregulation made it more difficult for governments freely to support the green agenda. The IPCC, a body comprising mainly scientists appointed by national governments, was formed in 1988 to play a less independent advisory role (see Box 1.1). In turn, Boehmer-Christiansen argued, the IPCC's influence eroded through its leaders' decision to adopt the pose of scientific neutrality and to redraw a sharp boundary between its own science and the world of policy. Insistence on science as an autonomous but capable tool for policy prompted science bureaucrats, as well as opponents of policy innovation, to focus on the figleaf of reducing uncertainty through more study. Boehmer-Christiansen argued that a more honest recognition of indeterminacy and the fuzzy boundaries and limits of science might have heightened the IPCC's influence while encouraging policy development.

More recent sociological analysis of the IPCC's use of global science (Shackley & Wynne 1996, Shackley et al. forthcoming) suggests that indeterminacies in climate-change knowledge (and perhaps in the climate itself) were indeed constructed by the IPCC and global climate modelers as determinate uncertainties. But to dismiss this process as merely serving scientists' interests misses the complexity of the hybrid world of science and decisionmaking. The IPCC leaders' actions were dominated by an overriding concern to generate a global consensus on the nature and magnitude of climate change risks. Furthermore, the IPCC was concerned not only with scientific but with policy consensus. It thus spent enormous energy on negotiating policy summaries of the science, involving government officials, industry lobbies, and environmentalist NGOs with scientists in the process. Although this frustrated many scientists, who felt that the diversity and sharpness of scientific stances were narrowed into an overly homogeneous account, it can be seen as an entirely necessary part of building useful knowledge in a culture that unites science and policy into a common worldview.[1] A question that opens up around this unprecedented institutional

---

1. As a point for reflexive analysis, constructing a state-of-the-art review of social science findings on science and public policy involves a similar blurring and flattening of disciplinary and individual perspectives. This problem is recognized by the participants in *Human choice and climate change.*

exercise is how this common science–policy culture relates to the other parts of the scientific and policy worlds.

The IPCC's efforts to provide usable knowledge resonated with the belief of sponsoring policy organizations that climate change is a manageable problem within the framework of existing institutions and cultures. IPCC experts engaged in long and often painfully self-searching attempts to reshape their own cognitive categories in order to meet the challenge, as in continuing debates over how to define the *global warming potential* (GWP) of greenhouse gases, whether to abandon the concept as unscientific or embrace it as a useful policy construct, and, if so, how to deal with the concept's indifference to historical responsibility for greenhouse gas emissions. Global warming potential served in this context as a kind of cognitive *boundary object* (Star & Griesemer 1989) facilitating communication across different cultures. Such efforts to construct new discursive objects at the nexus of scientific and other cultural domains are an important, and often overlooked, dimension of stabilizing scientific knowledge for use in policy.

Going public: the cultural shaping of credibility

Given the local and contingent character of most scientific knowledge, how does the public come to accept scientific claims—especially the universalizing claims relevant to climate change policy—and their legitimacy as a basis for policy? Although social construction, standardization, and the discursive strategies of modernity tell parts of this story, other lines of research are also needed to explain how the public understands and contextualizes scientific knowledge offered by experts and how different political and cultural contexts shape the look and content of policy-relevant knowledge.

Public understanding and perception of science is a key to supporting the authority of modern political institutions, since these derive their legitimacy from experts' framings of problems and policy options (Ezrahi 1990, Beck 1992). Interpretive work on the public understanding of science has begun in recent years to challenge the naïve, binary formulation of the problem that still dominates much policy, and much quantitative survey research: the public either understands or does not understand science, as measured by criteria deemed applicable by scientists. (See Ch. 4 for a more extensive discussion of the lay/expert dichotomy.) A more complex account emerges from sociological work that examines the issue of scientific understanding from the standpoint of its capacity to sustain social relations and social identities. Political and institutional analyses of science for policy offer a useful supplement. They underscore the role of political culture in foregrounding particular styles of scientific inquiry and interpretations of science, within which tacit social values may be privileged or reinforced. Public rejection or indifference may thus arise not from misunderstanding but from a dissonance with framing commitments and moral visions embedded in such scientific and policy definitions. How consensus in policy-relevant knowledge is formed and maintained across different scientific cultures and political regions has emerged as an important problem for social science analysis.

Public understanding of science

The public's understanding of science has been investigated in part through quantitative studies of the way lay people perceive technological risks. Influential psychometric studies by Fischhoff et al. (1978, 1981) and other colleagues (Slovic et al. 1980, 1985, Slovic 1991) suggested that public risk perceptions are correlated with such factors as the respondents' prior experience with the risk (e.g., its novelty or familiarity), the voluntariness of the exposure, and the dread quality of the risk (e.g., its suddenness or its magnitude). A widely cited conclusion from these studies is that the public's relative ranking of risks differs from that of experts, who are assumed to have a truer perception of the real possibilities and magnitudes of risks associated with hazardous activities. The wide-ranging implications of these studies were reflected in varied ways in US environmental policy through the 1980s and 1990s: a turn toward using relative risks to set federal and state policy priorities (US EPA 1987); a growing emphasis on risk communication, designed to bring lay and expert risk perceptions into closer alignment (US NRC 1989); and a call for delegating risk decisions to trained experts in place of the lay public and its elected representatives (Breyer 1993).

Despite its impact on policy, the psychometric approach to studying risk perception is subject to several important criticisms. Although perceptions of voluntariness may affect people's responses to information about risk, there is growing evidence that these perceptions are themselves socially constructed in relation to people's historical experiences (Krimsky & Plough 1988) and their expectations of order and accountability in public life (Wynne 1987). Whereas the psychometric approach takes the factors that shape public response to be objective attributes of a given risk, interpretive work on public understanding indicates that the fundamental framing of what counts as a risk is shaped by factors such as the social experience that people have of the institutions that control the risks (Rayner & Cantor 1987). Through ethnography, participant observation, and in-depth interviews, research on the public understanding of science has sought to avoid the a priori assumptions of psychometric studies about what constitutes actual risk or real science. Research in this genre shows emphatically that people always encounter science imbued with social interests of some kind—for example, in the way risk is framed as an object of investigation—regardless of the motives of its producers and disseminators.

In efforts to characterize people's mental models of climate change, researchers found that respondents held a mixture of correct and incorrect beliefs. For example, they tended to confuse stratospheric and tropospheric ozone, misidentified stratospheric ozone depletion with the greenhouse effect, and showed little awareness of carbon dioxide from burning of fossil fuels as the primary cause of climate change (Bostrom et al. 1994, Read et al. 1994). Although such studies provide useful first cuts at characterizing public understanding, the focus on individuals' correct versus incorrect beliefs misses the complexity of ethical and social commitments underlying people's concerns about the environment (Shackley & Wynne 1994; also, see Ch. 4). Dickens (1992), for example, examined the effect of fatalism upon people's appetite for scientific knowledge and their judgment of the worth of that knowledge. After the hurricane that hit the south of England in October 1987, he found that many people rejected scientific weather forecasting on the grounds that it represented excessive confidence and control over matters that should be recognized as essentially uncertain. Dickens argued that people tacitly accepted limits on agency through the moral stance that too much control of nature was bad medicine, and risky. Their rejection of forecasting thus represented less a passive condition of ignorance than an active moral position, countering what was seen as an irresponsible culture of scientism.

The finding that public scientific knowledge embodies social relational norms as if they were natural is highly significant to public understanding of scientific knowledge. It implies that no one can define the boundary between public views of nature and culture or between the domains of natural knowledge and social–cultural knowledge. Hence, it reinforces the problematic nature of the models of science and policy discussed in above. Many constructivist analyses converge on this key point, whether they see scientific knowledge as a vehicle for central domination of marginal cultural identities (McKechnie 1996), as a scientistic reduction of kinship relations and cultural patterns to laboratory manipulability (Strathern & Franklin 1993), as a risk of being ensnared in nuclear propaganda (Michael 1992, Wynne 1992a), as an alien culture of assumed control and standardization (Wynne 1992b), or as a tacit imposition of unacceptable social and familial relations (Martin 1987, Layton et al. 1993). Public readiness to understand science is fundamentally affected by whether the public feels able to identify with what it takes to be science's unstated prior framing of social relations. This is directly relevant to the question posed earlier about how scientific knowledge and policy agendas co-produce the framing of such issues, but in forms that may lack resonance with various publics.

The work of Wynne and others in the field of public risk perception (Wynne 1980, 1987, 1992b, Freudenberg 1992) has borne out the existence of socially laden meanings embedded in scientific communication, as well as the un-reflexive nature of science in relation to the public's understanding of these meanings. The scientific framing of a natural discourse about objective risk magnitudes often conceals founding assumptions about the trustworthiness of the controlling institutions. Yet public groups can usually access historical experience of relevant institutional behavior and thus test the tacit framing assumptions of science. Public reactions that policymakers or their expert advisers see as subjective or irrational may represent a legitimate rejection of science on many grounds different from technical ignorance: lack of trust, irrelevance, and different models of agency (Krimsky & Plough 1988, Wynne 1995).

Trust

Sociologists have long recognized the pervasiveness of trust relations in society (Garfinkel 1963, Gambetta 1988, Shapin 1994). Research on public responses to science and technology and public risk perceptions asserts the relevance of a trust relationship to acceptance of scientific knowledge. The basic framework of public responses depends largely upon the experience and perception of the trustworthiness of relevant institutions or social actors, not upon the under-standing of technical information framed in ways that implicitly take trust for granted (Wynne 1980, 1982, 1992a, Rayner & Cantor 1987, Renn 1992). People seem capable of informal scientific savvy (Prewitt 1982, Brown 1987) when it is attuned to their own concerns and needs. From this vantage point, the public's apparently confused identification of aerosol cans and industrial pollution as causes of climate change (see above) appears not as mere ignorance or misconception but as the extension of a generalized, historically grounded, distrust of industry (see Ch. 4).

Relevance

Lay people may ignore scientific knowledge because they regard it as irrelevant, even though experts assume it ought to be central to them. Emergency information around hazardous facilities is routinely ignored, even ridiculed, by ordinary people because to them it is naïve and unrealistic about real conditions that would prevail after a major accident (Wynne 1989b, Bradbury et al. 1994). Lambert & Rose (1996) found that lay patients suffering from high cholesterol dismissed medical advice about dietary fats because the advice was not clear enough about different kinds of fats in a way that they found relevant. Wynne (1992a) noted that sheepfarmers in northern England were offered (for them) useless whole-body monitoring of radiation when they had asked for their water supplies to be analyzed after the Chernobyl accident; the scientists' failure to produce knowledge on which the farmers could reasonably act adversely influenced the farmers' judgment of the credibility of the controlling institutions. Prewitt (1982) observed that scientists' own unreflective social assumptions about what is relevant to lay people are built into scientific knowledge for public communication, and equally into the design of survey instruments to test public understanding. For these reasons Layton et al. (1993) questioned whether such surveys test public scientific literacy, or whether they measure only the degree of the public's social conformity to the stereotype held by many scientists and survey researchers.

Models of agency

Lay people often have no social freedom or power to use available scientific knowledge in the ways experts assume they can. In other cases they may deliberately eschew the freedom even if they have it, or they may be uncertain whether or not they have it and therefore be unwilling to risk the consequences of testing their power. In other words, tacit models of social agency (having the ability to affect choice) underlie assumptions about what people understand, or are capable of understanding, about science. If available knowledge is useless, or even (socially) dangerous, there may be no point in taking on the often considerable costs involved in assimilating it. Furthermore, these contours of social agency become so much a part of people's very identity that they shape the boundaries of recognizable natural knowledge. As Michael (1992) observed, people who are always uncertain about whether they can act on the scientific knowledge presented to them find the relevance or usability of that knowledge problematic. They may thus calculate how much understanding they are willing to own, negotiating agency in the process. This often hidden process may then be recorded, misleadingly, as simple ignorance or resistance.

In many public encounters with science, this basic cultural–epistemological conflict is obliquely played out between, on the one hand, scientists' assumptions of certainty, control, and management and, on the other hand, popular assumptions of intrinsic indeterminacy, need for adaptation, and the dangers of control. These are conflicts not merely over what scientific knowledge is capable of controlling but what scientific knowledge should be expected to control.

Social construction of ignorance

Social analysis has explored the roots of public indifference to science. Using discourse analysis, Michael (1992) examined how lay people reflected on various possible relationships between themselves and science, as well as various meanings of the word "science". Interview data showed a rich and active reflection on people's own social position (and agency) in relation to what they took to be science. This underlying relational process shaped the scope of their interest in the cognitive content of science and their sense of trust in or identification with it. As Michael observed, people's reflexive social positioning in relation to science took different forms, depending on circumstances. In some cases it resulted in distrust and deliberate avoidance of radiation science because it was thought to be imbued with the interests of promoting nuclear power. Ignorance was actively constructed and maintained, even though some respondents were scientifically qualified. It was part and parcel of the dynamic construction of social identity.

In other instances ignorance was constructed with a more positive purpose. For example, Wynne et al. (1990) found that volunteers in a program for monitoring household radon levels constructed in effect a collaborative division of labor with the scientists conducting the study, having offered their homes as laboratories in the public interest. Their vicarious participation exempted them from having to understand the technical details. Their elected scientific ignorance was not a mere vacuum of knowledge, but a construct built on a particular tacit model of social relations and identity.

In the case of radiation workers at the Sellafield nuclear reprocessing plant, the same authors found a similarly unsuspected positive social construction of ignorance. The researchers expected that these workers would have an especially powerful self-interest in understanding the science of radiation risks, but they found that this was not the case. Indeed, the workers vigorously justified their ignorance on several grounds. First, there was plain economy—if they started to follow the disputed scientific arguments, they would never get to a resolution of those arguments. Second, to follow the science would only mean they had to confront endemic uncertainties, which would not only be unsettling but perhaps even dangerous. Finally, they emphasized that there were already several groups of experts in their own company and in regulatory bodies whose job it was to know the science and to fold it into design and working procedures. Thus, to show an active interest in understanding the scientific knowledge of radiation risks would be a direct threat to existing social arrangements, signalling distrust of those actors and arrangements that were meant to protect them.

Technical ignorance became in this case a reflection of *social intelligence*, with science being understood in terms of its institutional dimensions rather than its factual content. Of course, the Sellafield workers were not naïve enough to imagine that they could trust existing social arrangements without any critical attention; in fact, relations between management and workers at the company were by no means totally harmonious. However, their attention was devoted not to the socially irrelevant science of radiation, but to the relevant social evidence for or against trust in the experts and other actors, on whom they knew they were inevitably dependent. These findings reinforce those of Rayner (1986) among hospital workers whose jobs involved the use or disposal of radioisotopes.

Public knowledge for public action

Research that relates the acceptance of science to forms of social and political organization challenges the notion that public attitudes to risk can be satisfactorily explained in terms of individual misunderstanding or competence deficits. On the contrary, the factors that influence people to seek varying degrees of proof and to accept different types of scientific evidence of risk appear to be neither entirely random and arbitrary nor matters of unconstrained individual choice (on the rejection of the *individualist fallacy*; see, for example, Schwarz & Thompson 1990). Social and political studies of environmentalism and environmental regulation interpret public risk perceptions and their uptake into policy as being deeply embedded in a social and historical context.

Cultural framings of environmental threats
Cultural theorists from Durkheim to Douglas have noted that beliefs about nature and society are encountered in some commonly recurring clusters that appear to correlate with forms of social organization. Three dominant belief systems about environmental problems have been described most often in the literature:

- catastrophist or preventivist (nature is fragile)
- cornucopian or adaptivist (nature is robust)
- sustainable developmentalist (nature is robust within limits) (Cotgrove 1982, Douglas & Wildavsky 1982, Jamison et al. 1990, Rayner 1991).

Thompson et al. (1990) contributed two additional myths, further differentiating the image of nature as cornucopian:

- lottery-controlled cornucopian (nature is capricious)
- freely available cornucopian (nature is resilient).

What unites these accounts is a belief that human views of nature, and associated views about human nature, are socially constructed, yet not infinitely variable. Such views grow out of a need to preserve important ordering elements in social relations, such as hierarchy within a community (*grid*) or the firmness of its demarcation from other communities (*group*) (Douglas 1970). For example, bureaucratic organizations (high-grid and high-group, in Douglas's terms) are most inclined to believe that nature, although not infinitely malleable, can be managed by means of appropriate, technically grounded and formally legitimated rules; in contrast, market or entrepreneurial cultures (low-grid and low-group) seem more likely to subscribe to a cornucopian view of nature—that is, the capacity of nature to rebound from assaults without active human intervention.

In reducing the complexity of human–nature interactions to a few fixed types, the categorizations of cultural theory run up against many theoretical hurdles. Institutions and their members appear to be inflexibly bound together in hard and fast belief systems, denying the ambivalence and plasticity of response uncovered in the literature on public understanding and risk perception (but see Rayner 1992). Cultural theory offers no systematic explanation for large-scale social and ideological changes, such as the shift from a pollution-centered to a sustainable developmentalist philosophy of environmental management in the 1980s. Science, technology, and expertise play a passive or subordinate role in this framework, as expressive or rhetorical resources to be enrolled by the dominant cultural types (see, for example, Thompson et al. 1986), rather than as centers of distinctive knowledges, discourses, and persuasive power. Nonetheless, this approach calls attention to the connections between social relations, beliefs about nature, and the choice of management strategies. In this respect, cultural theory offers a useful counterpoint to the approach of Lave & Dowlatabadi (1993), in which scientific uncertainty is first generated by scientific inquiry and then is accorded different weights and values by optimistic, pessimistic, or moderate publics.

Empirical studies such as the Thompson et al. (1986) account of Himalayan deforestation militate against taken-for-granted, naturalistic explanations of environmental risk phenomena. This perspective helps to illuminate how scientific problem definitions and paradigms may be framed in ways that reflect underlying cultural presuppositions, including different beliefs about the resiliency of nature (optimism versus pessimism). Thus, culturally preconceived ideas about human agency and the impact of human actions on the environment may tacitly shape understandings that appear to have been objectively given by scientific inquiry.

Risk, science, and political culture
Historical and comparative studies of the risk policies of industrialized nations also contradict the assumption that environmental policy evolves according to a universal model of progress, in which uncertainties are gradually reduced and increasing knowledge sustains more and more sophisticated policy. The very

methods by which states garner and sort the information that guides their social policies depend on their forms of organization and their internal divisions of power. Thus, Porter (1992, 1995) described how the production of objectivity through the standardization of weights and measures in the nineteenth century went hand in hand with the liberalization and centralization of the state. In Britain, for historical and cultural reasons (pragmatism, class considerations, lack of resources), nineteenth-century inspectors settled upon persuasion rather than prosecution to enforce safety requirements against powerful factory owners; one result was that local, case-by-case negotiations came to substitute for objective, quantitative, and legally enforceable standards in some regulatory programs (Brickman et al. 1985, Vogel 1986). Institutional developments in the twentieth century continued to reflect these historical dispositions, particularly in British policymakers' skeptical attitude toward developing uniform technical standards and formal decisionmaking methodologies.

Jasanoff's (1986, 1987, 1989) comparative studies of chemical risk management illustrate the interdependence of politics and technical expertise in the making of regulatory policy. Decisionmakers in political cultures with open access to government and high public expectations of accountability display a greater preference for formal and quantitative decisionmaking techniques than their counterparts in more closed and consensual societies (Brickman et al. 1985, Vogel 1986). The heavy US reliance on mathematical modeling and other statistical tools in assessing and managing the socioeconomic impacts of environmental pollutants is an example of this phenomenon. Cultures that rely more on informal relations within institutions and networks for problem solving create fewer demands for formal methodologies to legitimate scientific findings relevant to policy. Credibility, both within and outside the networks, is secured through relations of personal trust or institutional credibility instead of through appeals to a higher scientific authority (see also Ch. 5).

Cultural differences among and within nations are also reflected in the relative willingness of state institutions to acknowledge the existence of scientific uncertainty. In general, policymakers may be more prepared to tolerate a fuzzy line between known and unknown if they are equipped to investigate uncertainty and manage it through scientific methods that are themselves subject to political negotiation (Jasanoff 1991a). Lacking such traditions and means of control, decisionmakers may be reluctant to admit uncertainty openly and to act only on the basis of knowledge deemed secure by experts. Technical uncertainty, in these settings, may be identified as an expression of social uncertainty or as a threat to social order. It follows that a society may elect to protect its centers of established authority in the guise of maintaining a sharp line between what is known and unknown about nature (Wynne & Mayer 1993).

For all of these reasons, the scientific constructs by which government agencies rationalize their policies comprise, in effect, some of the most significant sociotechnical hybrids produced by modern societies. Negotiations among competing visions of nature, culture, human agency, and the objectives and boundaries of rational inquiry, underlie every stage in the production of regulatory science (Jasanoff 1990, 1991a). Yet, when it comes to generating *public* authority, the same processes are also generally effective in separating this world of troublesome hybrids and boundary objects into distinct, uncontaminated domains of science and policy (Douglas 1966, Jasanoff 1990, Latour 1993).

The environmental knowledge of social movements
Social movements and nongovernmental organizations (NGOs) have begun to play an increasingly visible and influential role in producing environmental knowledge, complementing the historically more entrenched collaboration between scientists and state institutions. Participation in policy by these relatively unstructured and dynamic groupings has not only created new facts and displaced earlier orthodoxies but has exposed anew the maneuverability of the boundary between nature and culture or science and society.

In their comparative study of environmentalism in three European countries, Jamison et al. (1990) argued that social movements beginning with a shared cosmology, grounded in an ecological worldview, ultimately diverged in their choices of emphasis, issue, and target. Sweden, for example, with its technocratic and socialist political tradition, was less receptive than Denmark and Norway to the themes of human domination of nature. Gottweis (1995) suggested that the meaning of biotechnology was deconstructed in Germany by social movements, who saw the technology, in the light of Germany's particular history, as embodying threatening and controlling approaches to the definition of truth, life, historicity, and otherness.

Working in the British tradition of sociology of scientific knowledge, Yearley (1991, 1995) pointed to the opportunities and dilemmas confronting environmental NGOs as they become not only alternative sources of scientific knowledge and expertise in industrial societies but also the targets of deconstruction and epistemological relativism (see also Beck 1992). By adopting greater technical expertise, environmental NGOs run the risk of undermining their role as authentic representatives of lay values and interests. The magnitude of this risk becomes apparent when one considers the levels of skepticism toward scientists uncovered in a 1989 Euro-barometer survey of European public attitudes: fewer than 50 percent of the responders "strongly agreed" or "agreed" that "scientists can be trusted to make the right decisions" (Topf 1993: 109). Nonetheless, the NGO role in making and certifying scientific knowledge is likely only to grow with time; its force, moreover, has begun to be strongly asserted in the international arena (Yearley 1996).

We have looked at the co-production of scientific knowledge and the elements of public acceptance or rejection of that knowledge. Analyses of both of these processes at the global level follow the general trend of developing environmental science in international organizations and tying the scientific knowledge so produced to potential policy responses of international organizations. Crossnational institutions, both formal and informal, are critically important to the internationalization process.

Knowledge without borders

Studies of the ways in which environmental science gains worldwide acceptance are still in their infancy, although such research could greatly enrich traditional game theoretic approaches to understanding international conflict and cooperation (see Vol. 3, Ch. 2). It would, for example, transcend a rigid separation of factual knowledge (assumed to be universally available) and values (defined, problematically, as independent individual preferences). This section looks at the topic of internationalization in several perspectives: the globalization of research systems and agendas; the formation of transnational knowledge/policy coalitions; and the creation of two specific international science programs, the International Biological Program (IBP) and its successor, the International Geosphere–Biosphere Program (IGBP).

The production of global knowledge

The process of globalization in such areas as climate change involves not only the international coordination of assessment and policies but also the difficult task of harmonization at the cognitive level. *Cognitive* here includes the ways in which the objects of research are defined, as well as the choice and detailed implementation of preferred methodologies, basic models, and concepts. A few insights into this process have begun to emerge from work now in progress (Elzinga 1993a,b,c). First, developments in the internationalization of science correspond quite closely to more general patterns of social construction and standardization of science noted in earlier sections. Second, aggregation at the global level—of disciplines, interests, resources, institutions, and so on—raises issues of trust, credibility, public understanding, and political assent similar to, although less well understood and perhaps more challenging than, corresponding issues encountered in national science policy domains. The particular manifestation of these issues in the context of computer simulation modeling is examined in detail later in this chapter; this discussion is complemented by the examination of integrated assessment models in Volume 3, Chapter 5.

Finally, supranational science programs present distinctive sites for observing the co-production of scientific and political order because their authority is still emergent and the processes through which order is being created are less thoroughly naturalized or socialized than in most national programs. What remains as a largely open question for now is whether, and how, international research organizations—which almost by definition stand somewhat apart from established national processes of producing public assent and trust—will be able to secure the public authority needed to channel their technical findings into policy prescriptions for a heterogeneous world.

The globalization of science on the organizational plane is motivated by the escalating costs of research programs, the need for cost sharing on megascience projects, the urge to win prestige for national research projects, and the desire to spread knowledge to scientifically less advanced countries. Transnational programs dependent on international funding contribute to the definition of needs and priorities, and international scientific associations and journals with international advisory boards bring additional structure to the emerging global forums for research and assessment.

However, the rhetoric of globalization and internationalization does not always harmonize with the actual commitments that prompt national governments and bureaucratic or policy cultures to join the globalization choir. Countries lagging in areas of advanced technology, for example, have a definite interest in promoting the rhetoric of internationalism in the hope of obtaining access to results produced in other nations. In practice scientific internationalism sometimes signifies its very opposite: a strategy of serving national political or economic interests or, in short, business as usual (Ancarani 1995). Even among industrial states, a considerable gap yawns between the ideal of internationalism articulated by academic scientists and the practical internationalism of the combined processes of commercial conglomerates and bureaucratic policy cultures in different countries. Studies of scientific collaboration between unequally placed partners, such as Brazil and Germany (Velho 1994), indicate that the dominant nation's research goals and priorities may be reproduced without change or challenge in the allegedly collaborative context.

International scientific research is influenced not only by dominant national interests and priorities but also, both organizationally and cognitively, by existing international research programs. Scientific internationalism is not simply a matter of cooperation across existing research agendas; in the context of climate change, there has been a reorientation of perspectives so as to reposition work in national investigative contexts as part of an emerging *Earth systems science*. Scientific practices in various countries are actively redesigned and linked together to define, in effect, problems and conceptual frameworks at what is construed as the international research front. Alternative concepts and approaches are thereby partially foreclosed as these alternatives also have to be marshalled and expressed at a fully international level. Increasingly, for instance, Antarctic processes are interpreted with the help of global models, that is, models of major Earth systems, each comprising a specific "sphere" (Elzinga 1993a,b,c).

For climate change research, common approaches are developed across disciplinary boundaries, taking as the object of study the atmosphere, troposphere, stratosphere, cryosphere (ice), biosphere, geosphere, lithosphere, and hydrosphere. Other approaches focus on various marine and terrestrial ecosystems and land use. Data from these systems are assembled into a variety of computer simulation models, with general circulation models (GCMs) at the top of the hierarchy of complexity. An important research objective is to determine the crucial parameters of global change and, if possible, to predict its dynamics. Predictive assessments, in turn, lay the basis for negotiating and elaborating international regimes to protect the climate and environment, thereby co-producing new forms of politics at the global level (Yearley 1996).

Key to the harmonization of cognitive perspectives is the notion of *system*, which plays a strongly regulative role in international research agendas for climate change. In biology, the systems approach is reflected in modeling of population ecology and behavior, ecological energetics, sociobiology, and ecosystems modeling. In molecular biology, research on the likely impact of new life-forms entails systemic approaches to risk assessment. In the Earth sciences, theories of plate tectonics and seafloor spreading provide a systemic and integrative basis for many previously unrelated fields—and some newer techniques (such as remote sensing from satellites) reinforce this trend. In climate research, GCMs and other models attempt to grasp the entire atmosphere as a system influenced by other dynamic Earth systems, such as the ocean and polar ice caps. State-of-the-art GCMs combine the dynamical interaction of oceans and the atmosphere in predictive simulations up to centuries into the future.

In turn, efforts to quantify and simulate Earth systems favor certain disciplines and approaches over others, for instance, by giving more weight to the present than the past, to near-term meteorological timescales over geological ones, and to physical processes (which may be more tractable at global levels of representation) than to biological parameters. Such influences on the perception and definition of the central objects of research in turn generate tensions between the pace-setting climatologists and certain more traditional categories of Earth scientists, with associated struggles over who should have priority in defining baseline data and key parameters for the models used. The use of technologically sophisticated methods such as computer simulations also give rise to political problems of inclusion and exclusion, particularly for viewpoints from less scientifically and technically resource-rich states and regions of the world (Gibbons et al. 1994; see also Ch. 5). Thus, globalization as a cognitive process involves many organizational changes and intellectual constraints which shape the scientific enterprise and its forms of political embedding.

The globalization of beliefs and worldviews, and their integration into transnational policy agendas, tended to fall outside the purview of academic work on international relations until the 1970s (see Ch. 5). Analysts have since recognized that, in view of the complex interdependencies in world politics, states neither possess complete information—thereby leaving the way open for political action by nonstate knowledge bearers—nor behave like rational individual actors (see Vol. 3, Ch. 3). Some scholars acknowledge that ideas play a functional role in promoting and maintaining international cooperation by helping states to identify their interests and establish agreements, around which expectations can converge (Adler 1987, Adler & Crawford 1991, Haas 1992, Goldstein & Keohane 1993). Environmental ideas, moreover, are increasingly seen as promoting new forms of association. Of particular relevance to climate change policy are epistemic communities and international institutions—two instruments by means of which the internationalization and diffusion of environmental knowledge can take place, as discussed in the international relations literature.

Epistemic communities as agents of policy change
Drawing on constructivist ideas in science and technology studies, a group of scholars has attempted to understand the role of consensual knowledge in securing international cooperation. These theorists argue that consensus about policy-relevant knowledge contributes to the formation of regimes;[2] especially in the environmental arena, emergent regimes are driven not only by state power but also by the scientific understanding of ecological systems. Accordingly, their work is marked by an emphasis on understanding how perceptions, beliefs, and knowledges shape the expectations and preferences of major actors, both within and across states (Haas 1992).

The research program focusing on *epistemic communities* rests on a broad collection of theoretical assumptions about knowledge production and international cooperation. Decisions, according to this analytic program, are taken by individual decisionmakers, who opt for procedural rationality and do not engage in continuous information searches about the state of the environment and the effectiveness of their own efforts. Changes in policy are therefore most

---

2. Defined as sets of implicit or explicit principles, norms, rules, and decisionmaking procedures around which actors' expectations converge in given areas of international relations.

likely to occur following well-publicized shocks or crises, at which times decisionmakers recognize major anomalies and pursue new policy patterns (see Ch. 5). Most important, however, is the assumption that scientific knowledge enjoys special status in the policymaking of modern nation states as a consequence of the post-Enlightenment faith in science, the functional needs of bureaucratic and administrative agencies, and the social authority conferred on professionals in industrial societies.

The growing importance of scientific knowledge in international politics accounts for the rise of epistemic communities, defined as networks of knowledge-based communities with an authoritative claim to policy-relevant knowledge within their domains of expertise (Haas 1992). However, these networks are also seen as carriers of particular value orientations toward the issues in question, thus as promoters of particular normative (policy) commitments, connected with this knowledge. Members, who are often professionals from different disciplines, are assumed to share the following characteristics:

- shared values or principled beliefs that provide a rationale for social action by the members of the community
- shared causal beliefs or professional judgments that provide analytic reasons or causal explanations to justify linkages to possible policy actions
- common notions of validity, consisting of intersubjective, internally defined criteria for validating knowledge
- a common policy enterprise, centering on a set of problems that have to be tackled, presumably out of a conviction that human welfare will be enhanced.

Often constituted in the wake of attention-focusing environmental disasters, epistemic communities are thought to promote effective environmental regimes, even in the absence of leadership by strong states, which realist international theorists long considered a necessary precondition for cooperation.

Political scientists differ in the amount of explanatory weight they are willing to grant to epistemic communities. One line of criticism, informed by Durkheimian sociology, argues that more important than the epistemic communities are the epistemes: deeply embedded, widely shared, and often unquestioned cultural beliefs are seen as constitutive features of a historical era and as driving forces for patterns of international behavior (Foucault 1970, Edwards 1996). Others believe that the epistemic communities approach pays insufficient attention to the influence of states over the formulation of the information acquired for policy. This line of work acknowledges the cognitive dimension introduced by Haas and others, but then reasserts the (sovereign) role of states and formal institutions in controlling the cognitive domain (Higgott 1992, Milner 1992, Risse-Kappen 1994). Still others have questioned whether common beliefs can be identified when members of scientific research programs simply

51

paper over differences in their beliefs for instrumental reasons. There are some disagreements as well about the long-term effects of consensual knowledge, specifically whether knowledge, once agreed on, will continue to be interpreted similarly over time, or whether decisionmakers will gradually diverge in response to different political needs and historical moments (Adler & Crawford 1991, Haas 1992). Finally, some have wondered whether epistemic communities should be seen as independent motivators of action, since they do not play a role in all instances of regime formation (Nollkaemper 1992, Risse-Kappen 1994).

Whatever their precise significance as players in the international arena, clearly epistemic communities not only form around many environmental issues of global concern, but they can impart a distinctive normative or political cast to debates on these subjects. Jasanoff (1996b) argued that understanding the potential role of epistemic communities for relations among states and citizens requires an examination of the social and cultural commitments and conditions that make such communities coalesce or cohere as political actors. In other words, epistemic communities should be understood within a framework of kinds of *social solidarity* (see Ch. 4). This approach is consistent with that of political scientists, who have suggested that, for analytic purposes, epistemic communities might better be seen as dependent than independent variables. But constructivist analysis goes further in proposing, in line with the co-production model, that epistemic communities represent the institutionalized vehicle for expressing alternative knowledges and value commitments that may have been systematically excluded by the formal knowledge-making and knowledge-utilizing machinery of modern nation states. That is, it coincides with the new emphasis given to informal networks and civil society associations in policy formation processes (see Ch. 5).

Science and technology studies point to various avenues through which communities of scientists may form and gain political influence. At the deepest level, Ezrahi (1990) attributes the rise of the modern liberal state to the instrumental use of science and scientific communities as a means for securing public assent to governmental authority. According to this analysis, a commitment to solving problems through science is woven into the democratic state's preference for self-justification through the common public witnessing of political actions—a form of legitimation that Ezrahi traces back to the rise of experimental science in the Enlightenment period (Shapin & Schaffer 1985). With greater historical specificity, studies in comparative environmental politics suggest that real or apparent epistemic convergences concerning particular causal paradigms may come about through independent developments in individual nation states (Brickman et al. 1985; see also Benedick 1991 for evidence of this dynamic in the formation of the Montreal Protocol); however, Jasanoff (1986) and Jamison et al. (1990), among others, cautioned that domestic politics can function as a source of epistemic divergence as well as convergence. Haas's comprehensive case study of the Mediterranean Action Plan suggested that the UNEP played a dominant role in fostering common research agendas, professional reward systems, and standardized measurement techniques; these activities drew scientists from many Mediterranean countries into a shared commitment to ecological thinking (Haas 1989, 1990). Mukerji's (1989) sociological account of US oceanography assigned a more self-conscious agency to the state, which in this case provided the resources for maintaining a reserve labor force of scientists to supply policy-relevant knowledge on demand.

Epistemic communities, then, cannot be explained simply as sharers in a common epistemologically driven project for the preservation of particular environmental values. Rather, international epistemic groupings appear to be held together in many instances by heterogeneous, often loosely coupled, interactions among emerging disciplines or ideas, detailed processes of socialization and professionalization, strategic allocation of public resources, and commitment to political values of decentralization and civic involvement. Such groupings may never achieve either the boundedness or the internal cohesion and common purpose that one intuitively associates with the term epistemic community. From a constructivist standpoint, these are contingent entities, representing temporarily stable but institutionally fragile conjunctions of social, ethical, and cognitive forces. Nonetheless, such networks can serve as effective levers for international agenda setting and policy coordination.

International institutions

International institutions are discussed in some detail in Chapter 5 and hence require only abbreviated treatment here. Nonetheless, they occupy a distinctive place in the model of co-production schematized in Figure 1.6. International institutions are quintessential cultural hybrids; they serve as meeting grounds for the exchange of knowledges, discourses, practices, and goals from each of the ideal cultural types engaged in the production of global environmental knowledge. This perspective points to a somewhat different interpretation of their role in linking science and collective decisions from that adopted in conventional political analyses of the international system.

Briefly, international institutions are ordinarily seen as agents whose primary purpose is to compensate for the lack of evenness on the playing fields of multilateral action. In a recent analysis of bodies active in the area of environmental decisionmaking (Haas et al. 1994), international institutions are credited with the ability to increase governmental concern, in part through the creation of knowledge; to enhance the contractual environment for bargaining, in part through monitoring of environmental quality and performance; and to build national capacity, in part through provision of technical expertise. Implicitly, in this model, international institutions are responsible more for harmonization and technology transfer than for policy innovation. Their main contributions are to facilitate negotiation, disseminate knowledge, create transparency, and improve the condition of the weakest players.

The constructivist approach points to an altogether more proactive and (cognitively as well as politically) more dynamic reading of international institutions in environmental decisionmaking. They, like epistemic communities, should be seen as additional sites for the production of new forms of knowledge, beliefs, and political action—not merely as cognitively passive agents that facilitate convergence toward some independently ordained, optimal end-point of international bargaining. The power of international institutions flows importantly, in this view, from their ability to reframe problems for collective solution, to and redefine the boundaries and parameters of relevant knowledge (and thus of imaginable policy action), and to determine the rules of participation in knowledge creation. These themes are elaborated below.

Three levels of internationalization

Brief histories of two international organizations provide illuminating windows on the dense intertwining of scientific, bureaucratic, economic, and social factors, at national as well as international levels, required to bring such programs into being, sustain them over time, and enable them to link into policy debates. These insights into how areas of scientific study obtain places on the national agenda, and how international organizations set boundaries and direction for research, are directly relevant to climate change, which now has its own place on national and international science and policy agendas.

The national origins of international science

The political recognition of ecology as the science of the environment began with a 1968 decision by the US Congress to endorse an American contribution to the International Biological Program (IBP). This initiative acknowledged the appropriateness of the big-science model for biological research through the establishment of the Biome projects, large-scale investigations of the structure and functioning of ecosystems with the help of computerized modeling (Kwa 1993a,b). But systems ecology had occupied only a marginal position within the life sciences up to this point. Why did the US Congress decide to promote this field in 1970, and what implications did this support have for the internationalization of ecology?

Ecology benefited from the intense awareness of pollution as a problem following the publication of Carson's *Silent spring* in 1962. Identifying ecology, and in particular systems ecology, as the kind of basic science needed to solve

54

environmental problems such as pollution proved to be of the utmost importance. Crucial hearings were held in 1967 by the House Committee on Science, Research, and Development, at which 16 experts testified on the desirability of funding the IBP. It was the image of ecology as a managerial science, capable of systematically understanding nature and warding off catastrophe, that most powerfully appealed to a newly sensitized Congress.

The overarching conceptual frame that emerged from the expert testimony before Congress was of nature as a system that could be controlled and managed and of ecology as the right scientific tool to do the job. According to the (then widely fashionable) cybernetic systems theory, a system should be in steady state or in homeostasis. If the system is in good order, enhancing productivity (or finding its limits) could be a goal of management; if the system is not, irreversible damage, or a catastrophe, could occur. Especially in the 1960s, politicians and bureaucrats were swayed by images of both nature and society as closed systems that could be manipulated and controlled from a position outside or superior to the system (Baritz 1985, Gibson 1986, Kwa 1994, Edwards 1996). The IBP and systems ecology evidently gave members of the US Congress a remarkably persuasive vision of how both social and natural systems could be brought under rational management and control.

Ecology's managerial claims, however, grew from modest beginnings that needed to be synchronized with more firmly institutionalized research agendas. Quantification and mathematization had occurred in ecology since the 1930s, but these approaches remained confined to small ecological systems of one or two species in the field of population ecology (Kingsland 1985). Odum and his fellow radiation/ecosystem/systems ecologists, although themselves naturalists by training, set out to invigorate what they considered an outdated discipline. Odum, in particular, launched ecosystem ecology, both in a synthesis of theoretical and methodological approaches and in formation of crucial linkages with the Atomic Energy Commission (AEC) and, later, to two ecologists at Oak Ridge National Laboratory (ORNL), Auerbach and Crossley, who appointed Odum as consultant in an effort to raise their own professional status within their institution.

In little more than a decade, the ecology groups at ORNL and the University of Georgia grew from small and insignificant to nationally known centers of ecology, with the AEC as their common patron. With the US government's funding of the Biome projects through the IBP, systems ecology, the product of this unexpected collaboration, finally gained national and international visibility. The internationalization of this scientific style shows how localized purposes and practices can be imported into standardized methods and natural knowledge systems, with influence far beyond their original point of development.

Defining an international field of practice

The IBP supplies an informative historical parallel for current global environmental science by showing how a transnational epistemic community of scientists emerged through a set of formal conversations or discourses linking knowledge about global phenomena to prescriptions for international political action. The ten-year effective life of the IBP can be broken down into three key periods for the purposes of this analysis: preparation (pre-1964), planning (1964–7), and implementation (1967–74).

During the first period, competing versions of the program were imagined, different topics proposed, and the range of possibilities reduced. In particular, this period gave rise to the IBP's preoccupation with *biological productivity*, a central metaphor of the kind Kwa (1987) found mediating between ecology and science policy in international biological research. A metaphor in this context is a linguistic figure that serves to abbreviate the distance between heterogeneous contexts, enabling analogies to be drawn between social and political ideas on the one hand and scientific knowledge on the other (Mitman 1988, Taylor 1988). It can be regarded as a boundary object in the sense described earlier (see p. 37), mediating not only between different subcultures within science but between scientific and policy cultures.

A focus on the discursive construction of the IBP at the planning stage is appropriate precisely because such documents as plans and scenarios were produced before the object that they purported to represent (here, the research program) had come into being. Latour & Coutouzis (1986) argued that such prospective representations at a time t_0 should be seen not as a forecast of the future at a later time t_1, but as instruments for achieving the future shape of the project, that is, for bridging t_0 and t_1. As linguistic tools, documents such as plans also permit observations to be abstracted and externalized from the immediate locus of production, and so to serve as instruments for building coherence across different contexts (for a discussion of the externalization of observation in scientific practice, see Pinch 1985).

Successive attempts to formulate the precise scope of the IBP led eventually to a definition of its target audiences and its position in relation to other programs of international research, most notably the projects of the International Council of Scientific Unions and of agencies in the United Nations system. Moving in a space already defined by other international organizations, international public opinion, national governments, and the scientific community, the IBP's early planners eventually elected to work on topics that would be:

- politically salient without being controversial
- at the forefront of research but not covered by any other international organization
- interdisciplinary in ways also permitting international comparison.

The productivity of biological communities was selected as the topic that would best meet all of these socioscientific criteria. For example, the fact that biological productivity could be represented in terms of energy flows (a measure of energy consumption by living beings) had three consequences: it allowed organisms of very different kinds to be compared within a common taxonomic system; it made measurement and comparisons at different locations possible; and it also facilitated international cooperation. This case thus provides an interesting parallel for decisions within climate change science to focus on concepts such as global warming potential, which similarly facilitate global comparison and exchange.

The early implementation of the IBP, then, can be seen as another example of co-production at several levels. First, the discursive framing of the program's objectives changed over time as different actors, with different backgrounds and interests, entered the negotiations. Second, the plans created at this stage aimed at and achieved a dual result:

- they provided a cognitive framework for the integrated interdisciplinary description of natural events at dispersed sites of investigation
- they drew a map for the development of international scientific (and in turn policy) collaboration.

The epistemic commitments of the IBP (i.e., its definition of objects and methods of research) and the shared internationalist values of its members reinforced each other at one and the same time through the development of common discursive interactions.

Institutionalizing global knowledge

The IGBP—particularly through its framework activity on global analysis, interpretation, and modeling—offers an instructive study in the joint formation of an international institution and the framing of global scientific knowledge. Conceptually, the IGBP is influential in harmonizing perspectives, linking and coordinating research efforts, standardizing datasets, and laying the groundwork for integrated analysis and assessment. A significant conceptual bottleneck is the lack of an agreed classificatory logic from which to identify model parameters relating to land use, vegetation cover, and the like. Agreement on classification, as noted in the earlier discussion of standardization, is an important element in building consensus (Running et al. 1994). Administratively, the IGBP's steering efforts are devoted to orchestrating interactions among four levels of activity and funding flows: individual researchers, the national effort of a given country, internationally designated IGBP core projects, the program as a whole (*Global Change Newsletter* 1994: 17). Activities at the conceptual and administrative levels inevitably build upon each other.

The IGBP is divided into six core projects. Each operates under a Scientific

Steering Committee whose chair is a member of the Scientific Committee of the Steering Committee of the IGBP, a body that includes scientists mainly from the industrialized world, especially the United States and Britain. A conscious effort is made to match national research activities in various countries to the IGBP core projects. In some cases, this may require a shift in perspective or a widening of the research focus flowing from established national priorities and commitments. For instance, "where there has been a strong impetus from meteorological departments, the emphasis is likely to be on `climate change' rather than the wider scientific issues of `global change'" (*Global Change Newsletter* 1993: 11).

Research under the IGBP umbrella is classified according to a three-tier system that determines what is considered central and what is more peripheral. "Core research" is that which falls directly within the domain of, and thus addresses the problems and goals of, one of the six IGBP core projects. "National or regional research" is deemed to be closely associated with the objectives of an IGBP research plan but may have other overall objectives coordinated at the national or regional levels. "Relevant research" has no formal affiliation with the IGBP but is expected to make indirect contributions to the IGBP agenda. All IGBP researchers are urged to acknowledge their affiliation in everything they publish, as part of a conscious visibility raising—but also community building—strategy; researchers are advised, for instance, that formal recognition that a project is part of the IGBP may assist in obtaining funding for such work in one's own country (*Global Change Newsletter* 1993: 15). The Scientific Steering Committees of the six core projects play an important part in the IGBP's cognitive boundary work by determining what is relevant to their particular core. Each committee has a Core Project Office; Australia, Britain, Germany, the Netherlands, Switzerland, and the United States each hosts an office.

Although the IGBP's structure appears to be top-down and strictly hierarchical, the six core projects evolved from relatively wide discussion in appropriate scientific communities. Thus, the operational plan for one core project was developed over a period of three years, with over 300 scientists participating in assorted workshops and meetings along the way. For the most part, important decisions are made without causing many ripples outside the immediate IGBP research community. Recently, for example, a distinction has been drawn between two possible approaches to orchestrating research, a distinction that could have significant consequences for global participation in the politics of climate research (Barron 1994). One approach, termed the *rich tapestry model*, conceives of the IGBP as a broad umbrella under which a host of national and individual contributions could take place, with an emphasis on communication and collaboration. The other, somewhat tighter, approach is the *flagship model*, which would involve clearer task delineation, closer integration, and far-reaching harmonization of perspectives, field experiments, and modeling—all of which would enhance the IGBP's visibility and standing as an autonomous international program. Significantly, the latter model would also imply a stricter form of dirigism that could widen the gap between those who belong and those who do not.

Observations such as this underscore the significance of the IGBP as a site of cognitive and normative co-production. Under the guise of elaborating a research program, scientist-politicians are (perhaps inevitably, given the magnitude of their project) laying the ground rules for cognitive and political participation. Yet, as research evolves and knowledge grows, such socioscientific framing choices will tend to grow less visible, unless of course they are brought to light through controversy, whether originating within the research community (Balogh 1991) or coming from outside.

Modeling environmental systems and climate change

Computer modeling of environmental systems and its connections with policy have received relatively little attention from the social sciences. Even less has been published on the specific problem of climate modeling, although work is in progress and some is in print (Messner et al. 1992, Edwards 1996, Shackley et al. forthcoming). To date, published work in this field (Crouch 1985, Bloomfield 1986, Taylor 1992, Kwa 1993a, Buttel & Taylor 1994, Oreskes et al. 1994, Shackley & Wynne 1996, Shackley et al. 1995, forthcoming, Wynne & Shackley 1994) corresponds well with the thematic issues raised in earlier sections of this chapter about the construction of authoritative knowledge and its influence on policy. The insights about problem framing and its relation to knowledge, as well as more focused issues about standardization and closure, for example, are equally applicable to formal computer simulation models. This section briefly reviews work on the emergence and critique of simulation models of ecological systems and Earth systems; it then analyzes the construction of climate models and related knowledge for policy.

As noted above, modeling of systems behavior is an important technique for attempting to overcome the problems of uncertainty for decisionmaking (the so-called trans-science problem). Models predicated on the analysis of physical and social systems hold out the promise of understanding, and hence being able to manage, unimaginably complex phenomena through the prediction and control of salient variables. Models reduce complexity to simplified prototypes that are thought to capture all relevant relationships among major contributing factors. The impetus for model building on a grand systematic scale is one of the markers of modernity. Social theorists have written about the scientific response to the breakdown of earlier certainties and the rise of insecurity in the modern period. Particularly in the social sciences (economics, demography, psychology), massive social dislocations and the concomitant growth of centralized state bureaucracies are associated with the emergence of scientific techniques of classification, measuring and modeling (Foucault 1978, 1979, 1980, Hacking 1983, Porter 1986, Nowotny 1990).

The relative opacity of physical systems modeling has hindered comparable research on the initial framing choices that guide the development of such methods. However, historical work such as Kwa's (1993b, 1994) on the IBP demonstrates that the very construction of the systems approach in environmental modeling is tied up with a variety of cultural–political contingencies. Ashley (1983), in his powerful critique of global systems models, drew attention to the invisibility of the initial framing assumptions once models are in place and operational within research communities. Although criticism remains robust, attention focuses on frame-internal questions and no longer grapples with the overarching presumption of centralized, all-comprehending knowledge and control (which Ashley—echoing Foucault 1980—called "the eye of power") that models simultaneously reflect and reinforce. Nor does such criticism reach into the covert transformations and manipulations of the social world brought about as a result of the inevitable dislocation between these integrative presumptions and the more disparate, pluralistic and autonomous worlds the models claim only to describe.

The application of computerized models to policy raises additional issues related to the relative invisibility of the underlying epistemological commitments. Synthetic environmental modeling reinforces particular orientations surrounding policy cultures. Such modeling is almost explicitly instrumental. It generates knowledge not simply with the aim of understanding and explaining the nature of the climate, or oceans, or whatever is to be modeled, nor simply as a way of organizing or systematizing what is known. Rather, modeling is routinely construed both by modelers and their governmental patrons as a means of determining what controls the behavior of a particular output variable or set of variables (e.g., methane emissions from paddy fields). Policymakers thereby hope to ascertain what steps may be taken to remedy the perceived environmental threat. Inherent in the modeling exercise, then, is the presumption that the system under study can be modified, managed, or controlled along pathways that the model makes visible; policy institutions that become linked to such an epistemic attempt link their own policy credibility to the avowedly apolitical credibility of such modeling knowledge cultures.

The ambiguity of models

Simulation models of environmental systems, including the effects of human interventions, use mathematical equations to represent and combine elements of system behavior in appropriate forms. Equations are then solved, using input data to reach simulated output states that represent predictions of the system, under assumed conditions, at a certain future point. The construction of such simulation models of environmental phenomena gives rise to several ambiguities. To begin with, such models not only use, but in effect define, the characteristics of input variables. Knowledge is drawn from different research contexts and is formalized through mathematical equations that are assumed to represent behavior across the system in question. For example, such a model might combine soil chemistry with atmospheric chemistry, atmospheric transport, hydrology, and plant physiology to produce simulations of the effects of acid aerial emissions from given sources on distant forests. This synthesizing effort may produce knowledge that appears more relevant and tractable to policy than the separate knowledges from all the original specialties involved. The building of such models also abstracts relevant behavioral relationships in numerical form from each context. Like any other similar scientific practice, such abstraction from a larger conceptual system can discard qualifying conditions and variances that may be part of the normal scientific currency of each contributing scientific subspecialty.

The definition of system boundaries, as well as the selection of what is fixed behavior as opposed to dependent relationships, reflects not only understandings of the objective properties of the system but also the interests and commitments of the analyst. Modelers' prior conceptions of feasible points of intervention and management, and assumptions about the active properties of system components, including human agents, are reflected in their models (see Taylor 1992 and the discussion of the IGBP above). The selection of end-points for modeling (e.g., climate warming, forest damage or soil erosion) may call for assumptions by scientists. Even when the end-points of interest to policy are clear, scientists exercise judgment about what precise model output variable (or combination of variables) adequately represents these end-points. Assumptions such as these may be discussed and intensely debated by members of the modeling community, but their discretionary choices may not be transparent to nonmembers, including policy-users, once the model is constructed. (This is a general predicament of science for policy (e.g., Ashley 1983, Jasanoff 1990) and is not confined to formal computer models.)

Possible variance and even indeterminacy of system response may be artificially suppressed in simulation models when relationships between variables that can be specified precisely and with confidence under a particular set of conditions are taken to stand as universal behavioral regularities (Taylor 1992, Cartwright 1994). In these ways, scientists' accounts and understandings of what is technically feasible to represent and model may influence policy-makers' beliefs as to what can reasonably be predicted or simulated through such models.

Cartwright (1994) noted that the term *model* suggests a more tentative attitude to the explanations in question than would be warranted in a fully fledged well-confirmed theory. She suggests that *theory* implies a set of covering laws that embody and determine the regularities observed in relevant parts of system behavior, whereas *model* implies a less comprehensive or imperialistic approach to explanation. A model is potentially a more pragmatic and instrumental tool, and one for avowed policy uses. Yet this introduces further important ambiguities concerning the understanding and interpretation of models within scientific and policy settings.

First, as noted earlier, the observation and mathematical simulation of behavioral relationships that are regular under certain conditions offers no guarantees that such regularity prevails universally, whether spatially or temporally. Yet the assumed universality is often built into modeling practice and science-policy discourse in such a way as to establish an assumption of determinism in system behavior. In theory, such assumptions should be tested and, if incorrect, revised by validation processes; in reality, validation can only be partial and incomplete, especially for large, complex models. Thus, modeling may inadvertently suggest that assumptions have been independently tested when they have been falsely confirmed. Therefore, a relevant question is whether, in the explicit treatment of (deterministic) uncertainties by systems modeling, deeper uncertainties concerning possibly less stable nondeterministic behavior are being overlooked and obscured from policy consciousness.

A second form of ambiguity concerns the intellectual status, role, and identity of formal computer models. In professional communication, models may be well understood to be only formal conventions bearing questionable relationship to the far greater complexity they seek to represent. As such, they may be represented as cognitive heuristics that help advance theoretical diagnosis and understanding by identifying discrepancies and anomalies. In policy settings, however, the same models may instead be treated as truth machines, capable of producing realistic representations and authoritative predictions for policy. Scientists engaged in formal computer modeling are sometimes ambiguous about the status and function of models when addressing policy audiences (Wynne 1984, Oreskes et al. 1994, Wynne & Shackley 1994). They may trade on the truth machine image in policy contexts where the demands of decision-making stifle free expressions of uncertainty; in less political situations, they may emphasize the model's more modest identity as a research heuristic.

This kind of discursive flexibility has been described as a commonplace of scientific communication (Gilbert & Mulkay 1984), but, in domains where science and policy are closely connected, the ambiguity of models may give rise to conflicting political interpretations. Many of the skeptical attacks on global warming predictions in the United States, for example, have gained political credence by debunking an overly deterministic vision of climate modeling (Balling 1992, Michaels 1992, Bailey 1993)—one that most modelers would reject anyway as a mere caricature of their more complex and highly deliberative professional activity.

Global systems models—a historical outline

The first systems models relevant to global environmental thinking came from a tradition different from that underlying modern climate models. Whereas the latter are principally concerned with interactions in the global biogeosphere, with human dimensions in some cases added on as exogenous variables of inputs and impacts or as separate models, the earlier tradition took human variables as endogenous and focused on simulating the interactive effects of different human actions on the global environment.

The Club of Rome's famous report, *The limits to growth* (Meadows et al. 1972), was the first published attempt to simulate the cumulative future impacts of separate trends in population growth, pollution, resource depletion, food production, energy use, and economic growth. Although its dire forecasts of impending environmental collapse had a powerful impact, it also encountered severe criticism on several fronts: for example, that the models used extremely crude indices of conditions such as pollution; that the model dynamics took no account of feedbacks representing human adaptive responses, but simply extrapolated trends into the future; that other adaptive responses such as technological innovation and resource substitution were ignored; and that unrealistically standardized regional averages were used to represent variables and processes known to be highly heterogeneous. The epithet "Malthus with a computer" was coined to satirize what were seen as false or implausibly pessimistic assumptions built into the models, even though they were presented as scientific (Cole et al. 1973).

Faced with criticism about using an unduly mechanistic model, the authors of *The limits to growth* emphasized that they had not been assuming no human response as a realistic scenario for the future, but that their computer predictions had been intended precisely to induce a policy response by showing the consequences of not changing course. This acknowledgement of the rhetorical role of confident scientific representations exposed the instrumentally constructed boundaries of science for policy (Jasanoff 1990, Gieryn 1995), but disclosure occurred only after the model's predictive capability had been publicly called into question. The authors displayed a greater appreciation of complexity in a later, more reflective review of modeling, aptly entitled *Groping in the dark* (Meadows et al. 1982). Ashley (1983) takes even this review to task for its failure to step completely outside the frame of predictive modeling; also see Bloomfield (1986) for an analysis of *The limits to growth* from a sociology of science perspective, calling attention to the mutual shaping of modeling techniques, objects of modeling, and the instrumentalities available for this purpose.

Similar complex linear-optimization models of global energy systems were developed over the same period, some of which attempted to incorporate environmental dimensions. The global energy model (or suite of coupled models) developed by the International Institute for Applied Systems Analysis (IIASA) was the leading example, supporting the scientific status of the policy conclusions drawn by the IIASA energy modeling group. In 1984 an ex-member of the modeling group published a critique showing that the claimed dynamic solutions of the models were in fact completely constrained by a few key input assumptions. The outputs could be generated from the inputs on a pocket calculator, leaving the hundreds of parameters and variables in the models doing little except creating an impression of dynamic complexity (Keepin 1984). Sensitivity analysis on model variables and parameters had not been performed, even though this was a recognized norm of good practice in this domain. Further, the coupling of the models had been so confidently expected and described that even fellow modeling specialists (potentially the best source of professional criticism) were unsure whether the coupled models were actually in operation rather than still only exogenously connected. Thus, both insiders and outsiders to the modeling process failed to realize the considerable amount of informal and unaccountable judgment and negotiation, including social and policy assumptions, that were necessary to interpret and construct the actually quite narrow and limited model results into policy-relevant scientific conclusions (Wynne 1984).

Modern forms of global modeling—integrating human and ecological dimensions but with a primary focus on human activities—also build on a basic systems approach. An important example is the IMAGE model of the Dutch RIVM research group (Rotmans 1990, 1992). This uses a far simpler model of climate than the state-of-the-art physical general circulation models, but by so doing is able to incorporate as model variables a much wider range of anthropogenic disturbances, such as detailed models of trace-gas emissions, models of economic effects and feedbacks, and a land-use model based on actual land uses. Such models are potentially more attractive to policymakers than GCMs because they make available more human variables both as drivers of the simulated system (potential policy levers) and as outputs or effects (potential focus for remedial or adaptive attention). These human variables offer possible focal points for policy implementation (see Vol. 3, Ch. 5).

Significantly, however, the modeling efforts built on GCMs have proved to be much more influential in policy arenas such as the IPCC and national legislative forums. This may well reflect the greater influence and prestige, as well as the greater historical and political institutionalization, of the epistemic tradition of physics and physical modeling (Friedman 1989, Wynne 1994, Edwards 1996), although the promise of even this tradition is still largely unrealized (see below).

Ecological models
Scientific modeling of ecological dynamics similarly incorporates representations of pastoralist practices and the scientific modelers' assumptions concerning the likely points of policy intervention. This is most clearly seen in the definition of system boundaries and the choice of essential system categories and units. These models also illustrate the reduction of complexity and flattening of variability that characterize modeling keyed to policy requirements.

Taylor's analysis of a systems model of African pastoralist ecology is instructive in this respect. After the drought crisis of the early 1970s, international aid agencies requested such a model in order to identify the kinds of management policies that could be adopted to avoid desertification, economic collapse, and starvation of that region's population. As Taylor notes (1992: 123), the model "was not simply representing the nature of the system, but rather [was] a science of representing in relation to someone's conception of possible interventions." In this case, the system boundaries took for granted, and thus naturalized, such external factors as international trade rules and the scope of intervention granted to international agencies. The behavior of internal actors such as pastoralists was assumed to be homogeneous and no different in principle from natural stimulus–response dynamics. This allowed the model structure to be specified in ways that, perhaps unwittingly, fixed various nature–society relationships that could have been represented instead as more flexible and indeterminate, following more complex and differentiated rules. For example, the model built in fixed relationships for rice farmers' encroachment upon river basin grazing by livestock, thereby objectifying and universalizing this relationship in the system under analysis. Yet, more socially informed examination would have revealed that this encroachment was influenced by contingent factors such as changing local tax arrangements and landownership patterns.

Second, the fact that fixed parameters (e.g., encroachment, per capita energy use) can be shown to be variables, whose values are influenced by further factors, reflects a very general problem of modeling. In practical modeling of ecological and other systems, choices must constantly be made about what to parameterize and what to specify as a variable dependent upon further causal connections (which then need to be estimated or observed enough to represent mathematically). This parameterization issue is also important in climate-system modeling and prediction. Even in much smaller models than GCMs, hundreds of parameters have to be put into the model. Yet as Oreskes et al. (1994: 641) observed about hydrogeological models, "the models that use these components are never closed systems. One reason . . . is that models require input parameters that are incompletely known . . . the embedded assumptions render the system open."

In other words, the very character of modeling leads to representing indeterminacy in system behavior as misleadingly deterministic or at best constrained within bounds that are not natural but inadvertent artifacts of modeling. A further point is that what the model output variables or end-points are sensitive (or insensitive) to is determined not just by scientific commitments and choices, but also by implicit policy choices—or assumptions about which choices matter; which can be suppressed or controlled; where human agency, contingency, and responsiveness must be revealed; and which policy users may act upon. In this sense even if the system is deterministic, the knowledge of it generated by the model is indeterminate by its very nature. In this way, the goals and knowledges of scientific and policy cultures fuse together, as outlined above in the model of co-production (Fig. 1.6). Decisions about where and how to attenuate the variation and complexity of behavioral representations is, in part, a pragmatic matter of the computing power available for calculating such escalating and branching chains of interaction. Equally, it reflects pragmatic policy relationships and interests that dictate how much time can be devoted to investigation and observation, and with what resources, skills, and methods.

Another important effect of parameterizations is that they may suppress the possibility of diversity and indeterminacy in outcomes of model runs. In the ecological–social systems analysis of the sub-Saharan pastoralists, the definition of a fixed model parameter, such as percentage of livestock sold per year, ignored heterogeneity in this factor across the system studied, and also took it to be objectively and universally determined. Taylor noted that historical complexity was pre-emptively ignored because of policy-analytical exigencies; for instance, an objectively fixed relationship was established between demographic pressure and intensification of grazing and resultant desertification, overlooking the importance of historical landownership patterns. Keepin & Wynne (1984) found a parallel in global energy modeling when they observed that fixed universal parameters for energy use per capita were taken from limited observations and built into such models, even though those observed values were only sustained by contingent cultural and institutional factors.

Observations such as these help explain why the empirical reality of model outputs, and of the resultant knowledge for policy, can so often be deconstructed by the equally empirical counterclaims of critics. In controversies among "dueling modelers" (Barnthouse et al. 1984), both sides tend to ignore the limitations built into modeling by the underrecognized exigencies of technical modeling practices, data constraints, and institutional resources.

The implicit construction of human agents is a third important issue in such models. The models analytically constrain and standardize the circumstances and behavior of human actors in the system. This is more than a merely analytical commitment, in theory open to correction; rather, the very structure of the model fixes the scale, standardization, and degree of mechanistic determination, as opposed to intelligent agency, imputed to different actors, such as the pastoralists in the sub-Sahara model. Knowledge so produced becomes normative to the extent that it is converted into policy interventions without appreciation of these contingent assumptions. In a further twist, the construction and dissemination of such implicit normative models of human subjects threatens to undermine policy credibility with the human agents whose behavior has been rendered so artificially determinate. This is not a predicament only of formal computer simulation models, as Wynne (1992a) has documented in a very different case involving ecological systems knowledge for policy. But the scale and integration of such epistemic constructs, and the widespread misunderstanding of their properties, make them more difficult to critique or remedy in the global climate case.

Earth science models
Earth science models, as for example in hydrogeology and geochemistry, raise issues very similar to those for ecological systems. The behavior of human agents may be less significant and variable in such models, but the typology of basic problems is identical. Oreskes et al. (1994) described the a priori determinism and artificial closure introduced by parameterization in hydrogeology, where such factors as storage coefficient, porosity, or conductivity were exogenously specified as fixed and universal. Such parameters are often constructed from estimates and submodels on the basis of nonexistent or very partial observational data; thus, further assumptions and inferences have to be made in order to construct a model at all. Even if it is known that a parameter does not represent the full range of behavior, it is often still used, because representing the possible underlying relationships dynamically is too difficult and might in any case result in the model's drifting uncontrollably or showing chaotic behavior.

As Oreskes et al. noted, overlaying multiple assumptions can have devastating effects on intellectual clarity and hinder the diagnosis and correction of inaccurate or mistaken cognitive commitments. For when the model predictions do not match observations (which are also laden with assumptions, perhaps not independent of those that constructed the model), it is impossible to know which assumptions have introduced the discrepancy. Orsekes et al. found that hydrological modelers adopted a specialized discourse and set of practices to correct for deficiencies in model runs. They acknowledged that model calibration needed additional refinements and forced empirical adequacy, and they performed ad hoc empirical tunings to have the model reproduce baseline conditions, sometimes to keep the model from disintegrating when it was run. In their analysis of flux adjustments in coupled ocean–atmosphere GCMs, Shackley et al. (1995) interpreted this major structural problem in GCMs as a product of the intersecting and mutually reinforcing social worlds of policy and science: flux correction is a necessary instrument for long-term climate prediction, demand for which is only expressed because (thanks in part to flux adjustment) such prediction can be deemed to be feasible.

Validation

Although modelers recognize the multilayered assumption-laden character of models, they generally assume that erroneous results can be corrected—or validated—by comparing predictions against observed system behavior. There are, however, some practical obstacles to validation. First, models by themselves do not always produce the final outputs of interest to policy users. There is often a further process of judgment and estimation, or separate, decoupled modeling, needed to reach the final outputs. Thus, comparisons of model outputs with perceived real-world conditions may be difficult or impossible to make directly. More seriously, when discrepancies are noted, it may not be at all obvious (especially to those outside the modeling community) which part of the model should be altered, because so many interacting assumptions or other ad hoc interventions have been made in the model or the specific model run.

Further, the observational data against which the model is tested or validated are themselves not free of theoretical commitments and assumptions. Climate models, for example, are validated by attempting to have them reproduce what modelers refer to as existing climatology, meaning a set of data on, say, sea-surface temperatures, pressures, and precipitation. But, as we have seen, such datasets themselves reflect implicit choices of what is important to measure, how and where data are recorded, what standardization methods are used, and so on. Many such validation sets are themselves generated by models. Particular partial or local criteria, such as whether the model can reproduce the El Niño circulation or the Gulf Stream, may be established as dominant evaluative standards for complex reasons, such as their representational clarity or their informally judged importance. Match (or mismatch) with existing climatology, like experimental replication (see Collins 1985) is inevitably a matter for negotiation.

For large and comprehensive models such as GCMs, datasets that are used as the standard against which to evaluate the model's performance may not be entirely independent of the model or the assumptions shaping it. One common validation practice with climate models is to have them run backward to see if they can reproduce past climate states (described in terms of selected variables and distributions, as noted above). However, the reconstruction of past climates, as we have seen, is an act of heterogeneous archaeology that combines analysis of physical phenomena (deep polar ice cores, fossilized pollen, tree rings, and the like) with at least superficially incommensurable social productions, such as parish records and other surrogate representations of temperature and other climate measures (see pp. 34–35). All these measures of past climate, in turn, depend heavily upon theoretical reasoning and inference. Theoretical commitments are needed to go from the measured variable to the variable of interest and to resolve the discrepancies between different samples and methods. Computerized GCMs are one of the important resources used in the very process of constructing credible time-series datasets of past climate states.

Thus, modelers cannot escape the intrinsic underdetermination of model outputs or predictions by independent data, and an inevitable element of circularity remains in validation attempts. This form of underdetermination has long been recognized by philosophers and sociologists of science such as Hesse (1974), Cartwright (1983), Hacking (1983), and Pickering (1990). Closure occurs around what is taken to be validated knowledge, thanks to overlap across intersecting fields of knowledge, while each field is itself underdetermined by independent natural evidence, its practitioners underestimate the uncertainty, or underdetermination, of its intersecting neighbor. This corresponds in general terms with the concept of the certainty trough (MacKenzie 1990) discussed above. Members of the specialist modeling community may be more aware of the uncertainties than their professional peers in the wider world of modeling. Complete outsiders, such as the lay public, may be most skeptical because they have neither the professional credentials nor the sense of participatory inclusion that might quell doubt and disbelief. We will return below to the policy implications of these and similar observations.

GCMs and the IPCC

Cartwright (1983) observed that models are a work of fiction in which some properties ascribed to objects will be genuine properties of the objects modeled, but others will be merely properties of convenience." One might add that convenience turns subtly into what appears to be objective necessity when such modeling is institutionalized as a policy tool. This may seriously mislead policy users if recognition of and critical reflection upon its instrumental and constructed origins is allowed to relax. Although a thorough and searching analysis of GCMs in the light of these observations remains to be undertaken, some important policy-related issues have already been identified (van der Sluijs 1997, Shackley et al. forthcoming).

First, the familiar IPCC estimate of average predicted global warming from a doubling of atmospheric carbon dioxide can be seen as a construct that more or less openly responds to the claims of both science and policy, although to recognize its constructed character is not to refute it or deny its robustness (see next section). The range usually given of 1.5°C to 4.5°C has remained remarkably stable for over a decade—a surprisingly long time, from before the establishment of the IPCC—and through some fundamental changes in modeling approaches and scientific understanding. This estimate is publicly assumed to be produced by the GCMs as a product of modeling; in that case, it would be reasonable to expect a quantified probability distribution across the range, with a most likely value (say, 2.5°C) somewhere in the middle, tailing off toward low values at the extremes. In practice, however, the range is not derived in this way, deterministically from the formal models, but is the result of less constrained and more diffuse expert judgment and negotiation among climate modelers. As one GCM expert involved in the IPCC process observed (quoted in Wynne 1996):

What they were very keen for us to do at IPCC, and modelers refused and we didn't do it, was to say we've got this range 1.5–4.5 degrees, what are the probability limits of that? You can't do it. It's not the same as an experimental error. The range is nothing to do with probability—it is not a normal distribution or a skewed distribution. Who knows what it is?

Comments such as this underscore the contingent and hybrid nature of the widely disseminated scientific range of global warming (see also Nordhaus 1994). The limits apparently were demarcated by means of a complex hybrid of scientific judgment and assumptions, combined with perceptions of policymakers' needs. This hybrid consensus-building process, giving rise to definitive statements of expert knowledge, is a legitimate and necessary approach to engendering robust scientific conclusions for use in policy.

The stability of the projected temperature range has helped to define a seemingly manageable problem for both science and policy, provided that one accepts the legitimacy of the process that led to its establishment. The chair of the Scientific Working Group of IPCC, Britain's Sir John Houghton (1994), reflected on the need for pragmatic limits on the framing of scientific forecasting when he observed:

> There are those who home on surprises as their main argument for action. I think that this is a weak case. No politician can be expected to take on board the unlikely though possible event of disintegration of the West Antarctic ice sheet. What the IPCC scientists have been doing is providing a best estimate of future climate under increased greenhouse gases— rather like a weather forecast is a best estimate. Within the range of possibility no change of climate is very unlikely. Sensible planning I would argue needs to be based on the best estimate, not on fear of global catastrophe or collapse.

Thus, what may appear to be the natural approach to producing climate knowledge is a complex exercise in which scientific judgment interacts with policymakers' needs for sensible and usable planning instruments; the domains of scientific knowledge production and policy use are fused into one. Although Houghton and the IPCC were rigorous in their attempt to deal with explicit scientific uncertainties and to communicate these to policymakers, some of these are recognized to be problematic, both within the frame of climate modeling and also surrounding the validity of that frame itself. Some of these uncertainties relate to the exclusion of various known feedbacks in global climate processes from the existing models and the need to estimate the consequences of these omissions in a highly subjective manner, albeit one conducted through collective deliberation and negotiation. Others have to do with the implications of the extensive parameterizations, as discussed earlier for simpler models.

In spite of these caveats, the IPCC process itself is significant as a means of marshalling scientific knowledge and making it useful in policy, and it adds an important normative dimension to gauging the validity of IPCC's scientific statements. The degree of organized, open, and accountable deliberation, extensive peer review, and explicit, rigorously applied rules for handling disagreements on the various working groups and writing teams positively influence the credibility of IPCC's output to wider professional audiences and other publics.

However, some problems are exposed by this elaborate and innovative attempt to reconcile scientific authority over such a broad and complex field with policy effectiveness at a global scale. First, the heroic efforts to generate consensus have resulted in a monolithic corpus of knowledge in which many key variations, conflicts, and complexities, in both the natural and social domains, have been rendered virtually invisible. Second, a major preoccupation of the IPCC has been to establish a consensus position on its scientific assessments as a necessary precondition of policy authority. This has been combined with a very particular vision of global policy—one that can reasonably be characterized as *global* or *corporatist*—which assumes that policy, like scientific knowledge, can be meaningfully coordinated at a global level. Global policy institutions, under this model, are presumed to possess effective authority to disseminate policy responses down to national and local levels. But the focus on institutions which would enact this global or corporatist policy order may, by default, force into the background a different vision: one in which a less anxiously constrained scientific consensus would allow a more openly diverse scientific research world to interact on many different fronts with diverse users in the policy world (see Ch. 5). Of course, pluralism exists to some extent even within the IPCC, but it does so in tension rather than in productive support with the monolithic vision linking global consensus science with global policy.

Reaction and backlash

Since the early 1990s, several well-publicized critiques of the scientific knowledge have underpinned the supposed consensus on climate change (Seitz et al. 1989, Balling 1992, Michaels 1992, Bailey 1993). Even the more strongly established consensus on the depletion of stratospheric ozone by chlorofluorocarbons has been the object of attempted deconstruction (Maduro & Schauerhammer 1992) that has won support from legislators in the US Congress. The critics point to what they claim are unwarranted assumptions and inferences threading the intellectual construction of the position that the great majority of mainstream scientists represent as natural knowledge. Given the prominence by such mobilizers of public opinion as the conservative US talkshow host Rush Limbaugh, the debate spilled out of expert circles into the less disciplined discourse of popular culture.

The outward form of this backlash follows well-known patterns of scientific controversy, as discussed in the literature on science and technology studies, centering on the interpretive flexibility of scientific observations of complex phenomena. For example, Michaels' (1992) attack on the scientific belief in anthropogenic greenhouse warming rehearsed various known deficiencies in the empirical basis for correlating increasing atmospheric carbon dioxide concentrations and the global average sea-surface temperature record. Michaels also pointed out the seeming arbitrariness of choices made by scientists as to which time-periods of data to use, and which not to use, in establishing a correlation. In particular, he criticized the American climate modeler James Hansen for manipulating data in his extremely influential testimony to Congress in 1988. Hansen had used in his presentation data from only the first and last ten years of the century, prompting Michaels (1992: 17) to assert that "throwing out 80% of the data to make a striking pronouncement hardly seems to be normal scientific procedure." At the same time, again following the well-attested pattern of scientific controversies (Gilbert & Mulkay 1994), Michaels defended his own skeptical position with facts that appeared to speak for themselves, unmediated by human interpretation: for example, he made the unqualified assertion that, if a carbon tax were adopted in the United States, "the mean surface temperature of the planet will be a quarter of a degree cooler in 2030 than it would be if the policy were not adopted" (Michaels 1992: xiv).

But the constructivist social science perspectives presented in this chapter account for more than the structure of the arguments advanced by opponents of climate change policy. The controversy also conforms to deeper historical and cultural patterns. It originates in the United States, where distrust of public agencies linked to a demand for rational decisionmaking most frequently propels political disagreements into the arena of technical debate (Jasanoff 1986, 1989, 1991b). Pluralism is the US norm in policy-relevant science as well as in politics, and this is reflected in the public prominence of climate change advocates such as Stephen Schneider of Stanford University and critics such as Richard Lindzen of MIT and Frederick Seitz of the Marshall Institute. In public debates among experts, the boundary between good science and mere politics becomes an important political resource (designed to discredit one's scientific opponents), but because of the transparency of American political institutions and their knowledge claims, even lay persons such as Rush Limbaugh can appropriate enough of the expert discourse to play an influential role in shaping public opinion. More open acknowledgment of the necessarily judgmental properties of policy-relevant science might ward off such challenges to expert authority, since the attacks are predicated to some extent on an exaggerated view of the certainty of such knowledge. Yet the very distrust that motivates the backlash also prevents US policymakers from taking refuge in forms of judgment that are expressly subjective, founded on specialized experience, and not available for continual public criticism (Jasanoff 1991a).

Such culturally specific tendencies toward deconstruction or cognitive agnosticism could be countered by powerful community-building forces operating across national boundaries, such as epistemic communities and international institutions of the kind that the IPCC has patiently attempted to build. Yet, for this dynamic to take hold, the international system has to be sensitive and responsive to the multiple and varied registers in which publics around the world express their need for legitimate and trustworthy political decisions.

Thus, in its first round of deliberations the IPCC proved vulnerable, at least in the eyes of distrustful US decisionmakers, to charges that it had systematically excluded respectable but uncomfortable expert opinions. US views of political legitimacy place particular stress on open engagement among disparate shades of opinion on contested issues. In the complex, heterogeneous, and institutionally unpracticed world of global environmental politics, it may be easier for international scientific bodies to lose credibility by excluding voices prematurely than to regain it in matters of far-reaching import.

Conclusion

The production and dissemination of scientific knowledge have played a crucially important part in the elevation of climate change to a topic of worldwide interest and political concern. The social science literature on science and public policy helps us to paint a finely textured and critically informed picture of this process of globalization by tracing scientific knowledge from its places of production and validation to its ultimate incorporation into policy. Constructivist approaches in the social sciences illuminate the extent to which our knowledge of the global environment is made by human agency, and not simply given to us by nature. In particular, interpretive analyses of the framing of policy problems, the production of scientific claims, the standardization of science and technology, and the international diffusion of facts and artifacts all focus attention on the co-production of natural and social order. Constructivist accounts provide important resources for explicating the factors that lead to scientific controversy as well as to consensus, as in the case of the American backlash against climate change and ozone science. Thus, they also provide a more textured and useful account of how scientific knowledge becomes (or fails to become) robust in policy contexts.

Work in this genre pinpoints the many locations at which the cognitive and the political domains connect with, support, or (at times) conflict with one another. Accordingly, it has also been instrumental in revealing that technical knowledge deemed suitable for public action is not exclusively a production of the scientific community, with its vigorous, but publicly invisible, forms of self-criticism. Rather, it is a sociotechnical hybrid whose authority depends on active communication and collaboration among multiple cultures or forms of life— including the bureaucratic, scientific, economic and social—each of which possesses its own distinctive resources for producing and validating knowledge.

Research in the social sciences has been especially helpful in explaining two sets of transpositions that are important for understanding the relationship between scientific knowledge and decisionmaking for the global environment: these are the moves from the particular to the universal in the domain of knowledge, ideas, and beliefs; and from the local to the global in the domain of political action and policy choice. Each move involves an intertwining of cognitive and social elements in ways that are well-illuminated by fine-grained interpretive analysis that would elude the lenses of quantitative survey research or of grand social science theories. But although constructivist studies have tended to stress the local, contingent, and particular aspects of knowledge creation and its use in policy, the wealth of case studies accumulated by researchers performing science and technology studies also reveals certain broad patterns of globalization and internationalization. These approaches provide a basis for addressing as yet inadequately understood questions about the sources and limitations of political authority in a fragmented but globalizing world.

With regard to the transposition of knowledge from the particular to the universal, several themes emerge as particularly significant for policymaking. These include the black boxing of contingency and the constraining of local freedom of action through the development of standard procedures, techniques, and devices; the importance of practices, discourses, and institutions in sustaining standard measures or methods; and the capacity of standardized science and technology to draw together quite heterogeneous cultures of belief. With regard to the transposition from local to global action, themes of particular relevance to the management of climate change include, perhaps foremost, a new emphasis on the importance of ideas and abstractions in building transnational communities. Hardly less important is the observation that the globalization of knowledge requires the production of trust and participation on a hitherto unprecedented scale.

Two of the most salient contributions of this body of work to the policy domain have been to disclose how the social world becomes embedded in the technical at many levels, and vice versa, and to show how the concepts of *good science* or *scientific validity*, with all traces of the social washed out, continually resurface as important resources in the justification of policy. Governmental institutions, such as courts and advisory committees, are everywhere deeply involved in the acts of re-representation that erase the social from the scientific and technical. But social actors, too, display a commitment to the objectivity of science, especially in skeptical, participatory cultures. We have seen that this tendency has potentially deleterious consequences for the credibility of ruling institutions, because it sets up questionable models of public understanding in the minds of experts and, at the same time, separates the methods and goals of scientific inquiry from people's felt needs and from lay systems of acquiring, testing and acting upon knowledge. These kinds of disjunctions were clearly visible in controversies over nuclear power and toxic chemicals, and to a lesser extent in the Green Revolution and the associated spread of a modern, internationalized agricultural science.

Constructivist social science research has also added depth and richness to the concept of uncertainty, both in science and in its ramifications within society. Uncertainty, like knowledge, is revealed as a deeply cultural product, reflecting such imperatives as the need to maintain particular models of human agency and causation, to safeguard valued social identities and relationships, to legitimate established political formations, and to assert moral sensibilities about the appropriate limits of controlling both human beings and nature. The ability (or inability) to acknowledge cognitive uncertainty—and its particular representation—surrounding issues in a given society is often a function of historical experiences with controlling social risks. The framing and control of environmental hazards, for example, reflects cultural features such as openness, diversity, civic participation, trust, and hierarchical control. Perhaps most significant in the context of climate change is the role played by various scientific institutions in appropriating domains of ignorance to study and control by scientific methods, thereby converting what was unknown into what is only uncertain, and hence in principle knowable. Scientific modeling is the increasingly encompassing vehicle through which the world's technical communities are seeking to bring what was formerly labeled trans-science—questions lying beyond the analytic reach of science—under rational and systematic control.

An overall observation of social science research on modeling is that judgments about what counts as an epistemically valid model incorporate judgments about prevailing institutional structures and policy assumptions. Implicit social commitments and assumptions are embedded within modeling practices and relationships—assumptions, for example, about the appropriate scale and distribution (global or local) of policy and institutions; about human rationality and agency; about appropriate degrees of control over human beings or nature; and about the purposes of knowledge making. These are shared across a hybrid culture of policy and science, and hence are often deployed and reproduced without explication or critical reflection, as if they were natural, that is, contained entirely within the realm of scientifically produced knowledge. Thus, particular forms of social order or culture, and particular forms of epistemic order mutually reinforce, construct, and validate one another at levels deeper than expressed scientific or policy choice.

A final, and in some ways paradoxical, conclusion relates to the potential vulnerability of policymaking institutions charged with responding to climate change. At one level of analysis, contemporary scientific research has been enormously successful in projecting the view that global risks can be deciphered, understood, and managed within the framework of existing institutions or institutional prototypes. In part, the standardizing and globalizing processes of science have been instrumental in promulgating this belief. Thanks to the power of laboratory-generated, depersonalized, and universal science, informal knowledge systems—together with their supporting social and cultural institutions, and even their physical environments—have been reformed in many instances to fit into emerging global systems. The visibility and prestige of institutions such as UNEP and the IPCC testify to the successes of modern science. At another level, however, these very achievements may hold the seeds of their own undermining, as discussed by theorists of modernity (e.g., Habermas 1975, Beck 1992).

By mastering the problem of trans-science, and by casting its net of presumed cognitive and predictive control over ever more complex and dispersed phenomena, the scientific study of climate change threatens to generate expectations that cannot be met and promises that may begin to strike many as illusory. The political backlash against the ozone agreements and against the emerging scientific consensus on global warming in the United States offer a sobering foretaste of this possibility of implosion. Further, the very process of globalization cuts science loose from its moorings in all those localized, historically warranted, social and cultural spaces where trust and credibility have been for so long been produced hand in hand with natural knowledge.

Where will the universal, hegemonic, yet institutionally weakly grounded science of climate change turn for authentic, globally effective legitimation and public authority? The view from the social sciences suggests that the solution lies partly in the patient construction of communities of belief that provide legitimacy through inclusion rather than exclusion, through participation rather than mystification, and through transparency rather than black boxing. The gathering social and cultural challenges posed by these observations are likely to carry intellectual consequences that still remain to be defined. This chapter has offered some important resources for the task.

References

Agarwal, A. & S. Narain 1991. *Global warming in an unequal world: a case of environmental colonialism*. New Delhi: Centre for Science and Environment.

Adler, E. 1987. *The power of ideology*. Berkeley: University of California Press.

Adler, E. & B. Crawford (eds) 1991. *Progress in postwar international relations*. New York: Columbia University Press.

Almond, G. & S. Verba 1965. *The civic culture*. Boston: Little, Brown.

Ancarani, V. 1995. Globalizing the world. See Jasanoff et al. (1995).

Anderson, B. 1991. *Imagined communities*, 2nd edn. London: Verso.

Anderson, J. R., R. W. Herdt, G. M. Scobie 1989. *Science and food*. Washington DC: World Bank.

Ashley, R. 1983. The eye of power: the politics of world modeling. *International Organization* **37**(3), 495–535.

Bailey, R. 1993. *Eco-scam: the false prophets of ecological apocalypse.* New York: St Martin's Press.

Balling, R. 1992. *The heated debate: greenhouse predictions versus climate reality.* San Francisco: Pacific Research Institute for Public Policy.

Balogh, B. 1991. *Chain reaction: expert debate and public participation in American commercial nuclear power 1945–1975.* New York: Cambridge University Press.

Baritz, L. 1985. *Backfire.* New York: Ballantine.

Barnes B. & D. Bloor 1982. Relativism, rationalism and the sociology of knowledge. In *Rationality and relativism*, M. Hollis (ed.). Cambridge, Massachusetts: MIT Press.

Barnthouse, L. W., J. Boreman, S. W. Christensen, C. P. Goodyear, W. Van Winkle, D. S. Vaughan 1984. Population biology in the courtroom: the Hudson River controversy. *BioScience* **34**, 14–19.

Barron, E. 1994. IGBP core projects: a "rich tapestry" or "flagship" model." *Global Change Newsletter* **17**, 2.

Baudrillard, J. 1983. *Simulations.* New York: Semiotext(e).

Beck, U. 1992. *The risk society: towards a new modernity.* London: Sage.

Beck, U., A. Giddens, S. Lash 1994. *Reflexive modernity.* Cambridge: Polity.

Benedick, R. 1991. *Ozone diplomacy: new directions in safeguarding the planet.* Cambridge, Massachusetts: Harvard University Press.

Bijker, W., T. Hughes, T. Pinch (eds) 1987. *The social construction of technological systems.* Cambridge, Massachusetts: MIT Press.

Bloomfield, B. 1986. *Modelling the world: the social constructions of systems analysts.* Oxford: Basil Blackwell.

Bloor, D. 1976. *Knowledge and social imagery.* Chicago: University of Chicago Press.

Boehmer-Christiansen, S. 1994. Global climate protection policy: the limits of scientific advice, parts 1 and 2. *Global Environmental Change* **4**(2), 140–59; **4**(3), 185–200.

Bostrom, A., M. Morgan, B. Fischhoff 1994. What do people know about global climate change? Part 1: mental models. *Risk Analysis* **14**, 959–70.

Bowker, G. 1994. How to be universal: some cybernetic strategies, 1943–1970. *Social Studies of Science* **21**(3), 107–127.

Bradbury, J., K. M. Branch, J. H. Heerwagen, E. B. Liebow 1994. *Community viewpoints of the chemical stockpile disposal program.* Washington DC: Battelle, Pacific Northwest Laboratories.

Brante, T., S. Fuller, M. Lynch (eds) 1993. *Controversial science: from content to contention.* Albany: State University of New York Press.

Breyer, S. 1993. *Breaking the vicious circle: toward effective risk regulation.* Cambridge, Massachusetts: Harvard University Press.

Brickman, R., S. Jasanoff, T. Ilgen 1985. *Controlling chemicals: the politics of regulation in Europe and the United States.* Ithaca, New York: Cornell University Press.

Broecker, W. 1992. Global warming on trial. *Natural History* **101**(April), 6–14.

Brown, P. 1987. Popular epidemiology: community response to toxic wastes-induced disease in Woburn, Massachusetts. *Science, Technology, and Human Values* **12**, 78–85.

Bush, V. 1945. *Science, the endless frontier.* Washington DC: US Government Printing Office. [Reissued 1980. New York: Arno Press.]

Buttel, F. & P. Taylor 1994. Environmental sociology and global environmental change. In *Social theory and the global environment*, M. Redclift & E. Benton (eds). London: Routledge.

Callon, M. 1986. Some elements of a sociology of translation: domestication of the scallops and the fishermen of St Brieuc Bay. In *Power, action and belief: a new sociology of knowledge?*, J. Law (ed.). London: Routledge & Kegan Paul.

——1987. Society in the making: the study of technology as a tool for sociological analysis. See Bijker et al. (1987).

Cambrosio, A., P. Keating, M. Mackenzie 1990. Scientific practice in the courtroom: the construction of sociotechnical identities in a biotechnology patent dispute. *Social Problems* **37**, 275–93.

Carson, R. 1962. *Silent spring*. Boston: Houghton Mifflin.

Cartwright, N. 1983. *How the laws of physics lie*. Oxford: Oxford University Press.

——1994. Ceteris paribus *laws and socio-economic machines*. Unpublished paper, Department of Philosophy, Logic, and Scientific Method, London School of Economics.

Chandler, D. 1977. *The visible hand: the managerial revolution in American business*. Cambridge, Massachusetts: Harvard University Press (Belknap).

Chubin, D. & E. Hackett 1990. *Peerless science: peer review and US science policy*. Albany: State University of New York Press.

Cobb, R. & C. Elder 1972. *Participation in American politics: the dynamics of agenda building*. Baltimore: Johns Hopkins University Press.

Cole, H. S. D.,C. Freeman, M. Jahoda, K. L. R. Pavitt (eds) 1973. *Thinking about the future: a critique of* The limits to growth. London: Chatto & Windus.

Collingridge, D. & C. Reeve 1986. *Science speaks to power: the role of experts in policy*. New York: St Martin's Press.

Collins, H. 1985. *Changing order: replication and induction in scientific practice*. London: Sage.

Conrad, J. (ed.) 1980. *Science, technology and risk*. London: Academic Press.

Cotgrove, S. 1982. *Catastrophe or cornucopia: the environment, politics and the future*. Chichester, England: John Wiley.

Crawford, E., T. Shinn, S. Sorlin (eds) 1993. *Denationalizing science*. Dordrecht: Kluwer.

Crouch, D. 1985. Biological effects of low level exposure to ionizing radiation. In *Radiation and health*, R. Russell-Jones & R. Southwood (eds). New York: John Wiley.

Dennis, M. 1985. Drilling for dollars: the making of US petroleum reserve estimates, 1921–25. *Social Studies of Science* **15**, 241–65.

Dickens, P. 1992. *Society and nature: towards a green social theory*. Philadelphia: Temple University Press.

Douglas, M. 1966. *Purity and danger: an analysis of the concepts of pollution and taboo*. London: Routledge.

——1970. *Natural symbols: explorations in cosmology*. London: Barrie & Rockliff.

——1985. *Risk acceptability according to the social sciences*. New York: Russell Sage Foundation.

Douglas, M. & A. Wildavsky 1982. *Risk and culture*. Berkeley: University of California Press.

Dryzek, J. 1990. *Discursive democracy – politics, policy, and political science*. Cambridge: Cambridge University Press.

Edwards, P. 1996. *The closed world: computers and the politics of discourse in Cold War America*. Cambridge, Massachusetts: MIT Press.

Ellul, J. 1964. *The technological society*. New York: Vintage Books.

Elzinga, A. 1993a. Antarctica: the construction of a continent. In *Denationalizing science*, E. Crawford, T. Shinn, S. Sorlin (eds). Dordrecht: Kluwer.

Elzinga, A. 1993b. Science as the continuation of politics by other means. In *Controversial science: from content to contention*, T. Brante, S. Fuller, M. Lynch (eds). Albany: State University of New York Press.

——(ed.) 1993c. *Changing trends in Antarctic research*. Dordrecht: Kluwer.

Elzinga, A. & A. Jamison 1995. Changing policy agendas in science & technology. See Jasanoff (1995).

Ezrahi, Y. 1984. Science and Utopia in late 20th-century pluralist democracy. See Mendelsohn & Nowotny (1984).

——1990. *The descent of Icarus: science and the transformation of contemporary democracy*. Cambridge, Massachusetts: Harvard University Press.

Fairhead, J. & M. Leach 1994. *Relics of colonial science: rethinking West Africa's forest–savanna mosaic*. Unpublished paper, Institute of Development Studies, University of Sussex.

Farman, J., B. Gardiner, J. Shanklin 1985. Large losses of total ozone in Antarctica reveal seasonal ClO_X/NO_X interaction. *Nature* **315**, 207–210.

Fischhoff, B., P. Slovic, S. Lichtenstein, S. Read, B. Combs 1978. How safe is safe enough? A psychometric study of attitudes towards technological risks. *Policy Sciences* **8**, 127–52.

Fischhoff, B., S. Lichtenstein, P. Slovic, S. L. Derby, R. L. Keeney 1981. *Acceptable risk.* Cambridge: Cambridge University Press.

Fleck, L. 1935. *Entstehung und Entwicklung einer Wissenschaftlichen Tatsache.* Basel: Benno Schwabe. [Translated by F. Bradley as *Genesis and development of a scientific fact.* Chicago: University of Chicago Press, 1979.]

Forman, P. 1971. Weimar culture, causality, and quantum theory, 1918–1927: adaptation by German physicists and mathematicians to a hostile intellectual environment. In *Historical studies in the physical sciences* (vol. 3), R. McCormmach (ed.). Philadelphia: University of Pennsylvania Press.

Foucault, M. 1970. *The order of things: an archaeology of the human sciences.* New York: Pantheon.

—— 1978. *The history of sexuality*, vol. I. New York: Pantheon.

—— 1979. *Discipline and punish: the birth of the prison.* New York: Random House.

—— 1980. *Power/knowledge: selected interviews and other writings 1972–1977* [edited by C. Gordon]. New York: Pantheon.

Freudenberg, W. 1992. Heuristics, bias and not-so-general publics. See Krimsky & Golding (1992).

Friedman, R. M. 1989. *Appropriating the weather.* Ithaca, New York: Cornell University Press.

Funtowicz, S. & J. Ravetz 1985. Three types of risk assessment: a methodological analysis. In *Risk analysis in the private sector*, C. Whipple & V. Covello (eds). New York: Plenum.

—— 1990. *Uncertainty and quality in science for policy.* Dordrecht: Kluwer.

—— 1992. Three types of risk assessment and the emergence of post normal science. See Krimsky & Golding (1992).

Gambetta, D. (ed.) 1988. *Trust: the making and breaking of cooperative relations.* Oxford: Basil Blackwell.

Garfinkel, H. 1963. A conception of, and experiments with "trust" as a condition of stable concerted actions. In *Motivation and social interaction*, O. Harvey (ed.). New York: Ronald Press.

Geertz, C. 1973. *The interpretation of cultures.* New York: Basic Books.

—— 1983. *Local knowledge.* New York: Basic Books.

Gibbons, M., C. Limoges, H. Nowotny, S. Schwartsman, P. Scott, M. Trow 1994. *The new production of knowledge.* London: Sage.

Gibson, J. 1986. *The perfect war: the war we couldn't lose and how we did.* New York: Vintage.

Gieryn, T. 1995. Boundaries of science. See Jasanoff et al. (1995).

Gilbert, G. & M. Mulkay 1984. *Opening Pandora's box: a sociological analysis of scientists' discourse.* Cambridge: Cambridge University Press.

Gillespie, B., D. Eva, R. Johnston 1979. Carcinogenic risk assessment in the United States and Great Britain. *Social Studies of Science* **9**(3), 265–301.

Goldstein, J. & R. Keohane (eds) 1993. *Ideas and foreign policy: beliefs, institutions, and political change.* Ithaca, New York: Cornell University Press.

Gore, A. 1992. *Earth in the balance: ecology and the human spirit.* Boston: Houghton Mifflin.

Gottweis, H. 1995. German politics of genetic engineering. *Social Studies of Science* **25**(2), 195–236.

Haas, P. 1989. Do regimes matter? Epistemic communities and Mediterranean pollution control. *International Organization* **43**, 377–403.

—— 1990. *Saving the Mediterranean: the politics of environmental cooperation.* New York: Columbia University Press.

—— (ed.) 1992. Knowledge, power and international policy coordination. *International Organization* **46**, 1.

Haas, P., R. Keohane, M. Levy (eds) 1994. *Institutions for the Earth: sources of effective international environmental protection*. Cambridge, Massachusetts: MIT Press.

Habermas, J. 1970. *Toward a rational society: student protest, science and politics*. Boston: Beacon Press.

—— 1971. *Knowledge and human interests*. Boston: Beacon Press.

—— 1975. *Legitimation crisis*. Boston: Beacon Press.

Hacking, I. 1983. *Representing and intervening*. Cambridge: Cambridge University Press.

Hajer, M. 1995. *The politics of environmental discourse*. Oxford: Oxford University Press.

Haraway, D. 1991. *Simians, cyborgs, and women: the reinvention of nature*. New York: Routledge.

Hazell, P. & C. Ramasamy 1991. *The Green Revolution reconsidered*. Baltimore: Johns Hopkins University Press.

Hesse, M. 1974. *The structure of scientific inference*. London: Macmillan.

Higgott, R. 1992. Pacific economic cooperation and Australia: some questions about the role of knowledge and learning. *Australian Journal of International Affairs* **46**(2), 182–97.

Houghton, J. 1994. Personal communication to S. Shackley, 3 August.

Houghton, J., G. H. Jenkins, J. J. Ephraums (eds) 1990. *Climate change: the IPCC scientific assessment*. Cambridge: Cambridge University Press.

Hughes, T. 1983. *Networks of power: electrification in Western society, 1880–1930*. Baltimore: Johns Hopkins University Press.

Jamison, A., R. Eyerman, J. Cramer 1990. *The making of the new environmental consciousness*. Edinburgh: Edinburgh University Press.

Jasanoff, S. 1986. *Risk management and political culture*. New York: Russell Sage Foundation.

—— 1987. Cultural aspects of risk assessment in Britain and the United States. See Johnson & Covello (1987).

—— 1989. The problem of rationality in American health and safety regulation. In *Expert evidence: interpreting science in the law*, R. Smith & B. Wynne (eds). London: Routledge.

—— 1990. *The fifth branch: science advisers as policymakers*. Cambridge, Massachusetts: Harvard University Press.

—— 1991a. Science, politics, and the renegotiation of expertise at EPA. *Osiris* **7**, 195–217.

—— 1991b. Acceptable evidence in a pluralistic society. See Mayo & Hollander (1991).

—— (ed.) 1994. *Learning from disaster: risk management after Bhopal*. Philadelphia: University of Pennsylvania Press.

—— 1995. *Science at the bar: law, science, and technology in America*. Cambridge, Massachusetts: Harvard University Press.

—— 1996a. Is science socially constructed—and can it still inform public policy. *Science and Engineering Ethics* **2**, 263–76.

—— 1996b. Science & norms in international environmental regimes. In *Earthly goods: environmental change and social justice*, F. Hampson & J. Reppy (eds). Ithaca, New York: Cornell University Press.

Jasanoff, S., G. E. Markle, J. Petersen, T. Pinch (eds) 1995. *Handbook of science and technology studies*. Newbury Park, California: Sage.

Johnson, B. & V. Covello (eds) 1987. *The social and cultural construction of risk*. Dordrecht: Reidel.

Keepin, W. 1984. Technical appraisal of the IIASA energy scenarios. *Policy Sciences* **17**, 199–275.

Kellogg, W. 1991. Response to skeptics of global warming. *Bulletin of the American Meteorological Society* **74**(4), 499–511.

Keohane, R. 1988. International institutions: two approaches. *International Studies Quarterly* **32**, 379–97.

Kiehl, J. 1992. Atmospheric general circulation modelling. See Trenberth (1992).

Kingdon, J. 1984. *Agendas, alternatives, and public policies*. Boston: Little, Brown.

Kingsland, S. 1985. *Modeling nature: episodes in the history of population ecology*. Chicago: University of Chicago Press.

Knorr Cetina, K. & K. Amann 1991. Image dissection in natural scientific inquiry. *Science, Technology, and Human Values* **15**(3), 259–83.

Kohler, R. 1994. *Lords of the fly: Drosophila genetics and the experimental life*. Chicago: University of Chicago Press.

Krimsky, S. & A. Plough 1988. *Environmental hazards: communicating risks as a social process*. Dover, Massachusetts: Auburn House.

Krimsky, S. & D. Golding (eds) 1992. *Social theories of risk*. London: Praeger.

Kuhn, T. 1962. *The structure of scientific revolutions*. Chicago: University of Chicago Press.

Kwa, C. 1987. Representations of nature mediating between ecology and science policy: the case of the International Biological Program. *Social Studies of Science* **17**, 413–42.

—— 1993a. Modeling the grasslands. *Historical studies in the physical and biological sciences* **24**(1), 125–55.

—— 1993b. Radiation ecology, systems ecology and the management of the environment. See Shortland (1993).

—— 1994. Modeling technologies of control. *Science as Culture* **4**(2), 363–91.

Lambert, H. & H. & Rose 1996. Disembodied knowledge? Making sense of medical science. In *Misunderstanding science*, A. Irwin & B. Wynne (eds). Cambridge: Cambridge University Press.

Latour, B. 1987. *Science in action*. Cambridge, Massachusetts: Harvard University Press.

—— 1988. *The Pasteurization of France*. Cambridge, Massachusetts: Harvard University Press.

—— 1990. Drawing things together. See Lynch & Woolgar (1990).

—— 1993. *We have never been modern*. Cambridge, Massachusetts: Harvard University Press.

Latour, B. & S. Woolgar 1979. *Laboratory life: the construction of scientific facts*. Princeton, New Jersey: Princeton University Press.

Latour, B. & M. Coutouzis 1986. Le village solaire de Frangocastello. *L'Année Sociologique* **36**, 113–67.

Lave, L. & H. Dowlatabadi 1993. Climate change: the effects of personal belief and scientific uncertainty. *Environmental Science and Technology* **27**(10), 1962–72.

Law, J. (ed.) 1986. *Power, action and belief: a new sociology of knowledge?* London: Routledge & Kegan Paul.

—— 1987. Technology and heterogeneous engineering: the case of Portuguese expansion. See Bijker et al. (1987).

Law, J. & M. Callon 1988. Engineering and sociology in a military aircraft project: a network analysis of technological change. *Social Problems* **35**(3), 284–98.

Layton, D., A. Davy, E. Jenkins 1986. Science for specific social purposes. *Studies in Science Education* **13**, 17–40.

Layton, D., E. Jenkins, S. MacGill, A. Davy 1993. *Inarticulate science?* Driffield, England: Studies in Education.

Leggett, J. (ed.) 1991. *Global warming*. London: Macmillan.

Lindzen 1990. Some coolness concerning global warming. *Bulletin of the American Meteorological Society* **71**, 288–99.

Lipschutz, R. 1991. Wasn't the future wonderful? Resources, environment, and the emerging myth of global sustainable development. *Colorado Journal of International Environmental Law and Policy* **2**, 35–54.

Lynch, M. & S. Woolgar 1990. *Representation in scientific practice*. Cambridge, Massachusetts: MIT Press.

MacKenzie, D. 1990. *Inventing accuracy: a historical sociology of nuclear missile guidance*. Cambridge, Massachusetts: MIT Press.

Maduro, R. & R. Schauerhammer 1992. *The holes in the ozone scare*. Washington DC: 21st Century Science Associates.

Mann, D. 1991. Environmental learning in a decentralized world. *Journal of International Affairs*

44(2), 301–337.

Martin, E. 1987. *The woman in the body: a cultural analysis of reproduction.* Boston: Beacon Press.

Mayo, D. & R. Hollander (eds) 1991. *Acceptable evidence: science and values in risk management.* New York: Oxford University Press.

McKechnie, R. 1996. Insiders and outsiders: identifying experts on home ground. In *Misunderstanding science*, A. Irwin & B. Wynne (eds), Cambridge: Cambridge University Press.

Meadows, D. H., D. L. Meadows, J. Randers, W. Behrens III 1972. *The limits to growth.* New York: Universe.

Meadows, D. H., J. Richardson, G. Bruckmann 1982. *Groping in the dark: the first decade of global modeling.* Chichester, England: John Wiley.

Mendelsohn, E. & H. Nowotny (eds) 1984. *Nineteen eighty-four: science between Utopia and Dystopia* [Sociology of the Sciences Yearbook VIII]. Dordrecht: Reidel.

Merchant, C. 1980. *The death of nature: women, ecology, and the scientific revolution.* San Francisco: Harper & Row.

Merton, R. 1973. The normative structure of science. In *The sociology of science: theoretical and empirical investigations*, R. Merton (ed.). Chicago: University of Chicago Press.

Messner, W., D. Bray, C. C. Germain, N. Stehr 1992. Climate change and social order: knowledge for action? *Knowledge and Policy* **5**(4), 82–100.

Michael, M. 1992. Lay discourses of science: science-in-general, science-in-particular, and self. *Science, Technology, and Human Values* **17**(3), 313–33.

Michaels, P. 1992. *Sound and fury.* Washington DC: Cato Institute.

Milner, H. 1992. International theories of cooperation among nations. *World Politics* **44**(3), 446–96.

Mitman, G. 1988. From population to society: the comparative metaphors of W. C. Allee and A. E. Emerson. *Journal of the History of Biology* **21**(2), 172–94.

Molina, M. & F. Rowland 1974. Stratospheric sink for cholorfluoromethanes: chlorine atom catalysed destruction of ozone. *Nature* **249**, 810–12.

Mukerji, C. 1989. *A fragile power: scientists and the state.* Princeton, New Jersey: Princeton University Press.

Nelkin, D. (ed.) 1992. *Controversy*, 3rd edn. Newbury Park, California: Sage.

Newby, H. 1993. *Global environmental change and the social sciences: retrospect and prospect.* Unpublished paper, Economic and Social Research Council, Swindon, England.

Noble, D. 1977. *America by design: science, technology and the rise of corporate capitalism.* Oxford: Oxford University Press.

Noble, D. 1984. *Forces of production: a social history of industrial automation.* New York: Knopf.

Nollkaemper, A. 1992. On the effectiveness of international rules. *Acta Politica* **1**, 49–70.

Nordhaus, W. 1994. Expert opinion on climatic change. *American Scientist* **82**(1), 45–51.

Nowotny, H. 1990. Knowledge for certainty: poverty, welfare institutions and the institutionalization of social science. In *Discourses on society: the shaping of the social science disciplines*, P. Wagner, B. Wittrock, R. Whitley (eds). Dordrecht: Kluwer.

O'Connell, J. 1993. Metrology: the creation of universality by circulation of particulars. *Social Studies of Science* **23**(1), 129–73.

Oreskes, N. K. Shrader-Frechette, K. Belitz 1994. Verification, validation and confirmation of numerical models in the earth sciences. *Science* **263**, 641–6.

O'Riordan, T. & J. Jäger 1996. *Politics of climate change: a European perspective.* London: Routledge.

Oudshoorn, N. 1994. *The making of the hormonal body: a contextual analysis of the study of sex hormones 1923–40.* London: Routledge.

Parson, E. 1994. Protecting the ozone layer. In *Institutions for the Earth: sources of effective international environmental protection*, P. Haas, R. Keohane, M. Levy (eds). Cambridge,

Massachusetts: MIT Press.

Pickering, A. 1990. Knowledge, practice and mere construction. *Social Studies of Science* **20**, 682–729.

Pinch, T. 1985. Towards an analysis of scientific observation; the externality and evidential significance of observational reports in physics. *Social Studies of Science* **15**, 3–36.

——1993. "Testing—one, two, three . . . testing!": toward a sociology of testing. *Science, Technology, and Human Values* **18**(1), 25–41.

Porter, T. 1986. *The rise of statistical thinking 1820–1990*. Princeton, New Jersey: Princeton University Press.

——1992. Objectivity as standardization: the rhetoric of impersonality in measurement, statistics, and cost–benefit analysis. In *Rethinking objectivity*, A. Megill (ed.). Durham, North Carolina: Duke University Press.

——1995. *Trust in numbers: the pursuit of objectivity in science and public life*. Princeton, New Jersey: Princeton University Press.

Prewitt, K. 1982. The public and science policy. *Science, Technology, and Human Values* **7**, 5–14.

Price, D. 1965. *The scientific estate*. Cambridge, Massachusetts: Harvard University Press.

Pyenson, L. 1985. *Cultural imperialism and the exact sciences: German expansion overseas, 1900–1930*. New York: P. Lang.

Rayner, S. 1984. Disagreeing about risk: the institutional cultures of risk management and planning for future generations. In *Risk analysis, institutions, and public policy*, S. G. Hadden (ed.). Port Washington, New York: Associated Faculty Press.

——1986. Management of radiation hazards in hospitals: plural rationalities in a single institution. *Social Studies of Science* **16**(4), 573–92.

——1991. A cultural perspective on the structure and implementation of global environmental agreements. *Evaluation Review* **15**(1), 75–102.

——1992. Cultural theory and risk analysis. See Krimsky & Golding (1992).

Rayner, S. & R. Cantor 1987. How fair is safe enough? The cultural approach to societal technology choice. *Risk Analysis* **7**(1), 3–9.

Read, D., A. Bostrom, M. Morgan, B. Fischhoff, T. Smuts 1994. What do people know about global climate change? Part 2: survey studies of educated lay people. *Risk Analysis* **14**, 971–82.

Redclift, M. & E. Benton (eds) 1994. *Social theory and the global environment*. London: Routledge.

Renn, O. 1992. See Krimsky & Golding (1992).

Richards, E. & B. Martin 1995. Scientific knowledge, controversy, and public decision making. See Jasanoff et al. (1995).

Risse-Kappen, T. 1994. Ideas do not float freely: transnational coalitions, domestic structures, and the end of the Cold War. *International Organization* **48**(2), 185–215.

Roan, S. 1989. *Ozone crisis*. New York: John Wiley.

Rotmans, J. 1990. IMAGE: *an integrated model to assess the greenhouse effect*. Boston: Kluwer.

——1992. ESCAPE: an integrated climate model for the EC. *Change* **11**(October), 1–4.

Rudwick, M. 1972. *The meaning of fossils*. London: Macdonald.

Running, S., T. Loveland, L. L. Pierce 1994. A vegetation classification logic based on remote sensing for use in global biogeochemical models. *Ambio* **23**(1), 77–81.

Rushefsky, M. 1986. *Making cancer policy*. Albany: State University of New York Press.

Sacks, H. 1984. Notes on methodology. In *Structures of social action: studies in conversation analysis*, J. M. Atkinson & J. Heritage (eds). Cambridge: Cambridge University Press.

Salter, L. 1988. *Mandated science: science and scientists in the making of standards*. Dordrecht: Kluwer.

Schaffer, S. 1992. Late Victorian metrology and its instrumentation: a manufactory of ohms. In *Invisible connections: instruments, institutions and science*, R. Bud & S. Cozzens (eds). Bellingham, Washington: Optical Engineering Press.

Schwarz, M. & M. Thompson 1990. *Divided we stand: redefining politics, technology, and social choice*. Brighton, England: Harvester Wheatsheaf.

Schwing, R. & W. Albers (eds) 1980. *Societal risk assessment: how safe is safe enough?* New York: Plenum.

Seitz, F., R. Jashrow, W. Nierenberg 1989. *Scientific perspectives on the greenhouse problem.* Washington DC: George C. Marshall Institute.

Shackley, S. & B. Wynne 1994. Climatic reductionism: the British character and the greenhouse effect. *Weather* 49(3), 110–11.

—— 1996. Representing uncertainty in global climate change, science and policy: boundary ordering devices and authority. *Science, Technology, and Human Values* 21(3), 275–302.

Shackley, S., J. Risbey, P. Stone, B. Wynne 1995. *Adjusting to policy expectations in climate change modelling: an interdisciplinary study of flux adjustments in coupled atmosphere–ocean general circulation models.* Unpublished paper, Centre for Science Studies and Science Policy, University of Lancaster.

Shackley, S., P. Young, S. Parkinson, B. Wynne forthcoming. Uncertainty, complexity and concepts of good science in climate change modelling: are GCMs the best tools? *Climatic Change*, in press.

Shapin, S. 1984. Pump and circumstance: Robert Boyle's literary technology. *Social Studies of Science* 14, 481–520.

—— 1994. *A social history of truth*. Chicago: University of Chicago Press.

—— 1995. Here and everywhere: sociology of scientific knowledge. *Annual Review of Sociology* 21, 289–321.

Shapin, S. & S. Schaffer 1985. *Leviathan and the air-pump: Hobbes, Boyle, and the experimental life.* Princeton, New Jersey: Princeton University Press.

Shiva, V. 1989. *The violence of the Green Revolution: ecological degradation and political conflict in Punjab.* Dehra Dun, India: Natraj Publishers.

Shortland, M. (ed.) 1993. *Science and nature* [BSHS Monograph 8]. Oxford: British Society for the History of Science.

Skolnikoff, E. 1990. The policy gridlock of global warming. *Foreign Policy* 79, 77–93.

Slovic, P. 1991. Beyond numbers: a broader perspective on risk perception and risk communication. See Mayo & Hollander (1991).

Slovic P., B. Fischhoff, S. Lichtenstein 1980. Facts and fears: understanding perceived risk. See Schwing & Albers (1980).

Slovic, P., B. Fischhoff, S. Lichtenstein 1985. Characterizing perceived risks. In *Perilous progress: managing the hazards of technology*, R. Kates, C. Hoheneuser, J. X. Kasperson (eds). Boulder, Colorado: Westview.

Sluijs, J. van der 1997. *Anchoring amid uncertainty: on the management of uncertainties in risk assessment of anthropogenic climate change.* Leiden: Ludy Feyen.

Smith, C. & N. Wise 1989. *Energy and empire*. Cambridge: Cambridge University Press.

Solingen, E. 1993. Between markets and the state: scientists in comparative perspective. *Comparative Politics* 26(1), 31–51.

Star, S. & J. Griesemer 1989. Institutional ecology, "translations" and boundary objects: amateurs and professionals in Berkeley's museum of vertebrate zoology, 1907–39. *Social Studies of Science* 19, 387–420.

Strathern, M. & S. Franklin 1993. *Kinship and the new genetic technologies: an assessment of existing research.* Report to the Commission of the European Communities (DG-XII), Human Genome Analysis Programme, Brussels.

Suchman, L. 1987. *Plans and situated actions*. Cambridge: Cambridge University Press.

Taubes, G. 1993. The ozone backlash. *Science* 260, 1580–83.

Taylor, P. 1988. Technocratic optimism, H. T. Odum, and the partial transformation of ecological metaphor after World War II. *Journal of the History of Biology* 21(2), 213–44.

—— 1992. Re/constructing socioecologies: systems dynamics modeling of nomadic pastoralists in sub-Saharan Africa. In *The right tools for the job*, A. Clarke & J. Fujimura (eds). Princeton, New Jersey: Princeton University Press.

Thompson, M. 1986. To hell with the turkeys! A diatribe directed at the pernicious trepidity of the current intellectual debate on risk. In *Values at risk*, D. MacLean (ed.), 113–35. Totowa, New Jersey: Roman & Allanheld.

Thompson, M., M. Warburton, T. Hatley 1986. *Uncertainty on a Himalayan scale*. London: Ethnographica.

Thompson, M., R. Ellis, A. Wildavsky 1990. *Cultural theory*. Boulder, Colorado: Westview.

Topf, R. 1993. Conclusion. In *The politics of expert advice*, A. Barker & G. Peters (eds). Edinburgh: Edinburgh University Press.

Trenberth, K. 1992. *Climate system modeling*. Cambridge: Cambridge University Press.

US EPA 1987. *Unfinished business*. Washington DC: United States Environmental Protection Agency.

US NRC [US National Research Council] 1983. *Risk assessment in the federal government: managing the process*. Washington DC: National Academy Press.

———1989. *Improving risk communication*. Washington DC: National Academy Press.

———1994. *Science and judgment in risk assessment*. Washington DC: National Academy Press.

Velho, L. 1994. Assessment of international scientific collaboration in Brazilian Amazonia. Paper presented at the ORSTOM/UNESCO Conference "20th-century science: beyond the metropolis," Paris, France.

Vogel, D. 1986. *National styles of regulation*. Ithaca, New York: Cornell University Press.

Weber, M. 1922. *Wirtschaft und Gesellschaft*. Tübingen: Mohr. [Translated by E. Fischhoff et al. as *Economy and society: an outline of interpretive sociology*. Berkeley: University of California Press, 1978.]

Weinberg, A. 1972. Science and trans-science. *Minerva* **10**, 209–222.

Wynne, B. 1980. Technology, risk, and participation: the social treatment of uncertainty. In *Society, technology and risk*, J. Conrad (ed.). London: Academic Press.

———1982. *Rationality and ritual: the Windscale inquiry and nuclear decisions in Britain*. Chalfont St Giles, England: British Society for the History of Science.

———1984. The institutional context of science, models and policy: the IIASA energy study. *Policy Sciences* **17**(3), 277–320.

———1987. *Risk management and hazardous wastes: implementation and the dialectics of credibility*. Berlin: Springer.

———1988. Unruly technology. *Social Studies of Science* **18**, 147–67.

———1989a. Frameworks of rationality in risk management: towards the testing of naive sociology. In *Environmental threats: social sciences approaches to public risk perceptions*, J. Brown (ed.). London: Pinter (Belhaven).

———1989b. Sheepfarming after Chernobyl. *Environment* **31**, 11–15, 33–9.

———1992a. Misunderstood misunderstanding: social identities and public uptake of science. *Public Understanding of Science* **1**(3), 281–304.

———1992b. Risk and social learning: reification to engagement. See Krimsky & Golding (1992).

———1994. Uncertainty and environmental learning. In *Ciencia, tecnologia y sociedad*, M. G. Garcia, J. A. L. Cerezo, J. L. L. Lopez (eds). Barcelona: Antropos.

———1995. Public understanding of science. See Jasanoff et al. (1995).

———1996. SSK's identity-parade: signing-up, off-and-on. *Social Studies of Science* **26**(2), 357–91.

Wynne, B., R. McKechnie, M. Michael 1990. *Frameworks for understanding public interpretations of science and technology* [End-of-award report to the Economic and Social Research Council, UK]. Unpublished report, Centre for Science Studies and Science Policy, University of Lancaster.

REFERENCES

Wynne, B. & S. Mayer 1993. How science fails the environment. *New Scientist* **138**(June), 33–5.
Wynne, B. & S. Shackley 1994. Environmental models—truth machines or heuristics? *The Globe* **21**, 6–8.

Yearley, S. 1991. *The green case*. London: HarperCollins.
—— 1995. The environmental challenge to science studies. See Jasanoff et al. (1995).
—— 1996. *Sociology, environmentalism, globalization*. London: Sage.
Young, O. & P. Stern 1992. Human dimensions of global change. *Environment* **34**(7), 2–3.

Zehr, S. 1994. Method, scale and socio-technical networks: problems of standardization in acid rain, ozone depletion and global warming research. *Science Studies* **7**(1), 47–58.
Zheng-Kang, C. 1990. Equity, special considerations, and the Third World. *Colorado Journal of International Law and Policy* **1**, 57–68.
Ziman, J., A. Rip, S. Cozzens 1994. *The research system in transition*. Boston: Kluwer.

CHAPTER 2

Population and climate change

F. Landis MacKellar, Wolfgang Lutz,
A. J. McMichael, Astri Suhrke

Contributors
Vinod Mishra, Brian O'Neill, Sanjeev Prakash, Lee Wexler

According to one school of thought (e.g., Myers 1993), population growth in less industrialized countries is the main cause of global environmental stress; according to another (e.g., Rahman et al. 1993), the major factor is the high level of personal consumption in the North. A hybrid view (e.g., Ehrlich & Ehrlich 1990) is that, given the tremendous difference in annual per capita levels of natural resource utilization, population growth in more industrialized countries, although slow, bears as much responsibility as rapid population growth in the South. This latter view has been marginalized in the debate, although there is no reason to do so a priori; at least the accounting that backs it up is sound. Thus, the population–consumption debate has remained essentially bipolar.

The most vehement authors in the climate policy debate (e.g., Agarwal & Narain 1991) speak openly of "blame"; others use the more neutral terms "cause," "responsibility," or "share." Even thus watered down, however, the population–consumption debate is still about the equity of proposed mitigation policies in view of the skewed distribution of resources and responsibility for past accumulation of atmospheric carbon dioxide. What synthesis of the positions has occurred has consisted merely of putting all three (especially the first two) views together and calling for sacrifices—forgoing both desired consumption and fertility—all around (e.g., Harrison 1992).

The population–consumption debate came to dominate public discussions of climate change and of global environmental stress more broadly despite the existence of at least two well-developed alternative framings of the issue. Commoner (1971, 1991) continues to blame neither population nor mass consumption, but rather the promotion by entrenched interests of large-scale, centralized, energy- and capital-intensive, highly polluting industrial technologies, as well as the encouragement via advertising of consumption habits (such as the *throwaway culture*) that depend on them. Orthodox neoclassical economists, for their part, have stood aloof from the population–consumption debate, for at least three reasons. First, they trust markets can defuse and mediate pressures on the environment whatever their origins; the issue, according to this interpretation, is the removal of impediments to markets, not reducing the scale of human population or its level of consumption. (Hence, Ch. 4 distinguishes this diagnosis as a distinctive voice in climate change discourse, focused on pricing and property rights.) Second, the population–consumption debate explicitly or implicitly makes a distinction—empty from the point of view of utility theory—between luxurious or wasteful consumption and virtuous or necessary consumption (Ekins 1991, Durning 1992). This distinction is found to be insupportable (see Ch. 3). Third, participants in the debate commit the elementary mistake (from the standpoint of utility theory) of making interpersonal utility comparisons. We cannot know (rigorously) whether the couple in a more industrialized country who forgo a desired second car are giving up more or less utility than a couple in a less industrialized country who forgo a desired birth.

In the international political arena, the population–consumption debate has become the focus of the broader debate about equity and fairness (see Ch. 4). For example, whenever Northern delegates at the UN Conference on Environment and Development (UNCED) in Rio raised the issue of rapid population growth in less industrialized countries, Southern delegates countered with the issue of overconsumption (Rowlands 1992). As a result, population issues were watered down: Principle 8 of the nonbinding Rio Declaration calls on states to reduce and eliminate unsustainable patterns of production and consumption and to promote to appropriate demographic policies, but this is purely hortatory. When delegates from less industrialized countries proposed even the modest step of monitoring consumption patterns, industrialized nations, led by the United States, not surprisingly vetoed the idea.

By focusing attention on responsibility for causing global climate change, the population–consumption debate diverts attention from the more important issue of coping with climate change. Obscured almost entirely in the debate is one of the most consistent findings to emerge from climate change research: that the populations most adversely affected will be poor, marginal populations in less industrialized countries who depend on ecologically fragile renewable natural resources. Only by focusing on means of adaptation can the needs of these seriously affected populations be addressed.

The first section of this chapter discusses the demographic situation and outlook, commenting on the decline in fertility now underway in less industrialized countries and the relative certainties: population will grow substantially beyond its current size, its distribution will continue to tilt toward less industrialized countries, and it will continue to age.

The second section assesses studies of the role of population in the global change debate and critically reviews the common model used in the population–consumption debate. This polarized debate adds little value to addressing the questions related to climate change and diverts attention from important issues of vulnerable populations and fragile ecosystems.

The third section extends the neoclassical economic model of population and the environment to incorporate poverty, insecurity, the low status of women, and the fragility of marginal environmental zones where many of the world's poor live. To use language introduced by Gunnar Myrdal in his classic An American dilemma (1944), this results in a vicious circle model in which societies find themselves captured in a high-fertility low-income trap. Because it is comprehensive and it addresses a range of concerns within a broadly orthodox neoclassical framework, this vicious circle model has become the dominant model for research on, and policy advice regarding, population–environment interactions in less industrialized countries.

The fourth and fifth sections assess the social science research related to two population-specific phenomena that might be associated with climate change, specifically climate warming: health impacts, and effects on land and water, leading to migration and conflict. Higher temperatures would lead to a direct increase in heat-related mortality, but the public health implications of this would be relatively small. Changes in climate conditions might also change the distribution of disease vectors, such as malarial mosquitoes, and alter host–parasite relationships, with implications for the distribution and severity of vector-borne diseases. Moreover, changes in the variability of weather conditions might lead to greater frequency of extreme climatic events, especially droughts and floods, and might make fragile renewable resource systems more prone to breakdown. The result might be an increase in the number of distress migrants or, as they have come to be known in the popular literature, environmental refugees. One school of thought holds that tensions over impaired natural resource systems might escalate into wars over natural resources.

The conclusion grapples with the question of why, in a world where virtuous ends outstrip scarce public means, policymakers should concern themselves with slowing population growth. The answer, often held to be so obvious in the public debate, is found in this chapter to be highly contingent on contexts and conditions, and ultimately on values. Current wisdom, embodied in the deliberations and Statement of the 1994 UN International Conference on Population and Development (ICPD), is deeply informed by vicious circle arguments. The new basis for international population policy is widening the choice set of women, children, and the poor, based on an uneasy coalition between advocates for women and the poor and the neoclassical economic orthodoxy.

A constructive criticism of the vicious circle argument shows that some themes are lacking. First, equity concerns have been framed in strictly neoclassical economic terms; this cannot help but weaken the coalition that must implement policies. Second, global ecological fragility and risk are not addressed; in short, the view that human population growth is a bad thing in and of itself, is missing. The chapter concludes with a plea that plural norms and values, which have been more or less missing or suppressed in the population debate, be recognized and allowed to form the basis of a constructive dialogue.

Population situation and outlook

This section summarizes the current demographic situation and describes the global demographic transition which is now entering its late stage. Human population growth results not from a mechanistic biological growth process but from human choices and, ultimately, human values. The key uncertainty, in part reflecting disagreements among researchers on the nature of the underlying model, is the speed of the fertility decline now occurring in less industrialized countries.

Demographic trends and outlook: a global summary

World population at present is approximately 6 billion. In 2050, according to population projections made by researchers at the International Institute for Applied Systems Analysis (IIASA; Lutz 1996), it is extremely likely to be in the range 7.1–13.3 billion, and in 2100 3.9–22.7 billion. These high/low bands reflect only extreme sets of mortality and fertility assumptions and should not be interpreted as probabilistic confidence intervals. By applying probabilistic methods, the IIASA researchers estimate that in 2050, the 95 percent confidence interval is 8.1–12.0, billion and in 2100 it is 5.7–17.3 billion. This level of uncertainty might be considered high by traditional scientific standards, but in the area of global environmental change, the population outlook is one of the more robust factors to be considered.

Demographic takeoff and transition
The dominant feature of the global socioeconomic landscape is the demographic contrast between the well-off populations of Europe, North America and Japan and the poor populations of Asia, Africa, the Middle East and Latin America. According to UN Population Division estimates (Table 2.1), the population of the industrialized countries is small in absolute numbers (1143 million in 1990) and expanding very slowly over time (0.40 percent per year growth between 1990 and 1995). That of the less industrialized, mostly agricultural, and commodity-producing countries is large in absolute numbers (4141 million in 1990) and expanding at a rapid rate (1.88 percent per year). The total fertility rate (TFR) in more industrialized countries is estimated to be 1.70, in less industrialized countries 3.48; life expectancy at birth for both sexes combined is 74.4 in the first group of nations and 62.3 in the second.[1]

---

1. Unless otherwise noted, "fertility rate" refers to the total fertility rate (TFR), defined as the average number of births per woman on the assumption that she survives to the end of her reproductive years. Mathematically, this is the integral from 15 to 45 of the age-specific fertility rates (births to women aged x divided by number of women aged x) observed in a given year. Life expectancy at birth is the number of years that would be lived by a hypothetical person who was born and passed through life, subject to the age-specific mortality rates observed in a given year; mathematically, it is the integral from zero to infinity of age-specific survival rates (one minus the age-specific death rate). Both the TFR and life expectancy are synthetic indices reflecting age-specific event rates in a given year; they do not give the actual number of births per woman or average age at death in a specific cohort.

Table 2.1 Demographic trends in the world since 1950.

	Total population (millions)			Growth rate			Life expectancy (both sexes)			Total fertility rate		
	1950	1970	1990	1950–55	1970–75	1990–95	1950–55	1970–75	1990–95	1950–55	1970–75	1990–95
World	2520	3697	5285	1.78	1.96	1.57	46.4	57.9	64.4	4.97	4.88	3.10
More industrialized	809	1003	1143	1.20	0.81	0.40	66.5	71.2	74.4	2.77	2.36	1.70
Less industrialized	1711	2695	4141	2.05	2.37	1.88	40.9	54.6	62.3	6.13	5.96	3.48
Africa	224	364	633	2.23	2.56	2.81	37.8	46.0	53.0	6.64	6.67	5.80
Asia	1403	2148	3186	1.90	2.27	1.64	41.3	56.3	64.5	5.86	5.06	3.03
Europe	549	656	721	0.96	0.60	0.15	66.1	70.8	72.9	2.56	2.14	1.58
Latin America & Caribbean	165	283	440	2.68	2.44	1.84	51.4	61.1	68.5	5.87	4.98	3.09
North America	166	226	278	1.80	1.10	1.05	69.0	71.5	76.1	3.47	2.01	2.06
Oceania	13	19	26	2.21	2.09	1.54	60.8	66.6	72.8	3.84	3.21	2.51

Source: UN (1994).

The term *less industrialized country* is so often taken as almost synonymous with the word "poverty" that a qualification is in order. Poverty in less industrialized countries is a bounded phenomenon. The proportion of the population of these countries living in poverty is estimated by the World Bank to have remained at about 30 percent between 1985 and 1990, with significant declines in East and Southeast Asia being offset by increases in Latin America, the Middle East, North Africa, and sub-Saharan Africa. The greatest incidence of poverty is in sub-Saharan Africa. Images of urban slums notwithstanding, roughly 70 percent of the world's poor live in rural areas and roughly 50 percent live in environmentally fragile rural areas. However, the urban share of the impoverished population is expanding. Just as the extent of poverty is overblown in the popular imagination, symmetrically, the size of the middle class is underappreciated. The World Resources Institute (1994) estimates that the top income class in India, containing 1.5 percent of the population, is as large as the population of Belgium.

Demographic takeoff   The second half of the twentieth century is a unique episode in the history of world population. Never before has the population multiplied at such a speed, and almost assuredly, in view of ecological constraints and human values, it will never do so again. Before world population took off in the eighteenth century, fluctuations in birth and death rates almost canceled each other out and on average resulted in slow population growth. It took all of human history, until 1800, for population to reach one billion (roughly equal to today's population of Europe and North America combined). It took 130 years, until 1930, to add the second billion. It took only 60 years, until 1960, to add the third billion. The fourth billion was added between 1960 and 1975 and the five billion mark was passed in 1987. At present rates of increase, the sixth billion should be added in 1997.

Simple extrapolation of the current world population growth rate gives rise to spectacular increases in human numbers: growing at the estimated global growth rate of 1.57 percent per year, compounded annually, population would more than double in 50 years, then more than double again in the next 50, reaching almost 30 billion by the year 2100. In fact, if birth and death rates remained frozen at current levels, world population could rise to the neighborhood of 700 billion by the end of the next century, because the high fertility, less industrialized countries would be accumulating a steadily growing weight.

But, to put it simply, since no one would choose to live in such a world, no one will live in it; the human population, in contrast to all other species, has the potential to control its own reproduction and is increasingly doing so. Although annual absolute increments to population continue to rise, the annual growth rate of world population has declined from its peak of 2.1 percent per year in the late 1960s and will decline further. The often-heard comment that the human population is *exploding* is in error; what is surprising is not how fast it is growing, but how decisively that growth is decelerating.

Demographic transition Writing at the end of the twenty-first century, historians will almost certainly consider the last decades of the twentieth century as those during which the world, considered as a whole, entered the terminal stages of the *demographic transition* which began in more industrialized countries the late eighteenth century and spread to less industrialized countries in the last half of the twentieth (Davis 1954, 1991, Coale 1973, Notestein 1975). The theory of the demographic transition predicts that, as living standards rise, first mortality rates decline and then, somewhat later, fertility rates decline. Perhaps we should qualify the term theory, because demographic transition theory is really just a generalization of events in what are now the more industrialized countries, where mortality rates declined comparatively gradually, beginning in the late 1700s, and then more rapidly in the late 1800s and where, after a lag of 75 to 100 years, fertility rates declined as well. We might also wish to use the plural, demographic transitions, because the long-term historical record shows that different societies experienced transition in different ways and from recent history that the various regions of the world are following distinctive paths (Tabah 1989). Nonetheless, the broad result was, and is, a gradual transition from a small, slowly growing population with high mortality and high fertility to a large, slowly growing population with low mortality and low fertility rates. During the transition itself, population growth accelerates because the decline in mortality precedes the decline in fertility.

The broad outlines of demographic transition in less industrialized countries can be seen in Table 2.1. Between 1950–55 and 1970–75, life expectancy increased from 40.9 to 54.6 years for both sexes combined, while fertility remained almost unchanged at a TFR of about 6. As a result, the population growth rate accelerated from 2.05 percent per year in the first five-year interval to 2.37 percent per year in the second. Between 1970–75 and 1990–95, however, the TFR fell by over 40 percent, to approximately 3.5. As a result, despite continued improvements in mortality conditions (life expectancy increased to 62.3), the growth rate of population in less industrialized countries declined to 1.88 percent per year. Underlying this average were, of course, very different regional patterns; for example, in Latin America the rate of population growth declined throughout the period, while in Africa it accelerated throughout the period.

Such regional differences remind us that blind extrapolation on the basis of cross-sectional data is risky. That is, it is not necessarily sage to assume that, just because the TFR is inversely correlated with level of income in cross-section, individual less industrialized countries will inevitably experience fertility decline as their economies grow. Nonetheless, trends have overwhelmingly confirmed the relevance of demographic transition theory, formulated on the basis of historical experience in more industrialized countries, to less industrialized countries. With the exception of pockets where religious or cultural beliefs are strongly pro-natalist, fertility decline is well advanced in all regions except sub-Saharan Africa and, even in that region, early signs of fertility decline can be perceived. In Southeast Asia and many countries in Latin America, fertility rates are on a par with those in more industrialized countries only several decades ago, and in extreme cases such as Taiwan and Korea, fertility is at subreplacement levels.[2] Thus, the assertion made at the beginning of the previous paragraph: taken as a whole, more and less industrialized countries together, the world is entering the later stages of the demographic transition that began in the eighteenth century.

The greatest difference between the demographic transition processes in the more and less industrialized countries has been the speed of mortality decline. Life expectancy in Europe rose gradually from about 35 in 1800 to about 50 in 1900, 66.5 at the end of the Second World War and 74.4 in 1995. In less industrialized countries, by contrast, life expectancy shot up from 40.9 at the end of the Second World War to 62.3 in 1995; that is, the increase that took more industrialized countries about one and a half centuries to achieve came to pass in half a century. As a result of the speed of the mortality decline, populations in less industrialized countries are growing much more rapidly today than did the populations of the present more industrialized countries at the comparable stage of their own demographic transition. The effect is compounded because, whereas mortality decline in more industrialized countries was relatively uniform over the age spectrum, mortality decline in less industrialized countries was heavily concentrated in infancy and early childhood. This has a pronounced multiplier effect on population growth, as females who would have died in childhood survive to bear children of their own. An important implication of this is that population growth in less industrialized countries is not only rapid, it is *very* rapid—three times the rate of growth in the present more industrialized countries during the comparable stage of their demographic transition.

---

2. Replacement-level fertility is the TFR which, if maintained over the long term, would result in an equilibrium in which each generation precisely replaced itself. Because of population momentum, discussed below, an instantaneous transition to replacement-level fertility would not immediately arrest growth in a population which has been expanding. The replacement-level TFR depends on the sex ratio at birth (which varies slightly from population to population) and the toll taken by mortality between infancy and the end of the reproductive lifespan. In countries that have undergone the initial mortality decline stage of the demographic transition, the replacement-level TFR is roughly 2.1.

Age structure, momentum, and near-term projections

Trends in population growth far into the future are already, to a large extent, embedded in the current population. Population growth is characterized by a momentum that arises from the persistence of a population's age structure; thus, even if age-specific fertility rates decline rapidly, the youthful age structure of a high fertility population ensures that it will continue to grow, albeit at a diminishing rate, for many years, as progressively larger cohorts of young women enter their reproductive years. Age structure is highly persistent, in turn, because *Homo sapiens* is what ecologists call a *K-species*, as opposed to an *r-species*: its evolutionary strategy revolves around physical robustness and behavioral complexity, that is, resistance to random shocks, not speed of reproduction following a random shock (MacArthur & Wilson 1967). One of the characteristics of K-species is a relatively long periodicity of generations; in the case of human beings, 25 to 35 years.

Differences in population age structure are illustrated in Figure 2.1, which compares two extreme cases—the young, rapidly growing population of Africa and the old, practically stagnant population of western Europe. Africa has more than twice as many children under the age of 5 than adults aged 20–25, four times more than those aged 40–45, and ten times more than elderly aged 65–70. In western Europe, the pattern is completely different and does not even resemble a pyramid. Because of very low fertility in recent decades, the pyramid becomes narrower at the base.

The narrowing of population pyramids at the base (from low fertility) and fattening at the top (from the aging of baby-boom cohorts and medical advances extend longevity) describes the phenomenon of *population aging*. As anyone who has followed political discussions regarding the uncertain future of social security systems can attest, population aging is an enormously important social phenomenon. Aging will continue in more industrialized countries and has already started in less industrialized countries, reflecting declines in fertility rates since the Second World War. Just as the speed of mortality improvements accentuated the implications of demographic transition for population growth rates, the speed of fertility decline in less industrialized countries will accentuate the aging phenomenon. In other words, not only will populations age in less industrialized countries, but they will age much more rapidly than did populations in more industrialized countries.

Just as engineers can predict the path of a braking vehicle with a relatively narrow margin of error because of inertia, demographers can project population several decades into the future with a fair degree of confidence. This does not arise from any methodological sophistication or particularly impressive insight; it is mostly because of the momentum of population; that is, the fact that

(a) Sub-Saharan Africa

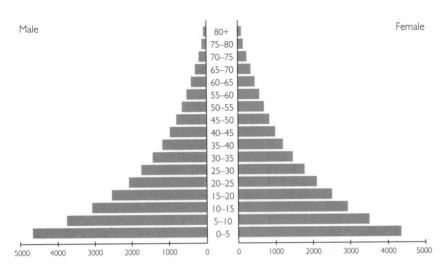

(b) Western Europe

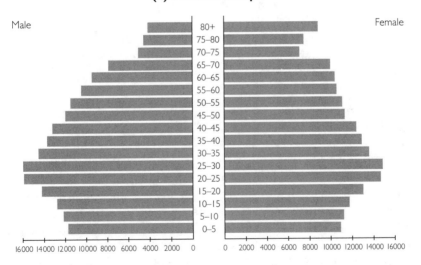

Figure 2.1 Differences in population age structure between a highly industrialized region and a less industrialized region.

a large part of the population which will be alive 25 years from now has already been born. Most, although not all, of the remainder will comprise the offspring of females who have already been born (i.e., we can estimate the number of potential mothers rather closely) and whose reproductive behavior is unlikely to differ drastically from that observed today.

Cumulated errors and long-term projections

Long-term projections, on the other hand, are another matter entirely. Because of the nature of the compounding process, small errors in the early years of a projection translate into massive inaccuracies in the outer years. Therefore, extremely long-run population forecasts are really little more than reasoned speculations. The wide high/low band and confidence interval cited above for the year 2100 arises mostly from uncertainty regarding fertility, not mortality. That the outlook is much more sensitive to variations in fertility than mortality is explained by the fact that, since high mortality in infancy and childhood has been substantially reduced in all regions and practically eliminated in some, variations in mortality rates do not make much difference in the numbers of women who survive to bear children. The striking fact is that, because of the nature of compounding, seemingly minuscule variations in the path of fertility over the next few decades will exert a disproportionate influence on the size of the population a hundred years from now.

The IIASA population projection

In this section, we take a detailed look at the assumptions and results of the population outlook whose global results were summarized above. Most citations to the research literature are suppressed because these are available in the original publication (Lutz 1996).

The cohort component method

In the cohort-component approach, an initial-year population by age and sex is *survived forward* according to assumed age-specific mortality, fertility, and migration rates. The size of the youngest age group is determined by age-specific fertility rates applied to the female population in reproductive age groups. Hence, the projected size and age structure of a population at any point in time depend exclusively on the size and age structure of the population in the initial year and on age-specific fertility, mortality and migration rates during the projection period. These four inputs—an initial year population and three sets of assumptions—are the inputs to any cohort-component population projection.

Most population projections are done by choosing assumptions which will result in a sensible range of forecasts; after the fact, the projections are labeled middle-, high- and low-growth variants. Usually the differences between base-line and alternative assumptions are fairly ad hoc. For example, until 1992, the UN Population Division's low-variant population projection assumed faster

100

fertility decline in less industrialized countries, but did not alter the assumed path of mortality rates. One school of thought held that faster fertility decline would be most likely to occur under conditions of accelerated development, in which case mortality would also be likely to decline more rapidly, tending to offset the deceleration of population growth arising on the fertility side. The problem is that differences of opinion regarding the causal models that underlie the components of demographic dynamics are too great to permit a systematic scenario approach. Thus, despite frequent misperceptions to the contrary, the high and low variants of most population projections cannot be interpreted as probabilistic confidence intervals; they simply represent alternative paths.

The IIASA population projection approach took the scenario approach one step further by asking an international panel of experts to make high/low variant assumptions for each of the three required sets of parameters for each of thirteen regions (see Tables 2.2 and 2.3 for mortality and fertility assumptions). The experts were instructed to construct assumptions in such a way that

Table 2.2 Alternative assumptions for life expectancy at birth in 13 world regions.

	1995	2000			2000–35			2000–85		
		L	C	H	L	C	H	L	C	H
Male										
North Africa	62.7	63.0	63.8	64.7	64.6	71.1	77.7	64.6	74.9	85.2
Sub-Saharan Afr.	50.6	49.6	51.1	52.6	43.1	54.4	65.6	43.1	58.1	73.1
China and CPA	66.4	66.9	67.2	67.4	70.2	72.0	73.9	70.2	75.8	81.4
Pacific Asia	63.1	63.1	64.1	65.1	63.1	70.6	78.1	63.1	74.4	85.6
Pacific OECD	76.1	76.6	77.1	77.6	79.9	83.6	87.4	79.9	87.4	94.9
Central Asia	65.1	65.6	66.1	66.6	68.9	72.6	76.4	68.9	76.4	83.9
Middle East	65.6	65.9	66.7	67.6	67.5	74.0	80.6	67.5	77.8	88.1
South Asia	59.7	59.7	60.5	61.2	59.7	65.3	71.0	59.7	69.1	78.5
Eastern Europe	67.3	67.8	68.3	68.8	71.1	74.8	78.6	71.1	78.6	86.1
European FSU	61.1	61.1	62.1	63.1	61.1	68.6	76.1	61.1	72.4	83.6
Western Europe	72.1	72.6	73.1	73.6	75.9	79.6	83.4	75.9	83.4	90.9
Latin America	66.3	66.8	67.3	67.8	70.1	73.8	77.6	70.1	77.6	85.1
North America	72.3	72.8	73.3	73.8	76.1	79.8	83.6	76.1	83.6	91.1
Female										
North Africa	65.3	65.6	66.4	67.3	67.2	73.7	80.3	67.2	78.7	90.3
Sub-Saharan Afr.	53.9	52.9	54.4	55.9	46.4	57.7	68.9	46.4	62.7	78.9
China and CPA	70.1	70.6	71.1	71.6	73.9	77.6	81.4	73.9	82.6	91.4
Pacific Asia	67.4	67.4	68.4	69.4	67.4	74.9	82.4	67.4	79.9	92.4
Pacific OECD	82.2	82.7	83.2	83.7	86.0	89.7	93.5	86.0	94.7	103.5
Central Asia	72.5	73.0	73.5	74.0	76.3	80.0	83.8	76.3	85.0	93.8
Middle East	68.0	68.3	69.1	70.0	69.9	76.4	83.0	69.9	81.4	93.0
South Asia	59.7	59.7	60.7	61.7	59.7	67.2	74.7	59.7	72.2	84.7
Eastern Europe	75.0	75.5	76.0	76.5	78.8	82.5	86.3	78.8	87.5	96.3
European FSU	72.8	73.3	73.8	74.3	76.6	80.3	84.1	76.6	85.3	94.1
Western Europe	78.6	79.1	79.6	80.1	82.4	86.1	89.9	82.4	91.1	99.9
Latin America	71.5	72.0	72.5	73.0	75.3	79.0	82.8	75.3	84.0	92.8
North America	79.1	79.6	80.1	80.6	82.9	86.6	90.4	82.9	91.6	100.4

Source: Lutz (1996).
L = low, C = central, H = high.

Table 2.3 Alternative assumptions for total fertility rates in 13 world regions.

	1995	2000			2000–35			2000–85		
		L	C	H	L	C	H	L	C	H
Male										
North Africa	4.35	3.92	4.13	4.35	2.00	3.00	4.00	1.54	2.04	2.54
Sub-Saharan Africa	6.18	5.56	5.87	6.18	2.00	3.00	4.00	1.44	1.94	2.44
China and CPA	2.00	1.60	2.00	2.40	1.50	2.25	3.00	1.37	1.87	2.37
Pacific Asia	2.88	2.30	2.65	3.00	1.70	2.35	3.00	1.29	1.79	2.29
Pacific OECD	1.53	1.22	1.53	1.84	1.30	1.70	2.10	1.24	1.74	2.24
Central Asia	3.35	2.68	3.34	4.00	2.00	3.00	4.00	1.45	1.95	2.45
Middle East	5.47	4.92	5.20	5.47	2.00	3.00	4.00	1.45	1.95	2.45
South Asia	3.77	3.39	3.58	3.77	1.70	2.35	3.00	1.20	1.70	2.20
Eastern Europe	1.66	1.33	1.66	2.00	1.30	1.70	2.10	1.39	1.89	2.39
European FSU	1.50	1.20	1.50	1.80	1.30	1.70	2.10	1.55	2.05	2.55
Western Europe	1.67	1.34	1.67	2.00	1.30	1.70	2.10	1.39	1.89	2.39
Latin America	3.10	2.48	2.79	3.10	1.70	2.35	3.00	1.60	2.10	2.60
North America	1.97	1.58	1.94	2.30	1.40	1.85	2.30	1.59	2.09	2.59

Source: Lutz (1996).
Notes: L = low, C = central, H = high. CPA = Centrally Planned Asia, FSU = Former Soviet Union.

their high/low variants represented a subjective 90 percent confidence interval. A ninth, central variant, set of assumptions was constructed by averaging high/low variant assumptions for mortality, fertility and migration. This implies eight alternative sets of forecast assumptions (high, low, and central) for fertility, mortality and migration. The IIASA approach, while still ad hoc, is somewhat more systematic, and it brings out explicitly the subjective probability distributions of experts in fertility, mortality and migration.

Experts' high/low assumptions were made for each five-year period out to 2030–35; these were then extrapolated to 2080–85. In the case of fertility, the endpoints chosen for 2080–85 were assumed to lie in the range 1.7–2.1, depending on the population density of the region. This procedure is ad hoc, but no more so than the common alternative, which is to assume that fertility falls (or rises, as the case may be) to replacement level and then remains fixed there. In the high mortality scenario, life expectancy was assumed to reach a maximum in 2030–35 and stay there; in the low mortality scenario, life expectancy continued to improve between 2030–35 and 2080–85. In the extremely long run, between 2080–85 and 2100, all rates are assumed to remain constant.

Tables 2.4, 2.5 and 2.6 present three sets of projection results. The scenario labeled Central (Table 2.4) combines central assumptions for fertility, mortality, and migration. The scenario labeled High (Table 2.5) combines high fertility rates with low mortality rates; migration rate assumptions are left at their central level. The scenario labeled Low (Table 2.6) combines low fertility rates with high mortality rates, again keeping migration at its central level. Thus, the two alternative scenarios give high/low growth bands. As discussed above, they have no probabilistic interpretation, but merely bound experts' assessments of

Table 2.4 Central scenario (central fertility, central mortality, central migration).

	Population by region (millions)		
	1995	2050	2100
More industrialized regions			
North America	297	406	467
Western Europe	447	469	413
Eastern Europe	122	109	77
European FSU	238	187	135
Pacific OECD	147	148	125
Total	1251	1319	1217
Less industrialized regions			
Latin America	477	906	1056
Central Asia	54	138	195
Middle East	151	517	738
North Africa	162	439	607
Sub-Saharan Africa	558	1601	1759
China and CPA	1362	1837	1796
South Asia	1240	2340	2202
Pacific Asia	447	776	783
Total	4451	8554	10353
World total	5702	9873	10228

For definition of regions, see Lutz (1996).

Table 2.5 High scenario (high fertility, high mortality, high migration).

	Population by region (millions)		
	1995	2050	2100
More industrialized regions			
North America	297	505	812
Western Europe	447	582	736
Eastern Europe	122	140	160
European FSU	238	246	289
Pacific OECD	147	181	217
Total	1251	1654	2214
Less industrialized regions			
Latin America	477	1169	2096
Central Asia	54	197	435
Middle East	151	685	1491
North Africa	162	593	1288
Sub-Saharan Africa	558	2390	4770
China and CPA	1362	2503	4055
South Asia	1240	3056	4701
Pacific Asia	447	1049	1688
Total	4451	11642	20524
World total	5702	13296	22738

Notes: CPA = Centrally Planned Asia, FSU = Former Soviet Union.
For definition of regions, see Lutz (1996).

Table 2.6   Low scenario (low fertility, low mortality, low migration).

	Population by region (millions)		
	1995	2050	2100
More industrialized regions			
North America	297	321	251
Western Europe	447	371	209
Eastern Europe	122	84	30
European FSU	238	139	51
Pacific OECD	147	118	65
Total	1251	1033	606
Less industrialized regions			
Latin America	477	687	454
Central Asia	54	92	70
Middle East	151	375	299
North Africa	162	311	227
Sub-Saharan Africa	558	1001	479
China and CPA	1362	1311	640
South Asia	1240	1743	872
Pacific Asia	447	550	289
Total	4451	6070	3331
World total	5702	7103	3937

Notes: CPA = Centrally Planned Asia, FSU = Former Soviet Union.
For definition of regions, see Lutz (1996).

possible demographic futures. Although the high and low scenarios bound probable futures, they also contain an inconsistency. If mortality is at its high assumption level, it is far more likely that fertility will also be at its high level; this scenario might be called slow demographic transition. Conversely, a rapid demographic transition scenario would combine low mortality with low fertility. These less extreme scenarios (from the standpoint of population growth) are given in Tables 2.7 and 2.8.

The rapid and slow demographic transition scenarios are more relevant for population policy than the more extreme high and low scenarios. This is because policies designed to accelerate fertility decline are also, to a large extent, policies that lead to mortality improvements. Policies to encourage population stabilization must, in this sense, cope with an internal contradiction that the faster fertility declines, the faster mortality declines as well. This also invests population policy with a more intense aging ratchet than is evident in the extreme low-growth (low fertility/high mortality) scenario. Although fertility reductions give rise to aging over the long term, reductions in mortality rates give rise to an aging effect in the immediate term as well, because older persons now alive survive longer.

Table 2.7 Slow demographic transition scenario (high fertility, high mortality, central migration).

	Population by region (millions)		
	1995	2050	2100
More industrialized regions			
North America	297	463	697
Western Europe	447	525	616
Eastern Europe	122	125	128
European FSU	238	209	217
Pacific OECD	147	164	183
Total	1251	1486	1841
Less industrialized regions			
Latin America	477	1080	1700
Central Asia	54	184	361
Middle East	151	610	1088
North Africa	162	519	912
Sub-Saharan Africa	558	1654	1827
China and CPA	1362	2321	3331
South Asia	1240	2558	2872
Pacific Asia	447	884	1136
Total	4451	9810	13227
World total	5702	11296	15068

Notes: CPA = Centrally Planned Asia, FSU = Former Soviet Union.
For definition of regions, see Lutz (1996).

Table 2.8 Rapid demographic transition scenario (low fertility, low mortality, central migration).

	Population by region (millions)		
	1995	2050	2100
More industrialized regions			
North America	297	360	318
Western Europe	447	424	278
Eastern Europe	122	97	45
European FSU	238	171	79
Pacific OECD	147	135	87
Total	1251	1187	807
Less industrialized regions			
Latin America	477	756	612
Central Asia	54	101	93
Middle East	151	426	453
North Africa	162	362	357
Sub-Saharan Africa	558	1437	1305
China and CPA	1362	1449	862
South Asia	1240	2098	1528
Pacific Asia	447	673	492
Total	4451	7302	5702
World total	5702	8489	6509

Notes: CPA = Centrally Planned Asia, FSU = Former Soviet Union.
For definition of regions, see Lutz (1996).

Forecast assumptions

Lutz (1996) contains chapters devoted to fertility, mortality and migration in less industrialized and more industrialized countries, as well as methodological chapters and special focus chapters on AIDS (discussed below and in Box 2.1) and the world food situation. In the following paragraphs, forecast assumptions are summarized in a few brief sentences.

Fertility   Because the overwhelming evidence favors further fertility decline in less industrialized countries, even high fertility variants in these regions generally call for fertility to be lower than it is today. One exception is China, where the high variant assumes that the one-child policy is relaxed to allow fertility more in line with desired fertility levels. The second exception is Latin America, where there is some evidence that fertility decline in some countries has stalled at a TFR of around 3.0, and desired fertility might rise again. High-variant fertility scenarios for other regions assume that the continuing fertility transition is retarded or stalled. That this can easily happen is illustrated by the important case of India, where fertility decline was arrested in the early 1980s at a TFR of about 4.0. Low-variant assumptions imply that fertility decline in less industrialized countries, as in more industrialized countries, does not stop at a TFR of 2.1 but continues to decline, carrying countries into the range of subreplacement fertility. The central assumptions that result from averaging high and low variants are slightly above replacement-level fertility in most less industrialized regions and substantially above it in sub-Saharan Africa.

In more industrialized countries, fertility rates rose through the mid-1960s, then declined to subreplacement levels in the 1970s. Southern European countries such as Spain and Italy lagged behind northern European countries such as Germany and Sweden in experiencing fertility decline, but the decline, when it came, was steeper. Fertility has recently turned up again in northern Europe, spectacularly so in Sweden, where provision of excellent daycare and other pro-natalist policies have encouraged childbearing. On the other hand, it is not clear that high fertility will persist. Similarly, it seems unlikely that the extraordinarily depressed fertility levels that have prevailed in eastern Europe and the former Soviet Union during the crisis of economic transition represent a long-term state of affairs.

Population forecasts have traditionally assumed that low fertility, more industrialized countries approach replacement-level fertility from below, just as less industrialized countries approach it from above. On the other hand, Westoff (1996a) has pointed out that there is no empirical basis for this assumption, and some observers (e.g., Bumpass 1990) see no end in sight to individuation and the low fertility that, practically by definition, it implies. Room for further decline exists, since, even in very low fertility societies, surveys reveal that a high proportion of pregnancies are unplanned. In view of the potential for further fertility decline, the low fertility variant assumption for the TFR was set at 1.4 in North America and 1.3 in all other more industrialized regions. The high fertility assumptions are 2.3 in North America and eastern Europe and 2.1 in western Europe and Japan and Australia.

Mortality Mortality decline in Europe, North America, and Japan came about over the course of two centuries as a result of reduced variability in the food supply, better housing, improved sanitation and, finally, medical progress. Mortality decline in less industrialized countries, by contrast, can be compared to one tremendous downward ratchet, made possible by the application of Western medical and public health technology to infectious, parasitic, and diarrheal diseases, since the Second World War. Apart from the acquired immunodeficiency syndrome (AIDS) epidemic (Box 2.1), there is every reason to expect the gap between life expectancy in more industrialized and less industrialized countries to narrow further.

The low mortality variant for Africa assumes that AIDS is brought quickly under control, in which case life expectancy is projected to increase at a rate of three years per decade. Under the most pessimistic AIDS conditions, life expectancy in Africa might fall by three years per decade. Thus, the central mortality assumption for Africa is no change in life expectancy. In South Asia and Pacific Asia, the high mortality variant assumes no increase in life expectancy because of AIDS mortality. The low mortality variant assumes that AIDS can be brought largely under control and mortality from other causes will continue to improve quickly.

Analysis of trends in age- and cause-specific mortality rates in more industrialized countries do not indicate an imminent leveling-off of improvements, so life expectancy is expected to continue rising in developed regions. Studies on occupational mortality differentials in Nordic populations, which are ethnically rather homogeneous, reveal substantial mortality differentials by socioeconomic status. This indicates that changes in lifestyle behaviors such as smoking and alcohol consumption may give rise to further reductions in mortality rates. The decline in male life expectancy, which was experienced since the 1970s by most eastern European populations and the population of the then Soviet Union, was caused in significant part by factors associated with the economic crisis and may be expected to reverse as these countries recover.

Controversy surrounds the question of whether there are biological limits to longevity and, if so, whether humans are anywhere near these limits. The traditional view sees aging as a process intrinsic to all cells of the human organism. Under this view, recent and future mortality improvements are interpreted as elimination of premature deaths and massing of mortality risk near the

---

Box 2.1   AIDS and Africa

Even today, it is sometimes heard that AIDS is "solving Africa's population problem." This is vicious nonsense. By subjecting members of the most economically active and productive groups to a wasting and premature death, AIDS is imposing an economic and social toll on Africa which is far in excess of any conceivable costs of rapid population growth (Ainsworth & Over 1994).

Yet, although the sheer numbers of deaths, and hence the magnitude of the AIDS epidemic on a human and social scale, is immense, the effects of AIDS on population growth rates is now known to be modest, even in Africa. Bongaarts (1996) estimates that by 2000, the AIDS death rate in sub-Saharan Africa will approximately equal the HIV seroprevalence rate (the number of cases based on diagnosis of blood sera), implying that seroprevalence will plateau. In the worst case, this results in an increase of the crude death rate by 10.7 deaths per 1000 members of the population; in the best case, 1.7 deaths per 1000 members of the population. Regarding (even modest) social response, a simulation analysis by Cuddington et al. (1994) finds that, in a typical African population, a rise in condom usage from zero to 10 percent cuts steady-state AIDS prevalence by over one-third, from 31 to 19 percent of the population.

In its 1992 round of population projections, the UN Population Division incorporated AIDS mortality into its national population projections for 15 of the most seriously affected African countries, with a combined population of 42 million in 1990. In these 15 countries, the UN estimates that AIDS mortality will reduce the average annual growth rate between 1990 and 2025 by 0.5 to 0.8 percentage points (roughly speaking, from 3 to 2 percent per year). In no case was the doubling time of a population, estimated to be on the order of 20–25 years without AIDS, found to be increased by more than two or three years by the effect of the epidemic.

How can it be that so devastating an epidemic can have only a limited effect on the population as a whole? The answer lies in the nature of AIDS mortality and the fact that the fertility rate in Africa remains very high. A woman infected with the HIV virus at 20 may not die of AIDS until 27, by which time she may have had five babies, only two or three of whom are seropositive. In other affected areas of the developing world, such as Thailand and India, much less is known about the possible effect of AIDS; however, it seems implausible that the impact on population growth would be relatively more serious than in sub-Saharan Africa, with its acutely elevated rate of seroprevalence.

---

biological limit of longevity. One study based on this view calculated a maximum lifespan of 115 years, with an average age at death of about 90 years. However, even this remarkable extension would imply a marked slowdown in the rate of gains in life expectancy which populations of most more industrialized countries have enjoyed in recent decades.

The alternative, and less orthodox, view, sees aging as a multidimensional process of interaction in which partial loss of one function in one organ can be compensated for by others, and only total loss of an organ system would result in death. Given improved living conditions and, possibly, direct intervention into the process of cell replication and aging, dramatically higher life expectancy could be attained. Small populations followed for short periods of time have been observed to have life expectancies well in excess of 90 years. Further supporting evidence can be found by studying changes in very old age mortality over time. Swedish data since 1900 show that mortality rates at 85, 90, and 95 have declined at an accelerating rate.

The traditional and orthodox views of old-age mortality conveniently bracket low mortality and high mortality assumptions for more industrialized countries. The high mortality assumption is that life expectancy for both men and women increases at a rate of one year per decade—that is, at a substantially slower rate than in the past. The low mortality variant assumes that life expectancy increases at a rate of three years per decade. The central mortality assumption is thus an increase of two years per decade in life expectancy. A special set of assumptions was made for eastern Europe to reflect the broader range of uncertainty and the recent deterioration in mortality conditions. If conditions continue to be unfavorable, life expectancy is assumed to increase by only half a year per decade; on the other hand, if conditions improve and, especially, if lifestyles change for the better, it will increase by four years per decade. Under the latter set of conditions, the gap between eastern Europe and more industrialized countries, which has broadened recently, will close again.

International migration   The future of international migration is particularly difficult to assess, for several reasons. First, reliable data are scarce and historical trends are very volatile. International migration tends to proceed in spurts, not as a continuous flow. Second, international migration depends closely on the prevailing economic, social, and political state of the world. Third, international migration is contingent on policy decisions in receiving regions. Low migration assumptions for all regions were set simply at zero, meaning that the number of in-migrants equals the number of out-migrants. High migration assumptions set the number of net in-migrants per year at 2 million in North America, 1 million in Europe, and 350000 in Japan, Australia and New Zealand. These migrants were distributed among sending regions using currently observed patterns of flows. In this section, only the central migration variant is discussed.

Results
If every region in the world followed the central fertility, central mortality and central migration scenarios—which are assumed to be the most likely ones as seen today—world population would increase from 5.7 billion in 1995 to 9.9 billion in 2050 and to 10.3 billion in 2100. Population would increase by another 4 billion before stabilizing around mid-century. The most extreme case of rapid population growth results from combining high fertility and low mortality assumptions in each region. In this bounding case, world population would double before mid-century and reach 22.7 billion by 2100. At the other extreme, if every region followed the path dictated by low fertility and high mortality

assumptions, world population would peak before mid-century (in about 2030; this cannot be inferred from the data presented in the table) and commence a steady decline. By 2100, it would have returned to its level in the early 1970s, a little short of 4 billion.

The extremes are not only unlikely by construction (experts were asked to make bounding assumptions) but somewhat lacking in meaning. For example, if fertility remains high in less industrialized countries, it is likely to be because economic and social progress have been slow, in which case it is more likely that mortality would be high, not low. Similarly, if rapid change results in low fertility, it is more likely that mortality would be low, not high. These alternative scenarios, rather than corresponding to rapid population growth and slow population growth, as above, would correspond to something that might be called slow demographic transition and rapid demographic transition. In the first case, world population would rise to 15.1 billion in less industrialized countries by 2100; in the second case, it would rise to 8.5 billion in 2050 before declining slowly to return to approximately its current level, 6.5 billion, in 2100.

Probabilistic extension

But all of these scenarios merely represent ad hoc combinations of assumptions; they have no probabilistic interpretation. The application of probabilistic methods to population projection is not conceptually simple (Lutz et al. 1996). The confidence intervals reported above result from fitting normal probability distributions to the high, medium, and low assumptions and combining assumptions randomly in a Monte Carlo simulation. These simulations also considered the possibility that fertility and mortality trends may be correlated within regions (e.g., high fertility in sub-Saharan Africa is more likely to go hand in hand with high mortality than with low mortality) and that regional trends may be either independent of each other (e.g., fertility in sub-Saharan Africa uncorrelated with fertility in Latin America) or correlated. As reported in the first paragraph of this section, the 95 percent confidence interval in 2050 is 8.1–12.0 billion and 5.7–17.3 billion in 2100. For regional results, the reader is referred to Lutz (1996).

It is often heard that world population will double in years to come. Yet world population doubles in only about one-third of the cases examined in the Monte Carlo simulation. This is the strongest evidence to date that at least the more extreme rhetoric in the international population debate is incorrect. To repeat, what is surprising is not how rapidly the human population is growing; it is rather how decisively that growth is decelerating.

Three certainties

However, three certainties emerge from the range of scenarios and from the Monte Carlo simulation:

- World population will increase substantially from its current level. Even in the lowest growth extreme scenario, population increases by close to 2 billion before starting to decline.
- The distribution of world population will continue to shift toward less industrialized countries. Even assuming rapid fertility decline and little improvement in mortality, less industrialized countries still account for a rising share of world population.
- The world population will continue to age. In the central scenario, the share of the world population aged over 60 is expected to rise from 9.5 percent in 1995 to 19.6 percent in 2050 and 26.8 percent in 2100. But even under the high fertility / high mortality (slow demographic transition) scenario, the share of the elderly rises to 14.7 percent in 2050 and 17.8 percent in 2100.

Sensitivity

Regarding the level of world population, fertility assumptions have a far greater impact on the outlook than do mortality assumptions. Holding fertility and international migration assumptions at their central values and allowing only mortality assumptions to vary, the forecast range for 2100 is between a population of 8.1 billion in the high mortality case and 12.7 billion in the low mortality case. Holding international migration and, this time, mortality assumptions at central values and allowing only fertility to vary, the range of variation is between 5.1 billion in the low fertility scenario and 19.0 billion in the high fertility scenario.

From the standpoint of long-run population aging, fertility assumptions also have the greater impact. Under central fertility and migration assumptions, the high mortality scenario implies 24.0 percent of the population aged over 60 in the year 2100, and the low mortality scenario implies 30.8 percent. Under central mortality and migration assumptions, the high fertility scenario implies 19.9 percent over 60 and the low fertility scenario implies 37.2 percent. Somewhat contrary to population wisdom, mortality and fertility trends are more important from the standpoint of population aging than are migration assumptions. Western Europe is a good example. Holding mortality and fertility assumptions at central levels and allowing only migration assumptions to vary, the forecast range for the proportion of the population aged over 60 is only from 34.1 percent in the low migration case to 36.5 percent in the high migration case.

111

Fertility decline in less industrialized nations

The rapid increase in the size of world population has always attracted the most attention, although population aging is arguably as important. And it is the far-reaching consequences of current fertility decisions for future population size that underlie the urgency permeating discussions, such as those at the 1994 ICPD in Cairo, of population policy in general, and family planning policy in particular. The regional focus on less industrialized countries stems from two causes: fertility levels in more industrialized countries are already at, and in many cases below, the replacement level and are unlikely to go much lower; second, less industrialized countries account for the largest share of world population. In terms of the size of global population, the most important uncertainties relate to the future path of fertility in less industrialized countries.

The literature on fertility in less industrialized countries is so vast—citations would be superfluous, since entire journals are practically devoted to the subject—that even an adequate summary is beyond the scope of this subsection. Much of the literature revolves around empirical data made available by three major data collection and analysis projects: the European Fertility Project, the World Fertility Survey (WFS), and its successor, the Demographic and Health Surveys (DHS). The first studied the European demographic transition; the latter two concentrate on less industrialized countries. In the paragraphs that follow, we concentrate on the question of what causes fertility decline. Insights into what sorts of programs and policies will accelerate fertility decline follow fairly closely from the answer. Whether fertility decline ought to be accelerated in the first place is a much thornier question.

Proximate determinants of fertility
The idea that parents in traditional settings aim at maximum family size is uninformed. In all but a handful of observed human populations, fertility is much lower than its theoretical maximum, which is on the order of 15 births per woman. The adoption of modern methods of contraception has, in some degree, simply involved the substitution of new methods for traditional ones. In some cases, it has occurred at the same time as the erosion of practices and mores, such as late marriage, prolonged breastfeeding (which lengthens the sterile period following a birth) and periods of postpartum sexual abstinence, which formerly depressed fertility (Tabah 1989).

The proximate determinants of fertility are age at marriage, prevalence and effectiveness of contraception, prevalence of induced abortion, and duration of postpartum inability to conceive, especially because of breastfeeding (Bongaarts & Potter 1983). Fertility decline must come through changes in one or more of the four proximate determinants. In fact, the adoption of contraception has been far and away the major source of fertility decline. Adoption of contraception has, in turn, been modeled as a diffusion process consisting of stages of awareness, information, evaluation, trial, and adoption.

Coale (1973) put the conditions required for fertility decline in a nutshell: fertility must be regarded as being within the realm of conscious choice, there must be advantages to lower fertility, and the means of fertility reduction must be available. More succinctly, couples must be willing, ready, and able. We do not devote attention to the first, important as it is (van de Walle 1992), because information technology has reduced the totally fatalistic attitude toward fertility to pockets, especially in sub-Saharan Africa.

This suggests three avenues from high to low fertility (Murphy 1993):
- rising availability of family planning technology and services, including maternal and child health programs, which reduce infant mortality
- changes in socioeconomic variables, mostly neoclassical economic costs and benefits arising from variables such as child labor, female participation in the labor force, and support in old age
- attitudinal and cultural changes, such as declines in the prestige value of children and improvements in the status of women.

In the first case, advantages to having fewer children were always present, but the means of fertility control were unavailable; in the second and third cases, the means were available all along, but advantages to having fewer children emerge. In economic language, the first case corresponds to one in which demand for fertility limitation is already present and what triggers fertility decline is an increase in the supply of family planning; in the last two cases, an adequate supply of the information and technology necessary to reduce fertility exists; what triggers fertility decline is a reduction in demand for children.

The proximate cause of fertility decline is not in dispute: in the less industrialized world it has occurred as more married women have adopted contraception (Weinberger 1994). The statistical association between various indices of family planning program effort and the prevalence of contraceptive practice is unquestioned at the national level. The problem is the fundamental chicken-and-egg ambiguity over causation: does family planning through national programs lead to lower fertility via increased adoption of contraception, or do parents' declining fertility desires, translated into demand for contraception, induce the supply response of a national family planning program (Box 2.2)? The difference between the positions was well captured by the rallying cries of delegates from more—and less—industrialized countries to the 1974 Population Conference in Bucharest: "Contraception is the best contraceptive," on the one hand, and "Development is the best contraceptive," on the other. A new position that emerged forcefully at the 1994 ICPD in Cairo, might be expressed as "Security and improved status of women are the best contraceptives."

Box 2.2   Fertility decline in Bangladesh.

The debate over sources of fertility decline has concentrated on Bangladesh, where the rate of contraceptive use grew from 3 percent in 1971 to 40 percent in 1991 and the TFR fell from 7 to 5 between 1975 and 1988. Cleland et al. (1994) argue that there was no conspicuous economic development or change in the standard of living for most of Bangladesh's households. In such conditions, they suggest, the explanation for reductions lies in supply side factors, including national commitment to deliver family planning services, as well as in nonspecific socioeconomic and cultural changes which can be subsumed under *ideational change*. In rejecting explanations primarily based on economic variables, they note that reproductive behavior has changed among all major social groups.

Kabeer (1994) argues against this view, seeing in fertility decline a neoclassical response to long-term erosion of the returns to family size brought about by growing population pressure against the resource base. Although both wealthy and poor individuals reduced fertility rates, their motivations differed. In wealthier households, investments in education and the quality of children offered a more diversified pool of assets, contracts, and opportunities. For poor and landless households the initially large dependency ratio, combined with an erosion of familial ties and intergenerational obligations, provided an incentive to reduce expenditures by having fewer children. Despite high risks of mortality caused by natural catastrophes, insecurity of property rights, and the persistence of economic dependency of women on men in Bangladesh, women from the poorest households showed the greatest willingness to use contraception, often without their husbands' permission (Kabeer 1985).

In the Matlab Family Planning Health Services District of Bangladesh, contraceptive prevalence is high relative to other areas of the country despite, the fact that income, status of women, and other typical explanatory variables are no higher. Cleland (1993) and Degraaf (1991) attribute this to aggressive provision of family planning services in the district. Thomas (1993) argues that the massive provision of public health assistance amounted to a reduction in insecurity and poverty. Robinson (1986) echoes Kabeer's view above by arguing that the explanation lies in the massive long-term decline in per capita income in the district. Finally, Pritchett (1994) pointed out that the that the level of expenditure per capita on family planning in the district was so high that fertility decline was virtually unavoidable, that is, that the example cannot be generalized.

The difficulties of generalization are highlighted by persistent disagreements among researchers, even within one intensively studied country.

There has been a natural, but unfortunate, tendency to treat these positions as straw men to be knocked down. All research suggests that fertility decline is complex, regionally differentiated, and context dependent. Generalizations are risky even within regions, let alone worldwide. Every truism has at least one counterexample. For example, fertility decline has sometimes occurred in the context of vigorous national family planning programs (e.g., Thailand) but it has also occurred in countries that have almost no national family planning policy at all (e.g., Brazil). Whereas economic growth has generally been a prerequisite for fertility decline, cross-sectional plots reveal outliers such as Sri Lanka and Mauritius, where fertility levels have long been much lower than would be predicted on the basis of per capita income alone. Finally, although fertility decline has sometimes occurred in the context of improving women's status (e.g., Kerala State in India), there are counterexamples (e.g., Indonesia) that experienced spectacular fertility decline with virtually no change in male/female inequality.

There is a clear synergism among the various factors; national family planning programs, combined with material and socioeconomic development, combined with improvements in the standard of living of the poor and empowerment of women, result in fertility decline.

The role of national family planning programs
From comparing fertility trends in broadly similar countries, such as Mexico and Colombia, and Pakistan and Bangladesh, Cleland (1996) has concluded that government attitudes toward family planning were a crucial variable. However, experience over several decades has shown that family planning programs have an impact only when desired fertility has already declined because of socioeconomic development and that they work best when integrated into other government policies in areas such as health, education and rural development (Concepcion 1996). The mere supply of contraceptive technology, backed up by government propaganda, is no guarantee of change; indeed, in Europe, marital fertility began to decline decades before modern contraceptive methods were available. Even in cases where fertility decline has occurred despite any evident change in economic variables or cultural values, scholars have argued that decline in infant mortality had triggered latent demand for lower fertility (Cleland & Wilson 1987, Cleland 1993). As a general proposition, national family planning programs are at best a necessary, but never a sufficient, condition for fertility decline. On the other hand, assuming that the socioeconomic preconditions for lower fertility are present, well-designed family planning programs can greatly enhance couples' ability to meet fertility goals and thus accelerate fertility decline.

Neoclassical economic costs and benefits
A reduction in the desired number of children can be described either in terms of shifting economic costs and benefits of fertility or evolving group norms and values; a third view stresses the barrier posed by poverty, insecurity and the low status of women in traditional patriarchal society. The economic benefits from children are of two types: old-age security and current income flows, which can arise from labor, from earnings turned over to parents, or from remittances sent by children who have left the household (Clay & Van der Haar 1993). Economic costs relate mostly to the costs of education and the opportunity costs of time expended in childbearing and childcare.

Fertility can be viewed as the outcome of a utility-maximizing decision made by parents in response to economic costs and benefits (Becker 1981, Becker & Barro 1988, Becker et al. 1991). Parents' well-being is considered to be a function of child quantity, child quality, and the level of consumption of a third, composite, good. The price of child quantity involves fixed costs, such as time expended in childbearing, and the price of child quality involves costs related to education and other investments in human capital. The availability of natural resources and environmental assets can be dealt with by adding these to the utility function, on the assumption that parents make a three-way tradeoff between number of children, material consumption, and state of the environment. Altruism can be added to the model by including well-being of the children as an additional argument in parents' utility function (Nerlove et al. 1987).

Fertility decline, according to the neoclassical model, results from a combination of increasing costs of child quantity (e.g., an increase in the formal-sector labor force participation rate of women, which raises the opportunity costs of time expended in childcare), and declining costs of child quality (e.g., increasing availability of opportunities for education). All else being equal, gains in income per capita associated with economic development would lead to increases in fertility, just as these gains lead to increases in the consumption of material goods. All else is not equal, however, as development is also accompanied by shifts in the relative prices of child quantity and quality. To these price-shifts must be added direct reductions in the economic rate of return on children as assets: modernization reduces the importance of child labor, and the opening of avenues for financial saving, and public social security schemes, reduce the value of children as pension and insurance assets. Shifts in relative prices and declines in the asset value of children combine to cause households to shift their consumption baskets away from child quantity in favor of child quality, as well as material goods.

However, empirical evidence for the neoclassical model is thin (Murphy 1992). Apart from various indices related to female education, measures of socioeconomic status as collected in survey data fail to disclose any significant associations with the number of children desired (Westoff 1996b). Multivariate cross-sectional analysis with national level data, as well as analysis of time-series data within countries, show only an ambiguous relationship between per capita income and fertility. This does not necessarily invalidate the model, because the shifts in relative prices that accompany rising per capita income are complex and hard to measure. Most evidence, however, shows that social and nonmaterial aspects of development play a larger role in fertility decline than simple increases in per capita gross domestic product (GDP).

116

Group norms and values

Although the neoclassical economic view is explicitly individualistic, a more sociological view encompasses group norms and values (see Box 2.3 for one model). From this perspective, high fertility in less industrialized countries can be regarded as a temporary, but stubborn, deviation from a pre-transition demographic regime in which high fertility was balanced out by high mortality (Cleland 1993). Although the biological imperative for high fertility has disappeared, the group norms and values derived from it have persisted. Worse yet, these high fertility norms have persisted while traditional practices that limited fertility have disappeared under the onslaught of modernization.

Norms and values can be purely ideational or have a strong material basis (Thomas 1993); in the latter case, they can blend with neoclassical economic

---

Box 2.3   Fertility and cultural values.

Simons (1986) related reproductive behavior in Europe to cultural values as measured by a questionnaire; he argues that, while economic considerations are important determinants of fertility, these are mediated and, ultimately, validated by cultural values. Simons situates countries in the quadrants formed by two axes: one runs from absolutism (absolute acceptance of norms dictated by the moral hierarchy) to relativism; the other from social collectivism (high value placed on the collective expectations of the community) to individualism. Loosely speaking, absolutism emphasizes prescribed norms, whereas relativism downplays them; individualism prizes standing out from the crowd, but collectivism prizes fitting in. Simons finds that countries with high fertility tend to combine moral absolutism and social collectivism; those with low fertility tend to combine moral relativism with social individualism.

Simons' model is essentially the same as that which emerges from cultural theory (Thompson et al. 1990), especially the closely associated grid-group typology introduced by Douglas (1978). Group refers to the individualist/collectivist dimension and grid to the personal/positional authority dimension. The combination of positional authority with collectivism establishes a *hierarchical* perspective in which persons are bound to socially imposed rules by strong group pressure, whereas the combination of personal authority with collectivism defines an *egalitarian* perspective in which individuals define their own norms but are under strong group pressure not to differentiate themselves from other group members. Individualism combined with personal authority gives rise to an *individualistic* perspective; individualism combined with positional authority defines a *fatalistic* perspective is which social norms are perceived to be absolute but their attainment is a matter of chance, not individual actions in response to group pressure. Interestingly, the gradient of high to low fertility lies not along the axis of group, as is conventionally assumed, but along the axis of grid. This suggests that fertility decline can perhaps be interpreted, not in terms of growing individualism at the expense of community identity and *belongingness*, but in terms of growing ethical relativism at the expense of moral hierarchies.

Van Asselt et al. (1995) have elaborated a comprehensive model of population policy in which views of nature, views of human nature, and attitudes toward desired number of children, contraception and abortion are classified according to the four perspectives of grid-group analysis. Global fertility outcomes, in this approach, are the aggregation of fertility outcomes in households falling into the four quadrants, each of whom set and meet fertility goals differently.

costs and benefits. Caldwell & Caldwell (1987) stressed material norms in arguing that, in traditional societies, a lifelong net flow of material resources from children to parents was maintained by rigorous adherence to the dictates of intramural and community hierarchies. Lesthaeghe (1983; see also Lesthaeghe & Meekers 1986) stresses nonmaterial norms, especially those related to individuation—the erosion of values that privilege the established order and the community over values that place the individual first. Ideational shift may be accelerated by government propaganda programs, education of girls, and so on, but the effectiveness of such programs will depend heavily on the prevailing cultural and normative context.

A vicious circle model: poverty, insecurity, and low status of women
The logic above implies that, in the normal course of events, development would give rise to changes in costs and benefits of children and to ideational evolution; these would combine to reduce demand for children. So long as adequate family planning infrastructure were available—a big "if", according to members of the international public health community—fertility decline would be more or less automatic. Why, then, does high fertility persist among many populations that appear to have access to the means of contraception? One interpretation is that high fertility is a rational response to insecurity, poverty, and the low status of women (Thomas 1993); this is the starting point for the vicious circle model, which will concern us often throughout the remainder of this chapter.

The link between women's status and fertility finds support in the fact that the strongest correlate (far stronger than income, occupation, labor force participation, and the like) of fertility has long been known to be female education (Cochrane 1979, Cleland & Wilson 1987, Cleland & Rodriguez 1988). Even when controlling for socioeconomic status, the independent effect of education tends to exceed that of any other socioeconomic factor (UN 1993). Although part of the effect of schooling is to raise age at marriage, the strongest link between female educational attainment and lower fertility is the greater likelihood that married women who were schooled as girls will use contraception. There are increasing returns (in terms of lowered fertility) as years of schooling rise, but women who have had even a few years of primary schooling are observed to be more likely to practice contraception. Education raises women's status within the household, enabling them to follow their own, usually lower, desired family size rather than that of their husbands; it also tends to shift values in favor of smaller family size by raising the probability that women will work outside the home. Parents' decisions to endow girls with even a modicum of education, as opposed to none at all, reflects a fundamental shift in the fairness with which women are treated. It sets in motion an irreversible shift in women's perceptions, ideals, and aspirations (Cleland & Wilson 1987).

The causal nature of the links between high fertility and low status of women has been studied most intensively by Lloyd (1994) and many collaborators. In addition to diluting household resources available to all children, high fertility has three effects that fall disproportionately on girls:

- an *opportunity effect*, that is, high fertility may lead parents to deny girls access to available public resources (such as schooling)
- an *equity effect*, that is, high fertility may make more unequal the distribution of available resources among household members
- an *intergenerational effect*, that is, high fertility may impede attitudinal change.

These and similar equity problems dominated the discussions of the 1994 ICPD in Cairo. The list of rationales for intervening to accelerate fertility decline is not a long one. One such rationale is that the preferences that underlie existing fertility preferences are unjust and iniquitous. This view, couched in neoclassical language which refers to broadening the choice set of women, prevailed in Cairo.

Conclusion

This section has identified three certainties in the world population outlook: further population growth, further tilt toward less industrialized countries in the world distribution of population, and further population aging. These follow from a sophisticated probabilistic population projection exercise that embodied the sectoral expertise of an international panel of researchers. It has identified one key uncertainty: the nature, and hence the speed, of fertility decline in less industrialized countries. The most recent discussions have stressed equity aspects of fertility, arguing that high fertility is a component of a vicious circle whose other components are poverty, insecurity, and subordination of women.

Population in the global climate change debate

Much of the discussion about the link between population and global climate change has taken the form of a population–consumption debate over the contribution to greenhouse gas emissions (and global environmental stress more generally). This section reviews the population–consumption debate and concludes that it polarizes discussions while adding rather little value. The impact = population × affluence × technology ($I=PAT$) model, which informs and in large part drives the debate, is seriously flawed. A more hopeful trend has been the emergence of an extended version of the vicious circle model described above into global change discussions. This has the effect of focusing attention, not on responsibility for global climate change, which may be in significant degree unavoidable, but on possibilities for strengthening the response capabilities of the populations most likely to be adversely affected.

The I=PAT model and the population–consumption debate

The population–consumption debate is indissolubly linked to the I=PAT model. "So entrenched is I=PAT," wrote one feminist critic (Hynes 1993: 3), "that critics and advocates alike debate from within it; like a mental boxing ring, it locks in those who take it on."

Demographic impact identities and I=PAT

I=PAT is a multiplicative *demographic impact identity* of the sort often used to characterize the effect of population on the environment. This model was introduced by Ehrlich & Holdren (1971):

$$I(t) = P(t) \times A(t) \times T(t)$$

where

     I = natural resources utilized or pollution generated (impact)
     P = population
     A = GDP per capita (affluence)
     T = natural resources used or pollution produced per unit output (technology)
     t = time.

In its original form, the equation was $I = P \times F$, where F was an unspecified function that measured per capita impact on the environment. F was conceived of as a complex function of the level of per capita consumption, the composition of the consumption basket, production technology and the level of population itself. For Ehrlich & Holdren (1971: 112), this complexity took the form of non-linear "disproportionate" impact of population on the environment. However, in order to operationalize the concept of environmental impact per capita, they abandoned the complex and unspecified function F in favor of a simple measure of material well-being or affluence, namely, income per capita. This resulted in the now-familiar I=PAT identity.

Using prime notation to denote annual growth rates, the I=PAT identity may be expressed in the following growth-rate approximation:

$$I' = P' + A' + T'$$

120

This simple linear expression lends itself to decomposition exercises in which global impact is divided into portions attributable to population growth, per capita income growth, and technical change. Such simple *I=PAT* decompositions have played a major role in the policy debate over global warming and environmental change more generally. Among authors who have presented allocations of responsibility based on *I=PAT* decompositions are Harrison (1992), Holdren (1991) and Bongaarts (1992). For example, the introduction of the *I=PAT* identity in 1971 set off a bitter dispute, carried on in the pages of the *Bulletin of the Atomic Scientists*, between Ehrlich & Holdren, who blamed environmental deterioration on rising population, and Commoner, who blamed the introduction of more polluting technologies (see Marden & Hodgson 1975).

An I=PAT decomposition of sources of growth in world energy consumption
The following paragraphs present an example of the sort of decomposition exercise that has become prominent in climate discussions. Although energy consumption is by no means the only link between population, economic activity, and climate change, it is arguably the most important. Tables 2.9–2.11 present the results of using the *I=PAT* model to decompose growth in global energy demand between 1970 and 1990 into demographic and economic components and to perform some simple simulations for 1990–2030.

Table 2.9 shows basic data on population, GDP, and energy utilization. The regions used are consistent those in Table 2.1. The key dynamics of the *I=PAT* framework are as follows:

- Population growth is concentrated in the less industrialized countries (2.2 percent per year over the period 1970–90, as opposed to 0.7 percent per year in more industrialized countries) where per capita energy consumption is low. On the other hand, equity considerations require that economic growth be concentrated in the same region where energy consumption per unit of GDP is high.

- Energy consumption is growing more rapidly than GDP in less industrialized countries; thus, the energy:GDP ratio rose from 0.466 to 0.611 between 1970 and 1990. It is growing more slowly than GDP in more industrialized countries. This is because energy demand is elastic with respect to GDP when economies are rapidly shifting away from agriculture and toward industry, but inelastic with respect to GDP when economies are moving away from industry toward services; in addition, within some sectors, less industrialized countries are substituting energy-intensive production methods for labor-intensive ones. Thus, change in the *T(t)* term in the *I=PAT* identity represents the combination of structural change in the form of changing sectoral shares in total economic activity, and technical change in the form of new production methods within sectors.

Table 2.9 Population, affluence and technology: *c.* 1970 and 1990.

	1970		1990
Less industrialized countries			
Population (millions)	2695		4141
Average annual change (%)		2.2	
GDP[a] per capita (1990 US$)	498		900
Average annual change (%)		3.0	
Energy consumption (mkoe[b])	625240		2277550
Average annual change (%)		6.7	
Per capita (koe[c])	232		550
Average annual change (%)		4.4	
Energy: GDP (koe/$)	0.466		0.611
Average annual change (%)		1.4	
More industrialized countries			
Population (millions)	1003		1143
Average annual change (%)		0.7	
GDP per capita (1990 US$)	10095		15000
Average annual change (%)		2.0	
Energy consumption (mkoe)	3797358		5715000
Average annual change (%)		2.1	
Per capita (koe)	3786		5000
Average annual change (%)		1.4	
Energy: GDP (koe/$)	0.375		0.333
Average annual change (%)		−0.6	

Source: Population, see Table 2.1

(a) GDP figures are based on market exchange rates (MERs) and thus exaggerate the income gap between less and more industrialized countries and, as a result, the energy-efficiency gap as well. Siddiqi (1994) discusses the possibly serious bias which may result from using MER instead of purchasing power parity (PPP) GDP estimates in energy analyses.
(b) Million kilograms of oil equivalent.
(c) Kilograms of oil equivalent.

Per capita GDP *c.* 1990 and growth rate of per capita GDP 1970–90 estimated by authors from United Nations Secretariat (1994).
Per capita energy consumption *c.* 1990 and growth rate of total energy consumption 1970–90 estimated by authors from United Nations Secretariat (1994).

Table 2.10 presents growth in energy demand in each of the two regions decomposed conventionally into growth in population, growth in income per capita, and change in the energy:GDP ratio. In both less and more industrialized countries, the growth rate of population was one-third as rapid as the growth rate of total energy consumption; following conventional logic, then, population growth accounted for one-third of the increase in energy consumption, holding all other factors constant. Growth in income per capita combined with structural economic change and shifts in production methods—in other words, economic change, broadly considered—accounted for the remaining two-thirds. Table 2.11 applies the growth rates in Table 2.9 to initial levels, so that the contribution to the absolute increase in world energy consumption can be judged. Between 1970 and 1990, world energy consumption grew by 178497 million kilograms oil equivalent (mkoe) per year, of which 82615mkoe (46.3 percent) represented increase in less industrialized countries and 95882 (53.7 percent) represented the increase in more industrialized countries.

As a crude way of estimating sensitivities, we can calculate the effect of freezing different variables at their initial year levels. Calculations employing the data in Tables 2.10 and 2.11 indicate that, if there had been zero population growth in more industrialized countries during the period in question, all other rates of growth remaining unchanged, the level of world energy consumption in 1990 would have been 8.8 percent lower than its actual observed value. If there had been zero population growth in less industrialized countries, the reduction would have been a roughly equivalent 9.9 percent, because per capita energy consumption is lower in less industrialized countries. If the level of per capita output in more industrialized countries had remained frozen at its initial-year level, but the energy:GDP ratio had continued to decline at 0.6 percent per year, world energy consumption in 1990 would have been 23.4 percent lower than the baseline observed level. If zero economic growth in more industrialized countries also meant no technical and structural economic change in the region, the reduction would be limited to 17.4 percent.[3] We do not consider the case of zero economic growth in less industrialized countries.

Table 2.10 Sources of growth of energy consumption, c. 1970–90 (average annual change, %).

	Growth rate of energy consumption (% per year)	Attributable to growth of population	Attributable to growth of income per person	Attributable to change in technology
Less industrialized countries	6.7	2.2 (32.8%)	3.0 (44.7%)	1.5 (22.4%)
More industrialized countries	2.1	0.7 (33.3%)	2.0 (95.2%)	−0.6 (−28.6%)

Source: Calculations based on data in Table 2.9.

---

3. Bartiaux & van Ypersele (1993) present a similar simulation over the period 1950–90 for carbon dioxide emissions, with more pronounced results partly because of the longer time period. Freezing more industrialized countries' population at their 1950 level growth reduces 1990 emissions by 22.9 percent vis-à-vis its 1990 observed level; freezing less industrialized countries' population effects an 18.2 percent reduction; freezing the carbon dioxide emissions per capita of more industrialized countries effects a 30.5 percent reduction.

Table 2.11 Sources of growth of energy consumption, *c.* 1970–90 (average annual absolute change; million kg oil equivalent).

	Population	Income and change in technology	Total
Less industrialized regions	27127 (15.2%)	55488 (31.1%)	82615 (46.3%)
More industrialized regions	31961 (17.9%)	63921 (35.8%)	95882 (53.7%)
Total	59088 (33.1%)	119409 (66.9%)	178497 (100.0%)

Source: Calculations based on data in Tables 2.9 and 2.10.

These back-of-the-envelope calculations give rise to two conclusions. First, if the numbers which emerge from the $I=PAT$ model itself are to be believed, the population–consumption data offer few guidelines for policies to reduce emissions, at least in the near term. The assumptions made above are extreme (population momentum makes it impossible to stop demographic increase in its tracks, and the chances are remote that policymakers in more industrialized countries would choose to limit economic growth substantially, let alone renounce it altogether). Yet even under these extreme assumptions, global energy consumption would still have grown substantially over the twenty-year period.

Second, if the discussion is to be couched in terms of blame, then blame must be shared all around. Both less and more industrialized countries have experienced rapid energy consumption growth, and both population growth and economic growth combined with changes in economic structure and technology have contributed to rising energy use. Even within the simplistic $I=PAT$ framework itself, there is no single "climate bomb" (Rahman et al. 1993).

Carbon dioxide emissions
The results above are for energy consumption, but some studies have looked directly at emissions of carbon dioxide. Among the various greenhouse gases, human links to carbon dioxide emissions are the most important in terms of global warming potential. While criticizing the conventional decomposition methodology employed above, MacKellar et al. (1996) assigned 41 percent of world growth in carbon-equivalent greenhouse gas emissions from industrial sources over the period 1965–90 to population growth. Working from the US Environmental Protection Agency's "No Response" scenario (Lashof & Tirpak 1990), Bongaarts (1992) assigned 50 percent of growth in global carbon dioxide emissions from fossil fuels between 1985 and 2025 to population growth. Over the entire simulation period (1985–2100), population accounted for 35 percent of growth in carbon dioxide emissions. Raskin (1995) used a modified decomposition procedure to analyze emissions of carbon dioxide only, and assigns to population growth a share of 32 percent for the period 1950–90 and 75 percent over the period 1990–2050 in the IPCC IS92a scenario.

Results vary depending on the definition of impact, on the time period being covered, and on the population scenarios employed. Some studies (e.g., Kolsrud & Torrey 1992) that have looked at mitigation strategies have found that future growth in energy consumption and carbon dioxide emissions is not very sensitive to reasonable alternative demographic assumptions. The reasons were summarized by Birdsall (1992: 13–15):

> First, differences in projections of population growth on a global scale are not that great. . . . Second, the potential for affecting future population size is greatest in those countries of the world where per capita emissions are currently lowest. . . . Third, it is likely that for given per capita income . . . a smaller population will produce somewhat higher per capita emissions, due to substitution of energy for labor.

The first point is especially important. Shares assigned in $I=PAT$ decompositions implicitly compare a baseline population growth scenario with one of zero growth (as in the illustrative energy example above). The policy-relevant comparison is, rather, one of projected baseline population growth to a reasonable alternative scenario. Population momentum alone is enough to ensure that the differences between the two are modest.

But reductions in population growth are only one way of meeting targets and may not be the preferred way. This is illustrated in Table 2.12, which combines three alternative IIASA population projections with three IPCC per capita greenhouse gas emissions scenarios (from commercial energy consumption only, in carbon-equivalent terms) to arrive at total emissions levels.[4] Looking only at the year 2100, holding per capita emissions at IPCC central scenario levels and allowing only the population scenario to vary, the range of global carbon dioxide emissions projections is from 12.4 gigatonnes of carbon in the rapid demographic transition (low mortality / low fertility) case to 28.5 gigatonnes in the slow demographic transition (high fertility / high mortality) case. Now holding population at levels implied by central fertility / central mortality assumptions, and allowing only the per capita emissions scenario to vary, the projection range is from 7.1 to 34.4 gigatonnes. Clearly, future emissions are much more sensitive to a reasonable range of variation in emissions per capita associated with economic growth, structural change and technical progress than to a reasonable range of variation in fertility and mortality rates. Reducing per capita emissions

---

4. Since the IPCC population assumptions differ from those the IIASA projection, the levels in Table 2.4 do not correspond to IPCC *total* emissions projections. There is nothing comparable about the magnitude of the differences in assumptions in the IIASA population projections and those in the IPCC high/low emissions scenarios. The example is meant only to be illustrative.

Table 2.12 Projected GHG emissions from commercial energy (GIC).

Demographic projections	Low (IS92c) 2020	2050	2100	Central (IS92a) 2020	2050	2100	High (IS92e) 2020	2050	2100
Low mortality/low fertility									
More developed	4.5	3.5	1.7	5.7	5.4	4.6	6.8	7.7	7.5
Less developed	3.2	4.0	3.2	4.3	6.6	7.8	5.6	9.5	14.4
Total	7.8	7.5	4.9	10.0	12.0	12.4	12.4	17.2	21.9
Central mortality/central fertility									
More developed	4.7	3.8	2.6	5.9	6.0	6.9	7.1	8.5	11.3
Less developed	3.4	4.7	5.1	4.5	7.7	12.4	5.8	11.2	23.2
Total	8.1	8.6	7.7	10.5	13.8	19.4	12.9	19.7	34.4
High mortality/high fertility									
More developed	4.9	4.3	3.9	6.1	6.8	10.5	7.3	9.6	17.1
Less developed	3.5	5.4	7.4	4.7	8.9	18.0	6.1	12.8	33.5
Total	8.4	9.7	11.3	10.8	15.7	28.5	13.4	22.5	50.6

from central to low levels can reduce total emissions in the year 2100 by about 60 percent; slowing the rate of population growth from that of the central IIASA scenario to that implied by the rapid demographic transition scenario can reduce emissions by only 36 percent.

A critical look at I=PAT

The discussion above suggests that there is less to the population–consumption debate than meets the eye. Flawed models often give rise to such unproductive debates, and in this section we critically review the shortcomings of I=PAT. Some of the shortcomings we find are technical and may be amenable to solutions such as more careful specification of the model, resolution of mathematical issues, and availability of finer-grained data. Others are essentially irremediable and point the way toward a better model.

Mathematical ambiguities

Some conceptually simple but intractable mathematical problems arise in I=PAT decompositions. Among these are the following:

- The commonly employed growth-rate expression of the I=PAT identity is only a mathematical approximation, and over long periods of time (or even over relatively short periods of time if average annual rates of change are very rapid), it can give rise to misleading results. To give a single-year example, if X and Y each grow by 10 percent, then their product XY grows, not by 20 percent, but by 21 percent. Cumulated year after year over time-frames on the order of a century, such errors become significant.
- When a global I=PAT identity is expressed as the weighted average of regional I=PAT identities, care must be exercised in choice of weights: for

example, fixed weights reflecting initial-year shares will give rise to misleading results in long-term scenarios.

- A related problem (Lutz et al. 1993) is that when the decomposition method is applied over long periods of time, and when the regions employed are characterized by different rates of population growth, the breakdown between population and economic factors at the global level (the column sums at the foot of Table 2.11) is highly sensitive to the number of regions employed. In other words, an analysis of more industrialized versus less industrialized countries would give a different result from an analysis of more industrialized countries versus low-, middle- and upper-income less industrialized countries. Bartiaux & van Ypersele (1993) pointed out that several works that are influential in the public debate, among them Ehrlich & Ehrlich (1990), UN Population Fund (1991), and Gore (1992) make similar elementary mistakes that arise from aggregating heterogeneous regions.

- Interpretation of decomposition results is difficult when terms on the right-hand side have different signs; that is, when changes in one variable are canceling out changes in another. The most common manifestation of this is when, as in the case of more industrialized countries in Table 2.10, the energy:GDP ratio is declining while the other two terms are rising. How can change in a term on the right-hand side account for a negative proportion of change in a term on the left-hand side; or account for more than 100 percent of change in a term on the left-hand side (which is possible if one of the terms on the right-hand side is negative)? The mathematics may be correct, but the meaning is ambiguous. When the terms canceling on the right-hand side are large relative to the term on the left-hand side, minor changes in rates of growth on the right-hand side can make for major changes in proportional allocations of responsibility (Box 2.4).

Box 2.4   Ambiguities arising from opposite signs

An example: in state of the world A, population grows at 1 percent per year, per capita GDP grows at 2 percent per year and the ratio of impact to GDP declines at 2 percent per year, making for a rate of growth of impact of 1 percent per year. According to conventional logic, population growth accounts for 100 percent of rising impact, economic growth for 200 percent, and changing technology for –200 percent. In state of the world B, impact per unit GDP declines by 1.5 percent per year, all else remaining equal, so that impact on the left-hand side grows at 1.5 percent per year. Population growth, again according to conventional logic, now accounts for 66.7 percent of rising impact, economic growth for 133 percent, and changing technology for –100 percent. A minor change in a variable on the left-hand side has completely changed results.

Ecological threshold and scale effects
The proportional rate of increase in environmental impacts is not of greatest concern, but their absolute magnitudes are: tonnes of carbon residing in the atmosphere, tonnes of topsoil washed away, tonnes of biomass lost through deforestation, and so on (Keyfitz 1992). By this logic, any discussion in terms of dimensionless growth rates is irrelevant. $I=PAT$ expressions in terms of growth rates can easily be translated back into absolute magnitudes, as in Table 2.11, but this is not always done in practice. If ecological discontinuities exist, non-linearities and threshold effects, then the log-linear $I=PAT$ identity will under-estimate scale effects.

Ecological complexity and feedbacks
The operational definition of impact as total utilization of natural resources or total emission of pollution (as opposed to Ehrlich & Holdren's original complex F) is straightforward when the natural resource is a nonrenewable one or the pollutant is one for which the environment has no assimilative capacity. However, this strategy amounts to carving up overall environmental impact, which is too complex to express in a tractable identity, into a series of linearly separable impacts: utilization of fossil fuels, utilization of copper, emissions of carbon dioxide, emissions of chlorofluorocarbons, and so on. A disadvantage of this divide-and-conquer strategy is that the effect of each individual impact on over-all environmental sustainability may not be linearly separable from the effect of other impacts; that is, there may be complex interactions that make the whole greater than the sum of the parts.

Ambiguities regarding the demographic unit of account
$I=PAT$ assumes that the individual, not the household or the community, is the relevant unit of demographic account (Box 2.5). Yet, to take energy consumption as an example, substantial economies of scale are possible at the household level.[5] Thus, all else (household income and the composition of the household consumption basket) being equal, a given percentage decline in household size

---

5. For references to studies in both more and less industrialized countries and a summary of findings, see MacKellar et al. (1996). To get an idea of the significance of such effects, US energy data from the end of the 1980s indicate that, not controlling for income, households consisting of two persons consume 58.1 percent more vehicle fuel and 37.6 percent more residential energy than households consisting of one person. Households consisting of three persons consume 30.4 percent more fuel and 15.1 percent more residential energy than households consisting of two persons, and economies of scale continue to grow as household size increases energy consumption. Based on a survey of studies, the authors conclude that energy consumption tied to the hearth and not the number of members of the household may account for up to 50 percent of residential energy consumption (including household transportation) in both more and less industrialized countries.

128

will be accompanied by a less-than-proportional decline in average household energy consumption. For a constant population, total energy consumption—average household consumption times number of households—will rise. Therefore, under conditions of declining household size, the share of environmental impact attributed to demographic factors will be higher if the demographic unit of account is the household than it will if it is the individual. Households versus individuals is not the only problem of demographic accounting; for example, calculations that take into account rapid urbanization in less industrialized countries, and differences in urban and rural energy consumption, give rise to dramatically different results than those that combine urban and rural populations (MacKellar et al. 1996).

Ambiguities regarding the economic unit of account
Fundamental accounting questions also arise about whether impacts should be considered in terms of impact per unit of GDP, gross output, domestic absorption, or some other unit. Impact per unit of GDP does not include production of intermediate goods. Impact per unit of gross output includes exported goods, the impact of whose production should reasonably be imputed to someone else's domestic absorption. Impact per unit of domestic absorption includes imports (weighted averages of impacts per unit of production in trading partners). Empirical difficulties aside, even the conceptual issues are not easily resolved.

Interrelationships between variables
The difficulties enumerated above are troublesome but are, in varying degree, amenable either to future research or to due diligence in the presentation and interpretation of results. But the greatest weakness of the $I=PAT$ approach, which is irremediable, is its lack of social science content. Shaw (1993: 190) put it this way:

How much attention should be devoted to apportioning blame to population versus other factors? Rigorous measurement of population impacts requires an appropriate explanatory framework, controls for variables other than population, testable hypotheses concerning population's direct and indirect effects, suitable data, a good understanding of multivariate analysis, and the inevitable round of debate over the accuracy of the findings. Some people are impatient with all this.

Thomas (1992) argues that authors who cite $I=PAT$ results as justification for favored policy interventions (e.g., UN Population Fund 1991) seem unaware that $I=PAT$ calculations arise from an accounting framework which is empty of causal or behavioral content.

Box 2.5   Population or households?

Between 1950 and 1990, average household size in industrialized countries underwent a decline which, in proportional terms, can fairly be termed massive, from 3.6 to 2.7. This decline was attributable more or less equally to changes in population age structure (mostly aging) and reductions in age-specific household headship rates. The latter reflect the weakening of the extended family, young persons moving away from home earlier and declining age-specific nuptiality rates, with consequent increase in mean age at marriage. In less industrialized countries, by contrast, average household size remained practically unchanged between 1950 and 1990, declining only from 5.0 to 4.8; in fact, if China is excluded from the total, average household size increased somewhat. Analysis indicates that, although age-specific household headship rates will presumably rise with modernization, changes in population age structure are likely to dominate changes in average household size. In the case of both regions, population aging will favor smaller household size. Perversely, the fertility decline that directly reduces environmental impact gives rise to smaller average household size through its effect on the age distribution, thus weakening the effect.

A study (MacKellar et al. 1995) which replicated the *I=PAT* decomposition presented in Table 2.10 in household terms (i.e., an *I=HAT* decomposition), assigned 58.3 percent of world energy demand growth in 1970–90 to demographic change, in the form of rising population combined with declining average household size, rather than 33.1 percent as in Table 2.10. Further research by the same team (MacKellar et al. 1996) found that the differences between household-based and population-based greenhouse-related emissions projections were significant. Because of population aging, with consequent decline in average household size, household-based estimates of total emissions were higher than population-based estimates. The scenarios also underscored the complications, in the form of changing age-structure of the population, which must be faced in translating different demographic scenarios into emissions estimates. Fertility decline reduces absolute population size, but the consequent rapid population aging tends to raise the number of households. For example, in the early years (until around 2020) the IIASA rapid demographic transition (low fertility/low mortality) scenario actually results in more households than the slow demographic transitions (high fertility/high mortality) scenario. Although fertility decline has no impact on the number of households for some 20 years, lower mortality at older ages results in an immediate increment to the number of households, in the form of aged persons living alone. Only in the longer term does the slower overall population growth in the rapid demographic transition scenario result in fewer households.

The lack of social science input may be expressed as a long list of ceteris paribus assumptions. Among these are the following:

- P *does not determine* P'   Population does not grow blindly as density and the resulting environmental impacts rise. Fertility, mortality and migration are all fundamentally density dependent.
- P *does not determine* A   Since research has failed to uncover a strong relationship between the rate of population growth and the rate of economic growth, this may not be an unreasonable assumption in the relatively near term. Over the long term, however, this assumption denies the possibility of the learning-by-doing and increasing returns to scale which are at the very heart of modern economic growth theory.

- A *does not determine* P   The relationship between fertility, mortality and per capita income is far from well understood (see above); indeed, the relationships may be so dependent on conditioning variables as to be well nigh incomprehensible. But the least likely theory is that there is no relationship at all, and it is this theory that informs $I=PAT$.

- P *does not determine* T   Economic structure and technology are, in large degree, responses to population pressure. For example, rapid population growth and the ensuing elevation of the population-to-land ratio may have the effect of concentrating output into the agricultural sector (Gilland 1986). On the other hand, neoclassical substitution mechanisms of the sort that underlie the Boserup (1965, 1981) model of agricultural intensification and technical change might lead to substitution of labor for scarce natural resources.

- T *does not determine* A   It seems a commonplace that the more efficiently materials can be transformed into economic product and the less noxious residuals are generated during the process, the higher will be the level of income. Indeed, the core result of the neoclassical economic growth model is that, in equilibrium, the rate of per capita economic growth will be given by the rate of technical progress, where the latter is defined as the rate of increase in economic output, the level of all inputs remaining the same.

- A *does not determine* T   It has been abundantly documented that economic structure varies predictably with level of development (Chenery & Syrquin 1975, Maddison 1989, Pandit & Cassetti 1989). Partly as a result, environmental impact per unit GDP either declines monotonically with level of development or first rises, then falls, that is, follows an inverted U-shaped path (World Bank 1992). This path reflects not only changes in economic structure but also the fact that rising income stimulates demand for environmental quality. The combination of changing economic structure and rising demand for environmental quality defines an *environmental transition* (Ruttan 1971, Antle & Heidebrink 1995) in which economic growth is associated with environmental deterioration when a country is poor but environmental improvement after a critical point in national economic development has been reached (Box 2.6). Carbon dioxide is, on first consideration, an apparent exception to the environmental transition model—international cross-sectional evidence indicates that emissions per capita rise monotonically with income over the entire range. When emissions are considered per unit GDP, however, the canonical inverted U-path reasserts itself.

Box 2.6   The environmental transition and its critics.

The empirical literature on the environmental transition is growing rapidly, as is criticism of the model. The principal background paper for this aspect of the 1992 World Bank *World development report* was Shafik & Bandyopadhyay (1992), who examined access to safe water, access to sanitation, urban atmospheric concentrations of particulate matter, urban atmospheric concentrations of sulfur dioxide, municipal waste per capita and carbon dioxide emissions per capita. In international cross-section, the first two declined monotonically with level of income; the second two followed an inverted U-curve peaking at a few hundred dollars in the first case and at just over $1000 in the second case. Antle & Heidebrink (1995) found an inverted U-curve relating to deforestation, as did Panayotou (1993) and Cropper & Griffiths (1994), and availability of national parks; the peak occurred at $1200–2000. Grossman & Krueger (1995) found inverted U-curves for a wide range of water and air pollutants and estimated turning points ranging from $2700 (dissolved oxygen content of rivers; this a trough rather than a peak) to $11 600 (cadmium). According to their estimation results, by the time per capita income reaches $8000, levels of virtually all pollutants fall with further economic growth. All prices are in 1985 Summers–Heston purchasing-power parity terms; for reference, GDP per capita in the early 1990s was roughly $1000 in India, $5000 in Mexico and $10000 in Spain.

Preston (1994) points out the importance of the interaction effect between per capita GDP and carbon dioxide emissions per unit GDP. He took advantage of the *I=PAT* model's log-linearity to express variance (across regions of the world) in the growth rate of carbon dioxide emissions as the sum of variances in the growth rates of GDP per capita, emissions per unit GDP and population; plus two times the sum of the pairwise covariances. He concluded, first, that variance in the rate of population growth was a negligible player (Birdsall 1992 makes the same observation); second, that even when the two covariances involving population were included in the calculation, variance in population growth rates could not be made to account for more than one-quarter of variance in emissions growth rates; and, third, the linear decomposition of variance is dominated by the huge negative covariance between the rate of per capita economic growth and the rate of growth of emissions per capita. Replication of the Preston decomposition using data at national level (MacKellar et al. 1996) has not only confirmed the basic thrust of these results, but suggests tentatively that the importance, not only of the A–T covariance, but of all pairwise interaction effects, has increased over time.

Arrow et al. (1995) have, however, expressed strong concern lest the environmental transition model be invoked as a panacea. It is relevant, they argue, only in the absence of ecological feedbacks and when local social and economic institutions can be counted on to respond to environmental damage. To some extent, Arrow et al. set up a straw man: although the policy document most heavily informed by the environmental transition model, the 1992 World Bank *World development report*, paid little effect to ecological instabilities, it in no way claimed that economic growth was a substitute for efficient and equitable institutions. Antle & Heidebrink (1995) are similarly cautious; Panayotou (1993) proposes that the environmental transition curve may shift up or down depending on the institutions in place. On the other hand, Arrow et al. evoked a strong comment from Ayres (1995) in which he expressed opposition to *any* further economic growth (including growth due to income-raising efficiency gains) which involves materials consumption or energy use.

Costs and benefits

Another aspect of the lack of social science content is that *I=PAT* contains no reference to the costs and benefits of various policies, which can be estimated only with economic prices that depend in part on values and tastes. For example, analyses based on *I=PAT* have generally found that the potential for abating emissions by policies to slow population growth in less industrialized countries is modest. Birdsall (1992), on the other hand, offers a solid rationale for such strategies despite the small magnitude of direct effects: the cost of fertility reduction attained by means of providing family planning services and female education is extraordinarily low. When this is taken into account, population policies in the less industrialized world compare favorably, in terms of the benefit–cost ratio, with carbon taxation policies. Wexler (1996) has estimated, on the basis of standard economic models of climate change (such as Nordhaus's DICE), large external economies to averting births, in which case Birdsall's logic would be further strengthened. We wrote above that, within the *I=PAT* framework, possibilities for mitigation of climate change appear modest, but when weighted by costs and benefits, the numbers may tell a very different tale. This failure to take account of human preferences places the *I=PAT* model in the same league with another framework which has often been invoked in the global environmental change debate—human carrying capacity of the Earth (Box 2.7).

The neoclassical economic tradeoff between utility from childbearing, from the consumption of goods, and from environmental quality, is absent from the *I=PAT* framework. Much argument based on the *I=PAT* model and virtually the entire population–consumption debate are based on the convenient assumption that people would really be happier if they either consumed less (mainly in more industrialized countries) or had fewer babies (especially in the case of less industrialized countries). One or both of these propositions may be true; a priori we do not know (see Ch. 4).

Conclusion

In this section we have analyzed a central tool used in the population–consumption debate, the *I=PAT* framework. This tool is not only weakened by conceptual and methodological problems, but it is flawed by its failure to take the social science perspective into account. A broader and more flexible view of population and the environment is necessary to avoid policy mistakes whose costs are potentially large. Although *I=PAT* and the population–consumption debate remind us that environmental impact arises from more than one factor, they do not provide a sound basis for policy discussions, let alone decisions.

Box 2.7 Human carrying capacity

Like the $I=PAT$ model, the concept of the human carrying capacity of the planet has played a large role in climate change discourse. The carrying capacity of an ecosystem is the largest population that can be supported without reducing the supportive capacity of the ecosystem, that is, supported in perpetuity. Carrying capacity is one of the simplest and most important models in ecology and the model has been extensively applied to laboratory and field populations.

Estimating the human carrying capacity of the Earth under various assumptions about natural resource consumption and efficiency in production is a perennial activity. Cohen (1995) has published an encyclopedic review of estimates made since the seventeenth century. With a few exceptions, these cluster in the range of 4 to 16 billion—by coincidence (but no more), a range very close to the range of population projections discussed earlier. Yet social scientists, especially but not only economists, have taken little interest in applying the carrying capacity concept to human beings. Hardin (1991) observes that the US National Research Council (US NRC 1986) report on population and development contains no reference to carrying capacity. This, he complains, is like an accounting textbook leaving out assets and liabilities. However, neoclassical economists are far from alone in criticizing the relevance of carrying capacity. Keyfitz (1990: 21) refers to it as "congenial to natural scientists and an irritation to social scientists." One obvious reason is that culture, institutions, accumulation and so on allow human beings to change the technical coefficients that must be assumed to calculate carrying capacity. Cohen (1995) argued, nonetheless, that a useful indicator might be a set of surfaces that define human carrying capacity—maximum supportable population as a function of efficiency in natural resource production and level of consumption per capita.

But indicator of what? Human carrying capacity, like $I=PAT$, takes no account of the welfare implications of a given set of assumptions (MacKellar 1996). For example, what are the opportunity costs implicit in best practice estimates where it is assumed that demand for the natural resource is squeezed to the bare minimum and factors of production are poured into the natural resource sector? These opportunity costs are a function of prices and thus reflect individual preferences and values as mediated through market mechanisms. To know the relevant prices, we would need to solve an economic general equilibrium model of a level of sophistication unlikely to be attained anytime soon, if ever.

One reply from an ecological perspective would be that the assumptions embedded in carrying-capacity calculations can be made to reflect aspects of wise stewardship that cannot be left to the price system; that is, cannot be left up to individuals to work out in the marketplace. A good example is to be found in the Daily et al. (1994) estimate that the optimal world population is 1.5–2 billion persons; among the factors considered are that the population should be large enough to support urban centers, which provide a critical mass for the arts, yet small enough to allow indigenous cultures breathing space to live in isolation. However, this example in itself shows how carrying capacity is contingent on cultural norms and values: it is based on a particular way of seeing human beings, their needs and wants, as well as a given view human beings' ability or inability to mediate impacts on the environment through institutions.

To argue the irrelevance of human carrying capacity (save perhaps at the local level for populations living on the edge of subsistence) is by no means the same thing as to argue the irrelevance of ecology.

Moving deeper into the analysis, we can see that the population–consumption debate stands in the way of a more constructive discussion because it suggests that unidimensional policies hold the key to responding to climate change. The reductionist nature of the debate comes as no surprise because it is informed by a reductionist model. A much more constructive school of research has focused on extending the vicious circle model of high fertility, introduced above, to encompass the environment. In this way, attention is focused on the vulnerable populations in less industrialized countries who are most likely to be adversely affected by global climate change, and on how societies cope with environmental stress.

Population and the environment

This section looks at the neoclassical economic model of population and the environment, and then extends it to encompass poverty, and environmental fragility, and high fertility. No model exists in a vacuum and the resulting vicious circle model is informed by a characteristically neoclassical view of nature, of human nature, and fairness.

A neoclassical framework

The elements of a flexible model of population and the environment were enumerated by Duncan (1959, 1961) in the POET model: the human population (P), socioeconomic organization (O), the environment (E), and technology (T). Early human ecologists (e.g., Ogburn 1922) treated the natural environment, social organization and technology as exogenous; the human population adapted and there was an end to the matter. Over time, however, the tendency has been increasingly to view population as active. Today, population is viewed as acting not only upon the environment, but also on technology (Boserup 1965, 1981) and social structure and organizations (McNicoll 1990, 1993). This is, however, an inherently challenging research area, and little is known about how population affects path-dependent technology and institutions. The challenge is to learn more about how population facilitates and impedes institutions of all kinds, including but not limited to the market, as they seek to mediate environmental stress. How does population affect the ability of human institutions to react to the stress that population inevitably places on the environment?

A framework for considering two-way links between population and the environment is shown in Figure 2.2. In the box at the top left are variables

135

describing the state of the population: its size, density, age and sex structure, and spatial distribution. These state variables reflect the operation of the underlying demographic processes of fertility, mortality, and migration. In the box at the lower right are variables describing the state of the environment: ambient concentrations of pollutants, biodiversity, soil fertility, and the like. These are caused by processes such as agricultural practices and industrial production.

Figure 2.2 shows proximate determinants, that is, factors that directly determine processes and through which other factors must work. The simplest example is fertility. The level of contraception is a proximate determinant of fertility. The level of socioeconomic development, which operates through contraception (as well as marriage rates and other proximate determinants), is an important influence on fertility, but it is not a proximate determinant. The same logic is applied in Figure 2.2 to environmental processes. A proximate determinant of deforestation is the clearing of new agricultural land; the rate of population growth and availability of alternative economic activities are more fundamental causes which work through this (and other) proximate determinants. Impacts upon proximate determinants are of two kinds: direct impacts, conveyed by the arrows at the top and the bottom of the diagram; and indirect impacts, which are mediated through what we have labelled the COST complex—cultural, organizational, socioeconomic, and technological factors.

Cultural values play an implicit role in models that seek to relate environmental impacts to population because many of the key concepts—such as environmental quality, security, population density—lie in the eye of the beholder. Perceptions are not static; they can shift over time. Whereas the natural scientific point of view privileges technological factors and often views technical coefficients as being fixed or rigid, the social scientific point of view privileges cultural, organizational, and socioeconomic processes which can either shift technical coefficients or promote adaptive attitudinal change when they cannot be changed. In economic analysis, the main mechanism of change is substitution in response to price signals.

The neoclassical economic model of population,
natural resources, and the environment

Analysts and researchers use and extend basic economics tools to study the relationships among population, consumption, and environmental effects. Underlying these tools are certain assumptions about human behaviors, natural resources and their use for human consumption, what is fair and equitable, and how markets mediate all these relationships. This section provides an introduction to how economic analysis is applied to issues of people and nature.

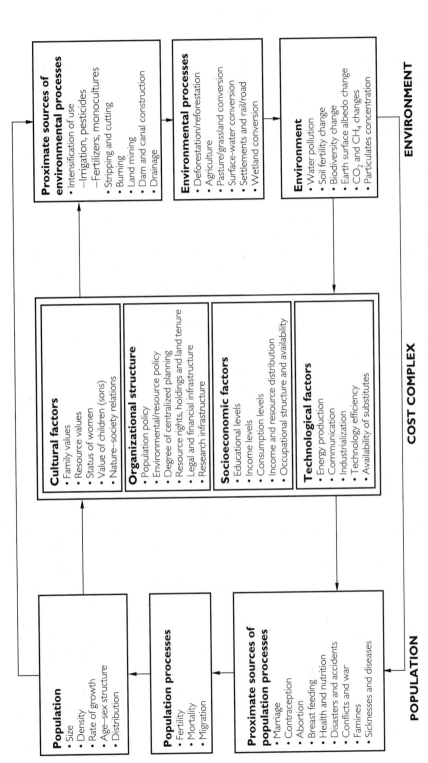

Figure 2.2 A conceptual framework for the study of population and environment.

POPULATION

Population
• Size
• Density
• Rate of growth
• Age–sex structure
• Distribution

Population processes
• Fertility
• Mortality
• Migration

Proximate sources of population processes
• Marriage
• Contraception
• Abortion
• Breast feeding
• Health and nutrition
• Disasters and accidents
• Conflicts and war
• Famines
• Sicknesses and diseases

COST COMPLEX

Cultural factors
• Family values
• Resource values
• Status of women
• Value of children (sons)
• Nature–society relations

Organizational structure
• Population policy
• Environmental/resource policy
• Degree of centralized planning
• Resource rights, holdings and land tenure
• Legal and financial infrastructure
• Research infrastructure

Socioeconomic factors
• Educational levels
• Income levels
• Consumption levels
• Income and resource distribution
• Occupational structure and availability

Technological factors
• Energy production
• Communication
• Industrialization
• Technology efficiency
• Availability of substitutes

ENVIRONMENT

Proximate sources of environmental processes
• Intensification of use
  – Irrigation, pesticides
  – Fertilizers, monocultures
• Stripping and cutting
• Burning
• Land mining
• Dam and canal construction
• Drainage

Environmental processes
• Deforestation/reforestation
• Agriculture
• Pasture/grassland conversion
• Surface-water conversion
• Settlements and rail/road
• Wetland conversion

Environment
• Water pollution
• Soil fertility change
• Biodiversity change
• Earth surface albedo change
• CO_2 and CH_4 changes
• Particulates concentration

Basic concepts

Economic analysis sees people as consumers who make consumption decisions based on their judgments of costs and benefits; judgments about the environment are made on this basis as well as decisions to purchase natural resources and man-made goods. Similarly, fairness, equity, and sustainability are interpreted through a cost–benefit lens. A well-functioning market, in which consumers have individually maximized utility and producers have individually maximized profits, gives rise to an economically efficient outcome. That is, since resources have been allocated over competing uses in such a way as to maximize total benefits minus total costs.

According to neoclassical economic theory, tradeoffs between population and quality of the environment may be understood in terms of the marginal economic costs and benefits (Kneese 1989, Cropper & Oates 1992). The survival of nature itself is not in question and nature is valued only to the extent that it is a source of utility to individuals. For example, if individuals derive more utility from highly developed national parks than from the existence of unspoilt wilderness areas, then it follows that existing wilderness should be developed for recreational purposes. At the limit of the neoclassical position lies Simon's (1981) critique of *The limits to growth* (Meadows et al. 1972) and *Global 2000* (CEQ 1980), and more recent work by Beckerman (1995). The term *exemptionalism* has been used (Dunlap 1983) to describe the view, implicit in the neoclassical model, that *Homo sapiens* is either exempt from ecological limits or, at least, is nowhere near having reached them.

Neoclassical economics has a distinctly unromantic view of human nature, focusing on how the individual gets ahead in material terms. At the heart of the neoclassical view is Adam Smith's celebrated invisible hand: individual self-interests give rise to a robust (in the sense of stable when disturbed) and efficient (in the sense of maximizing total output minus total inputs) equilibrium. The social system is permeated by the operation of an efficient marketplace in which price signals of scarcity are transmitted and appropriate responses are elicited. Some of this occurs within the economic sphere per se; for example, as copper becomes scarce and its price rises relative to other materials, producers turn to alternatives in manufacturing, investors allocate funds to exploring for and developing new copper sources (thereby profiting from the rising price), recycling becomes attractive, consumers substitute away from goods containing a great deal of copper, and so on. Other responses may be social and organizational in nature; for example, as income rises, demand for environmental quality rises and voters insist on policies and programs to achieve it. Shifting prices induce technical progress by alerting the research and development community to profitable avenues of technology development.

Sustainability is defined in terms of intergenerational transfers: fertility and natural-resource consumption decisions in the present period are sustainable if the natural environment bequeathed to the next generation is not inferior in value to that inherited by the present generation. A less restrictive, hence less eco-friendly definition by Solow (1991) is that the value of the entire capital stock (natural, human, and man made) should not diminish in value over time. The key phrase is "in value," which opens the door to the expression of individual preferences via the marketplace. An intergenerational allocation of environmental assets may be ethically abominable and yet sustainable according to the strict neoclassical definition of the term (Dasgupta & Heal 1979).

The neoclassical definition of sustainability opens the door for discounting—the systematic devaluation of future costs and benefits by a factor that reflects preference for consumption now, as opposed to consumption later. Discounting is often assailed by critics of neoclassical economics, but many problems become analytically intractable without discounting. For example, without discounting, the value of the stream of future disbenefits arising from any environmental damage (however slight) in the present is infinite. Therefore, the debate over discounting is best limited to the rate of discount, not to the practice itself (Pearce et al. 1990).

Some neoclassical economists would argue that the discount rate employed to analyze the costs and benefits of public investment projects ought, in accordance with the principle of consumer sovereignty, to be identical to that of consumers. Outside the ranks of these hardliners, however, discomfort with the extension of consumer sovereignty to time preference has always been acute (Robinson 1990). The very founders of modern welfare economics, while universally accepting time preference as a fact of human nature, have described it as "impatient and greedy" (Marshall) and "a polite expression for rapacity and the conquest of reason by passion" (Harrod; see Robinson 1990 for citations and many more quotes). Others have referred to time preference as characteristic of "children," "laborers," and "savages." Pigou (1920: 29) spoke of "irrational discounting":

> It is the clear duty of Government, which is the trustee for unborn generations as well as for its present citizens, to watch over and, if need be, by legislative enactment, to defend, the exhaustible natural resources of the country from rash and reckless spoliation.

This is a lucid statement of the stewardship ethic prevalent among ecologists. Although the discount rate can be derived analytically from economic models, these attempts have failed to displace the more qualitative definition of the discount rate as an expression of society's subjective values: its concern for the well-being of future generations. If households' values lead them to discount the welfare of the next generation heavily, then the economically optimal

139

consumption path will bear heavily on resources and the environment in the present.

The neoclassical model uses economic market concepts to describe the relationship between humans and their environment. Natural resources, in this model, are goods subject to market transactions and scarcity. Scarcity signals, in turn, will prompt various market responses, including technical improvements. Population plays a role, obviously, in what responses to scarcity are chosen; not so obviously, population growth may cause or contribute to market failures, although the research on this question does not provide clear answers. This section briefly explores each of these issues.

Scarcity signals
Natural resource supply and demand are mediated through markets, with prices providing the scarcity signals that elicit substitution, exploration and conservation behaviors. Partly because the share of primary goods (especially food) within the consumption basket falls as consumer income rises, the share of natural resources in economic output as a whole declines. Economic growth does not place pressure on the resource base because it generates a rising surplus (in the form of output and income outside the primary sector) which can be used to promote sustainability. That the surplus will be thus deployed is guaranteed by the fact that, as per capita income rises, so does demand for environmental quality.

The cornerstone of neoclassical natural resource and environmental economics is that all natural resource prices include a scarcity rent which grows exponentially at the financial rate of interest (if not, why would the owner not liquidate the resource stock and invest in bonds?). This reduces demand in the present period so as to conserve supplies for the future. The higher the discount rate, the lower the present price relative to the price in the future; hence, the more aggressively the resource is consumed.

The emphasis on prices reflects a fundamental assumption of neoclassical economics: scarcity is a relative concept, reflecting the ease with which one good can be substituted for another in production and, ultimately, in consumers' utility functions (Box 2.8). If scarcity is absolute—at least one good exists that has no substitute and the constraint is near enough to be relevant—then neoclassical economists would be the first to admit that their paradigm is inappropriate.

The key effect of population in the neoclassical model, absent market failure, is to drive up scarcity rent and raise the price of natural resources relative to the price of labor, thus shifting the distribution of income against resource consumers in favor of resource owners. In poor countries, redistribution of income from wages to profits may be (and probably is) distributionally vicious, but

---

Box 2.8   Ecological economics: an alternative

Ecological economics, which has emerged over the past quarter century based on the writings of economic mavericks such as Nicholas Georgescu-Roegen, Mancur Olson and Kenneth Boulding, combines elements of economics, ecology, and a deep concern with distributional issues. The theory tells a story of increasing scarcity with the threat of collapse. When the scale of total human activity—number of persons times per capita output or impact—was tiny relative to the size of the ecosystem, economic growth passed for progress and, based on the fact that each generation was better off than the last, appeared to offer a panacea for social ills. Now, the signs are multiplying that ecological limits have been exceeded (Goodland 1992). Total throughput of the natural system must be stabilized, or even better, reduced.

Because further growth is impossible, the theory holds, economic progress and, indeed, political security, can be achieved only by enhancing equity. Since equity is an explicitly normative concept, ecological economics is a self-professed postnormal science (Duchin 1994, Funtowicz & Ravetz 1994), driven by environmental values and combining advocacy with analysis. The advocacy element places ecological economics on the periphery of the economics discipline along with radical political economy.

Scale (and hence aggregate population size) is virtually irrelevant in neoclassical economics; it is absolutely crucial in ecological economics. The disagreement may be ascribed to fundamentally different pre-analytic visions of scarcity. Scarcity in neoclassical economics is relative—scarcity of good A relative to good B—which drives allocative decisions (e.g., allocation of investment resources between sectors A and B), which in turn balance out relative scarcities. Although the allocative focus implicitly recognizes that each individual human activity has an optimum scale (allocation of productive resources to agriculture versus industry, for example), there is no such thing as an overall optimum scale of human activity. By extension, there is no such thing as an optimum size for the human population.

The pre-analytic vision of scarcity in ecological economics is not relative, but generalized (e.g. Daly 1977), driven by growing scarcity of energy. Under conditions of relative scarcity, the potential to substitute abundant materials for scarce ones is practically infinite (Goeller & Weinberg 1976, Goeller & Zucker 1984). Under conditions of generalized scarcity, the price of virtually all goods would rise relative to the price of labor. Forced to allocate an ever-larger share of productive resources to eking food and materials from ever more costly sources (and cleaning up pollution), society would find itself caught in a vicious circle. Rapid population growth obviously worsens generalized scarcity, so ecological economists, in contrast to neoclassical economists, are deeply concerned by current population trends.

---

there is nothing economically inefficient about it. Governments are, in the event, free to tax winners and compensate losers if they so wish.

Technical progress

Population growth will also, by putting pressure on the natural resource base, give rise to technological innovation and progress which will permit that resource base to be used more intensively and more efficiently (Boserup 1965, 1981). According to Boserup's classic study, population pressure was responsible for the spread of the institutions that facilitated agricultural intensification and technological change in Europe. As population grew, more land was

141

brought under cultivation and fallow periods decreased. Ultimately, fallow periods were abandoned altogether in favor of continuous cultivation. New methods were developed to replace the soil's capacity to regenerate naturally. These consisted, first, of increased labor input, followed by organic fertilizer and animal traction, followed by artificial fertilizer and mechanical power. Intensive agriculture both required and facilitated the development of infrastructure for marketing, transportation, and storage. Thus, population growth led first to agricultural extensification, then to intensification, resulting at first in reduced soil productivity, to which farmers responded by introducing technical change.

According to one line of thought, population growth is the single most important factor driving technical progress (Simon 1981). At least at the national level, population can also give rise to economies of scale (efficiencies as the level of production rises) and agglomeration economies (efficiencies that are gained when more than one firm is able to locate in the same place because of the size of the market).

Market failures

The question at the core of the neoclassical economic view of population, natural resources, and the environment is whether population factors give rise to market failures or worsen the effects of already existing ones. The most important of these market failures revolve around the impact of population on externalities, public goods, and the tragedy of the commons:

- Externalities are costs or benefits that arise from production or consumption decisions, but which are not borne by the decisionmaker. For example, eroded soil (and the chemicals it contains) inflicts damages downstream which are external to the farmer. The farmer will fail to take these damages into account when making profit-maximizing decisions; thus, the level of erosion, although economically optimal from the farmer's point of view, will be too high from the point of view of society as a whole.

- Public goods, such as existence of species and a stable global climate, are goods for which indivisibilities in consumption exist; that is, the amount consumed by person A does not diminish the amount consumed by person B. The definition of a public good is inherently cultural; for example, although police protection is regarded as public in more industrialized countries, private neighborhood militias are widespread in less industrialized countries. In other cases, most importantly climate and the quality of the atmosphere, technical factors make the good indisputably public. This gives rise to the free-rider problem: people with relatively low demand for public goods attempt to free-ride at the expense of people with higher demand. Thus, the marketplace (and the election process) will lead to the production of a socially suboptimal supply of public goods.

- The tragedy of the commons has been a powerful metaphor since the publication of Hardin's (1972) much-cited article of that title. Although the tragedy of the commons is often associated with common-property natural resources, it is important to note that many resources (e.g., communal grazing lands in semi-arid regions), while held in common, are utilized only according to strictly enforced rules. Failure to control access, not common ownership, is the key. In fact, merely being a common-property resource is neither necessary nor sufficient for the tragedy of the commons: many tropical forest areas that are experiencing deforestation are, in theory, owned by the government, but the owner fails to restrict access.

In all three cases, research has concluded that the role of population is complex and/or heavily conditional on other factors:

- In the area of externalities, neoclassical economists frequently invoke the Coase theorem, according to which under suitable conditions (universality of property rights, absence of transactions costs, absence of wealth effects, and symmetric information), the pursuit of economic self-interest will give rise to bargaining and negotiation processes that will tend to eliminate externalities. Population might enter the Coase negotiation process in several ways. By giving rise to specialization and fragmentation of interests, population might raise transaction costs. If social and political institutions are better equipped to deal with moderate change than rapid change, then the Coase negotiation process might work better under conditions of slower demographic increase. If demographic factors lead to the emergence of an impoverished, disenfranchised subpopulation, then asymmetries of information would probably be worsened. However, imagining all of these problems arising on the national and subnational scale is easier than seeing them at the international level. On the international scale, rapid population growth may accelerate the Coase process by raising the stakes for all parties concerned.
- Population size and rate of growth do not alter the fundamentally public nature of goods such as the global climate, which arises from indivisibilities and the impossibility of limiting consumption. In other words, if supply of the public good is fixed, and if population grows, per capita consumption of the good remains as it was; its scarcity or abundance is unaffected. On the other hand, when supply of a public good is not fixed; for example, if the global climate can be stabilized by means of an ambitious investment program, then it is cheaper on a per capita basis to produce the public good in a large than in a small population. This point is

closely associated with economies of scale in supplying infrastructure, a theme developed by Simon (1981) and elsewhere. The same theme is important to installation of emissions-reducing equipment, provision of agricultural extension services, research and development, and other areas relevant to global climate change.

- Population size and, by extension, rate of growth exacerbate the tragedy of the commons by increasing the number of hands grabbing for a slice of the pie. Population pressures do not, however, give rise to common -property open-access problems where there were none before; on the contrary, they encourage privatization of formerly common-property resources and the evolution of rules limiting access to resources still held in common (Hayami & Ruttan 1991 for an example from the Philippines). This process may be distributionally troublesome, as elites may be able to lay exclusive claim to renewable natural resources that were formerly open to the poor (Jodha 1989 for the case of India) or provided an economic occupation of last resort (Stevenson 1989 for the case of wood fuel gathering in rural Haiti). Some writers (e.g., McNicoll 1984, 1990) have suggested that tenure systems are less likely to evolve toward sustainability under conditions of rapid population growth. The point is speculative, but plausible, and has become a standard feature in the literature. The US National Research Council (US NRC 1986) came close to saying the same thing when it stressed that slower demographic growth would give policymakers more breathing room in which to make politically difficult allocational decisions. Lee (1990b) has also identified a second tragedy of the commons (really an externality) as follows. Say a common property resource is optimally managed, meaning access is controlled and a user fee is charged. An additional birth raises the value of the resource and hence the user fee. The resource is still optimally managed, but now all couples—not just parents of the newborn—are paying the higher user fee.

On its face, an externality argument suggests that public programs to encourage lower fertility are a sound investment for climate-change mitigation (Box 2.9). On the other hand, the problems of estimating costs and benefits in climate change are notorious, a range of policies such as emission permits can also be used to correct the externality, and the greenhouse-related emissions externality is only one of the market failures in which population plays a (sometimes positive) role.

In summary, the neoclassical model suggests that, if markets and other social institutions work well, then a world of more rapid population growth will be one in which natural resources and environmental assets are more highly priced relative to other goods and services. If global climate change makes some natural resources, such as agricultural resources, scarcer and, what amounts to the

---

**Box 2.9   Population and greenhouse-related emissions
from a neoclassical economic point of view**

Application of neoclassical model to the problem of population and greenhouse-related emissions would give rise to the following analysis. Leaving aside implications for the atmosphere, economists agree that no common-property or public-good problem affects the consumption of fossil fuels; in no other area are property rights more extensively elaborated or minutely assigned. The idea that the finiteness of fossil fuel supplies is a rationale for slower population growth has practically disappeared from the literature; in part because of the obvious fact that, on the assumption that the resource endowment is ultimately exhausted, total utilization is invariant to the rate of population growth (Dasgupta & Heal 1979). Whether a path in which many persons consume the resource now and few later (rapid population growth) is preferable to one in which few consume now but many later (slow population growth) is a question of the discount rate.

The heart of the matter lies, rather, in the public-good aspect of the global atmosphere, in the external cost imposed on other countries by within-country fossil-fuel combustion and land-use changes and in the external benefit of within-country emissions control and the elimination of subsidies on the combustion of coal. From the discussion here, it seems unlikely that population plays a major direct role in worsening or alleviating the market failures that give rise to the accumulation of greenhouse-related gases in the atmosphere. However, by adding urgency to resolution of the problem and strengthening the bargaining position of less industrialized countries ("Share with us your wealth or we will share with you our poverty . . ."), rapid population growth in less industrialized countries may have hastened the onset of negotiations.

Wexler (1996; see also Appendix 4.5 of MacKellar et al. 1996) evaluates the external costs an average newborn will place on society through its projected emissions of greenhouse-related gases. A serious global warming scenario under which the marginal damage from carbon emissions was valued at $180 per tonne, evaluated at a 2 percent discount, rate yields a $20000 per birth cost in the more industrialized countries and a $13000 per birth cost in the less industrialized countries. A more optimistic scenario, assuming marginal damage costs of only $10 per tonne, evaluated at a 5 percent discount rate, yields a $620 per birth cost in the more industrialized countries and a $180 per birth cost in the less industrialized countries. To the external cost in the form of greenhouse gas emissions (and any other environmental externalities) must be added external costs, which arise from dilution of the available supply of public goods (such as schools). On the other hand, the birth gives rise to external benefits mediated through tax revenues, payments into the public pension system, and so on. Balancing out external costs and benefits is difficult and highly dependent on assumptions made, including the noneconomic external benefits of children. On its face, however, the externality argument makes a case for alleviating climate change through averting births.

---

same thing, raises the costs of burning fossil fuels, then these effects will be magnified under conditions of rapid demographic increase. Such effects can have distressing distributional consequences, but under the assumption of well-functioning markets, economic efficiency in the sense of allocating goods and services so as to maximize the present value of total costs minus total benefits will be unaffected. Dealing with the distributional consequences of more rapid population growth (and, for that matter, of climate change) is the task of political and social institutions and, ultimately, rests upon human values. It is impossible to say, on welfare-theoretic grounds, that one population scenario is preferable to another.

On the other hand, if markets do not work well, or if institutional arrangements impede response and the development of coping strategies, then rapid population growth is likely to exacerbate the effects of market failure. Under such conditions, and setting aside for the moment the strict standard imposed by welfare theory, slower population growth will be preferable to more rapid population growth. Moreover, the possibility must be considered that rapid population growth at the macro level and high fertility at the micro level may themselves impede the smooth functioning of markets and other institutions.

Population and renewable resources

Since the seminal US NRC (1986) study, researchers have placed special emphasis on links between population and renewable resources. The debate over population and agricultural resources mirrors the broader debate. The two polar positions are those of Thomas Malthus and Ester Boserup. Malthus proposed that a geometrically growing population tends to outrun an arithmetically growing food supply. Over the long run, population and agricultural resources remain in a state of equilibrium mediated by the available technology of food production and the prevailing living standard. The agricultural resource base is assumed to be fixed, and no allowance is made for technological change. Boserup (1965, 1981), on the other hand, argued that increasing population pressure itself induces technological change, leading to a more intensive use of land. A refinement on the Boserup model is Hayami & Ruttan's (1971, 1987, Ruttan & Hayami 1991) induced innovation model, according to which constraints imposed by an inelastic supply of labor are offset by advances in mechanical technologies, whereas constraints imposed by an inelastic supply of land are offset by biological technology. The examples of the first situation are typical of industrialized countries; examples of the second type are found in many less industrialized countries in general.

Boserup argued that opportunities for land extensification (i.e., rural to rural migration) are exhausted before intensification commences. Only when no more land is available do further increases in population density lead to substitution of more labor-intensive farming practices and modernization (such as mechanization and application of fertilizers and pesticides). The empirical evidence, however, is that land intensification does not necessarily wait for an exhaustion of land extensification opportunities. Pingali & Binswanger (1987)

146

argue that medium- and large-scale government-induced infrastructural investments, which facilitate land intensification at the farm level, become essential long before all potentially cultivable land is brought under the plow. They distinguish between farmer-based innovations and science- and technology-based innovations. The farmer-based innovations include changes in land use, land investments, development of organic fertilizer use, and the evolution of the tool systems. Science- and technology-based innovations include development of agricultural industry, science-based induced technological change, and development of agricultural research institutions. The authors argue that farmer-based innovations can only support slowly growing populations. In order to accommodate rapid population growth, science- and technology-based innovations are necessary as well.

Complicating the picture is the fact that the distribution of benefits from technical change is affected by policy interventions, such as export taxes and food consumer subsidies, of the sort almost universally applied in both highly industrialized (Alston et al. 1988) and less industrialized (Anania & McCalla 1995) countries. Some of these policy interventions are effectively endogenous; for example, rapid urbanization combined with failure of the agricultural sector to develop may lead almost inevitably to some form of consumer subsidy. Thus, there is a perhaps crucial, and unstudied, link between population growth and the impact of technical change. If population growth were to encourage policies that reduce the benefits of technical progress to those who must implement it, this would pose a serious obstacle to coping with demographic increase.

Theories and case studies of vicious and virtuous circles are derived from this debate over the role of population in resource use and the environment.

A vicious circle model

In this section we describe a vicious circle model, which combines the neoclassical model above with the fertility–poverty trap model which we discussed previously. Poverty, insecurity, and low status of women, although not market failures per se, give rise to similar problems. Much environmental damage in less industrialized countries occurs in disadvantaged local areas, which are characterized by acute deprivation: inequitable access to resources of all kinds, including land, credit to finance investments, and insurance to cover risks; insecurity; poor governance; and lack of opportunities for alternative economic activities or out-migration. The pernicious impact of poverty upon the operation of the price system was one of the major themes of the 1992 World Bank *World development report* focusing on environment and development, and the importance of market failures arising from poverty and insecurity has been

147

explored by many researchers: a general framework is given by Bilsborrow (1987) and among case studies embodying the approach are Stonich (1989) and many others.

Women are more adversely affected than men across the board, and impoverished insecure households living at the margin of survival are likely to deplete surrounding natural resources and environmental assets with little heed for future consequences. Even if such households desired to safeguard their surroundings, however, their room for maneuver, in the form of the types of substitution, adaptation, and behavioral change that are at the heart of the neoclassical economic model, would be painfully restricted. For example, when poor households intensify agricultural production to cope with rapid population growth, they are unable to afford the investment and inputs necessary to conserve soil. The smooth neoclassical substitution mechanisms mediated through the market are unlikely to operate under such conditions. Thus, poverty, insecurity, and low status of women are not only morally wrong, they are barriers to neoclassical economic efficiency as well.

The most influential work in this area is the unified theory of fertility and the environment developed by Dasgupta (1993). In this model, population places pressure on the renewable resource base, say the supply of wood fuel. Poverty prevents substitution of alternative fuel sources; the low status of women and girls devalues the rising amount of time and effort that they must devote to daily wood gathering (Agarwal 1994, Sen 1994). As the value of hands around the house rises, fertility decline is impeded both directly (the value of child labor rises; for example, Feldman 1990) and indirectly (attitudinal change, which might occur through education of girls, is blocked because girls are kept home to help their mothers). The result is yet faster population growth, yet further degradation of the renewable resource base, and yet further erosion of women's position. Poverty, depletion of renewable natural resources, high fertility, and low status of women have combined in a vicious circle which, at best, forms a poverty trap and, at worst, may lead to local ecological breakdown.

But the key to the vicious circle is that it is contingent on the local historical, social, and cultural context. A range of research verifies the existence of virtuous circles as well, in which population pressure leads to environmentally benign intensification of renewable resource exploitation, development of alternative economic activities, and so on.

A virtuous circle model

Land intensification, properly implemented, is a virtuous process; it involves maximizing the productivity of existing land resources. Research in the Machakos district of Kenya (Tiffen & Mortimore 1992, Tiffen et al. 1994) and in semi-arid northern Nigeria (Mortimore 1993) has described the virtuous cycle in which population pressure gives rise to farm-level innovations, elicits policy responses in the form of agricultural extension services, stimulates the growth of nonagricultural activities and off-farm employment, and the like. Before the Second World War, when population growth in Machakos was slow, agricultural productivity was low and there was widespread land degradation in the district. But after the war, when the population of the district grew much more rapidly, this growth was accompanied with improved food production and considerable improvements in land degradation.

This virtuous circle model is almost directly opposed to the vicious circle model. The Machakos example has become so celebrated that it has been pointed out that not all types of soils are able to support such intensification. However, further evidence that demographic increase can stimulate productivity growth comes from the unlikely case of Bangladesh, where high-density rural districts had higher agricultural wages than low-density ones and, over time, the rate of population growth was positively correlated with the rate of change of real agricultural wages (Boyce 1989). The key question facing researchers is to identify the types of institutions that promote healthy response to environmental stress (Box 2.10).

Conclusion

The vicious circle model described here represents the state of the art in population–environment research related to global environmental change. It incorporates flexibility, in the form of neoclassical responses to scarcity; equity in the form of the recognition that poverty, insecurity, and low status of women impede healthy responses; and ecology, in the form of stressing the fragility of marginal environmental zones. As a basis for policy dialogue it is a great improvement over $I=PAT$, in that it focuses attention on response to climate change rather than on responsibility for avoiding climate change, which may be in significant degree unavoidable. It is an improvement over the basic neoclassical model in that it recognizes that markets must function in a possibly hostile social and historical context. It focuses attention on those populations that are simultaneously most likely to suffer consequences of climate change and least able to adapt. And finally, it focuses researchers' attention on the crucial question of what sorts of policies strengthen and erode the ability of institutions of all kinds to cope with environmental stress.

Figure 2.3 represents an attempt to distill some of the themes developed here while moving beyond a strictly economic framework. Economic, social, and

---

Box 2.10   Virtuous and vicious circles

When does virtuous Boserupian intensification *not* occur? This is the focus of work by Bilsborrow (1987) and many collaborators (Bilsborrow & Geores 1994, Bilsborrow & DeLargy 1991). Among the contextual factors on which intensification is contingent are the existing level of living, availability of potentially cultivable land, availability of off-farm employment opportunities, size and distribution of landholdings, potential for labor and technological intensification, rural fertility level, rural and urban population distribution, and existing crop structure. Crucial to the success of the virtuous cycle is the intervention of supportive and responsive institutions, especially in the public sector. Under pessimistic sociopolitical and institutional conditions, the result of population pressure will not be Boserupian intensification, but either predatory cultivation of existing land resources or a vicious extensification in which inequitable access to land causes poor families to crowd onto marginal lands whose low productivity exacerbates, in turn, the problem of poverty. Lele & Stone (1989) documented such outcomes in six sub-Saharan African countries, and pointed out that a major impediment to agricultural intensification is that, whereas the economic gains to large families are low, the social gains, in terms of community status and the like, are high. Cleaver & Schreiber (1993) described an African population, agriculture, and environment nexus which might be called Boserup in reverse: a vicious cycle of rapid population growth, agricultural stagnation, and environmental degradation. The conclusion is that a policy-led intensification is needed to supplement the demand-driven (autonomous) intensification suggested by Boserup. Case studies from Asia and Central America have illustrated the vicious combination of population pressure, poverty, and inequitable access to land which forces cultivators onto marginal lands (Cruz et al. 1992), and the UN Secretariat (1991) concluded that there is reason to question the relevance of the Boserup model for many less industrialized countries in the late twentieth century.

---

political institutions mediate pressures on the natural resource base and the conflicts to which they give rise. In line with the nature of the discussion above, most of the sources of stress shown in the figure have to do with market failure, but this is not the end of the story. Ideational shift and ecological surprises are other sources of stress. The functioning of institutions is informed by their perceived ethical legitimacy, in particular whether they are perceived to be fair (e.g., du Bois 1994 for equity in water management). By definition, populations cope in one way or another with environmental problems. They may cope in environmentally virtuous ways; they may become trapped in a vicious circle; they may use various strategies, a mixture of benign and destructive. The means of coping will, in turn, affect the nature of institutions. In the case of the strategies associated with the vicious circle model, this may amount to institutional fracture and atrophy; in the other cases, it may amount to institutional deepening and strengthening. The means of coping may also directly affect the ecosystem under consideration, and it may alleviate or worsen sources of stress.

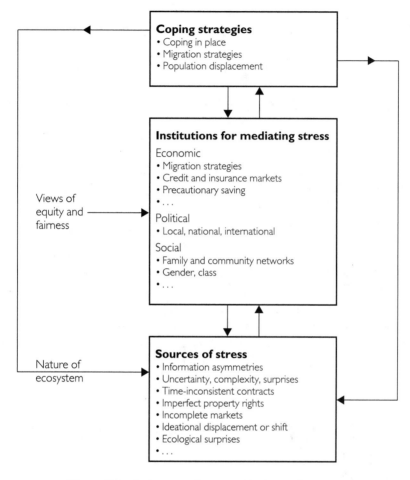

Figure 2.3 Environmental stress and institutional response.

Health

The previous sections have looked at the interactions between climate change and population issues as they relate to economic well-being and the state of the environment. Less well researched, but potentially important, are the possible impacts of climate change on human health.

The health profile of a human population is an outcome that integrates many inputs, some of which are outside human control and some of which, such as social and individual responses to disease, and perceptions of good health, depend on human behavior. Population is related to health in several ways:

- In societies marked by high and closely spaced fertility, the health of women and children tends to be impaired. Some evidence even suggests that the impact of family planning programs on women's health is greater than the impact on fertility.

- In rapidly growing populations, the scarce public health resources are strained. On the other hand, government health expenditures per capita are largely uncorrelated with health outcomes such as infant mortality and life expectancy. Dilution effects are a far less important policy problem than inefficiencies and inequities in the distribution of available health and education resources; for example, to urban-based curative hospital care at the expense of rural primary healthcare, to boys at the expense of girls, and so on (Jiminez 1989).

- In low fertility societies, population aging places special demands on the health system. It is cause for concern that, in both more and less industrialized countries, health systems will have to cope with any stresses arising from global climate change at the same time that they cope with the challenges posed by population aging.

The vicious circle paradigm is applicable to health insofar as good health and holistic well-being are fundamental human assets. Poverty is inimicable to health, and poor health is, in turn, a form of impoverishment. Poor health of rural workers, for example, is a significant barrier to rural development.

Global climate change: a new, fundamental, and complex health challenge

The sustained health of populations depends absolutely on maintaining climate variables within a range of tolerable extremes, protection from solar ultraviolet radiation, adequate supplies of food and fresh water, and (for various reasons) the continued existence of diverse species and their genes. Global climate change would pose a new, fundamental, and complex type of hazard to human health (Last 1993, McMichael 1993, Epstein 1995). As "new," "fundamental," and "complex" are words liable to overuse, this characterization is important to explore.

The hazard is new because, during two centuries of urbanization and industrialization, public health hazards have emerged primarily within geographically localized contexts, reflecting local demography, culture, technology, and wealth. Thus, patterns of infectious diseases, chemical pollutants, occupational exposures, and, more recently, the rise of affluent, risk-bearing behaviors (e.g. consumption of tobacco, alcohol, and processed foods; automobile transport) have mainly originated and been countered on a local scale. However, the disruption of Earth's natural systems associated with global environmental change poses a new, supra-population scale of health hazard. The hazard is fundamental because these systems together comprise a general life-support system which underpins the long-term biological health of all species.

Complexity arises because forecasting these potential health impacts entails multiple uncertainties, nonlinearity, and a long time-horizon (McMichael & Martens 1995). The first two of these characteristics pose challenges to prevailing modes of scientific data assembly and analysis and, subsequently, to the process of scientific inference. The long time-horizon suggests that much of the research will not be amenable to conventional hypothesis testing (and certainly not within the timeframe of relevance to social decisionmaking). Because of the complexity of the ecological and geophysical disturbances attendant on climate change, we should expect some surprise outcomes (Levins 1995).

The hazard is new also because the extent and rate of some of the predicted changes would fall outside the range of recorded human experience. Conventional epidemiological research relies on collecting data that describe current or past experiences of populations or groups, calculating risks, and elaborating models which explain variations in risk. By extension, the conventional prediction of health risks (i.e., formal health risk assessment) entails applying empirically derived exposure–response relationships to current populations with a known or presumed exposure profile. Thus, both the exposure–response and population risk parameters are real, or at least realistic. However, assessment of the health impacts of global environmental change entails the prediction of future health risk from scenarios of future population exposures. Such exposures may be qualitatively different from past experience, because they will reflect changes in a range of background variables, such as changes in nutrition and the distribution of disease-bearing vectors (e.g. ticks, mosquitoes, and fleas). Few historical data directly encompass the projected exposure scenarios.

The risks are not merely more of the same—more heatwaves or more air pollution, for instance. Rather, they would arise substantially via indirect pathways; in particular, by disturbance of natural systems such as the ecology of infectious agents, food production, and freshwater supplies. Researchers have long been aware that global warming may have both direct and indirect effects on human health (WHO 1990). Nutritional status, disease incidence, and morbidity/mortality outcomes are, in turn, related by complex, incompletely understood processes (Murray 1994). Another indirect effect would arise if coping with impacts of global environmental change diverted public and private resources away from health. Difficult as direct effects are to model and predict, the challenge posed by indirect effects is greater, because these effects are contingent on a wider range of assumptions. The further the scenario moves from the empirical epidemiological record, the more tenuous the prediction and the greater the likelihood of surprises.

Because of these difficulties, the impact of global warming on human health is uncertain, at best, and perhaps, in part, unforeseeable. This difficulty is compounded by uncertainties about regional patterns of environmental change, and by variations in the vulnerability of populations in those different regions. However, the bulk of research has concluded that, although some changes are likely to be beneficial, the net impact of global warming on human health is likely to be negative (McMichael et al. 1996), with indirect effects being more significant than direct ones in the long term. In other words, most of the health impacts of global warming, especially those mediated by disturbances to ecological systems, would be adverse. Among these possible negative impacts on health may be the following:

- increased morbidity and mortality because of more extreme events, particularly heatwaves, fires, cyclones, and flooding
- changes in infectious disease epidemiology, particularly increases in the spread and activity of a variety of vector-borne diseases
- health impacts of changes in nutritional status arising from changes in agricultural productivity
- disruption of freshwater supply, and perhaps sanitation, because of sea level rise
- extensive population movements, some involving distress of the sort associated with the environmental refugee model discussed in the next section
- health impacts of social stresses associated with global environmental change and its impact on the economy.

In this section, we focus on two health impacts that are most likely to prove significant and which have been most intensively examined: the direct effects of increased frequency of thermal extremes, and indirect effects mediated through alteration of the distribution of vectors which transmit certain infectious diseases. Although the first is much better understood, the second is likely to involve the greater impacts, because of the greater size and vulnerability of the population exposed to heightened risk, and the more limited resources available for response and adaptation.

Background conditions

Just as a fairly typical transition from high to low fertility can be discerned in the historical record, so can an epidemiological or mortality transition be described. In more industrialized countries, this transition was marked first by increased resistance to disease as a result of improved living conditions, then by mortality declines owing to improved sanitation, then by declines resulting from medical advancements such as vaccinations and antibiotics (McKeown 1988). The effect of these developments was to concentrate mortality into older ages where degenerative, rather than infectious and parasitic, diseases predominate. The most recent phase of the mortality transition has been reductions in some of these causes of death, such as cardiovascular disease and cancer. However, despite advances in high-technology, high-cost medical interventions, mortality rates in industrial countries are more closely associated with the equity of the income distribution than income level itself (Wilkinson 1994).

In less industrialized countries, the transition has been rather different, since modern medical technology became available before countries had undergone improvements in living conditions. Thus, as discussed in the early pages of this chapter, the mortality decline that took 200 or more years to occur in the industrialized countries has occurred in the less industrialized countries in 50 years. One result has been a gap within the Third World in the medical care available to the rich and the poor (World Bank 1993); for example, in countries where rural areas often lack basic maternal and child healthcare facilities or sanitation systems, the capital city may possess an up-to-date center for cardiac surgery. Although the urban/rural gap in healthcare is still the main concern, so is the gap between the urban middle class and poor, and between those elite workers with access to the public health system through membership in social security schemes and the rest of the population (McGreevey 1990). Good health is perhaps the most fundamental aspect of human capital, and reforming health systems to eliminate inequities and improve the health of the poor is one of the most promising opportunities for combating poverty (World Bank 1993). Steep health gradients across socioeconomic class are not, however, a concern limited to the Third World (Frank & Mustard 1994).

Health transition in rural areas of less industrialized countries must be placed in the context of continuing agricultural intensification. Growing use of machinery, fertilizers, and pesticides (often under conditions that would be considered unsafe in industrial countries), and the impacts of large dam projects are examples of factors that may affect health, as do more general agronomic practices (e.g., mosquito breeding is affected by how often ricefields are drained). One of the chief characteristics of health transition in urban areas is exposure to elevated levels of both traditional pollutants (e.g., particulates from woodfuel or charcoal burning, or sulfur dioxide and urban smog; Romieu et al. 1990, Pope et al. 1995) and of new pollutants, such as toxic substances. Rapid industrialization has not been accompanied by the development of institutions and regimes to ensure proper disposal of the harmful wastes generated by industries (Ludwig & Islam 1992 for Bangladesh, Asante-Duah & Sam 1995 for

West Africa). Marquette (1995) has written of the urgent need for improved information-gathering and planning mechanisms to cope with environmental health hazards in rapidly industrializing countries and in the transition economies, as well as of the need for a greater focus on the urban environment in a rapidly urbanizing world.

Several major components of the world health situation stand apart from the mortality transition model in its unadorned form. Recent years have seen a resurgence of infectious diseases and the emergence of new viruses (Morse 1991). Examples include the emergence of the human immunodeficiency virus (HIV), emergence of new vector-borne viral infections in the Americas, discovery of a new and spreading strain of cholera, the resurgence of diphtheria in Russia, and the emergence of various antibiotic-resistant microbes, including the malaria parasite (especially in Asia) and multidrug-resistant tuberculosis strains (among urban populations in the northeastern United States). Also well publicized is the upward ratchet in mortality in the transition economies of central and eastern Europe (Feachem 1994, Potrykowska & Clarke 1995). Some of these, such as the appearance of HIV, are classic surprises, whereas others, such as the development of antibiotic-resistant bacterial strains, fall within the range of experience and could have been predicted by models that accounted for the ecological complexity of disease.

The major deviation from the mortality transition model is, of course, the widespread increase in HIV infection and ensuing AIDS mortality. Studies discussed in Box 1.1 have concluded that the effect of AIDS mortality on population growth, although significant, is likely to be modest. On an individual and societal level, on the other hand, the AIDS epidemic is an epochal event, roughly on a scale with the 1918 influenza pandemic. In Africa, the social effects of AIDS are exacerbated by the fact that the persons at highest risk are in the prime productive years and belong, moreover, to skilled urban elites (Ainsworth & Over 1994). Thus, although other diseases such as tuberculosis and malaria account for more deaths, the economic impact of AIDS is greater. In all regions, AIDS is placing stress on public health budgets and, more generally, is increasing the share of total resources that must be devoted to health (e.g., placing claims on savings of affected families and raising insurance premiums).

Thermal extremes

The main thermal hazards of global warming would result from increased frequency and severity of heatwaves, defined often as five days in a row in which the daily ambient temperature exceeds the normal body temperature of 36°C (98.6°F). Prolonged heat stress can lead after several days to heat exhaustion characterized by dizziness, weakness, and fatigue. More acutely, heat stroke, in which body temperature exceeds 41°C (106°F), may occur, often resulting in unconsciousness and sometimes death.

Minor changes in temperature and humidity evoke both physiological and behavioral responses. Healthy persons cope with moderate rises in ambient environmental temperature and, within certain limits, thermal comfort is thus maintained. Further physiological acclimatization develops after several days, thus minimizing heat stress. However, frail or ill individuals with lower physiological resilience adapt less well. Hence, heat stress is a greater health hazard in elderly persons, infants, and in persons suffering from cardiovascular or other disorders.

Higher summer temperatures and accompanying heatwaves would increase rates of heat-related illness and death in both temperate and tropical regions, but reliable dose–response estimates exist only for the first. Historical analogues may be found in events such as the extremely hot summers experienced in Missouri during the early 1980s, when temperatures were 2–3°C higher than normal, and heat-related deaths occurred at seven times their normal rate (Centers for Disease Control 1989). The pattern of deaths from all causes in relation to daily summer temperature in New York City indicates a nonlinear relationship with a threshold of approximately 33°C, above which overall death rates increase sharply (Kalkenstein 1993b). However, other studies in the United States indicate that 20–40 percent of such heat-related deaths during heatwaves represent a displacement or early harvesting effect; that is, deaths that would have occurred within several weeks under normal temperature conditions. From studies done in heat-sensitive northern US cities (those where heatwaves are infrequent) it has been estimated that, under climate scenarios accompanying a doubling of carbon dioxide concentration, heat-related deaths in such populations would increase by a factor of five or six (Kalkenstein & Smoyer 1993). Cities with naturally warmer weather would be less affected, because their inhabitants are better adapted to prolonged bouts of summer heat.

Excess mortality related to heatwaves is greatest in crowded inner urban environments, owing to the heat island effect, and in communities lacking air conditioning and proper ventilation. Before the advent of air conditioning in industrialized countries, excess mortality during heatwaves was much more pronounced than it is at present. Data from heatwaves of similar magnitude in Los Angeles in 1939, 1955, and 1963 indicate a sharp drop in excess mortality between the second and third episodes, probably because of the advent of residential air conditioning (Goldsmith 1986).

Just as global warming would be expected to increase heat-related mortality, it would, to some extent, reduce winter-time mortality by reducing the extent and frequency of extreme cold weather (Kalkenstein 1989, 1993a,b, Langford

& Bentham 1993). Excess winter mortality is predominantly attributable to influenza, other respiratory infections such as bronchitis and pneumonia, and coronary heat disease.

Temperature and other climatic variables affect the respiratory tract (Ayres 1990). Bronchitis and emphysema are typically exacerbated during winter, whereas asthma and hay fever tend to break out during summer, perhaps because of pollen release. Hot dry summer weather increases the pollen count, whereas summer rain stimulates the release of fungal spores. Thus, global warming may reduce winter bronchitis and pneumonia and increase summer asthma and hay fever.

Fossil fuel combustion, which is the principal cause of rising atmospheric carbon dioxide concentration, is accompanied by increases in the ambient concentration of other pollutants in the urban atmosphere, such as sulfur dioxide and nitrous oxides. The urban atmosphere in industrial countries has generally improved as a result of more effective environmental policies (OECD 1991); however, most less industrialized countries lack such policies. Higher summer temperatures would also stimulate the chemical reactions that give rise to photochemical smog. Bufalini et al. (1989) estimated that a 4°C increase in average summer temperature in the San Francisco Bay area would triple person-hours of exposure to concentrations of atmospheric ozone in excess of the current air quality standard. Exposure to such pollutants reduces lung function, thus increasing susceptibility to infection, heat stress, and chronic lung disease, with consequences for mortality and morbidity from a wide range of causes.

Some direct effects in addition to those mediated through thermal extremes also deserve mention. Disasters give rise to an entire class of public health problems (Gregg 1989), and to the extent that global climate change includes greater frequency of floods, storms, and other extreme weather events, the frequency of such problems will rise. Among these, in addition to direct weather-related mortality, are outbreaks of diarrhoeal disease when water sources are contaminated by fecal material, problems associated with runoff of toxic materials (Thurman et al. 1991, 1992), and increases in some vector-borne infectious diseases as a result of flood conditions (Hederra 1987, Cotton 1993). Even without flooding, increased rainfall and higher temperatures would also be favorable to the bacteria and protozoa that cause diarrhoeal diseases, including cholera.

Vector-borne diseases

Most infectious disease transmission mechanisms are affected one way or another by climatic factors (Bradley 1993), and the link to climate is especially close in the case of vector-borne infections. Most vector-borne diseases have at least three, and usually four, components (Longstreth 1990): the infectious agent (e.g., to take the case of Rocky Mountain Spotted Fever, *Rickettsia ricketsii*), the vector (*Dermacentor variabilis*), an intermediate host (woodland birds and animals) and an ultimate host (humans). Changes in climate can affect any one of these components.

The maintenance of a vector-borne infectious disease agent requires an adequate population of the vector and favorable environmental conditions for both vector and parasite (Koopman et al. 1991, Shope 1991, Herrera-Basto et al. 1992, Bouma et al. 1994, Loevinsohn 1994). Slight changes in climate can affect the viability and geographical distribution of vectors. To take one example, and probably the most important one, the *Anopheles* mosquito, which transmits malaria, does not survive easily where the mean winter temperature drops below approximately 15°C, and it survives best where the mean temperature is 20–30°C and humidity exceeds 60 percent (Martens et al. 1995a). Higher temperatures accelerate the developmental cycle of the malaria parasite (Burgos et al. 1994). Further, the malarial parasite (*Plasmodium*) cannot survive below a critical temperature: around 14–16°C for *P. vivax* and 18–20°C for *P. falciparum*. By improving conditions for both vector and parasite, unusually hot and wet weather in endemic areas can cause a marked increase in malaria (Loevinsohn 1994). Many other vectors, parasites and microbes generally thrive in warmth and moisture (Gillet 1974 for parasites, Shope 1991, Nicholls 1993 for the case of rodents); thus, climate changes over the coming century could promote vector-borne and other infectious diseases. Although these cannot necessarily be ascribed to climate change, occurrences have already been noted of dengue fever in new areas and of malaria at higher latitudes than previously observed (Levins et al. 1994); these may arise from complex changes in regional climate, local ecological systems, and the distribution of the human population (Epstein 1995). Studies in Mexico have shown that incidence of dengue fever increases several-fold in years with rainy seasons of above-average warmth (Koopman et al. 1991).

A simple model, which related annual average temperature and rainfall to malaria incidence, predicted that incidence in Indonesia might increase 25 percent over 80 years as a result of climate change (Asian Development Bank 1994). Another model employing the same approach but worldwide found that five different climate change scenarios gave rise to increases ranging from 7 to 28 percent in the land area affected by malaria (Martin & Lefebvre 1995).

A detailed epidemiological model has been developed (Martens et al. 1994, 1995a,b) in which development, feeding frequency and longevity of the mosquito and the maturation period of the parasite within the mosquito are endogenous variables. The prevalence of public health control measures is exogenous; thus, the model's predictions refer only to potential alterations in the geographic range of transmission; their significance for alterations in disease incidence must be interpreted in relation to local conditions and public health control measures. Model simulations based on an assumed increase of 3°C in global temperature by 2100, holding population size and public health responses fixed, indicate a doubling of potential malaria incidence in tropical regions and a tenfold increase (from a very low base) in temperate regions.

A core finding of the study was that, although malaria would be worsened in all currently endemic regions, the effect would be more severe in currently low-endemicity areas, not in areas where prevalence is already elevated. Included among areas that might become endemic are highland urban areas, such as Nairobi and Harare, or parts of the Andes and mountainous western parts of China, which are currently situated above the mosquito line. The vulnerability of newly affected populations would initially lead to high case-fatality rates because of their lack of natural immunity. Worldwide, the model predicts a climate-induced increase of around 25 percent in malaria cases.

The re-emergence of malaria in formerly malarious areas, such as parts of the southern United States, is unlikely. Longstreth (1990), interpreting results of model simulations by Haille (1989) as well as other research, wrote that only a rather unlikely combination of events could lead to the re-emergence of malaria as a serious public health problem in the United States: a breakdown in the effectiveness of vector-control programs or establishment of a pesticide-resistant strain of *Anopheles*, plus establishment of a large infected human population that went untreated for an extended period of time.

Malaria is only one of many vector-borne diseases whose distribution may extend and whose intensity may be increased by warmer, more humid conditions (Rogers & Packer 1993). Others include trypanosomiasis (African sleeping sickness and American Chagas disease), filariasis (elephantiasis), onchocerciasis (river blindness), schistosomiasis (bilharzia), hookworm, guinea worm, and various tapeworms. Vector-borne viral infections such as dengue fever, yellow fever, and rodent-borne hantavirus are also affected by temperature and surface-water distribution (McMichael et al. 1996).

Climate change would also tend to increase various infectious diseases that are not vector borne, such as cholera, salmonellosis, other food- and water-related infections, and diseases caused by large parasites such as hookworm and roundworms. This would be most likely in tropical and subtropical regions, because of the effect of changes in water distribution and temperature upon micro-organism proliferation. Dobson & Carper (1992) have put it simply: parasites and disease will do well on a warmed Earth.

Conclusion

Assessing and countering these hazards is one of the main long-term challenges facing those concerned with the health of human populations (Powles 1992). Cost-effective public health responses can minimize the impacts described above. For example, in the case of malaria these would include surveillance, improved treatment, open-water management and applications of pesticides (although the acceleration of parasites' lifecycle allows quicker development of resistant strains). The range of measures available is broad: improved and extended medical care services, environmental management, protective technology (such as housing and water purification), public education directed at personal behaviors, and appropriate professional and research training. Bradley (1994) has classified responses in the case of tropical diseases as follows: pesticides, chemotherapy, vaccines, and environmental management. Better and larger-scale public health monitoring systems are also needed (Haines et al. 1993). Interventions need not be designed directly to reduce incidence of the disease, but rather to reduce its impact on the community. For example, where malaria eradication is infeasible, interventions designed to improve the nutritional status of an undernourished population may be more appropriate than vector-control interventions. As in the case of agriculture, the importance of local capacity and institutions must be stressed.

Most research has concluded that, given the possibility for response, the health impacts of climate change in more industrialized countries will probably be modest. In less industrialized countries, on the other hand, where populations tend to be more vulnerable (both socially and biologically) and public health spending is limited by available resources, mortality and morbidity conditions are likely to worsen as a result of global climate change. Both conclusions must be conditioned by the uncertainties and complexities discussed in the first paragraphs of this section.

Refugees, migration, and resource conflicts

The potent combination of poverty, natural resource scarcity, demographic pressure, ignorance, and ethnic hatred was evoked by Kaplan (1994) in a piece whose message was summed up by its title: "The coming anarchy." According to this school of thought, the pressure of impoverished populations against renewable natural resources is becoming one of the leading causes of population displacement, internal conflict between different ethnic and interest groups and, ultimately, international conflict (Homer-Dixon 1991, Homer-Dixon et al.

161

1993); if present trends continue, it will be one of the major international security problems of the next century.

The Kaplan scenario has some basis in economic theory: when renewable common property natural resources such as land, water, and forests, become more scarce, elites may claim them and thus worsen an already inequitable distribution. Much of the focus is on Africa, where drought and desertification have already exacted a heavy toll and where the situation might worsen under conditions of global climate change. South Asia, particularly sensitive border areas such as the territory between India and Bangladesh, is another area of concern. Jodha (1989) has documented such a process at work over the long term in India. Global climate change may be joined to the list of potential causes of conflicts. If land becomes uninhabitable or nonproductive, people will migrate to more desirable locations.

Environmental refugees

The term *environmental refugees* brings population–environment linkages forcefully home to policymakers, evoking images of human misery and social chaos. In the following paragraphs, by deflating some of the more expansive claims that have been made, we are able to focus more clearly on problems of environmental distress migration; that is, migration in which the deterioration of the natural resource base is a significant push factor. Such environmental migration can be dealt with in the much more familiar framework of international migration for economic reasons.

Minimalists versus maximalists

Although there is a substantial literature on the consequences of migration for the environment, there is much less research on the effects of environmental factors on migration. Yet two different and opposing perspectives can be identified. In one, the *minimalist* view, environmental change is a contextual variable that can contribute to migration, but analytic difficulties and empirical shortcomings make it difficult to draw reliable conclusions. The other perspective is a *maximalist* view, which holds that environmental deterioration is a direct cause of large-scale population displacements.

Minimalists (e.g., Bilsborrow 1987, Kritz 1990) are drawn principally from the ranks of economists, demographers, and geographers specializing in migration studies. A neoclassical strand of thought within the minimalist school considers the decision to migrate as the outcome of a cost–benefit calculation in which expected economic well-being is the variable of interest. A poor state of the environment, according to this model, is only one of many push variables;

its effect is to reduce utility directly by making the environment less healthy, to reduce expected income by reducing the productivity of agricultural land, and to increase risk by raising the variance of agricultural yields. Costs of household production related to the renewable resource base—that is, gathering wood and fetching water—are increased as the resource base becomes less productive.

In a strict neoclassical interpretation, out-migration is seen as the result of a smoothly functioning response mechanism which offers the potential migrant a wide choice of options and strategies. In a neo-Marxist interpretation, however, decisions to move are made in the context of a powerful set of historical, institutional, and cultural factors that tilt the playing field against the potential migrant. Environmental deterioration, in this interpretation, is closely tied to poverty and exploitation; out-migration is best understood as an uprooting of households who are denied access to the resources that would allow them to ameliorate deteriorating environmental conditions.

In either of the minimalist interpretations, environmental change is not the simple direct cause of out-migration. Maximalists, by contrast, claim that substantial numbers of migrants in less industrialized countries represent households which have been directly displaced by deteriorating environmental conditions, and they forecast that the situation is bound to worsen. A seminal study in this vein stated, "All displaced persons can be described as environmental refugees, having been forced to leave their original habitat (or having left voluntarily) to protect themselves from harm and/or seek a better quality of life" (El Hinnawi 1984), and Myers (1994) offers a similarly broad definition of environmental refugees as people who can no longer earn a secure livelihood in their erstwhile homelands because of drought, soil erosion, desertification, and other environmental problems. Jacobson (1988) limited the definition to persons displaced by drought, flood, toxification, and rising sea level, but widened the umbrella by adding deforestation.

As a result of the expansive (practically, in the case of El-Hinnawi, all-inclusive) definition of the word "refugee", the numbers of people potentially involved are enormous. Westing (1992, 1994) estimated that there were 10–15 million displaced persons, mostly in Africa, and that the number is increasing by some 3 million per year. There being no discernible rise in warfare or persecution, he assigns the increase to environmental deterioration. Myers (1994) calculates that, by the year 2050, the number of environmental refugees may rise to 150 million people (89 million of them from China, India, Bangladesh and Egypt; some 1.5 percent of projected world population as opposed to the 0.2 percent that Myers estimates to currently qualify as environmental refugees).

Flexible definitions invite speculation at best and abuse at worst. To rehabilitate the term environmental refugee, we first return to the generally accepted definition of the term refugee and, second, situate the population displacements associated with environmental distress along a continuum, with refugee flight at one end and normal migration at the other. Refugees, in common sociological usage, flee involuntarily and in haste; they are powerless and vulnerable in their new place of residence. Although not in strict accordance with international law,[6] the term might reasonably be applied to persons displaced by a flood which was, in turn, exacerbated by environmental deterioration.

Migrants, by contrast, move of their own volition in response to a combination of disagreeable conditions (push factors) and in anticipation of a better life (pull factors); once installed in their new residence, they typically relate to the host society from a much stronger position than do refugees. The members of a household that relocates after months of struggling to cope with worsening environmental conditions are, by reasonable definition, environmental migrants, not environmental refugees. Similarly, the World Bank estimates that, from 1985, to 1995 80–90 million persons in less industrialized countries have been forced to move by infrastructural development projects, most involving either irrigation or transportation (Cernea 1995). Although they often suffer profound consequences, these displaced persons are not refugees.

A synthesis of the minimalist and maximalist lines of thought is possible along the following lines. Marginal deterioration of environmental conditions will, under normal circumstances, give rise to various responses, out-migration prominent among them. If conditions continue to deteriorate, and if households choose not to or are unable to alleviate the underlying environmental problem, then the importance of the out-migration response will grow. In the worst scenario, households do not address the problem of environmental deterioration and orderly out-migration is impeded; then pressure will build up until there is a classic ecological collapse and a resulting wave of environmental refugees. In the following section, we discuss responses and strategies likely to be invoked in order to avoid this extreme outcome.

Demographic and social responses to environmental stress
Since environmentally induced population movements are most pronounced in the rural areas of less industrialized countries, we may gain some insight by looking at the case of preindustrial Europe. The typical case examined is a run of bad harvests in an agricultural community. As summarized by Lee (1990a), among the responses that have been identified are the following. Vulnerable members of the population, particularly the aged, exhibit increased frailty and

---

6. According to the 1951 United Nations Convention on the Status of Refugees and Stateless Persons, to be considered a refugee, a person must be outside his or her country of origin for reasons of "persecution" based on "race, religion, nationality, membership of a particular social group or political opinion."

die as a result of normal morbidity conditions. Men may leave the community to seek work in adjoining agricultural regions or in the city; the ensuing spousal separation leads to a reduction in fertility. As financial assets are deployed to purchase food, marriages are delayed, reducing the number of first births. Fecundity may be somewhat reduced by poor diet and, more significantly, if there is a shortage of weaning supplements, infants will be breastfed more intensively for a longer period, with consequent reduction in fecundity. Davis (1963) long ago coined the term *multiphasic response* to refer to this dynamically complex demographic reaction to stress. Dyson (1991) found a proactive demographic response in South Asia, where famines were preceded by extended periods of worsening adversity, during which fertility declined.

When the harvest recovers, adaptation behaviors change. Children inherit land from those who died during the bad harvests, and young couples can thus marry. Returning male migrants are reunited with wives who have ceased breastfeeding infants conceived before the crisis and are fecund as a result. With the frailest members of the population having died, age-specific mortality rates may even be lower than normal. From beginning to end, the demographic response to a subnormal harvest requires about four years to run its course. This pattern, although first recognized for the case of preindustrial Europe, appears to be relevant to non-European populations. Lee (1990) discussed research findings from Bangladesh, China, India, Taiwan, and preindustrial Japan, all conforming to the pattern. Other studies have looked at a broader range of responses.

In drought-prone regions, seasonal or temporary migration of some household members may already be an established means of coping with periodic food shortages; when disaster strikes, households resort to the coping strategy with which they are most familiar. This was the case during the 1980s drought in the Sahel, during which Hill (1989) found that the most prevalent coping strategy was to move. Findley (1994) found that in Mali the drought did not cause an increase in migration per se, but led rather to a dramatic shortening of the periodicity of circular migration, concluding that the appropriate policy response is to facilitate the migration. Caldwell et al. (1986) looked at coping strategies employed by households in drought-prone south India during an especially severe episode. By far the most common response was eating less (to some extent in all households; to the point of hunger in one-third of households), followed by reductions in discretionary spending (a little under one-fifth of all households), followed at some distance by securing loans, selling assets and changing employment. Famine mortality in South Asia consists not of persons actually starving to death but of a massive expansion of normal seasonal mortality patterns, especially mortality caused by malaria (Dyson 1991). In northern Mali, an acutely drought-prone area, population expanded relatively smoothly throughout the twentieth century, despite periodic catastrophes (Pederson 1995).

As population pressure rises and the productivity of the renewable resource base declines, a bifurcation point is reached (Mortimore 1989, Tiffen et al. 1994). One branch corresponds to the environmental refugee scenario: worsening environmental deterioration, growing food scarcity, starvation and distress out-migration, dependence on international relief, and so on. The other branch, which shares the spirit, if not the particulars, of the Boserup model of agricultural intensification (Boserup 1965), is characterized by land-saving investment, adoption of improved agricultural practices, development of non-agricultural economic activities, and diversification of income sources. So, once again, we return to the theme of a vicious circle and a virtuous circle.

Which path is taken in response to environmental stress will depend in part on local conditions (e.g., the nature of land tenure rights) and on the enabling or impeding role of the state. The role of public policy is illustrated by Warrick's (1980) examination of the changing impact of recurrent droughts in the American Great Plains states. Great droughts in the 1890s and 1910s provoked large-scale out-migration; however, it was much less pronounced in the 1930s and 1950s, because public policies and programs were in force to encourage adaptation in place. International early warning systems and emergency assistance responses have improved over the years, but they remain unable to deal with situations in which civilian food supplies are destroyed or interdicted in the course of military conflict (Chen & Kates 1994).

Droughts, which tend to extend over several years and are periodic, give societies time to evolve a range of adaptive responses. Floods, being one-off events, are much more likely to provoke population dislocation. On the other hand, because floods are rare events, displaced populations are likely to re-implant themselves once the waters recede. Thus, although floods are more likely to produce environmental refugees than are droughts, their status as refugees will not necessarily be permanent or even long term. Although droughts cause less dislocation in the near term, they can cause more significant long-run social change because of their persistence.

Sea level rise

All estimates of the number of potential environmental refugees consist in part of persons displaced by rising sea level. Although the most dramatic effect of sea level rise is inundation, the loss of land area to the sea, sea level rise has a range of less profound impacts, such as intrusion of salt water into aquifers. These effects and possible responses are discussed extensively in Volume 2. Rising sea level lies midway between drought and floods, in that its effects are felt only over the long term, but when they are felt they take the form of more frequent flooding of low-lying coastal areas. The severity of damage will depend more on local conditions than on the precise extent of sea level rise (Smil 1990). If coastal areas come under assault by the sea, and if countermeasures are not taken, then these areas will be gradually lost to human habitation. If countermeasures are taken, the effects of sea level rise can be in significant degree mitigated; the price will be forgone investment in other areas. The experience of low-lying countries such as the Netherlands is relevant, although the models that predict sea level rise also predict that it will occur much more rapidly than ever in historical experience.

Concern has been focused on the inundation of densely populated low-lying areas, such as the Nile Delta, and on coastal cities; in fact, because the value of land is so high in such regions, these are precisely the areas least likely to be abandoned to the sea. For example, the Nile Delta region is in no sense a natural delta in geophysical equilibrium; it has long been an area managed by ceaseless human intervention (Stanley & Warne 1993). The effect of sea level rise in areas of relatively low population density, by contrast, could be devastating to the populations affected. In a survey of South Pacific islands, Pernetta (1989) sorted countries into five categories, ranging from countries that might conceivably cease to exist (Kiribati being the most populous of these) to those where impacts would be only locally severe (Papua New Guinea, Guam, and Western Samoa among them). In the latter, planning responses could significantly ameliorate damages within existing social, demographic and agricultural structures. However, neither national nor international environmental policy communities seem to be reacting very effectively to the threat of sea level rise in the South Pacific (Pernetta 1992).

Some speculative damage estimates (e.g., Broadus 1993) have been made on the basis of land prices. Yohe et al. (1995) pointed out that, in a perfect world, sea level rise would be mediated through a forward-looking real-estate market in which prices are discounted to reflect hazards. (See the discussions in Vol. 2, Ch. 3 and Vol. 3, Ch. 1.) Taken to the limit, this logic would imply that sea level rise would be Pareto neutral (i.e., no one can become better off without making another worse off), with sellers of land losing while purchasers gain. Although extreme, the example serves to remind us that the real-estate market will serve a crucial function in defusing the economic costs of sea level rise. In California, for example, high real-estate prices in coastal neighborhoods, a function in part of rapid past population growth, have moved the focus of demographic increase to inland neighborhoods of coastal counties, that is, areas that would be less seriously affected by sea level rise (Van Arsdol et al. 1995). However, the real-estate market deals only with economic costs and benefits; for example, it will do nothing to mitigate the unambiguous loss that would occur if the cultural heritage of a small Pacific island were eradicated through sea level rise.

Some writers have stressed the enormity of the costs of sea level rise in low-lying coastal areas of developing countries; however, these calculations should be taken with a grain of salt. For example, Myers (1994) cited research indicating that engineering countermeasures in Bangladesh (which would not necessarily negate the problem altogether) would cost $10 billion. Since Bangladesh's total gross national product (GNP) is only on the order of $25 billion, this seems at first glance to be an impossible task. However, the capital investment requirement is a stock concept, whereas GNP is an annual flow. Assuming that total GNP remains fixed at $25 billion (which is exceedingly unlikely), a $10 billion investment project can be completed over 20 years by diverting 2 percent of GDP every year. On the other hand, once installed, public engineering works must be maintained; if the depreciation rate is 5 percent, further costs of $1 billion per year, again 2 percent of GNP, would be incurred. However, the diversion of 4 percent of GDP every year to investment in flood control, as opposed to other projects, would be a heavy blow; it would not spell the end of economic development in Bangladesh. The calculation errs, moreover, on the pessimistic side, because of the constant GNP assumption and because it takes no account of economic activity generated by the investment program.

International migration

If environmental conditions are regarded as an additional push factor encouraging migration, then environmental migration can be placed in the broader context of international economic migration. Although accurate data are hard to find because of the volume of illegal migration, there is little doubt that the volume of economic migration has risen and continues to rise (Böhning & Oishi 1995). International migration is a crucial variable in any global environmental change scenario because, depending on the policy regime, it either provides or is prevented from providing a means of adjustment to changing climatic conditions. A climatically changed world, which has effected adjustment in the institutional context of relatively free international movement of labor, is bound to be very different from one that has adjusted in the context of closed borders. The pessimistic scenario described above, in which a virtuous out-migration response is stifled, leading to environmental collapse at the local level, can easily be broadened to the national scale.

Refugees tend to move within countries or across neighboring borders; economic migrants tend to move either from less industrialized poor countries to highly industrialized rich countries, or into regional immigration poles such as Abidjan or Singapore. Immigration is everywhere a complex and emotional issue: it brings about global efficiency gains, but there are local winners and losers; moreover, it involves social and cultural dislocations for receiving and sending regions, and perhaps most of all for migrants themselves. Neoclassical economic theory describes how, in a two-region world, there are aggregate welfare gains in both regions when factors are free to move from one to the other (Simon 1989, Layard et al. 1992). Unimpeded, labor will flow from the low-wage, labor-abundant region (i.e., the region characterized by a low capital-to-labor ratio) to the high-wage capital-abundant region, whereas capital will flow in the opposite direction. Economic scarcities are thus abated, with resulting increases in welfare in each region. The problem is that each region has winners and losers; the scarce factor loses and the abundant factor wins. The greater internal economic rigidities, the greater the imbalance. When the analysis moves to the macroeconomic level, there is less clarity; for example, a recent survey of US studies found no consensus on the burning political question of the fiscal impacts of immigration (Rothman & Espenshade 1992).

Thus, the policy debate over immigration has largely been driven by interest-group politics; for example, in the United States, organized labor has generally opposed free immigration, whereas the business community has generally favored it. The dispute cuts across other axes as well: socioeconomic class (unskilled workers lose from the import of cheap, unskilled labor; skilled workers may benefit), location (workers in border regions lose more than workers in further-flung regions from competition by cheaper labor). There is also a neglected generational aspect: older workers and retirees benefit economically from immigration because it strengthens the social security system; younger (typically less skilled) workers lose from competition in the labor market and from the fact that immigrants represent co-claimants on the social security system (as well as on public goods such as the school system). Assessing the net impact of immigration on younger persons is difficult, because without immigration, social security taxes would have to be higher to support pensioners, and this higher tax on labor would encourage employment of capital as opposed to labor. Even if younger people gain from immigration, however, clearly they do not gain as much as older workers and retirees.

On the other hand, international migration cannot be reduced to simple economics, because it is driven not only by economic disparities but also by more diffuse social and cultural factors. The diffusion of industrial culture raises the demand for an industrial lifestyle; the rise of individualism demands mobility. Similarly, opposition to immigration is not entirely a matter of economic interest-group politics; it also reflects a genuine fear that local cultural traditions will be eroded with the loss of homogeneity. All in all, it is likely that the social consequences of immigration are far greater than the economic consequences.

Several imbalances and inequities exist in the current international migration process. First, whereas intercontinental migration provided a major escape route from Europe during its period of rapid demographic expansion, people from less industrialized nations have so far benefited much less from migration (Emmer 1993). Second, whereas policy reforms since the mid-1970s have substantially reduced barriers to the flow of capital from industrialized countries to the South and to the East, the barriers to the flow of labor into industrialized countries have, if anything, increased (van de Kaa 1993). Policymakers in less industrialized countries, including the former socialist bloc, have put in place comprehensive policy regimes to facilitate capital inflows, whereas governments in industrialized countries have not yet adopted complementary policies in the area of immigration (Bade 1993 for the case of Germany).

Under conditions of climate change, if current research, which assigns the most serious agricultural and health impacts to developing countries, is correct, South–North migratory pressures will increase. To the extent that less industrialized countries are able to adjust smoothly to changing climate conditions, these pressures will be smaller, but perfect adjustment is an ideal that is unlikely to be attained. As in many other areas explored in this chapter, adjustment in the industrialized nations to these pressures can be either virtuous or vicious. In the latter case, immigration policy will remain essentially ad hoc, confusing, and inequitable, in which case the inevitable confusion is likely to bring about an increase in the number of illegal immigrants. Newcomers will not be integrated into host societies, and broader domestic policies that relate to problems such as structural unemployment will not be implemented, resulting in xenophobia and resentment. In the virtuous case, countries will elaborate comprehensive immigration policies, which respect national priorities while preserving equity and transparency, immigrants will be integrated into their destination, and societies and policies will be found to address the problems of vulnerable groups, such as unskilled workers.

Renewable natural resource wars

Since environmental change forces choices, which amount to the weighing and contesting of competing claims, conflict per se is essential to human adaptation and change (Stern et al. 1992). Violent conflict is only one of a range of means by which competing claims to scarce resources can be settled. Early research indicated, not surprisingly, that population pressure (density) was related to violent international conflict only by a complex chain of intervening causal variables (Choucri 1974). However, the model by which population pressure causes violence has received a new lease on life in the view that, if renewable natural resource systems are impaired by overuse in the context of global environmental change, risks of acute conflict and war will be increased (Westing 1986, Gleick 1989, Renner 1989).

Many of the root causes that make countries prone to violent conflict also make them prone to degradation of the renewable natural resource base, but this is not necessarily a simple cause–effect relationship. For example, Engleman & Leroy (1995) all but endorsed the hypothesis that recent violent internal conflicts in Rwanda, Somalia, Yemen, and Haiti are attributable in significant degree to food scarcity exacerbated by rapid population growth; in the first case, Bonneaux (1994) has blamed "demographic entrapment". Myers (1989, 1993) and Homer-Dixon et al. (1993) argued that competition for natural resources, worsened by demographic pressure, were to blame for the 1969 Soccer War between El Salvador and Honduras, and water scarcity has been the cause of small-scale regional conflicts in Central Asia (Smith 1995 for citations) and the Middle East (see Lonergan & Kavanaugh 1991 for citations). Competition for natural resources is often along ethnic lines (e.g., Hazarika 1993 for the case of Bangladesh and Assam). A series of case studies (Howard & Homer-Dixon 1995, Kelly & Homer-Dixon 1995, Percival & Homer-Dixon 1995) have broadened the application of the basic model of environmental scarcity and violent conflict. At the same time, the model has been subjected to a strong critique from within political science and international relations (Levy 1995a,b), and just as spiritedly defended (Homer-Dixon & Levy 1995).

If social and political institutions for conflict resolution, including the market, prove inadequate to the rising demands placed upon them, then regional environmental change associated with global climate change might increase the frequency of skirmishes over impaired renewable resource systems. However, a principal conclusion of Suhrke (1993) was that environmental degradation, at least to the extent that it gives rise to displacement of people, is more likely to lead to exploitation and structural low-level conflict than to acute conflict, let alone war. Although access to renewable resource systems spanning national boundaries will be an important component of any country's foreign policy, various options will be explored before a country resorts to war. Faced with the choice of obtaining food through trade or war, it is difficult to conceive of a country choosing the latter. Issues of national pride, as well as the pressures brought to bear on national policymakers by the local populations affected by resource scarcity, may be severe, and peace will stand or fall on the strength of conflict resolution mechanisms.

By far the largest body of research dealing with conflict over natural resources has dealt with water (Falkenmark 1989, Starr 1991, Anderson 1992, Gleick 1993, 1994). Gleick (1992) identified four factors that determine a country's vulnerability to disruption of shared water resources: scarcity of water, the extent to which water is shared, the degree of dependence on shared water, and the relative power of states that share rivers and other watercourses. In judging whether disruption is likely to lead to conflict, these considerations must be placed in a broader context of perceived interests, internal and external power relations, and so on. The possibility of relatively (at least with respect to war) low-cost internal adjustment mechanisms must not be forgotten. For example, Beaumont (1994) stressed the tremendous inefficiency with which water is employed in much of the Middle East and arrived at a conclusion captured parsimoniously in the title of his article, "The myth of Middle Eastern water wars." In a quite different reading of the evidence, however, Lonergan & Kavanaugh (1991: 281) forecast "desperate competition and conflict" in the near future. Indeed, so pessimistic was their view that they discounted the effects of climate change, which are long-term in nature.

When the costs of internal adjustment are too high, countries will have recourse to mechanisms for the international mediation of claims. The body of law regulating the interregional and international allocation of scarce water resources is simply massive, as is the body of accumulated experience (Biswas 1992, Chitale 1995). The relevant principles (Smith 1995) consist of three norms and three obligations. The three norms are equitable use, prevention of significant harm to other states and shared management of international rivers; the three obligations are to notify and inform, to share information and data, and to resolve disputes peacefully.

As yet, no international framework exists for resolution of water disputes, but work toward such a framework has begun (International Conference on Water and the Environment 1992). Mageed & White (1995) and Grover & Howarth (1991) review existing institutional arrangements. Regional organizations, such as the Interstate Coordinating Commission for Water Resources (ICCW) in Central Asia and the Middle East Water Commission (MWC) currently provide the natural institutional setting for the development of such regimes; some experts (Grover & Biswas 1993, Chitale 1995) have called for the constitution of an integrated World Water Council. The potential of water scarcity to serve as a focus of conflict cannot be denied, but neither can the distinct unlikelihood that violence will be casually resorted to.

Conclusion

The concept of environmental refugees has attracted wide interest precisely because it has been expansively and loosely used. A more careful reading indicates, however, that the term contains a grain of truth: rising environmental pressures are a push factor encouraging out-migration, and, if a virtuous out-migration response is stifled, then rapid environmental deterioration and resulting distress migration are possible. A similar observation applies to violent conflicts over natural resources: scarcity invariably gives rise to conflicts between stakeholders; if these are not resolved by institutions, including the market, then violent conflict becomes a distinct possibility. However, it is premature to conclude that global environmental change is ushering a century of massive refugee movements and violent conflicts. A more sober reading is that the stresses associated with global change will intensify the pressures that already drive international migration, and that policymakers and societies will be forced to come to terms with these rising pressures, one way or another.

How will they do so? Environmental stress is mediated by institutions whose functioning is contingent on their perceived ethical legitimacy, in particular whether they are perceived to be fair. By definition, populations cope in one way or another with environmental problems. At one end of a continuum is successful coping-in-place; at the other is population displacement under highly distressed conditions; somewhere in the middle lies a wide and complex variety of migration strategies. The means of coping will, in turn, affect the nature of institutions. In the case of population displacement, this may amount to institutional fracture and atrophy; in the other cases, it may amount to institutional deepening and strengthening. The means of coping may also have a direct effect on the ecosystem under consideration, and it may alleviate or worsen sources of stress.

Finally, we need to develop a more flexible model of human security and the environment. Virtually all the key concepts in this area—security, poverty, displacement, equity, conflict, and even environmental deterioration itself— are open to differing views. Policies to promote response to environmental stresses associated with global change should acknowledge such ambiguities and recognize that such differing views can be complementary and the dialogue between them constructive.

Conclusion: population policy and global change

After a review of the world demographic situation and prospect, this chapter has concentrated on links between population, global climate change, and the possible effects of global climate change. In looking at the relationship between population and climate change, we stressed tradeoffs between policies to decelerate the rate of growth of population, on the one hand, and, on the other hand, policies impinging on the economy, technology, and the capacity of institutions to adapt to environmental stress. A recurring theme was the neoclassical economic tradeoff between children, the level of material consumption, and quality of the environment. Unidimensional models such as $I=PAT$ act as if reducing environmental impacts were a strictly linear matter; in fact, the factors that give rise to environmental stress are interrelated in ways that are incompletely understood.

A second theme stressed was an institutionalist one. Population gives rise to scarcity of natural resources and environmental assets; it always has and it always will. Human society brings all of its institutions to bear on resolving conflict one way or the other. The resolution of one conflict, however, may simply engender another. The point is that resolution can be virtuous or vicious. We have tried to bring out that a key theme for research is how population pressure impedes or facilitates virtuous responses, and in what sorts of institutional contexts.

A third theme we have stressed is that population is more than simply a scale factor. In particular, it has an age distribution, and the difference between an aged and slowly growing population and a young and rapidly growing one is at least as important, socially speaking, as the difference between a small sparse population and a large dense one. It cannot be overstressed that global change includes global aging; the challenges of the next century will have to be met by a population that is older, with all that is implied for health systems, world savings, and so on.

The vicious circle model and the state of the art

We have come a long way since the population bomb literature of the 1960s. The chapter has revolved, in large part, around a vicious circle model, which represents the state of the art in research on the relationships among population, environment, and development. It incorporates flexibility, in the form of neoclassical responses; equity, in the form of recognizing the pernicious impacts of poverty, insecurity and low status of women; and ecology, in the form of recognizing the fragility of marginal environmental zones. It is constructive in that it focuses attention on response to climate change rather than responsibility for avoiding climate change. It is fair in that it focuses attention on those populations that are simultaneously most likely to suffer consequences and least able to adapt.

In the process leading up to the 1994 ICPD in Cairo, and in the conference itself, members of the public health orthodoxy defended the importance of family planning programs, orthodox neoclassical economists defended the virtues of overall socioeconomic development, and women's advocates challenged the policy community to make both family planning programs and socioeconomic development policies more relevant to women. What emerged was a women-first prescription for population policy which stressed its role in broadening opportunities for women (McIntosh & Finkle 1995, McNicoll 1995), as well as children and the poor more generally. At the heart of this policy is the vicious circle model, both with and without its environmental component.

The rationale for slowing population growth

Many scholars and policymakers strongly affirm the desirability of slowing world population growth, consistent, of course, with human rights. But such assertions ought to be examined within a social science perspective, so we should ask the question: Why, in view of what we have learned in this chapter, deploy scarce public resources to slow population growth?

The list of rationales is limited:

- Parents in less industrialized countries really want fewer children but cannot achieve fertility targets; this rationale is based in altruism. But parents in less industrialized countries (and in more industrialized countries as well) want a great many things and cannot get them. Why should policy favor low fertility over, say, clean water?

- Parents' desire for many children reflects only private costs and benefits; parents do not consider the external costs imposed on society and the world as a whole. This is an empirical question: how important are externalities to childbearing? Is lowering fertility a better way of correcting the externality than other means, such as carbon taxes or emissions permits? Closely related to the externality question are matters related to inadequate information. Perhaps high fertility is even now placing ecological systems, even the world as a whole, at risk of catastrophic collapse. Whether this is so or not is, again, an empirical question, albeit one beset by complexities and uncertainties.

- High fertility changes the way in which social systems and institutions work in ways that are inimicable. For example, high fertility may give rise to market failures that would not have occurred with low fertility. Or it may limit the choice set over which preferences are defined. This is, in part, an area for empirical research: does high fertility really give rise to market failure? Does it really impede the functioning of institutions? Such questions rest on a normative foundation, namely, a value judgment as to the way systems and institutions ought to work. The Cairo ICPD reflected one value judgment, namely an individualistic approach to the welfare of women and children.

- Parents' desire to have many children is immoral. All empirical research shows that high fertility is inversely correlated with a range of welfare indicators for women and children. A utility theory argument might run that parents, including wives, know this and maximize utility nonetheless by having many children, half of them destined to second-class status on account of their sex. But arguments based in utility theory can always be trumped by an ethical card—in this case, the conviction that behaviors inimical to the welfare of women and children (as perceived, of course, from the perspective of the moralist) are wrong.

Following the Cairo conference, it was sometimes said that the new "women-first" direction for population policy represented a consensus view. This is simply untrue: what was attained was a coalition between methodologically individualistic economists, concerned that high fertility limits the options of women, children and the poor; and moralists concerned with much more general issues of empowerment. This coalition replicates the international development policy orthodoxy, which stresses removing barriers that prevent the poor from participating in free-market based economic development.

The vicious circle model: what is left out

However, some parties are excluded from the Cairo coalition. Among these, and attracting the most attention, were religious traditionalists, whose idea of equity has nothing to do with freedom to maximize individual utility. Their influence has been waning; the Catholic Church is increasingly marginal in the population policy debate, and Muslim fundamentalism has done little to stem the rising practice of contraception among Muslim women. More important is the fact that, even within the Cairo coalition, empowerment issues have been subjected to a rather Procrustean reframing in neoclassical economic terms, and that the view that human population growth must be slowed at all costs to avoid global catastrophe has largely disappeared from population policy discourse.

Policies are shaped by models, so we look at these two matters, and others as well, in terms of the vicious circle model. The goal is not to invalidate the model, which is far better than others that have been proposed, but, first, to point out areas in which it can be strengthened, and second, to identify areas where further disputes in international population policymaking can be expected.

Equity according to whom?

Does the vicious circle model truly address equity concerns or merely co-opt them in neoclassical economic terms? An egalitarian view of human nature might hold that the fundamental human urge is not to maximize consumption but to belong to a nurturing community among whose members risks and burdens are shared equitably. (See Ch. 3 for a fuller discussion.) Prevailing institutions, economic arrangements and technology, according to this view, have encouraged materialism at the expense of fairness, placing the ecosystem at risk in the process. Fairness, in turn, would be defined not in terms of process, as in economics, but in terms of the justice of the outcome. The definition of sustainability would be broadened to encompass not only the commitment to maintain the value of assets as they are passed from generation to generation, but a commitment to justice within each generation as well.

The vicious circle model only partly meets the concerns of this point of view, because poverty, insecurity, and women's status, all of which reflect values, have been couched in less ideational, more material terms. Insecurity has been interpreted in terms of the old-age security motive (Cain 1983, Nugent 1985 and Nugent & Anker 1990 for reviews of the literature) and also seen as representing a means of diversifying income sources or as a lottery process in which parents gamble that one son may be highly successful (Bledsoe 1994). If parents had adequate access to alternative forms of saving, insurance, and income, it is implied, high fertility would be unnecessary. Poverty is interpreted as an impediment to the smooth functioning of neoclassical economic substitution mechanisms; elevated fertility is seen as a survival strategy pursued by the poor because they have no other options (Birdsall & Griffin 1988, Ahlburg 1994). Low status of women consists either of unequal weighing of neoclassical costs and benefits that are specific to men and women (Lloyd 1994) or arises from intra-mural market failures such as information asymmetries between men and women (Palmer 1991).

The vicious circle model is so popular in part because it delivers the agreeable message that doing anything is better than doing nothing. Because the feedback effects in the model are so dense, any policy that improves the status of women, alleviates environmental stress, or reduces poverty is bound to have positive repercussions throughout the system. But the rather sanitized terms of reference above are some ways removed from the existential outrage with which many people view poverty and the exploitation of women. Jackson (n.d.), far from seeing the vicious circle model as serving women's interests, sees it as a means of co-opting women's legitimate gender interests in a way congenial to the established policy orthodoxy. Birdsall (1994) used the expression "win–win" in the context of fertility and poverty; the vicious circle model in current form extends this to win–win–win–win by adding women's status and the environment to the circle, but the fundamental question, "Win according to whose rules?", should not be overlooked.

For example, women's status and girls' education are treated as nearly equivalent, despite fact that women's status is a complex, multidimensional variable that cannot be adequately represented by a single proxy variable (Balk 1994). It is difficult to escape the conclusion that education of girls receives disproportionate attention because it can be so easily translated into targets and indicators—female literacy rate, female enrollment rates, and so on. A similar cautionary note was sounded by Wolf & Ying-Chang (1994) in the case of female labor for participation. In summarizing their finding that fertility in a district of rural Taiwan from 1905–80 did not vary according to women's agricultural labor force participation, they write, "It does not suffice for women to be involved in labor if they are involved only as laborers. Their fertility is only affected when women control or earn what they produce" (Wolf & Ying-Chang 1994: 433) Once again, attention seems to have been focused on an easily quantifiable variable, in this case, the female labor force participation rate.

The lack of reflexivity in the definition of equity applies also to a range of other variables as they are currently discussed. Security, poverty, displacement, equity, conflict, and even environmental deterioration itself are open to differing views. For example, equity may be interpreted in terms of priority, proportionality or strict equality (Young 1993; see the extended discussion in Ch. 4). In the area of population and the environment, views of fairness hinging on equality of opportunity in the present generation, equity of outcome in the present generation, and a just intergenerational distribution of risk have been identified (MacKellar 1997). Policies to promote response to environmental stresses associated with global change should acknowledge such ambiguities and recognize that such differing views can be complementary and the dialogue between them constructive.

How significant are individual causal effects within the vicious circle?
Is the sum really greater than the whole of the parts? Empirical research, limited as it is, has suggested that piecemeal causal effects, which comprise the vicious circle model (in particular, the deleterious effect of high fertility on children's well-being) are significant but nonetheless modest. The belief that these piecemeal effects add up, through synergy, to a whole that is greater than the sum of its parts is based as much on faith as empirical evidence. The empirical evidence (apart from correlation studies) that would lead policymakers to choose, say, female education over reforestation schemes, is thin. If female education is to be chosen over reforestation, it should be because it is an inherently good thing, and for no other reason.

How about the urban population and population aging?
One pressing need is for extension of vicious circle reasoning to the urban and industrial setting. An interesting contribution along this line (Hogan 1995) found that the workers who profited from highly paid industrial jobs in an intensely polluted city were often short-term migrants or long-distance commuters. The long-term resident impoverished population of the city lost more, in terms of impaired health and losses of public goods, than they gained in terms

of well-paid jobs. They formed the potential constituency for political pressure to alleviate pollution, but they were impoverished by pollution, just as rural women are impoverished by renewable resource degradation. Also neglected is the problem of impoverished rural aged persons living in environmentally fragile zones. When the young and healthy migrate out, the process of population aging is accelerated many times at the local level.

What about global ecological risk?

As mentioned in the opening pages of this chapter, the World Bank estimates that one-third of the population of less industrialized countries live in poverty and one-half of these live in environmentally fragile zones. The full vicious circle model applies, therefore, only to one-sixth of the population in less industrialized countries, less than one-seventh of the total world population. Even the half of that population in poverty represent only 40 percent of the world population. Policies to encourage fertility decline among these sub-populations are of limited impact in terms of stabilizing world population growth. If drastic actions to curb demographic increase are to be taken, a rationale beyond the vicious circle model will have to be found.

Post-Cairo population policy is decidedly oriented toward the welfare of the individual; it takes little stock of the concerns raised by modern, discontinuous, and complex ecology (Holling 1994). Neoclassical economics is based on smooth substitution mechanisms, which are expressed in classical Newtonian mechanics; ecologists, on the other hand, are trained to expect discontinuities. These are the stock in trade of statistical mechanics, according to which where you move next stands in no fixed relation to where you are now. In such dynamic systems, seemingly small alterations in the present period can have dramatic consequences in later periods. Thus, ecology is filled with examples of surprises, that is, events that fall outside the boundaries of prediction based on prior experience and theory.

Where economists see individuals making finely tuned tradeoffs between consumption, fertility, and the state of the environment, ecologists are more likely to see blind material and genetic overexuberance. Thus, instead of individual liberty to choose, the theme of prudent stewardship is most likely to be encountered in writings from the ecological school. So long as the human/nature balance is in local equilibrium, the *gradualist* model by which small changes in human impacts are predicted to lead to small changes in the state of the system will be valid. If these impacts are pushed too far—and the gradualist model is incapable of predicting what "too far" is—the system will experience a catastrophic collapse. Individuals and the policymakers who speak for them act as though they lived in a world consisting of only a few easily understood interdependencies. They fail to grasp the true underlying model, which is complex, uncertain and nonlinear; therefore, decisions that are rational according to the simple neoclassical calculus of the individual are irrational at the macro level (Boyden & Dovers 1992), and may give rise to ecological catastrophe (Catton 1982, 1984, Dunlap 1982). The only way to avoid disaster is to impose wise guidance on the individual or, what amounts to the same thing, ensure prudent stewardship of nature.

However, the ecological critique of neoclassical economics is not itself above criticism. Scale need not always be an exacerbating factor. Prevailing institutional arrangements, where much of the explanation for environmental trends is to be found, are in significant degree scale-dependent. Just as scale need not be exacerbating, prudence can cease to be a virtue when its opportunity cost is staggeringly high. Simply citing the possibility of (low probability) catastrophic events is not enough to convince policymakers to divert scarce resources from competing uses.

Where is the institutional dynamic?

The key aspect of the social coping process is that it is dynamic and path-dependent (McNicoll 1989). The vicious circle model, although providing a useful guide for policy interventions so far as it goes, recognizes only an economic–ecological dynamic at the local and household level; it takes little stock of the ability of institutions to adapt and change. The next step for research in this area is to examine the contextual variables that promote institutional robustness and evolution. For example, it is often asserted, quite plausibly but with no rigorous foundation, that rapid population growth impedes institutions' ability to react (US NRC 1986) or that population dynamics may reduce the capacity of the social system to adapt without violent conflict (Sirageldin 1994).

Closing thoughts

This chapter has been largely economic in orientation. The rise of rational actor models (especially at the household level, in the form of various economic models) in the field of population has, to be honest, been at some expense of research into the role of norms, values, and culture. "Demand," we learn in the first lecture of an undergraduate economics course, is a function of income, prices, and tastes. But "tastes" is a euphemism for values, which get short shrift in economic analysis (after the first lecture). The preceding analysis makes no claim to have gone much beyond a conventional economic analysis of population. But even within that orthodox paradigm, it emerges that population policy has too often been based on the easy, specious logic of "You would be happier if you had fewer children." Time and again in this chapter, we have found that this assertion is difficult to back up with rigorous social scientific evidence. The real underlying logic has often been "I would happier if you had fewer children."

This simply represents a set of values. What sort of world population do we wish to see in the twenty-first century? Our choice set is limited because of population momentum, but then human choices made by our forebears brought us to where we are now, and human choices made in the present and future will determine where we end up, given the degrees of freedom available to us, so it all boils down to choice. The more frank and open the dialogue about human values, the more constructive the discussion will be and the more successfully we shall be able to attain the population future which we choose.

References

Agarwal, B. 1994. The gender and environment debate: lessons from India. In *Population and the environment: rethinking the debate*, L. Arizpe, M. Stone, D. Major (eds). Boulder, Colorado: Westview.

Agarwal, A. & S. Narain 1991. *Global warming in an unequal world: a case of environmental colonialism*. Delhi: Centre for Science and Environment.

Ahlburg, D. 1994. Population growth and poverty. In *Population and development: old debates, new conclusions*, R. Cassen (ed.). Washington DC: Overseas Development Council.

Ainsworth, M. & M. Over 1994. AIDS and African development. *The World Bank Research Observer* 9(2), 203–40.

Alston, J., G. Edwards, J. Freebairn 1988. Market distortions and benefits from research. *American Journal of Agricultural Economics* 70, 281–8.

Anania, G. & A. McCalla 1995. Assessing the impact of agricultural technology improvements in developing countries in the presence of policy distortions. *European Review of Agricultural Economics* 22, 5–24.

Anderson, E. 1992. The political and strategic significance of water. *Outlook on Agriculture* 21(4), 247–53.

Antle, J. & G. Heidebrink 1995. Environment and development: theory and international evidence. *Economic Development and Cultural Change* 43(3), 603–623.

Arrow, K., B. Bolin, R. Costanza, P. Dasgupta, C. Folke, C. Holling, B-O. Jansson, S. Levin, K-G. Mäler, C. Perrings, D. Pimentel 1995. Economic growth, carrying capacity, and the environment. *Science* 268, 520–21.

Asante-Duah, D. & P. Sam 1995. Assessment of waste management practices in sub-Saharan Africa. *International Journal of Environment and Pollution* 5(2/3), 224–42.

Asian Development Bank 1994. *Climate change in Asia: Indonesia country report*. Manila: Asian Development Bank.

Asselt, M. B. A. van, J. Rotmans, M. den Elzen, H. Hilderink 1995. *Uncertainty in integrated assessment modeling: a cultural perspective-based approach*. GLOBO Report Series 9 (no. 461502009), National Institute of Public Health and Environmental Protection [RIVM], Bilthoven, the Netherlands.

Ayres, J. 1990. Meteorology and respiratory disease. *Update 1990* 40, 596–605.

Ayres, R. 1995. Economic growth: politically necessary but not economically friendly. *Ecological Economics* 15, 97–9.

Bade, K. 1993. Immigration and integration. *European Review* 1(1), 75–9.

Balk, D. 1994. Individual and community aspects of women's status and fertility in rural Bangladesh. *Population Studies* **48**(1), 21–45.

Bartiaux, F. & J-P. van Ypersele 1993. The role of population growth in global warming. In *Proceedings of the International Population Conference Montreal 1994* (vol. 4). Liège, Belgium: International Union for the Scientific Study of Population.

Beaumont, P. 1994. The myth of Middle Eastern water wars. *Water Resources Development* **10**(1), 9–21.

Becker, G. 1981. *A treatise on the family*. Cambridge, Massachusetts: Harvard University Press.

Becker, G. & R. Barro 1988. Reformulating the economic theory of fertility. *Quarterly Journal of Economics* **103**, 1–25.

Becker, G., K. Murphy, R. Tamura 1991. Human capital, fertility and economic growth. *Journal of Political Economy* **98**(5), S12–37.

Beckerman, W. 1995. *Small is stupid: blowing the whistle on the Greens*. London: Duckworth.

Bilsborrow, R. 1987. Population pressures and agricultural development in developing countries: a conceptual framework and recent evidence. *World Development* **15**(2), 182–203.

Bilsborrow, R. & M. Geores 1994. Population, land use and the environment in developing countries: what can we learn from cross-national data? In *The causes of tropical deforestation*, D. Pearce & K. Brown (eds). London: UCL Press.

Bilsborrow, R. & P. DeLargy 1991. Land use, migration and natural resource deterioration: the experience of Guatemala and the Sudan. In *Resources, environment and population*, K. Davis & M. Bernstam (eds). New York: Oxford University Press.

Birdsall, N. 1992. *Another look at population and global warming*. Working Paper WPS 1020, Population, Health and Nutrition Policy Research, World Bank, Washington DC.

—— 1994. Government, population, and poverty: a "win–win" tale. See Lindahl-Kiessling & Landberg (1994).

Birdsall, N. & C. Griffin 1988. Fertility and poverty. *Journal of Policy Modeling* **10**(1), 29–55.

Biswas, A. 1992. Water for Third World development. *International Journal of Water Resources Development* **8**(1), 3–9.

Bledsoe, C. 1994. "Children are like young bamboo trees": potentiality and reproduction in sub-Saharan Africa. See Lindahl-Kiessling & Landberg (1994).

Böhning, W. & N. Oishi 1995. Is international economic migration spreading? *International Migration Review* **29**(3), 794–9.

Bois, F. du 1994. Water rights and the limits of environmental law. *Journal of Environmental Law* **6**(1), 73–84.

Bongaarts, J. 1992. Population growth and global warming. *Population and Development Review* **18**(2), 299–319.

—— 1996. Global trends in AIDS mortality. *Population and Development Review* **22**(1), 21–45.

Bongaarts, J. & R. Potter 1982. *Fertility, behavior and biology*. New York: Academic Press.

Bonneaux, L. 1994. Rwanda: a case of demographic entrapment. *The Lancet* **344**(December), 1689–90.

Boserup, E. 1965. *The conditions of agricultural growth*. Chicago: Aldine.

—— 1981. *Population and technological change: a study of long-term trends*. Chicago: University of Chicago Press.

Bouma, M. E., H. E. Sondorp, H. J. van der Kaay 1994. Climate change and periodic epidemic malaria. *The Lancet* **343**, 1440.

Boyce, J. 1989. Population growth and real wages of agricultural labourers in Bangladesh. *Journal of Development Studies* **25**(4), 467–85.

Boyden, S. & S. Dovers 1992. Natural resource consumption and its environmental impacts in the Western world: impacts of increasing per capita consumption. *Ambio* **21**(1), 63–9.

Bradley, D. 1993. Human tropical diseases in a changing environment. *Ciba Foundation Symposium* **175**, 146–62.

—— 1994. Agriculture and health. In *Health and sustainable agricultural development: perspectives on growth and constraints*, V. Ruttan (ed.). Boulder, Colorado: Westview.

Broadus, J. 1993. Possible impacts of, and adjustments to, sea level rise: the cases of Bangladesh and Egypt. In *Climate and sea level change: observations, projections and implications*, R. Warrick, E. Barrow, T. Wigley (eds). Cambridge: Cambridge University Press.

Bufalini, J., P. Finkelstein, E. Durman 1989. Air quality. In *The potential effects of global climate change on the United States*, J. Smith, & D. Tirpak (eds). Report EPA-230-05-89-050, Environmental Protection Agency, Washington DC.

Bumpass, L. 1990. What's happening to the family? Interactions between demographic and institutional change. *Demography* 27(4), 483–98.

Burgos, J., S. Curtos de Casas, R. Carcavallo, I. Galíndez Girón 1994. Global climate change influence in the distribution of some pathogenic complexes (malaria and Chagas disease) in Argentina. *Entomologia e Vectores* 1(2), 69–78.

Cain, M. 1983. Fertility as an adjustment to risk. *Population and Development Review* 7, 435–74.

Caldwell, J. C., P. H. Reddy, P. Caldwell 1986. Periodic high risk as a cause of fertility decline in a changing rural environment: survival strategies in the 1980–83 South Indian drought. *Economic Development and Cultural Change* 34(4), 677–701.

Caldwell, J. & P. Caldwell 1987. The cultural context of high fertility in sub-Saharan Africa. *Population and Development Review* 131(3), 409–37.

Catton, W. 1982. *Overshoot: the ecological basis of revolutionary change*. Urbana–Champaign: University of Illinois Press.

——1984. Probable collective response to ecological scarcity: how violent? *Sociological Perspectives* 27(1), 3–20.

Centers for Disease Control 1989. Heat related deaths—Missouri, 1979–1988. *Morbidity and Mortality Weekly Report* 38, 437–9.

CEQ [Council on Environmental Quality] 1980. *The Global 2000 report to the President*. Washington DC: US Government Printing Service.

Cernea, M. 1995. Social integration and population displacement: the contribution of social science. *International Social Science Journal* 143, 91–112.

Chen, R. & R. Kates 1994. World food security: prospects and trends. *Food Policy* 19(2), 192–208.

Chenery, H. & M. Syrquin 1975. *Patterns of development, 1950–70*. Oxford: Oxford University Press.

Chitale, M. 1995. Institutional characteristics for international cooperation in water resources. *Water Resources Development* 11(2), 113–23.

Choucri, N. 1974. *Population dynamics and international violence*. Lexington, Massachusetts: Lexington Books.

Clay, D. & J. Van der Haar 1993. Patterns of intergenerational support and childbearing in the Third World. *Population Studies* 47(1), 67–83.

Cleaver, K. & G. Schreiber 1993. *The population, agriculture and environment nexus in sub-Saharan Africa*. Washington DC: World Bank.

——1993. Equity, security and fertility: a reply to Thomas. *Population Studies* 47, 344–52.

——1996. A regional review of fertility trends in developing countries: 1960 to 1995. See Lutz (1996).

Cleland, J. & G. Rodriguez 1988. The effects of parental education on marital fertility. *Population Studies* 42(3), 419–42.

Cleland, J. & C. Wilson 1987. Demand theories of the fertility transition: an iconoclastic view. *Population Studies* 41(1), 5–30.

Cleland, J., J. F. Phillips, S. Amin, G. M. Kamal 1994. *The determinants of reproductive change in Bangladesh*. Washington DC: World Bank.

Coale, A. 1973. The demographic transition. In *Proceedings of the International Population Conference* (vol. 1). Liège, Belgium: International Union for the Scientific Study of Population.

Cochrane, S. 1979. *Fertility and education: what do we really know?* Baltimore: Johns Hopkins University Press.

Cohen, J. 1995. *How many people can the Earth support?* New York: W. W. Norton.

Commoner, B. 1971. *The closing circle*. New York: Knopf.

——1991. Rapid population growth and environmental stress. In *Consequences of rapid population growth in developing countries*, G. Tapinos, D. Blanchet, D. E. Horlacher (eds). New York: Taylor & Francis.

Concepcion, M. B. 1996. Population policies and family planning in Southeast Asia. See Lutz (1996).

Cotton, P. 1993. Health threat from mosquitoes rises as flood of century finally recedes. *Journal of the American Medical Association* **270**, 685–6.

Cropper, M. & W. Oates 1992. Environmental economics: a survey. *Journal of Economic Literature* **30**(2), 675–740.

Cropper, M. & C. Griffiths 1994. The interaction of population growth and environmental quality. *American Economic Review* **84**(2), 250–54.

Cruz, M. C., C. A. Meyer, R. Repetto, R. Woodward 1992. *Population growth, poverty, and environmental stress: frontier migration in the Philippines and Costa Rica*. Washington DC: World Resources Institute.

Cuddington, J., J. Hancock, C. Rogers 1994. A dynamic aggregative model of the AIDS epidemic with possible policy implications. *Journal of Policy Modeling* **16**(5), 473–96.

Daily, G., P. Ehrlich, A. Ehrlich 1994. Optimum human population size. *Population and Environment* **15**(6), 469–75.

Daly, H. 1977. *Steady state economics: the economics of biophysical equilibrium and moral growth*. San Francisco: W. H. Freeman.

Dasgupta, P. 1993. *An inquiry into well-being and destitution*. Oxford: Oxford University Press.

Dasgupta, P. & G. Heal 1979. *Economic theory and exhaustible resources*. Cambridge: Cambridge University Press.

Davis, K. 1954. The world demographic transition. *Annals of the American Academy of Political and Social Science* **237**, 1–11.

——1963. The theory of change and response in modern demographic history. *Population Index* **29**(4), 345–66.

——1991. Population and resources: fact and interpretation. In *Resources, environment and population: present knowledge*, K. Davis & M. Bernstam (eds). Oxford: Oxford University Press.

Degraaf, D. 1991. Increasing contraceptive use in Bangladesh: the role of demand and supply factors. *Demography* **28**(1), 65–81.

Dobson, A. & R. Carper 1992. Global warming and potential changes in host–parasite and disease–vector relationships. In *Global warming and biological diversity*, R. Peters & T. Lovejoy (eds). New Haven, Connecticut: Yale University Press.

Douglas, M. 1978. *Cultural bias*. Occasional Paper 35, Royal Anthropological Institute, London. [Reprinted in *In the active voice*, M. Douglas. London: Routledge, 1982.]

Duchin, F. 1994. Structural economics: toward a post-normal science of ecological economics. Paper presented at the Biennial Meeting of the International Society for Ecological Economics, San José, Costa Rica.

Duncan, O. D. 1959. Human ecology and population studies. In *The study of population*, P. M. Hauser & O. D. Duncan (eds). Chicago: University of Chicago Press.

——1961. From social system to ecosystem. *Social Inquiry* **31**, 140–49.

Dunlap, R. 1982. Ecological limits: societal and sociological implications. *Contemporary Sociology* **11**(2), 153–60.

——1983. Ecologist vs exemptionalist: the Ehrlich–Simon debate. *Social Science Quarterly* **64**, 201–203.

Durning, A. 1992. *How much is enough?* Washington DC: Worldwatch Institute.

Dyson, T. 1991. On the demography of South Asian famines, part II. *Population Studies* **45**(2), 279–97.

Ehrlich, P. & J. Holdren 1971. Impact of population growth. *Science* **171**, 1212–17.

Ehrlich, P. & A. Ehrlich 1990. *The population explosion*. New York: Simon & Schuster.

Ekins, P. 1991. The sustainable consumer society: a contradiction in terms? *International Environmental Affairs* **3**(4), 243–58.

El-Hinnawi, E. 1985. *Environmental refugees*. Nairobi: United Nations Environment Programme.

Emmer, P. 1993. Intercontinental migration as a world historical process. *European Review* **1**(1), 67–74.

Engleman, R. & P. LeRoy 1995. *Conserving land: population and sustainable food production*. Washington DC: Population Action International.

Epstein, P. 1995. Emerging diseases and ecosystem instability: new threats to public health. *American Journal of Public Health* **85**, 168–72.

Falkenmark, M. 1989. Middle Eastern hydropolitics: water scarcity and conflicts in the Middle East. *Ambio* **18**(6), 350–52.

Feacham, R. 1994. Health decline in Eastern Europe. *Nature* **367**, 313–14.

Feldman, A. 1990. *Environmental degradation and high fertility in sub-Saharan Africa*. Working Paper 36, Morrison Institute for Population and Resource Studies, Stanford University.

Findley, S. 1994. Does drought increase migration? A study of migration from rural Mali during the 1983–1985 drought. *International Migration Review* **28**(3), 539–53.

Frank, J. & J. Mustard 1994. The determinants of health from a historical perspective. *Daedalus* **123**(4), 1–19.

Funtowicz, S. & J. Ravetz 1994. Uncertainty, complexity and post-normal science. *Environmental Toxicology and Chemistry* **13**(12), 1–5.

Gilland, B. 1986. On resources and economic development. *Population and Development Review* **12**(2), 295–305.

Gillett, J. 1974. Direct and indirect influences of temperature on the transmission of parasites from insects to man. In *The effects of meteorological factors upon parasites*, A. Taylor & R. Muller (eds), 79–95. Oxford: Blackwell Scientific.

Gleick, P. 1989. Climate change and international politics: problems facing developing countries. *Ambio* **18**(6), 333–9.

—— 1992. Effects of climate change on shared freshwater resources. In *Confronting climate change: risks, implications, and responses*, I. Mintzer (ed.). Cambridge: Cambridge University Press.

—— (ed.) 1993. *Water in crisis: a guide to the world's fresh water resources*. New York: Oxford University Press.

—— 1994. Water and conflict: fresh water resources and international security. *International Security* **18**(1), 79–112.

Goeller, H. E. & A. M. Weinberg 1976. The age of substitutability. *Science* **191**, 683.

Goeller, H. E. & A. Zucker 1984. Infinite resources: the ultimate strategy. *Science* **223**, 456–62.

Goldsmith, J. 1986. Three Los Angeles heat waves. In *Environmental epidemiology: epidemiological investigation of community environmental health problems*, J. Goldsmith (ed.), 73–81. Boca Raton, Florida: CRC Press.

Goodland, R. 1992. The case that the world has reached limits: more precisely that current throughput growth in the global economy cannot be sustained. *Population and Environment* **13**(3), 167–82.

Gore, A. 1992. *Earth in the balance: ecology and the human spirit*. Boston: Houghton Mifflin.

Gregg, M. B. 1989. *The public health consequences of disasters*. Atlanta, Georgia: US Center for Disease Control.

Grossman, G. & A. Krueger 1995. Economic growth and the environment. *Quarterly Journal of Economics* (May), 353–77.

Grover, B. & A. Biswas 1993. It's time for a World Water Council. *Water International* **18**, 81–3.

Grover, B. & D. Howarth 1991. Evolving international collaborative arrangements for water supply and sanitation. *Water International* **16**, 146–52.

Haille, D. G. 1989. Computer simulation of the effects of changes in weather patterns in vector-borne disease transmission. In *The potential effects of global climate change in the United States* (appendix G), J. B. Smith & D. Tirpak (eds). Washington DC: Environmental Protection Agency.

Haines, A., P. Epstein, A. McMichael 1993. Global health watch: monitoring the impacts of environmental change. *The Lancet* **342**, 1464–9.

Hardin, G. 1972. The tragedy of the commons. *Science* **162**, 1248.

—— 1991. Paramount positions in ecological economics. In *Ecological economics: the science and management of sustainability*, R. Costanza (ed.). New York: Columbia University Press.

Harrison, P. 1992. *The third revolution: environment, population and a sustainable world*. London: I. B. Tauris.

Hayami, Y. & V. Ruttan 1971. *Agricultural development: an international perspective*. Baltimore: Johns Hopkins University Press.

—— 1987. Rapid population growth and agricultural productivity. In *Population growth and economic development: issues and evidence*, D. G. Johnson & R. D. Lee (eds), 57–104. Madison: University of Wisconsin Press.

—— 1991. Rapid population growth and technical and institutional change. In *Consequences of rapid population growth in developing countries*, G. Tapinos, D. Blanchet, D. E. Horlacher (eds). New York: Taylor & Francis.

Hazarika, S. 1993. *Bangladesh and Assam: land pressures, migration and ethnic conflict*. Occasional Paper Series, Project on Environmental Change and Acute Conflict, American Academy of Arts and Sciences (Boston) and Peace and Conflict Studies Program, University of Toronto.

Hederra, R. 1987. Environmental sanitation and water supply during floods in Ecuador (1982–83). *Disasters* **11**, 113–16.

Herrera-Basto, E., D. Prevots, M. Zarate, J. Silva, J. Amor 1992. First reported outbreak of classical dengue fever at 1700 meters above sea level in Guerrero State, Mexico. *American Journal of Tropical Medicine* **46**, 649–53.

Hill, A. 1989. Demographic responses to food shortages in the Sahel. In *Rural development and populations: institutions and policy*, G. McNicoll & M. Cain (eds). New York: Oxford University Press. [Supplement to *Population and Development Review* **15**.]

Hogan, D. 1995. Population, poverty, and pollution in Cubatao, Brazil. See Potrykowska & Clarke (1995).

Holdren, J. 1991. Population and the energy problem. *Population and Environment* **12**(3), 231–55.

Holling, C. 1994. An ecologist view of the Malthusian conflict. See Lindahl-Kiessling & Landberg (1994).

Homer-Dixon, T. 1991. On the threshold: environmental changes as causes of acute conflict. *International Security* **16**, 2.

Homer-Dixon, T., J. Boutwell, G. Rathjens 1993. Environmental change and violent conflict. *Scientific American* **268**(February), 38–45.

Howard, P. & T. Homer-Dixon 1995. *Environmental scarcity and violent conflict: the case of Chiapas, Mexico*. Washington DC: American Association for the Advancement of Science.

Homer-Dixon, T. & M. Levy 1995. Correspondence: environment and security. *International Security* **30**(30), 1890–98.

Hynes, H. 1993. *Taking population out of the equation: reformulating I=PAT*. North Amherst, Massachusetts: Institute on Women and Technology.

International Conference on Water and the Environment 1992. *The Dublin statement on water and sustainable development*. Dublin: Conference Secretariat.

Jackson, C. n.d. Questioning synergism: win–win with women in population and environment policies? In *Environment and population change*, B. Zaba & J. Clarke (eds). Liège: Ordina.

Jacobson, J. 1988. *Environmental refugees: a yardstick of habitability*. Washington DC: Worldwatch Institute.

Jiminez, E. 1989. Social sector pricing policy revisited. *Proceedings of the World Bank Annual*

Conference on Development Economics 1989. Washington DC: World Bank.

Jodha, N. 1989. Depletion of common-property resources in India: micro-level evidence. In *Rural development and populations: institutions and policy*, G. McNicoll & M. Cain (eds). New York: Oxford University Press. [Supplement to *Population and Development Review* **15**.]

Kaa, D. J. van de 1993. European migration at the end of history. *European Review* **1**(1), 87–108.

Kabeer, N. 1985. Do women gain from high fertility? In *Women, work and ideology in the Third World*, H. Afshar (ed.). London: Tavistock.

——— 1994. Re-examining the "demand for children" hypothesis in the context of fertility decline in Bangladesh. In *Poverty reduction and development cooperation: report from a conference.* Working Paper 94.6, Centre for Development Research, Copenhagen.

Kalkenstein, L. 1989. The impact of CO_2 and trace gas-induced climate change upon human mortality. Appendix G in *The potential effects of global climate change on the United States*, J. Smith & D. Tirpak (eds). Report EPA-230-05-89–057, Environmental Protection Agency, Washington DC.

——— 1993a. Global warming and human health. In *International implications of global warming*, L. Kalkenstein & J. Smith (eds). Cambridge: Cambridge University Press.

——— 1993b. Health and climate change: direct impacts in cities. *The Lancet* **342**, 1397–9.

Kalkenstein, L. & K. Smoyer 1993. The impact of climate change on human health: some international implications. *Experientia* **49**, 469–79.

Kaplan, R. 1994. The coming anarchy. *The Atlantic Monthly* (April), 44–76.

Kelly, K. & T. Homer-Dixon 1995. *Environmental scarcity and violent conflict: the case of Gaza.* Washington DC: American Association for the Advancement of Science.

Keyfitz, N. 1990. Population and development within the ecosphere: one view of the literature. *Population Index* **57**(1), 5–22.

——— 1992. Seven ways of making the less developed countries' population problem to disappear – in theory. *European Journal of Population* **8**, 149–67.

Kneese, A. 1989. The economics of natural resources. In *Population and resources in Western intellectual traditions*, M. Teitelbaum & J. Winter (eds). New York: Cambridge University Press.

Kolsrud, G. & B. Torrey 1992. The importance of population growth in future commercial energy consumption. In *Global climate change*, J. White (ed.). New York: Plenum Press.

Koopman, J., D. Prevots, M. Marin 1991. Determinants and predictors of dengue infection in Mexico. *American Journal of Epidemiology* **133**, 1168–78.

Kritz, M. 1990. Climate change and migration adaptations. Working Paper 2.16, Population and Development Program, Cornell University.

Langford, I. H. & G. Bentham 1993. *The potential effects of climate change on winter mortality in the UK.* Working paper GEC 93-25, Centre of Social and Economic Research on the Global Environment [CSERGE], University of East Anglia and University College London.

Lashof, D. & D. Tirpak (eds) 1990. *Policy options for stabilizing global climate (including technical appendix).* Washington DC: Hemisphere.

Last, J. 1993. Global change: ozone depletion, greenhouse warming and public health. *Annual Review of Public Health* **14**, 115–36.

Layard, R., O. Blanchard, R. Dornbusch, P. Krugman 1992. *East–West migration: the alternatives.* Cambridge, Massachusetts: MIT Press.

Lee, R. 1990a. The demographic response to economic crisis in historical and contemporary populations. *Population Bulletin of the United Nations* **29**, 1–15.

——— 1990b. Comment: the second tragedy of the commons. *Population and Development Review* **16**, 315–22.

Lele, U. & S. W. Stone 1989. *Population pressure, the environment and agricultural intensification: variations on the Boserup hypothesis.* MADIA Discussion Paper 4, World Bank, Washington DC.

Lesthaeghe, R. 1983. A century of demographic and cultural change in western Europe; an exploration of underlying dimensions. *Population and Development Review* **9**(3), 411–35.

Lesthaeghe, R. & D. Meekers 1986. Value changes and the dimensions of familism in the

European community. *European Journal of Population* **2**, 225–68.

Levins, R. 1995. Preparing for uncertainty. *Ecosystem Health* **1**, 47–57.

Levins, R., T. Awerbuch, U. Brinkman, I. Eckhardt, P. R. Epstein, N. Makhoul, C. Albuquerque de Possas, C. Puccia, A. Spielman, M. E. Wilson 1994. The emergence of new diseases. *American Scientist* **82**, 52–60.

Levy, M. 1995a. Time for a third wave of environment and security scholarship? Issue 1 (44–6), Environmental Change and Security Project Report, Woodrow Wilson Center, Princeton University.

—— 1995b. Is the environment a national security issue? *International Security* **20**(2), 35–62.

Lindahl-Kiessling, K. & H. Landberg (eds) 1994. *Population, economic development, and the environment*. Oxford: Oxford University Press.

Lloyd, C. 1994. Investing in the next generation: the implications of high fertility at the level of the family. In *Population and development: old debates, new conclusions*, R. Cassen (ed.). Washington DC: Overseas Development Council.

Loevinsohn, M. 1994. Climate warming and increased malaria incidence in Rwanda. *The Lancet* **343**, 714–18.

Lonergan, S. & B. Kavanaugh 1991. Climate change, water resources, and security in the Middle East. *Global Environmental Change* **1**(4), 272–90.

Longstreth, J. D. 1990. Global warming: clues to potential health effects. *Environmental Carcinogenesis Reviews* **C8**(1), 139–69.

Ludwig, H. F. & A. Islam 1992. Environmental management of industrial wastes in developing countries: Bangladesh case study. *International Journal of Environment and Pollution* **2**(1/2), 76–86.

Lutz, W. (ed.) 1996. *The future population of the world: what can we assume today?* London: Earthscan.

Lutz, W., C. Prinz, J. Langgassner 1993. World population projections and possible ecological feedbacks [*POPNET* 23 (Summer)]. Laxenburg, Austria: International Institute for Applied Systems Analysis.

MacArthur, R. H. & E. O. Wilson 1967. *The theory of island biogeography*. Princeton, New Jersey: Princeton University Press.

MacKellar, F. L. 1996. On human carrying capacity: a review essay on Joel Cohen's *How many people can the Earth support? Population and Development Review* **22**(1), 145–56.

—— 1997. Population and fairness. *Population and Development Review* **23**(2), 359–76.

MacKellar, F. L., W. Lutz, C. Prinz, A. Goujon 1995. Population, households, and CO_2 emissions. *Population and Development Review* **21**(4), 849–65.

MacKellar, F. L., W. Lutz, L. Wexler, B. O'Neill 1996. *Population and global warming*. Unpublished paper, International Institute for Applied Systems Analysis, Laxenburg, Austria.

Maddison, J. M. 1989. *The world economy in the 20th century*. Paris: Organisation for Economic Cooperation and Development.

Mageed, Y. A. & G. F. White 1995. Critical analysis of existing institutional arrangements. *Water Resources Development* **11**(2), 103–11.

Marden, P. G. & D. Hodgson 1975. *Population, environment, and the quality of life*. New York: AMS Press.

Marquette, C. M. 1995. Population and environment in industrialized regions: some general policy recommendations. See Potrykowska & Clarke (1995).

Martens, W. J. M., J. Rotmans, L. W. Niessen 1994. *Climate change and malaria risk: an integrated modelling approach*. GLOBO Report Series 3, Report 461502003, Global Dynamics and Sustainable Development Program, National Institute of Public Health and Environmental Protection [RIVM], Bilthoven, the Netherlands.

Martens, W. J. M., L. Niessen, J. Rotmans, T. H. Jetten, A. J. McMichael 1995a. Potential impact of global climate change on malaria risk. *Environmental Health Perspectives* **103**, 458–64.

Martens, W. J. M., T. H. Jetten, J. Rotmans, L. W. Nielsson 1995b. Climate change and vector-borne diseases: a global modelling perspective. *Global Environmental Change* **5**(3), 195–209.

Martin, P. H. & M. G. Lefebvre 1995. Malaria and climate: sensitivity of malaria potential transmission to climate. *Ambio* **24**(4), 200–7.

McGreevey, W. P. 1990. *Social security in Latin America*. Discussion Paper 110, World Bank, Washington DC.

McIntosh, A. & J. Finkle 1995. The Cairo Conference on Population and Development. *Population and Development Review* **21**, 223–60.

McKeown, T. E. 1988. *The origins of disease*. Oxford: Basil Blackwell.

McMichael, A. J. 1993. Global environmental change and human population health: a conceptual and scientific challenge for epidemiology. *International Journal of Epidemiology* **22**, 1–8.

McMichael, A. J. & W. J. M. Martens 1995. Assessing health impacts of global environmental change: grappling with scenarios, predictive models, and uncertainty. *Ecosystem Health* **1**, 15–25.

McMichael, A. J., A. Haines, R. Sloof, S. Kovats (eds) 1996. *Climate change and human health*. Geneva: World Health Organisation.

McNicoll, G. 1984. Consequences of rapid population growth. *Population and Development Review* **10**(2), 177–240.

——— 1990. Social organization and ecological stability under demographic stress. In *Rural development and population: institutions and policy*, G. McNicoll & M. Cain (eds). New York: Oxford University Press.

——— 1993. *Malthusian scenarios and demographic catastrophe*. Working Paper 49, Research Division, Population Council, New York.

——— 1995. On population and revisionism. *Population and Development Review* **21**, 307–340.

Meadows, D. H., D. L. Meadows, J. Randers, W. W. Behrens III 1972. *The limits to growth*. New York: Universe.

Morse, S. S. 1991. Emerging viruses: defining the rules for viral traffic. *Perspectives in Biology and Medicine* **34**(3), 387–409.

Mortimore, M. 1989. *Drought and drought response in the Sahel*. Background paper prepared for the Committee on Human Consequences of Global Change, National Research Council, Washington DC.

——— 1993. Northern Nigeria: land transformation under agricultural intensification. In *Population and land use in developing countries*, C. J. Jolly & B. B. Torrey (eds). Washington DC: National Academy Press.

Murphy, M. 1992. Economic models of fertility in post-war Britain – a conceptual and statistical reinterpretation. *Population Studies* **46**(2), 235–58.

——— 1993. The contraceptive pill and women's employment as factors in fertility change in Britain 1963–1980: a challenge to the conventional view. *Population Studies* **47**, 221–43.

Murray, J. 1994. Nutrition, disease and health. In *Health and sustainable agricultural development: perspectives on growth and constraints*, V. Ruttan (ed.). Boulder, Colorado: Westview.

Myers, N. 1989. Population, environment, and conflict. In *Resources, environment and population: present knowledge*, K. Davis & M. S. Bernstam (eds). Oxford: Oxford University Press.

——— 1993. Population, environment and development. *Environmental Conservation* **20**(3), 205–16.

——— 1994. Environmental refugees in a globally warmed world. *BioScience* **43**(11), 752–61.

Myrdal, G. 1944. *An American dilemma*. New York: Harper.

Nerlove, M., A. Razin, E. Sadka 1987. *Household and economy: welfare economics of endogenous fertility*. New York: Academic Press.

Nicholls, N. 1993. El Niño–Southern Oscillation and vector-borne disease. *The Lancet* **342**, 1284–5.

Notestein, F. 1975. Population policy and development: a summary view. In *The population debate: dimensions and perspectives: papers of the World Population Conference, Bucharest, 1974*. New York: United Nations.

Nugent, J. B. 1985. The old age security motive and fertility. *Population and Development Review* **11**, 75–97.

Nugent, J. B. & R. Anker 1990. *Old age support and fertility.* Working Paper 172, Population and Labor Policies, International Labour Organisation, Geneva.

OECD 1991. *The state of the environment.* Paris: Organisation for Economic Cooperation and Development.

Ogburn, W. F. 1922. *Social change: with respect to culture and original nature.* New York: Viking Press.

Palmer, I. 1991. *Gender and population in the adjustment of African economies: planning for change.* Geneva: International Labour Office.

Panayotou, T. 1993. *Empirical tests and policy analysis of environmental degradation at different stages of economic development.* Working Paper WEP 2-22/WP.238, World Employment Programme, International Labour Office, Geneva.

Pandit, K. & E. Cassetti 1989. The shifting patterns of sectoral labor allocation during development: developed versus developing countries. *Annals of the Association of American Geographers* **79**(3), 329–44.

Pearce, D. W., E. Barbier, A. Markandya 1990. *Sustainable development: economics and environment in the Third World.* Cheltenham, England: Edward Elgar.

Pederson, J. 1995. Drought, migration and population growth in the Sahel: the case of the Malian Gourma: 1900–1991. *Population Studies* **49**, 111–26.

Percival, V. & T. F. Homer-Dixon 1995. *Environmental scarcity and violent conflict: the case of South Africa.* Washington DC: American Association for the Advancement of Science.

Pernetta, J. C. 1989. Projected climate change and sea-level rise: a relative impact rating for the countries of the Pacific Basin. In *Implications of expected climate changes in the South Pacific: an overview,* J. C. Pernetta & P. J. Hughes (eds). Regional Seas Reports and Studies 128, United Nations Environment Programme, Nairobi.

——— 1992. Impacts of climate change and sea-level rise on small island states: national and international responses. *Global Environmental Change* **2**(1), 19–31.

Pigou, A. 1960 (1920). *The economics of welfare* [reprint]. London: Macmillan.

Pingali, P. & H. Binswanger 1987. Population density and agricultural intensification: a study of the evolution of technologies in tropical agriculture. In *Population growth and economic development: issues and evidence,* D. G. Johnson & R. E. Lee (eds). Madison: University of Wisconsin Press.

Pope, C. A., D. V. Bates, M. E. Raizenne 1995. Health effects of particulate air pollution: time for reassessment. *Environmental Health Perspectives* **103**, 472–80.

Potrykowska, A. & J. I. Clarke (eds) 1995. Population and environment in industrialized regions. *Geographica Polonica* **64** [special issue].

Powles, J. 1992. Changes in disease patterns and related social trends. *Social Science and Medicine* **35**, 377–87.

Preston, S. 1994. Population and environment. From Rio to Cairo. IUSSP Distinguished Lecture on Population and Development, International Union for the Scientific Study of Population, Liège, Belgium.

Pritchett, L. 1994. Desired fertility and the impact of population policies. *Population and Development Review* **20**(1), 1–55.

Rahman, A., N. Robins, A. Roncerel (eds) 1993. *Population versus consumption: which is the climate bomb?* Castle Cary, England: Castle Cary Press.

Raskin, P. D. 1995. Methods for estimating the population contribution to environmental change. *Ecological Economics* **15**, 225–33.

Renner, M. 1989. *National security: the economic and environmental dimensions.* Worldwatch Paper 89, Worldwatch Institute, Washington DC.

Robinson, J. 1990. Philosophical origins of the social rate of discount in cost–benefit analysis.

Milbank Quarterly **682**, 245–65.

Robinson, W. C. 1986. High fertility as risk assurance. *Population Studies* **40**(2), 289–98.

Rogers, D. T. & M. J. Packer 1993. Vector-borne diseases, models and global change. *The Lancet* **342**, 1282–4.

Romieu, I., H. Weitzenfeld, J. Finkelman 1990. Urban air pollution in Latin America and the Caribbean: health perspectives. *World Health Statistics Quarterly* **43**, 153–67.

Rothman, E. S. & T. J. Espenshade 1992. Fiscal impacts of immigration to the United States. *Population Index* **58**(3), 381–415.

Rowlands, I. H. 1992. North–South politics, environment, development and population: a post-Rio review. In *Environment and population change*, B. Zaba & J. Clarke (eds). Liège: Ordina.

Ruttan, V. W. 1971. Technology and the environment. *American Journal of Agricultural Economics* **53**, 707–717.

Ruttan, V. W. & Y. Hayami 1991. Rapid population growth and technical and institutional change. In *Consequences of rapid population growth in developing countries*, G. Tapinos, D. Blanchet, D. E. Horlacher (eds). New York: Taylor & Francis.

Sen, G. 1994. Women, poverty and population: issues for the concerned environmentalist. In *Population and the environment: rethinking the debate*, L. Arizpe, M. P. Stone, D. C. Major (eds). Boulder, Colorado: Westview.

Serageldin, I. 1995. Water resources management: a new policy for a sustainable future. *Water Resources Development* **11**(3), 221–2.

Shafik, N. & S. Bandyopadhyay 1992. *Economic growth and environmental quality: time series and cross-country evidence*. Policy Research Paper WPS 904, World Bank, Washington DC.

Shaw, P. 1993. Review of Harrison (1992). *Population and Development Review* **19**(1), 189–92.

Shope, R. 1991. Global climate change and infectious diseases. *Environmental Health Perspectives* **96**, 171–4.

Siddiqui, T. A. 1994. Implications for energy and climate-change policies of using purchasing-power-parity-based GDP. *Energy* **19**(9), 975–81.

Simon, J. 1981. *The ultimate resource*. Princeton, New Jersey: Princeton University Press.

—— 1989. *The economic consequences of immigration*. Boston: Basil Blackwell.

Simons, J. 1986. Culture, economy and reproduction in contemporary Europe. In *The state of population theory: forward from Malthus*, D. Coleman & R. Schofield (eds). Oxford: Basil Blackwell.

Sirageldin, I. 1994. Population dynamics, environment and conflict. What are the connections? In *Population–environment–development interactions*, J. I. Clarke & L. Tabah (eds). Paris: Centre International de Recherche sur l'Environnement et la Développement [CIRED].

Smil, V. 1990. Planetary warming: realities and responses. *Population and Development Review* **16**(1), 1–29.

Smith, D. R. 1995. Environmental security and shared water resources in post-Soviet Central Asia. *Post Soviet Geography* **36**(6), 351–70.

Solow, R. 1991. *Sustainability: an economist's perspective*. Woods Hole, Massachusetts: Marine Policy Center.

Stanley, D. J. & A. G. Warne 1993. Nile Delta: recent geological evolution and human impact. *Science* **260**(30 April), 628–34.

Starr, J. R. 1991. Water wars. *Foreign Policy* **70**(2), 17–36.

Stern, P., O. Young, D. Druckman (eds) 1992. *Global environmental change: understanding the human dimensions*. Washington DC: National Academy Press.

Stevenson, G. 1989. The production, distribution and consumption of fuelwood in Haiti. *Journal of Developing Areas* **24**(1), 59–76.

Stonich, S. C. 1989. The dynamics of social processes and environmental destruction: a Central American case study. *Population and Development Review* **15**(2), 269–96.

Suhrke, A. 1993. *Pressure points: environmental degradation, migration and conflict*. Occasional

Paper Series on Environmental Change and Acute Conflict, Peace and Conflict Studies Program, University of Toronto.

Tabah, L. 1989. From one demographic transition to another. *Population Bulletin of the United Nations* **28**, 1–24.

Thomas, N. 1992. Review of UNFPA, *Population, resources, and the environment: the critical challenges. Population Studies* **46**(3), 559–60.

——1993. Economic security, culture and fertility: a reply to Cleland. *Population Studies* **47**, 353–9.

Thompson, M., R. Ellis, A. Wildavsky 1990. *Cultural theory*. Boulder, Colorado: Westview.

Thurman, E. M., D. A. Goolsby, M. T. Meyer, M. S. Mills, M. L. Pomes, D. W. Kolpin 1991. Herbicides in surface waters of the United States: the effect of spring flush. *Environmental Science and Technology* **25**, 1794–6.

——1992. A reconnaissance study of herbicides and their metabolites in surface water of the mid-western United States using immunoassay and gas chromatography/mass spectrometry. *Environmental Science and Technology* **26**, 2440–47.

Tiffen, M. & M. Mortimore 1992. Environment, population growth and productivity in Kenya. *Development Policy Review* **10**(4), 359–87.

Tiffen, M., M. Mortimore, F. N. Gichuki 1994. *More people, less erosion: environmental recovery in Kenya*. New York: John Wiley.

UN 1993. Synthesis of the Expert Group Meeting on Population, Environment, and Development. *United Nations Population Bulletin* **34/35**, 19–34.

United Nations Population Fund 1991. *Population, resources, and the environment: the challenges ahead*. New York: United Nations.

United Nations Secretariat 1991. Relationships between population and environment in rural areas of developing countries. *Population Bulletin of the United Nations* **46/47**, 52–69.

——1994. Population and environment: an overview. In *Population, environment and development: proceedings of the United Nations Expert Group meeting on population, environment and development*. New York: United Nations.

US NRC [US National Research Council] 1986. *Population growth and economic development: policy questions*. Washington DC: National Academy Press.

Van Arsdol, W. D., D. J. Sherman, A. Constable, J. Wang, L. Rollin 1995. Impacts of global sea level rise on California coastal population resources. In *Population–environment–development interactions*, J. I. Clarke & L. Tabah (eds). Paris: Comité International de Coopération dans les Recherches Nationales en Démographie.

Walle, E. van de 1992. Fertility transition, conscious choice and numeracy. *Demography* **29**(4), 487–502.

Warrick, R. 1980. Drought in the Great Plains: a case study of research on climate and society in the USA. In *Climatic constraints and human activities*, J. Ausabel & A. Biswas (eds). New York: Pergamon Press.

Weinberger, M. B. 1994. Recent trends in contraceptive use. *Population Bulletin of the United Nations* **36**, 55–80.

Westing, A. H. (ed.) 1986. *Global resources and international conflict: environmental factors in strategic policy and action*. New York: Oxford University Press.

——1992. Environmental refugees: a growing category of displaced persons. *Environmental Conservation* **19**, 201–207.

——1994. Population, desertification, and migration. *Environmental Conservation* **21**(2), 110–15.

Westoff, C. F. 1996a. The return to replacement fertility: a magnetic force? See Lutz (1996).

——1996b. Reproductive preferences and future fertility in developing countries. See Lutz (1996).

Wexler, L. 1996. *The greenhouse externality to childbearing*. Unpublished manuscript, International Institute for Applied Systems Analysis, Laxenburg, Austria.

WHO 1990. *Potential health effects of climate change: report of a WHO Task Group*. Geneva: World Health Organisation.

Wilkinson, R. G. 1994. The epidemiological transition: from material scarcity to social disadvantage? *Daedalus* **123**(4), 61–77.

Wolf, A. P. & C. Ying-Chang 1994. Fertility and women's labor: two negative (but instructive) findings. *Population Studies* **48**(3), 427–33.

World Bank 1992. *World development report 1992: development and environment*. Washington DC: World Bank.

—— 1993. *World development report 1993: investing in health*. Washington DC: World Bank.

World Resources Institute 1994. Natural resource consumption. In *World Resources 1994–95*. New York: Basic Books.

Yohe, G., J. Neuman, H. Ameden 1995. Assessing the economic cost of greenhouse-induced sea level rise: methods and application in support of a national survey. *Journal of Environmental Economics and Management* **29**, S78-S97.

Young, P. 1993. *Equity in theory and practice*. Princeton, New Jersey: Princeton University Press.

CHAPTER 3

Human needs and wants

Mary Douglas, Des Gasper,
Steven Ney, Michael Thompson

Contributors
Russell Hardin, Shaun Hargreaves-Heap, Saiful Islam, Denise Jodelet,
Hélène Karmasin, Ota de Leonardis, Judith Mehta, Sanjeev Prakash,
Zofia Sokolewitz, Thanh-dam Truong

Discussions of the underlying causes of climate change focus on two villains: one is population growth in the less industrialized world; the other is mindless consumption in the rich industrialized nations (see Ch. 4). Clearly, the issue of human needs and wants lies at the heart of the whole debate. Family and lifestyle shape population patterns and deplete natural resources. Aspirations to live well influence the selection of technologies and the rate of their adoption.

The study of human needs and wants appears to offer opportunities for policy to design means of reducing greenhouse gas emissions. To do this, policymakers have to know what human needs and wants are. So, they turn to the social sciences to provide answers to questions about wants and needs. Yet, surprisingly, attention has not been directed to these problems, neither by social scientists addressing global environmental change, nor by those who have specialized in needs theories. In default, needs and wants tend to have been subsumed under headings such as economic growth and technological change or, at best, as attitudes and beliefs about material goods (Stern et al. 1992). Within the international discourse on climate change, the distinction between needs and wants is used to justify different targets and burdens for emissions reductions in less industrialized and industrialized countries (see Chs 4 and 5). Yet, fundamental questions that need to be posed about the relationship between human needs and global climate change are not yet articulated.

The main question we will ask of human needs theories is, can they be of any use to policymakers concerned with global climate change? We will look at some of the assumptions that underpin theories of human needs and wants. We will show that there are grave difficulties in the way of making a coherent theory of poverty or affluence. Finally, we will propose a new approach: a cultural theory of human needs and wants that should be able at least to pose the questions relevant to the global climate change debate.

Wants and global climate change

It seems fair enough to pin responsibility for massive greenhouse gas emissions on human efforts to satisfy their wants. The branch of the social sciences where wants as such are studied is economics, and in economics "wants" have a specialized meaning. An agent, later to be known as "the consumer," was originally invented to solve theoretical problems about the market. Strictly speaking, the theory of consumer demand is not about wants at all, but is a technical device to explain market behavior. Sociology has a theory of needs, but it hardly connects at all with the market theory of wants.

In the history of economics the theory of demand completed the model of

196

flows and equilibria. The balance of power was an old idea in politics, and the balance of pain and pleasure an elementary idea in psychology. The idea of self-balancing counterflows of bullion and goods was used by eighteenth-century physiocrats against the protectionist policies of mercantilists. Hume (1711–76) using the hydraulic analogy ("All water, wherever it communicates, remains always at a level."), described international trade as a self-regulating balance achieved by flows of precious metals acting automatically on domestic price levels. This was the first systematic account of equilibrium based on prices (Hume 1777: 312).

So far, the idea of consumer demand had not appeared. Ideas of diminishing marginal utility were in the air, but not been applied to consumers: the Swiss mathematician, Bernouilli (1700–1782) proposed that the utility of wealth increases at a marginally decreasing rate (this in connection with probability calculations of risk); the theory of diminishing marginal returns was applied by Ricardo (1772–1823) to factors of production, but not to consumption; both the principle of market equilibrium and the principle of diminishing marginal utility were ready, but it took a hundred years after Hume to put them together into one system.

In the early 1870s economists in three different countries independently produced a model of the economy in which the wheels of trade are moved by buyers' demand, with prices as the pivot of interaction. In the model, producers' supply decisions are triggered by a comparison of marginal revenue with marginal cost, both of which ultimately depend on consumers' demand for the commodity in question and workers' supply of labor (balanced by their demand for leisure). Thus, diminishing marginal utility permeates the market-based model of the economic system. Without it the market theory would collapse in a jumble of arbitrary absurdities, and without the market theory the idea of demand for leisure or of satisfied demand would not be formulated.

If wants were unruly and irrational the market would not work, nor would it be possible to explain how it works. The central idea of diminishing marginal utility is simply that people split their expenditure between different items rather than plunging wildly from one to another, and that they split it consistently. This minimal rationality of humans is needed to make calculations about price movements, and that is all that it is needed for.

A highly technical concept of rationality might not have become the dominant principle of contemporary social theory had not those in favor of individual freedom and free markets won against those in favor of tariffs. The winners bequeathed to future generations the principle that the proper start for social theory is the rational individual. Wants are the desires of a rational being: they are ordered logically in a hierarchy of claims on resources. The ordering has no guaranteed connection with needs. The economists do not have an official doctrine as to how wants arise. This would fall outside their professional tasks and beyond their sphere of competence. To be telling the people what they ought to want, or what they should not want, to make any judgments about wants beyond the effect on market behavior, would be preaching. The economist exercises political and moral judgment to the best of his ability, but his techniques of enquiry are tools; they are not supposed to carry a normative bias.

Almost by default, wants are supposed to be based on subjective preferences, an idea that links consumption theory to the Benthamite hedonistic psychology and to the political philosophy of individual freedom. It leads to the guiding principle of concern for the happiness of the greatest number. By this circuitous route a particular theory of consumer behavior has become entrenched in economics and politics.

The ignoble spirit of emulation

The usual model of the representative consumer in economic theory has been one of a hedonist whose choices refer to private wants and private satisfactions. This is largely the result of the academic professionalism which takes care not to poach on other preserves or to make assumptions about choices and preferences that might import hidden political or moral judgments. But interestingly, if the economic literature ever does pay unguarded attention to social influences on consumption, the social factor is taken to be display in social competition, and disapproved as often as not. So, the vacuum left unfilled because the professional economists consider it improper to impose private moral judgments (i.e., the empty space where their model says nothing about interpersonal relations) was filled by standardized moral judgments against keeping up with the Joneses.

For example, Marshall implied that the principle of diminishing marginal utility applied only to physical wants when he said, "man's capacity for food is limited by nature, but not his craving for distinction." In this ignoble craving he finds the "source of the desire for costly dress" (Marshall 1890). Here, when utility theory reached its complete formulation, we find a split that separates physical and social wants. There is nothing in utility theory itself to support this, but implicitly consumer choices have to satisfy two kinds of wants: one natural kind, which is subject to diminishing marginal utility, and one social kind, which is subject to inordinate competitive drives.

Some environmentalists blame insatiable consumption habits for the depletion of the globe's resources, including its capacity to absorb atmospheric carbon. Commentators from less industrialized countries distinguish between their own *survival emissions* of greenhouse-related gases, originating from the satisfaction of basic needs, and the *luxury emissions* of the industrialized world, originating from unrestrained consumerism (Agarwal & Narain 1991). By definition such consumption is deemed irrational, if not also immoral. We look in vain for a social science theory that explains how wants escape from rational control. For the utilitarian, human wants are rationally ordered and competition between them is reduced by awareness of budget constraints. Social constraints on consumption fall through the theoretical gap, but, as we shall see, social constraints can be very strong, and, if we want to connect wants with depletion of environmental resources, it will have to be by bringing into the picture the influence of other people on individuals.

In practice, most economists are professionally more worried about under-consumption than overconsumption. This, in fact, is a major point of contention between different camps in the global climate change debate. Some more radical environmentalists (Kemp & Wall 1990, Rainbow 1993, Meyer 1994a) maintain that environmental protection in general and protecting the atmosphere in particular are at odds with an economic approach committed to perpetual growth. Their opponents, notably economists such as Nordhaus (1991) and Pearce (1991), argue that halting climate change would require immense resources, and that these can be raised only by continued economic growth. The social factors in judgment and choice have been inadvertently relegated, and the discussions of climate policy limp along with an impoverished definition of the self and a theory of rationality that does not involve negotiating with other selves.

Subsistence goods and luxuries

All of this makes it unsurprising that the difference between needs and wants is not drawn in utility theory. Far be it for the economist to pronounce on which expenditures are necessary and which unnecessary. There is, however, a long tradition that distinguishes between subsistence and higher wants. It goes back at least to the Malthusian theory that workers' consumption would always tend to press on subsistence because of excessive population. Robbins, discussing this distinction between subsistence and other wants, quoted a passage from Ricardo that he felt was not sufficiently known (quoted in Robbins 1952: 78):

> The friends of humanity cannot but wish that in all countries the laboring classes should have a taste for comforts and enjoyments, and that they should be stimulated by all legal means in their exertions to procure them. There cannot be a better security against a superabundant population. In those countries where the laboring classes have the fewest wants, and are

contented with the cheapest food, the people are exposed to the greatest vicissitudes and miseries.

Thus, from the earliest foreshadowing of the population–consumption debate over climate change, two kinds of consumption were recognized: subsistence and the rest, necessities and luxuries, both dependent on what will make the individual contented. The distinction has given rise to a modern version of an antique psychological theory, according to which the individual person is composed of a spiritual element in an animal body. The two parts can be distinguished and they generate different kinds of motivations: the animal requirements are primary and must be satisfied before ethical, artistic, and spiritual pleasures can receive attention. This composite being is able to attend to higher needs only when the belly is full. First, see to it that there is bread in the belly, and then art and altruism will follow. Values fit into an evolving hierarchy.

In Victorian times implanting a desire for higher satisfactions would be the antidote to the fecklessness of the laboring masses. Malthus himself considered that divinely implanted *mind growth* would halt population growth and attendant misery. Nowadays the hierarchy of values is used to explain the same thing. Our contemporary equivalent of mind growth would explain why well-to-do individuals and countries are allegedly more deeply engaged with higher and other-worldly issues than poorer people and nations; they are altruistic because they are comfortable enough to attend to their higher needs.

Even if it were intuitively plausible that the poor are too pressed by hunger and other wants to worry about these higher wants, the theory does not explain why so many of the rich are not interested in environmental causes. And although it may be plausible in industrialized society, in other parts of the world it does not hold good. The poor recognize the claims of the environment when their livelihood immediately depends on certain resources (Ostrom 1990), but not always. People do run down their resources, and are known to move on, leaving a land laid waste. (Vol. 3, Ch. 1 discusses ethnographic and historical examples of care for the sustainability of the environment.)

There is no heading for *luxury* in *The new Palgrave: a dictionary of economics* (Eatwell et al. 1987). But economics has developed an excellent definition of luxury that conforms exactly to practice, which implies no moral judgment, and which uses information only about purchases. This idea for how to make a distinction between necessities and luxuries came from outside of utility theory.

The German statistician Engel (1821–96) analyzed the household expenditures of Belgian coalminers in collaboration with the French sociologist, Le Play. He found a steady relationship between level of income and expenditure on food, such that households with higher incomes spend more on food but that the share of food in the budget goes down as the income level goes up (Houthakker 1957, Eatwell et al. 1987). Some goods are income inelastic (as income rises, the budget share of these goods goes down, because they are necessities). Others are income elastic (as income rises their budget shares also increase); they are the luxuries that we can do without when times are hard. Necessities are food and rent, and other things slide according to local cultural demands toward or away from the luxury end of the household expenditures.

This discovery, known as Engel's law, introduces a link between household behavior and the market. It does economics the service of grounding the analysis of demand in an empirically established connection. The Engel curve is a powerful analytic tool which just gives facts about the market that the theory of market can use. The interesting thing is that it lends support to the idea that some needs are more basic than others, and that the basic needs have physical satisfaction, of which the paradigmatic example is the need for food. Being able to distinguish necessities from luxuries on a statistical basis, economists are relieved of the burden of philosophizing about human vanity. They have several instruments that work well on the assumption that wants can be hierarchized, starting with biological needs.

Where do wants and preferences come from?

According to the anthropologists' assumptions, wants and needs do not come from inside the person, nor are they ordered according to private preference (Douglas 1986). This is the most unrealistic item in the box of conjuring tricks. It treats the abstracted individual consumer as if no one else were there, as in a film studio where Tarzan might be swinging in front of a painted rainforest backdrop. The stage hands and mechanical props are invisible, everything around him is unreal. Only he and his urges are seen as authentic, and they respond to internal demands, on the model of hunger and thirst.

The theory of wants will one day come to terms with the theory of society. Then the inherent sociality of the person will be restored. Without that, economists can have no theory about why people want to buy goods, or why they buy what they buy, or wherein value resides.

A minute's reflection is enough to demonstrate that other people impose ordering on individual wants. Other people make demands on Ego's time and resources. Ego hurries along, or slows down, in response to other people's definition of the short and the long term. Principles of reciprocity limit how far one can go. Social life is a continuous negotiation of acceptable demands.

Scientists have had their gaze fixed upon the wrong elements. If researchers had only been looking at people's relations with each other and recognized that physical objects only mediate the negotiations, they could have had a social theory of exchange. Watching the florist and the post office might tell more than watching the bakery.

A person wants goods for fulfilling personal commitments. Commodities do not satisfy desire; they are only the tools or instruments for satisfying it. Goods are not ends. Goods are for distributing, sharing, consuming or destroying publicly in one way or another. To focus exclusively on how persons relate to objects can never illuminate desire. Instead research should focus on the patterns of alliance and authority that are made and marked in all human societies by the circulation of goods. Demand for objects is a chart of social commitments, graded, and timetabled for the year, or the decade, or the lifetime. As Douglas (1976) remarks, restricting consumption of goods restricts participation in the extended social conversation for which they are used.

The traditional priorities are violated by suggesting that consumption is first for other people. This shift in the explanation of why people want goods transforms conventional utility analysis (but it could be adapted). The main objective of consumption is the desired pattern of social relations. The material objects only play an ancillary role; goods are battle standards; they draw the line between good and evil, and there are no neutral objects.

Advertisers are shocked to learn that taste formation does not depend on childhood learning so much as on current interaction with other people. Individuals adopt their tastes in accordance with their relationship to the larger continuing system in which they live. As they contemplate their wants and needs, they negotiate with others about how to set the standards.

The forms of society are also being negotiated by the same people who are standardizing their tastes. Society and tastes are co-produced. It is a loop: as people try to form a kind of society, they make the list of wants and needs they are going to consider acceptable, and set themselves to procure what will satisfy them. It does not matter where researchers start to unravel the circle; when they discover the system of feedbacks, they can check whether they have got it right if a change at one point sets off waves in all the channels. If people want an unpolluted environment, they will change their laws, and changing these will change the pattern of wealth and income distribution, and this will change the flows of goods and people on birthdays, anniversaries and weddings, retirements, funerals, sick visiting, and ordinary Sunday family gatherings.

Enough has been said to indicate that economics does not have a theory about human wants and that the economic theory of individual preferences is not primarily about preferences. It is a mistake to take it for a theory of human wants, or of motives, self-interested or other. It is first and foremost a theory about how markets behave, about quantities, profits and losses, loans and debts. What it has to say about the psychology of wants is very indirect.

The practitioners of a powerful technical apparatus for market analysis, however neutral their philosophy, would be more than human if they never invoked it to support the normative principles that appeal to them. And paradoxically, the intention not to enter on one side or another of the central normative debate of one's own culture is almost impossible to implement. In the more general case, by conflating wants and needs into the demand curve, the economist breaks a lance on the side of the libertarian view. But the Engel curve as the basis of econometric research supports the idea that physical wants (food especially) make a more imperative demand on income than others, and so it breaks a lance for welfarism. This makes the discipline seem to be essentially neutral, since either side can invoke its authority. But a heavy bias weighs in favor of libertarian principles because of the economics definition of human wants and preferences.

Through the meshes

Since the economic analysis of wants must take tastes as given, there are many things that it cannot explain. The person defined for market analysis is not a social being. Without a theory of social persons we cannot start to use the distinction between basic and higher needs. The behavior of famine victims who die because they will not go to the clinic without proper clothes has to be dismissed as irrational. Women in Bangladesh who do not wish to abandon purdah practices find themselves in such a predicament at the time of flood disasters. Crisis undoes the social bond, but it is rationality, not irrationality, that catches the victims in desperate dilemmas.

Another challenge for the more simple-minded kinds of economics is that different societies take different attitudes to the accumulation of wealth. The hunter in the rainforest, who believes that goods are for sharing, is totally mystified by capitalist accumulation, supposing that only a lonely person would accumulate possessions. How goods make the social bond is the second thing that the economist in a professional capacity can say nothing about. A third is why people ever save for the next generation or, in terms of climate change, why we would consider large current expenditures to prevent damage to those yet unborn. A fourth is why sometimes a whole community or nation throws calculation to the winds and goes for a wild and prolonged spending bout, living way beyond its resources, in a style to which none of the market assumptions about rational choice would seem to apply. Paradoxically, this charge, which conventional economists would describe as irrational behavior, is used by environmentalists and Southern observers to characterize the behavior underlying greenhouse gas emissions from industrialized countries. Because the theory does not take social pressures into account, social scientists still have no theoretical framework for explaining why the budget constraint does not always constrain spending.

These are not quaint and trivial gaps in a theory that otherwise works well enough. They arise in a fundamental philosophical inadequacy that disbars the social sciences from speaking coherently about affluence, and, by the same token, about poverty. Economics cannot but define poverty as a lack of things and so automatically, alleviation of poverty is treated as a restoration of necessary things.

Pierre Bourdieu's vast tome, *La misère du monde* (1994), is an angry fist shaken at contemporary professional approaches to poverty. In French *la misère* means poverty, whereas English has separated the concepts, using many words, such as misery, for unhappiness, and many other words about lack of material things, for poverty. Six hundred pages of interviews gives a heartbreaking picture of loneliness, isolation, humiliation and lost autonomy: this is what poverty feels like, underlying and causing a lack of things, a lack of persons in the right place at the right time. Plenty is said about want and needs, but it does not hold together and it does not apply to the problem in hand. At the root of the failure is the idea of the person, defined as an isolate and not as a social being whose most explicit and urgent needs are in respect of other people. Let us now see how well this deficiency is compensated in the branches of the social sciences that focus upon the idea of need.

Human needs and global climate change

The concept of needs is cited by the World Commission on Environment and Development (also called the Brundtland Commission; WCED 1987) as one of the two key concepts defining sustainable development. A theory of human needs is expected to offer a useful basis for global climate change policy. For example, it could be used for determining which resource claims are justified in need and which claims are substitutable wants. Further, a theory of human needs might help in deciding how the burden of reducing greenhouse gas emissions could be distributed in order to meet "the needs of the present without compromising the ability of future generations to meet their own needs" (WCED 1987: 10).

If needs theories are going to underpin climate change policy, we should examine them closely and consider the claim that human needs theories are an improvement on the economist's model of wants. In this section, we will see how the term need is defined and then, moving from the abstract, three broad approaches will be evaluated in terms of their relevance to global climate change policy: psychological approaches, basic material needs approaches, and ethical needs theories.

Defining human needs

The idea of need in general appears intuitively obvious. In fact, at least in most European languages, the word "need" permeates day-to-day use at every level. With many senses, it carries an idea of obligation. A baby needs milk, a person may need to buy bread from the shops, politicians need to understand their voters, and the news repeatedly reminds us of the needy people at home and in other places.

So, what are human needs? Even human needs theorists have different answers. However, there is a negative consensus: needs are not wants, or, more precisely, not all wants are needs. Among social scientists concerned with human needs, there is near-universal insistence on a sharp distinction between needs and wants (Bay 1968, 1990, Clark 1990, Doyal & Gough 1991, Plant 1991, Ramsay 1992). Galtung (1990: 303) was representative when he declared that "a need should be distinguished from a want, a wish, a desire, a demand. The latter are subjectively felt and articulated; they may express needs, but they also may not; and there may be needs that are not thus expressed."

The fact that needs and wants are often conflated reflects that on other occasions the English word "want" can mean need, lack, or requirement, as in the phrase "to live in want." Of the meanings for want in the *Collins English dictionary* (1979), seven are about families in want, and another eight concern individually felt wishes, desires, or needs. The nine everyday meanings given for need are much more uniform: eight contain no mention of feelings, and of these six concern requirements and the others concern distress and extreme poverty or destitution.

Wants are not needs because they are not rationalized in the same way. A need can be justified as something required for functioning in some approved way, that is, "needs in their socially evaluative use" (Braybrooke 1987: 77). The individual may not know or feel the need that others can recognize, and conversely, "perceived or felt need . . . may or may not correspond to or overlap with real [justified] need" (Bay 1968: 242). In contrast, wants are consciously felt: they are "demonstrable dispositions to desire or prefer something" (Ramsay 1992: 10). We may rationalize a want in terms of our narrow subjectivity or, of course, not at all: in any case, it is argued, a want is not necessarily grounded in social norms.

Further, as Galtung's definition implies, needs are not necessarily felt or conscious. However, they may still be justified. For example, environmentalists assert that access to a healthy environment, including a stable climate, is a human need (Kemp & Wall 1990, Leggett 1990) and that this is so irrespective of whether or not the individual person expresses it as a want or a desire. Plant (1991) summarized an extensive literature that corroborates this needs/wants distinction through analysis of English-language usage; Livingstone & Lunt (1992) presented similar findings from interviews.

As to the question of how wants arise, needs theorists appear to be as little interested as the economists. Wants, it is maintained, are a cultural phenomenon; this makes wants rather uncomfortable elements of a theory with claims to universality. However, some approaches, notably Marcuse's (1964) or Bay's (1968), suggest that there can be wants, or false needs, generated by oppressive socioeconomic systems.

Beyond this and in contrast to our everyday understanding of needs, social scientists find the term very difficult to pin down. Needs researcher Mary Clark noted, "the abstract word, needs, is never clearcut" (1990: 37). Its ambiguities and many meanings with even more connotations make for an instant headache in the world of social science. This may be attributable to the circumstance that, as Lederer (1980) pointed out, needs are theoretical constructs and are not open to direct observation. To illustrate the difficulties in finding a workable definition we have drawn some examples from the human needs literature.

Gillwald (1990: 115) proposed an all-embracing definition of human needs; for her, "needs are all the exigencies of human existence and are an important driving force thereof." Not only do needs somehow define the entire human condition, but they also influence behavior; human needs map out the boundaries of what it means to be human and they also determine how we go about this.

Other theorists stress the element of necessity or requirement. They define basic needs as those goals that must be satisfied as the precondition for an individual to achieve any other goal. Friedman (1990) built on this idea by defining human needs as a conscious or unconscious recognition of a lack of something indispensable for a state of personal equilibrium, physical or emotional. Here she has added the idea of equilibrium to the notions of human existence and necessity. A need maintains equilibrium not of the market, as in economic theory, but of the human person.

Matters are complicated when yet other theorists assign a more dynamic role to human needs. Bay (1968, 1990) understood needs as inferred objective requirements for individual safety, well-being, and growth. Similarly, Sandole (1990: 60) referred to basic needs as "necessary conditions to basic survival and further physical and psychological development." Not only do needs point out what is necessary for maintaining humans in some stable state, but they also show the way for further development.

206

What can we glean from these broad definitions? So far, we can say that needs express necessities of being and developing as a human and that these requirements are the same for all humans. Needs are necessities that, in Ramsey's words (1992: 13) "... all human beings by virtue of their nature must share ..."

"Necessity for what?" Galtung (1990: 303) asks, and promptly answers by stating that needs are requirements "for the person to be a human person ... One aspect of "need" is thus tied to the concept of necessity, which means that we have an image of what is necessary to be human—or at least, of what it is to be non-human." A concept that casts needs as "any behavior tendency whose continued denial or frustration leads to pathological responses" (Bay 1968: 242) is too broad to help in drafting greenhouse gas reduction strategies.

To illustrate the human aspect of needs, Clark introduces a *needs spectrum*. At one end of the spectrum we all need food, water and shelter. "Yet," she continues, "these are not specifically 'human' needs; they are shared by other life forms" (1990: 37). At the other end of the spectrum, needs are defined by a particular culture; the example cited is that southern Californians claim to need cars. But, according to Clark, these too are not human needs but so-called derived needs. Evidently, human needs can be found in a space somewhere between physiological needs and derived needs: they are specifically human, as opposed to animal, and are independent of culture.

Already we can see the potential problems of applying human needs theories to the global climate change issue. Although the semantic variability and flexibility of the word "need" may be a positive characteristic in everyday language, it is ill suited to clear, precise and unambiguous concepts. For social scientists, the apparently commonsensical idea of needs turns into a very elusive and complex concept. It is not clear from these definitions whether a healthy environment in general can be classified as a human need or a derived, culturally specific want. At this point in our discussion, social science definitions of human needs appear too abstract to be relevant to the policy process for global climate change.

The semantics of human needs

Trying to make sense of the different meanings of the term human need, Taylor (1959) identified four sets of meaning. First, needs may be a requirement for satisfying a law; for instance, in most of the world, one needs to pass a driving test by law to be allowed to drive a car. Need may further refer to a requirement for satisfying a given end; for example, a person may need wood to build a fire. The third set of meanings relates needs to wants and desires; the superstitious sports person may need a talisman to ensure good performance. Last, need may refer to a justified or priority requirement such as a constitutional claim for freedom of speech to be a good citizen.

Since the first meaning is a specialized case of the second, they can be merged to leave us with three sets of meaning of the word "need". These form the columns of Table 3.1. Column A represents the set of meanings that relate needs to wants or desires. Column B shows the meanings of need that relate needs to requirements for satisfying a given end, and column C shows the meanings of need with an overtly normative content. Related meanings are placed in the rows where possible. As the table shows, there are over 30 different meanings of the word "need."

To complicate matters further, the three different types are interrelated. Type B needs describe positive linkages: "I need a drink to relax," "I need coal to heat my house," or "I need a car to travel." In each case the need and the means to

Table 3.1 Some different meanings given to "needs" as a noun.

A	B	C
Related to wants or desires	Requirements for meeting a given end	Justified or priority requirements (Taylor 1959)
Equated to wants or desires	Requirements for meeting wants	Requirements for avoiding harm
Those wants felt earlier than others	Requirements for survival	Requirements for survival, when justified
Wants whose nonfulfillment results in (significant) suffering	Requirements for avoiding suffering	Requirements for avoiding excessive/unjustified suffering
Strong wants		Requirements for minimum decency
Behavior tendency whose continued denial results in pathological responses (for Bay 1968, if criteria of pathology are not culturally relative, e.g., death)	Requirements for satisfaction, fulfillment	Justified requirements for desirable satisfactions Requirements for flourishing or "the good life"
Behavior tendency whose fulfillment results in satisfaction		
Factors (e.g., drives or instincts) that (are claimed to) underlie and generate wants	Requirements for participating in a given way of life	Justified requirements of a way of life Requirements of a justified way of life
Human potentials (not all are desirable)	Requirements for fulfilling (a conception of) the human essence (Springborg 1981: 109)	Justified requirements for fulfillment of desirable human potentials
	Requirements for pursuing very many (or even any) other ends or ways of life	Justified requirements for pursuing very many (or even any) other ends or ways of life
	Requirements for meeting a law	Requirements that should be ensured by state action
		Basic rights

satisfy it are tangible (a glass of wine, coal, and an automobile). This meaning underlies the two other categories. On the one hand, it provides the logical format for justified needs since a justified need is something that is required to achieve a normatively important end.

On the other hand, the link between type A and type B usages is more complex. People, according to other people's expectations, will typically want whatever they require to, for example, survive or fulfill their desires or avoid suffering, or be fulfilled, or satisfy the rules and requirements of the way of life of the group(s) to which they belong, and so on. However, as we have seen above, people do not always know or want what they need in those senses; and much work is required to understand what influences actual wants.

The relationship between type A and type B meanings would seem to be of crucial importance for the issues of global climate policy. As we have seen, Clark and other needs theorists seek to differentiate between universal human needs and needs derived from a specific culture and lifestyle. For policymakers looking for areas to cut greenhouse gas emissions, it would be very useful to know which needs are truly human needs and therefore must be met, and which needs are derived and therefore potentially manipulable.

Maslow's hierarchy of needs

Maslow (1943) proposed that needs can be organized in a hierarchy. Drawing from observations of mentally ill patients, Maslow's work represents an early and very influential attempt to specify human needs. Maslow attempted to describe the drives that influence human behavior. The original version consisted of five types of needs: physiological needs, safety needs, belongingness and love needs, esteem needs, and self-actualization needs, to which Maslow later added aesthetic and cognitive needs. The needs progress in the scale from the lower to the higher, starting with physiological needs at the bottom (Fig. 3.1).

Physiological needs refer to the "basic internal deficit conditions that must be satisfied to maintain bodily processes" (Fisher 1990: 91). When in danger, an individual experiences safety needs. Social relationships satisfy belongingness needs, whereas self-esteem needs are met by achievement and personal competence. The last set of needs, self-actualization needs, represent the ultimate motivation and are satisfied by fulfilling one's potential.

Maslow ordered these needs in a hierarchy where one need becomes pressing only after the preceding lower need has been satisfied. Figure 3.1 shows what is known as Maslow's pyramid of needs. The prepotency approach, meaning that higher needs can only be tended to after lower needs have been satisfied, is compatible with a range of evidence, like the so-called Easterlin

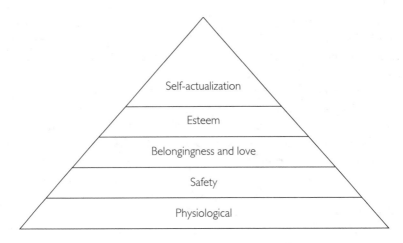

Figure 3.1 Maslow's needs pyramid (adapted from Maslow 1943).

paradox, according to which people in rich countries do not appear happier than those in poor ones, which could suggest that new needs have emerged which the rich are now struggling to meet (Kamarck 1983). This applies to the Maslow model, which is often used to suggest that needs for cultural expression increase with income level.

In fact, much of environmental policy at any level shows that the idea of a hierarchy of needs is, at least implicitly, widespread. Whether proposed by nongovernmental organizations, national governments, or international organizations, environmental policies attempt to link environmental protection to physical survival in one way or another (Kemp & Wall 1990, UN 1993, Greenpeace 1994). One could argue that this is an attempt to prioritize environmental policy, particularly global environmental policy, as a more pressing need than other justified needs (such as the provision of housing, employment, and cultural goods).

However, prepotency is not clearcut, there are no sharp target levels after which one urge disappears and the next suddenly appears. Needs are complementary, and transition may be gradual. Besides, many argue that a need of self-actualization may in fact be the most fundamental, and not a late starter. Lea et al. (1987) note that attempts to go beyond impressionistic evidence have so far found little support for Maslow's five or seven different levels of need, rather than just two or three; in fact, they find much co-occurrence of needs.

The implication that needs can be divided into lower needs, usually satisfied by material goods, and higher needs, satisfied by nonmaterial means, has proved particularly contentious. Ethical needs theorists find that Maslow's idea of hierarchy legitimizes a distribution of power in favor of intellectuals and those who specialize in nonmaterial needs, such as ascetics (Galtung 1990).

Maslow's theory is at once acultural and culturally biased. The notion that the human experience can be broken down, compartmentalized, and ordered into a universal hierarchy, bears the hallmarks of Western rationalism. Other cultures may view the human condition more holistically, or turn the pyramid the other way up.

Scitovsky (1992), a psychologist, notes that our central nervous system automatically focuses attention (which is always selective) on whatever is currently identified as most urgent or threatening. What it selects might indicate a prepotent hierarchy of organismic needs; but in fact culture and individual experience also influence these selections. Needs analyses understate the centrality of culture by treating it as something supplementary rather than intrinsic.

Maslow's hierarchy of needs appears to offer several attractive opportunities for enhancing the political importance of the global climate change issue. If it were possible to construe reductions in greenhouse gas emissions or reforestation as meeting one of the lower needs, a strong case could be made for moving climate change to the top of political agendas worldwide. However, within Maslow's framework, this is not possible. The nature of his typology of needs makes it very difficult to associate global climate change directly to lower needs, such as physiological needs and safety. Since climate change is a problem of global proportions that has (as yet) only indirect effects on the individual, the individualist bias reflected in Maslow's needs typology does not apply readily to the effects of climate change. It is too easy to claim that there is another more urgent need to satisfy.

The opposite could be argued: hierarchical conceptions of lower and higher needs could conceivably provide a justification for postponing environmental policy. Arguably, the lower, more pressing needs for adequate nutrition and shelter must be dealt with before turning to more distant issues such as global climate change, thus supporting the belief that reduction of greenhouse gas emissions is essentially a matter for rich industrialized countries.

The process of claiming that a policy problem involves a lower need is very tendentious; between competing policy claims the existence of a hierarchy becomes dubious. In order for Maslow's system to legitimate a global climate change policy, the different types of need would have to be fairly robust and somewhat impermeable. They should not be seen to be socially constructed or subject to cultural influence. If it is admitted that needs are politically defined, the claim to objectivity that would justify policy founded upon meeting them would evaporate.

Improving Maslow: basic human needs

One may very well ask why we have given Maslow so much space if he has been widely discredited. One reason is that he has been so influential in this subject. Another is that, apart from the historical significance of Maslow's theory, his typology shows up the pitfalls for any theory of human needs. If we take Maslow as the starting point, the discussion about human needs has branched out in two directions: one conversation concerned with basic needs and another about higher needs. Like any field in the social sciences, basic needs are a very complex and wide area of study: to cover all approaches would be beyond the limits of this chapter. Instead, we will concentrate on the historical development of two different types of basic needs theories and how these apply to the global climate change debate: basic material needs (BMN) approaches and basic human needs (BHN) approaches.

Although the International Labour Office (ILO) World Conference in 1975 was the first to address BMN, the idea had grown since the late 1960s as a reaction to the relative failures of development policies. Why, policymakers asked, are poverty and destitution so widespread in the less industrialized world despite elaborate development strategies that, in some cases, have resulted in handsome economic growth? The answer was that the basic needs of the poorest have not been met by economic development.

The advent of BMN approaches heralded, so it was thought, the end of the discredited classical economic dogma. Up to that point, development had been synonymous with maximizing GDP and modernization had meant maximizing investment. When the trickle-down effect promised by classical economics had not materialized, policymakers looked to a new approach: BMN. The postwar economic wisdom whereby the less industrialized world was to mimic the Western process of industrialization (only faster) was to be replaced by a new paradigm of which BMNs were to be the new organizing principle: poverty was to be tackled by meeting the basic physical needs of the poorest.

Champions of BMN approaches, such as the ILO and the Food and Agriculture Organisation (FAO), rejected the absolute status that had been accorded to economic accumulation in development processes. Green (1976) argues that this practice had resulted in sacrificing the minimum standard of living for the growth of productive forces: this was clearly unacceptable to advocates of the new paradigm. BMN approaches aimed to fulfill five broad targets (Green 1976: 7–8):

- to provide basic consumer goods such as food, clothing, housing, basic furnishing, and other socially defined necessities
- to provide universal access to basic services such as education, water, primary and curative healthcare

- to secure a right to productive employment that pays enough for each household to meet basic personal consumption out of its own income
- to provide an infrastructure capable of providing goods and services as well as a surplus to finance basic communal services
- to guarantee mass participation in decisionmaking on proposals to meet basic needs.

The BMN paradigm was designed to remodel development policy. Although it was production oriented, it was not essentially materialistic; for example, productive employment was not just a means for economic accumulation but also an end in itself. More controversially, the BMN approaches implied a major redistribution of income, assets and power (Green 1976: 8). Adding to this the commitment to mass participation in decisionmaking, BMN approaches envisaged politically revolutionary change in the developing world.

Supposing it were to be used as more than a rhetorical tool, the problems of such an approach are similar to those of the Maslovian model. The flow of goods that would satisfy basic needs differs from country to country, from culture to culture, and according to the level of development. BMN approaches face two equally unappealing options: either theorists specify what commodities fulfill basic needs and so run the risk of introducing culturally unsuitable goods (one example would be introducing food proscribed in a country, such as beef products in India), or they provide abstract definitions that are virtually unusable (such as the UN's recommendations for daily calorific intake).

BMN approaches also rely on expanding consumption according to northern consumption patterns of industrialized countries (Lederer 1980). The BMN paradigm was in part conceived as a reaction to arguments of the late 1960s that set limits on growth. It has, however, now become clear that expanding consumption in the less industrialized world according to lifestyles in the industrialized world would lead to unacceptable increases in greenhouse gas emissions. For example, China ranked second in the table of carbon emitters for 1995 but was much lower on the per capita table. Without a radical change in electricity-generating technology, simply providing every Chinese household with a refrigerator will lead to significant increases in China's total emissions. Without going so far as to say that poverty and destitution should be tolerated for the sake of reducing greenhouse gas emissions, policymakers are aware that less industrialized countries cannot copy the industrialization process of Europe, North America, and Japan (see, for example, the UN Framework Convention on Climate Change: UN 1993). Attractive though the BMN concept may be, it does not provide a workable approach to the global climate change issue. Basic needs, just like human needs, appear to be not easily defined. There are several common senses of basic need. The term means fundamental needs, which may be because those needs are felt first or because they are the most justified. The different senses are often not distinguished, leading to ambiguous usage, as with the word "need" itself. One commonsense meaning refers to fundamental or general urges underlying particular felt needs, which we can call source needs. Since we largely lack highly specific animal instincts, these general needs (if they exist—for example, perhaps a need for achievement) would be actualized and specified differently in different situations, as particular needs and desires. Some actualized needs-cum-desires could reflect a distortion or frustration of the more basic needs.

Linking this sense to the format for prerequisites from Table 3.1, we generate three levels for analysis:

- source need (that is, felt first, such as hunger)
- actualized need, the concretization of the source need in a given context (e.g., we need grain to make bread)
- satisfier, a means to fulfill an actualized need in the given context (e.g., the loaf of bread ready to eat).

How to use this hierarchy remains a question. The source-need notion is a crude summary of complex plural causes. The problems of this hierarchy are the same as for the Maslovian system: its objective is to create a basis for rational argument, but first the premises have to be agreed on.

Other senses of basic need form a separate group:

- survival needs (often also prepotent needs)
- prepotent needs, those felt before any others. Survival needs are part of prerequisite needs, those that must be satisfied in order to do other things (e.g., good health is a prerequisite for much else).

The next sense concerns:

- fundamental prerequisites, those required for very many or all activities, or prerequisite for fundamentally valued outcomes
- needs that a government or society must (is morally obliged to) try to ensure are satisfied.

Gasper (1991) summarized some of the proffered criteria for fundamental normative importance:

- for an individual to be able to participate fully or adequately in the way of life of the society (This cannot stand as a criterion if no limits are set on what is an acceptable way of life, for example, if slavery or genocide is permitted.)
- to be able to fulfill or pursue one's life plan (Again this is too permissive if it pays no attention to what is unacceptable as a life plan.)
- to avoid serious harm (Doyal & Gough 1991), where serious harm may mean death, abnormal/deranged functioning, or, more specifically, inability to fulfill basic social roles (e.g., parent, householder, worker, citizen, according to Braybrooke 1987); or failure to achieve (mental and

214

physical) health and autonomy (Doyal & Gough 1991)

• to achieve a fulfilling life, human flourishing, or full development of positive potentials. (Only a narrow consensus can be expected on such criteria; Braybrooke (1987) argued that needs ethics should not try to cover all of life, but instead complement other ethics.)

Basic needs ethics are deliberately restricted in scope, in order to fulfill the role Braybrooke identifies of obtaining sufficient consensus in plural societies. They are intended to face the challenge of plurality. The reference universe of different versions varies, from a nation to a group of nations (e.g. Braybrooke refers to Europe and the Americas) or all humanity.

Ethical needs as basic human needs (BHN) of individuals

On the grounds of not having any ethical or scientific basis and of being too focused on the commodity level, BMN approaches are rejected by contemporary ethical needs researchers (Lederer 1980, Sen 1994).

Instead, ethical needs theories are designed to answer questions such as "What does it mean to be a human being? Are there irreducible qualities which all peoples predictably require in their lives?" (Rader 1990: 231). In effect, BHN approaches are a quasi-Kantian exercise: ethical needs theories attempt to specify what the minimal preconditions for human action are and thereby provide a rational and moral basis for discussing policy issues. Human needs theories are intended to act as "a guideline for monitoring conditions adequate to human existence, irrespective of cultural differences all over the world" (Lederer 1980: 9).

Rather than attempting to compile a list of commodities that satisfy basic human needs, ethical needs theorists aim to construct parsimonious models of universal human needs. By arguing that certain categories of human needs apply to everyone, while their satisfiers (i.e., the goods that fulfill needs) are culturally determined, BHN theorists avoid the problems that confounded earlier approaches. Galtung (1990: 303) argued that it is futile to determine beforehand what commodities satisfy basic needs. However, he continued, ". . . it does make sense to talk about certain classes of needs . . . and to postulate that in one way or the other human beings everywhere and at all times have tried and will try to come to grips with something of that kind, in very different ways."

Max-Neef (1991) explicitly repudiated any notion of hierarchy in needs; all needs are necessary, all equally necessary. He found nine fundamental human needs: freedom, identity, idleness, creation, participation, understanding, affection, protection, and subsistence. Each need occurs at four different levels of activity—being, having, doing, and interacting. The means of satisfying any need may be highly variable, but the need is the same everywhere. Max-Neef's analysis then classified different kinds of satisfiers: some promise, but do not satisfy; some satisfy one but inhibit another; some satisfy one need but ignore others; and some meet several different needs (analogous to so-called double dividend policies that address, for example, climate change and air pollution). If Max-Neef was correct, policymakers could evaluate policy instruments with regard to whether they meet universal needs, for example for protection and subsistence, and what type of satisfiers they are.

A multitude of approaches vary widely both in the number of human needs they identify and the conceptual basis they exploit. We have drawn some examples from the literature to illustrate the variety and complexity of the field.

Sites (1990) based his system of human needs in psychology. Drawing on Kemper's four primary human emotions (fear, anger, depression, and satisfaction), he understood them to be analogues to human needs: the need for security corresponds to the emotion of fear, the need for meaning to the emotion of anger, the need for self-esteem to depression, and the need for latency to satisfaction. Emotions produce feelings of pleasure and displeasure. These feelings in turn condition human responses to avoid, ameliorate or prolong the pleasure or displeasure. The responses to emotions require satisfiers and hence, Sites argued, humans have needs. Given that emotions are characteristics of all human beings, even though triggers and display-rules differ widely across cultures, those four needs are also universal.

Clark (1990: 39), arguing from a biological perspective, maintained that human evolution was only possible because early man was an intensely social animal. However, her notion of sociality was idiosyncratic: humans have been what she calls hard-wired "with a desire [sic] to *belong*, not to *compete*" (original italics). From this premise she deduced that "the greatest human need that we all have is for social bonding." She qualified this by adding the human need for meaning: not only is the bonding crucial, but the quality of the social bond (its meaningfulness) is also important.

In support of her position, Clark produced a catalogue of psychological, physiological and social disorders that result from an unrealized social bonding. But what does she think holds a person back from fulfilling this deepest instinctual need? As so often, institutions turn out to be the culprit: "When conflict arises within a society, it is almost always because this biologically based need for bonding among its members is being thwarted by one or another social arrangement" (Clark 1990: 49). Clark suggested that, by accepting social bonding as a biological and evolutionary prerogative, people can overcome their blindness "to the kind of society that satisfies our deepest human needs" (Clark 1990: 36).

Johan Galtung's system has four classes of human needs based on two sets of distinctions. On the one hand, Galtung drew a line between whether a need is satisfied by an actor or by social structures. On the other hand, Galtung looked at two different types of satisfiers: material and nonmaterial. In this way, Galtung established a fourfold typology of needs (Fig. 3.2).

	Actor-dependent need satisfaction	Structure-dependent need satisfaction
Material	Security (violence)	Welfare (misery)
Nonmaterial	Freedom (repression)	Identity (alienation)

Figure 3.2 Galtung's fourfold typology of human needs (adapted from Galtung 1990).

Galtung (1990: 311) explicitly rejected the Maslovian idea of hierarchy. It limits the potential of a needs theory, namely "to serve as a basis for revealing . . . social malconstructions or cases of maldevelopment and to indicate other possibilities." But where do these maldevelopment and social malconstructions originate? Again, culture and social structures turn out to be the enemies. Does this indicate a cultural bias? Although Galtung (1990: 313) explicitly acknowledged the role of socialization as a formative factor, it "raises the problem that people may be socialized into trying to satisfy some needs that will stand in the way of others trying to satisfy theirs—these others being present and future generations."

Ethical needs of social beings

Unlike other needs theorists, Doyal & Gough (1991) incorporated the social dimension into their model. Explicitly Kantian, they asked what the minimal individual and social preconditions are for successful human action. Individual human needs are given in abstract form by two sets of pairs: survival–health and autonomy–learning. For viable social and individual life, Doyal & Gough argued, four societal preconditions must be met: production, reproduction, culture–communication, and political authority. These two needs complexes interact to produce social and human existence. Doyal & Gough maintained that different social systems emerged from efforts at optimizing both the societal and individual needs. The implication is that if both sets of needs were fully optimized, humans would be liberated from unjust social relations: thus, justice and liberation become involved in basic human need.

Doyal & Gough distinguished five levels in analysis of basic needs:

(a) a level of universal human interests, specified as avoidance of serious harm or minimally impaired functioning, but also sometimes as human liberation

(b) a level of basic needs required for the universal goal(s), posited as health (physical and mental) and autonomy (which may refer to both action and values, that is, in both agency and critical capacity); these needs correspond to Sen's word "capabilities"

(c) intermediate needs, that is, certain sets of characteristics (e.g., shelter) necessary for fulfillment of level (b) basic needs/capabilities, specified as nutritional food and clean water, protective housing, nonhazardous work and physical environments, appropriate healthcare and education, security in childhood, significant primary relationships, physical and economic security, and safe birth control and child-bearing

(d) specific satisfier commodities (inputs) to fulfill the intermediate needs; these will vary according to culture, context, and the person concerned

(e) societal preconditions (or conducive factors) for providing satisfiers that fulfill the above.

For levels (b), (c) and (e), Doyal & Gough concertized and enriched the theory through empirical indicators drawn from the work on social indicators, and analyzed the results. They further addressed questions about how to operationalize the theory in terms of political and social process and organization.

Differences in the criteria at level (a) will give different conceptions of needs. This is clear too from our earlier table on meanings of needs (Table 3.1). Similarly, indicators and target levels will be variously set in different political communities according to their own resources and decision processes.

In contrast to the source-need hierarchy, ethical needs theories do not claim to describe a real structure; rather they provide a frame-for-work in arguing intelligently about priorities. They do not require a commitment to controversial grand theories of behavior or satisfaction. In sum, ethical needs theories attempt to establish a rational framework for argumentation. In this sense they are as relevant to the global climate change issue as to any policy domain: it is a question of what level of policymaking is being discussed.

Some criticisms

In terms of the climate change policy debate there are two broad criticisms of ethical needs theories. On the one hand, they have not been designed to provide a policy tool, so it is understandable that they should be somewhat unhelpful for resolving the immediate concerns of global climate change policymakers. However, even in their intended role of philosophical clarification, ethical needs theories are not very clear. Furthermore, their high degree of abstraction makes them difficult to apply. As Galtung (1990) and Lederer (1980) note, it is very difficult to operationalize the idea of universal human needs without falling into the same pitfalls as beset the BMN approaches. If categories are too broad, they run risk of being all-inclusive: again a result that would not help global climate change policymakers.

Ethical needs theories are aimed at the meta-policy level. They offer a broad reference point for discussion, a bottom line that all policy actors can agree on. The idea is to frame the policy problems and sort out priorities. Yet it is doubtful whether a needs theory with a consumptionist and anthropocentric orientation could raise broad support in all camps of the global climate change policy debate. For example, environmentalists often speak of the needs of the planet quite independently of human needs (Kemp & Wall 1990, Rainbow 1993, Richardson 1995). Global climate change debates sometimes come to a halt on whether to accept a conception of nature in which the environment is seen as a means for human needs satisfaction. (See Ch. 4.)

The point here is not to discredit needs theorists as anti-environmentalists, which their literature shows to be far from the case. The problem is that ethical needs theories will not be accepted as the rational grounding for policy argumentation about global climate change so long they are at variance with the position laid out in the Framework Convention on Climate Change. Needs theories are focused on protecting humans, and the convention focuses on the need to protect the climate system from humans generating greenhouse gas emissions.

For example, in the Sites approach, concern for the environment seems to be neither a basic nor a universal need; no emotional analogue can readily be found to accommodate environmental concerns. Fear may be a possibility: we are fearful of the consequences of climate change and hence we need security from adverse effects of atmospheric change. However, this only captures one particular motivation that drives climate policy actors. The environmentalists, for example, see global climate policy as a question of fairness (see Ch. 4 for a fuller discussion; also Kemp & Wall 1990, Leggett 1990, Meyer 1994b). National governments and international organizations speak repeatedly of our responsibility toward future generations (WCED 1987). We have to conclude that, according to the Sites model, the concern for the environment is a composite need: important, but not basic.

The same applies to Galtung. His echo of the Brundtland Commission's findings may seem to be a hopeful sign to climate change policymakers. However, the problems become apparent when Galtung (1990: 308) provided a list of basic needs that "may be of some use as a checklist to discuss problems of Western societies" (Box 3.1). In his category of welfare needs, we find the need to be protected against the environment and climate: the satisfiers listed are clothes and shelter. The protection of the environment *from* human intervention is not a basic need; it only enters as a socialized or derived need or even a subjective

---

Box 3.1   A list of basic human needs: a working hypothesis.

Security needs (survival needs)—to avoid violence
Against . . .
* individual violence (assault, torture)   Police
* collective violence (wars, internal, external)   Military

Welfare needs (sufficiency needs)—to avoid misery
For . . .
* nutrition, water, air, sleep   Food, water, air
* movement, excretion   Physical freedom
* protection against climate, environment   Clothes, shelter
* protection against diseases   Medical treatment
* protection against excessive strain   Labor-saving devices
* self-expression, dialogue, education   Schooling

Identity needs (needs for closeness)—to avoid alienation
For . . .
* self-expression, creativity, praxis, work   Jobs
* self-actuation, for realizing potentials   Jobs and leisure
* well-being, happiness, joy   Recreation, family
* being active and subject; not being passive, client, object   Recreation, family
* challenge and new experiences   Recreation
* affection, love, sex; friends, spouse, offspring   Primary groups
* roots, belongingness, support esteem: association with similar humans   Secondary groups
* understanding social forces; for social transparency   Political activity
* partnership with nature   Natural parks
* a sense of purpose, of meaning with life; closeness to the transcen-   Religion, ideology
  dental, transpersonal

Freedom needs (freedom to; choice, option)—to avoid repression
Choice . . .
* in receiving and expressing information and opinion   Communication
* of people and places to visit and be visited   Transportation
* in consciousness formation   Meetings, media
* in mobilization   Organizations, parties
* in confrontations   Elections
* of occupation   Labor market
* of place to live   ?
* of spouse   Marriage market
* of goods and services   (Super-) market
* of way of life   ?

Source: Galtung (1990).

---

want. In that case, the need to protect the environment may stand in the way of more basic needs. If ethical need theories help us to prioritize, then we must concede that, according to these theories, the protection of the environment is not a priority for humans.

Finally, the acultural nature of ethical needs theories makes them unsuitable for the global comparisons that are necessary in the policy debate about global climate change. In an attempt to shed the Western legacy of rational thought, ethical needs theories go to great lengths to maintain the universality of human needs. But it is precisely this insistence on universal validity that leaves them locked in the modernist paradigm: their bias intrudes the more uncomfortably the more global the domain of application becomes. We will return to this later. For the time being suffice it to say that needs theories are still harnessed to the thought of Maslow. And they are still culturally innocent, that is, they are still unaware of any bias in the Western tradition.

Human needs in the Western tradition

The previous section shows that human needs and wants, as presently conceived in the social sciences, do not provide a useful focus for looking at global climate change issues. They have been classified and reclassified, but not theorized in a way that would meet the hopes of the Brundtland Commission. It is in a way unfair to have expected that this body of thought could be extended beyond the cultures for which it was made. The problems are not local theoretical difficulties that can be smoothed out by further application; rather, they are symptoms of a deeper complex of assumptions that lies deep in the rationalist tradition of the West. Its concealed assumptions pervade the social sciences and thereby impose its values. This is how local culture works, and local culture is in for shocks and contradiction when it tries to generalize in a global context.

Can there be a universal theory of human needs and wants?

Galtung (1990: 313), in his BHN approach, dealt at length with a phenomenon he called Westernization. He defined Westernization as:

> a process that shapes anything in a Western direction. It is seen as a social code that leaves its imprint on whatever comes its way, transforming it so that the result is compatible with the code.

He went on to say that Westernization implies the adoption of a Western cosmology and a Western social structure (Box 3.2). Galtung appeared to be worried that the process of Westernization was impinging on people's ability to fulfill their human needs.

Box 3.2 Johan Galtung's concept of Westernization

The Western social cosmology is characterized by:
• a Western-centered, universalist, conception of space
• a unilinear, present-centered, conception of time
• an analytic rather than holistic conception of epistemology
• a man-over-man conception of human relations
• a man-over-nature conception of relations to nature.

The Western social structure is characterized by:
• a vertical division of labor favoring the center
• a conditioning of the periphery by the center
• marginalization, a division between social inside and outside
• fragmentation, separation of individuals from each other
• segmentation, separation inside individuals.
Source: Galtung (1990).

What Galtung offered is a neat summary of the effects of Western thought systems on traditional forms of life. He is in good company, whether in studies of alienation by Marx, Lukàcs, and the Frankfurt School, or of normalization by Nietzsche, Heidegger, and the French postmodernists, or in company with Emile Durkheim's analysis of social anomie. The atomizing and alienating effects of modern forms of discourse have been well documented.

Galtung imagined that there can be a non-Western theory of human needs and wants. But a candid look at the assumptions of the Western tradition reveals that the whole project of providing a theory for human needs and wants is embedded in it. Theories of human needs and wants have been devised to meet questions raised alongside of the philosophic and scientific enquiries of the European Enlightenment. The exact terminology—whether this framework is called modern, Western, or occidental—does not matter: there is a historical European framework in which the project of providing a universal theory of human needs and wants was devised. They draw their explanatory power from the same assumptions and make no sense apart from them.

Subject and object radically disjoined

The Enlightenment project is based on the distinction between subject and object, which is the formative and defining element of modernity. It pervades all levels of the Western tradition. It provides the organizing principle for scientific theories and methods and also selection criteria for both expert and everyday decisionmaking; in short, it provides the criterion for truth and even for morals.

Enlightenment thought, in a continuation of the ancient Greek tradition, attributed subjectivity to beings capable of reason. As a result, the natural world was relegated to a world of soul-less, albeit well-behaved, objects. After centuries of discussion, animals had been defined by Aristotle as lacking the capacity for reason (Sorabji 1993). Objects in the natural world obeyed natural laws that were open to reason. If subjects could uncover these laws, they could control and manipulate objects to suit their own, subjective ends. The Enlightenment told a story of a natural world that was no more than a series of objects waiting to be conquered by the rational subject. In this tradition, "the environment . . .," argued Banuri & Apffel Marglin (1993: 18), "becomes either the source of gratification for the individual, or a constraint to such gratification."

However, the split between the subject and the object was more than a means to distinguish humans conceptually from their natural surroundings. The dualism is evident in the structure of reason itself. Adorno & Horkheimer saw reason (they focused specifically on Kant's idea of reason), as drawn in two directions. On the one hand, reason offers to humans liberation from the yoke of irrational political repression, such as absolutism, and freedom from want, by allowing the subject to master the natural world. On the other hand reason is:

> the court of judgment of calculation, which adjusts the world for the end of self-preservation and recognizes no function other than the preparation of the object from mere sensory material in order to make it the material of subjugation. (Adorno & Horkheimer, quoted in Held 1980: 150)

Following this line of thinking, the more that reason was applied to the social and natural world in order to free humans, the more the environment, and humans, were subjected to rational control and manipulation. Seeking to replace old forms of repression by liberating reason, the Enlightenment instituted a new form of rational domination.

In practice, the radical separation of subject from object meant that the relationship between humans and their environment was fundamentally changed. The Western tradition replaced any intrinsic value of nature with utility. Hence, the rise of an instrumental attitude toward nature: from then on, subjects could fulfill their needs and wants by manipulating, controlling and dominating the natural world (which, of course, includes humans). As we shall see below, this contrasts sharply with the more immediate and symbiotic human–nature relationships that characterize more traditional forms of social interaction. Prigogine & Stengers (1984), eminent scientists, summarized the Enlightenment model of nature: "[Classical] science . . . revealed to men a dead, passive nature, a nature that behaves as an automaton which, once programmed, continues to follow the rules inscribed in the program" (quoted in Banuri & Apffel Marglin 1993: 19).

Economic theory, the theory of wants, grew out the Enlightenment sciences. Economists would never disclaim the Western origin of their theory and by the same token it has a valid claim to be universal: it offers a systematic means of understanding market behavior and the flow of goods in any economy, regardless of culture, geographical location, or historical period. Economists, in keeping with the Enlightenment premises, assume that their objects of inquiry are well behaved: markets obey laws that can be understood by reason.

The subject/object dualism makes economic theory possible. At the center of economic theory we find the rational economic agent that deals with the objects in the market. Although most would agree that the laws of the market are based on very complex social arrangements, these find no mention in economics textbooks, and for good reason. If the social dimension of market operations is not faded out, market behavior cannot appear as an unconscious process ruled only by natural laws (much like gravity in physics; Habermas 1962); only when it is abstracted from any social matrix can economists speak of an invisible hand ruling market behavior and contrast its natural-like operations with government interference.

If the social world comprised by market exchange is nothing but a series of objects obeying rational laws, then a rational theory of the market makes sense; if subjects can master these economic laws, they can control their economic environment.

A similar scheme embraces the natural environment. Nature in economics is a series of goods that have or could have an abstract exchange value. In the policy debate over global climate change, this is brought home vividly by shooting at the favorite target—environmental cost–benefit analysis. The technical ins and outs of this approach are dealt with in greater detail in Volume 3, Chapter 1. Suffice it to say at this point that environmental cost–benefit analysts aim at establishing, among other things, an exchange value for goods in the natural world. For example, people are asked what they would be willing to pay for, say, an unpolluted atmosphere.

The very idea that monetary values could be placed on the natural environment inflames the tempers of radical environmentalists; for example, Meyer (1994c) and other not so radical environmental researchers (e.g., Adams 1994) argued that such a monetary valuation of the natural world is impossible. For example, how can an inhabitant of Amazonia put a monetary value on a stretch of the rainforest that is the resting ground of his ancestors and the focus of spiritual values for his village? While the problem of monetizing values to which the monetary convention has not been applied is seen by economists as a technical challenge, the radical critic turns it into a comparison of spiritual versus material values and reasserts the greater value of the subject over the object. Both show how deep the shared perspective has been dug, and willy nilly, when the debate takes this turn, it entrenches the Enlightenment project more firmly than ever. Is it fair to attack economists for something they would agree with? The economic discourse is explicitly situated in the occidental tradition. Is it fair to point out that the same is the case for theories of human needs?

Subject and object in human needs theories

BHN approaches are often intended to counter the inherent market-oriented bias of economics. Normative needs discourses arise when people reject the market as arbiter of all valuation, and hold that some goods have a prior claim, for example, health, shelter and literacy for all. As we saw, some needs theorists go further: Nudler (1980) and Galtung (1990) sought a theory of needs that was not based on the Western tradition. Aware of the dangers of reification, needs theorists attempt to construct human needs models where the continuity with the Western tradition is less obvious, but, nonetheless, they cannot escape from the dualism of the subject and object, and its implications reach deep into their theorizing.

As Rist (1980) showed in his criticism of BHN approaches, the idea of need mediates narrowly between the individual and the natural world. When the theory admits only the concept of individual need, the theory is one more model of instrumental exploitation. Rist provided a diagram (Fig. 3.3) which shows how in human needs theories the individual subjects objectify the world so that both institutions and people and the natural environment are seen only under the sign of their capacity to satisfy individual needs.

The continuity with the Western tradition becomes even more striking in the case of satisfiers (the means by which needs are met). Human needs theorists carefully emphasize that satisfiers are culturally determined: culture provides the selection criteria to match satisfiers to need. Satisfiers are still objects without meaning apart from the fulfillment of individual need. The cultural and social arrangements that define them are loosely tacked on to the general theory.

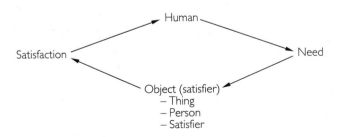

Figure 3.3   Rist's diagram of human needs.

Rist agreed that there is more to be said about culture than merely providing a local variation to a general theme. Humans communicate and make sense of their surroundings by using symbols: goods have a meaning beyond utility (Douglas & Isherwood 1979). Rist (1980: 237) saw that:

> reducing food in a functionalist way to a sheer satisfier of a need called "hunger" overlooks the fact that people almost never eat just to be fed, but also to communicate with others (to share bread and salt, to share bread and wine, etc.).

The reference to functions is written into the definition of need; as the previous section explains, needs are objective and they enable objectively valid statements to be made. Whereas it is proposed that wants are subjective and specific to the individual, needs are viewed as universal to all humans. In BHN approaches, human needs are those elements of the human condition that humans cannot influence either because of genetic programming (Clark 1990), psychological set-up (Sites 1990) or the structure of the human brain (Sandole 1990). In short, needs are the objects inside the subjects. As objects, needs, and the humans who have needs, are open to rational investigation. Rader (1990: 220) saw in the study of human needs the analysis of "the humanization process, the ways people struggle for their liberation from dehumanizing forces." The recognition of human needs allows the comparison of subjects; it gives license to ignore all cultural differences and to assume that people are roughly all the same. Whatever they may desire, someone else knows what they really need. The final twist in emancipating the theory of human needs from the Enlightenment is to turn humans into objects.

In this manner, human needs theorists venture where economists dare not tread. For economists, individuals know best what is good for them. Economists are not interested in why people want what they want, so long as they express wants by preferences; this is the realm of the rational individual subject, and economists have no business peeping through the keyhole. Human needs theorists breach this stronghold of subjectivity, but at the cost of fading out the factors that make people different, that is, that make people individual subjects. The tension between two opposing ideas of the Enlightenment, identified by Adorno & Horkheimer is reproduced in the structure of human needs theories.

Happiness of human subjects

The distinction between the subject and the object has consequences not only for the way social sciences conceptualize the natural world but also how humans are perceived. Western rationalism saw the rise of the transcendental Ego as the basis of social theory. But who is this Ego from whom the theories start? The diffuse, aggregated individual is adopted as a convenience for statistical sampling. It produces quite robust results for economists studying markets, but it blurs the differences that interest moralists and policymakers.

The sociologist remedies this by introducing distinctions based on administrative categories. Administration calls for information on births and deaths, the numbers of children attending school, the admissions to hospitals and lunatic asylums, the claimants of old age pensions, and whether all these are male or female. Accordingly, the aggregated individual is disaggregated by gender, age, and health status. The further information researchers might need for a theory of consumption is based on age, household composition, educational level, income, and gender.

The census makes an implicit assumption that apart from these lifecycle differences and certain forking paths of entry to the labor market, individuals are all the same. If they do not have the same set of preferences within these broad categories, the differences are concealed by the way the research data are collected.

The incidental result of thus narrowly framing what can be said about wants is to promote the materialist bias. Inevitably, partly because of theoretical interests, and partly in default of other information, the indicators of standards of living were first based on physical needs. The *level of living index* (Drenowski & Scott 1966) used a typical table of components and indicators of welfare. Components were presented in three groups: basic physical needs, basic cultural needs, and higher needs. In the first were indicators of nutrition, shelter and health; in the second, education, leisure and security. The most serious flaw in the scheme is that higher needs are assumed to be met with only surplus income (a dubious concept in itself, which suggests that most people never satisfy their higher needs).

Researchers have recognized and sought to counter the limitations of the materialist bias. Allardt (1975) developed an alternative approach to the Swedish model of welfare research, which focused on levels of living indicated by the individual's command over resources; this, he felt, relied too heavily on material factors. He grouped welfare needs into three kinds: *having* (meaning control of material and impersonal resources), *loving* (love, companionship and solidarity), and *being* (self-actualization). His focus was on the necessary conditions for human development (Allardt 1993).

The Institute of Applied Research in Oslo developed a concept of the *inner quality of life*, with four groupings of components: the rating for a high quality of life goes up the more the person is active, has self-esteem, has a mutual and close relationship and a sense of togetherness, and has a basic mood of joy

(Naess 1979, summarized in Erikson 1987). It may be perverse to suggest that not everyone wants a mood of joy all the time, or that some even relish the tragic sense of life. A member of a contemplative religious order can question the universal need for constant activity. "A sense of togetherness" may be a poor translation, but the idea starts from subjective mood, and some definitely like to select the company they are in. In this research the bogey of objectivity has been defied.

Although Erikson (1987) gives the nonbasic needs lower and Allardt gives them higher value, in both cases wants emerge after the basic needs have been satisfied. Furthermore, both wants and needs remained attributes of the individual subject: the person may need other people, may want love and sympathy, but these are wanted for personal development as a human being. What does self-actualization mean, without a concept of self? A theory of personal development that is not based on a coherent theory of what constitutes a person falls back on normative (local, culturally innocent, and far from universal) judgments of what a person needs.

The problems common to most current survey work on public attitudes follow from the traditional bias of psychology, which assumes that wants emanate from individuals and that basically individuals are the same the world over. In the philosophy of welfare economics, the study of the quality of life shares this same weakness (Sen 1993). The human person is taken here too as the aggregated rational individual, and the idea of a good life is universalized.

If in practice there are many ideas of the good life, when they are blurred together it is not surprising that, as Sugden said in a review of Sen's work on inequality, "The concept of a good life is objective but fuzzy; there is no single, clearly correct view about the relative values of different functionings" (Sugden 1993).

Scarcity and affluence

Given the intention of supplementing or improving upon economic theory, scarcity would not be expected to be an element in human needs theory. Rader (1990: 232), herself convinced of the value of human needs theory, nevertheless lamented that its central assumption is a "derivation from an industrial mode of thinking, with its focus on scarcity." In practice the preoccupation with social justice has affected the idea of human needs so that it has come to imply that the satisfiers are in short supply. Human needs theories, we have argued, are concerned with the just distribution of a certain class of goods: those that fulfill a justified human need. Scarcity is an artifact of a distributional problem.

In economics the assumption of scarcity is the fundamental motor of the model of market behavior. Scarcity creates costs and this puts price tags on goods. The rational individual sorts wants according to price tags. Without scarcity of goods and services, market behavior would be inconceivable or, at least, untheorizable, and so would valuations, exchanges, transactions, profits.

The anthropologist Sahlins (1968) challenged the assumption that the creation of wealth and its distribution are inherently influenced by the principle of scarcity. Rather, scarcity is a result of a kind of organization and a kind of evaluation; primeval hunter–gatherer societies would not necessarily have known scarcity: the oxymoron, *savage affluence*, may often reign. Sahlins gathered together the reports of many anthropologists to demonstrate that, on any definition of affluence, those societies poorly endowed with material things would normally have experienced it at a high level. The telling symptom of poverty in industrial societies is being obliged for long hours to do grinding work, with no time to satisfy what we saw above were classed by the early economists as higher wants. It now turns out that hunter–gatherers are able to spend their time pursuing just those leisure activities that possession of wealth is supposed to endow. After hunting for a few days, the rest of the time in these societies was free for cave painting, cosmetics, recitation, dancing, ritual, and other self-expressive activities.

This is very subversive news for bread-in-the-belly theorizing about the hierarchy of wants. It was a large stone thrown into the theoretical pond of needs theories. The idea has never been exploited, and no wonder, for it exposes the incoherence of the whole exercise. Needs are supposed to be the objective part of individual wants. But the individual is defined in isolation, and wants are derived on a functional model from biology. Needs are requirements for intentions to be fulfilled. But where do the intentions come from? And where do definitions come from? From the standpoint of needs theory it is impossible to think of definitions except as individually made, and since this is patently wrong, needs theory is obliged to take them as given. Forest or savanna peoples who have defined their wants for shelter, food, and drink at a low level, and their wants for leisure and the arts at a high level, ought to be a challenge to needs theory and its claims to objectivity.

Needs of individuals make sense only in terms of the institutions of sharing and caring and argumentation. The needs theory that starts in the air will stay up there. Modernist objectivity was held to be a capacity for discerning the facts out there. Another form of objectivity in the social sciences requires an explanation of behavior to be founded in a credible system of interacting elements. The tests of truth would not be intuitive, but testing of the alleged systematic connections that call forth different responses.

Reaching for objectivity about needs, theorists would line up the relevant influences and try to draw a circle of connections in which living and arguing together about needs generates classifications, with certain needs classified as legitimate; then the needs thus classified, and met, exemplify the classifications and show what it means to be living together the right way. A good needs theory should have feedback loops. It should bowl along with the individuals defining their needs collectively, defining them up or defining them down, arguing with one another about the best institutional arrangements for satisfying them. Needs theory cannot but be a theory of society.

Power and violence in the Western tradition

The social sciences have an unreal needs theory that is unconnected with any theory of production and which lacks any social theory. Although carrying the banner for social justice, the theory of needs separates the individual from the society in which the individual should expect to be judged and to receive justice. But what are researchers complaining about? Have not modern science and technology raised the standard of living by eliminating disease? Have they not reduced the toil from work, and generally made life easier? Does not the liberal political system strive continuously to ensure that individual civil liberties are respected? What is wrong with an academic tradition that resists coordination?

The view from the South

As long as our view is limited to the affluent North, the answer is, "Nothing is wrong." However, should we include the fate of the South, we have a different story. Southern commentators, such as Banuri & Apffel Marglin (1993), Guha (1990), or Nandy (1988), attack the Western tradition from a different perspective: the destruction of the natural world and the violence committed to both people and culture are more visible in the Southern Hemisphere.

Banuri & Apffel Marglin (1993: 1) traced environmental problems to the power and violence inherent in the Western tradition. To illustrate this, they chose an approach that looks at systems of knowledge. The Western tradition, they surmised, gives rise to systems of knowledge that are described by their "disembeddedness, universalism, individualism, objectivity and instrumentalism". Conversely, "embeddedness, locality, community, a lack of separation between subject and object, as well as a non-instrumental approach" are hallmarks of nonmodern knowledge systems.

Such a focus on the politics of knowledge aims to reveal the domination of one form of knowledge over all others as the root of the environmental crisis in the South. Rather than assuming that there is a unique reality that can be understood by reason, Banuri & Apffel Marglin (1993: 9) argued that there are multiple ways of defining reality: there is a multiplicity of knowledge communities. Each community has its own cosmology; they:

> ... embody different systems of knowledge, different ways of understanding, perceiving, experiencing, in sum, of defining reality, which includes the notion of one's relationship not only to the social milieu but also to the natural environment.

The problem, as Banuri & Apffel Marglin described, is that the dominant system of knowledge, the Western tradition, confers considerable communicative power to those who work within it. Like most other systems of knowledge, the Western tradition has a very specific and narrow conception of what counts as knowledge. Thus, with the yardstick of reason and rationality, Western scientists relegate all other forms of knowledge to the status of myth. Their claims to universality and objectivity cannot tolerate the existence of other systems of knowledge: like a jealous husband preventing his wife from having other male friends, the Western system of thought suppresses all other forms of truth. What that leaves us with, argue many of the Southern commentators, is an instrumental and exploitative approach to nature, alien to traditional social forms.

Colonial legacy

Southern critics, for example Guha and Nandy, consider the dominance of the Western tradition in the less industrialized world as both a hangover from colonialism and a sign of the continuing dependence on industrialized nations. In terms of modern technology, Nandy (1988: 7) refers specifically to nuclear power; India has adopted "shop-worn Western models which have often been given up in the West itself as too dangerous or ecologically unviable." Apart from the obvious environmental hazards, Nandy stresses a more insidious effect: Indian middle classes "expect this technology to allow the country to tackle its basic political and social problems and thus ensure the continued political domination of an apolitical, that is, technocratic elite over the decisionmaking process, defying the democratic system."

Nandy bewails the fact that modern science and technology have become the ultimate justification for the Indian state: modern science and technology, paraded as the answer to all of India's problems, legitimates the new Indian elites. Scientific experts in India "can lay claims to the charisma which in some other political cultures belongs exclusively to god-kings." These scientists:

... are the ones to assess and pass final judgment on Indian culture, on what is good in it and what is defective. Generally it turns out that what is good in the Indian civilization, according to these specialists, is exactly what is good for modern science and what is defective in the civilization is exactly that which impedes modern science. (Nandy 1988: 8)

This is perverse indeed, since by definition an expert is a specialist, and so is the last person to give moral and political advice.

This effect is found not only in the developing world. Habermas (1962, 1973, 1981) has warned that the advanced capitalist state is shifting decisionmaking responsibilities away from the public sphere and into the hands of technical experts: policymaking has become a technical activity in which only those who have mastered the right kind of knowledge can take part. (See Ch. 1.)

So, what is new?

Several qualifications can be made regarding this line of criticism. First, it is true that when production, communication and transport are efficient, so of course are the means of coercion more effective. Although there is nothing new in that, the fact has ramifications. It is not new that imperial rulers have subjugated conquered peoples and ruled them from a distance. It is not new that remote foreign rulers have kept decisionmaking in their hands, excluded local opinion, and made decisions according to their commercial or strategic interest.

There is no need to invoke the Enlightenment to explain what was happening in the Indian Forest Department (Box 3.3): the story lies straight in the middle of the traditional political analysis and would only surprise one who thinks that collusion of industry and government is unusual. The remedy would not be a change of thought-system so much as an old-fashioned improvement in the system of representation, so that other interests are given voice. The Chipko movement is a lesson about a cause that has no constituency and lacks a lobby strong enough to fight for it in the circles of power.

In the age-old story of colonialism, the Enlightenment is responsible for the impetus it gave to science and industry, which made the political effectiveness of colonial powers so much greater, and the more sinister. But as a system of thought among others, it would be hard to maintain that it is more flattering to its supporters and more destructive to its enemies than other historical systems of thought.

What may be new is to compare the intellectual and moral hold of the Western tradition to the mixture of coercion and free commitment that is normal in the history of world religions. In times past, the West applied violence to make

232

Box 3.3   Forest management in India

The power of the Western tradition lies in its ability to create consensus and dismiss other forms of knowledge. When consensus is not forthcoming, the Western tradition uses violence both on the cultures and on people, regardless of their cherished wants and needs. Forest management, especially of the tropical forests of the less industrialized world, is often discussed as a policy option for sequestering atmospheric carbon. The history of forest management practices in the Indian district of Uttarakhand demonstrates how needs and wants of individuals are seen as part and parcel of the productive system, and how the exported occidental philosophy justifies denying local peasants the control over their environment that is necessary for them to meet their needs in traditional ways.

Banuri & Apffel Marglin (1993) pointed to the history of forest management practices and identified three problem areas. First, the Western knowledge system allows the exploitation of the object of knowledge: here it is the forest and the people that live from it. Second, the word "scientific" all too often hides short-run commercial interests. Last, the universalism inherent in the Western discourse facilitates direct state control of forests and with it corruption, inefficiency, and waste.

Guha (1990, 1993) showed how the application of Western knowledge has damaged the ecosystem and provoked civil unrest and violence. The advent of scientific forestry practices dates back to the middle British colonial rule in India. As soon as the commercial profitability of the Indian forests was realized, one-fifth of the Indian land area was brought under state control with the Indian Forest Act of 1878. German experts were sent in by the British government to set up a forest department to oversee the exploitation of India's timber resources. The "imperatives of colonial forest management," argues Guha (1993: 83), "were essentially strategic"; the Indian forests were to feed the imperial demand for timber between the world wars, as well as to provide a constant stream of revenue for the Exchequer.

From the start, the Forest Department had a commercial orientation. The mixed forests of India's northern hill districts were to be transformed into profit-yielding stands of conifers. As a result, the peasantry's access to the forest was severely proscribed: the Forest Department levied heavy fines for what it termed misuse of forest resources, the misuse being no more than the former livelihood of the peasants.

With the creation of the Forest Department, a linguistic shift took place that represented a shifting attitude toward the forest. Scientific terminology was employed to describe the forest; the forest was turned from a life-giving entity, the way inhabitants viewed the forest, to an object of economic value. Guha (1993: 85) observed that:

> the terms "valuable" and "desirable," for example, commonly used to describe certain species (especially conifers), were in every instance euphemisms for "commercially valuable and profitable," while the prefix "inferior" (used mainly to refer to oaks) bore no relation to the ecological and other functions the species thus described may have performed for the surrounding countryside.

The 1878 Indian Forest Act also changed the way the inhabitants were viewed: it "made the customary users of the forest its enemies" (Guha 1993: 83).

233

From the outset, the changes were opposed by the peasantry. Widespread and continuous social unrest accompanied the introduction of scientific forest management. Fearing not only for their livelihood but also for their way of life, peasants organized labor strikes, refused to cooperate with the Forest Department, and even resorted to arson. For the most part, these uprisings met with harsh measures. The "most celebrated of the moments" occurred at Rawain, where government troops opened fire on unarmed peasants.

Guha argues that the peasant resistance to the Forest Department was motivated by a clash between two fundamentally different views of the forest. Guha (1990: 88) notes that:

> the ideology of "scientific" forestry proclaimed that the imposition of state control was a logical corollary of the lack of "scientific" management practices among the population that lived in and around the forest.

In fact, the traditional forms of social interaction of the forest peasantry reveals the existence of a highly sophisticated system of conservancy.

Forest management practices continued after Indian independence. Led by Nehru, India's leaders opted for fully fledged industrialization. The consequence has been ecological degradation and social unrest. Timber out-turn has increased in the Uttarakhand district. Road-building projects that were supposed to bring industry to the area just led to more timber exports, with less employment for the population of the woodlands and further destruction of the environment. Local people, again seeing their way of life under threat, struck back and formed the now famous Chipko movement.

the closed hierarchies of the Orient open their doors to trade. But now military coercion is not the only means. Who needs to be induced by fear of military retaliation, so long as there is hope of capital loans?[1] Converts who embrace the faith for love of consumer goods do not need to be coerced.

It is not very telling to accuse the Enlightenment of bad things that have been done in its name that were formerly done in the name of other worldviews. Though it is perfectly true that the Western tradition dismisses dissident beliefs, the contempt of other cultures as mythical nonsense is normal for any well-embedded ideology. A thought system becomes strong by resisting incompatible ideas. World religions tend to be defensive and, although reprehensible, there is nothing unique about Western thought in that respect. For the same reasons and with the same evidence of standardized opinions (see Ch. 1), it is doubtful that the consensus-building capacity of the Enlightenment is more effective than that of the world religions in times past.

What is shocking is the surprise—the contrast between what Northerners say to each other about individual freedom of thought and speech and the standardized opinions they evince. If they are so free to think what they like, why do they tend to think the same? The real trouble with the Enlightenment

---

1. Hence, the dispute between North and South over the issues of additionality and conditionality of funding provided to less industrialized countries through the Global Environmental Fund; see Chapter 5.

project lies with the same inhibition of self-criticism that shackles all ideologies. Its praise of freedom raises expectations of understanding, but its methodological individualism blocks the questions.

The economists assume that needs and wants are ordered, the psychologists and philosophers suggest how they are ordered, but all have been crippled by an ego-focused model of the psyche and all lack a theory about the relations between Ego and Ego's universe of others. To the several listed disadvantages of the view from Ego, we can add another: since all humans are supposed to be alike in all essentials, and all are rational beings, the nature of disagreement has to be attributed to lack of information or to poor reasoning ability. (See Ch. 4 for an account of this in the climate discourses.) Theorizing, then, does not include the possibility that persons in discord will simply dig their heels in, regardless of the information they could tap. An inability to understand fundamental disagreement about the environment is one of the shortcomings of the model of the person.

Intransigence and being impervious to new facts is simply not accounted for as rational behavior. Refusing to believe the opponents' arguments, rejecting a priori what the opposition contends—this is very much the state of the art in debates about climate change and, indeed, the environment more generally. Yet the legacy of the Enlightenment teaches the experts to dismiss such behavior as irrational. The puzzle of *contradictory certainties*, as Thompson (1986) has put it, is not one that this frame of ideas can deal with.

The critics named above used the metaphor of disembeddedness, as if they believed that, in accordance with the Enlightenment ideals of objectivity, ideas and theories are actually freed from their old institutional matrices. They present the Western tradition as a culture disembedded from all moral and social obligations. Well, yes, indeed, disembedding of that kind has certainly been going on. But their criticism is strengthened if it allows that re-embedding is happening at the same time. Although certain obligations are being discarded, others are being learnt. As our minds are being freed from the claims of local ties, they are more deeply embedded in the moral and social principles of the market system. It is easier for us to be market minded than to be village minded, easier to be sensitive to professional than to family censure.

These caveats do not imperil the theses of the Southern commentators outlined above. On the contrary, they are sharpened by the admission that we are disabled from seeing past our local blindspots. For these reasons we do not notice that science and technology have a more intimate connection to their own social structures than their self-image projects (see Ch. 1). Schmutzer (1994) demonstrates how science and technology provide a means to establish social consensus. Historically, he argues, changes in scientific knowledge have always shadowed changes in social structure. The Enlightenment tradition emerged when medieval forms of social interaction were under pressure from the burgeoning capitalist system: the dialectic scripture-based science of scholasticism could no longer provide social consensus. It was replaced by the monologic and universalistic science of the Enlightenment, which provided a basis of argumentation and means of agreement for atomized individuals. When transposed to different social forms, such as those in the less industrialized world, its limitations become more blatant, but its consensus-building function, as Nandy demonstrates, is the same and just as efficient as that of the pre-Enlightenment religions.

So, we can return to the question: what else is new?

A new term has entered the vocabulary of politics. Human needs are to be taken into account; all parties now refer to basic human needs. Guha (1993: 100) himself frames his diagnosis in these terms: "It was the lack of fulfillment of the basic needs of education, health and employment, coupled with the continuing denial of traditional forest rights, that found expression through the medium of Chipko." Needs of the people, needs of the forest, needs of the economy to supply the needs of the people: it is not necessarily something to rejoice over when the protagonists make the protection of needs into one more set of claims and counterclaims. The very vagueness of the theorizing has merely shifted the language so that either side now needs to monopolize respect for needs, as well as justice and human rights.

It would be another new thing if the West recognized its own ideology as violent and oppressive: traditionally it is presented as supremely tolerant, unideological, and pragmatic. Its supporters never compare its sense of complete rightness and virtue with world religions; in this culture, thought is supposed to be free, the individual can live as he or she likes. The day will come when the cultural constraints are made visible. Usually that happens when the culture is being disembedded by new institutional forms. Before the advent of that day, researchers can try to create a way of talking about needs that meets the current demands of objectivity, impersonality, and impartiality.

Measuring the needs of social beings

The critical reader may justifiably argue that tearing down is far easier than building up: as long as there are no alternatives, social scientists should, in keeping with Karl Popper's prescription of piecemeal tinkering, try to improve the theories they have. In what follows, we take up this challenge.

We have seen so far that the social sciences are not coordinated. Excellent work conducted inside one compartment does not help the scholars in another. This is why, as previous sections have shown, social science conceptualizations of human needs and wants do not impinge effectively on the policy issues concerning global climate change. We then showed how current theories of human needs and wants are embedded in the Western intellectual tradition in their focus on individuals. We shall now briefly describe important international research, which switches focus from the individual to the communal level, a major development. First, work on social capital allows for the individual person's dependence on the efforts of others and, second, work on the responsiveness of government institutions to their publics overrules the suspicion of institutions entrenched in the history of the social sciences.

International comparisons of well-being provide a solid basis on which to build an assessment of how human needs and wants may constitute a danger to the global atmosphere. Comparisons are also necessary to move discussions of international equity in climate policy away from simplistic caricatures of rich and poor countries (see Ch. 4). We shall describe three approaches that do not rely on information about the atomized individual to measuring and comparing well-being across countries. In all three accounts the interest of the analysis is in the quality of the exchanges in which the individual can take part. In each of them a background of inherited possibilities is foregrounded. Attempts are made to assess the relation of each individual to these opportunities. This has involved a huge shift from the theories listed above.

The human development index (HDI) clearly owes much to Sen's idea of *entitlements* (Sen 1981, 1993). Admittedly, Sen tends to present his theory of poverty as if it were a question of measuring a penumbra of potential achievements around each person, always understanding that the individual is at the center of the scheme, the bull's eye of the concentric circles dear to *Homo economicus*. But when the measurements are studied closely we discover that the individual is kept offstage and all the focus of the measuring is on the supporting cast, the props, and machineries.

Statistics of poverty and well-being

The process of collecting statistics for international comparisons of poverty and welfare has been transformed. The human development index (HDI) harks back to the ILO statistics for the League of Nations. It was first produced by the United Nations Development Program (UNDP) in 1990. The title shows how much the idea of the good life has gained over old-fashioned comparisons of material welfare and subsistence levels. Subsequent annual editions have amended the original concept, but the central idea has remained the same. Instead of national income figures, which hide the distribution of income in a country and do not give other important information, the object is to provide a comparison of human development. This means studying the "enabling environment" in which people can "enjoy long, healthy, and creative lives." Well-being improvement is the "process of enlarging people's choices" (UNDP 1990: 9).

The three selected influences on choices are life expectancy, education, and access to resources needed for "a decent standard of living" (UNDP 1990: 10). Three additional factors are political freedom, guaranteed human rights, and personal self-respect. Briefly, the concept of human development is "a participatory and dynamic process" which works on two levels: wider choice and achieved well-being. Persons with good health, education and expectation of a long life also need the opportunity to use their acquired capabilities. For example, they need the opportunity to employ their talents, be active in political organization, take part in social life, and so on.

Three indicators are used for this information (UNDP 1990: 12):

- life expectancy at birth
- literacy rates
- purchasing-power adjusted GDP per capita (in logarithmic form).

The first two indicators are expressions of the supporting infrastructure on which the individual's life unfolds. Life expectancy is a good indicator of public health; it results from clean water, sewerage, medical practice, and nutritional status. Literacy is a good indicator of the spread of education and access to information. Purchasing power indicates the individual's prospects of acquiring "the good things."

The UNDP arrives at the HDI via a human deprivation index, which is amended and updated every year. This index measures the relative deprivation of individual countries on a scale where maximum deprivation is equal to 1 and minimum deprivation, the target of development, is set at 0. However, for real-life comparisons, the ordinal values must refer to statistical data from the sample countries. The UNDP obtained the minima from the lowest measured value for each indicator in 1987. The lowest expectancy of life after birth was taken from Afghanistan, Ethiopia and Sierra Leone, and was 42 years; Somalia's 12 percent provided the lowest literacy rate; Zaire had the minimum PPP-adjusted GDP at US$220 per capita. These values represented 1 on the human deprivation continuum.

The target values for each indicator were obtained in the same way. For life expectancy at birth, Japan set the target with 78 years; the value for literacy was set at 100 percent; target income was taken from average poverty-line figures of nine industrialized countries: Australia, Canada, Germany, the Netherlands, Norway, Sweden, Switzerland, the United Kingdom, and the United States.

The UNDP proceeds to rank individual countries on the human deprivation continuum (0 to 1) for each indicator; the average over the three indicators provides the overall deprivation index. The HDI was obtained by subtracting the latter from 1. Figure 3.4 illustrates the difference between the HDI and the

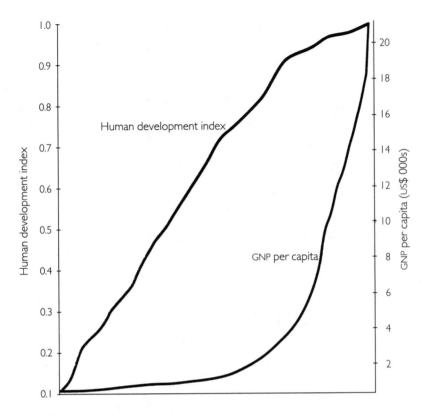

Figure 3.4 The HDI compared to income as a measure of development; 130 countries ranked. The two curves reveal that the disparity among countries is much greater in income than in human development. There is no automatic link between the level of per capita income in a country and the level of its human development.

conventional GDP measures. This shows that the disparity of incomes between countries is much greater than HDI differences, but lest this encourages complacency other information is added: for example, rapidly growing less industrialized nations (e.g., Brazil) have been less than successful in controlling gross human deprivations. Similarly, the inability of rich industrialized countries to halt homelessness, the spread of AIDS, and growing illegal drug-use, illustrates that high national income does not immunize them from human deprivation.

The annual balance sheets between progress and deprivation are ingeniously drawn up. On nutrition, for example, in 1992 "Daily caloric intake is now about 110% of the overall requirement (compared with 90% some 25 years ago)," but "Over 100 million people were affected by famine in 1990. More than a quarter of the world's people do not get enough food, and nearly one billion go hungry" (Box 3.4).

239

Box 3.4   The HDI balance sheet, 1991: human development in developing countries

Progress	Deprivation
Life expectancy	
• Average life expectancy increased by over one-third between 1960 and 1990—and is now at 63 years	• 10 million older children and young adults, and 14 million young children, die each year—most from preventable causes
Health	
• The proportion of people with access to health services has risen 63 per cent	• 1.5 billion people still lack basic health care • Over 1.5 billion people do not have safe water, and over 2 billion lack safe sanitation
Education	
• Adult literacy rates increased between 1970 and 1985, from 46 to 60 per cent	• Over 1 billion adults are still illiterate • 300 million children are not in primary or secondary school
Income	
• Income per head grew in the 1980s by almost 4 per cent, and by 9 per cent in East Asia • More than one person in four in the 1980s lived in countries with growth rates above 5 per cent	• More than 1 billion people still live in absolute poverty • Income per head has declined over the past decade in Latin America and sub-Saharan Africa
Children	
• Under-five mortality rates were halved over the past three decades • Immunization coverage for one-year olds increased dramatically during the 1980s, saving an estimated 1.5 million lives annually	• Over 14 million children die each year before reaching their fifth birthday • 180 million children under five suffer from serious malnutrition
Women	
• Primary school enrolment for girls increased between 1960 and 1988 from 79 per cent to 87 per cent • Women's enrolment in tertiary education has increased almost everywhere, and has achieved near-equality with men in Latin America and the Caribbean	• Half the rural women over 15 are illiterate • Women are often denied the right to decide whether or when to have children; half a million women die each year from causes related to pregnancy or childbirth • Women are often legally (or effectively) denied the right to own, inherit, or control property
Rural and urban areas	
• The proportion of people living in rural areas with access to adequate sanitation has doubled over the past decade • 88 per cent of urban dwellers have access to healthcare, and 81 per cent have access to safe water	• Only 44 per cent of the rural population have access to healthcare • There are 2.4 people per habitable room, three times the average in the North; one urban dweller in five lives in the nation's largest city

Source: UNDP (1992).

The development of this index is a great achievement: it transforms the idea of human needs. The index is a highly sophisticated attempt to assess the infrastructure of the individual's life. The individual person is not left dangling in mid-air, without support or clues as to what might realistically be possible at that time or place. A person's chances of schooling, nutrition, life expectancy, and income, say much more about well-being than straight comparisons of income, and they give more than answers to questions about individual happiness. The index is also more informative than the abstract systems of needs described earlier.

There is scope for some suggestions about the chosen indices. Literacy, for example: will it not need one day soon to be updated to numeracy? Computer competence can presumably be added, when absence of facilities and training clearly put a severe limit on the individual's capabilities and functioning in a computer-literate community. The ratio of telephones to population, and of personal computers and e-mail networks, will be eventually needed to assess whether inhabitants of poor countries are excluded from communication with each other and with the rich. Douglas & Isherwood (1979) have argued that the distribution of technology of communication sums up the meaning of the other indices of well-being (Islam 1991).

Living is a production process: Dasgupta's idea of commodity needs

The UNDP's human development index achieves objectivity by sticking to commensurables. What is measured are clues to the supporting institutions which enable an individual to achieve his ends. This follows Sen's lead in emphasizing *positive freedom*, the freedom to achieve and fulfill a personal potential. The techniques of assessment are a tool; the commentaries and accompanying theories lead to revisions of the tool. The next stage in the history of the idea of well-being was to include *negative freedom* in the assessment.

First of all, can welfare be evaluated without bringing the idea of freedom into consideration? Utilitarians resolve it summarily by arguing that for someone else to decide what is good for one evinces a lack of freedom. Since only individuals can know best what is good for themselves, claim the utilitarians, evaluations of well-being ought to be based on the individual's revealed wants, and not on general principles (see Ch. 4). Nonutilitarian theories invariably lead to paternalism because someone else is choosing the ideal; individual choice and individual autonomy must be the basis of evaluation. At the other end of the spectrum, proponents of freedoms-based approaches anticipate that utilitarianism implies unacceptable tradeoffs: they fear that, if inviolable rights are not the basis of well-being, then power-hungry regimes can always point to this

year's economic growth to justify postponing democratic elections or implementing strategies to reduce greenhouse gas emissions for yet another year.

Dasgupta started to respond to this debate with the dictum that there is "no
one type of freedom that is real freedom" (1993: 42). He found the HDI measures
to be "... an inadequate index of well-being which neglects primary negative
liberties." On the other hand, if the state is limited to securing negative freedoms, the lack of positive freedoms may make the individual's claim to life,
liberty, and property look absurd: "A person dying of starvation may well be
negatively free; but the foreclosure on his freedom to do anything is terminal"
(Dasgupta 1993: 42). Consequently, he looked for a concept of welfare to incorporate both.

Dasgupta also questioned the assumption of applied welfare economics that
public policy should serve an aggregate of individual utility. The connection
between personal choice and the individual's perception of the good is not
straightforward. In poor countries, individual well-being is often forfeited for
the well-being of institutions. (We would add that this is not only true for poor
countries.) Norms such as female circumcision in Africa or expectations that
women or the old should place their own well-being, or even their survival, after
that of their family, as repulsive as this may seem to Western sensibilities, are
internalized to such an extent that the liberal criteria of injustice are not applicable: these people are not always forced, nor do they necessarily dislike their
social responsibilities. Moreover, to say that their freedom needs or identity
needs (Galtung 1990) are not being satisfied may be true in a very general sense,
but since it bears no relation to what we will call the cultural realities, it is
meaningless. This suggests a rupture between individual utility and individual
advantage: well-being is not necessarily synonymous with fulfillment of
private wants (Galtung 1990: 59).

Although Sen did not say as much, his concept of well-being treated the
activities and achievements of individuals as outputs from some production
process which provides the necessary conditions (such as public health and
education). Dasgupta took this further, reckoning that the individual's achievements should be counted as further inputs on their own account. This breaks
the conventional distinction between producer and consumer: the consumer is
also a producer, because living is productive. In Dasgupta's model of well-being
the whole of human life is a complex production process that calls for inputs,
and produces outputs, which themselves influence the next stage of input.

Inputs are the commodities humans consume: at the most basic level these
are food, water, shelter, and so forth, which are indicated by "... crude
measures of commodity availability" (Dasgupta 1993: 38). These are what needs
theorists would call basic material needs. Inputs in the physiological production process are transformed into utilities and individual functioning such as

survival, health, and exercise of skills. Outputs are aggregate welfare and "the extent to which certain real, vital interests of persons are being served and promoted" (Dasgupta 1993: 39). The outcomes of social interaction include positive freedoms. For this reason, Dasgupta included background conditions in his model. These are the political and civil liberties to which an individual has access in a given society.

Background conditions: the negative freedoms

First, Dasgupta (1993) evaluated the commodity determinants of well-being: these were the inputs in his approach. His three broad indices of well-being included the individual's current and prospective real income, including non-marketable goods. Income enables individual access to commodities and contributes to enjoyment. From these Dasgupta constructed four socioeconomic criteria:

- income per capita (GDP)
- life expectancy at birth
- infant survival rate
- adult literacy rate.

Income represents the input vector of the human productive process, whereas the other three measures are outputs of this process, and correspond to the idea of positive freedom which is so prominent in Sen's thinking. So far, he was not doing anything very different from the HDI.

He then combined these four socioeconomic measures with something to indicate the presence of political and civil liberties, that is, something to indicate the presence of negative freedom, freedom from arbitrary interference. He was interested in the extent to which citizens can take part in the decision of who governs and by what laws; and in the freedoms an individual enjoys vis-à-vis the state, such as freedom of speech and the independence of the judiciary. These two negative freedoms indicate the social institutions that confer value on commodities, allocate them fairly or unfairly and permit their peaceful and safe enjoyment.

Once Dasgupta set up the comparisons, he interrogated the results with the question of whether or not democratic freedoms are a luxury of the rich Western countries. In modern contract theory, political and civil liberties outline a sphere of human interaction, the public sphere, at the same time as they protect and promote socioeconomic rights; they are therefore not to be counted as luxuries. His empirical results confirmed this. When the four socioeconomic indicators were correlated to the two sociopolitical measures, he could start to make comparisons of political culture.

By these means Dasgupta made a major advance. He explicitly shifted the focus of well-being research from the individual to the social mechanisms of allocation. Whereas Sen's approach to the enabling environment of individual well-being emphasized positive freedom, Dasgupta's attended to the production of both positive and negative freedom. He did away with the idea that consumption is a process that starts with shopping and ends at dinner time in the domestic unit. He taught that consumption actually produces the kind of society in which the consumer lives. As a process of transformation it has something in common with Marx's notion of food transformed into labor power, not to mention Marx's framing notion of the unity of production and consumption.

Dasgupta's approach ingeniously confronted the philosophical difficulties that beset most welfare theories. The process of transforming commodities into well-being is a long way from a list of commodities that are supposed to satisfy the individual's basic needs. At the same time it is more concrete and capable of systemic comparisons than the abstract systems of needs proffered by ethical needs theories. It might be clearer if the two kinds of background were treated as inputs in a feedback model (see Fig. 3.5).

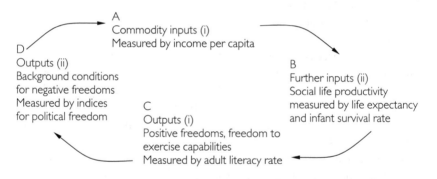

Figure 3.5 Commodity needs: a dynamic feedback loop.

The line of continuity goes thus: first Sen shifted the conversation from utilitarian individualism to the infrastructures provided by society. Although Sen's method seems formally to be focused on the individual, he actually uses a concept of social capital and his work with the HDI has shown a method for measuring it. Dasgupta took up the measure of positive freedoms and includes negative freedom into the comparison. For Sen the infrastructure (education, transport, communications, public health, or whatever the researcher cares to measure) gives the individual a supporting environment of opportunity for self-realization. For Dasgupta another set of background conditions indicates freedom from arbitrary despoilment and misrule. In each case the individual is nominally to the fore, and the rest of society is at the rear—but only nominally, for the measures assess the institutional support for the individual. Another name for this is social capital. The next stage will be to bring the background forward, so as to give direct attention to institutions that establish the individual's scope for fulfillment by creating social capital.

Institutional performance

Putnam (1993) evaluated the same ideal of well-being in terms of institutional performance. He compared the performance of Italian regional governments from their inception in 1970 until the mid-1980s. For that period, he found that some regions ". . . have been consistently more successful than others"; they were "more efficient in their internal operations, more creative in their policy initiatives, more effective in implementing those initiatives" (Putnam 1993: 81). Predictably, the regional governments of northern Italy outperformed their counterparts from the south. By analyzing institutional responses to real policy demands, Putnam looked at how needs are structured, articulated and responded to by social networks.

Putnam attributed the variation to social structure. In other words, he agreed that what Dasgupta calls background conditions are prime factors in providing welfare. In southern Italy, which is marked by vertical structures that encourage patronage and isolation, regional government performed poorly. By the same token, in the north, more egalitarian and less traditionalist cultures did better. These regions have established horizontal networks of civic interaction, thanks to which the community "values solidarity, civic engagement, cooperation, and honesty: government works" (Putnam 1993: 115).

Putnam's ideals of social life date back to the Renaissance republican thought of Machiavelli. The core of this approach is not the individual but the civic community. Whereas liberalism stresses individual rights, the republican approach emphasizes the obligations of the citizen to the civic community; the pursuit of collective goals is a conscious endeavor, not the byproduct of self-interest. According to Putnam, although individuals in the civic community are not "selfless saints", self-interest is defined in terms of the community itself, rather than being myopic or turned in. For Putnam the civic community has three defining qualities. First, civic engagement in public affairs is evident. Institutional success depends on the interaction of institutions and citizens. Second, citizens enjoy political equality. This equality is ensured by horizontal relations of reciprocity and cooperation: norms of trust, solidarity and tolerance mark public life in the civic community. Last, the civic community is associational: citizens are not isolated individuals but take part in diverse forms of organizations and associations in which individuals are educated in the art of citizenry and learn to appreciate the quest for collective goals.

Good government in the civic community means interaction between government and citizen. Participation in public affairs fosters civic virtues (trust, tolerance, solidarity). Unlike the classical liberal model, civic virtues are not inherent in the individual. They can only be acquired by the individual in his or her social settings, or in the terms of the following chapters, through social solidarities.

To measure government performance, Putnam constructed 12 indicators (Box 3.5). The indicators 1–3 refer to the policy process, 4 and 5 are concerned with policy substance, and measures 6–12 show the level of policy implementation. These 12 indicators provided Putnam with measures of well-being. Good performance in each area represents a high level of well-being. Figure 3.6 shows the comparative well-being of Italian citizens between 1970 and the mid-1980s.

Since differences in well-being in a region depend on the level of *civic-ness*, which we shall refer to below as the level of civility, Putnam (1993: 96) relied on four further indicators to assess the presence of civic virtues:

- the level of preference voting in a particular region
- the voter turnout for referenda (since voting in general elections is mandatory in Italy)

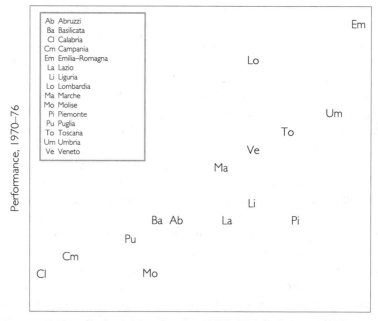

Figure 3.6 Comparative government performance in Italy (Putnam 1993).

Box 3.5   Twelve performance indicators.

1. Cabinet stability: the ability of local governments to form lasting coalitions.
2. Budget promptness: the ability of the regional government to deliver the budget on 1 January each year.
3. Quality of the statistical and information services available to regional governments.
4. Reform legislation: the extent to which regional governments adopt new legislation.
5. Legislative innovation: the speed at which a regional government adopts creative legis-lation from other regions.
6. Number of daycare centers for children.
7. Number and quality of family clinics.
8. Use of industrial policy instruments.
9. Agricultural spending capacity.
10. Local health unit expenditure.
11. Housing and urban development.
12. Bureaucratic responsiveness.

Source: Putnam (1993).

- newspaper readership
- associational membership: the number of civic associations (football clubs, choral societies, rotary clubs, and so on) per citizen.

Figure 3.7 shows how these indicators correlate with the level of institutional performance.

In Putnam's account, high scores for institutional performance depend on high scores for civility; the more civic virtues, the higher the level of institutional performance and the higher the level of individual well-being. Indeed, Putnam found that citizens living in the high scoring regions were more satisfied with life than citizens of less civic regions (Fig. 3.8): Thus, "happiness is living in a civic community" (Putnam 1993: 113).

If we were to use Dasgupta's terminology we would say that Putnam found measures for outputs and background conditions. The emphasis on the civic virtues and structures of civic interaction is more detailed and articulate than in Dasgupta's approach. Putnam has put the background conditions into the foreground. In his work they were so vital to well-being that they have become synonymous with well-being itself. Whereas Dasgupta limited himself to objectively measurable standards (constitutional freedoms, stated policies, and so on), Putnam tried to assess the more elusive normative factors such as trust and solidarity. However, as the indicators for civility reveal, Putnam also held on tight to a Western ideal of democracy, including voting procedures, in the indicators. Hardly surprising, since he was after all talking about modern Italy. In applying such an institutional analysis to a non-Western political system, such a criterion may not be suitable.

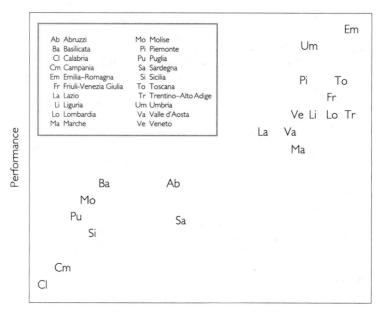

Figure 3.7 Civic virtues and government performance (Putnam 1993).

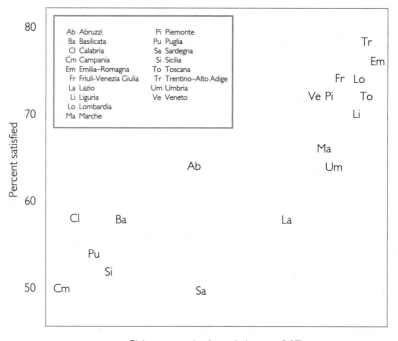

Figure 3.8 Satisfaction with life and the civic community (Putnam 1993).

Putnam played down the input side of human well-being; all Italian regions had the same amount of financial resources available. He also explicitly rejected the claim that is sometimes made that socioeconomic modernity and the associated growth in income explain differences in institutional performance in Italy. Rather, it was the other way round; he argued that the normative structures determined the input side of Dasgupta's equation: "civic traditions may have powerful consequences for economic development and social welfare, as well as for institutional performance" (Putnam 1993: 157).

If we try to compare the two approaches, we start by noticing that Putnam does not take any interest in commodities. His diagram would be very similar, except that his first input is Dasgupta's second output, government performance, for which he invented the 12 indices. The first output flows from this factor in the form of civility, individual practice and enjoyment of positive freedoms. This has a pervasive influence on the production process. And these outputs flow straight to the background conditions, so the circle is completed; the snake's tail has been put into its mouth.

Neither Dasgupta nor Putnam took into account that the social process feeds back directly on the demand for commodities and indirectly results in levels of greenhouse gas emissions. The social process not only produces people, it also defines them, and what they need and want. The means by which those needs and wants are satisfied shape a society's greenhouse gas emissions profile.

Instead of commodities or material conditions, Putnam offered an institutional analysis of well-being. This is bold, because institutions are out of intellectual fashion. However, he was right; institutions embody historical decisions and shape politics (see Ch. 5 for a fuller discussion). As he said, they influence outcomes because they shape actors' identities, power, and strategies, or, as Sen had it, they define the individual's capabilities. Choice at any one time is limited and conditioned by preceding choices that have affected the structure of institutions. This finds its analytic expression in the idea of social capital. Putnam defined social capital as "the features of social organization, such as trust, norms, and networks, that can improve the efficiency of society by facilitating coordinated action" (Putnam 1993: 167).

The concept of social capital is an attempt to explain how successful social interaction can resolve the prisoner's dilemma (Vol. 3, Ch. 2) and avoid the tragedy of the commons. Like physical and financial capital, social capital is productive: it aids spontaneous cooperation and creates moral resources. Successful social arrangements for the management of common pool resources depend on the level of social capital that can be mobilized and on the norms that facilitate implementation. However, since social capital is a public good, it is usually undervalued and undersupplied, and, since institutions have for a long time been out of favor in academic circles, their study has been fogged in bias.

Questions about the cultural dimension

These three initiatives of the HDI, Dasgupta, and Putnam, take humans as essentially social beings contributing to each other's welfare by providing an infrastructure of mutual aid and communication. Although very relevant to the theory of needs, they are held in conceptual frameworks that cannot address questions about why lifestyles and consumption patterns are changing so fast that they press upon global climate change. The popular idea is that consumer demand is so insistent that bankers and industry must rake the Earth's resources for more goods for consumption. Certainly, consumption goods have multiplied; certainly consumer demand is an effective despoiler of forests and land. But there is no theory about why consumers are sometimes content to live as they always did, honoring the ways of their ancestors, and why they sometimes go on wild spending sprees, when no amount of money is enough, no amount of goods will satisfy.

In economics the budget constraint is supposed to constrain spending, but borrowing is possible. Why do some kinds of societies condone living on borrowed resources? What are these kinds of societies, where impatience is the norm, and what has happened to the virtue of waiting? What undoes the old constraints? From an individualist basis there is no way to answer these questions. The social sciences can compile information about trends, but even if the scientists were agreed about future effects of consumption on the environment, the social sciences cannot bring out of their dispersed expertise any answers to the questions that are in the forefront of lay and media speculation. Will consumption patterns continue to disrupt old social forms? Will the consuming public come to take the responsibilities for climate change so much to heart that constraint will win the day?

Needs in a unified social theory

It seems irrelevant, even frivolous, to talk about culture and the theory of the person in a serious conversation about human needs and their consequences for climate change, and yet we must say something about both.

Utilitarian writings refer to other persons only sporadically as they enter and leave Ego's orbit. Copernicus had the same kind of problem. Studying the sky with the Earth at the center of the Universe, astronomers found it difficult to construct a systematic view of the relations of the planets and did not recognize that the systematic view would help. Social scientists need a new way of talking about the person as a social being. This means a way of talking about the person who has needs and wants as immersed in a culture co-produced with other persons, a culture arising out of social solidarity that gives an array of entrenched ideas. With such a concept, researchers could save the theory of wants and needs from being bandied about in climate politics and give it more bite in the current debates.

We have listed blank places, which are kept blank in diverse branches of the social sciences. Two are in economics, which for its own theoretical purposes defines rationality without culture and, following from this, adopts a solipsist model (based on a belief that only the self can be known) of the rational being. The other social sciences, for quite different theoretical purposes, also avoid the inherent sociality of the human being. Why does cognitive psychology start with the isolated individual thinker? Why too does needs theory start with the needs of an individual? Why are social needs only tacked on at the end of the account? If a being is social, the sociality is inherent from the beginning. It is neither intellectual laziness nor simple-minded keeping up with the Joneses in the economics departments. The explanation is cultural. In fact, the very thing social scientists do not want to talk about, the rejected element in all their analyses, that is, culture based on social solidarity, explains why the theorizing falls short.

Cultural difference is a subject that Anglo-Saxon thinkers have good reason to evade. If only humans all had the same culture, that is, the same ultimate values, it would be all right, but Western society is trying to live in a cultural melting pot, trying to find grounds for laws that are not founded in religion (because religions are different), trying to find principles of justice that do not depend on revelation (because revelations are different), trying hard to make it possible for Muslims and Hindus to live along with Jews and Africans under the same laws with atheists and Christians. The solution is to label certain areas of enquiry as no-go areas, as if the differences of belief are so insignificant that they can be ignored. One of these unsystematizable topics is the person.

Why the homogenized person?

The philosophers of the industrialized world have had good reasons for making the person a topic that can be talked about freely but not systematized. The wish to put important sensitive topics outside the scope of intercultural conflict arises from negative experiences with dictators and religions imposing their definitions of the human person. For these reasons the mind is stripped bare by theories, and plunged naked into the statistical cauldron, while influences from other minds are systematically disregarded.

So a homogenized person enters the statistical tables and there creates a paradox. Why do the social sciences describe the self as if it were not a social being? The empty idea of the person perhaps avoids negative experiences of imposed needs, but the same empty idea paradoxically allows experts to tell us what our true needs are. But then the wish to avoid coercion does explain why the theories of needs are placed harmlessly at the level of meta-discourse, unapplied and unapplicable to practical issues such as climate policy.

Every culture has its blind spots, this by definition. A culture is like a cognitive sieve that sorts information flooding into the rational beings trying collaboratively to organize their lives. Some information is accepted and allowed to pass through the meshes, and some is rejected. In this active process, anything that comes through and reaches good standing as a piece of knowledge then joins the work of testing future knowledge. The sifting of information goes on not in secluded libraries but in practical cooperation and competition. The tests of new information include compatibility with what is there already. Future possible information has to fit well with the existing set of ideas, and the whole has to work in the business of practical living. That is why social scientists cannot borrow piecemeal here and there attractive bits of non-Western theories of needs and of persons. If they want to correct their own theoretical apparatus, a social model of the self should not smell of oriental mysticism. It would have to satisfy compatibility conditions.

A self for the social sciences

The history of the Anglo-Saxon discourse about needs and wants requires that any new ways of describing the self must be empirical, scientistic, and parsimonious. A person has desires, but scientists must not say in advance what they are. The person has to be rational, to have theories about the world, how it works and what to do about fulfilling those desires. And, to be a social being, the person has to have theories about other people's behavior and be able to interpret it in terms of their beliefs and desires.

This social person will fit to the consumer whom humans know personally much better than to the model of the solipsist sovereign rational consumer of economic theory whose own shopping is for his or her own consumption. The social person's shopping will be planned to make markers in the week and the year, using goods to mark other people as friends and relatives, and watching to see if the others reciprocate or not. This person will be dependent on the goodwill of neighbors and colleagues. This person will save for the long term if everyone else in the vicinity expects as much, and will be as free with criticisms of profligacy as they are—and no more. This person will of course use the normal accounting of costs and benefits, should be expected to make the normal moves in coalitions and games, should display trust and distrust in assessment of risk (see Vol. 3, Chs 1–3).

There may be nothing new here, except for one thing. With some such concept of the rational social being, social scientists can start to have a social theory of needs and wants, because the other persons are talking to each other and trying to cajole and threaten in the name of the good society.

For these purposes a model is at hand already. Dennett developed it to bridge various sciences dealing with mind, artificial intelligence, game theory, psychology, and philosophy. These uses of his model guarantee that a needs theory based on it, whatever other trouble it may run into, will not be dismissed as oriental mysticism. In his all-purpose minimal model, the person is just an *intentional system*. For his limited theoretical purposes, persons are rational beings whose actions can be understood in terms of their intentions, and these can be construed from the logical relations between their beliefs and desires.

An abstract model

Dennett's intentional system has three necessary conditions: rationality, intentions, and a reciprocal stance toward and from other intentional systems. *Intentionality* is the capability to have intentions that persons ascribe to each other. A person takes the intentional stance, which means expecting to be able to predict how other persons are going to behave, and makes this knowledge the basis for strategies in fulfilling intended goals (Dennett 1988). A person's primary activity is to interact with other persons. This means that the person must be capable of awareness of the relations of self to other selves and always sensitive to the pressures of others. By definition the person is continuously engaged in interpreting, responding and looking for response from other persons—the process of creating and dissolving social solidarity.

One benefit of the model is that from the beginning social interaction is written into the account. Another is that the model can be complicated by incorporating one intentional system inside another, as a neuron in a person's body, a person in a village, a village in a municipality and so on. So their sociality can be thought of as layered or differentiated in several dimensions. A person is defined as open to influences from these ambient other persons.

If researchers adopt this approach, they do not have to introduce social needs additively at the end of the list of needs and wants, for other persons are there from the start; they may be counted necessary for survival as well as for enjoyment, near other persons may be more significant that distant ones, or the other way round. For understanding wants it is a distinct benefit to have inherent sociality restored to the idea of the intrinsically human being, and restored in a sense that invites counting and measuring of influence from other persons.

Since intentionality is the primary characteristic of a person, we can presume that in interaction with other persons the individual has an overall objective, to protect the ability to formulate, negotiate and achieve his or her own intentions. Keeping some options free, trying to hold on to choice, would be one prior need, so that social intercourse can go on. The less obvious but necessary rider is that the person engaged in safeguarding his or her own choices is watching out for threats to independence. So, this definitionally minimal person would adapt quite comfortably to the definitions in quality of life and capabilities theorizing to which we have referred to above (Sen & Nussbaum 1993).

It would be as if a little constitutional monitor inside the head warns Ego when the demands of other persons are going to change the higher-level inclusive intentional system into one that Ego cannot control. The requirement of staying in control is so basic to the model that we can go further and expect that the person will subordinate many—no, most—wants and needs to it. This invites us to pay special attention to the capability of rejecting information, and draws us back to the first chapter of this volume in which structures of ignorance were cited as a normal part of scientific work.

The model of a rational self engaged with other selves should be quite simple. All it needs is a body that contains a set of neural networks exchanging inputs and outputs, and a context of other networks with which it makes external exchanges. Much is unattractive about this minimal idea of a social person, its lack of color, undescribed emotions and weaknesses, lack of passion and capability for love. But this is because it is abstract. The rest can be filled in according to the guidelines, depending heavily on what other people are doing in the social environment. It would be possible to use this model of the self as a scheme for recording all the exchanges into which the person has entered or is capable of entering in the course of a lifetime. It provides a way of assessing the variety of relationships persons are capable of sustaining. The accepted definitions of wants and needs will depend on the quality of these relationships. Even the definitions of the basic constituents of personhood will depend essentially on the social experience. The persons talk; they try to persuade and coerce each other; they are busy justifying what they do in terms of grand principles that will appeal to the other persons who can be helpful, or a threat. Justification is the basis of culture.

Culture

Every form of organization is also a form of culture. Its cultural side provides the justifications and explanations for what is being done. It allocates blame and judgments of guilt. This is clearly seen in the political discourse about the causes of climate change. Every culture has its implicit theory of the person, a theory of the right way to behave to enable all right-minded people to collaborate, for example, to mitigate or adapt to climate change according to the agreed principles. And at least implicitly, the theory of the person is a theory of wants and needs, for it is the kind of society that generates the lists of acceptable wants. The model of the inclusive system of intentional systems would have to be amended to allow for feedback upon intentions changing its whole direction.

We do not suppose that culture is static, nor that there is only one kind of culture in a community. Rather, there are at least three types of culture always potentially present in any group of persons, all three at war with one another and each tipping behavior toward one or another type of organization. We say three, not because three types are all that there are, but for the sake of having a parsimonious model of social organizations. For explanatory value, three, four, or five types of social organization are enough to generate three, four, or five explanatory cosmologies, which stabilize three, four, or five kinds of ideal person. For we assume that each person is gathering clues about what the world is like from the others in their ambit, and learning how to behave, which means learning how to think and choose conformably.

In each case, the shopping baskets are different; shoppers are not merely buying to satisfy their families' needs. Modern, or traditional, original or conformist, puritan, or hedonist, they are not personal choices, but choices that register persons' allegiance to their own cultural situations (Douglas 1992).

As described by Thompson et al. (1990), cultural theory posits five social beings or five forms of social solidarity, each of which will be found (in varying strengths and patterns of interaction with the other four) in any social system. It then goes on to predict the distinctive household *consumption styles* that will accompany and uphold each of those solidarities:

- the *cosmopolitan* style of the individualist (for whom the world is his oyster and a thing of beauty, a joy for a fortnight)
- the *traditionalist* style of the hierarchist (who anchors his stratified collectivity in the weight of history)
- the *naturalist* style of the egalitarian (who, in rejecting artifice and excess, seeks to bring human demands down within nature's frugal limits)
- the *isolated* style of the fatalist (for whom nature operates without rhyme or reason, suggesting therefore that there is no point in trying to manage needs and resources in any way)
- the *conviviality without coercion* style of the hermit (who is careful not to get drawn into all the coercion that is entailed, in one way or another, in the other four styles).

Only the "onward and upward" style of the individualist conforms to the economist's *nonsatiety requirement*: that a person always prefers a larger bundle of goods to a smaller one (Awh 1976). The other four, each in its distinctive way, transgress this requirement. Such nonconforming households, therefore, are not economically rational, but they are still culturally rational: their consumption behavior helps strengthen the solidarities (the patterns of social relations together with the distinctive sets of beliefs and values that justify those relations), of which they are the vital parts (see Ch. 4). Economic rationality, too, is cultural, in that it supports the sort of ego-focused networks that promote a life of bidding and bargaining: the individualist's solidarity.

Dake & Thompson (1993) tested this fivefold scheme on a sample of 220 British households. Households, they found, do indeed fall into these five styles, each of which is quite thick on the ground, and each of which works its way through into a set of purchasing preferences—a shopping basket—that is markedly different from those to which the other four give rise (Box 3.6). The much relied-upon notion of national per capita consumption becomes statistically invalid if each nation comprises five distinct consumption populations. Indeed, it would make more sense to aggregate each consumption population across nations than to lump them all together as American consumers, Chinese consumers, Indian consumers, and so on.

With a moratorium on the use of national per capita consumption (who, after all, would want to be caught committing the statistical sin of homogenizing heterogeneity?), attention can then shift to the styles: their impacts on one another and the possibility of changing some of the items that at any time are defining those styles (they're changing all the time anyway) for others that are less environmentally harmful—although what is considered to be environmentally harmful will vary with the social construction of nature that accompanies and supports each solidarity. For instance, those who are not egalitarians are unlikely to be convinced that they need a whole new relationship with nature but they can readily latch onto the desirability of eating lower on the food chain. Many of the highest earning and best educated Americans are doing just that, not (if they are individualists) to save the world but in the pursuit of healthy living and personal success. At the same time, of course, many of the poorest and least well-educated Americans have moved themselves (or, in the case of that high proportion who are fatalists, have found themselves moved) up the food chain. All of which suggests that education and productive employment—fatalism reduction, in other words—would be worthwhile policy goals in relation to global climate change.

This is not a facetious suggestion. The multiplier effect—it takes 30 kilograms of grain to produce just 1 kilogram of meat—means that a quite small shift down the food chain in America (say) translates into a massive (and carbon sequestering) global shift in land use and land cover. Much the same holds for other

---

Box 3.6   Household consumption styles

The Dake & Thompson survey (1993) revealed five styles of consumption at the household level:

- Individualists are fashion conscious, like to look successful, prefer a tidy garden and don't join clubs. They do not go in for vegetarianism, biodegradable products or informality, nor do they allot specific chores within the household or go out of their way to avoid fascist vegetables and the like—the products, as the survey put it, of "oppressive institutions."

- Hierarchists formalize gender differences at their dinner parties (different wines for the ladies and the gentlemen, for instance). They use traditional ingredients, have their own places at table, are sticklers for punctuality, and wash their clothes on "wash day," having first sorted them out according to color and fabric. They do not boycott certain products, nor do they find that work often runs late, nor do they go in for take-away meals. They are not prepared to put up with broken furniture, nor are they comfortable with a house that is untidy.

- Egalitarians are about as opposed to both individualists and hierarchists as it is possible for them to be. Communality, together with unprocessed foods and biodegradable products (which, moreover, should be made by institutions that are not oppressive), is what they look for: an informal, joining, vegetarian sort of a life, in a pleasantly scruffy house filled with furniture that is not new and surrounded by a garden that is far from tidy. Egalitarians, unlike hierarchists and individualists, are not brand loyal, nor are they fashion conscious, nor do they wash their clothes on the same day each week, or sort them out into separate piles before they put them into the washing machine.

  Already the power of this sort of approach appears. For instance, if an organization is thinking of siting a nuclear waste repository somewhere that is geologically ideal, and the people round about turn out not to sort their washing out into separate piles, the organization would be well advised to site it somewhere else.

- Fatalists make few long-term plans, find it difficult to save money, and are much addicted to take-away meals. They do not have regular routines or allotted household tasks or their own places at the table. Indeed, their take-away meals are likely to be eaten in front of that quintessentially fatalist piece of technology—the television set.

- The questionnaire said little about the hermit households because it has not yet been developed to the point where it can tap into the autonomous solidarity. But hermits work hard to distance themselves from all the consumptive positions that the other four social beings dig themselves into, and so it should not be too difficult to design some questions for future surveys that will capture this deliberate and carefully judged reticence.

---

changes in behavior that the members of the various solidarities can pick up from one another: choosing a house, next time a person moves, that is nearer the workplace than the present house, for instance, or letting the forest grow back on a Scottish hillside instead of keeping it as a bald monoculture optimized for deer stalking. BMW funding a study of how to reduce the number of private cars in the center of Munich is another example of this sort of constructive interplay: a culturally plural and responsive citizenry interacting with reflexive policymaking so as to find better ways of living together in a particular locality. This is not to say that there is no role for global-level actors. Of course there is, but the anti-homogenizing lesson is best learned at the local level and then transferred to the global (see Ch. 5).

Much the same heterogeneity of consumption styles is evident in the South. Gadgil & Guha (1995) have focused on the consumption of natural resources in India and have identified three distinct populations: the *omnivores* (the development-aided class of modern consumers), the *ecosystem people* (the traditional subsistence farmers and fisherfolk) and the *eco-refugees* (those who have neither the social contacts nor the entry fee to join the omnivores and, at the same time, have been unable to maintain their viability as ecosystem people). The omnivores, clearly belong to the individualist solidarity, the ecosystem people (somewhat idealized) belong to the egalitarian solidarity, and the eco-refugees are the excluded fatalists. The interactions of these three solidarities, thanks to the interventions of the hierarchy (national government and international development assistance) are not constructive. Indeed, what we have in India, according to Gadgil & Guha, is almost the opposite of what has been happening in virtuous Munich.

They identify six root causes of this unconstructive interaction:
- The ecosystem people are being deprived of the natural capital on which they depend.
- The ecosystem people are denied access to human-made capital by virtue of their not being much involved in the formal economy.
- The process of building human-made capital is itself inefficient and destructive of natural capital.
- The omnivores, unlike Adam Smith's market actors, do well even when others do not benefit. This is because their consumption of natural capital is subsidized by the state.
- Because of the omnivores' monopoly over human-made capital, the ecosystem people and the eco-refugees have no incentive to invest in the quality of their offspring; only quantity brings them any benefit.
- The concentration of human-made capital in a few urban centers (where it is fueled by imported technology) has led to the mining of natural capital elsewhere, a process that is exacerbated by the omnivores dumping their wastes on those who are not omnivores.

These two heterogenizing examples—one from the industrialized world, one from the less industrialized world—share the same typology of social solidarities, and they begin the task of opening up the sorts of dynamics—sometimes virtuous, sometimes not—that are at work at the various scales: household, village, nation, and so on. Together, they suggest that policy monocultures—approaches that insist that people are all the same (all insatiable, all with the same basic needs, or whatever)—are not what policymakers need for dealing with global climate change. Indeed, they are what policymakers don't need. The idea of consumption as a moral activity—a way of supporting and strengthening a social solidarity—is therefore the first essential in getting to grips, in a useful way, with human needs and wants.

If researchers knew the kind of culture, they would know the kinds of persons who subscribe to it. So, now we turn to the questions about tastes and preferences, xenophobia, trust, impatience, high priority for environmental safety. The argument is that these are not matters that start and end in the unanalyzable individual psyche. The person lives inside a nested set of inclusive intentional systems that organize the incoming information, and align the moral issues. This is a theory about mutual persuasion, not about cultural determination. If the person wants to earn a living in a particular type of organization, the easiest thing would be to accept the culture that goes with it.

Conclusion

What can we summarize from this chapter? Clearly, human needs and wants play a role in changing global climate. Lifestyles certainly do give rise to consumption patterns that certainly do deplete resources. However, as we have shown, the dominant social science conceptualization of human needs and wants provides little help for formulating global climate change policy. Social sciences dealing with needs and wants remain firmly bound to the individualist tradition, thus weakening the analysis. The abstract and universalistic claims of social science in general and ethical needs theories in particular do not impinge on those questions relevant to the global climate change debate.

This is not to say that the focus on human needs and wants should be abandoned for research into global environmental questions. It means that, unlike current theorizing, the social and cultural dimensions of human needs and wants must be included in the theoretical approaches. Human needs and wants are generated, articulated, and satisfied in an institutionalized feedback system. They do not appear from thin air but are created by the social interactions that comprise the civic community. The idea of social capital offers an approach to look at how different institutional systems generate human needs and wants. Rather than postulating universal categories of human needs, the social capital approach urges us to include the social dimension from the outset.

Including the social dimension also allows us to see why the present social science conceptualization of human needs and wants sits awkwardly in the global climate change debate. The issue of global climate change is not built into the institutional processes for the civic society, whether at local, national or global level. Neither the local environment nor the global climate system is included in any theory for identifying or meeting human needs and wants; they fall outside the institutional feedback loop and are not a constituency in any political system (see Ch. 5).

The questions surrounding global climate change must be incorporated into the institutions of social accounting. The major obstacles to this lie in the socio-economic system itself. The premises of the capitalist system are individual and do not allow for the environment being easily built back into the institutional feedback loop.

References

Adams, J. 1994. Alternative policies for reducing dependence on the car. Paper presented at Leeds Environmental Action Forum Conference, Leeds.

Agarwal, A. & S. Narain 1991. *Global warming in an unequal world: a case of environmental colonialism*. New Delhi: Centre for Science and Environment.

Allardt, E. 1975. *Att ha, alska, att vara, om valfard i Norden* [*Having, loving, being, on welfare in Nordic countries*] Borgholm, Sweden: Argos.

——— 1993. Having, loving, being: an alternative to the Swedish model of welfare research. In *The quality of life: a study prepared for the World Institute for Development Economics Research of the United Nations University*, A. Sen & M. Nussbaum (eds). Oxford: Oxford University Press.

Awh, R. 1976. *Microeconomics: theory and applications*. New York: John Wiley.

Banuri, T. & F. Apffel Marglin 1993. *Who will save the forests?* London: Zed.

Bay, C. 1968. Needs, wants and political legitimacy. *Canadian Journal of Political Science* **1**(3), 241–60.

——— 1990. Taking the universality of human needs seriously. See Burton (1990).

Bourdieu, P. 1994. *La misère du monde*. Paris: Minuit.

Braybrooke, D. 1987. *Meeting needs*. Princeton, New Jersey: Princeton University Press.

Brundtland Commission. See WCED (1987).

Burton, J. (ed.) 1990. *Conflict: human needs theory*. New York: St Martin's Press.

Clark, M. 1990. Meaningful social bonding as a universal human need. See Burton (1990).

Dake, K. & M. Thompson 1993. The meaning of sustainable development: household strategies for managing needs and resources. In *Human ecology: crossing boundaries*, S. Wright, T. Dietz, R. Borden, G. Young, G. Guagnano (eds). Fort Collins, Colorado: The Society for Human Ecology.

Dasgupta, P. 1993. *An inquiry into well-being and destitution*. Oxford: Oxford University Press.

Dennett, D. 1988. *The intentional stance*. Cambridge, Massachusetts: MIT Press.

Douglas, M. 1986. *How institutions think*. Syracuse, New York: Syracuse University Press.

——— 1992. In defence of shopping. In *Produktkulturen: Dynamik und Bedeutungswendel des Konsums*, R. Eisendle & E. Miklautz (eds). Frankfurt: Campus. [Reprinted as "On not being seen dead: shopping as protest," in *Thought styles*, M. Douglas (Thousand Oaks, California: Sage, 1996).]

—— 1976. Relative poverty – relative communication. In *Traditions of social policy*, A. H. Halsey (ed.). Oxford: Basil Blackwell.

Douglas, M. & B. Isherwood 1979. *The world of goods*. New York: Basic Books.

Doyal, L. & I. Gough 1991. *A theory of human need*. London: Macmillan.

Drenowski, J. & W. Scott 1966. *Level of living index*. Report 4 (44–5). Geneva: United Nations Research Institute for Social Development [UNRISD].

Eatwell, J., M. Milgate, P. Newman (eds) 1987. *The new Palgrave: a dictionary of economics*. London: Macmillan.

Erikson, R. 1987. *The Scandinavian model, welfare states and welfare research*. Armonk, New York: M. E. Sharpe.

Fisher, R. 1990. Needs theory, social identity and an eclectic model of conflict. See Burton (1990).

Friedman, Y. 1990. The role of knowledge in conflict resolution. See Burton (1990).

Gadgil, M. & R. Guha 1995. *Ecology and equity: the use and abuse of nature in contemporary India*. London: Penguin.

Galtung, J. 1990. International development in human perspective. See Burton (1990).

Gasper, D. 1991. *Equity, equality, and appropriate distribution*. The Hague: Institute of Social Studies.

Gillwald, K. 1990. Conflict and needs research. See Burton (1990).

Green, R. 1976. Basic human needs. *IDS Bulletin* **9**(4), 7–11.

Greenpeace 1994. *Climate time bomb: signs of climate change from the Greenpeace database*. Amsterdam: Greenpeace International.

Guha, R. 1990. *The unquiet woods*. Delhi: Oxford University Press.

—— 1993. The malign encounter: the Chipko movement and competing visions of nature. See Banuri & Apffel Marglin (1993).

Habermas, J. 1962. *Strukturwandel der Öffentlichkeit*. Neuwied, Germany: Luchterhand.

—— 1973. *Legimitationsprobleme im Spatkapitalismus*. Frankfurt: Suhrkamp.

—— 1981. *Theorie des kommunikativen Handelns*. Frankfurt: Suhrkamp.

Held, D. 1980. *Introduction to critical theory*. Berkeley: University of California Press.

Houthakker, H. 1957. An international comparison of household expenditure patterns commemorating the centennial of Engel's law. *Econometrica* **25**(4), 532–51.

Hume, D. 1777 (1985). *Essays and treatises on several subjects* [1889 edn: *Essays: moral, political and literary*, edited by E. Miller, 308–326]. Indianapolis: Liberty Classics.

Islam, S. 1991. *The 1.5gW society*. Munich: Max Planck Institute.

Kamarck, A. 1983. *Economics and the real world*. Oxford: Basil Blackwell.

Kemp, P. & D. Wall 1990. *A green manifesto for the 1990s*. London: Penguin.

Lea, S., R. Tarpy, P. Webley 1987. *The individual in the economy: a survey of economic psychology*. Cambridge: Cambridge University Press.

Lederer, K. (ed.) 1980. *Human needs: a contribution to the current debate*. Cambridge, Massachusetts: Oelgeschlager, Gunn and Hain.

Leggett, J. (ed.) 1990. *Global warming: the Greenpeace report*. Oxford: Oxford University Press.

Livingstone, S. & P. Lunt 1992. Everyday conceptions of necessities and luxuries. In *New directions in economic psychology*, S. Lea, P. Webley, B. Young (eds). Cheltenham, England: Edward Elgar.

Marcuse, H. 1964. *One-dimensional man*. London: Routledge & Kegan Paul.

Marshall, A. 1890. On wants and their satisfaction. In *Principles of economics* (vol. III, pt 2). London: Macmillan.

Maslow, A. 1943. A theory of human motivation. *Psychology Review* **50**, 370–96.

Max-Neef, M. 1991. *Human scale development*. New York: Apex Press.

Meyer, A. 1994a. *Climate change, population and the paradox of growth*. London: Global Commons Institute.

——— 1994b. *Global climate change and the noose of equity and survival*. London: Global Commons Institute.

——— 1994c. *Pay now – live later*. London: Global Commons Institute.

Naess, S. 1979. *Om å ha det gedt i byen og på landet* [*On well-being in the city and the country*]. Oslo: Institute of Applied Social Research.

Nandy, A. (ed.) 1988. *Science, hegemony and violence: a requiem for modernity*. Bombay: Oxford University Press.

Nordhaus, W. 1991. To slow or not to slow: the economics of the greenhouse effect. *The Economic Journal* **101**, 920–37.

Nudler, O. 1980. A holistic model of human needs and wants. See Lederer (1980).

Nussbaum, M. & A. Sen (eds) 1993. *The quality of life: a study prepared for the World Institute for Development Economics Research of the United Nations University*. Oxford: Oxford University Press.

Ostrom, E. 1990. *Governing the commons: the evolution of institutions for collective action*. Cambridge: Cambridge University Press.

Pearce, D. (ed.) 1991. *Blueprint 2: greening the world economy*. London: Earthscan.

Plant, R. 1991. *Modern political thought*. Oxford: Basil Blackwell.

Prigogine, I. & I. Stengers 1984. *Order out of chaos: man's new dialogue with nature*. New York: Bantam.

Putnam, R. 1993. *Making democracy work: civic traditions in modern Italy*. Princeton, New Jersey: Princeton University Press.

Rader, V. 1990. Human needs and the modernization of poverty. See Burton (1990).

Rainbow, S. 1993. *Green politics*. Oxford: Oxford University Press.

Ramsay, M. 1992. *Human needs and the market*. Aldershot, England: Avebury.

Richardson, T. (ed.) 1995. *The green challenge: the development of green parties in Europe*. London: Routledge.

Rist, G. 1980. Basic questions about basic needs. See Lederer (1980).

Robbins, L. 1952. *The theory of economic policy in English classical political economy*. London: Macmillan.

Sahlins, M. 1968. *Stone Age economics*. London: Tavistock.

Sandole, D. 1990. The biological basis of needs in world society: the ultimate micro–macro nexus. See Burton (1990).

Schmutzer, M. 1994. *Ingenium und Individuum: eine sozialwissenschaftliche Theorie von Wissenschaft und Technik*. Vienna: Springer.

Scitovsky, T. 1992. *The joyless economy: an inquiry into human satisfaction and consumer dissatisfaction*, 2nd edn. Oxford: Oxford University Press.

Sen, A. 1981. *Poverty and famines: an essay on entitlement and deprivation*. Oxford: Oxford University Press.

——— 1993. Capabilities and well-being. In *The quality of life*, M. Nussbaum & A. Sen (eds). Oxford: Oxford University Press.

Sites, P. 1990. Needs as analogues to emotions. See Burton (1990).

Sorabji, R. 1993. *Animal minds and human morals: the origins of the Western debate*. London: Duckworth.

Springborg, P. 1981. *The problem of human needs and the critique of civilization*. London: George Allen & Unwin.

Stern, P., O. Young, D. Druckman (eds) 1992. *Global environmental change: understanding the human dimensions*. Washington DC: National Academy Press.

Sugden, R. 1993. Welfare, resources, and capabilities: a review of "Inequality reexamined" by Amartya Sen. *Journal of Economic Literature* **31**(4), 1947–62.

Taylor, P. 1959. "Need" statements. *Analysis* **19**(5), 106–111.

Thompson, M. 1986. *Uncertainty on a Himalayan scale*. London: Ethnographica.

Thompson, M., R. Ellis, A. Wildavsky 1990. *Cultural theory*. Boulder, Colorado: Westview.

UN 1993. *The United Nations Framework Convention on Climate Change*. London: HMSO.

UNDP 1990. *Human development report*. New York: Oxford University Press (for the United Nations Development Program).

——1992. *Human development report*. New York: Oxford University Press (for the United Nations Development Program).

WCED [World Commission on Environment and Development] 1987. *Our common future*. Oxford: Oxford University Press.

CHAPTER 4

Cultural discourses

Michael Thompson & Steve Rayner

Contributors
Luther P. Gerlach, Michael Grubb, Denise Lach, Steven Ney,
Mathew Paterson, Adam Rose, Peter Timmerman

Who talks about climate change? The experts on climate change, obviously, but also ordinary folk; "lay people," as those who study citizens' grasp of things climatic call them. Our discussion begins with a detailed look at some of the recent studies that have framed the climate change discourse along the lines of an expert/lay dichotomy of understanding. This includes studies that have used a mental models approach and others that have used a sociodemographic framework to examine perceptions of global change in relationship to variables such as age, class, and gender.

These approaches, it turns out, are Procrustean, and have to cope with the plurality of views that characterize the discourses by reducing or oversimplifying the data. The trouble stems from two hard-to-avoid assumptions that are built into the expert/lay distinction: first, that experts are all the same and are different from lay people (who are also all the same) and, second, that the experts have a clear understanding of climate change and the laity are rather confused about it. Neither of these assumptions, as we will see, is able the stand up for long, but at least this oversimple expert/lay distinction does enable us to get started on the important business of discourse analysis. Once we have started, we can learn where the initial assumptions are invalid and cast about for other, less simple, assumptions that better fit the heterogeneity that exists within each realm of discourse—expert and lay—and the remarkable isomorphisms that exist between those two realms.

That, in essence, is the structure that underlies this chapter: a structure that carries us from the oversimple assumptions that are embedded in the conventional expert/lay distinction, through the problems that are encountered when this distinction is applied to a more complex understanding of the essential heterogeneity of climate change discourse (expert and lay). Competing ideas about nature and about equity inform climate change policy debates at all levels from the family hearth to the international negotiation of the Framework Convention on Climate Change (FCCC). The chapter argues that, rather than being obstacles to be overcome, the uneasy coexistence of different conceptions of natural vulnerability and societal fairness is a source of resilience and the key to the institutional plurality that actually enables us to apprehend and adapt to our ever-changing circumstances.

Expert and lay perceptions of climate change

Recent surveys have shown that public support for environmental protection is strong, particularly in the industrialized countries where there is an expressed willingness to pay for products that do not harm the environment

(Harris et al. 1989). Many people say they have witnessed the deterioration of their local environments in their lifetimes and therefore have a direct experience of environmental problems. In the same vein, Hays (1987) has noted that concern for the local environment and for personal health is an important factor in support for local environmental protection schemes. Such observations fit well with what is called the *knowledge-based approach*, the assumption that people worry about the things that are worth worrying about: a commonsense assumption which, as we will see, does not hold up well.

A contrasting approach sees the rising curve of environmental concern as stemming from changes in ethical frameworks. White (1967), for instance, argues that the moral basis for environmental protection derives from the animistic religions of small traditional cultures that are still closely dependent on the land, but not from the Judeo-Christian tradition which, he claims, is anthropocentric and supportive of the view that humanity can transcend and dominate nature. On this argument, the protection of nature under the moral framework of the Judeo-Christian tradition would be justified only as *resource management*. Others, Berry (1988) and Rolston (1988) for instance, reject White's claim, arguing that the Judeo-Christian tradition can (and should) accord nature an intrinsic value. Nash (1989) has pointed to many instances where the Western tradition has had no great difficulty in recognizing nature's intrinsic rights.

The knowledge-based and ethical approaches, of course, are not mutually exclusive, and Heberlein (1972), taking a social psychological approach, has combined them as a way of explaining the upsurge of environmental concern that swept across the United States in the 1960s. Public awareness of the effects of pollution, he argues, together with the pinning of blame on those responsible for that environmental harm, helped to develop a *land ethic*, a concept borrowed from Leopold. According to this view, a thing is right when it tends to preserve the integrity, community and beauty of the natural environment. It is wrong when it tends otherwise. Dunlap & Van Liere (1977), however, have taken Heberlein to task, pointing out that his research is concerned only with the harm that environmental destruction does to humans, not to nature. Heberlein, they argue, has not grasped the land ethic, nor has he found evidence of any environmental norms that are consistent with such an ethic. All he has done is trace out, through some environmental linkages, the old rule, "Do unto others as you would have them do unto you." Explaining environmental concern, clearly, is not a straightforward business.

A consideration that looms large for many people (but by no means all) is the welfare of future generations. They are concerned that, if we mistreat the environment, the quality of life of their children and grandchildren will diminish. Their discount rate, economists would say, is low or even negative. MacLean

267

(1983: 194) has sought to explain this by arguing that meaning and happiness determine the quality of life, and that "a commitment to securing resources and opportunities for future generations . . . is an appropriate way of expressing our belief that the society and culture that matters to us are important enough to survive into the future." This explanation, in contrast to both the knowledge-based and ethical approaches, centers on the need to hold together something shared: a form of *social solidarity*. It does not require that the environment actually be deteriorating (only the shared perception that it is or may be), nor does it have to invoke a value shift (an uncaused cause) from anthropocentrism to ecocentrism. It also holds out the possibility of explaining why it is that not everyone shares this concern for future generations: they may be upholders of different forms of solidarity—the solidarity, for instance, that sustains those high-discount-rate characters who are careful to take no thought (anxious or otherwise) for the morrow. Such an approach is anti-Procrustean; it encourages us to recognize and respect the different perceptions that people (both lay and expert) have of how things are, why they are that way, and what if anything can and should be done about it.

Research focused more specifically on climate change has led to two main results. The first is that global climate change has become a concern not just among experts but also among lay people (Whyte & Harrison 1981, Doble et al. 1990, Löfstedt 1991). US figures reveal that, between 1982 and 1989, the percentage of people believing the "greenhouse effect" to be a "very serious problem" increased by roughly 30 percent (Dunlap 1991). The second is that lay people confuse global warming with other environmental problems such as ozone depletion (Henderson-Sellers 1990, Kempton 1991). That much is clear. The trouble starts, as we have already seen with environmental concern generally, when we attempt to account for this increased concern over climate change.

Those who subscribe (wittingly or unwittingly) to the knowledge-based approach focus, not surprisingly, on the various means by which the public acquire or fail to acquire their knowledge about global warming. The media's role in translating concerns from the natural sciences to the wider public receives much attention. So does the public's willingness and ability to acquire knowledge about climate change, and the related question of how and when that knowledge, once acquired, translates into a search for alternative courses of action. Public perception studies that have been framed in this knowledge-based way have tended to attribute the public's confusion to misguided public information campaigns and to the issuing of contradictory statements by policymakers.

Studies from around the world—Australia (Hedges 1991), Austria (Löfstedt 1993), Britain (Hedges 1991), Sweden (Löfstedt 1991), and the United States (Kempton 1991, Bostrom et al. 1994, Read et al. 1994, Kempton et al. 1995)—have all shown that many respondents do not distinguish between global warming and the thinning of the ozone layer: a potential source of communication difficulty for those who are endeavoring to inform the public.

Kempton et al. (1995) found that their subjects already had four clusters of knowledge—around the issues on stratospheric ozone depletion, tropospheric air pollution, plant photosynthesis, and seasonal and geographic temperature variation (to use very much the expert's terminology)—and that these were being used to sift and categorize new information. They suggest that these four pre-existing *mental models* explain why it is difficult to introduce a new concept—global warming or the greenhouse effect—to a lay person's *cognitive map*. Kempton et al. suggest that, because of all this sifting in terms of their pre-existing mental models, the accuracy of the detailed information that members of the public are receiving from media discussion or public awareness campaigns is largely irrelevant. The messages, rather, need to be designed in such a way that they can get through those sifting devices and onto the lay person's cognitive map.

Bostrom et al. (1994) found that many lay people (in the United States, that is; we should not necessarily expect these findings to hold true in India, say) believe that the climate has already become significantly warmer over the past few decades. Their study also found that the main causes of this perceived global warming are commonly identified by lay people to be aerosol spray cans, industrial emissions, automobiles, and general pollution. The term *greenhouse effect* has conjured up an image of a hot and steamy climate in the minds of the lay public, and very often there seems to be confusion between stratospheric ozone depletion and the greenhouse effect, and between weather and climate.

The effects of global climate change and stratospheric ozone depletion are similarly conflated, with perceptions ranging from increased rates of skin cancer to changes in agricultural yields. Some lay respondents, when asked what should be done about climate change, proposed that an artificial ozone layer should be created along with the development of an alternative fuel source for cars. Respondents tended to focus on regulating industrial emissions, restricting automobile use, and applying general methods of pollution control, whereas links to carbon dioxide and energy use were rarely mentioned. Lay respondents also appeared to be unfamiliar with recent international agreements and regulations, such as the phase-out of nonessential uses of chlorofluorocarbons. Other perceptions included the notion that space programs and the generation of electricity from nuclear power have contributed to global climate change.

The distinction between weather and climate is not easily grasped. Studies of public perceptions that set off from a clear distinction between weather and climate run into difficulties when, as soon happens, they come up against respondents who think of them as the same thing. Kempton's findings, in supporting the view that people are capable of directly perceiving weather but not climate, raise problems for those who would like the demand for action to be based on the perception that it is the climate that is changing. In seeking to address these problems, Kempton asked three questions:

- How do people make, and then draw conclusions from, casual weather observations?
- Would the average person notice if the climate began to change?
- Is the claim that climate change is caused by anthropogenic gases plausible to most lay people?

Only in the case of his third question did he approach a clear answer. His findings suggested that people (US people, that is) tend to believe that the weather is affected by human activities, particularly those human activities that are carried out in the atmosphere and that might be regarded as unnatural or immoral or both: for instance, space shots, atomic bombs, and pollution.

Farhar (1977) has shown that some Americans certainly object to deliberate attempts to change the weather (by cloud seeding, for instance), which comports with Kempton's inference that the perceived unnaturalness of the behavior is at the heart of much public concern. Farhar found that, among the same group, there is also a widespread belief that weather patterns have changed, a belief that the respondents say is based on their own observations (that the winters are warmer than they used to be, for instance).

Ludlum (1987) reveals that, during the colonial period in the United States, there was a widespread belief that the weather was warmer and less harsh than that described by earlier generations. One popular explanation was that the increased human activities—the felling of trees, in particular—had allowed more temperate winds from the coast to reach farther inland, and that the newly bared soil was receiving and holding more solar heat (Williamson 1771). Increased heating of buildings and smokepot rings were also seen as compounding the warming caused by deforestation. All in all, this is remarkably close to the present expert understanding of climate warming. Farhar et al. (1979) showed that, two centuries later, many Americans are still convinced that things are warming up. And, when asked how they knew this, the majority of respondents said it was through their direct observation of the weather.

Kempton (1991: 193) concluded that "we have a historical propensity to perceive weather change, whether or not it is occurring, and to attribute it to human perturbations." The present publicity and scientific concern about global warming therefore comport with the lay propensity to attribute changes in weather patterns to human activity, and it is this combination, Kempton et al. (1995: 85) suggested, that explains why "a potentially implausible hypothesis—that human activities will warm the entire planet—has been so readily picked up by the general public." Nor, we should note, is it safe to assume, as the expert/lay distinctions encourages us to assume, that this propensity is confined to lay people. Sir John Houghton (1995)—the eminent British scientist who chairs the IPCC Working Group I—even goes a step further and sees the catastrophes that are about to befall us as divine retribution.

Conclusions derived from the expert/lay distinction

Questionnaire research by Morgan et al. (1992) and Bostrom et al. (1992, 1994) indicated that lay people have what Read et al. (1994) called a "nonspecific mental model" of environmental risks in general and climate change in particular; a conclusion that is also supported by studies by Kempton (1991) and Kempton et al. (1995) and McDaniels et al. (1995). Morgan & Bostrom and their colleagues listed problems that they see lay people as facing, thanks to their nonspecific mental model:

- widespread belief that climate change is caused by general pollution (e.g., ozone in cities, toxic waste and dumping in the oceans) and that green regulatory policies and actions will prevent it
- failure to appreciate that carbon dioxide will be the primary cause of global warming if it occurs
- failure to understand that the main cause of carbon dioxide emissions is the burning of fossil fuels, that is, coal and oil
- confusion between the problems of stratospheric and tropospheric ozone
- confusion in differentiating between causes and actions specific to the climate change issue and more general good environmental practices
- belief, among 10–20 percent of the respondents to their questionnaires, that nuclear power and the space program contribute to global warming.

Further problems were revealed by the responses to more general questions about environmental change:

- belief, among 37 percent of respondents, that human action has changed the environment and the belief, among a further 61 percent, that it is "somewhat likely" that it has
- disparity between many lay people, who believe that global warming to date has exceeded 2°C, and many scientists, who believe that it has not exceeded 0.5°C (The IPCC predicts that global warming will occur at a rate of 0.3°C per decade if greenhouse gas emissions continue at their current levels. Respondents believed that the increase in temperature would be far more dramatic and the median from the survey was 2°C per decade, with 4°C in 50 years' time. Some estimates were as high as 20–30°C!)

The survey showed that the respondents (177 reasonably well-educated

Pittsburghers) clearly were concerned about global climate change and believed it was a significant threat requiring policies and regulations to prevent or reduce its effects. However, the different levels of understanding, and the varying perspectives on the problem, yielded a variety of mitigation strategies, which seems to suggest that the actions people are currently taking to prevent climate change may be misguided: that people will avoid using products such as spray cans, but will not change their patterns of energy consumption.

These conclusions, of course, assume that reasonably well-educated Pittsburghers are typical of the wider (global) population, that the experts have got it right, and the lay people have got it wrong, and that it's not possible to do the right things for the wrong reasons. Even so, the researchers are dismayed by the reluctance of decisionmakers to incorporate the findings of these public perception studies into practical public policy. Several reasons have been advanced as to why these findings are ignored (Weinberg 1966, Stern 1986, Schipper et al. 1989, Kempton 1993, Löfstedt 1995):

- The relationship between what people say in opinion surveys and what they actually do is tenuous, and the studies cannot act as accurate predictors of how the respondents will really behave.
- Policymakers tend to perceive the public as being concerned primarily with their economic situation. Thus, regardless of people's perception of global warming, policymakers adhere to the view that high energy prices are an effective restraint against inefficient and environmentally damaging energy use.
- Some decisionmakers hold the view that technology will solve environmental problems (e.g., fuel-efficient cars).
- Policymakers who propose a technological fix as the answer to global climate change problems are concerned that social scientists and their public perception studies will lead to a call for reduced lifestyles, which might discredit current energy conservation efforts.

Even so, those who view science's role in policy as one of speaking truth to power argue that well-designed studies of public perception can be helpful to policymakers. The frequent failures of large public environmental awareness campaigns, for instance, have led many policymakers to conclude that such campaigns should be abandoned. However, Löfstedt (1995) argued that such campaigns can be effective, and that those that fail do so because they are poorly designed. Careful survey work, he argued, can help put things right. A recent example is Britain's "Helping the Earth Begins at Home" campaign, which cost £6.2 million and was part of an effort by the government to stabilize Britain's carbon dioxide emissions in the year 2000 at the level that prevailed in 1990.[1] An evaluation of the campaign showed that its newspaper and television advertisements had failed to raise public awareness of global climate change and had no effect on energy efficiency in the homes of the British public. Yet the Hedges Report (commissioned by the Department of the Environment, which also managed the "Helping the Earth Begins at Home" campaign) showed that the British public were increasingly concerned about environmental problems but that they did not understand the linkages among diminishing natural resources, environmental hazards, and energy consumption.

Small wonder, Löfstedt pointed out, that the campaign failed; it was doomed from the outset because it ignored this basic public misunderstanding about the issue. However, such a conclusion like all the conclusions that are drawn from these public perception studies, rests on the assumption that there are right (expert) and wrong (lay) perceptions of climate change.

Alternative interpretations of lay (and expert) understandings

Rather than simple confusion of climate change and stratospheric ozone depletion, it may be that the distinction between them is not salient to a public that is concerned with human insult to the atmosphere or even to the more general environment. For many lay people, the climate change issue is perceived as part of a wider problem concerning humankind's disturbed relationship with nature. In this sense, climate change and ozone depletion are the same thing: they are members of the category of environmental insults deriving from industrial society. If industrial society is the problem, and if climate change and ozone depletion are interchangeable symbols or prototypes of the problem, then the specific etiology of each simply may not be relevant to the respondents to these surveys. Such an interpretation would be consistent with the notion that, over the past few decades, there has been a widespread ethical shift from materialistic to *postmaterialistic values* (Inglehart 1977, 1990) or to *the new environmental paradigm* (Steger et al. 1989). Possibly perception and concern for the environment rest on these general value orientations, rather than on knowledge about the explicit problems (Steel et al. 1990). Consequently, relevant knowledge for lay people is not composed solely of facts about the dynamics of climate change. Jaeger et al. (1993: 208) urged communication beyond the facts:

> Communicating the insights of natural scientists about climatic risks to a large public may be more effective if natural scientists consciously try to develop these insights in an ongoing dialogue with social scientists, philosophers, artists, etc. interested in the human dimensions of global change (Jaeger et al. 1993: 208).

---

1. These government efforts, it seems, were not necessary, because Britain is now on track to meet this emission target, thanks to the massive switch away from coal in the wake of the privatization of the energy industry.

This is not to say that people who have environmental concerns do not know what they are talking about; their concern is positively associated with knowledge about environmental problems. We suggest, however, that both variables—knowledge and concern—depend on underlying cultural orientations. The failure of public information campaigns may be attributable to their simplistic assumptions of public ignorance: assumptions that result in campaigns designed to displace the holistic concerns of the public with the scientific details involved in the etiology of specific problems. And if this is what is happening, then we should not be surprised if such campaigns miss the mark.

Disaggregating "the public" (and "the experts")

The simple expert/lay dichotomy encourages us to regard the public as an undifferentiated blob—an amorphous mass of homogeneous individuals— and it encourages survey research methods that tend to smear out systematic variations in public perceptions and values. Where differentiation is sought, it is usually assumed that it will be in the standard demographic variables: variables of the sort suggested by the behavioral tradition of social science. Thus, most research to date shows that the higher the level of education of an individual, the higher their degree of concern for the environment. Age appears to decrease an individual's level of environmental concern (Van Liere & Dunlap 1980, Samdahl & Roberston 1989), although Jaeger et al. (1993) found that it goes the other way in Switzerland. The influence of education on environmental concern can perhaps be explained by the fact that education enables individuals to gather and interpret science-based information. The effect of age on environmental concern, possibly, has to do with different generational expectations, and with events that have shaped these expectations differently over the past century. Steger & Witt (1989) also noted that women tend to be more concerned about the environment than men are, which may be attributable to gender-specific value orientations. However, each of these determinants is rather a weak predictor of environmental concern. After extensively reviewing the existing literature and their own social research data, Samdahl & Roberston (1989: 57–8) concluded that:

> traditional variables (sociodemographic characteristics, residence and political ideology) are largely inadequate in explaining the variance in perceptions of environmental problems or ecological behavior. Further research might benefit most by exploring underlying belief structures rather than demographic characteristics of the population.

This is likely to be the case increasingly as environmental concern becomes less of a research focus than actual environmental behavior (Ester & van der Meer 1982, Gray et al. 1985, Diekmann & Preisendörfer 1992). Research on the emergence of a so-called new environmental paradigm has already been quite successful in relating environmental behavior to underlying belief structures (Cotgrove 1982, Van Liere & Dunlap 1983, Dunlap & Van Liere 1984). This approach views industrial society as having had a specific set of basic beliefs about the world and humankind's place in it: a paradigm whose dominance is now being challenged by one that highlights the ways in which humankind is grounded in an ecological context that human beings must respect and understand. This, of course, is the *ethical shift* approach that we have already contrasted with the *knowledge-based* approach, and we should take great care to ensure that it is not invoked as an uncaused cause—a deus ex machina that gets us all from where we used to be to where we are now.

Instead of one homogeneous traditional blob, miraculously transformed into an equally homogeneous modern (or postmodern) blob, we need the idea that we always have been and always will be heterogeneous, with different social solidarities (and their supporting perceptions, discount rates and preferred solutions) pulling in different directions. The relative strengths of these solidarities will change over time, as will their patterns of interaction, and it is in these dynamic and structured contentions and transformations that we should seek to anchor our explanations.

For example, Jaeger et al. (1993) executed an ambitious project that recapitulates the line of argument we have been developing in this chapter. They began by setting up three models: one in which the flow of information from the natural sciences to the public is the crucial process (the knowledge-based approach), one in which the focus is on demographic variables such as age and sex (the standard behavioral approach) and one in which attention is centered on sociocultural processes (the ethical shift without the deus ex machina approach). Their project, in other words, put the various approaches in competition with one another—a commendably scientific procedure that is all too frequently shunned by social scientists. These three models were then brought down to Earth—to one specific part of the Earth, the Surselva Alpine region of Switzerland (Box 4.1).

The first model revealed, yet again, that knowledge about the risk of anthropogenic climate change among lay people leaves considerable room for improvement. But, instead of assuming that the closing of this knowledge gap was the obvious way to proceed, the study examined the relationship between education and relevant environmental action. Knowledge about the risks from climate change did have a positive effect, but it was not statistically significant. Much more important in providing and sustaining environmental action was

---

Box 4.1   The Surselva study—
a comparison of three explanatory frameworks

Jaeger et al. (1993) distinguished three models by different independent variables that might influence commitments to act on the problem of climate change:
• knowledge-based, focused on ability to provide accurate scientific information
• sociodemographic, based on variables like age and gender
• cultural networks, based on rule sharing and interpersonal contacts.

Jaeger et al. tested their hypothesis with three logit models that they formulated and tested with data gathered from the Surselva Alpine region in Switzerland. The Surselva was identified as a suitable region to study the possible effects of climate change for two reasons. The first is that severe winter storms have affected the region and damaged large tracts of mountain forest, there are fears that climate change could increase the frequency and severity of these storms. The second reason is that the region relies on pre-Christmas snowfall for its winter tourism and in recent years the snowfall has diminished. There are fears that climate change could affect the region in this regard as well. The Surselva region is also exposed to the discussion of global climate change in the national and international media.

The researchers distributed a questionnaire to a representative sample of 230 participants taken from the Surselva population, which totals about 23000. The questionnaire was designed after qualitative interviews were conducted with some of the region's inhabitants, so that a suitable format and focus could be found. The questionnaire followed a multidimensional approach to environmental concern (Maloney & Ward 1978). It contained eight items that were used to assess whether an individual was adopting climate-relevant environmental action. These included energy saving as well as political actions related to climate change. A distinction was made between knowledge and concern about global climate change.

The hypothesis of the researchers emphasized sociocultural variables following the work of Burns & Flam (1978) and Boyd & Richerson (1989), which regards culture as a dynamic set of interrelated rules. The new environmental paradigm and value orientations like post-materialism (Inglehart 1977) can be regarded as specific subsets of these rules. The survey contained items that queried whether or not a person "is exposed to cultural rules favoring climate-relevant environmental action among friends and relatives. The study focused on rules relevant to specific social contexts because they tend to be implemented in interpersonal relations (Shotter 1984). The researchers, recognizing these relations as social networks (Wellman & Berkowitz 1988), assessed people's involvement in networks where climate change issues are important.

The knowledge-based model
To the survey, 91 percent of the respondents replied that they had heard about the threats associated with climate change and 80 percent affirmed they had heard of the greenhouse effect. The survey established that there was a clear majority of people who had heard of the specific risks associated with climate change in the Surselva region. As shown in Figure A (Jaeger et al. 1993: 204), a large majority in the region considered the problem of climate change to be a matter for serious concern. The findings revealed that levels of concern did not necessarily equate to understanding of the basic scientific information (Fig. B). For example, only 28 percent of the survey respondents identified carbon dioxide as the main greenhouse gas. The other 72 percent said either that they did not know, or identified gases often mentioned in discussions about air pollution and global change.

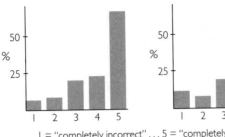

1 = "completely incorrect" . . . 5 = "completely correct"

"I think that climatic change due to human activities will have catastrophic effect."

"Human folly with regard to our environment will lead to huge climatic changes."

Figure A   Concern about the risk of climate change in Surselva, Switzerland.

Answer to the question: "Which one of the following substances is especially relevant for the greenhouse effect?"

Multiple-choice responses: "Don't know / carbon dioxide / nitrogen oxide / ozone / sulphur dioxide."

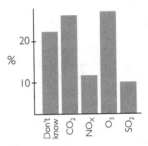

Figure B   Knowledge about the greenhouse problem in Surselva, Switzerland.

The survey established that the influence of education on climate-relevant environmental action is still unclear. Knowledge about the specific risks from climate change has a positive, but not statistically significant, effect. Playing a far more important role in provoking and sustaining environmental action in response to climate change is an underlying general concern about the global climate issue and, to a greater extent again, higher education. The latter may enable people to seek out and disseminate information about global climate change to a greater extent. However, it may simply be one of many sociodemographic characteristics that influence attitudes such as environmental concern and establish the inclination to take climate-relevant environmental action.

The sociodemographic model
The sociodemographic-focused model fares better than the knowledge-focused model. In this model, women are shown to be more likely to take climate-relevant environmental action than men, but gender is still a weak determining influence. Age is a stronger influence, and the findings of this study contradict the starting assumption that younger people are more likely to take environmental action relevant to climate change (Van Liere & Dunlap 1980, Samdahl & Robertson 1989).

Instead, the Jaeger et al. study shows that older people are more likely to take climate-relevant environmental action. This seems to be attributable to the nature of the community in the Surselva region, where it is likely that the older people have stronger emotional ties to their surrounding environment than do members of the younger generations, who are attracted to a modern urban existence. The study also found that occupational status influenced the dependent variable.

The cultural network model

The third model with sociocultural variables fares better than either the sociodemographic or knowledge-focused models. In order to assess their selection of variables, the researchers compared them with the widely discussed variable, postmaterialism (Inglehart 1977, 1990).[1] The findings showed that there was a significant impact on climate-relevant environmental action when postmaterialism was the only independent variable. However, when an independent variable for postmaterialism was added to the sociocultural model, the parameters of the variable were practically insignificant. Jaeger et al. subsequently posited that the statistical association between postmaterialist attitudes and climate-relevant environmental action suggested an effect that could be grasped by considering the three predicates—network density, interconnectedness, and rule sharing—used the sociocultural model (Jaeger et al. 1993: 207):

> Climate relevant environmental action definitely seems to depend on cultural rules and social networks related to the issue of climate change. However, the strong effect of political interest shows that rules and networks with a more general content can also have a clear impact.

---

1. Jaeger et al. (1993) treated postmaterialism as a continuous variable in order to facilitate comparisons with pre-existing literature on the subject.

a general underlying concern about the global climate change issue.

The demographic (or behavioral) model fared better than the knowledge-based model. Women were a little more likely than men to take climate-relevant environmental action, and older Swiss people are considerably more likely to do this than are younger Swiss people (this contradicts the starting assumptions of Van Liere & Dunlap 1980 and of Samdahl & Roberston 1989). However, Jaeger et al. concluded that it is differences in solidarity rather than differences in age that are responsible. The older Surselvans are deeply attached to each other and to their rural surroundings; the younger ones are more attracted to a nomadic and essentially urban existence.

The sociocultural model fared better than the other two. Climate-relevant environmental action, Jaeger et al. (1993: 207) concluded, "seems to depend on cultural rules and social networks related to the issue of climate change." Moreover, "rules and networks with a more general content can also have a clear impact."

By putting the three approaches in competition with one another, Jaeger et al. were able to draw some useful conclusions. First, the climate change issue for lay people was seen as part of a wider problem: humankind's disturbed relationship with nature. Second, relevant knowledge for lay people, in consequence, was not composed solely of facts about the dynamics of climate change. Third, information (drawn from the traditions of natural science, from cultural attitudes, and from a locally grounded common sense) that adds to their knowledge about the relationship between human beings and their environment would be most relevant for lay people.

Our discussion so far has shown that different people perceive the global climate change issue in different ways. We have examined some of the problems that this raises for public policy and have presented the arguments that are most visible at the surface of the climate change debate:

- Lay responses to surveys often do not distinguish climate change from other environmental issues such as stratospheric ozone depletion. Although some researchers interpret this as public confusion over scientific facts, it may be more valid to see such results as indicative of concern for a broad category of environmental issues: humankind's disturbed relationship with nature.
- The assumption of homogeneity in the categories of the expert/lay dichotomy overlooks the evidence that very different positions can be distinguished within each category.
- Variations in public perceptions and values relevant to climate change are better explained by the sociocultural variables of network density, interconnectedness, and rule sharing, than by either traditional demographic variables or general notions of postmaterialism.

These considerations suggest that social scientists seeking to interpret the societal conversation about climate change need to look beyond the expert/lay dichotomy. Our discussion now turns to theories that seek to do this by focusing on the sociocultural dynamics that both sustain and transform the various positions from which the global change discourse is conducted. These theories seek to capture this underlying plurality into typologies that are less Procrustean than the expert/lay distinction.

Collective representations of nature

Differing views of nature and of the proper relationship between people and the environment have been evident throughout history (e.g., Nash 1967). Early this century, the celebrated conflict between John Muir and Gifford Pinchot over the grazing of sheep in the US national forests set the tone for a protracted societal debate between preservationists, who wanted natural resources preserved intact for their own sake, and conservationists, who sought managed exploitation of such resources. In Britain, by contrast, the wilderness ideal has proved less attractive, with the national parks crystallizing around Gray's ideal of a landscape in which man is an essential: one in which "all is peace, rusticity and happy poverty in its neatest and most becoming attire" (quoted in Wordsworth 1810: 70). Since the formation of the Club of Rome in 1968, there has been a persistent parallel contrast in America and Europe between *catastrophists*, who advocate limited growth, steady state economics, and the regulatory preservation of the environment, and *cornucopians*, who advocate unrestricted economic growth and a laissez-faire attitude in which the market determines when and where the natural environment should be preserved or modified (Meadows et al. 1972, Cotgrove 1982, Bloomfield 1986).It is to these that we now turn. Table 4.1 shows the elements of the cornucopian and catastrophist paradigms.

Table 4.1   Elements of the cornucopian and catastrophist paradigms (Cotgrove 1982: 27).

	Dominant paradigm	Alternative environmental paradigm
Core values	Material (economic growth) Natural environment valued as resource Domination over nature	Nonmaterial (self-actualization) Natural environment intrinsically valued Harmony with nature
Economy	Market forces Risk and reward Differentials Individual self-help	Public interest Safety Incomes related to need Egalitarian* Collective/social provision

Polity	Authoritative structures
	  (experts influential)
	Hierarchical
	Law and order
		Participative structure
		  (citizen/worker involvement)
		Nonhierarchical*
		Liberation*

Society	Centralized Large-scale Associational Ordered	Decentralized Small-scale Communal Flexible*
Nature	Ample reserves Nature hostile/neutral Environment controllable	Earth's resources limited Nature benign Nature delicately balanced
Knowledge	Confidence in science and technology Rationality of means Separation of fact/value, thought/feeling	Limits to science Rationality of ends Integration of fact/value, thought/feeling

* Some environmentalists want a return to small-scale communities because they provide a traditional organic order—differentiated, hierarchical, and stable.

Cornucopians, Cotgrove (1982) argued, are entrepreneurial types who view nature as intrinsically robust and overflowing with an abundance of readily exploitable resources. On the other hand, catastrophists are represented by the modern environmental movement. Their view of nature is that it is fragile and vulnerable to the plundering actions of the cornucopians. Cotgrove examined the underlying assumptions of both groups and found that, beyond their conflicting views of nature, the catastrophists and the cornucopians have fundamentally different views on social relations, organization, science and technology, and that their core values and moral judgments are in conflict with one another. Cotgrove (1982: 28) described the ethos of the cornucopians as follows:

> The creation of "wealth" for the industrialists is a moral imperative. And if wealth is the name of the game, then the rules for winning that game follow: rewards for enterprise and risk, a free market, and creating a climate in which individuals are motivated to look after themselves and not to turn to others.

In comparison, he argued, the catastrophists

> not only challenge the importance attached to material and economic goals, they by contrast give much higher priority to the realization of non-material values—to social relationships and community, to the exercise of human skills and capacities, and to increased participation in decisions that affect our daily lives.

The catastrophist/cornucopian dichotomy is a variation on a dualistic typology that has long prevailed in the social sciences as a way of explaining social diversity and competing worldviews. More commonly, the traditional typology has defined the differences between market-driven values, and the regulatory structures of a hierarchical system. The market/hierarchy dichotomy has been elaborated upon in many ways (e.g., Williamson 1975, Lindblom 1977), and as worldviews they are perhaps most readily identifiable, thanks to the conflictual discourse between market incentives and social sanctions that they so readily provoke. Cotgrove's analysis differed from this traditional typology in that his conflictual discourse was between the market view and that of the modern environmental movement. The value orientation of the catastrophists that Cotgrove described introduces a different range of strategies from either market-driven interests or regulation-prone hierarchies, and tends toward a more egalitarian set of beliefs about nature and social organization, one in which people come together in respecting nature's rights, rather than to manage nature (which is the hierarchy's aim) or to commoditize it (which is the market's aim). However, the reduction of societal diversity and complexity to the dichotomy that Cotgrove defined is a simplification that does not capture some other interesting and equally valid positions in the social discourse about the problems of global change.

In their study of cultural orientations and environmental perspectives among the American public, Kempton et al. (1995) described three sets of general environmental models. The first set concerns nature as a limited resource upon which humans rely. The second set relates to notions of nature as balanced, interdependent and unpredictable. The third set are the cultural models relating to society and nature. In particular, Kempton et al. focused on the market's devaluation of nature and the accompanying societal alienation from nature which leads to it being appreciated less but, in some instances, idealized more. They argued that the models of nature they described are applicable to all environmental problems, not just those associated with global change, and that they form the basic underpinnings of public perception of the environment:

> They are used to understand global environmental problems, they reinforce and justify environmental values, and they are the basis for reasoning that leads to preferences for some environmental policies over others. (Kempton et al. 1995: 39)

Based on their survey work, Kempton et al. (1995) suggested that the dependence of humans on the environment is often expressed, in its most survival-conscious form, as a health concern. For example, people link pollution, chemicals, and human interference in the environment with diseases and with psychosocial as well as physical health problems. Kempton's study also showed that people were more likely to identify examples of pollution that could be seen, and that they perceived the Earth as a closed system, vulnerable to the effects of human activity. This perception is closely linked to the notion of the environment as being home, which differs from the alternative notion of home as a sanctuary against a wild and threatening nature; a notion that was in decline but not extinct.

The Kempton et al. study also revealed an expectation of significant changes in the environment if factors such as species loss, climate change, and increased pollution were to occur. Often, respondents referred to the "balance of nature," which they clearly considered to be quite delicate, and referred to the interactions between humans and the environment as "chain reactions." However, they also revealed a perception of nature as resilient, and to some extent self-healing, in response to small perturbations. Larger perturbations, however, were viewed as more likely to be catastrophic. In addition, there were those who perceived nature as unpredictable in its response to human-induced change and took a conservative stance about altering or intervening in the natural system in any way.

Here, we see the heterogeneity begging to be revealed and Kempton, for his part, giving it a helping hand. If people have different perceptions of nature, and if some people, in consequence, denounce behavior that others see as eminently reasonable, then we can begin to see how it is that different opinions emerge in environmental debates. Once again, in defiance of the expert/lay dichotomy, the Kempton et al. findings closely match the *myths of nature* that have been identified by theoretical ecologists (Holling 1986).

Nature myths and narratives

In social science parlance, myths are not fictions or fanciful tales. Certainly, they do not represent falsehoods, but they are stories that embody fundamental truths underlying our assumptions about everyday or scientific reality. Conventionally, myths, like histories, take a narrative form because it "is the chief literary form that tries to find meaning in an overwhelmingly crowded and disordered reality" (Cronon 1992: 1349). Also, like histories, myths are selective. They achieve coherence only by excluding those elements that do not contribute to the tale. "In the act of separating story from non-story, we wield the most powerful yet dangerous tool of the narrative form. . . . Whatever its overt purpose, it cannot avoid a covert exercise of power: it inevitably sanctions some voices while silencing others." (Cronon 1992: 1349–50).

Cronon, an environmental historian, traced four quite distinctive narrative histories of the Great Plains, focusing on the Dust Bowl events of the 1930s. Each of these histories recounts essentially the same events, but each tells a fundamentally different story about nature and humanity and the relationship between them. Two of these accounts are *progressive* histories of immigrant pioneers domesticating a wild and empty landscape. They differ essentially in the degree to which nature is a passive resource to be shaped like a vessel out of clay or an active antagonist that resists its own improvement.

Both of the remaining accounts are *declensionist* in that they describe how human intervention in a fragile ecosystem led to degradation of the land. One of these is unremittingly catastrophist. It is that of the Crow Indian chief, Plenty Coups, who wrote, "When the buffalo went away the hearts of my people fell to the ground, and they could not lift them up again. After this nothing happened." (Linderman 1930: 311). This was truly the end of nature and the end of history. However, the second declensionist narrative has a happier ending with the managerial intervention of the New Deal. According to this version, the destruction of the Plains ecosystem resulted from people continuing to tell themselves the wrong story. Having settled their lands in an anomalously wet interlude, the new inhabitants regarded the return of the more prevalent dry conditions as a drought anomaly and they failed to migrate or adapt. In the end, the Great Plains and their hapless inhabitants were rescued in the nick of time by the scientific planning and technology-based intervention of the state, which tapped vast underground water resources for irrigation.

Each one of these narratives contains true elements, yet each is a coherent story only because of what it doesn't tell, but the others do. Attempting to tell all four stories simultaneously leaves us with only an incoherent chronology and a contradictory set of messages. Mythological narratives can also be condensed or compressed into icons that simultaneously represent the essential elements of a story. Icons vary from the immensely sophisticated and complex public representations of Renaissance painting to simple diagrams used in technical communication within scientific disciplines. A potent example of such compression is the iconography devised by ecologist Holling to describe the assumptions about nature underlying the seemingly disorganized and contradictory spruce-budworm control strategies practiced by Canadian foresters. Holling discerned that there was a consistent pattern in these diverse interventions. The problem he faced was that if the managers were irrational there would be no discernible patterns to what they did; if they were all conventionally rational, they would all do the same. Hence, Holling asked himself, what are the minimal representations of reality that must be ascribed to each managing institution if it is to be granted the dignity of rationality? He found that he needed at least three representations, which he called *myths of nature*, each of which could be compressed into a little picture of a ball in a landscape (Holling 1986). Figure 4.1 illustrates these myths of nature.

The myth of a *benign* nature purports that the natural environment is favorable toward humankind. It is supportive of the concept of global equilibrium, that is, no matter what humans do to their environment, it will renew, replenish and re-establish its natural order without fail. No matter which way the ball is

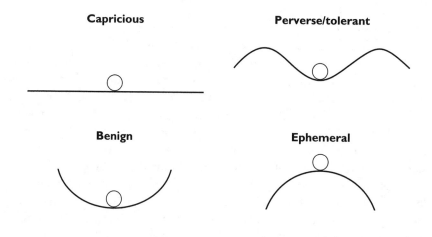

Figure 4.1 The four myths of nature (Thompson 1987).

knocked, the steeply sloping sides of the basin always return it to its secure starting point. It is a myth that supports a level of confidence in action, it both encourages and justifies a trial-and-error approach and experimentation in the face of uncertainty. Consequently, the learning and knowledge selection that is achieved within the framework of this myth justifies managing the natural environment as an intrinsically robust system.

The countermyth to the view that nature is benign, is the myth that it is *ephemeral*. Far from being stable, the natural environment is seen to be in a precarious and very delicate state of balance. The least disturbance or upheaval may trigger a complete collapse in the system. The ball is precariously balanced on the top of an upturned basin, where the slightest movement will cause irreparable damage. This myth supports a cautious approach in managing nature. It suggests a more reactive than proactive learning and knowledge selection process, which supports the notion that nature is vulnerable and therefore requires protection.

The illustration of the third myth, that of nature *perverse/tolerant*, might appear to suggest that it is a hybrid of the two myths above. However, it is very different. Although it acknowledges a certain degree of uncertainty as being inherent in the system, it assumes that management can limit any disorder and that a state of equilibrium can be maintained. Subsequently, the learning and knowledge selection processes that occur within the framework of this myth support neither the unbridled experimentation maintained by the myth of nature benign, nor the cautious, restrictive behavior encouraged by the myth of nature ephemeral. Instead, it maps and manages the boundary lines between these two approaches. Certainty and predictability are the main goals that drive the learning and knowledge selection process of the nature perverse/tolerant myth.

To those three, Thompson (1987) added a fourth, that of nature *capricious*, represented by a ball on a flat surface, liable to move unpredictably in response to any perturbation. It is likely that Holling did not encounter this myth among forest managers, for the same reason that it plays only a minor role in debates about climate change. That is because the myth of nature capricious is associated with a fatalistic world outlook that does not actively engage in management or debates about managing natural resources, which are, to those who hold this myth, in principle unmanageable (see Fig. 4.1).

Timmerman (1986) argued that myths of equilibrium (nature benign and nature perverse/tolerant) have prevailed in the industrialized world and that this has seriously affected the adoption of strategies to cope with phenomena such as global change. The equilibrium myths tend to disregard questions of instability and to ignore the unpredictable, and this has supported a way of thinking that is focused on control and stability seeking.

Such a line of reasoning suggests that the need to explain the concept of social order has led economics to support the myth of an ideal historical equilibrium; the notion that the social system is approaching, and will arrive at, a point of perfect stability. From the perspective of fairness, this would be the condition of Pareto optimality (Box 4.2). An additional weakness, Timmerman argued, has been the intolerance of this mythical model to externalities and its rulings out of alternatives that it cannot capture (but other myths can). The significant challenge to this myth of stability is that the system is approaching crisis, not equilibrium (e.g., Marxist thought). The idea that nature is fragile (nature ephemeral) and cannot be treated as a bundle of resources to fuel the market system also forms the basis for much of the modern environmental movement and

---

Box 4.2   Pareto optimality

The foundation of the neoclassical approach to welfare is consumer sovereignty, according to which the goal of policy is to enable households to maximize their satisfaction in accordance with their given set of preferences. Welfare comparisons are possible only between populations of identical size—in a world of 6 billion people, the social welfare function (presumably comprising aggregated individual utility functions) may be $U(X)$ where X is the range of available goods, but in a world of 12 billion people it might be $U'(X')$—which immediately invalidates the idea of optimum population size. There may be no end of reasons why a world of 12 billion is inferior to a world of 6 billion, but they are not to be found in utilitarian welfare theory or in the neoclassical economics that it supports. Interpersonal welfare comparisons are impossible, so the only practical criterion is that of Pareto optimality.

In a Pareto optimal (or Pareto efficient) world, no one party can be made better off without making another party worse off. Thus, there are no slack resources in the system. Pareto efficiency is quite compatible with inequality; for example, a society consisting of a king and a slave is as Pareto efficient as a world consisting of two middle-class persons, so long as you could not make one party better off without making the other party worse off. An intertemporal allocation of natural resources and environmental assets is Pareto efficient if no redistribution between generations could make one generation better off without making another generation worse off—all subject to time discounting.

When called upon to address the problem of morally repugnant Pareto optimal distributions, the reply of neoclassical economics is that the choice of income distribution is really up to the moral hierarchy—loosely speaking, the bundle of beliefs and institutions that can force you to do something against your own strict self-interest and impose harsh consequences if you do not—to establish through the political process. Many things in the world, skewed income distributions among them, are morally wrong, but not necessarily economically inefficient.

The view of fairness that prevails in neoclassical economics is based on an open, flexible, and unbiased market in which each participant is free to maximize utility, subject to given references. It is a disciplinary commonplace that a perfect market gives rise to a Pareto-optimal outcome; less obvious is that, in a Pareto-optimal world, since all utility-increasing trades have taken place, the market must have been open, flexible, and unbiased. In other words, and underappreciated by economists, Pareto optimality embodies a very particular view of fairness. Whether a market is "fair" or not, that is, whether it is an open and level playing field or not, is an empirical and hence a positive question, but whether or not markets should be used to redistribute benefits is a value-based question..

for the value system that Cotgrove describes in his definition of catastrophists.

Holling (1986) treats the states of stability and instability in slightly different terms, and in so doing leads us back to questions of sustainability and the appropriateness of policy responses to the surprises that global environmental change may present. A policy actor's view of nature, Holling points out, is not something that can be changed at will; whether it be perverse/tolerant, ephemeral or benign, it is supplied by his (or her) solidarity with other policy actors, and thus his strategy is fixed. However, explanations for the complexities of the natural system as it functions, organizes, and copes with internal and external change are to be found in the continuous interaction of these diverse, competing rationalities. Holling cites several examples of apparently chaotic and destructive forces serving as mechanisms for the renewed growth and sustainability of natural ecosystems (in particular, the action of forest fires in creating new growth and maintaining the long-term viability of certain types of forest environments). Humankind has intervened in this process, with the result that, when the controlling factors falter or fail, the magnitude of the disruption created can defeat the regeneration process entirely. Thus, within the extreme scenarios of nature as either unstable or stable, there lies the reality of nature functioning in a resilient and adaptive fashion. Resilient nature is not a perspective that is captured by any one of the myths of nature alone; it is best interpreted through a collective plurality of views. Humankind's response to change and surprise can thereby reflect the operation of the natural system (Holling 1986: 311):

> Just as ecosystems have their own inherent response times, so do societal, economic, and institutional systems. How long an inappropriate policy is successful depends on how slowly the ecosystem evolves to the point when the increasing fragility is perceived as a surprise and potential crisis. The response to such surprises is alarm, denial, or adaptation and is similarly related to the response times of different groups in society and of the management institutions.

Consequently, for the organization of human action in relation to global change, time and context prove to be important factors affecting the selection of strategies for action.

Those theoreticians who grapple with the concept of cultural plurality, and with the diversity of worldviews that make up social organization, have to balance on a knife-edge (or, rather, an Occam's razor-edge). They have to make sense of the variation in a parsimonious way without simplifying it to such an extent that it proves incapable of capturing the range and diversity of forms and meanings that actually exist. Svedin (1993) argued that adding the dimension of time captures the extent to which views and perceptions of nature and the world have changed and progressed, a view with which many cultural historians would concur. However, Sörlin (1993), in recounting the findings of John Evelyn, a member of the Royal Society of London, seem to suggest that perceptions and concerns have not changed drastically over the centuries. Evelyn's findings were presented to King Charles II in a 1661 volume entitled *Fumifugium, or The inconvenience of the aer and smoak of London dissipated*, which documented the effects of pollution on human health and mortality rates. Although his agenda for action, presented to parliament in 1662, was never acted upon, Evelyn's investigation and recommendations were remarkably similar to the research and activity that is generated by today's global change discourse. Agendas that are designed in response to pollution and climate change seem to be affected, as were Evelyn's, by perceptions of the problem's severity and by the unexamined assumptions of the institutions that instigate, organize and support action for change. Even so, time *does* matter (Sörlin 1993: 129):

> The cumulative damage and the accumulated knowledge reinforce one another in an interesting way. Knowledge alone, or the damage alone, would not have had the same effect.

So, is there nothing new under the sun or does the world get made afresh each morning? The answer, of course, is both. As Heraclitus put it, "We step and do not step into the same river," from which we may safely conclude that achieving a close global climate change shave with Occam's razor is not going to be easy. But then, as an Australian prime minister once said, "Life wasn't meant to be easy."

Myths of nature and views of climate change

Perhaps we should pause at this point and consider where we have got to in this chapter and where we are going:

- Are the conflicts and discourses over global climate change that we are caught up in today really different from conflicts and discourses about knowledge and social organization as they have occurred throughout history?
- Are the patterns of social organization and the perceptions of nature that, we argue, are framing the discourse particular to certain cultures or nations (or even to reasonably well-educated Pittsburghers) or are they instances of broad crosscutting themes that endlessly replay themselves in human perception and organization on a global scale?

288

Our review of the state of play so far suggests that differing perceptions in the climate change debate are deeply embedded and firmly held, and that these recurrent regularities do transcend the particularities of both time and space. We would add, in the same breath, that the particularities of time and space should not be disregarded when it comes to understanding the ways in which these universalities work their way through into specific localities at specific moments in history. Two more questions now arise:

- Is the discourse reflecting a debate that goes deeper than the surface issue of climate change, a debate that is fundamentally among different world-views and competing value systems?
- If it is, how do we relate surface to substrate, how do we recognize and understand these underlying features, and how can we measure them?

The points of conflict in the climate change debate, and the way in which they tend to resurface through all attempts at resolution, indicate that there *are* different underlying and fundamental perspectives jostling for position. And others can be identified by their inactive role in the debate or by their absence from it. On the question of access—how to recognize, understand and measure this substrate—we suggest that the answer lies in casting about for the other values that help each of these solidarities to cohere and, at the same time, distance itself from the others. In that way, a clearer and more complete picture of these depths—the myths of nature and their holders—can be drawn.

Climate change diagnosis and prescriptions

Environmental debates (at both the international and domestic levels) tend to be dominated by a particular set of themes that establish a rhetorical framework to which the representation of rival views must be adapted if they are to be accepted into the discourse. Rayner (1994) referred to these dominant themes as *hegemonic myths*. The usage, as with the myths of nature we have just discussed, is an anthropological one, designating fundamental propositions or assumptions that are unquestionable within the context of a particular discourse. It does not carry any implication as to their truth or falsity.

In contrast to the approach adopted by Haas (1990), hegemonic myths do not represent the triumph of a shared episteme or worldview. Rather, they set the rhetorical terms within which rival views and myths continue to compete, although in a more subdued manner. Arguments based on rival myths are likely to accept the general rhetorical assertions of the hegemonic myth while providing for specific elaborations or exceptions that effectively undermine it—a "Yes, but . . ." approach to debate.

What a rival myth cannot do is directly challenge a hegemonic myth and expect to remain a credible participant in the dialogue. For example, President Bush's environmental rhetoric was directed toward reassuring his domestic free-market business constituency. He emphasized scientific uncertainty in climate models and the vulnerability of the global economy to the perceived costs of preventive action, which brought him into direct conflict with the hegemonic myth of global fragility (described in detail below). As a result, the United States was left relatively isolated in international negotiations. In contrast, while remaining even more aggressively dedicated to the free-market system, Margaret Thatcher donned the green mantle in 1989 and placed the British government in the mainstream. Upon taking office, the Clinton administration followed the Thatcherite path, adjusting its environmental rhetoric while remaining firmly committed to a free-market strategy with respect, for example, to the North American Free Trade Agreement and the General Agreement on Tariffs and Trade, both of which were largely opposed by American environmentalists.

The myth of global vulnerability and fragility is the hegemonic myth that has emerged in the course of both the climate change debate and the broader global environmental change debate of which it is a part (Cantor & Rayner 1994). For example, the principal architect of the Montreal Protocol on that Deplete the Ozone Layer wrote (Benedick 1991: 199):

Perhaps the most poignant image of our time is that of Earth as seen by the space voyagers: a blue sphere, shimmering with life and light, alone and unique in the cosmos. From this perspective, the maps of geopolitics vanish, and the underlying interconnectedness of all the components of this extraordinary living system—animal, plant, water, land, and atmosphere—becomes strikingly evident.

This immensely powerful symbol consists of three elements. First, the imagery of the Earth itself emphasizes fragility. The adjectives "blue," "shimmering," and "light" all evoke, and are designed to evoke, a delicate object, easily broken. "Alone" and "unique" stress another aspect of vulnerability: that the object, once lost or shattered, never can be rescued or restored. The second element in this symbol evokes the complexity and interdependence of the systems of life on Earth. Interestingly, in addition to land, water, and atmosphere, which are clearly visible in such photographs, the writer supplies the details of plant and animal life, which are not observable, as if they are part of the visible image at the global scale. The third component of this symbol emphasizes the claim that human divisions, "the maps of geopolitics," are somehow artificial illusions of local ethnic, political, and economic independence that vanish once the quintessential truth of environmental interdependence is grasped. What is presented as a simple perception of reality is really a carefully constructed mythic vision of a fragile system of natural interdependence endangered by our own hubris.

According to a rival myth—the Gaia hypothesis—the Earth may be a dynamic self-adjusting system in the process of developing greater capacity to absorb carbon. Certainly, we know that there is a carbon fertilization effect that stimulates biomass growth in the presence of elevated carbon dioxide levels. In contrast, the myth of global vulnerability and fragility assumes a static biosphere, except where perturbed by human agency, and it conveniently ignores the fact that, according to the climate models, we should already be experiencing a detectable increase in global average temperatures greater than the 0.3–0.5°C that has occurred over the past century (Houghton et al. 1990). The myth of global vulnerability and fragility also excludes consideration of potential benefits accruing from global warming. If—admittedly a huge "if"—we are entering a period of natural global cooling which is being offset by anthropogenic warming, the sustainability of significant human populations may depend on elevated emissions of greenhouse gases.

It is important to realize how pervasive the myth of global vulnerability or fragility is within the environmental sciences, especially when we recall that the concept of global carrying capacity (the nature ephemeral myth that gives us the fixed pie) is imported directly from ecology. In fact, however, ecologists often bemoan the absence of any established theoretical principle that would permit them to make predictions about large-scale ecosystem behavior on the basis of micro-scale observations. Yet the same ecologists who explicitly state that they are unable to assess the ecological health of the globe by aggregating or otherwise extrapolating from individual instances of ecosystem degradation also claim that the Earth is headed for cataclysmic destruction if we do not radically change industrial behavior within the next 30–100 years. Their intuition, not their science, drives the myth of global vulnerability and fragility.

We are no better off in assessing the overall vulnerability of human society to environmental fluctuation. Not only is this a matter of controversy, it might even be a misleading question, given the many dimensions of vulnerability, the change evident in both natural and human systems, and the value judgments implicit in selecting specific indicators. Although it is clear that the burdens of environmental degradation fall disproportionately on marginal peoples, especially the landless poor, there is once again no clear theoretical connection between climate change and food security issues. The extension of the notion of carrying capacity from individual ecosystems to the level of global socioeconomic systems can be justified only by faith (Box 4.3).

The prospect of spectacular global catastrophe is not the only basis for

Box 4.3   Prevention, adaptation and sustainable development

Schelling (1983) was one of the earliest commentators who attempted to define the terms of the societal discourse concerning climate change response strategies as a debate between advocates of *prevention* and of *adaptation*. Prevention was favored by those who saw climate change as a clear and immediate threat to both nature and society. Adaptation was embraced both by skeptics, who did not invest prophesies of impending climatic disaster with much credibility anyway, and by fatalists, who viewed the planetary commitment to global warming as already being irreversible.

We can begin to see how these defining cleavages are themselves formed from opportune hybridizations of the fundamental myths of nature we have just described. Adaptation, for instance, unites (for a time, that is) skeptics (who are convinced that nature is benign) and fatalists (who are convinced that nature is capricious). Prevention similarly provides the basis for a temporary alliance between those who feel that we are (or are in danger of) approaching operating beyond the limits (nature perverse/tolerant) and those whose myth (nature ephemeral) insists that there are no safe limits. Pairwise alliances such as these are always open to surprises from those parts of the natural system that are working in ways that those alliances have ruled out, and they can also be caught off-balance by unexpected human actors whose myths they have excluded: Greenpeace's helicopters, for instance, landing on the Brent Spar oil platform as it was being towed toward what both Shell's managers and the British government's scientific advisers had agreed should be its final resting place. These sorts of perturbations impart an erratic trajectory to the entire debate and to the policy process that it feeds into.

Prevention versus adaptation, although it provided a means by which two pairwise alliances could be formed, put development very much on one side (the adaptation side) and sustainability very much on the other (the prevention side), which was not an acceptable way of framing things to those, such as Mrs Bruntland, who wanted the two to go together. Accordingly, in the 1980s, a third position emerged, focused on *sustainable development*—a hybridization of two of the fundamental myths, one (nature perverse/tolerant) from the *prevention* side and one (nature benign) from the *adaptation* side. Each of these approaches was supported by its own characteristic moral imperative and pair of myths. These three positions then described the extreme boundaries of the debate. Of course, a variety of less extreme positions could be identified within the two-dimensional space they defined (Rayner 1991), all of which could be reached from one or other of the three positions by adjusting the heights and depths of the basins representing the two fundamental myths from which it was formed (see Fig. 4.1).

In its most extreme form, the prevention strategy was compared to that of the positions of the Reagan administration on drugs and of the American religious Right on teenage pregnancy (Rayner 1991). All that was necessary to prevent the unwanted consequence was to persuade people to "just say 'No,'" and modify their behavior accordingly. Proper choices in this scenario would be reinforced by regulation and legal sanctions. From this standpoint, discussion of adaptation to climate change was viewed with the same distaste that the religious right reserves for sex education in schools. That is, both constitute ethical compromises that in any case will only encourage dangerous experimentation with the undesired behavior. The preventivist strategy is underpinned therefore by a conviction that it is morally wrong to distort natural processes by human behavior. The nature myth here is that of a fragile environment easily subject to irreversible catastrophic change: a ball precariously balanced on an upturned basin. The managing institutions must treat the system with great care.

The second strategy was that of adaptation. The extreme form of this view saw global environmental change as presenting new opportunities for human ingenuity that would be revealed through the workings of the marketplace. The ethical imperative driving this position was that it is morally wrong to curtail economic development and condemn the poor people and nations of the Earth to permanent deprivation of the benefits of modern industrial society. The nature myth underpinning adaptation is that which sees the environment as flexible, resilient to change, and cornucopian in its ability to provide resources for human use: a ball inside a basin. No matter what knocks we deliver to the system, the ball will return to the bottom of the basin. Managing institutions can afford a laissez-faire approach.[1]

In response to this dialectical thesis and antithesis, a predictable synthesis emerged, represented by the ideal of sustainable development. According to this third view, you can have your cake and eat it: global catastrophe can be avoided by careful stewardship of the limited opportunities that nature provides for controlled growth. The ethical imperative here is to preserve choice for future generations. The nature myth is that of a system that is resilient within knowable limits that must not be transgressed. "Its world is one that is forgiving of most events, but is vulnerable to an occasional knocking of the ball over the rim" (Schwarz & Thompson 1990: 5). These three positions crudely summarize the political rhetoric of climate change in the 1980s. In the 1990s the positions have become more sophisticated and, at first sight, more closely reconciled around a general scientific consensus that climate change is indeed a real prospect. However, the appearance of convergence is deceptive, resulting from the hegemonic status of the myth of global vulnerability and fragility described above.

---

1. In each of these extreme cases we see the pairwise alliance lurching all the way to the more extreme of the fundamental myths from which it is formed: nature ephemeral is the preventionist case and nature benign is the adaptationist case.

advocating reductions of greenhouse gases. Even without a major global perturbation, it is likely that moderate changes in weather patterns will lead to more poor people, largely in less industrialized countries, going hungry, getting sick, and dying prematurely. However, the specter of global disaster provides a stronger justification for implementing whatever remedy is preferred by one or another of the voices that can be heard in the debate than can be derived from predictions of more misery among the already poor.

Since the construction of nature as fragile represents a hegemonic bound on the climate change debate, any voice that does not acknowledge the idea that nature is fragile abdicates its claim to legitimacy in the conversation. However, beyond that level of formal agreement, the climate change discourse moves rapidly from an initial consensus that there is a "climate change problem" to profound disagreement about the nature and definition of that problem, the forces underlying it, and the appropriateness of potential solutions. The conditions for the viability of the capitalist system itself provide the debating ground and stage the rhetorical conflict.

Following Rayner (1991), the climate change policy debate can be described as constituting a tri-polar policy space defined by competing institutional voices, each representing a different policy bias (Fig. 4.2). The first is the activist voice that identifies *profligacy* in resource use as the underlying problem. The

Population

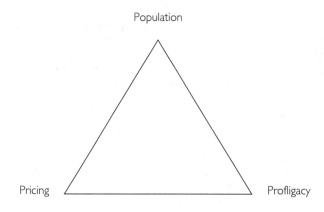

Pricing   Profligacy

Figure 4.2   A tri-polar policy space.

second voice blames economic inefficiency resulting from incorrect *pricing* or allocation of *property rights* for energy and forest resources. This voice is raised in disagreement with the first voice and the third voice, which diagnoses rapid growth in *population* as the principal culprit behind climate change. As well as asserting its diagnosis of the factors underlying and driving climate change, each voice offers its own solutions—frugality, price reform, and population control, respectively.

Each voice can be heard to some degree in almost all institutions and at all scales from household decisionmaking to international negotiations. Approaching these debates at the level of discourse, rather than through the classifications conventionally used in policy analysis (the state, national governments, pressure groups, etc.), captures the idea that institutions or even individuals are not unitary actors that can unambiguously represent (still less implement) a particular policy. Voice should not be equated with person. The speaker who uses only one voice is likely to be marginalized. Single individuals may use several voices. Indeed, speakers must adjust their rhetoric if they are to be fully heard within any particular institutional framework. As we describe in more detail later in this chapter, an institution is most often a pluralistic system in which competing and contradictory interests jockey for position.

The profligacy diagnosis

According to one voice in the debate, humankind is standing on the very edge of the abyss of environmental catastrophe. This voice urges policymakers not to delay action until further scientific evidence is available. This same voice identifies the capitalist mode of production and the level of consumption in

294

industrialized countries as the cause of climate change. It takes issue with the capitalist imperative for continuous economic growth because infinite growth cannot take place in a finite ecological system such as planet Earth: there are real limits to economic growth (Die Grünen 1980, Kemp & Wall 1990, Meyer 1994). These limits are seen as increasingly tangible in the form of the threats associated with global climate change.

The critique of profligate growth holds that the well-being of the citizen has been compromised by the profit motive (Leggett 1990). To maintain profit margins, unsound environmental practices are pursued by vested interests, regardless of the cost to the natural world. That is why cars and power stations will continue to emit irresponsible levels of carbon dioxide, and banks will continue to invest in deforestation so long as the balance sheet shows a positive value. The inequitable consumption level associated with industrial capitalism is also singled out as a cause of climate change. In 1988, the share of gross carbon dioxide emissions was two-thirds for the industrialized world and one-third for the less industrialized countries and per capita emissions are about eight times higher in the industrialized countries. Kemp & Wall (1990) argued that such a level of consumption has potentially ecocidal effects. Current lifestyles in industrialized countries, including frequent air and motor travel, high meat intake, use of many electrical appliances, and air conditioning are, we are told, unsustainable.

The profligacy diagnosis challenges conventional politics, both on a conceptual level and on the level of policy. According to this view, it is not the dramatic increase in world population that matters, nor is it governmental distortions of market mechanisms; it is the mode of production and consumption of the rich industrialized nations. Present and historical carbon dioxide emissions from the less industrialized countries are dramatically lower than those of the industrialized world, underpinning the case for focusing on economic growth and the imbalance of consumer wants as the primary cause of climate change. Unlike traditional political voices, which are intrinsically anthropocentric, this voice purports to speak for the planet on which we live. Since all life on Earth is connected in a self-sufficient biosphere, it follows that humans have no special status outside nature (Richardson 1995). Humankind is an integral part of nature and its actions directly impinge upon the natural world. That is why, this voice argues, human activity must be viewed in a holistic context; the destruction of nature means the destruction of mankind (Die Grünen 1980, Kemp & Wall 1990, Richardson 1995).

Social and cultural phenomena are related in a similar way. That is why the protest against profligacy addresses the whole spectrum of social and cultural activity (Rainbow 1993, Richardson 1995). The profligacy diagnosis requires us to apply a holistic view to social and economic problems, a view that fixes on the close connection between the destruction of the natural world and wider socioeconomic problems. Environmental degradation is a symptom of social imbalance. The way we treat the environment reflects the failures of our industrialized society. Social structures and cultural values that allow for the abuse of nature are also responsible for gender discrimination, racism, xenophobia, social alienation, crime, and poor health (Die Grünen 1980, Kemp & Wall 1990). As a result, it is argued, the environment can be protected only if these social imbalances are redressed in favor of equality and justice.

This criticism of industrial society turns attention to human needs and wants (see Ch. 3). The thesis is that industrial society has failed to meet real human needs. Since human life is bound into the cycles of the ecosystem, real human needs are the needs of planet Earth (Die Grünen 1980, Kemp & Wall 1990, Rainbow 1993). Real human needs are defined as both material (food, shelter, clothing) and spiritual (such as self-realization, personal development, and harmony with nature). However, this voice maintains that the citizens of industrial societies have been badly betrayed. Consumerism's promise of endless want satisfaction is condemned as an ideological distortion. Wants, according to this argument, are mere chimeras shaped by commercial interests and packaged by advertising agencies. These chimerical wants then function to ensure continued economic growth by creating demand for unnecessary and wasteful products such as bottled water. Thus, rises in real income and standards of living do not signify an improvement in the quality of life. Quite the opposite, this voice continues. Personal living environments have been destroyed. Social and psychological mass suffering have become the norm. The satisfaction of consumer wants has replaced the fulfillment of real human need. Real human needs cannot be met in a system that is based on the exploitation of the natural world and, by implication, mankind.

Within this framing, climate change is treated as a symptom of underlying social and economic imbalances. Ecological problems can be solved only if the question of equality, both national and international, is properly addressed. To halt climate change, industrial societies must reform themselves according to two principles: decentralization and grass-roots democracy. Decisionmaking must be decentralized into small and self-sufficient economic and administrative units. Local autonomy and codetermination will then ensure that economic development is sustainable (Die Grünen 1980, Kemp & Wall 1990, Rainbow 1993).

Less industrialized countries must also be involved in international decisions, on an equal footing. The structural dependency of the nonindustrialized world on the industrially advanced countries is seen as a severe impediment to climate change policy. Institutions such as the International Monetary Fund, where voting rights are distributed according to capital contributions, must be reformed to allow the less industrialized world to enter as equal partners (Die Grünen 1980, Kemp & Wall 1990, Leggett 1990).

The profligacy diagnosis leads to a comprehensive set of responses to climate change, including immediate adoption of the precautionary principle: "Do not emit a substance unless you have proof that it will do no harm to the environment" (Leggett 1990: 459). This voice demands that investment in research for renewable energy sources and energy efficient products be massively increased. Eventually, it envisages a low-energy future supplied by renewable resources. Above all, this voice calls for immediate cuts in carbon dioxide emissions and a total ban on chlorofluorocarbons (Leggett 1990, Kemp & Wall 1990).

This same voice reminds us that responsibility for arresting climate change does not reside with policymakers alone. Individuals in the industrialized world must become more conscious of their consumption habits. Halting climate change implies changing values. Rainbow (1993: 21) maintained that:

> . . . if real change is to occur, then we must look beyond conventional changes of guard at the level of the State and begin to change the way people think and what they value, i.e., the dominant cultural patterns in society must be transformed.

According to this view, individual choices matter; decisions about heating, lighting, and insulation make a difference to the global climate change problem. This voice urges us to exercise our consumer discretion over producers. By not recycling household waste, or by insisting on using the car to go shopping, we worsen the global climate change dilemma. If we continue to consume, regardless of the warnings, this voice maintains, we make ourselves morally responsible for the destruction of the biosphere.

It follows that the profligacy diagnosis views sustainable development in terms of social and cultural change. For development to be sustainable in both industrialized and less industrialized countries, social structures and values must change (Rainbow 1993), real human needs must be met, and chimerical wants must be discarded. Vested interests must shed power, political elites have to take action, and individuals will have to change their lifestyles. The voice raised against profligacy advocates an alternative future: the "conserve society". Based on a mutual partnership of nature and mankind, the conserve society would be driven by essential needs. Consumption would be limited by the use-what-you-need principle, thus avoiding waste of scarce resources (Die Grünen 1980, Richardson 1995). In sum, if profligacy and social inequality are the problem, frugality and equality must be the solution. Sustainable development, on this view, amounts to the abdication of capitalism in its present form.

The pricing and property rights diagnosis

Whereas the profligacy diagnosis is an explicitly moral argument, the policy bias that is focused on the price mechanism and property rights essentially views climate change as a technical problem. This diagnosis sees the climate debate in terms of scarcity and costs. Historically, market prices have not accurately reflected the full social cost of natural resources. As a result, scarce natural resources such as the atmosphere, the world's forests, and the seas have been overutilized to the brink of exhaustion. This diagnosis identifies distorted resource prices, usually resulting from misguided economic policy, as the prime culprit. Although the normative content of the climate debate is acknowledged, this diagnosis argues that a successful climate policy can be implemented by technical adjustments to existing institutions (Pearce et al. 1989, IBRD 1992).

The ideas underpinning this diagnosis originate in economic theory. In a world of changing climate, carbon sinks become increasingly scarce, which means they should be increasingly highly valued. This scarcity would influence decisionmakers if it were accurately reflected in relative market prices, because the market forces of substitution, technical innovation, and structural change would be effective. To compete in the marketplace, decisionmakers have to adapt their strategies and change their behavior. Conversely, if scarcity is not reflected in relative market prices, the resource is relatively inexpensive and will be overused (Pearce et al. 1989, IBRD 1992).

Economic theory assumes human wants are rational (see Ch. 3). According to price theory, the individual decisionmaker is able to perceive, rank, and tradeoff wants that are expressed as buyer's preferences, which influence market prices. According to the profligacy diagnosis, wants are manipulated by vested interest, but here they represent the rational self-interest of the individual.

In consequence, the idea of the individual decisionmaker is at the center of the pricing and property rights diagnosis and the natural world is treated as a means of fulfilling human wants. Although environmental degradation is a problem for humans—economic productivity suffers, human health suffers, and human amenity values are affected (Pearce et al. 1989, IBRD 1992)—nature, in the pricing diagnosis, has no intrinsic value. Arguments for the intrinsic value of nature, it is pointed out, are, in the last instance, made by humans who are expressing their preferences.

Contrary to the profligacy diagnosis, the pricing and property rights diagnosis considers markets and economic growth essential to environmental protection. Economic growth is seen to be the primary source of environmental protection for two reasons. First, for the global climate change problem to be tackled, industrialized countries will have to clean up their industries, which will be a very costly process. Second, industrialized countries will have to bear the costs of technological and economic development in the less industrialized world. Both of these will require resources that can be procured only by economic growth (Pearce 1991). Furthermore, the World Bank rejects the idea that economic growth invariably leads to environmental degradation; there are strong win–win options for environmental protection and economic growth because of the structural flexibility of capitalism (e.g. IBRD 1992). The German Environmental Agency (Umweltbundesamt) maintains that market economies have shown great flexibility in the change from manufacturing to service economies and suggests that this flexibility be used for the ecological restructuring of market economies (e.g. Umweltbundesamt 1993). Economic growth is seen as neutral; harnessed properly, it can act in the interests of environmental protection.

From this standpoint, distortions of relative resource prices are the cause of climate change. The costs of global warming have not been reflected historically in energy prices. If a resource or good is undervalued, it will be overutilized. Unfortunately, economic policymaking has failed to take due account of environmental costs, and failure in this respect has resulted in environmental degradation. If the true value of the environment were known, we would not degrade it as much (Pearce 1991).

According to the pricing and property rights diagnosis, state intervention represents one of the major obstacles to the achievement of sustainable development because of the present structures of subsidy, tax and pricing policies that exist in varying degrees in virtually all countries. Institutional interferences with market prices often serve as disincentives to environmentally friendly behavior by providing access to resources at less than their full marginal cost of production, thereby encouraging overuse and the eventual degradation of the resource.

For example, the World Bank estimated that over half of eastern Europe's air pollution is attributable to price distortions (IBRD 1992). Energy subsidies in less industrialized countries, it estimated, amounted to $230 billion in 1992, of which the former USSR and eastern Europe accounted for $180 billion. However, resource price distortions are not limited to the command economies of the former Eastern Bloc. Fossil energy subsidies are substantial in many industrialized Western economies. Deforestation is also blamed on misguided government policy. Subsidies on land that encouraged mass settlement in the Amazon rainforest led to the massive forest fires of the late 1980s (DOE 1990).

If the underlying cause of climate change is price distortions, the solution is simple: get the prices right. Policy instruments that work with the grain of the competitive free market are more efficient than administrative regulations (CBI 1995). The World Bank has spelled out three policy responses with positive externalities for the environment: liberalization of world markets, clarification of property rights, and the introduction of competition (IBRD 1992). These policies, it believes will harness the positive relationship of economic growth to environmental protection. This implies that what is good for market efficiency is good for the environment; increased efficiency means less waste and a more careful use of resources. The proper role of government, therefore, is to create a framework for market forces to develop. Market-friendly policies consist of investment in capital, both physical and human. Governments should provide education, health, nutrition, and family planning, to increase individual productivity (IBRD 1992). Furthermore, according to the pricing and property rights diagnosis, government involvement should be limited to setting minimal environmental standards (CBI 1995) and removing economic uncertainty. The latter involves clarifying legal structures and removing market rigidities (IBRD 1992).

The two remedies most commonly associated with the pricing diagnosis are a carbon tax and tradeable emission rights. A carbon tax—levied on the price of fossil fuels—is designed to make the user (the polluter) bear more of the costs associated with its use. Market rationality postulates that users will stop burning fossil fuels if they have to carry the full cost. Proponents of the carbon tax argue that both net damages and abatement costs would be minimized since the market efficiently allocates costs and resources (e.g. Barrett 1992). An alternative to the carbon tax is the concept of tradeable emission rights, whereby the regulator sets the absolute level of emissions reduction. Market mechanisms are then allowed to determine the price. This occurs because the regulator issues emission permits or rights, which are then traded on some form of exchange; the price of the permit, which would be determined by market forces, would be equivalent to the tax (Markandya 1991).

Proponents of the market solution do not just take a technical approach to sustainable development; they define it technically. Development is sustainable if the value of natural capital (K_n) and man-made capital (K_m) does not decline over time. This means that the stock of total capital ($K_n + K_m$) inherited by one generation should not decrease in value for the next generation as a result of human activity (Pearce et al. 1989, Pearce 1991, IBRD 1992). This notion assumes that natural and man-made capital can be fully traded off. Once natural capital is correctly valued, sustainable development is simply a matter of maintaining value.

To summarize the pricing and property rights diagnosis: distortions of relative resource prices cause global climate change. The problem stems from misguided government policies and can be overcome by removing price distortions and privatizing resources. The pricing and property rights position rejects the radical conclusion that is arrived at by the adherents of the profligacy diagnosis. Global climate change can be addressed solely in terms of the market.

300

The population diagnosis

Official statements agree that the world's population is increasing and that it is a threat to the global environment. According to the UK government, the "... world's population doubled between 1950 and 1987" and this "rate of population growth is exacerbating environmental pressures" (DoE 1990: 49). In the same vein, Klaus Kinkel, the former German foreign minister, held that "the population explosion is a threat to the planet's equilibrium" (G7 Leaders 1993: 902). Vice President Gore (1992: 380) agreed that "no goal is more crucial to healing the global environment than stabilizing human population."

The population diagnosis holds that human beings have a moral responsibility to take care of the planet Earth. The British government spoke of "mankind's duty to look after our world prudently and conscientiously" (DoE 1990: 8–10). President Clinton referred to "our obligations as custodians of this planet" (G7 Leaders 1993: 899). Nature, although it serves to satisfy human needs and wants, is not infinitely resilient. Although individual choices may be rational, the overall outcome of economic activity could be detrimental to the environment. Rational management of the economy and environment, therefore, will ensure that the destructive effects of economic activity do not become excessive.

The population diagnosis offers an account of human needs and wants that differs from those emanating from the other two apexes of the policy space (Fig. 4.2). Its idea of human needs is driven by the practical problems of administration and management. First, needs are fixed at every level of economic development. Second, the levels of development are assumed to be irreversible, at least in the short and medium terms. Third, needs are defined in per capita terms. The assumption that underpins this account is that human needs are an integral part of human existence: needs are immutable and must be met.

Texts and speeches advocating the population diagnosis argue for a balanced view on economic growth. On the one hand, economic growth is necessary for environmental protection. In the less industrialized world, poverty must be defeated so that population issues and environmental issues can be addressed. In industrialized countries, economic development is required to finance the greening of society (DoE 1990, Umweltbundesamt 1993). On the other hand, the destructive potential of economic growth is apparent and must be addressed. For this reason, economic growth should be embedded in carefully designed policies for economic and environmental management: development must be sustainable.

Since needs are defined by the population diagnosis in per capita terms (see Ch. 3), it follows, as surely as night follows day, that the more people there are with fixed needs, the more the environment will be put under pressure (see

Ch. 2). The effect of population growth "on economic development is not neutral. Neither is its linkage with the environment neutral" (Wirth 1993: 405). Problems arise when societies that have "learned over the course of hundreds of generations to eke out a living within fragile ecosystems are suddenly confronted—in a single generation—with the necessity of feeding, clothing, and sheltering two or three times as many individuals within those same ecosystems" (Gore 1992: 380). Similarly, the UK government averred that as "populations increase, so do demands for food, fuel, water and land" (DoE 1990: 49). Consequently, an increase in population means more mouths to feed and more demands on more agricultural land. If "per head emissions of greenhouse gases grow too rapidly in developing countries, the effects will be devastating, regardless of the benefits any steps which developed countries such as Britain may take" (DoE 1990: 50).

On this view, responsibility for global climate change lies with the developing countries. Rapid expansion of population, which is particularly their case, will lead to a level of aggregated need that will exceed the sustainability threshold. The crisis is not yet upon us but it is certainly on its way. By implication, economic activity to date has been more or less sustainable. Hitherto the world was living on income rather than eroding its capital, as it is about to do (DoE 1990). Britain's Royal Society and the US National Academy of Sciences (Royal Society 1992: 375) also focus on population growth:

> if current predictions of population growth prove accurate and patterns of human activity on the planet remain unchanged, science and technology may not be able to prevent irreversible degradation of the environment or continued poverty for much of the world.

Responsibility for environmental degradation is shared between industrialized and less industrialized worlds, but, according to the population diagnosis, the onus of taking action lies at the door of the latter (DoE 1990). Failing this, Gore predicts that the rate of population growth will nullify "all of the potential reductions in greenhouse gases coming from even extraordinary advances in technology . . ." (Gore 1992: 381).

The solution strategies of this diagnosis only treat the climate change problem symptomatically. Gore suggests three measures: increased resource allocation to literacy programs (education is statistically related to smaller families); reduction of infant mortality, which would improve expectations of rearing all the children born; and increased availability of birth control (Gore 1992: 383). The Clinton administration's seven-point plan comprises (Clinton & Gore 1993: 404):

- the right to determine the size of the family

- access to the full range of "... quality reproductive healthcare"
- public and private sector commitment to family planning
- the empowerment of women
- access to primary healthcare
- environmental protection
- support of sustainable development.

Similarly, the UK government policy aims at providing birth control and education to encourage the industrialized world's "own efforts to restrain population growth to levels which are consistent with their resources ... [by] ... alleviating poverty, promoting economic and social development and directly helping to meet demand for family planning" (DoE 1990: 50).

The definition of sustainable development in the population diagnosis reflects the normative and technical dimensions of the population argument. Sustainable development is about meeting human needs over time. Accordingly, the Brundtland Report (WCED 1987) maintained that sustainability means "meeting the needs of the present without compromising the ability of future generations to meet their own needs." This definition implies that economic growth is necessary to meet human needs, but that development can be, and must be, managed.

Contradictory certitudes

We have seen how the three voices diagnose the global climate change problem differently. Each voice suggests different prescriptions to resolve the climate change issue. These diagnoses and prescriptions compete with each other for acceptance by policymakers and the public, and this competitive process is marked by the mutual discrediting and assimilating of arguments. The different constituencies have their characteristic rhetorical styles. The profligacy diagnosis and the solution of egalitarian frugality is delivered in impassioned sermons, urging strong moral imperatives. Advocates of the pricing and property rights diagnosis and the market solution seem to speak in algebra, their case quantified and presented in equations, but efficiency underlies the rational calculus as a moral imperative. The population diagnosis combines a narrower moral imperative than the profligacy diagnosis with a simpler technical logic than that of the pricing position. The result is that the languages employed in the climate debate are so different that one might never guess that any one set of treatises is provoked by and is developed in response to the other sets.

The advocates of egalitarian frugality seek to persuade with explicitly moral arguments. By blurring the conventional distinction between fact and value, their holistic worldview ties environmental degradation to the immorality of industrial society. The profligacy diagnosis is a critique of ideology. Its voice claims to see through the ideological veil of industrial society and to be able to uncloak real objectives. In general, this voice accuses the others of cynicism in the face of environmental catastrophe. Rather than addressing the root causes of environmental degradation, national governments merely tinker because they lack the political will to confront vested interests (Kemp & Wall 1990, Leggett 1990).

The profligacy diagnosis levels a particularly acrid criticism at proponents of the pricing diagnosis and its market solution. It accuses economists of living in an Alice-in-Wonderland world because of their continued endorsement of open-ended economic growth (Kemp & Wall 1990, Meyer 1994). The profligacy position accuses economic sciences of deliberate ideological obfuscation (Kemp & Wall 1990, Leggett 1990, Meyer 1995) in order to maintain the inequitable and unjust capitalist system. The advocates of egalitarian frugality maintain that market arguments ignore the issues of power and equality. At its most vehement, this voice accuses practitioners of environmental cost–benefit analysis, which allots carbon dioxide emissions according to income (such as the Nordhaus or Pearce approaches), of economic genocide and ecological suicide (Meyer 1995; Box 4.4). In sum, the profligacy diagnosis singles out economists and industrialists as the ideological standard bearers of the destructive economic system. It also attacks the population account of climate change for its fundamental misunderstanding of the environmental issue. Uncontrolled population growth is a symptom of environmental and social imbalances, not the cause. The explanation offered by the population diagnosis is denounced as monocausal and simplistic (Kemp & Wall 1990, Meyer 1994). From this standpoint it is paradoxical and hypocritical that less industrialized countries are encouraged to reduce population growth, whereas the industrialized world is concerned about its dwindling national populations.

The pricing diagnosis attempts to convince policymakers and the public with technical arguments. Implicitly, proponents of the market policy bias claim a superior knowledge of the mechanisms that affect individual choice. They dismiss the profligacy diagnosis as being unrealistic, alarmist, and irresponsible. Growth is necessary to achieve sustainable development (Pearce et al. 1989, IBRD 1992, CBI 1995) and any argument that does not accept this premise is utopian (CBI 1995); the capitalist system is reality. They denounce the normative approach of the advocates of egalitarian frugality as wrong-headed and hysterical, as failing to grasp the elementary fact that social imbalances are not a result of economic growth, but a result of the lack of economic development. According to the pricing diagnosis, the market provides us with the most effective technical means of allocating resources and is thus the only way that effective and efficient environmental protection can be achieved. Changing the

---

Box 4.4   The value of human life

Climate change is likely to kill more people in poor countries than in rich countries, and the estimates of damage are therefore very sensitive to the assumed "value of life." Economic calculations such as those of Nordhaus (1991) and Fankhauser (1992) assume a "value of life" roughly in proportion to national per capita GDP. A direct clash on this point has already occurred between that particular school of Western economists and others, when various groups objected to this approach being taken in a (draft) report by the IPCC Working Group III. The Global Commons Institute launched an international campaign against a calculus that "values a European as equal to ten China men."[1] The issue reached its height when the Indian environment minister, Kamal Nath, wrote to other heads of delegations at the first meeting of the Conference of Parties to the Convention, in which he flatly rejected:

> the absurd and discriminatory global cost/benefit analysis procedures propounded by economists in the work of IPCC WG-III . . . we unequivocally reject the theory that the monetary value of people's lives around the world is different because the value imputed should be proportional to the disparate income levels of the potential victims . . . it is impossible for us to accept that which is not ethically justifiable, technically accurate or politically conducive to the interests of poor people as well as the global common good.[2]

The issues are not straightforward. Whatever one's ethical stance, it is clear that countries do not—cannot—value lives equally. It would indeed be absurd for India to try to put resources into modern medical services at the level prevailing in the United States, when so many more basic threats to life and health remain potent. As long as health and related decisions of nations remain essentially separate, therefore, there is nothing necessarily immoral in valuing life differently in different places; it is simply a reflection of reality. But climate change concerns impacts by some nations on others and, in aggregate, by rich nations on poorer ones. Whose value of life should then be used in evaluating the damages?

---

1. Letter, *Guardian*, 4 July 1994.
2. Open letter from Kamal Nath, Minister of Environment and Forests, India, dated 24 March 1995.

---

institution of the market would inevitably do more harm than good.

The population diagnosis comes under attack from the pricing diagnosis in terms of inefficiency. Government intervention in markets is seen as the main contributor to climate change. If correct policies that would facilitate wealth accumulation were in place, the population problem would not be as severe. Governmental management of the environment and the economy distorts markets.

Finally, the population diagnosis employs both normative and technical arguments to persuade. It is morally imperative to protect the environment, but this must occur within established institutions. The profligacy diagnosis, according to this view, is right to point to the normative dimension, but the solutions it urges are impractical. Indeed, they would make things worse. Rational management, not social upheaval, will secure sustainable development. And blaming the industrialized world diverts attention from the unsustainable population growth in the less industrialized world, which is the heart of the problem. From the standpoint of the population diagnosis, the market solution is right in emphasizing efficiency but is castigated for being hopelessly optimistic about the rationality of the market and the plausibility of uncontrolled growth. Individual rational decisions, proponents of the population diagnosis aver, can amount to irrational outcomes even if markets are unrestrained (DoE: 1990). However, rational management and limited growth will ensure sustainable development.

From all of the foregoing discussion of myths of nature and irreducible heterogeneity, and of the robustly triangular policy space that they give rise to, we draw two conclusions that close off all those ways forward that require us to decide who is right and that point us firmly in an opposite, and much more reflexive, direction:

- These are contradictory certitudes—they cannot be reconciled because each position actively defines itself in contradistinction to the others.
- Issues of diagnosis and prescription are compounded when viewed through the lens of equity.

Equity issues in climate discourses

Equity issues entered the climate change discourse in the late 1980s, arising out of the realization that certain nations or regions may actually gain from the impacts of change, whereas others would be disadvantaged (Kasperson & Dow 1991). For example, growing-seasons in high latitudes could be extended while lower latitudes experience drought. Ports previously icebound throughout the winter months might become accessible year round, while major navigable rivers elsewhere could be closed to traffic during the summer because of reduced streamflow. At this time there was relatively little interest in climate change among the less industrialized tropical nations, whose elites regarded it as a problem created by and affecting the wealthier nations of temperate latitudes.

However, the discussion was soon extended beyond the equity implications of impacts themselves to the potential effects of actions that countries could or should take to prevent climate change or to adapt to its consequences. The implications of measures to reduce greenhouse gas emissions on the development trajectories of the less industrialized nations became a prominent concern, leading their government representatives to dilate on the historical responsibility of the industrialized countries for greenhouse gas emissions and on the current disparity in per capita emissions between North and South. At the same time, rapidly rising trends in Southern emissions caught the attention of Northern analysts, who emphasized to their policymakers that their own efforts to control emissions would be fruitless without the participation of nations undergoing economic and technological development (Fulkerson et al. 1989). Southern interest in climate change increased drastically with the opportunity to make cooperation conditional upon Northern economic and technological support for their development aspirations. Hence, the first principle in Article 3 of the 1992 Framework Convention on Climate Change (FCCC) states that:

> The Parties should protect the climate system for the benefit of present and future generations of humankind, on the basis of equity and in accordance with their common but differentiated responsibilities and respective capabilities. Accordingly, the developed country Parties should take the lead in combating climate change and the adverse effects thereof.

The language employed in this claim represents a classic diplomatic formulation that permits all parties to enjoin equity, that is, fairness or justice, while retaining quite different notions of what would actually be fair and what duties obligations or commitments fairness would entail. The duties actually entailed in leadership by the industrialized country parties are left similarly vague. They will probably have to remain so with respect to guiding principles, about which, this chapter will argue, it may be more difficult to obtain agreement than to negotiate practical measures.

In a series of articles, Shue (1994) breaks the issue of fairness in climate change policy into four questions:

- What is a fair allocation of the costs of preventing the global warming that is still avoidable?
- What is a fair allocation of the costs of coping with the social consequences of the global warming that will not in fact be avoided?
- What background allocation of wealth would allow international bargaining (about issues such as the two above) to be a fair process?
- What is a fair allocation of emissions of greenhouse gases over the long term and during the transition to the long-term allocation?

The third item on this list, background allocation, is perhaps the least familiar area of discussion, and yet it provides for the basis of a fair process for determining the other three kinds of allocation. As a practical matter, background allocation concerns not only resources currently available to the negotiating parties but also their reasonable and secure expectations of future resource availability without climate change. Two well-known models of procedural equity are relevant for the negotiation problem: Coase's model of social cost and Rawls's criterion for social welfare.[2]

The Coase (1960) prescription for bargaining requires complete identification of the externalities of resource use, and consequently, of the winners and losers in decisionmaking. Disputes are resolved, and economic efficiency is restored, either by winners compensating losers for environmental damages or by losers bribing winners not to pollute. Thus, the discovery and clarification of information about the distribution of environmental outcomes are fundamental inputs to a Coasian bargain.

The Achilles' heel of the Coase strategy is its assumption of equal bargaining power among participants and equal distribution of the costs of making the bargain. In the philosophical literature, the ability of participants in a negotiation to bargain on equal terms is fundamental to what has been called "an ideal speech situation" (Habermas 1981): that is, a situation where dialogue and decisionmaking are free from inappropriate constraints. For instance, one of the most important sources of power in the climate negotiations is scientific information. It is well known that the present ability of a less industrialized country to engage in the scientific process that is critical in making the Framework Convention work is limited by insufficient information, insufficient communication, limited human resources, limited institutional capacity, and limited financial resources (IPCC 1990).

This means that there will be formidable obstacles to taking inventory, monitoring, and policing local activities. That is, even if countries sign agreements, how can they ensure that these are lived up to, even with the best will in the world? The role played by international institutions in providing climate information and adjudicating claims is suddenly highlighted as an ethical issue. The lack of an adequate scientific infrastructure, which appears on the surface to be an issue of pure and neutral information gathering, turns out to involve justice. This is only one example of how fact and value are inextricably intermingled in the case of climate change. To apply the Coasian strategy successfully in the real world of climate damages, we need a better understanding of how to equalize bargaining power among participants.

In contrast to Coase, the Rawlsian strategy uses the veil of ignorance about winners and losers to entice participants to strike a fair bargain (Rawls 1971). Since no participant can guarantee that he or she will not suffer a devastating outcome, risk-averse players will want to minimize such possibilities. Thus, fair and impartial bargains are more likely to occur in an information-poor envi-

---

2. These models were originally developed to address problems related only loosely to bargaining among economic agents (in fact, the Coase paper ignores the process of bargaining, and Rawls was concerned with the distribution of social welfare). However, they have come to represent, either implicitly or explicitly in the recommendations of policy analysis, different paradigms underlying strategies for making international environmental bargains.

ronment. Ignorance, not active discovery of information, is a valuable motivator for the Rawlsian bargain. Because information can be suppressed, intentionally or passively, Rawlsian agreements may be subverted by free riding and cheating. (Cheating may be a factor for the Coasian strategy as well, and it is likely to be exacerbated by poor information discovery.) Innovations for enforcement and compliance mechanisms that do not rely on winner and loser information will be necessary to make this strategy effective.

A more familiar playing field for struggles over background allocation is, of course, institutional representation, whether it be on the Commission for Sustainable Development, or in the continuing efforts to ensure that the Global Environment Facility (GEF) is "appropriately restructured" to have an "equitable and balanced representation of all Parties within a transparent system of governance" in accordance with Articles 11 and 21 of the FCCC (see Ch. 5). Again, equity issues involve not just seating arrangements but the provision of adequate resources to make the most of one's presence at the negotiating table.

Diplomatic language is only one acknowledgment that the demand for equity is universal. As Shue (1995: 385) pointed out, "People everywhere understand what it means to ask whether an arrangement is fair or is instead biased toward some parties over other parties." However, practical experience tells us that the answer to the question of whether any particular arrangement is fair is seldom glaringly obvious or universally agreed upon. It depends very much on both the interests and the procedural preferences of the respondent.

Philosophers, political theorists, sociologists, and economists have drawn up many overlapping typologies of distributional and procedural principles, which could be used to elucidate alternative solutions to each of Shue's allocation problems (Box 4.5). However, at the crudest level of aggregation, three basic sets of distributional and procedural preferences can be gleaned from the literature:

- libertarian (market utilitarian)
- contractarian (administrative utilitarian)
- egalitarian (anthropocentric and nature centric).

Distributional principles and allocational issues

Three principles, parallel to those of Shue, which can be applied to resolve practical problems of making fair allocations of resources, emerged from the work of mathematician Peyton Young (1993). These are *proportionality, priority,* and *parity.* Rayner (1995) employed the same terms slightly differently from Young to examine alternative proposals for allocating emissions rights.

Young used proportionality to describe the Aristotelian principle of allocat-

Box 4.5 Tradeable permit allocation criteria

In a series of analyses, Rose & Stevens (Rose 1992, Rose & Stevens 1993, 1998) identified ten equity criteria applicable to marketable emissions permit schemes. Three of these—*ability to pay, sovereignty, egalitarian*—apply to the initial allocation of permits. Three others—*market justice, consensus, Rawls' maximin*—apply to the negotiation process. The remaining criteria apply to the final outcome of the implementation of a permit scheme, that is, to the net welfare impacts following trading and greenhouse-related emissions mitigation. The set of outcome-based criteria encompasses *horizontal, vertical, compensation,* and *environmental* principles.

Rose's alternative equity criteria for global warming policy			
Criterion	Basic definition	General operational rule	Operational rule for CO_2 permits
Market justice	The market is fair	Make greater use or markets	Distribute permits to highest bidder
Compensation	No nation should be made worse off	Compensate net losers	Distribute permits so that no nation suffers a net loss of welfare
Sovereignty	All nations have an equal right to pollute and to be protected from pollution	Cut back emissions in a proportional manner across all nations	Distribute permits in proportion to emissions
Horizontal	All nations should be treated equally	Equalize net welfare change across nations (net cost of abatement as proportion of GDP equal for each nation)[1]	Distribute permits to equalize net welfare change
Vertical	Welfare changes should vary inversely with national economic well-being	Progressively share net welfare change across nations (net cost inversely correlated with per capita GDP)[1]	Progressively distribute permits
Ability to pay	Mitigation costs should vary inversely with national economic well-being	Equalize abatement costs across nations (gross cost of abatement as proportion of GDP equal for each nation)[2]	Distribute permits to equalize abatement costs
Consensus	The international negotiation process is fair	Seek a political solution promoting stability	Distribute permits in a manner that satisfies the (power weighted) majority of nations
Rawls' maximin	The welfare of the worst-off nations should be maximized	Maximize the net benefit to the poorest nations	Distribute the largest proportion to poorest nations
Egalitarian	All people have an equal right to pollute and to be protected from pollution	Cut back emissions in proportion to population	Distribute permits in proportion to population

Environmental	The environment should receive preferential treatment	Cut back emissions to maximize environmental values	Limit permits associated with vulnerable ecosystems (e.g., forests)

1. Net cost equal to the sum of mitigation benefits *minus* abatement costs *plus* permit sales revenues *minus* permit purchase costs.
2. Gross cost refers to abatement cost only.

In Shue's system, the first three criteria would be considered libertarian (market utilitarian), four through eight would be contractarian (administrative utilitarian), whereas nine and ten are essentially egalitarian. It should not be surprising that administered solutions are more numerous than either market or egalitarian ones, neither of which require explicit calculation or valuation of difficult tradeoffs.

So far as final outcomes are concerned, Rose & Stevens calculated that the actual distributions after trading would be consistent with the Coase theorem, which states that, provided that property rights are clearly delineated and transaction costs and income effects can be avoided, an efficient allocation of resources will result through trading, irrespective of how initial property rights are distributed. Hence, only permit transaction payments or receipts differ according to equity principles (i.e., only one of the three parts of the net benefits equation differs among equity rules). However, the major exception to this is the egalitarian principle, which gives the lion's share of permits to countries such as India, China, and Indonesia.

ing benefits according to contribution. He distinguished this from priority, which is allocation based on the strongest claim, for example, need in the case of kidney transplants or seniority in avoiding job layoffs. However, it seems that contribution, seniority, and need are all bases for claims that are intended to be settled by administrative allocations made by an adjudicating authority. Hence, Rayner used proportionality to indicate a distributive outcome in which benefits are allocated in accordance with an administrative determination of rank, contribution, or need.

This usage frees the term priority to be applied to distributional outcomes that are achieved through successful competition, in other words, first in time, first in right. This principle is well established in frontier conditions and today remains the basis of water law in the western United States. It is also a principle enshrined in the patent system, first introduced in England in 1623 (Headrick 1990). Patents are the origin of intellectual property rights, designed to concentrate the benefits of innovation on the inventor, so as to stimulate and reward intellectual competition. The overall societal benefits of that increased competition are supposed to include greater volume and velocity of technological innovation and also incentives for wider dissemination of innovation through benefits of scale in production.

The third principle of distribution is parity. This can be understood as the egalitarian principle of equal shares to all claimants. This is relatively simple to apply on an individualistic basis to divisible goods. However, with goods that are harder to divide, parity can lead toward the creation and maintenance of common property systems. Parity embodies the principle that each inhabitant of the Earth has the right to an equal use of the atmosphere. Hence, a fair allocation of emission rights to nation states would be one based on per capita population (Box 4.6).

This argument has been most steadfastly articulated by the nations of the South. Yet, within those nations, per capita parity is seldom, if ever, the operational distributional principle. Brazil's economy resembles Spain's in every important respect save the distribution of wealth. India has a middle class larger than the entire population of many Northern countries, although a recent estimate in the *Washington Post* of 240 million clearly includes many people that Americans (say) would have difficulty in recognizing as middle class. If we make the conservative assumptions that the affluent middle class is only twice

---

Box 4.6   Parity proposals—equal per capita entitlement

The specific proposal most widely cited for allocation in the literature is that derived directly from egalitarianism, suggesting that all human beings should be entitled to an equal share of the atmospheric resource. With minor variations, this takes two general forms: contemporary and historical per capita allocations. The net effect in all cases would be to give less industrialized countries, with their much lower per capita emissions, a substantial excess entitlement, while the industrialized countries, with per capita emissions well above the global average, would have a deficit (Grubb 1995).

Equal contemporary entitlement—allocation in proportion to national population—is the route proposed by Grubb (1989), Bertram (1992), Epstein & Gupta (1990), and Agarwal & Narain (1991), among others. These proposals are an intrinsically egalitarian way of deciding how to distribute a global, public, and hitherto free resource. The major objections to this approach are based partly on ethical and practical "comparable-burden" type arguments (since it would imply a huge adjustment burden on industrialized countries, to which they are unlikely to agree), and partly on grounds of concern that such allocation might reward population and population growth. Proponents tend to argue that any such effect is negligible compared to other factors influencing population; but, to avoid any inducement to population growth, Grubb suggested that the population measure should be restricted to population above a certain age. This ratification has been criticized for discriminating against children (although of course, like all international allocation proposals, it says nothing about discrimination within countries). Grubb et al. (1992) noted a wider range of possibilities for avoiding any incentive to population growth, including lagged allocation (related to population a fixed period earlier); apportionment to a fixed historical date; or the inclusion of an explicit term related inversely to population growth rate.

As Grubb (1995) pointed out, the international transfers implicit in equal per capita allocations would be much larger still in proposals for equal historical or stock entitlement. Fujii (1990), Ghosh (1993), and Meyer (1995) proposed that everyone should have an equal right to identical emissions regardless of country and generation. Fujii and Meyer took the equitability of this allocation as self-evident; Ghosh argues that it can be derived from a range of diverse ethical principles.

---

the size of India's MTV audience (around 31 million) and is as energy efficient as the average Japanese citizen (2.5 tonnes of carbon per capita per annum), the carbon dioxide emissions of the Indian middle class alone would exceed the total emissions of Australia—one of the industrial villains who would be required to cut industrial consumption by factors of 10–20 within a few decades (Rayner 1994).

From this standpoint, it seems that the vast numbers close to destitution rescue the middle classes (the "local North," as they are sometimes called) of many less industrialized countries from the same accusations of per capita overconsumption that they themselves level at industrialized countries. Furthermore, although far from equal, the actual distribution of wealth within the nations of the North is far closer to the per capita average than in the nations of the South. Hence, from a Northern perspective, claims based on the parity principle, that the North has a moral responsibility to take the lead in cutting consumption, may not be compelling. The so-called *survival emissions* of poorer countries may, in practice, translate into the *luxury emissions* of their elites. Claims that international equity should be established on the parity principle would be seen as more compelling in the North if mechanisms were established to ensure that, for example, a carbon tax does not simply reduce the welfare of the poor in the North, to benefit wealthy elites in the South (a criticism that has long been leveled at international aid). However, such mechanisms are likely to be viewed by those elites as unacceptable violations of national sovereignty.

Parity, among commentators from the less industrialized countries, is essentially an anthropocentric principle according to which the fragility of nature reflects and is exacerbated by societal inequality (Box 4.7). However, so-called *deep ecologists* in the industrialized world go further than enjoining nature to their cause. They advocate extending the principle to nonhuman attributes of nature, giving equal rights to animals and legal standing to plants and morphological features of the Earth's surface (Stone 1972). This extreme application of the parity principle has been described elsewhere as an *Earthrights* model which turns away from immediate and sole concern with human well-being, and attempts to argue on behalf of all beings on the Earth, as well as, in some versions, the Earth itself (or herself). Human activities are seen as already cutting deeply into the remaining space available for many other species on the planet. Various calculations have been made, for example, of the amount of the Earth's net primary productivity (NPP) from photosynthetic activity now being harvested by human beings for their own benefit—we are now taking approximately 25 percent, which will rise to 40 percent as the population doubles. Given the trends, unless the burden of human activities drops substantially, the deep ecologists warn, the already steep curve of species extinction will only grow steeper.

Box 4.7   Natural fragility and societal inequality

"Who cares about coral reefs?" I often heard in the corridors of the UN buildings in Geneva and New York, when the red wines seeps into the head, reality sets in and diplomacy is no longer in full play.

I care. I listen to the cries of millions of polyps that makes up the corals. Why, because there is much more at stake for us all than just the death of polyps and corals.

What is causing corals to die lies at the core of the way we humans live, especially in OECD countries. Dead corals are the victims of the injustices we continue to ignore, of greed, of selfishness and of the abdication of moral and ethical responsibility. It is an act of genocide against the corals and so against species who depend on them, including ultimately, humans.

The coral polyps's own world mirrors the human experience—the cries for freedom from the foreign debt, poverty, starvation, the cries to change lifestyles, not the climate, the cries to stop burning fossil fuels! To ignore the death of coral reefs is, I believe, to ignore the cries of many of the world's people of today, at the peril of our future generations and our planet.

It is for this reason, Mr Chairman, that time and time again, we have urged the international community to hear the cries of the corals as well as our own.

Statement by NGOs to the Plenary, COP I, Berlin, 30 March 1995 (delivered by Pene Lefale, Climate Action Network Pacific)

Parity is by no means the only basis advanced in the argument over allocation of emissions rights or so-called *environmental space*. In fact, advocates of market principles, mostly in the North, have invoked the *priority* principle to argue that, far from incurring a debt to the South by its historic carbon emissions, the North was merely exercising its right of *first in time* (Box 4.8). Such a view is reinforced by the *realist* perspective in political science and by neoconservative economic assumptions that powerful nations will in any case demur at the prospect of implementing any arrangement that flies in the face of their perceived national self-interest (see Ch. 5).

Box 4.8   Priority principles—status quo

On the priority principle view, not only should past emitters be held blameless, but their current rate of emissions constitutes a status quo established by past usage and custom (Young & Wolf 1991). Analogies are drawn with the common-law principles of adverse possession, such as "squatter's rights." Ghosh (1993) not only disputed the ethical acceptability of this but also commented that "pollution rights have no common law sanction." However, drawing on fisheries analogies, Yamin (1995) suggested that the industrialized countries' use of the climate system at present-day rates could be presented as a basis for a claim in the absence of stronger challenges to such use by developing countries.

A strict status quo allocation, proportionate to current emissions, has received widespread attention as a basis for analysis taking a pragmatic or game theoretic approach, in that it is the default allocation that would arise in the absence of agreement (and hence a focal point), and is the only specific suggested allocation basis that does not automatically impose large burdens upon industrialized countries (Barrett 1992).

Total cost minimization (also describable as efficiency or a refusal to waste scarce resources) is an ethical mainstay of the priority position. Another is a prohibition on making external moral assessments of what people ought to desire. The preferences of individuals are what matter, as expressed through willingness or ability to pay for what they prefer, as adjudicated by the market. Hence, this approach to climate policy emphasizes maximizing present-value utility, measured as ratio of the future benefits of present actions (see Vol. 3, Ch. 1).

Such analyses embody bold assumptions in the face of widespread uncertainty, some of which include emissions mitigation costs, future discounting, unmeasured externalities, a nature with no intrinsic value, and a relatively smooth period of onset of climate change. Under this paradigm, allocation is primarily assumed to be market-based, and that means allocation by preference and ability to pay.

Associated with this model is the position that delaying the response to climate change until more information becomes available is the most rational option (e.g., discussed extensively in Manne & Richels 1992). There will be more income in the future deriving from more productive kinds of investment, which can then be spent on more efficiently targeted abatement strategies. This position has received support, in part, because of the uncertainties associated with the scientific models. Within the same position, however, it can be argued that there is a waiting cost for delay—among other things, the future costs for greatly increased responses will be substantially higher. Shue (1994) also notes, with reference to the same position, that those who will be most able to accumulate the resources today to cope with climate change tomorrow are unlikely to be those who are the worst hit.

By analogy with the argument that patent rights result in increased general welfare through concentration of initial benefits, the priority principle is also defended on the basis that the industrial development of the North has resulted in a global increase in welfare. Hence, a fair allocation of emission rights would be one that recognizes the historical dependence of the industrialized countries on fossil fuels and would allocate emissions rights to nation states on the basis of GDP. Clearly, this approach violates the *parity* principle.

The third proposal is typically *proportional* in that it seeks to devise a formula that will transcend claims based on parity and priority. This is the *contractarian* or administrative–utilitarian approach. This allows for economic efficiency, but subordinates it to a larger goal, along lines analogous to the management of a trust. The argument is that people are trustees of the Earth, and as trustees people have a responsibility in each generation to preserve the planet's natural and human heritage (Weiss 1989).

This approach shares with the advocates of extending parity principles to nature the idea that some things are beyond price. However, they are more likely than the Earthrights proponents to include human artifacts in the category of priceless objects. For example, such treasures as the ceiling of the Sistine Chapel, the physical documents upon which Magna Carta and the US Constitution are written, are examples of entrusted objects whose loss is possible, but irreparable. In other words, pricelessness is socially constructed, with different and competing constructions at each of the three apexes of the policy space (an argument developed at some length in Thompson 1979).

The model of a fiduciary trust consistent with proportionality implies (among other things) the conservation of options (defined as preserving the diversity of the natural and cultural resource base), conservation of quality (defined as leaving the planet no worse off than it was received), and conservation of access (defined as equitable access to the use and benefits of the legacy); as well as a strong risk-averse strategy, especially for potentially irreversible damages, and the application of precautionary and prudential principles. A notion of responsibility is also introduced (Weiss 1989).

What is not clear in this approach is where the boundaries for this invocation of entrusting are, and this is especially important for the demarcation of what is to be kept outside of economic considerations. Alternatively: exactly what is being entrusted when we say we are committed to a "planetary trust"? Is it a specific trust that is being identified, or a general worldview within which even economics must function in a subordinate role? Is it some portion of the Earth's surface, or just certain species? Or is it rather the capacity of the Earth to sustain itself or to sustain human life at least at our current level of flourishing?

With respect to reductions in greenhouse gas emissions, the proportionality principle is essentially the *contractarian* approach. For example, such a formula might seek to combine population and GDP to provide a fair distribution of emissions rights for each nation state (Box 4.9).

This example also illustrates that a contractarian approach is the only one of the three that does not prefer clearly asymmetrical principles for losses and gains, because it is driven by the imperative of maintaining system stability rather than by imperatives to promote growth or equality. Contractarians tend to favor deep-pocket solutions (Calabrese 1970) as fair mechanisms for distributing liabilities, not so much out of a desire to move toward strict equality, but to avoid destabilization of the general welfare. In this way contractarian arguments advocate redistributive mechanisms, such as taxation, to apportion liabilities in a way that seems to them to be least disruptive, not to the whole society perhaps, but certainly to those constituencies whose stability they see as critical. Just as contractarians prefer to transfer losses through the system, they symmetrically prefer a system of allocating benefits where they best reinforce the accepted structures.

Libertarians (market utilitarians) tend to favor *loss spreading* in which market

---

Box 4.9   Proportionality proposals—mixed systems

The number of specific single-criterion proposals for emission allocation is rather limited. A comparative study by Burtraw & Toman (1992) considers just the two main dimensions of equal per capita entitlement and equal percentage cuts. There are of course many other proposals that approach the question directly in terms of "who should pay"; some of these explore the possibility of combining different criteria (Grubb 1995).

Wirth & Lashof (1990) proposed allocations based on an equal (50:50) mix of population and GDP, and Cline (1992) proposed an alternative allocation, which consists of a weighted combination of population, GNP, and current emissions. An approach other than historical egalitarianism, in which historical contributions are considered as a determinant of emissions allocation, is a scheme examined by Grübler & Nakicenovic (1994), in which countries have to cut back from current levels in direct proportion to their responsibility for past increases. In a sense, therefore, this is a mixed system. In requiring cutbacks from all countries, albeit more from the richer countries, it is probably inconsistent with some ethical principles, although modifications could be considered to address this (Grubb 1995).

Grubb et al. (1992), supported by Shue (1993), examined a mixed system in more detail, and an almost identical formulation was proposed independently by Welsch (1993). These authors suggested an allocation that combines egalitarian and status quo (comparable burden) principles in the form of a combination of population and current emissions measure, but did not specify an equal weighting of these components. Rather, they argued that the weighting accorded to population should increase over time toward pure per capita allocation. Grubb et al. suggested that the weighting would have to be determined on the basis of negotiation, reflecting in part the strength of competing equity arguments employed; Welsch proposed a 50-year transition from current emissions in the year 2000 to per capita allocation in the year 2050, and presented sample calculations of the distributions of the costs this could involve.

A wholly different quantified approach to the question of who should pay for abatement was provided by Chichilnisky & Heal (1994), who applied the concepts of classical economics to construct a strictly utilitarian formulation that seeks to maximize global utility, and concluded that the fraction of income that each country allocates to carbon emission abatement must be proportional to that country's income level, and the constant of proportionality increases with the efficiency of that country's abatement technology. This, they argued, is the only distribution of abatement effort, for a given global total abatement and set of welfare weights, in which no country can be made better off without making another worse off—Pareto optimality. The result in turn implies that the total resources each country should put toward abatement would increase as the square of the national income.

---

systems such as insurance and reinsurance determine who bears losses (Calabrese 1970). When pure market solutions are not available, advocates of this position attempt to reproduce what the market would have done if it had not been impeded by high information or transaction costs. For example, the Price–Anderson Act was designed to limit the liability carried by nuclear plant operators in the United States in favor of diverting the costs to the population in general. This is asymmetrical to the principle that allows the individual risk initiator to collect any gains that may accrue.

In contrast with both of the broadly utilitarian approaches, egalitarians seek a moral determination of liability that appeals directly to egalitarian values. This is a strict-fault system (Calabrese 1970) that makes those who are seen as responsible for imposing the risk directly responsible for the costs, making the polluter pay (Box 4.10). By this means, egalitarians aim to eliminate incentives to cut corners on safety, or even to continue with the activity at all. The strong preferences of egalitarians for allocating costs to guilty parties is asymmetrical to their communal principle of the broadest spread of gains. Thus, the argument in favor of parity in the distribution of emissions rights goes hand in hand with the argument that the North should bear the costs of climate change policies because it is responsible for the bulk of historical greenhouse gas emissions. However, this argument raises fundamental issues about principles of procedural fairness. These preferences for distributional outcomes are summarized in Table 4.2.

Box 4.10   Polluter pays principle

A general basis for responsibility may be considered in terms of the "polluter pays principle" (PPP). The Organisation for Economic Cooperation and Development (OECD) formally adopted a form of PPP in 1974 as a guide to environmental policy in stating that, if measures are adopted to reduce pollution, the costs should be borne by the polluters.[1] This is an economic principle that says essentially that polluters should bear the cost of abatement without subsidy. The principle does not explicitly state that all polluters of a common pollutant should pay in proportion to their emissions, and in fact the literature seems remarkably opaque about how the principle should be applied in a context such as climate change (Grubb 1995). The principle clearly points toward responsibility-based rather than burden-based criteria, proportional in some way to emissions. The polluter should pay, but on what basis: who should receive payment and for what purpose?

A critical distinction that is rarely clarified is whether the principle applies to gross payment or net payment. Burtraw & Toman (1992) assume that it applies to net payment, so that each country should pay for abatement in proportion to its contemporary emissions; this, they note, would be regressive against national income, thus bound to spark developing country opposition, and Chichilnisky & Heal (1994), among others, have pointed out that such allocation of payment may be neither efficient nor fair. Other authors assume that the principle means that gross payments should be proportional to emissions, leaving open the matter of how the resulting revenues should be distributed as a separate question of efficiency and equity; and they also consider different bases for payment (Grubb 1995).

1. OECD Council, 14 November 1974.

Table 4.2   Outcome fairness and asymmetry of losses and gains according to three ethical positions.

	Libertarian	Contractarian	Egalitarian
Principle for gains	Priority	Proportionality	Parity
Principle for losses	Loss spreading	Deep pocket	Strict fault
Outcome for gains	Narrowest	Greatest good	Broadest
Outcome for losses	Broadest	Least harm	Narrowest

Procedural fairness in climate change

There are many approaches to the issue of procedural fairness: whether the means by which an outcome is reached is considered to be fair and reasonable, regardless of whether the outcome is preferred. One that has been used quite effectively in the analysis of societal responses to technological hazards is that which focuses on preferred procedures for obtaining consent to risk (MacLean 1980, Rayner & Cantor 1987). Institutional preferences for valid principles of consent are summarized in Table 4.3.

Table 4.3 Valid consent as framed by three ethical positions.

	Libertarian	Contractarian	Egalitarian
Consent	Revealed	Hypothetical	Explicit

With respect to consent, decisionmakers in a market individualist context favor a *revealed preference* approach (Thaler & Rosen 1975), sometimes called *implicit consent* (MacLean 1980). For example, if the price differential between three ladders reflects only the degree of safety built into each one and a consumer selects the mid-price ladder, that consumer is deemed to consent to the additional risk that results from not purchasing the costliest ladder. At the same time the consumer is revealing that he or she does not consent to the increased risk that would result from purchasing the cheapest ladder. This principle allows market forces to determine planning priorities and the degree of risk that people are prepared to accept. The rationale is that people's preferences for one solution or another will be reflected accurately in how they spend their money (which, of course, assumes they have some).

The contractarian principle for obtaining consent is sometimes called *hypothetical* consent (Rawls 1971). The citizen is assumed to have entered into a contract with the decisionmaking institution, whereby he or she may be deemed to assent to decisions made through rational procedures of that institution, even though he or she may not like the particular outcome. For example, people pay income tax because they accept the legitimacy of the government's claim on their money, rather than because they agree with the amount that it charges them or the particular pattern of spending the government chooses. Contractarian appeals to procedural fairness in obtaining consent are likely to be compared to the constitutional procedures for decisionmaking.

Explicit consent is the only legitimate form of consent for egalitarians. The use of any surrogate for consent undermines the basic premise of egalitarianism, that all are the same and have equal say. This gives rise to particular difficulties in assigning responsibility to the present generation for the acts of our forebears, as well as for obtaining consent from future generations.

Consider the claim that the North bears a special obligation to pay for climate policies based on the historical dimension of global resource use (Box 4.11). It seems that there are two plausible lines of reasoning here. One is that children do indeed inherit the liabilities of their parents along with their assets. The other is that the historical behavior of the North has created a current condition of structural dependency of the South upon the North.

Box 4.11   Historical responsibility and natural debt

Smith et al. (1993) proposed that responsibility for paying should be determined on the basis of the "natural debt," i.e., in proportion to total cumulative emissions since a specified date. Because this in itself would result in all countries bearing some responsibility for paying (although very much less for developing countries), they modified this by suggesting a lower threshold for basic needs emissions, consistent also with the arguments of Agarwal & Narain (1991) and others.

The principle of using cumulative historical emissions directly as a component in determining payment (or future emissions allocation) was considered by these authors as a natural and important matter of equity, and many others also argue the central equity importance of historical emissions in more general terms (Grubb 1995). Some of these authors recognized a variety of potential practical difficulties: how far back the emission estimates should go; whether (and if so how) the natural decay (re-absorption) of emissions should be taken into account; which gases should be included, given the highly variable quality and in some cases complete absence of data; and how to relate the emissions to scale (e.g., cumulative population or current population). In part these complexities reflect different potential definitions of the natural-debt concept; in assessing responsibility indices, for illustration, Smith et al. consider total industrial CO_2 emissions since 1950 by country, with a range of lower threshold levels.

However, at the same time as espousing intergenerational egalitarianism, Ghosh (1993) criticizes the natural debt concept as a basis of historical responsibility on the grounds that it is an abstract environment-centered focus that does not acknowledge responsibility to others for one's actions and does not relate to fairness across human beings.

Historical responsibility as an equity principle has strong support in the literature, and politically in less industrialized countries, but there are also valid counterarguments (Grubb 1995). These include:
• ignorance of past generations about the consequences of their actions
• ambiguities in tracing responsibility for emissions
• the spread of benefits of emissions beyond the emitters.

Smith et al. and Ghosh rejected such objections as partly inaccurate, but mostly irrelevant to the Fujii (1990) principle of equal historical per capita entitlement, since it is based not upon fault, blame or compensation but upon an egalitarian principle of access. In fact, the disagreements illustrate several different dimensions of the debate about historical responsibility.

With respect to the principle of historical obligation, it is easy to reconcile the principle that the North has liabilities toward the South, based on past resource extraction, if the relevant entities of the North and the South are judged to be legally immortal hierarchical institutions, such as corporations or nation states.

This would be quite consistent with the contractarian principle of hypothetical consent, where the individual is deemed to consent to the decisions of legitimate institutions, even though he or she might individually dissent. But under egalitarian principles, an individual can incur a debt only by explicit informed consent and cannot be held liable for the debts of his or her forebears. Also the claims of individuals take precedence over those of hierarchical entities such as states. However, the preferred asymmetry of losses and gains enables the egalitarian to reconcile the contractarian argument about inherited liabilities with the egalitarian principle of parity, which is advocated in the per capita allocation of greenhouse gas emissions to states.

Equity, institutions and solidarity

What is fair may be the subject of disagreement, but the demand for fairness arises only because, as John Donne put it, "No man is an island." It is very hard to imagine what fairness would mean if people did not live and work together in families, communities, firms, nations, and other social arrangements that persist over time. The whole issue of fairness arises out of the establishment of public (i.e. shared) expectations for the conduct of community relations (*procedural* equity) and the distribution of rights over resources within and among communities (*distributional* equity). In other words, fairness is integral to the establishment and maintenance of social solidarity at every level of social institutions from the micro to the macro, from the local to the global (Rayner 1995). Protest and defection from institutions result when public expectations for procedures or for the outcomes of allocations are repeatedly violated or people cannot be persuaded to embrace emergent alternatives (Hirschman 1970). Family members may argue or leave home. Where religious reform fails, people switch religious denominations or give up church altogether. If scientists' letters to scholarly journals fall on deaf ears, they may cancel their subscriptions to professional societies. Disgruntled employees walk off the job singly or en masse. Nations withhold ratification of treaties and protocols or financial contributions to international bodies and may withdraw from them altogether.

Issues of equity in climate change highlight the central importance of the concept of social solidarity to understanding the social and political discourses about climate. They suggest that these discourses are inextricably institutional in nature and are not simply the rational expressions of preformed individual preferences, as assumed by the self-interest paradigm that has dominated economic and political analysis throughout most of the twentieth century.

Since the Second World War, political theorizing has been dominated by so-called noninstitutional perspectives. Noninstitutional theories can be characterized as follows (March & Olsen 1989):

- methodological individualist—political outcomes are more likely to be seen as resulting from the sum of individual actions, rather than being attributed to rules or structural factors
- utility maximizing—individuals are more likely to be seen as acting in accordance with what they determine to be their best interest, rather than as responding to perceived responsibilities and roles
- instrumentalist—politics is more likely to be seen as action—the making of decisions and the distribution of goods and services—rather than as a process of creating meaning
- functionalist—the historical development of a society is likely to be seen as a process of successful adaptation such that, over time, it reaches its own unique and stable configuration; dysfunction, instability, and similitude are not the focus of attention.

Such theories include those concerned with competitive rational agents (e.g., realism, rational choice, nonrepetitive game theory and its variants) and those concerned with the temporal sorting of problems, solutions, decision-makers, and choices, such as Kingdon's (1994) *stream model* of the flow of policy events.

However, by these very assumptions, noninstitutional approaches identify themselves with the individualist libertarian ethical stance that underpins market style institutional arrangements. They fit comfortably with the benign view of nature—the ball in the basin. As long as we all do our own exuberant individualistic things, this myth tells us, a hidden hand—the uniformly downward slope of the basin's inner surface—will lead us to the best outcome. From this point of view, we interfere with this process at our peril. Denying the institutional nature of human interaction is itself an institutional stance.

Managing climate change has to take place through institutional arrangements. Any attempt to conceptualize climate change will involve an institutional framework of one kind or another. Similarly, how responses to climate change are identified, evaluated, and enacted can only take place through the medium of institutional behavior. This is the starting point for those sociologists, political scientists, economists, and anthropologists who espouse the so-called *new institutionalism* and the field of *cultural theory*. Although, as we shall shortly see, they do not stay together, these two approaches do set off together by vigorously rejecting, in interestingly different ways, the so-called noninstitutional approach.

New institutionalism and cultural theory

According to the new institutionalism, it is rules, not the individual calculations of rational actors, that are the dominant force guiding political actions. Rules in this usage are "The routines, procedures, conventions, roles, strategies, organizational forms, and technologies around which political activity is constructed" (March & Olsen 1989: 22–3). This concept of rules also encompasses "the beliefs, paradigms, codes, cultures, and knowledge that surround, support, elaborate and contradict those roles and routines." Rules transcend individuals and can persist in an institution despite significant changes in the membership of the institution. Furthermore, individuals will adhere to rules even when such behavior does not appear to be in their immediate self-interest.

Rule-based behavior is shaped by a logic that differs from that assumed by the rational-actor, utility-maximizing approach. "To describe behavior as driven by rules is to see action as a matching of a situation to the demands of a position" (March & Olsen 1989: 23); that is, behavior is supported by a logic of appropriateness, rather than a logic of consequences.

Stated another way, the behavior of the calculating actor is anticipatory action, whereas rule-based behavior is obligatory action. In the anticipatory-action model, the actor asks questions about choices available, his or her values, and the consequences of the latter for the former, before selecting the action expected to generate the most preferred outcome. In the obligatory-action model, the actor first assesses the nature of the situation and his or her identity, considers the appropriateness of various actions for him- or herself in this particular situation, then selects the most appropriate action.

To describe most behavior as rule-based is not to say that the behavior is routine. "The number and variety of alternative rules assure that one of the primary factors affecting behavior is the process by which some of those rules, rather than others, are evoked in a particular situation" (March & Olsen 1989: 24).

The institutional view of politics differs significantly from that offered by many recent political theories. Rules play a central role in political behavior (March & Olsen 1989: 38):

> A calculus of political costs and benefits is less important; a calculus of identity and appropriateness is more important. Learning as recorded in history-dependent routines and norms is more important.

From the institutional perspective, institutions shape politics through the construction and elaboration of meaning. "Expectations, preferences, experience, and interpretations of the actions of others are all constructed within political institutions" (March & Olsen 1989: 39). This approach poses a serious challenge to theories of political action that assume that individuals act rationally in accordance with their *prior* preferences, since preferences emerge alongside political action, not in advance of it.

The new institutionalism perspective also has significant implications for conventional assumptions about institutional transformation. If routines and meanings are constructed and altered by institutions, active efforts to change an institution into another particular form are likely to encounter difficulty. This is not to say that deliberate transformation is impossible. Intentional change can be implemented in several ways, all of which can be discerned in our examination of the discourses of climate change:

- use adaptive processes already found in the institution
- exploit the incompleteness of institutional rules and routines
- shock the institution into change.

However, the transformation cannot be expected to go precisely as intended by those who sought it, if only because the intentions themselves are not unitary (March & Olsen 1989: 65–6):

> Understanding the transformation of political institutions requires recognizing that there are frequently multiple, not necessarily consistent, intentions, that intentions are often ambiguous, that intentions are part of a system of values, goals, and attitudes that embeds intention in a structure of other beliefs and aspirations, and that this structure of values and intentions is shaped, interpreted, and created during the course of the change in the institution.

Cultural theorists take this last point rather more seriously than do new institutionalists, who appear to hold out the prospect of eventual convergence on a single rationality—structure of values and intentions—through a combination of aggregative and integrative political processes (March & Olsen 1989: 118):

> Political institutions combine aggregative and integrative processes. In an aggregative process, the will of the people is discovered through political campaigns and bargaining among rational citizens, each pursuing self-interest within a set of rules for governance through majority rule. In an integrative process, the will of the people is discovered through deliberation by reasoning citizens and rulers seeking to find the general welfare within a context of shared social values.

Cultural theorists suggest that a single collective will can never be achieved by a complex society. Whereas March & Olsen seem ultimately unwilling to jettison at least the vision or goal of a universally shared rational consensus, for cultural theorists, turbulent patterns of disagreement are the only unchanging feature of the political landscape, as institutions and societies engage in a perpetual process of social learning, dissolving and reforming patterns of social solidarity in response to shifting endogenous and exogenous pressures without ever achieving a stable equilibrium, which would imply a single institutional pattern of solidarity that had decisively eliminated all alternatives.

Viewed in this way, the climate change discourse itself is an institution of societal management, and the society that it manages is diverse and pluralistic. Institutions do not merely create meaning; the process of constructing and elaborating meaning simultaneously creates the patterns of solidarity that constitute institutions. As it operates, discourse frustrates and complements government regulation, market exchange, and community pressure (Gerlach 1993a) to generate a series of crises, each of which serves to promote the competing organizational goals of the various groups involved and thus creates fresh problems. Groups are then mobilized to join, lobby, or criticize these problem-solving exercises and, in the process, add values and differing interpretations to expand and elaborate even the smallest problems. Such societal turbulence or disorder is characteristic of building and managing complex institutional arrangements, not of institutional confusion (Gerlach 1993b: 276):

> These large and small crises and related conflicts are understood as moments of disorder, partly because they are and partly because calling them disorder legitimates reorder.

The actions of individuals and groups in the discourses can be seen as orderly, and even to some extent predictable, through the respective cultures of interest, identity, and meaning to which they subscribe and adhere. Their interactions are also orderly in that their values prescribe strategies and exchanges characterized by rhetorical discourse. Subsequently, society and culture are changed as the discourse develops, with new debates taken up in the contexts of the old.

The contemporary focus of this kind of reconstitutive discourse is on the effects of technology, social action, and cultural interpretation of the biophysical environment as a natural resource. Subsequently, the issues that are framed by the discourse shape and alter the social and cultural contexts from which the resource definitions, uses, and systems of management arose. But, it is clear from this account that it is more than mere ideas that are being reordered—the relations of social solidarity themselves are rearranged.

Three forms of solidarity

More than 150 years of social theory—spanning legal history, sociology, anthropology, psychology, economics, and political science—indicates that institutions (solidarity) can be built in many ways and across different scales, from families to federations of nation states. This variation has often been presented as an evolutionary dichotomy: an inexorable historical journey from state A to state B, but (as we will see) with the theorists often selecting their As and their Bs very differently.

Dichotomous distinctions have proved to be very durable in the history of social theory. In the mid-nineteenth century, the legal historian Sir Henry Maine (1861) distinguished social solidarity based on *status*, in which actors know their place in hierarchical structures based on the idiom of the family, from solidarity based on *contract* in which agents freely associate by negotiated agreement. Later in the century, the German sociologist Tönnies (1887) distinguished between *Gemeinschaft*, where societies are bound by ties of kinship, friendship, and local tradition, and *Gesellschaft*, where social bonds are created by individualistic competition and contract. At the turn of the century the French anthropologist Durkheim (1893) distinguished human societies based on *mechanical solidarity*, in which agents bind themselves to others on the basis of sameness, from those built upon *organic solidarity*, in which agents are bound together by the interdependence of specialized social roles. Each of these grand dichotomies was viewed by its author in evolutionary terms that continue to resonate in contemporary social theorizing, such as that of Bennett & Dahlberg (1990), who, echoing Durkheim, detected in the development from preindustrial to industrial society, a shift from *multifunctionalism*, where everyone can do everything, toward *specialization*. For the most part, however, more recent approaches dispense with the unidirectional evolutionary assumption. Educational sociologists have identified *positional* families, in which behavior is regulated by appeals to hierarchical authority, and *personal* families, in which behavior is regulated by appeals based on individual preferences (Bernstein 1971). Major contemporary political scientists and economists such as Lindblom (1977) and Williamson (1975) focused on the different characteristics and dynamics of coexisting and competing social systems based on the social bonds created through participation in *markets* and those based on the solidarity of *hierarchy*.

We have already seen some of these grand dichotomies being used in connection with the public's understanding of environmental risk: Cotgrove's distinction between catastrophists and cornucopians, for instance (which contrasts the value orientations of the modern environmental movement with those of both the market and the hierarchy). Parsimony requires that we reduce this rich diversity to the minimum number of basic modes or patterns of solidarity that can be distinguished usefully. It is also desirable to have a basis for distinction that would hold across the board, from micro to macro scales of social organization.

Although there is a great deal of overlap among the grand dichotomies of social theory, they are far from perfectly congruent and they seem not to be reducible to fewer than three. In other words, if we are not to exclude some of those masters, we are going to have to allow one more solidarity than the two they themselves variously saw as fundamental (Table 4.4).[3]

Table 4.4 Characteristics of three kinds of social solidarity as described in classic social science literature.

Market	Hierarchical	Egalitarian
Gesellschaft	Gemeinschaft	Gemeinschaft
Organic solidarity	Organic solidarity	Mechanical solidarity
Specialized roles	Specialized roles	Multifunctional roles
Personal authority	Positional authority	Personal authority
Contract relations	Status relations	Status relations

First, solidarity can be expressed through the market, characterized by the features of individualism and competition associated with Gesellschaft. Solidarity is achieved in two ways, most obviously through contracts, but also through individual consumption choices that establish identity with fellow consumers and differentiation from those who follow different consumption patterns. As manifestations of Gesellschaft, market forms of solidarity are directly orthogonal to both of the other basic modes of solidarity, described below, which share the stronger community boundaries typical of Gemeinschaft solidarity.

Second, solidarity can be expressed through orderly differentiation in hierarchies, the rules for which establish identity through careful gradations of status based on explicit characteristics such as age, gender, educational attainment, professorial rank, and so on. This form of positional authority is directly orthogonal to the emphasis on personal freedom shared by both markets and the third form of social solidarity.

Third, solidarity can be expressed through egalitarian homogeneity; that is, by operating rules of equality that keep each participant at the same status. In this respect, egalitarianism is a manifestation of mechanical solidarity and multifunctional roles that is directly orthogonal to both hierarchies and markets, which both favor organic specialization of labor.

This synthesis creates a two-dimensional space within which multiple

---

3. For a discussion of how each master's work relates to this threefold typology, see part II of Thompson et al. (1990).

possibilities for institutions can be located. This has several methodological and pragmatic advantages over dichotomous frameworks. It is satisfying because it systematically encompasses the spectrum of dichotomous distinctions that, over a century and a half, have informed a wide range of empirical social sciences. This inclusiveness suggests that the three basic types are fairly robust.

The endogenous dynamic qualities of the two-dimensional framework are also methodologically appealing. Each kind of solidarity exists only in distinction from the other two, which means that instability and conflict are inherent to the framework, as they are in real life, and do not require the action of an exogenous agent for changes in social organization or the values that support it. The potential for endogenizing social change may have important implications for long-term policy modeling, which presently is unable to deal well with changes in societal preference functions, such as the demographic transition.

The dynamic quality of this triangular space contrasts with the evolutionary dichotomies, which are like a pipe with a nonreturn valve that permits fluid to flow in only one direction. The unidirectional flow metaphor may be an appropriate one for pollution entering the environment, but it will not do for social development. Furthermore, even if we dispense with the evolutionary assumptions associated with dichotomous schemes, we are still left with an overly simple switching model, one in which only two states are possible. If the system is not in state A, it must be in state B, and vice versa. By contrast, the triangular system is a complex framework, in that not being in state A does not automatically imply state B. It is therefore a nondeterministic framework.

This framework explicitly focuses on the modes by which people bind themselves to each other in social institutions and, in so doing:

- shape their epistemological and moral relationship with nature
- develop preferences for distributional equity
- establish principles of procedural fairness
- establish principles for intergenerational equity.

We have already explored the first three issues in this chapter as they have brought us to the understanding of discourse as building different kinds of solidarity among the living. Hence, we now turn to the issue of building solidarity among the living and the dead and the unborn—the issue of intergenerational equity.

Solidarity and intergenerational equity

The argument about historical debt invites us to address intergenerational equity as an issue of solidarity across generations—how we bind ourselves to our ancestors and to our descendants. Table 4.5 summarizes the effects of each

Table 4.5 Time, intergenerational responsibility, and discount rates as framed by three kinds of solidarity.

	Market	Hierarchical	Egalitarian
Time perception	Short term	Long term	Compressed
Intergenerational responsibility	Weak	Balanced	Strong
Discount rate	Diverse high	Technically calculated	Zero or negative

kind of social solidarity on expectations of the future, responsibility to future generations, and determination of the discount rate.

In market institutions, expectations of the future are likely to be strongly focused on deadlines (Rayner 1982). Competitive success depends largely on timing; planning for shifting market tastes, clinching deals at the right price, meeting delivery deadlines, or knowing when to sell pork-belly futures. The emphasis is on short-term expectations and immediate returns on activities and investments. Long-term planning is a feature of hierarchical institutions which, in principle, are immortal. Market individualists don't have time for such long-term considerations. Hence, market institutions pay little heed to intertemporal responsibility. They tend to assume that future generations will be adaptive and innovative in dealing with the legacy of today's technology, just as our generation has had to be in response to the legacy of the industrial era. So far as consent is concerned, it is assumed that future generations will make decisions on current market conditions and will therefore accept similar conditions of predecessors. The emergence of future liabilities can be left to market forces when they occur and will, in fact, provide the stimulus for future enterprise. Under these conditions different discount rates apply simultaneously for different goods or at different times for the same good. The discount rates also tend to be high.

In hierarchical institutions, history is strongly differentiated. Anniversaries of great events in the past are celebrated collectively and provide models for discriminating epochs of the future. Clear recognition of age-sets and generations, which are the basis for establishing seniority in the present, also engenders clear expectations of an ordered future. The regimes of distinguished leaders (whether kings or company directors) also contribute to an ordered expectation of the future. Intergenerational responsibility therefore tends to be strong but balanced by the needs of the present. It is also likely to be safeguarded by the longevity of institutions. Consent is based on the assumption that future generations will recognize the legitimacy of present institutions. The apparent discount rate, therefore, tends to be lower than where market solidarity applies. Furthermore, hierarchies are the most likely of the three kinds of solidarity to be concerned with the bureaucratic determination of a standardized rate that can be applied across the board.

In egalitarian groups also, history tends to be viewed as epochal but, because of the problems of resolving disputes in institutions that are reluctant to recognize dispute resolution by claims to seniority, competitive leadership, or established procedures, such groups are prone to frequent schism (Rayner 1986). Hence, the group's crusading mission may lead to a sense of historical self-importance that results in the view that the present epoch is a decisive historical moment. Under these conditions, intergenerational responsibility is very strong, but trust in formal institutions is weak. If consent cannot be obtained from future generations, and our descendants cannot force long-dead decisionmakers to pay for their errors, then we have no right to accept risks on behalf of those descendants. Under these conditions the apparent discount rate used for environmental and intergenerational calculations is very close to zero, possibly even negative.

The different perceptions of time and expectations of the future engendered by each kind of solidarity seem to be critical factors in the perception of the costs and benefits of climate change policies. Market-oriented decisionmakers focus on costs because they are primarily concerned about the needs of the current generation. Furthermore, the desired asymmetry of losses and gains leads those same decisionmakers to defer costs into the future where they may be capable of being dispersed more widely throughout society. Hence, there is a strong incentive in market solidarity to postpone policy responses to the threat of climate change.

The low discount rates of egalitarians, combined with high levels of intertemporal responsibility and the impossibility of obtaining explicit consent from future generations, focus decisionmakers' concern on potentially high, possibly catastrophic, future costs. This provides a powerful incentive to take action now, which in keeping with the desired asymmetry of costs and benefits, also places the burden on the parties actually responsible for the current emissions that may impact on future generations. Hence, egalitarian solidarity leads to an emphasis on rapid implementation of policies designed to prevent the onset of climate change.

The technocratic approach to discounting and the overriding concern for system maintenance in hierarchical solidarity lead toward a middle course: limiting responses only to the no-regrets strategy of implementing climate change policies that make sense for other reasons while attempting to improve understanding of the extent of present and future costs, and when they might arise.

A two-dimensional map of institutional discourse and human values

In the preceding sections we have summarized a wide range of social science insights into the three most basic ways in which people bind themselves to each other in social institutions and, in so doing:

- establish principles for intergenerational equity
- diagnose the underlying social causes of climate change
- develop preferences for distributional equity
- establish principles of procedural fairness.

These summaries provide us with a basic two-dimensional map of the climate change discourse as framed by the diversity of human values (Fig. 4.3). The triangle is equivalent to the territorial borders of a conventional geographical map. Using the same outline, separate maps can be drawn for each element

Hierarchical institutions

Myth of nature: perverse/tolerant
Diagnosis of cause: population
Policy bias: contractarian
Distribution: proportionality
Consent: hypothetical
Liability: deep pocket
Intergeneration responsibility: present > future
Discounting: technical standard

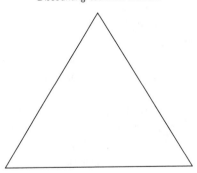

Market institutions

Myth of nature: benign
Diagnosis of cause: pricing
Policy bias: libertarian
Distribution: priority
Consent: revealed
Liability: loss spreading
Intergeneration responsibility: present > future
Discounting: diverse/high

Egalitarian institutions

Myth of nature: ephemeral
Diagnosis of cause: profligacy
Policy bias: egalitarian
Distribution: parity
Consent: explicit
Liability: strict fault
Intergeneration responsibility: future > present
Discounting: zero/negative

Figure 4.3 A two-dimensional map of institutional discourse and human values (Rayner 1995).

of equity, just as atlases contain maps of precipitation, vegetation, population, and other variables of interest that are superimposed on the land surface. Often, several maps can be overlaid to give a composite picture, as in Figure 4.3. This analogy with geographical maps is helpful precisely because such maps always tie the variable of interest to a particular location having specific geological characteristics that support the variable. In other words, precipitation, vegetation, population, and so on, are not free floating but are tied to specific places on the land surface. Similarly, the map of human values is not just a free-floating suite of policy biases and ethical options. It locates packages of values and ethical priorities in specific places in the social landscape; that is, within the discourse among institutions exhibiting various mixtures of market, hierarchical, or egalitarian solidarity.

The analogy with geographical maps is also useful in that maps can be drawn at different scales. Similarly, the map of discourse and human values can be drawn at a variety of scales. The family, the workplace, and the community all depend on the creation of solidarity among individuals. The corporation, the nation state, or the global community of nations are examples where solidarity is built among larger aggregations of people bound to each other in various ways. Ultimately, the issues of climate change and global sustainable development are a challenge to create and maintain solidarity at all of these levels. The two-dimensional map provides us with a richer analytic framework than do one-dimensional approaches for understanding and intervening in ethical disputes in the formation of treaties, the implementation of national policies, the shaping of consumer demand, and the modification of behavior at the micro level of firms and families.

Another feature of geographical maps drawn to scale is that they enable a navigator to locate his or her position in relation to other locations and to measure how close or far that is from various objectives. Systems of mathematical measurement of market, hierarchical, and egalitarian solidarities already exist at the level of communities and organizations (Gross & Rayner 1985) and of households (Dake & Thompson 1993). Similar measurement schemes have been adapted for measuring solidarities among larger units such as nation states (Grendstad & Selle 1997). Negotiators can use the map of values to locate their own positions, to select the direction in which they want to move in any dimension of equity, and to measure, on multiple criteria, the distance between their own positions and the goals of other participants in a negotiation process.

At the very least, use of the map could lead to technical improvements in the kind of benefit–cost analyses already being performed within the IPCC framework. For example, the map of human values rests on the processes of creating and maintaining social solidarity in both space and time. Hence, it provides a theoretical basis for developing predictive models of institutional differences

332

in principles of intergenerational obligation and social discount rates, which are key to the success of welfare economics, but into which welfare economics itself provides no insight.

In fact, welfare economics as a prescriptive value system has its own place on the two-dimensional map. The dominant concern for efficiency, embodied in the drive to achieve Pareto optimality, is characteristic of market solidarity. However, within welfare economics the market orientation is modified by hierarchical concerns to apply the efficiency criterion to administrative determinations of fairness. This locates welfare economics along the left side of the triangle, between market and hierarchical approaches. Thus, the triangular map graphically reminds us to consider the alternative utility functions: those that value equality over efficiency and refuse to discount future costs. Although some economists may be tempted to argue that such egalitarians are too few to matter in the grand scheme of things, those who study the dynamics of scientific and technological disputes will attest to the effectiveness of such parties in slowing or preventing the implementation of a variety of projects and programs, including hazardous waste facilities, nuclear power programs, and genetic engineering research development and marketing (Johnson & Covello 1987).

By focusing on the construction and maintenance of institutional solidarities, rather than on the preferences of individuals, the map also provides a basis for developing models of changes in societal preference functions. Furthermore, by making the form of solidarity the unit of analysis, and by allowing that an individual may be part of several solidarities, we can appreciate how it is that the individuals can make radical shifts in their individual preference functions. We no longer have to resort to the conclusion that they are either irrational or acting in bad faith. For example, a negotiator from a developing country elite may invoke the parity principle in international negotiations, the proportionality principle in apportioning budgets in his or her domestic bureaucracy, and the priority principle in making his or her own domestic private sector investments. Rather than cynically switching values in the pursuit of naked self-interest, the map suggests that the same individual may simply be involved in building different kinds of solidarity in different spheres of activity. Different kinds of solidarities expressed in different kinds of institutions stabilize each set of principles for defining needs, preferences for distributional outcomes and procedures, responsibilities to future generations, and obligations with respect to nature. By focusing on the form of solidarity, and not on the psychophysiological entity, we are able to cope with that most micro of institutional realities, the *dividual*, a term coined by Marriott (1967) to convey the point that there is nothing socially indivisible about the individual.

Furthermore, as Rose (1990: 927) observed, although there is good consensus among welfare economists on Pareto optimality as the best efficiency criterion, "there is no consensus on a 'best' equity principle." The two-dimensional map enables us to refine this observation; that is, we probably should not even attempt to find a best equity principle, but should focus instead on achieving practical agreement about joint action among parties upholding quite different, even incommensurable, principles of equity. And, of course, embedded in the Pareto principle is one fairness principle—priority. In other words, the IPCC should shift its sights from a *technocratic* goal of providing decisionmakers with the best possible prescription for fairness toward the more modest goal of providing decisionmakers with the best tools for essentially *political* negotiation among competing prescriptions. As Rose (1990: 934) concluded:

> The fact that there are several alternative definitions of equity should not give cause for dismay but, rather, should stimulate further study. In principle, nearly all nations subscribe to some concept of fairness, and thus its potential as a unifying principle should not be neglected.

The view that equity can be a rallying point in climate negotiations was echoed by several authors,, including Hahn & Richards (1989), Toman & Burtraw (1991), and Rose & Stevens (1993). A concept of fairness that acknowledges diversity across more dimensions than distributional outcome alone seems more capable of engaging diverse actors than a one-dimensional conception that may require participants to violate their values and preferences on other dimensions of equity.

This conclusion is consistent with the advice of decision theorists, that parties seeking agreements on actions should seek to include a wide range of dimensions in their negotiations (Fisher & Ury 1981, Raiffa 1982). To design win–win solutions in negotiations, we need to be able to recognize what counts as a win to the parties involved. Winning consists of more than just the bottom line from a single transaction; building communities at the local and global scales is a highly valued goal of human behavior. For instance, the US State Department often argues that participating in international environmental agreements enhances US leadership and credibility in the international community. This desire to promote goodwill and solidarity among nations may well override concerns for the domestic costs of participation (Hahn & Richards 1989). The map of human values provides a systematic tool for exploring multiple dimensions of fairness in the search for practical agreements.

Conclusions

We have described a moral landscape, and an approach to mapping it, that presents a picture of the equity concerns that are likely to influence the conduct of climate negotiations and efforts to implement climate change policies. This landscape is more complex than the one-dimensional analytic framework that currently dominates discussions of equity. However, it remains reasonably parsimonious and has clear practical implications for the conduct of research and negotiations, and for the implementation of climate change policies.

In navigating this moral landscape, we recognize that climate change provides an arena for debating a wide variety of social, economic, and political issues that society finds difficult to address directly. These include the unequal distribution of wealth within and among nations, and the tension between the imperatives of independence and interdependence at all levels of social organization. Much of the debate about equity in climate change mitigation is an extension of the broader debate about international economic development and political empowerment.

Clearly, there is social benefit to be obtained from the existence of an arena in which potential changes in the socioeconomic and political status quo can be explored as deriving from natural imperatives rather than human agency. This enables parties to advance agendas for change without directly and immediately threatening deeply entrenched political and financial interests.

But the situation also presents potential dangers for human society. On the one hand, it is plausible that the opportunity costs of debating significant social and economic change in a surrogate arena may reduce our capacity to make desirable changes. For example, if we allocate significant economic and political resources to mitigating climate change as a way of enhancing the development of less industrialized countries, we may be reducing the level of resources actually available to fight poverty, hunger, and ignorance. On the other hand, our use of the opportunity that a potential natural crisis provides for social reform to pursue a socioeconomic agenda may lead us to ignore or override signals from the natural system that nature is, indeed, about to use its veto over human behavior.

These are important questions that are seldom addressed directly by policymakers engaged in the climate change discourses. Unfortunately, policymakers and decisionmakers often seem to fear that making the implicit and underlying dimensions of the discourse an explicit object of reflection will undermine political will to act in accordance with their own policy preferences. If so, there is no basis for such fear in the kind of social science analysis presented here. Recognizing epistemological and ethical diversity does not lead inexorably to agnosticism and political paralysis. Rather, it provides a realistic perspective from which to participate in debate with a heightened ability to listen to and understand the arguments and standpoints of other participants, as well as to be aware of the role played by one's own institutional bias.

Furthermore, climate change is widely seen as part of a broader problem of humankind's relationship with nature. However, views of what that relationship should be are diverse and deeply rooted in our social relationships—in social solidarity. How we bind ourselves to each other shapes the way we bind ourselves to nature. Social and cultural variables of network density and interconnectedness, and of rule sharing, account better for variations in environmental perceptions and behavior than do standard demographic variables such as age and sex.

Important policy differences with respect to diagnosis and treatment of that syndrome reflect these differences in ways that fundamentally shape political and administrative proposals for its solution. The conceptual map of human values is a useful and parsimonious device, both for social scientists to identify and track the strength of support for alternative positions and for policymakers seeking to identify opportunities for effective intervention in the debates.

The assumption of homogeneity of perspectives in the expert/lay dichotomy obscures significant variation in the perceptions and preferences of both. It also obscures the fact that real people are not consistently experts or lay people. There are no universal experts and, in the civic arena, even the most modest lay person has some relevant expertise. Relevant knowledge brought to bear in the climate discourses is not composed solely of scientific facts about climate chemistry, dynamics, and impacts, but also derives from various experiences of social change and societal responses to natural change.

The expert/lay dichotomy also structures communication as a unidirectional process in which expert knowledge is passed to the public either to alleviate its ignorance or redress its misperceptions. In this mode, decisionmakers are often stopped in their tracks by recalcitrant populations who rightly insist that they have not been heard and that their expertise (what anthropologists call local knowledge) has been ignored. The suggestion that expert discourses are structured by the same elements of social organization as lay discourses redirects efforts at communication from simply overcoming ignorance to creating shared frames of reference and opportunities for shared action. Public information campaigns that assume that discrepancies between lay and expert accounts of climate change are simply attributable to knowledge deficiencies are bound to fail. Effective communication about climate change issues requires understanding of the frames of reference being used by all participants.

Finally, we observe that climate discourses are complex and turbulent. Many voices join in, and they are often inconsistent, even self-contradictory, but not randomly so, nor in a way that can simply be ascribed to naked self-interest.

However, plurality is not always easy to discern, because the vocabulary of one voice or another may define the debate, for a time, on its own terms. Under these conditions of hegemonic discourse, dissenting voices may not be heard clearly, because they are forced to use the terminology of the hegemonic voice. For example, it is very difficult to reject explicitly the egalitarian claims of equal per capita emissions rights in international negotiations, even though the resulting allocation of those rights to nation states would have no discernible effect on promoting individual equality. The point here is not that the egalitarian position is necessarily wrong, but that society's ability to explore alternative formulations and solutions is constrained under conditions of hegemony, and important opportunities for solutions may be lost.

The climate discourse, whether in formal negotiations among states or in the creation of informal alliances among social movements, actually constitutes the institutional arrangements for political action. By labeling the present state of affairs as disorderly, each voice seeks to legitimate the reordering of society along its own preferred principles. How these institutional arrangements are structured and how they operate in the climate change arena are the topic of Chapter 5.

References

Agarwal, A. & S. Narain 1991. *Global warming in an unequal world: a case of environmental colonialism*. New Delhi: Centre for Science and Environment.

Barrett, S. 1992. "Acceptable" allocations of tradeable carbon emission entitlements in a global warming treaty. In *Combating global warming*. Geneva: UNCTAD.

Benedick, R. E. 1991. *Ozone diplomacy: new directions in safeguarding the planet*. Cambridge, Massachusetts: Harvard University Press.

Bennett, J. W. & K. A. Dahlberg 1990. Institutions, social organization, and cultural values. See Turner et al. (1990).

Bernstein, B. 1971. *Class, codes, and control*, vol. 1. London: Routledge & Kegan Paul.

Berry, T. 1988. *The dream of the Earth*. San Francisco: Sierra Club.

Bertram, G. 1992. Tradeable emission permits and the control of greenhouse gases. *Journal of Development Studies* **28**(3), 423–46.

Bloomfield, B. P. 1986. *Modelling the world: the social constructions of systems analysts*. Oxford: Basil Blackwell.

Bostrom, A., B. Fischoff, M. G. Morgan 1992. Characterizing mental models of hazardous processes: a methodology and an application to radon. *Journal of Social Issues* **48**, 85–100.

Bostrom, A., M. G. Morgan, B. Fischoff, D. Read 1994. What do people know about climate change? Part 1: mental models. *Risk Analysis* **14**(6), 959–70.

Boyd, R. & P. Richerson 1989. *Culture and the evolutionary process*. Chicago: University of Chicago Press.

Burns, T. R. & H. Flam 1987. *The shaping of social organization*. London: Sage.

Burtraw, D. & M. A. Toman 1992. Equity and international agreements for CO_2 constraint. *Journal of Energy Engineering* **118**(2), 122–35.

Calabrese, G. 1970. *The cost of accidents*. New Haven, Connecticut: Yale University Press.

Cantor, R. & S. Rayner 1994. Changing perceptions of vulnerability. In *Industrial geology and global change*, R. Socolow, C. Andrews, F. Berkout, V. Thomas (eds). Cambridge: Cambridge University Press.

CBI 1995. *The CBI's statement of principles for business and sustainable development*. London: Confederation of British Industry.

Chichilnisky, G. & G. Heal 1994. Who should abate carbon emissions? An international viewpoint. *Economic Letters* **44**, 443–9.

Clark, W. C. & R. Munn (eds) 1986. *Sustainable development of the biosphere*. Cambridge: Cambridge University Press.

Coase, R. H. 1960. The problem of social cost. *Journal of Law and Economics* **3**, 1–44.

Cline, W. 1992. *The economics of global warming*. Washington DC: Institute for International Economics.

Clinton, W. & A. Gore 1993. US national population policy: an official statement. *Population and Development Review* **19**(2), 403–406.

Cotgrove, S. 1982. *Catastrophe or cornucopia: the environment, politics and the future*. Chichester, England: John Wiley.

Cronon, W. 1992. A place for stories: nature, history, and narrative. *Journal of American History*, **78**, 1347–76.

Dake, K. & M. Thompson 1993. The meanings of sustainable development: household strategies for managing needs and resources. In *Human ecology: crossing boundaries*, S. D. Wright, T. Dietz, R. Borden, G. Young, G. Guagnano (eds). Fort Collins, Colorado: Society for Human Ecology.

Die Grünen 1980 (1989). *Bundestagsprogramm*. In *The greens in West Germany: organisation and policy making*, E. Kolinsky (ed.). Oxford: Berg.

Diekmann, A. & R. Preisendörfer 1992. Persönliches Umweltverhalten: Diskrepanzen zwischen Ansprich und Wirklichkeit. *Kölner Zeitschrift für Sociologie und Sozialpsychologie* **44**, 169–93.

Doble, J., A. Richardson, A. Danks 1990. *Science and the public: a report in three volumes*. Vol. 3: *global warming caused by the greenhouse effect*. New York: Public Agenda Fund.

DoE [Department of Environment] 1990. *This common inheritance* [Cmd 1200]. London: HMSO.

Dunlap, R. E. 1991. Trends in public opinion toward environmental issues: 1965–1990. *Society and Natural Resources* **4**, 285–312.

Dunlap, R. E. & K. D. Van Liere 1977. Land ethic or golden rule: comment on "land ethic realized" by Thomas A. Heberlein. *Journal of Social Issues* **33**(3), 200–207.

——1984. Commitment to the dominant social paradigm and concern for environmental quality. *Social Science Quarterly* **4**, 1013–1028.

Durkheim, E. 1893. *De la division du travail sociale: étude sur l'organisation de sociétés supérieurs*. Paris: Alcan.

Epstein, J. & R. Gupta 1990. *Controlling the greenhouse effect: five global regimes compared*. Washington DC: Brookings Institution.

Ester, P. & F. van der Meer 1982. Determinants of individual environmental behavior: an outline of a behavioral model and some research findings. *The Netherlands Journal of Sociology* **1**, 57–94.

Fankhauser, S. 1992. The economic costs of global warming: some monetary estimates. In *Proceedings of the IIASA workshop on the costs, impacts, and benefits of CO_2 mitigation*, Y. Kaya, N. Nakicenovic, W. D. Nordhaus, F. Toth (eds). Laxenburg, Austria: International Institute for Applied Systems Analysis.

Farhar, B. C. 1977. The public decides about weather modification. *Environment and Behavior* **9**(3), 279–310.

Farhar, B. C., J. A. Clark, L. A. Sherretz, J. Horton, S. Krane 1979. *Social impacts of the St Louis*

338

urban weather anomaly. Final Report (vol. II), Institute of Behavioral Science, University of Colorado.

Fisher, R., & W. Ury 1981. *Getting to yes: negotiating agreement without giving in.* Boston: Houghton Mifflin.

Fujii, Y. 1990. *An assessment of the responsibility for the increase in the CO_2 concentrations and intergenerational carbon accounts.* Working Paper WP 05 55, International Institute of Applied Systems Analysis, Laxenburg, Austria.

Fulkerson, W., R. M. Cushman, G. Marland, S. Rayner 1989. International impacts of global climate change. Testimony to House Appropriations Subcommittee on Foreign Operations Export Financing and Related Programs (ORNL/TM-11184), Oak Ridge National Laboratory, Tennessee.

G7 Leaders 1993. G7 Leaders' voices on population at the UN General Assembly 1993. *Population and Development Review* **19**(4), 899–902.

Gerlach, L. P. 1993a. Negotiating ecological interdependence through societal debate: the Minnesota drought. In *The state and social power in global environmental politics*, R. D. Lipschutz & K. Conca (eds). New York: Columbia University Press.

——— 1993b. Crises are for using: the 1988 drought in Minnesota. *The Environmental Professional* **15**, 274–87.

Ghosh, P. 1993. Structuring the equity issue in climate change. In *The climate change agenda: an Indian perspective*, A. N. Achanta (ed.). New Delhi: Tata Energy Research Institute.

Gore, A. 1992. On stabilizing world population. *Population and Development Review* **18**(2), 380–83.

Gray, D. B., R. J. Borden, R. H. Weigel 1985. *Ecological beliefs and behaviors, assessment and change.* Westport, Connecticut: Greenwood Press.

Grendstad, G. & P. Selle 1997. Cultural theory, postmaterialism and environmental attitudes. In *Culture matters*, R. Ellis & M. Thompson (eds). Boulder, Colorado: Westview.

Gross, J. & S. Rayner 1985. *Measuring culture.* New York: Columbia University Press.

Grubb, M. 1989. *The greenhouse effect: negotiating targets.* London: Royal Institute of International Affairs.

——— 1995. Seeking fair weather: ethics and the international debate on climate change. *International Affairs* **71**(3), 463–96.

Grubb, M., J. Sebenius, A. Magalhães, S. Subak 1992. Sharing the burden. In *Confronting climate change: risks, implications, and responses*, I. M. Mintzer (ed.). Cambridge: Cambridge University Press.

Grübler, A. & N. Nakicenovic 1994. *International burden sharing in greenhouse gas reduction.* Research report RR-94-9, International Institute for Applied Systems Analysis, Laxenburg, Austria.

Haas, P. 1990. *Saving the Mediterranean: the politics of international environmental cooperation.* New York: Columbia University Press.

Habermas, J. 1981. *Theory of communicative action.* Boston: Beacon Press.

Hahn, R. W., & K. R. Richards 1989. The internationalization of environmental regulation. *Harvard International Law Journal* **30**(2), 421–46.

Harris, L., V. L. Tarrance, C. C. Lake 1989. *The rising tide: public opinion, policy and politics.* Washington DC: Americans for the Environment.

Hays, S. P. (in collaboration with B. D. Hays) 1987. *Beauty, health and permanence: environmental politics in the United States, 1955–1985 .* Cambridge: Cambridge University Press.

Headrick, D. R. 1990. Technological change. See Turner et al. (1990).

Heberlein, T. A. 1972. The land ethic realized: some social–psychological explanations for changing environmental attitudes. *Journal of Social Issues* **28**(4), 79–87.

Hedges, A. 1991. *Attitudes to energy conservation in the home.* London: HMSO.

Henderson-Sellers, A. 1990. Australian public perception of the greenhouse issue. *Climatic Change* **1**, 69–96.

Hirschman, A. O. 1970. *Exit voice, and loyalty: responses to declines in firms, organizations and states*. Cambridge, Massachusetts: Harvard University Press.

Holling, C. S. 1986. The resilience of terrestrial ecosystems. See Clark & Munn (1986).

Houghton, J. 1995. Me and my god. *Sunday Telegraph*, 10 September.

Houghton, J., G. J. Jenkins, J. J. Ephraums (eds) 1990. *Climate change: the IPCC scientific assessment*. Cambridge: Cambridge University Press.

IBRD [International Bank for Reconstruction and Development] 1992. *World development report*. Oxford: Oxford University Press.

Inglehart, R. 1977. *The silent revolution: changing values and political styles among Western publics*. Princeton, New Jersey: Princeton University Press.

——1990. *Culture shift in advanced industrial society*. Princeton, New Jersey: Princeton University Press.

IPCC [Intergovernmental Panel on Climate Change] 1990. *Report of the Special Committee on the Participation of Developing Countries*. Nairobi: UN Environment Programme.

Jaeger, C. G. Dürrenberger, H. Kastenholz, B. Truffer 1993. Determinants of environmental action with regard to climate change. *Climatic Change* **23**, 193–211.

Johnson, B. B. & V. T. Covello (eds) 1987. *The social and cultural construction of risk: essays on risk selection and perception*. Dordrecht: Reidel.

Kasperson, R. & K. Dow 1991. Development and geographical equity in global environmental change: a framework for analysis. *Evaluation Review* **15**(1), 149–71.

Katama, A. (ed.) 1995. *Equity and social considerations related to climate change* [papers presented to IPCC Working Group III Workshop]. Nairobi: ICIPE Science Press.

Kemp, P. & D. Wall 1990. *A green manifesto for the 1990s*. London: Penguin.

Kempton, W. 1991. Lay perspectives on global climate change. *Global Environmental Change: Human and Policy Dimensions* **1**(3), 183–208.

——1993. Will public environmental concern lead to action on global warming? *Annual Review of Energy and the Environment* **18**, 217–45.

Kempton, W., J. S. Boster, J. A. Hartley 1995. *Environmental values in American culture*. Boston: MIT Press.

Kingdon, J. 1984. *Agendas, alternatives, and public policies*. Boston: Little, Brown.

Leggett, J. (ed.) 1990. *Global warming: the Greenpeace report*. Oxford: Oxford University Press.

Lindblom, C. 1977. *Politics and markets: the world's political and economic systems*. New York: Basic Books.

Linderman, F. 1930. *Plenty Coups: chief of the Crows* [reprinted 1962]. Lincoln: University of Nebraska Press.

Löfstedt, R. E. 1991. Climate change perceptions and energy use decisions in northern Sweden. *Global Environmental Change* **4**, 321–4.

——1993. Lay perspectives concerning global climate change in Vienna, Austria. *Energy and Environment* **4**, 140–54.

——1995. Why are public perception studies of the environment ignored? *Global Environmental Change* **5**(2), 83–5.

Ludlum D. M. 1987. The climythology of America. *Weatherwise* **40**(October), 255–9.

MacLean, D. 1980. *Risk and consent: a survey of issues for centralized decision making*. Center for Philosophy and Public Policy, College Park, Maryland.

——1983. A moral requirement for energy policies. In *Energy and the future*, D. MacLean & P. Brown (eds). Totowa, New Jersey: Rowman & Littlefield.

Maine, H. S. 1861. *Ancient law*. London: John Murray.

Maloney, M. P. & M. P. Ward 1978. Ecology: let's hear from the people. *American Psychologist* **28**(7), 583–6.

Manne, A. & R. Richels 1992. *Buying greenhouse insurance: the economic costs of carbon dioxide emissions limits*. Cambridge: MIT Press.

Markandya, A. 1991. Global warming: the economics of tradeable permits. In *Blueprint 2: greening the world economy*, D. Pearce (ed.). London: Earthscan.

March, J. & J. Olsen 1989. *Rediscovering institutions*. New York: Free Press.

Marriott, M. 1967. Hindu transactions: diversity without dualism. In *Transaction and meaning*, B. Kapferer (ed.). Philadelphia, Pennsylvania: Institute for the Study of Human Issues.

McDaniels, T., L. J. Axelrod, P. Slovic 1995. *Lay perceptions of ecological risks from global climate change*. Report, Westwater Research Center, University of British Columbia.

Meadows, D. H., D. L. Meadows, J. Randers, W. W. Behrens III 1972. *The limits to growth*. New York: Universe.

Meyer, A. 1994. *Climate change, population and the paradox of growth*. London: Global Commons Institute.

—— 1995. The unequal use of the global commons. See Katama (1995).

Morgan, M. G., B. Fischoff, A. Bostrom, L. Lave, C. J. Atman 1992. Communicating risk to the public. *Environmental Science and Technology* **26**, 2048–2056.

Nash, R. 1967. *Wilderness and the American mind*. New Haven, Connecticut: Yale University Press.

—— 1989. *The rights of nature: a history of environmental ethics*. Madison: University of Wisconsin Press.

Nordhaus, W. 1991. To slow or not to slow: the economics of the greenhouse effect. *The Economic Journal* **6**, 920–37.

Pearce, D. (ed.) 1991. *Blueprint 2: greening the world economy*. London: Earthscan.

Pearce, D., A. Markandya, E. Barbier 1989. *Blueprint for a green economy*. London: Earthscan.

Raiffa, H. 1982. *The art of science and negotiation*. Cambridge, Massachusetts: Harvard University Press (Belknap).

Rainbow, S. 1993. *Green politics*. Oxford: Oxford University Press.

Rawls, J. 1971. *A theory of justice*. Cambridge, Massachusetts: Harvard University Press.

Rayner, S. 1982. The perception of time and space in egalitarian sects: a millenarian cosmology. In *Essays in the sociology of perception*, M. Douglas (ed.). London: Routledge & Kegan Paul.

—— 1986. Politics of schism: routinisation and social control in the International Socialists / Socialist Workers Party. In *Power, action and belief: a new sociology of knowledge*, J. Law (ed.). London: Routledge & Kegan Paul.

—— 1991. A cultural perspective on the structure and implementation of global environmental agreements. *Evaluation Review* **15**(1), 75–102.

—— 1994. Governance and the global commons. Discussion Paper 8, Centre for the Study of Global Governance, London School of Economics. [Reprinted in *Global governance: ethics and economics of the world order*, M. Desai & P. Redfern (eds) (London: Pinter, 1995).]

—— 1995. A contractual map of human values for climate change decision making. See Katama (1995).

Rayner, S. & R. Cantor 1987. How fair is safe enough: the cultural approach to technology choice. *Risk Analysis: an International Journal* **7**(1), 3–9.

Read, D., A. Bostrom, M. G. Morgan, B. Fischoff, T. Smuts 1994. What do people know about climate change? Part 2: survey studies of educated lay people. *Risk Analysis* **14**, 971–82.

Richardson, T. (ed.) 1995. *The green challenge: the development of green parties in Europe*. London: Routledge.

Rolston, H. 1988. *Environmental ethics: duties to and values in the natural world*. Philadelphia, Pennsylvania: Temple University Press.

Rose, A. 1990. Reducing conflict in global warming policy: the potential of equity as a unifying principle. *Energy Policy* **18**, 927–48.

—— 1992. Equity considerations of tradeable carbon entitlements. In *Tradeable carbon emission entitlement*, S. Barrett et al. (eds). Geneva: UN Conference on Trade and Development [UNCTAD].

Rose, A. & B. Stevens 1993. The efficiency and equity of marketable permits for CO_2 emissions. *Resource and Energy Economics* **15**, 117–46.

—— 1998. *The marketable permits approach to global warming policy*. Chicago: University of Chicago Press.

Royal Society & National Academy of Sciences 1992. On population growth and sustainability. *Population and Development Review* **18**(2), 374–6.

Samdahl, D. & R. Robertson 1989. Social determinants of environmental concern: specification and test of the model. *Environment and Behavior* **1**, 57–81.

Schelling, T. 1983. Climate change: implications for welfare and policy. In *Changing climate* [report of the Carbon Dioxide Committee, National Academy of Science]. Washington DC: National Academy Press.

Schipper, L., S. Bartlett, D. Hawk, E. Vine 1989. Linking lifestyles and energy use: a matter of time. *Annual Review of Energy* **14**, 273–320.

Schwarz, M. & M. Thompson 1990. *Divided we stand: redefining politics, technology, and social choice*. Hemel Hempstead, England: Harvester Wheatsheaf.

Shotter, J. 1984. *Social accountability and selfhood*. Oxford: Basil Blackwell.

Shue, H. 1993. Subsistence emissions and luxury emissions. *Law and Policy* **15**(1), 39–59.

—— 1994. Avoidable necessity: global warming, international fairness, and alternative energy. In *Theory and practice*, I. Shapiro & J. W. DeCena (eds). New York: New York University Press.

—— 1995. Equity in an international agreement on climate change. See Katama (1995).

Smith, K., J. Swisher, D. Ahuja 1993. Who pays to solve the problem and how much? In *The global greenhouse regime: who pays? Science, economics and global politics in the North–South convention*, P. Hayes & K. Smith (eds). London: Earthscan.

Sörlin, S. 1993. The nature contract: a transformation of the view of nature and the new ethics of nature. In *Views of nature*, L. Lundgren (ed.). Stockholm: Swedish Council for Planning and Coordination of Research and Swedish Environmental Protection Agency.

Steel, B. S., D. L. Soden, R. L. Warner 1990. The impact of knowledge and values on perceptions of environmental risk to the Great Lakes. *Society and Natural Resources* **4**, 331–48.

Steger, M. A. E. & S. L. Witt 1989. Gender differences in environmental orientations: a comparison of publics and activists in Canada and the US. *Western Political Quarterly* **4**, 627–49.

Steger, M. A. E., J. C. Pierce, B. S. Steel, N. P. Lovrich 1989. Political culture, postmaterial values, and the new environmental paradigm: a comparative analysis of Canada and the United States. *Political Behavior* **3**, 233–54.

Stern, P. C. 1986. Blind spots and policy analysis: what economics doesn't say about energy use. *Journal of Policy Analysis and Management* **5**, 200–227.

Stone, C. D. 1972. Should trees have standing: towards legal rights for natural objects. *Southern California Law Review* **45**, 450.

Svedin, U. 1993. The view of nature as seen in the mirror of history and comparative cultural analysis. In *Views of nature*, L. Lundgren (ed.). Stockholm: Swedish Council for Planning and Coordination of Research and Swedish Environmental Protection Agency.

Thaler, R. & S. Rosen 1975. The value of saving a life. In *Household production and consumption*, N. Terleckyi (ed.). New York: National Bureau of Economic Research.

Thompson, M. 1979. *Rubbish theory: the creation and destruction of value*. Oxford: Oxford University Press.

—— 1987. Welche Gesellschaftsklassen sind potent genug, anderen ihre Zukunft aufzuoktroyieren? In *Design der Zukunft*, L. Burchhardt (ed.). Cologne: Dumont.

Thompson, M., R. Ellis, A. Wildavsky 1990. *Cultural theory*. Boulder, Colorado: Westview.

Timmerman, P. 1986. Myths and paradigms of interactions between development and environment. See Clark & Munn (1986).

Tönnies, F. 1887. *Gemeinschaft und Gesellschaft*. Darmstadt: Wissenschaftlich. [Translated by C. P. Loomis as *Community and society*. East Lansing: Michigan State University Press 1957.]

Toman, M. & D. Burtraw 1991. Resolving equity issues: greenhouse gas negotiations. *Resources* **103**, 10–13.

Turner II, B. L., W. C. Clark, R. W. Kates, J. F. Richards, J. T. Mathews, W. B. Meyer, et al. (eds) 1990. *The Earth as transformed by human action*. New York: Cambridge University Press.

Umweltbundesamt 1993. *Jahresbericht 1993*. Berlin: Bundesdruckerei.

Van Liere, K. D. & R. E. Dunlap 1980. The social bases of environmental concern: a review of hypotheses, explanations and empirical evidence. *Public Opinion Quarterly* **2**, 181–97.

—— 1983. Cognitive integration of social environmental beliefs. *Sociological Enquiry* **2/3**, 333–41.

WCED [World Commission on Environment and Development] 1987. *Our common future*. Oxford: Oxford University Press.

Weinberg, A. M. 1966. Can technology replace social engineering? *University of Chicago Magazine* **LIX**(October), 6–10.

Weiss, E. B. 1989. *In fairness to future generations: international law, common patrimony, and intergenerational equity*. Dobbs Ferry, New York: Transnational Publishers.

Wellman, B. & S. D. Berkowitz 1988. *Social structures: a network approach*. Cambridge: Cambridge University Press.

Welsch, H. 1993. A CO_2 agreement proposal with flexible quotas. *Energy Policy* **21**(7), 748–56.

White, L. 1967. The historical roots of our ecological crisis. *Science* **155**(10), 1203–207.

Whyte, A. V. T. & M. R. Harrison 1981. *Public perception of weather and climate change: report on a pilot study in Ontario*. Ottawa: Atmospheric Environment Service.

Williamson, H. 1771. An attempt to account for the change of climate which has observed in the Middle Colonies in North America. *Transactions of the American Philosophical Society* **1**, 272–8.

Williamson, O. 1975. *Markets and hierarchies: analysis and antitrust implications*. New York: Free Press.

Wirth, D. A. & D. A. Lashof 1990. Beyond Vienna and Montreal – multilateral agreements on greenhouse gases. *Ambio* **19**, 305–310.

Wirth, T. 1993. US international population policy: an official statement. *Population and Development Review* **19**(2), 403–406.

Wordsworth, W. 1810. *Guide to the lakes* [1977 edn]. Oxford: Oxford University Press.

Yamin, F. 1995. Principles of equity in international environmental agreements with special reference to the Climate Change Convention. See Katama (1995).

Young, H. P. & A. Wolf 1991. Global warming negotiations: does fairness count? *Brookings Review* **10**, 2.

Young, P. 1993. *Equity in theory and practice*. Princeton, New Jersey: Princeton University Press.

CHAPTER 5

Institutional frameworks for political action

Timothy O'Riordan, Chester L. Cooper,
Andrew Jordan, Steve Rayner, Kenneth R. Richards,
Paul Runci, Shira Yoffe

Contributors
Daniel Bodansky, Urs Luterbacher, Ronald Mitchell,
Kal Raustiala, Ian Rowlands, Paul Samson, Detlef Sprinz

Chapter 4 established the view of discourse, implicit or explicit, across a range of social sciences, as both the social glue and the solvent that we use to create and rearrange the social order, building and dismantling bonds of social solidarity among individuals, communities, and other institutions across both space and time. This chapter focuses on the political actions and frameworks for action that arise from and nourish the discourse about climate change and the rearrangement of societal solidarities around the climate change issue at all levels of human society. Thus, the focus of this chapter is on political action as institutional action.

The concept of institution is very broad. In many respects, it is an example of what Gallie (1955) termed an *essentially contested* concept; an idea that can be clarified only through regular argument, that is, through discourse. The notion of institution applies to both organizations with leaders, memberships, clients, resources, and knowledge, and also to socialized ways of looking at the world as shaped by communication, information transfer, and patterns of status and association.

Understanding and managing climate change has to take place through institutional arrangements. Any effort to identify the causes of that change, or to adapt to its consequences, must also address the medium of institutional behavior. Institutions permeate all aspects of society, both formal and informal. Society simply would not exist in the absence of institutional arrangements.

Climate policy is shaped by formal organizational structures, as well as by informal networks of communication that, in turn, are the products of values, norms and expectations. These institutions range from the formal deliberating bodies engaged in treaty making to the informal liaisons among policy analysts and policy executives, regulatory agencies, and the day-to-day actions of billions of people. Both the extent and the impacts of climate change will be determined by the willingness of those billions of decisionmakers to change their ways. This change of behavior could be achieved by persuasion, command, education, taxation, moral arguments, or changes in the notion of property rights (see the discussion of policy instruments, p. 401 ff.). Any combination of these responses involves institutional change, ranging from incremental adjustment to profound transformation.

No matter how chaotic all the relationships among climate policy actors may seem, they could not function without some sort of order and guiding principles of social solidarity. This solidarity is the essence of social institutions and it forms the basis of the analysis provided by this chapter.

The Blackwell encyclopaedia of political science defines an institution as a "locus of regularized or crystallized principle of conduct, action or behavior that governs a crucial area of social life and that endures over time" (Gould 1991: 290). In different disciplines, however, the term carries particular nuances. For sociologists, the study of institutions is central to understanding the organization and functioning of all societies. Indeed, within the functionalist paradigm, sociology *is* "the science of institutions" and other "social facts" (Durkheim 1895: 1). Social theorists regard the concept of an institution as a socially organizing set of relationships that govern the basic problems of ordered social life. Eisenstadt (1968) visualized the characteristics of institutions as sets of normative rules that are shared by a society so as to retain cohesion and control, and also as patterns of behavior that operate according to norms and expectations, and in so doing give order and meaning to social life and government. Giddens (1986: 8) referred to institutions as "commonly adopted practices which persist in recognisably similar form across generations." "A society," he explained, "is a cluster, or system, of institutionalised modes of conduct . . . [which are] . . . modes of belief and behavior that occur and recur . . . across long spans of time and space." Smith (1988: 91) visualized institutions as "stable, valued, recurring patterns of behavior," a definition that encompasses fairly concrete organizations, such as governmental agencies, but also cognitive structures, such as the patterns of rhetorical legitimation characteristic of political discourse and belief systems. Although the term has been used in the field of international relations to refer specifically to formal structures, such as the United Nations, or specific treaty arrangements (e.g., Haas 1964), more recent scholars of international relations employ the term in a more sociological fashion (Haas et al. 1993).

Gould (1991) warned against confusing repeated or habitual activity with the more formal rules that are devised to regulate it. An activity may take place through informal arrangements, for example through kinship patterns or the evolution of expected codes of conduct. Examples would be the emergence of a car-pooling culture to cut driving needs, or the coordination of village communities in Bangladesh to provide single-band radios, platforms of refuge, and food redistribution schemes in the event of coastal flooding (Rahman 1996). These activities need no formal structure or external regulation, but they are most certainly institutions (Wynne 1993). Thus, despite disciplinary differences there seems to be convergence on a core set of ideas about institutions and their importance (Box 5.1).

It has been fashionable in recent years to regard institutions as mechanisms for offloading routine low-level day-to-day thinking that leaves the individual mind free to weigh important and difficult matters (Schotter 1981). However, Douglas (1986: 111) took the opposite view that "The individual tends to leave important decisions to his institutions while busying himself with tactics and details." From this standpoint, institutions are vital in the processes of identifying and responding to threats to survival or to conflict and social order. The mechanisms of predicting outcomes, of organizing response, of preparing for possible danger, and of accommodating to stress or hardship, are constitutive

---

Box 5.1   The concept of institutions

At the very heart of the meaning of institutions are some highly interrelated concepts:
- Institutions *regulate* behavior via socially approved mechanisms such as the rule of law and the accountable exercise of power.
- Institutions have a degree of *permanence* and are relatively stable. They are, for Giddens (1984: 24), "the more enduring features of social life." Institutions are *patterns of routinized behavior.*
- Institutions are continually being *renegotiated,* in the continuing interplay between human agency and wider social structures.
- Institutions are *cognitive* and *normative structures* that stabilize perceptions, interpretations, and justifications.
- Institutions determine what is *appropriate, legitimate,* and *proper;* they define obligations, self-restraints, rights, and immunities, as well as the sanctions for unacceptable behavior.
- Institutions *structure* the channels through which new ideas are translated into policy and new challenges receive a government response.
- Institutions *confer identity* on members through belonging and on others through allocation to categories that are institutionally established. "Similarity is an institution" (Douglas 1986: 55).
- Institutions *remember* and *forget.* "The competitive society celebrates its heroes, the hierarchy celebrates its patriarchs, and the sect its martyrs" (Douglas 1986: 80). Similarly, each kind of institution forgets information that challenges its organizational principles.

---

of the political debate about global climate and other environmental change. This is why institutions have to involve rules, regulation, and legitimacy—or social justification of the exercise or denial of authority—for the social good. It is also why institutions are constantly changing, adjusting subtly and sometimes turbulently to the needs of the times as interpreted by society in myriad ways. The direction of change is random or unpredictable. Change can be analyzed in terms of the existing relationships of values and norms, of social and political organization, of the jockeying for power and of the constant interchange between internal views of the world and external forces that are not always controllable by those in power.

In this chapter on institutions and climate politics we first identify those aspects of contemporary social science theory that cast light upon international institutional arrangements through which independent sovereign states conflict and cooperate on the issue of climate change and other global environmental issues. Following that discussion, we focus on institutional variation as manifest in national policy networks and policy styles.

This chapter recognizes the multiple dualisms inherent in political action. As discussed in Chapter 4, political action can be the means of both creating and dissolving bonds of social solidarity at individual and institutional levels. Political action can be both aggregative and integrative; it can also be instrumental (designed to achieve explicit goals) and expressive (communicating shared values and building solidarity). It can be anticipatory (rationally planned in the expectation of future events or actions) and reactive (responsive to new situations as they develop). It can be self-interested and altruistic. It can be optimizing (seeking the best conceivable solution) and satisficing (seeking a solution that is just good enough). This list is by no means exhaustive, but it can serve to remind us that political reality is far more multivalent than the purely instrumental perspective of *realpolitik* would suggest.

Disciplinary social science tends to separate out particular aspects of political action for attention and to downplay others. For example, political science tends to focus on politics as an instrumental, rational, goal-oriented activity, usually rooted in self-interest. It emphasizes formal structures of bargaining and negotiation bound by existing property rights, which determine power and responsibility; principles, which form the basis of accepting or rejecting facts and, hence, bargaining positions; norms or ethically accepted standards of behavior, which govern expected bargaining games; risks or decisionmaking principles, which shape final agreements; and decision-implementation procedures which influence the acceptability of an agreed outcome and, hence, the likelihood of compliance (e.g., Krasner 1983).

Economics shares this instrumental approach, but emphasizes the role of self-interest in the production of optimum outcomes for the whole system, rather than the accretion and exercise of power in an anarchical world. The economics approach presupposes rationality, or predictable order, in decisionmaking procedures, based on a clear set of preferences, a consistent valuation and prioritization approach, and goal-seeking behavior. Despite the fairly obvious pitfalls of contradictory rationalities summarized in Chapter 4, this approach still has appeal to both analysts and policymakers. Downs (1957) suggested that it is widely liked because it fits a yearning for predictability and simplicity of analysis.

Sociology often homes in on issues of recruitment to political movements and parties, and the mobilization of resources within them. These issues have been translated into interest-group behavior via several models. For instance, Dalton (1994) usefully summarized the combination of resource mobilization and new social movement theories. The resource mobilization approach is rooted in theories of organizational behavior on the grounds that actions are determined by the interests of, and expectations associated with, particular groups. In the case of climate change, the fossil fuel lobby predictably funds scientists to challenge the orthodoxy of the Working Group I of the Intergovernmental Panel on Climate Change (European Science Forum 1996), and the well-resourced road-transportation lobby promotes the use of more freeways and road haulage in the face of concern about carbon dioxide emissions. In such instances the lobbies not only mobilize information, they also develop networks and contacts with which to influence opinion.

Social movement theory presumes that society continually creates patterns of interests around issues of social justice or themes that require public attention, because they are not, or perhaps cannot, be resolved through existing institutional arrangements. Self-help groups form around a host of issues connected to racism, health, minority rights, freedom of information, and the environment in an egalitarian style of participation (see Ch. 4). Thus, although resource mobilization tends to reinforce existing patterns of power, social movements tend to expand policy coalitions by generating fresh perspectives (Freeman 1983). The debate over value-of-life calculations, discussed in Chapter 4, is an example of this process at work in climate politics. It captured the attention of interests that had not previously been mobilized in the climate debate.

Psychology often approaches politics in individualistic terms of personality types and attitudes. The foundations of this approach were laid by Lasswell in his classic work *Psychopathology and politics* (1930), although the most widely known example of this type of analysis is Adorno's *The authoritarian personality* (1950). (More recent applications were reviewed in Knutson 1973.) Other psychologists emphasize individual perception and judgment in political negotiation and decisionmaking (e.g., Jervis 1976). Social psychologists, taking a different approach, focus specifically on issues of constructing solidarity through cooperation around environmental and resource management issues (e.g., Stern 1978) and perspectives such as interdependence theory (Kelley & Thibaut 1978, Kelley 1984).

Anthropology is also host to a variety of perspectives on political activity. Traditionally, political anthropology has focused on politics outside the context of the modern nation state (e.g., Mair 1962) or on the confrontation of traditional politics with the state (see Balandier 1967). More recently, anthropologists have analyzed the role of social solidarities on the political controversies surrounding energy and other potentially hazardous technologies (see Chs 1 and 4; also Douglas & Wildavsky 1982, Rayner 1984, Gerlach 1987, Schwarz & Thompson 1990).

Sachs (1993) implied that the local focus of much political anthropology may be unexpectedly pertinent to global environmental issues. Echoing Wynne's highlighting of *local knowledge* (Wynne 1996; see also Ch. 1), Sachs cautioned against the *ecocratic* universalism of most environmentalists, which (like the economic universalism of development professionals) elides consideration of the rights and responsibilities of local communities to manage their resources. Sachs argued that the aggregated economic preference functions of state-centered rational-decision models at the heart of green globalism actually destroy the cultural enclaves that represent the social and political diversity lying at the heart of sustainability.

Political action is also the outcome of activities that occur across a multitude

350

of scales from micro to macro, from the individual to the nation state to supranational organizations, such as the European Union or the United Nations. Similarly, the repercussions of action taken at one level may reverberate throughout the global social, political, and economic system. Hence, the traditional focus of political science (particularly international relations) on the nation state, or sociology's concentration on social movements within the state, both leave important gaps in our understanding of the articulations among and between local and global actions (Gerlach 1991). Climate change forces the social sciences to a renewed consideration of their traditional division of labor.

Scholarly attention to the politics of climate change has mostly focused on the traditional political actors—the nation states. The challenge of political action is conventionally presented on the one hand as coordinating government policies through diplomacy and international law and, on the other hand, as efficiently implementing coordinated government policies domestically (see, for example, Paterson 1993). Countless scholarly papers and articles (e.g., those summarized by Thomas 1992) scrutinize past diplomatic and legal initiatives to derive lessons from past negotiations on both environmental and non-environmental issues to guide the actions of states on climate change. However, almost none of these writings questions basic assumptions about the centrality of the state in climate politics.

The conventional international relations literature remains "severely under-theorized" in this regard (Paterson 1996: 59):

> Most of the literature on the international politics of global warming either simply makes prescriptions for international action in one form or another or, where theoretical material is used, rather crudely presses it into service in order to support one or another normative position.

On the other hand, Saurin (1996: 81) identifies a rapidly growing theoretical literature on environmentalism and political thought (e.g., Dobson 1990, Pepper 1986, Atkinson 1991, Eckersley 1992, Merchant 1992, O'Neill 1993) almost all of it "written as if there were no international world, nor even a globalized social world." Climate change, by its very nature, challenges the social sciences to reconceptualize the relationship between the high politics of the nation state and the politics of everyday life as experienced in families, firms, and communities.

Indeed, these forms of everyday *solidarity* (as defined in Ch. 4) provide the metaphors that we use to think about negotiating international agreements. In the inaugural issue of the journal *International Negotiation* (1996), the contributors explore kinship, friendship, community, and diplomacy as models for international relations, as well as the centrality of solidarity-building concerns—equity, social learning, and collective representation—to those relations.

By framing the issue of political action in terms of social solidarity, we can begin to smooth out some of the discontinuities of scale and focus identified by the contrast between the literatures on international relations and environmental politics. Framed in this way, the concerns of international relations studies with treaty and regime formation, and the development of international law, can be conceptualized as the challenges of building horizontal solidarity among nation states. The concerns of political science with policy implementation can be viewed as the challenges of building vertical solidarity within nation states. The concept of solidarity also provides a consistent framework within which we can recognize the action of nongovernmental entities, such as technical and scientific institutions, the private sector, and the voluntary sector, in building horizontal connections directly across national boundaries as well as diagonal ties between nongovernmental entities and multiple governments. Intergenerational issues may be best understood in terms of institutional commitments to solidarity across time.

Hence, this chapter will initially consider the institutional basis of climate change politics as the attempt to build international solidarity among nation states around the theme of a global environmental threat, before proceeding to discuss the opportunities and constraints upon political action in different institutional settings and the range of policy instruments available for addressing climate change issues.

International relations theory and the changing political landscape

In describing the politics of climate change, the primary focus of both social scientists and journalists has been at the level of diplomacy among states in pursuit of international agreements. Saurin (1996: 77) described this approach as one in which ". . . the whole range of environmental concerns is theoretically and practically subordinated to, and dependent upon, the predetermined 'character' and 'interests' of the state." Furthermore, the proper lens through which the politics of global environmental change is to be viewed is one that firmly focuses on the way in which states manage the Earth among themselves or through formally recognized international organizations (Thomas 1992). Some of these authors explicitly frame the problem of climate change within an overall framework of solidarity among nation states, including the co-optation of nonstate entities. For example, Hurrell & Kingsbury (1992: 1) proposed that the central question underlying the analysis of worldwide political actions on the environment is, "Can a fragmented and often highly conflictual political system made up of over 170 sovereign states and many other actors achieve the high (and historically unprecedented) levels of cooperation and policy coordination needed to manage environmental problems on a global scale?"

Hurrell & Kingsbury distinguished their own framing of the issue of international solidarity from two alternative opposing formulations: first, the creation of a supranational authority endowed with power to coerce individual states into cooperation (e.g., Ophuls 1977; see also Ostrom 1990); and, second, the wholehearted decentralization of responsibility and power to manage ecosystems to the local communities that most directly depend upon them (see Dryzek 1987). Hurrell & Kingsbury, in company with many international relations scholars (e.g., List & Rittberger 1992), rejected these alternatives on both the practical grounds that the state has successfully fended off challenges to its sovereignty from above and below, and on the normative claims of the state to moral authority.

These widely differing perspectives on the state reflect the rapidly changing realities of the global political landscape of the twentieth century, in which political scientists sometimes seem to share the fate of generals condemned to open each new war with the weapons and strategies that won the previous one (Dyer 1985).

The global political landscape within which contemporary governments operate has changed substantially from that left behind by the Second World War. Perhaps as good a way to appreciate these changes is to put oneself in the place of the foreign minister or secretary of state, of, say, the United States, Egypt, China, the United Kingdom, or Brazil in the summer of 1945. Then, His Excellency had few more than three score colleagues on the six continents. Of these, only about a dozen would wield much influence beyond their immediate region. Now, 50 years later, assuming the requisite amount of time, energy and inclination, he or she must treat with 200 of his or her peers.

Furthermore, today's foreign ministers everywhere must address not only traditional bilateral and regional security concerns, and economic and political issues, but also treat with matters that had not yet found their way onto political agendas only a decade ago (Box 5.2). These matters include a host of considerations focusing on, and affected by, threats to the global environment and to the physical and institutional sustainability of societies everywhere.

The formation of many new official international bodies, mostly under the United Nations umbrella, has accompanied the multiplication of nation states during the postwar period. Several of these bodies deal, directly or indirectly, with climate change issues.[1] In addition, a few international groups, such as the World Climate Programme, the Advisory Group on Greenhouse Gases (AGGG), and the Intergovernmental Panel on Climate Change (IPCC), were established specifically to address the climate change issue.

The myriad sovereign nations and international bodies, the growing breadth

> **Box 5.2   Kaleidoscopic changes in the world scene**
>
> Not only has there been an explosion in the number of sovereign countries and in accompanying bilateral and multilateral complexities, there have also been changes in the nature and structure of the international issues at play. From the perspective of an historian in 2050, the latter half of the twentieth century may well appear kaleidoscopic (Sagasti & Colby 1993: 175–6):
>
> - ". . . a rapidly shifting political environment: a post-bipolar world in which East–West differences no longer matter as much as they did . . .; the spread of political pluralism, participation, and democratic movements on all continents; and a reduction in the political control of nation states over economic, social, environmental, and technological phenomena."
> - ". . . transformation in the patterns of world economic interdependence: the globalization of financial markets; the emergence of the Pacific Rim as the world's largest trading area; the shift from commodities trade to high-technology services and manufactured products; economic union in western Europe; conversion to market economies in eastern Europe and the former Soviet Union; economic turmoil in the Middle East; the Latin America debt crisis; and the decline of Africa."
> - ". . . cultural transformations: the growth of religious fundamentalism as a political force; tension between pressures to homogenize values and aspirations versus the desire to preserve cultural identity; and the emergence of moral and ethical issues at the forefront of choices about both inter- and intragenerational equity . . ."
> - ". . . the accelerating pace and increasing complexity of scientific advances and technological change: advances in computer science and informatics have changed the way new scientific knowledge is generated . . ."
> - ". . . the challenge of environmental sustainability: poverty and population growth in developing countries can be seen as both causes and effects of environmental/resource degradation, while the effects of excessive, often wasteful, resource consumption habits in the industrial countries on poorer countries received little attention. Climate patterns are not the only type of global environmental change putting future generations' livelihoods and quality of life at risk: The extinction of genetic resources in the form of biodiversity, stratospheric ozone depletion, the spread of toxic chemicals, and deforestation, among others, are now global issues . . ."

and complexity of the issues involved, and the awesome increase and speed of global telecommunications and international travel (Box 5.3) have helped to produce a new network of vocal and influential participants in the foreign affairs arena in addition to official government bodies. New players, such as the international nongovernmental organizations (NGOs), have grown in number and importance since the 1960s.

NGOs, especially those in America and western Europe, have had long experience on the international stage, but, following the Second World War, most

---

1. For example, the United Nations Development Programme (UNDP), the Food and Agricultural Organization (FAO), the United Nations Educational, Scientific and Cultural Organisation (UNESCO), the World Meteorological Organisation (WMO), the United Nations Environment Programme (UNEP), and the Global Environment Facility (GEF), which is managed jointly by UNDP, UNEP, and the World Bank.

Box 5.3   Increased velocity of information

Revolutionary developments in transportation and communication during the past century have forever transformed the global political landscape. Indeed, "technology has, in effect, shrunk the planet" (Bryant 1994: 42). Sometimes the proposition that the world is getting smaller is put forward as a proud boast, sometimes as a dire warning, sometimes as a tired and tiresome observation. But however phrased, the smaller world means that people everywhere soon know and are affected by whatever happens virtually anywhere. The international community must reckon with this reality.

During the past few decades, diverse events and developments in remote corners of the world have become the stuff of daily news programs in Boston, Beijing, and Beirut. Statesmen's foibles, epidemics, foreign exchange crises, oil shocks, droughts and floods, nuclear accidents, ethnic conflicts—all find their place, virtually simultaneously, on prime ministers' agendas in London, Taipei, and Nairobi. In the early nineteenth century, US Secretary of State John Quincy Adams, in reminding his minister in Spain that he had not heard from him in over a year, is reported to have written: "If I don't hear from you during the course of the next year, I will assume all is well." Isaac Asimov (1990: 36), commenting on the progress of communications, observed that "it took five months for Queen Isabella to learn of Columbus' voyage; two weeks for Europe to learn of President Lincoln's assassination; and 1.3 seconds for the world to witness Neil Armstrong's first steps on the Moon."

---

of them were engaged in welfare and development activities, such as famine relief, disaster aid, and technical assistance. As new reports began to surface in the 1980s about global environmental concerns, many US and European environmental groups extended their coverage from local and national concerns to include environmental issues overseas—often forming cooperative relationships with developing country NGOs in the process (Livernash 1992). In addition, large-scale international NGO coalitions have emerged, connecting groups within Asia, Africa, the Arctic region, western Europe, and North America (Princen & Finger 1994).

At the 1972 Stockholm United Nations Conference on the Human Environment, only 10 percent of the 134 NGOs attending were from less industrialized countries. In contrast, at the United Nations Conference on Environment and Development (UNCED, informally referred to as the Earth Summit), held in Rio de Janeiro in 1992, there were more than 1400 accredited NGOs—one-third of which were from the less industrialized world—sharing their knowledge, advocating their views, and networking the system (Haas et al. 1992).

Corresponding to the swelling in the ranks of NGOs has been a rise in their influence. For instance, NGOs played a leading role in the formulation and strengthening of the 1987 Montreal Protocol on Substances that Deplete the Ozone Layer. NGOs' effective targeting of key producers of chlorofluorocarbons and direct participation in the preparatory and actual negotiation processes cast them onto the international diplomatic stage as major players (Princen & Finger

1994). Subsequently, in the negotiations leading up to the UNCED at Rio, NGOs provided information and advice to participants in the negotiations and were instrumental in increasing the transparency of governments' actions.

On the other hand, many governments, especially those in developing countries, view NGOs with distrust. In part, this is because the NGOs of industrialized nations, having greater finance, expertise, experience, and numbers than their counterparts in less industrialized countries, tend to dominate international conferences. NGO effectiveness at negotiations is further hampered by poor coordination and duplication of effort. Moreover, there is a conspicuous lack of NGO accountability and legitimacy—who speaks for whom (Blackford 1994)?

Nevertheless, by the time of UNCED, NGOs in less industrialized as well as highly industrialized countries had become increasingly adept at forming coalitions and at networking among themselves for greater impact in the negotiation process. NGO representatives were even included as members of 15 nations' official government delegations (Box 5.4).

On the eve of the third millennium, all nations are aware that economic integration, technological advances, and growing awareness of transboundary environmental problems are altering the dynamics of international relations. On the one hand, these currents are leading to unprecedented levels of international cooperation and to the realization that national governments must act together to address the environmental, economic, and security interests of the international community. On the other hand, this same set of drivers is helping to empower ethnic and nationalist groups around the world, to facilitate the disintegration of nation states, and to spawn a host of influential, nontraditional players in world politics (Ignatieff 1993, Conca 1994, Rosenau 1995).

Clearly, the time when governments could direct their attention solely to narrow domestic or security issues has passed. And, yet, still only 70 or 80 hours remain each week for even the most diligent senior official to ponder, decide, plan, negotiate, implement, and monitor the myriad matters in his or her portfolio. It is no wonder that, despite greater worldwide sensitivity to environmental concerns, such considerations as global climate change—gradual in effect, costly to avert, uncertain in timing and extent—tend to be residual claimants for the time and attention of government leaders seized, in their own minds at least, with more urgent and important problems. And so, despite the lofty rhetoric that characterizes international gatherings addressing global climate change, it is fair to say that most governments will have to be convinced that the challenge is soon, certain, serious, and soluble, before they will actually commit substantial resources to deal with the matter (Ingram et al. 1990).

Although nation states are still central political actors in international relations, they are becoming "increasingly enmeshed in a network of collaborative arrangements or regimes that are creating a very different international political

---

Box 5.4   NGOs as policy advisers in global climate change negotiations

Many governments, particularly those in the less industrialized world, often do not have resources sufficient to provide expertise on how to address climate change. There is great uncertainty over their proper response, given some level of uncertain (yet expected) change. Many NGOs have devoted attention to this issue. In climate negotiations they have made use of their access to provide government delegations with extensive policy analyses and recommendations, as well as critiques of proposed policies. For governments that lack resources and expertise in this area, especially the smaller, less industrialized states, the NGOs provide useful information that is relatively costless. In addition, NGOs are often well placed to discover and suggest innovative solutions to bargaining impasses between delegations, expediting negotiations, and improving outcomes. They also frequently serve as a voice for the voiceless and thereby seek, in their own view, to provide both a human face and a concern for justice to the often technocratic and abstract process of negotiation (Tolbert 1991). Just as often, however, they are voices for the powerful.

Members of NGOs have appeared on several government delegations, and have acted as official and unofficial consultants for governments. Raustiala (1996) described one of the most prominent examples: the relationship between the London-based Foundation for International Environmental Law and Development (FIELD) and the Association of Small Island States (AOSIS). Members of FIELD, all international lawyers, consulted extensively with members of AOSIS, appeared on their delegations and, at times, acted as the delegation of certain AOSIS members. The tiny member governments of AOSIS, which often lacked any indigenous expertise about climate change and the policy possibilities, became a more powerful negotiating force in conjunction with FIELD.

NGOs are political actors. To varying degrees they provide political pressure on governments, and may threaten to scuttle agreements at home (or try to) if their demands are not adequately addressed. Governments respond to these pressures to varying degrees as well, depending on the type of government, the size of the NGO, and its type (business or public interest). Indeed, the political power of environmental NGOs—and the access they have gained in the climate negotiations—have stimulated the activities of "counter" NGOs and of business interests more broadly. Although environmental NGOs may be more prominent at international meetings, business NGOs are often very important players in the domestic context.

---

world than the one that existed in recent centuries" (Zacher 1992: 100). The nesting of states in regimes and other networks, and the challenges to state authority that sub- and transnational groups pose, appear to be constraining state power and sovereignty. Environmental issues in particular are altering the nature of national sovereignty, at once strengthening it on some levels and undermining it on others (Conca 1994). Most scholars maintain that the nation state is no longer the sole appropriate unit of analysis in world affairs in an era of *post-international* politics (Rosenau 1995). Although some scholars feel that the extent to which the state has declined has been overstated, they concede that the relative power of once clearly dominant states could be in decline as other nations rise in economic, military, or political stature (e.g., Huntington 1993, Jervis 1993, Layne 1993). The major European countries, especially France and the United

Kingdom, have lost much of their pre-war economic and political pre-eminence. Similarly, following the collapse of the Cold War bipolar balance, the Soviet Union's successor states appear to have failed to retain the substantial power, prestige, and influence of the USSR.

In the world of the 1990s and well beyond, Asia, rather than Europe, and (a somewhat less influential) America appear likely to dominate international affairs; Japan, Korea, and China may succeed Germany, France, and Great Britain as key political players.

Although many factors are at work in this dynamic restructuring of the international system, the rapid ascent of environmental issues has lent negotiating power and international prominence to those less industrialized countries whose natural resources—rainforests, coal and oil reserves, and wildlife—have global importance. Thus, Indonesia, Brazil, and Mexico also play important roles in international deliberations on economic and environmental issues. In short, "a world once dominated by one or a few nations has yielded to one in which economic power and influence are widely shared" (Bryant 1994: 43). It is hardly surprising that such a complex and rapidly changing landscape should spawn a variety of theoretical perspectives on international affairs.

Theories of international relations

The study of international relations as a social science discipline unto itself is a fairly recent phenomenon. Until the end of the First World War, foreign affairs was the territory of the professional diplomat, the historian, the international legal scholar, and, to some extent, the political philosopher. After the war, however, many of those concerned with international affairs began to study such matters in a more systematic manner, with the explicit and prescriptive purpose of preventing recurrences of such horrific events. Some (mainly American and British) intellectuals staked out a new field for social science concern, optimistic that they could study relations among states scientifically, and confident that their findings could preserve the hard-won peace. Although these scholars did not naïvely believe that states would act altruistically, they were idealistic in thinking that the engagement of the world's nations in international institutions such as the League of Nations—as a means of mediating conflict and fostering collective security—would prevent war.

Their optimism was short lived. Almost immediately after its conception, the League of Nations—a keystone to the structure of the new international system—was stillborn. Hardly a decade passed before Hitler rose to power, and the war machine began to turn again. The new *idealism*, championed by leaders such as Woodrow Wilson (a former professor of political science), appeared dashed as the looming war with Germany prompted the international community to embrace, once again, the more pessimistic, pragmatic tenets of real-politik. The school of thought that this engendered, known broadly as *realism*, dominated international relations thought throughout the Cold War. Realism, in contrast to idealism, suggested that the prospects for dramatic transformation in the international system were bleak. Relations among nations, realists maintain, are a continuous struggle for power in an anarchical world. Realism and *institutionalism* (the heir of Wilsonian idealism) are today the leading—and contending—schools of international relations. These schools of thought, and those that have arisen in response to them and to the changing political landscape—*dependency theory* and other current perspectives—are discussed below.

Realism and neorealism

The works of several influential theorists helped to secure the prominent position of realist thought in the period following the Second World War. Two of the defining scholarly works of this period are *Politics among nations* (Morgenthau 1948) and *Man, the state, and war* (Waltz 1959). Realism and associated bodies of theory (notably, neorealism and structural realism) remain thriving elements of the international relations discipline. In similar fashion, game theory frequently draws on the basic assumptions of realism in constructing formal (logic-based) theories of politics. Volume 3, Chapter 2 discusses game theoretic approaches in detail.

Since the mid-1970s, *neorealists* have elaborated many of the basic assumptions of traditional realism (Waltz 1979, Keohane 1986). As part of the neorealist research program, some scholars have extended the approach from traditional security questions to the domain of international political economy (Rowlands 1996). Although still pessimistic about the prospects for cooperation, some scholars have nevertheless argued that international cooperation on world economic dilemmas might be possible if a single actor with superior power exists and is willing to use its power resources (Kindleberger 1973, Gilpin 1975). This actor is identified as a *hegemon*. The theory of *hegemonic stability* (Keohane 1980) predicts that the degree of international cooperation will be directly proportional to the degree to which one actor dominates international politics. Acting either benevolently or malevolently (Snidal 1985), the hegemon has the resources to transform international structures so that coordinated policies result. Work within this tradition continues today (e.g., Grieco 1990, Lake 1993).

An international relations realist looks to the distribution of power among the world's states in order to assess prospects. Given the nature of the climate change issues, however, it is difficult to ascertain what is the most appropriate measure of power (Rowlands 1996). Certainly, the possession of military strength could still be relevant; one actor may be able to issue threats and cajole another into reducing activities that contribute to climate change. Indeed, war has often been used as a means to achieve foreign policy goals related to natural resource issues (Westing 1986). Similarly, economic power could well be pertinent. An economically powerful nation or coalition might threaten to use trade sanctions against a climate violator. This kind of economic action has already occurred on other environmental issues, for trade restrictions are key components of three major international agreements (the Montreal Protocol, the Basel Convention, and the Convention on International Trade of Endangered Species of Flora and Fauna). In the field of global climate change, power may originate from the ability to transform the atmosphere and thereby alter the climate. Therefore, major greenhouse gas emitters, such as the United States and China, hold a potential veto over any efforts toward cooperative measures (see Porter & Brown 1991).

Institutionalism

Although conflict and the distribution of state power are the most important factors in the anarchical world of realists, especially in the field of international security, institutionalists have mainly aimed to explain the emergence and endurance of cooperation in the international political economy and in international environmental policy.

The modern institutionalist school took shape in the 1950s and 1960s, as more and more theorists began to question the realist perspective of international relations, and particularly its rejection of the necessity—and the reality—of cooperation and interdependence among nations (Haas 1964). The boundary between neorealism and institutionalism is not always clearly discernible. Some scholars hold fast to the self-interest assumptions of nation states while tracing the realization of that self-interest through the workings of international institutions that modify traditional realist assumptions of anarchy (Keohane & Nye 1977, Keohane 1984).

Institutionalists insist that, besides the role of national governments in international relations, international institutions play an important role by intervening between *basic causal variables* (power and interests); being simultaneously caused, with behavior and outcomes both resulting from basic causal variables; or even being basic causal variables themselves (Krasner 1983).

The resurgence of institutionalism became most prominent under the label of *international regimes*, which have been most commonly defined as "sets of implicit or explicit principles, norms, rules, and decisionmaking procedures around which actors' expectations converge in given areas of international relations" (Krasner 1983: 2). This definition is rather broad and ambiguous in delimiting whether phenomena fall under the rubric of international regimes in empirical research. It includes both formal international governmental organizations (such as the various UN agencies) and regularized forms of policy coordination on a specific issue (Young 1989).

International institutions, it has been argued, will provide a network of interactions which "once established, will be difficult either to eradicate or drastically to rearrange" (Keohane & Nye 1977: 55)—a position that is in stark contrast to realist predictions, which belittle the independent role of international institutions and largely describe them as instruments at the disposal of powerful countries. Thus, although major powers may provide international regimes as public (and partially private) goods, these institutions are likely to outlive the eventual decline of the countries that originally created them (see Keohane 1984). This permanency adds predictability to the interactions among nations, especially by providing or creating (Rowlands 1996):

- public and government concern for an international problem, such as global climate change
- physical and logistical facilities
- rules of interaction or procedure (a public good by itself, which reduces the costs of interaction)
- an enhanced time horizon for interaction (thus reducing the scope for being exploited in sequential interactions)
- resources for operational and redistributive purposes (e.g., technology transfer or interregional redistribution of costs)
- information provision, validation, intercalibration, and dissemination
- property rights
- linkage of issues (perhaps, but not always, enhancing the prospects for arriving at international agreements)
- monitoring of compliance with agreements
- enforcement mechanisms (including negative media attention, trade sanctions).

Although international regimes have proven effective in managing environmental problems in some cases and can confer many long-term benefits beyond their intended scope, the prospects for a successful regime addressing climate change are not necessarily promising. Although a climate regime could potentially enhance the international policy environment by instituting any and all of the factors listed above, the contending interests and costs accruing to many powerful actors through such action could prove prohibitive to regime formation on a global scale. As Haas et al. (1993) note, international institutions may raise concern and build capacity for addressing environmental problems, and strengthen the international contractual environment, but strong government and industry constituencies may successfully resist if they perceive their power and interests to be unduly compromised or constrained by institution formation.

Marxism and dependency theories

In a similar vein to the institutionalist school, dependency theory arose in the 1950s and the 1960s in response to realist interpretations of the failure of Third World economic development after decolonization. The basic premise underlying dependency theory is that the underdevelopment and continued poverty of the less industrialized countries resulted from Western colonialism and continued suppression of the economic, social, and political development of newly independent states by biases inherent in the international capitalist system. Theorists in this school, many of whom have economics or sociology backgrounds, include Frank, Wallerstein, Galtung, and Evans.[2] Although dependency theory has been criticized from various ideological and empirical standpoints, it has provided "a rational counterpoint to the prevailing liberal orthodoxy and, as such, a rallying focus for Third World political activity" (Maddock 1992: 114).

Other critical perspectives (Baylis & Rengger 1992) have emerged, primarily since the 1980s, in response to current strands of the dominant realist and institutionalist schools. These critiques include *interpretation, Marxism, critical social theory, poststructuralism, postmodernism, postpositivism,* and *feminism* (see, for example, Lapid 1989, Rengger & Hoffman 1991, Linklater 1992). These critical perspectives represent an eclectic mix. Although sharing a basis in Marxist writings and a tendency toward historically sensitive interpretive methodologies (Baylis & Rengger 1992), they differ in their conceptual approaches, methodologies, and foci (e.g., Ashley & Walker 1990, Peterson 1992, Neufeld 1993). Exponents of these perspectives criticize the methodologies of prevailing theoretical approaches and argue for a restructuring of international relations theory. In particular, criticism focuses on the failure of prevailing international relations theory to adequately address the changing landscape of international relations in the period following the Second World War (George & Campbell 1990, Luard 1990), including changes in the nature of state actions, and the increasing role of nonstate actors in international affairs (e.g., Lipschutz 1992, Princen & Finger 1994).

---

2. For further elaboration, see Cardoso & Faletto 1979, Palma 1978; for a study of the dependency movement as a whole and its influence on several scholarly fields, see Packenham 1992.

Cognitive and cultural approaches

A fourth set of approaches directs attention to the ways in which actors receive, process, interpret and adapt to new information about their environment and each other (Rowlands 1996). Cognitive factors, its proponents argue, are the keys to understanding the decisionmaking process. Those who are perceived to have control over or privileged access to knowledge are highly valued during times of political uncertainty and may be given greater access to decisionmakers. Therefore, to explain international cooperation on climate change, we should look to those who control knowledge and the ways in which they interact with decisionmaking circles. Although such theories have gained significant prominence only relatively recently, the basic ideas date back to the interparadigm debate of the 1970s and 1980s (Deutsch 1966, Steinbruner 1974, Banks 1985). Cognitive explanations have attracted considerable interest among those studying international cooperation on climate change and other environmental issues, since these are often remarkably complex and are accessible only to those with expertise in particular branches of the natural sciences. Consequently, considerable reliance may be placed on experts to assist policy decisions, and the cognitive approaches suggest that transnational networks of scientists and policymakers would exert particularly strong influence on writing international rules (Litfin 1994).

Significant changes in the world of politics following the demise of the Cold War have given renewed salience to cognitive approaches and theories (Lipschutz 1992). In particular, the heightened prominence of global environmental problems on the world political agenda has prompted many theorists to re-examine the nature of political power itself (e.g., Lipschutz & Conca 1993). Although traditional military and economic measures of power remain relevant, others, such as the ability to frame issues and shape international discourse, may be equally important. Knowledge, many theorists argue, is the emerging measure of state and social power on a political landscape that is increasingly dynamic and diffuse (Rosenau 1990).

The international system of states is but one set of social relations that have global breadth. Consequently, any efforts to understand what we have (perhaps mis-) labeled international relations must be cognizant of the whole range of social relations, including global commodity production and exchange, global culture, and other factors, which all together make up world society (Sklair 1991, 1994, Shaw 1994). Leading logically from these efforts to conceptualize a global sociology, many scholars focus upon social movements as key agents of any change (Yearley 1994), an analysis that has particular relevance for international environmental issues (Gerlach 1991). Finally, cultural theorists (see Verweij 1995) have argued that multiple rationalities can exist simultaneously (for sustainable development, see Thompson 1993). They maintain that the "participation of governments in treaties is likely to be influenced by the relative strengths of each type of institutional culture in the national decisionmaking arena, as well as by the more obvious factors of political and economic self-interest" (Rayner 1991: 92).

Whereas the cognitive and cultural theorists criticize the mainstream, the more traditional international relations theorists have, in their turn, criticized all of these approaches for lacking concrete alternative interpretations or understandings supported by clear empirical research programs (Keohane 1988, 1988, Biersteker 1989, Young 1992).

The growing role of environment in international politics

The growing criticisms of traditional international relations theory reflect changes in the global landscape that they are constructed to interpret. Environmental issues represent a part of that change; however, current mainstream international relations theories are ill equipped to address them. As new theories are developed amid change in the international system—a concept that is itself in question—a key set of variables concerns the interrelationships between the global environment and social institutions.

Although, as Lipschutz & Conca (1993: 14) noted, environmental issues have until recently been treated as "lower than low politics," this situation has been changing. In the mid-1980s, many students of politics began to theorize about international dimensions of environmental and natural resource management issues, as it became apparent that the environment was under increasing anthropogenic stress. The literature on international regimes, in particular, began to concern itself with the challenge of international cooperation for environmental problems in the late 1980s. Much of the stimulus for this growing sensitivity to environmental issues can be related to domestic considerations (e.g. pressure groups, crises, and legislation). It was from these national roots that concern for environmental protection was elevated to the point where, by the 1980s, issues such as ocean pollution, erosion of the ozone layer, threats to the Earth's biodiversity, acid rain, and global climate change were becoming standard fare on international economic and political agendas.

At least three factors helped to realize this transition: an increase in the absolute amount of pollution being discharged worldwide, widespread public awareness, and advances in scientific knowledge. It was becoming clearer, year to year, that actions taken by one state within its own boundaries could have a direct impact on other states, not only along its borders but much farther away.

Acid rain was one of the first problems of transboundary pollution to be addressed in this way. Caused by the airborne transportation of sulfur dioxide from coal-burning electric power and other industrial plants to lakes, forests and farmlands hundreds of miles away, the issue became a matter of international contention in the late 1960s (Caroll 1988: 2):

Through both the broad dissemination of scientific findings and the vociferous complaint of the people of Sweden, Canada, and other nations, the world first became aware of the growing concern over a phenomenon called acid rain. With this concern came the knowledge that serious and complicated transboundary, transnational environmental problems of a size and complexity not before seen would characterize an ecologically uncertain future and could further becloud already inscrutable international diplomatic relationships.

In recent years, acid rain has generated tensions between the United States and Canada, between Great Britain and the Scandinavian countries, and between Germany and eastern European nations.

In the late 1960s, Swedish scientists demonstrated that the increased acidification of Swedish lakes was linked to sulfur dioxide emissions originating beyond Sweden's borders. Unilaterally, Sweden was unable to address the problem. Sweden therefore proposed and offered to host, as part of an effort to place the issue of long-range transboundary air pollution on the international agenda, the first worldwide environmental conference—the 1972 United Nations Conference on the Human Environment.

The conference, which was convened in Stockholm in 1972, "marked a watershed in international relations. It legitimized environmental policy as a universal concern among nations, and so created a place for environmental issues on many national agendas where they had been previously unrecognized . . ." (Caldwell 1990: 21).

The conference marked the first milestone in what has since become a pattern of international involvement in large-scale environmental issues. "On an abstract level, it helped to advance the vision that the human world and the natural Earth could not necessarily be divorced from one another" (Caldwell 1990: 21). Policymakers further accepted the proposition that at least some environmental problems needed to be addressed at the international level. The conference also produced the Declaration on the Human Environment (also known as the Stockholm Declaration)—a set of 26 principles, which, although not legally binding upon states, have served as a guide and a foundation for subsequent development of international environmental law.

Two new institutions emerged at Stockholm that were to have a significant influence on international environmental protection. The first was a large, multinational, vociferous, and effective group of NGOs. The second, was a new United Nations agency, the United Nations Environment Programme (UNEP). The NGOs, representing public concerns among a large number of countries and a variety of relevant and irrelevant interests, by and large played a constructive role in focusing international attention on environmental issues.

Another accomplishment of the Stockholm conference was an implicit recognition that international environmental concerns could not be effectively addressed in the absence of consideration for economic development issues. This view, in fact, paved the way for UNCED 20 years later.

It was more than a decade after the Stockholm conference before the international scientific community was able to direct the attention of policymakers and the media to an environmental development potentially more menacing than acid rain. This threat was global rather than regional in scale. It was more complex in cause and more costly in effect. Long and difficult international negotiations would be necessary to hold it at bay. If the threat actually emerged, it would be irreversible over the course of centuries. And so, whereas the occurrence and impacts of acid rain were the driving force at the 1972 Stockholm conference, the threat of a significant change in the global climate was a centerpiece of Agenda 21 of the 1992 Earth Summit (Box 5.5; also Haas et al. 1992, Jordan 1994).

Box 5.5   Agenda 21

In addition to conventions on climate change and biodiversity, a major output of the Rio Conference was an 800 page statement of principles entitled, *Agenda 21*. A blueprint to implement sustainable development in both the industrialized and developing regions of the world, this document outlines goals and priorities on issues across the international environment and development agenda: climate change, forests, freshwater resources, biodiversity and biotechnology, institutional mechanisms, and legal and financial instruments. Although not legally binding upon national governments, the intense negotiations surrounding many sections accentuate Agenda 21's possible influence and importance as a soft law instrument.

The increasing national awareness and growing pressures of actual and potential environmental problems between 1972 and 1992 can be noted in a quantitative comparison between the two UN meetings. Stockholm was a gathering of 114 nations but was attended by only 12 heads of state; Rio represented an assemblage of more than 150 nations, including over 100 heads of state. The 134 nongovernmental organizations at Stockholm were dwarfed by the 1400 nongovernmental organizations and more than 8000 journalists from 111 countries who attended the Rio conference (Haas et al. 1992).

Until the late 1980s the prospect of global climate change was a concern primarily of researchers and modelers. By the autumn of 1988, however, the issue began to appear on the national political agendas of the United States and many other industrialized countries, and quickly moved into an ever wider national arena. By the time of the Rio conference in 1992, approximately 160 countries were, with varying degrees of enthusiasm and expertise, participating in discussions of greenhouse gas emissions and global climate change.

Porter & Brown (1991: 93) commented that:

> [the] global warming issue, like that of ozone depletion, had a relatively long history before being officially introduced into the international political process, mainly due to the lack of sufficient awareness of the scientific aspects of the issue to impel international action. This lack was largely because the case for a future threat of global warming rests on modeling rather than on scientific proof.

However, the discovery of the Antarctic ozone hole and confirmation that it resulted from emissions of chlorofluorocarbons was widely regarded as justifying the drastic international action agreed in the 1987 Montreal Protocol on Substances that Deplete the Ozone Layer. Initially, public political concern about climate change rode on the coat-tails of the ozone issue (Bodansky 1994).

North America's extremely hot and dry summer of 1988 can hardly be regarded as providing the requisite "scientific proof." Even as a signal of climate change it did not begin to approach the significance of the ozone hole. Nonetheless, many public policy analysts and environmental writers have credited the weather during that period with at least some responsibility for calling the attention of policymakers in the United States to the work of the climate change research community. According to Bodansky (1993: 461), the heatwave and drought of 1988 "gave an enormous popular boost to greenhouse warming proponents." Porter & Brown (1991) claimed that the media and the Congress regarded climate change scenarios more seriously because of the heat of 1988.

Although the sunstrokes, heat exhaustion, and forest fires of 1988 focused attention on warnings of global warming, the global climate change issue was already becoming a familiar one to influential communities outside the laboratories. Several international meetings addressed the issue between 1985 and 1988. In 1985, the World Meteorological Organization (WMO) and UNEP introduced the prospect of global warming onto the international agenda. Their conference in Villach (Austria) was marked by a scientific consensus that greenhouse warming should be taken seriously. In 1986, a report by WMO, the National Aeronautics and Space Administration (NASA), and several other US agencies, concluded that "climate change was already taking place at a relatively rapid rate" (Porter & Brown 1991: 93). And in 1988, just about the time when America was experiencing its record-breaking heatwave, the World Conference on the Changing Atmosphere was convened in Toronto, Canada, in an effort to engage both decisionmakers and scientists in a serious discussion of global climate change. The conference concluded that stabilizing the atmospheric concentration of carbon dioxide emissions required reductions of more than 50 percent from 1988 levels. A 20 percent reduction by the year 2005 was proposed as an initial goal, along with the development of a global framework convention to protect the atmosphere and the establishment of a world atmosphere fund, financed in part by a tax on fossil fuels (Jäger 1992).

The year 1988 also marked a watershed in the emergence of the climate change regime, in that the climate change issue had been dominated up to that point by nongovernmental actors—primarily environmentally oriented scientists. Although some were government employees, their actions did not reflect official national positions. In 1988, however, climate change emerged as an *intergovernmental* issue (Bodansky 1996).

International solidarity through science

The first step toward a global agreement on the climate change issue was initiated in 1988 when several national governments requested the WMO and UNEP to establish the Intergovernmental Panel on Climate Change (IPCC). The IPCC was to provide policymakers with a complete report about the state of scientific consensus on the issue (see Ch. 1). Earlier international assessments, prepared by various groups within the scientific and environmental communities, primarily from countries in the Organisation for Economic Cooperation and Development, were viewed with suspicion in some governmental circles, especially within less industrialized countries. There was considerable criticism that conclusions reflected environmental activism rather than sound science. The IPCC, however, was a UN-sponsored initiative, composed of scientists selected by member-state governments and intended, in part, to reassert governmental control over what was becoming an increasingly sensitive political issue (Bodansky 1993).

The production and use of scientific knowledge are widely recognized as essential elements of environmental standard setting (see Ch. 1; also Wynne 1987, Salter 1988, Jasanoff 1990). Although this is increasingly true of international activities, few social scientists have thought seriously about the implications of the internationalization of science. Among those who have, scientific accord is most often thought to promote convergent behavior among states. Certainly, scientists, diplomats, and politicians view the role of science as providing them with information, with common understanding upon which solidarity can be built. This view is exemplified in accounts of the acid rain issue and the stratospheric ozone negotiations (Carroll 1988, Benedick 1991). The apparent impartiality of science offers a welcome point of purchase to parties who are reluctant to trust the more obviously self-interested and fallible institutions of politics, diplomacy, and even law. Thus, Haas (1990), writing about the crafting of the Mediterranean Action Plan (Med Plan), argued that scientific consensus, shared with politicians and diplomats, constitutes an *epistemic community*, which forms the basis of intergovernmental trust and solidarity (see Ch. 1).

The concept of epistemic communities and their role in developing international solidarity around environmental issues has been contested by a few critics on the basis that common understanding of cause and effect is not a prerequisite for agreement on a common course of action. In fact, the existence of a multitude of plausible problem frames can bring more parties into agreement on action, each for individual reasons, and demand for scientific consensus can actually force parties who do not agree with the diagnosis to withdraw from common action.

Conventionally, the IPCC is viewed as providing the basis for an epistemic community of scientists, diplomats, and politicians around the climate change issue (Skea & Boehmer-Christiansen 1994). Certainly, Working Group I has developed an impressive track record in doing just that. This record is not entirely surprising, as IPCC scientists were nominated by government officials who were themselves concerned with climate change. Scientists strongly skeptical of climate change concerns were unlikely to be selected for nomination, unless they were willing to face a perpetual uphill struggle with those pursuing a climate change agenda. In other words, the notion of the IPCC as an epistemic community may overstate the extent of overall consensus within the scientific community as a whole.

The extent to which an epistemic community really represents a consensus between scientists and policymakers may also be controversial. In the case of the Med Plan, politicians basically operated with a bathtub model of the sea, throughout which pollution diffused evenly, imposing a uniform externality on the countries bordering it. Scientific experts were aware that this was not the case, that pollutants concentrate in certain areas, and that the status quo ante Med Plan would have had winners and losers. That scientists, who had their own good reasons to encourage passage of the Med Plan, did not promulgate this knowledge with their political partners raises questions about the institutional significance of a shared episteme.

A tension has also been observed between the process of consolidating scientific claims and the process of reaching international agreements (Jasanoff 1998). The consolidation of scientific theories and technological artifacts into robust claims involves the institutional process described by sociologists of science as *black boxing*, which conceals conflict and uncertainty from those not directly involved in the process. The resulting facts are extremely resistant to scrutiny and subsequent deconstruction (see Ch. 1; also Callon & Law 1982, Callon 1986, Latour 1987). On the other hand, *transparency*, the accessibility of information to state and nonstate actors alike, has been observed to be conducive to effective regime formation. Ironically, although individual scientists involved in the scientific assessment of climate change are themselves aware of the uncertain and contingent nature of their art, they are driven by institutional pressures toward expressing consensus in their findings. Although diplomats and lawyers seek transparency, they tend to exhibit a low tolerance for scientific uncertainty. As a result, the black boxing of climate change science may be exacerbated. Probably the greatest challenge to the process of scientific assessment as a means of creating solidarity among nation states is reconciling the imperatives of scientific practices with those of diplomats and lawyers.

Nonetheless, these considerations should not lead us to underestimate the contribution of the IPCC's scientific assessment to international solidarity on the issue of climate change. At least as important as providing a common scientific basis for negotiations, the process by which the IPCC has conducted its assessment has made a significant contribution to building trust and confidence among the participating nations. In particular, many of the less industrialized countries have limited scientific resources of their own and find it difficult to prepare well to participate in international negotiations. Briefing delegates requires a scientific infrastructure capable of advising on the technical aspects of environmental policy, which many countries do not have to an adequate degree. Participation in the scientific assessment process of the IPCC has raised not only the level of consensus among scientists from different countries but also trust among the national delegations to political negotiations. In short, the process of joint scientific assessment may be at least as important to building international solidarity at both the governmental and nongovernmental levels as the formal scientific outputs of that process. Furthermore, as Jasanoff (1998) pointed out, scientific assessment is a crucial element in monitoring compliance with international environmental agreements.

The Framework Convention on Climate Change

Although we include a brief background and summary of the Framework Convention on Climate Change (FCCC), our purpose here is not to provide a detailed narrative of the process of negotiating and implementing a climate treaty by governments, industries, or interest groups. Even if a single narrative could be definitive, climate politics remains, by any account, such a turbulent field that any summary of the state of play will date rapidly. Rather, our goal here is to review the frameworks for cooperation and competition among relevant institutions and the kinds of public sector and private sector policy instruments that presently and potentially constitute political action on climate change and related environmental issues.

The FCCC opened for signature at the 1992 UNCED in Rio and subsequently signed by 155 nations, is the centerpiece of international instruments designed to address global climate change. The FCCC was to some extent the culmination of the work of the IPCC and the Intergovernmental Negotiating Committee (INC), which established a foundation for the Framework Convention and may have helped to reduce the time necessary for its negotiation. The elapsed time between the initiation of the formal treaty-making process and the entry into force of the FCCC, amounted to little more than three years—an impressive feat for an international environmental agreement of such broad scope, albeit one requiring rather limited commitments.

The INC was established by the UN General Assembly in December 1990 to negotiate a convention containing "appropriate commitments" in time for signature at Rio in June 1992. Initially, negotiators for the convention considered two alternative models for addressing climate change: a general framework agreement on the law of the atmosphere, modeled on the 1982 UN Convention on the Law of the Sea, which would have recognized the interdependence of atmospheric problems and addressed them in a comprehensive manner; and a convention and protocols specifically on climate change, modeled on the Vienna Ozone Convention and Montreal Protocol (Zaelke & Cameron 1990). The second approach prevailed, as memories of the unwieldiness of the Law of the Sea negotiations compared unfavorably with fonder ones of the relatively swift step-by-step approach invoked successfully in the creation of the ozone regime (Tolba 1989, Sebenius 1991, Bodansky 1993).

Two main conflicts characterized these negotiations (see Mintzer & Leonard 1994). The first, between the United States and other industrialized nations, arose over the setting of a quantified target for emission reductions. Behind the United States' refusal to set a target were cost considerations as well as a level of skepticism about the nature of scientific evidence for climate change. In a compromise solution, dates were set for emission reductions, but with wording sufficiently ambiguous that the agreement did not elicit binding commitments from its signatories.

The second conflict developed between the industrialized and less industrialized nations over the issue of funding for emissions abatement measures. After they had agreed on two responsibility issues. Both considered the climate change problem to stem principally from the historical actions of the industrialized countries. In addition, because the industrialized countries had both the financial and technological capability to enable the less industrialized countries to limit their future emissions, responsibility for technological transfer also fell to the industrialized nations. Although this was accepted, on the whole, by the industrialized countries, conflict arose over additionality—the amounts of financial compensation from the North to the South—and conditionality—limits on how such financial resources are spent (Box 5.6).

The FCCC establishes an infrastructure of institutions and legal mechanisms that are intended to create a long-term process to address the climate change problem, rather than to impose strict obligations (Box 5.7). Thus, despite early hopes that the FCCC would contain a clear commitment to stabilize or even reduce greenhouse gas emissions, the convention contains only a statement regarding the intention of industrialized countries to return to their 1990 emissions levels by the end of the decade. Both of its principal obligations—the preparation of national reports and, for OECD countries, the provision of financial assistance to developing countries for preparing reports—are essentially procedural; they encourage rather than require national action to combat climate change.

Like other multilateral environmental conventions, the FCCC is designed to be an evolving institution, laying the groundwork for increasingly specific agreements and commitments over time (Hahn & Richards 1989). As a framework convention, the FCCC outlines both important principles and general obligations, leaving more substantive actions on the part of signatories to the FCCC to be adopted through protocols or other legal instruments. Opportunities to revise obligations based on new information are built into the provisions of the FCCC and administered through meetings of the Conference of the Parties (COP), established by FCCC article 7 (Box 5.8). The COP, which meets annually unless it decides otherwise, is, in short, responsible for the process of implementing the Framework Convention.

Strengths and weaknesses of the convention-protocol approach

The strength of the convention-protocol approach, upon which the FCCC is structured, is that it is a gradual process enabling states to participate at the outset without making commitments to specific actions (Susskind & Ozawa 1992). In other words, solidarity among nation states is built through piecemeal confidence-building activities (Vogler 1995). For example, countries would not initially agree to specific greenhouse gas reduction targets immediately because of other political and economic priorities, but would, and did, agree on a

---

Box 5.6 Additionality and conditionality

Additionality and conditionality involve economic and political issues that go well beyond the issues surrounding global climate change. One of the most contentious issues raised at UNCED in June 1992 was the proposition, advanced by the less industrialized countries, that the OECD countries should, individually or collectively, pay the costs of measures undertaken by developing countries to tackle global environmental problems and make the transition to sustainable development as outlined in *Agenda 21*—a document that lays out a blueprint for sustainable development. This proposal came to be known as *additionality* because the less industrialized countries have insisted that the compensation should be in addition to all financial aid currently being transferred from the North to the South.

The matter of additionality came to be regarded as a make-or-break issue for the success of the Rio conference. Nonetheless, the debate about additionality is not new; it started long before UNCED and is continuing long after. UNCED, however, provided a showcase for the issue. Thus, at the very outset of the UNCED negotiations, the less industrialized countries made no secret of their intent to support agreements under discussion only if provisions were made for significant quantities of additional financing from the rich industrialized countries.

Conditionality is the other side of the coin. It is a codeword that encapsulates the industrialized world's rejoinder to the demands of the less industrialized. According to this view, the industrialized countries are not necessarily obligated, either morally or legally, to compensate less industrialized countries for contributing to preserving the global environment, which, after all, the latter share. But, according to this view, if funds are provided, it would be on the condition that they be used for projects related to international environmental protection, rather than as a supplement to existing foreign economic assistance or even as funding for national environmental projects (e.g., local sewage disposal).

The dialogue (or argument) does not end here, which is why additionality–conditionality discussions tend to reach an impasse. For the less industrialized nations, the proposition of conditionality arouses the shibboleths of "infringement of sovereignty," "linkages," "assistance with strings attached," and "neocolonialism." According to Jordan (1994), resources for environmental protection should be both new and additional; they should be disbursed on a grant or concessional (low-interest loan) basis; and they should be free of conditionality—the strings often attached to financial aid. Yet additionality is often difficult to calculate or prove in practice, conditionality is enormously contentious, and it would be politically naïve to expect all finance to be provided on concessional terms.

If the success of an international program to delay or reduce the severity of a worldwide change in climate depends on the transfer of vast sums to the less industrialized world from all or some OECD countries, the outlook for an international accord is grim. Unless there is a dramatic change in both the mood and the economic situation in the OECD community, nothing like the amounts being discussed by the representatives of the developing countries are likely to flow to the South. If, indeed, an effective climate change regime is to be established, a more innovative approach may be required.

---

program of scientific research and data collection. The start-up phase of the convention process created a momentum that encouraged commitment and cooperation. As demonstrated in the FCCC, the signing of conventions and their following protocols can be hastened by the accumulation of scientific evidence, strong public support, and international opinion.

Box 5.7   The Framework Convention on Climate Change

The following principles and obligations are included in the FCCC: an overall objective of stabilizing atmospheric concentrations of greenhouse gases at a "safe" level; general principles to guide future work, including principles of equity, precaution, and cost-effectiveness; a process intended to improve our information base, to encourage national planning and response measures, and to produce more substantive standards should scientific evidence continue to mount that human activities may change the Earth's climate; and institutions to oversee the implementation and development of the Framework Convention.

Bodansky (1995) summarized the key provisions of the FCCC are as follows.

Objective
Stabilize atmospheric greenhouse gas concentrations at a level that would prevent dangerous anthropogenic interference with the climate system, within a timeframe to allow ecosystems to adapt naturally, protect food production, and allow sustainable economic development.

Principles
Intra- and intergenerational equity, differentiated responsibilities and respective capabilities, right to sustainable development, precaution, cost-effectiveness, and comprehensiveness.

Commitments
Three levels of commitment are embodied in the treaty:
• *All countries*   General commitments to develop national emissions inventories; formulate national mitigation and adaptation programs; promote and cooperate in scientific research, education, training and public awareness.
• *Industrialized countries and countries with economies in transition* (listed in Annex I)   Recognize that a return to earlier emission levels of carbon dioxide and other greenhouse gases by the end of decade would contribute to modifying long-term emission trends, and aim to return to 1990 emission levels.
• *OECD countries* (a subset of Annex I countries listed in Annex II)   Commitments to fully fund less industrialized country inventories and reports; fund the incremental costs of agreed mitigation measures; provide assistance for adaptation; and facilitate, promote and finance technology transfer.

Institutions
Conference of the Parties, Secretariat, Subsidiary Body for Scientific and Technological Advice, Subsidiary Body for Implementation, and Financial Mechanisms.

Reporting
• *All countries*   Emissions inventories; steps taken to implement the Convention.
• *Industrialized countries (Annex I)*   Detailed description of policies and measures to limit emissions and enhance sinks, and a specific estimate of their effects on emissions.
• *OECD countries (Annex II)*   Details of financial and technological assistance measures.

Review mechanism
Reviews of the adequacy of commitments every three years, based on the best available scientific information.

Box 5.8   Conference of the Parties (COP)

The functions of the Conference of the Parties include review of the FCCC on a regular basis; assessment of its implementation and effectiveness; promotion and facilitation of the exchange of information on measures adopted by parties; facilitation and coordination of action between two or more parties on measures to address climate change and its effects; promotion and guidance of refinements of methodologies on greenhouse emissions, sinks, sources, and so on; ensurance of publication of reports on convention implementation; mobilization of financial resources; and other functions required for achievement of the objectives of the Framework Convention.

The mechanism of establishing a Conference of the Parties has become an established feature of the conventions and protocols approach to international environmental agreements, such as the 1989 Basel Convention on the Control of Transboundary Movement of Hazardous Wastes and their Disposal and the 1992 Biodiversity Convention.

Nonetheless, the current convention protocol approach has been criticized, both from within the perspective of conventional state-centered international relations theory and from the perspectives of other disciplines, many of which are less wedded to the state-centered approach. The hard bargaining style of the convention-protocol approach has been described by many as unwieldy, inflexible, and often detrimental to developing long-term relationships of trust and solidarity among nations. Rather than a creative approach, where parties brainstorm about best ways to reach agreement, the negotiation process can be reduced to a battle of wills and a series of standoffs, much as envisaged by the realist perspective. Negotiators are often wary of openly exploring novel options in negotiations, lest exploratory positions be misconstrued, or later invoked, by other parties as if they were commitments. As Susskind & Ozawa (1992: 150) have observed, ". . . when negotiators are in the business of trading concessions (rather than engaging in genuine problem solving) . . . an inordinate amount of time is wasted performing the 'concessionary dance'."

Another problem associated with the convention protocol approach is that, in the effort to reach an agreement, the negotiation is often reduced to accepting the weakest position among the parties, even though it may fall well short of perceived scientific necessity (Susskind & Ozawa 1992). The FCCC seeks to overcome this problem by recognizing three different levels of obligation:

- by all of the signatories
- the industrialized countries listed in Annex I
- the smaller subset of OECD countries listed in Annex II.

Critics also charge that delays in signing a convention followed by delays in the negotiation and signing of the protocols can act as a stalling mechanism for politicians and governments. Conventions thus provide window dressing, while the parties continue with business as usual. In the case of the FCCC, different parties tend to view the urgency of the problem quite differently. The AOSIS urges prompt emissions reductions, whereas the Organization of Petroleum Exporting Countries (OPEC) counsels against precipitate action. Both charges of stalling and of adopting the lowest common political denominator have been levelled against the FCCC, but usually from nongovernmental sources frustrated with the pace of negotiation (see Mintzer & Leonard 1994 for a full analysis).

In contrast to the above, institutionalist theorists might adopt a more optimistic outlook with regard to the convention protocol approach. Although the protocol process is admittedly slow and complex in the case of climate change, the routinization of interaction and information exchange among policymakers, scientists, nongovernmental organizations, and others may form a durable foundation of trust on which more ambitious negotiations and treaties might be based in the future; the very act of negotiating can provide *transaction benefits* (Richards 1996) through repeated opportunities to build trust and legitimacy around the FCCC process, a necessary function for reaching solidarity (Feldman 1992). Furthermore, the heterogeneity of actors and interests involved may provide important advantages, as recent research suggests. That is, the differential capabilities and desired outcomes of actors involved might provide a rich basis for negotiation and compromise and need not serve as a barrier to collective action on global environmental problems.

As proponents of cognitive approaches to international relations suggest, the framing of issues for the negotiation process is an expression of political power. In the climate change negotiation process, power might be conceived as the ability of actors to bound the international debate in terms advantageous to themselves or consonant with their worldviews, and to persuade others to buy into their framing. The most powerful states might be viewed as those that succeed in codifying their desired realities via the climate change convention (Litfin 1994).

Increasing the number of parties to a negotiation is known to exacerbate the problems of achieving, monitoring, and complying with agreements (Raiffa 1982, Touval 1989, Hampson 1990). Scholars disagree about whether the issue of climate change is one that requires universal or limited participation (see, for example, Szasz 1991, Dowdeswell & Kinley 1994). Others suggest that since the lion's share of greenhouse gases are emitted by a handful of states (see Vol. 2, Ch. 4), if the principal goal of climate change politics is really the instrumental one of emissions reduction, then limiting participation to the states with the most bargaining power would seem to offer the most efficient and expeditious solution. For example, the United States and the European Union were the primary negotiators of the Montreal Protocol. On the other hand, if climate change politics have become the expressive peg on which many issues, such as structural adjustment, resource consumption, and population management, have been hung, then clearly the negotiations need to be equally accessible to all potential parties. Commentators recognizing the dualistic nature of the climate negotiations have proposed various accommodations, including recognition of the symbolic importance of a universal treaty while pursuing smaller formal and informal multilateral actions (Rayner 1991) and a system of representative constituency groupings such as AOSIS, ASEAN (Association of Southeast Asian Nations, CANZ (Canada, Australia, and New Zealand), the European Union, and so on, thus allowing all countries to participate, although not directly (Dowdeswell & Kinley 1994).

Whatever the underlying goal of a treaty or protocol, its credibility depends on striking a believable balance between the desire to attract relevant parties to join and the likelihood that the actions required in the treaty will achieve its goals. Credibility is also a matter of effectiveness. For international environmental agreements in particular, which require, in effect, individual citizens to alter their behavior, effectiveness is not merely a matter of signatures, but whether support exists for ratification of the treaty, the desire and capability to carry out treaty provisions, and adequate monitoring of compliance to support the legitimacy of the treaty.

As the climate change regime develops, its effectiveness will become an increasing focus of concern. What commitments governments have accepted will become less important than the degree to which they and their citizens have adopted new behaviors to fulfill those commitments and the degree to which those new behaviors have prevented climate change; in other words, the ability of the regime to create and maintain solidarity around climate change concerns. Eventually, the FCCC will be evaluated against many standards and evaluation criteria (Box 5.9; also Underdal 1992, Levy et al. 1994). Much of the professional literature suggests that a treaty's problem-solving effectiveness depends on at least four factors (Mitchell 1996):

- Were the treaty's goals adequate to solve the environmental problem?
- Were the treaty's goals achieved?
- Did the treaty cause the accomplishment of those goals?
- Even if the treaty did not accomplish its goals, did it cause environmental improvements that would not have happened otherwise?

A necessary, but not sufficient, condition of problem-solving effectiveness is the treaty's ability to induce positive behavioral change, or behavior-changing effectiveness (Young 1992). Behavior-changing effectiveness incorporates common notions of treaty implementation and compliance; treaties should induce states to promulgate laws, regulations, and policies and make their behavior conform with specific rules (Nollkaemper 1992). We should also deem a treaty effective if it induces positive behavioral changes that fall short of full

---

Box 5.9   Evaluating regime effectiveness

One commonsense standard for judging success would use the criteria of problem-solving effectiveness, that is, to what extent global warming was averted and whether the regime was the cause of that accomplishment (Mitchell 1996). Less stringently, a counterfactual standard for success could demand that the treaty caused environmental improvements that would not have happened otherwise, even though they fall short of completely solving the problem, as if the FCCC delayed climate change by several decades but failed to avert its eventual arrival (Young 1992). This latter standard highlights that the convention, especially initially, may be only partially effective in solving the problem, but will thereby provide insights into its own improvement Or the treaty may succeed at achieving compliance and its stated goals, but not solve the true environmental problem, because of shortcomings in those goals themselves reflecting scientific uncertainty, failures of political will, or other factors. For example, even if the Convention on International Trade in Endangered Species completely eliminates trade in threatened wildlife, nontrade factors, such as habitat destruction, may still frustrate the ultimate goal of protecting endangered species (Mitchell 1996).

---

compliance (partial or good faith compliance); comply with the spirit but not the letter of the treaty; or exceed treaty-mandated standards (overcompliance).

International implementation mechanisms

Implementation is conventionally viewed as the process by which a national government carries out its obligations under a treaty. In that respect, it is very much a process of domestic solidarity building on the part of government elites. In a liberal democracy, any government will, of necessity, have begun this process before signing a treaty.

However, three mechanisms for implementation of the FCCC require close intergovernmental coordination or, sometimes, coordination between governments and nongovernmental entities in other countries, such as firms or environmental groups. These methods are Joint Implementation, tradeable permits, and financial and technological assistance through the Global Environment Facility (Box 5.10). Debate over these issues illustrates the multiple solidarities that constitute the international global climate change regime and the attempts to develop institutions to bridge those differences (see Victor & Salt 1995). Despite the theoretical attractiveness of Joint Implementation schemes—which permit countries to receive credit for emissions reductions they achieve outside their territorial boundaries—they have proven to be controversial from the viewpoints of both industrialized and less industrialized countries (Box 5.11). The Joint Implementation debate reflects an important political tension between the economic goal of minimizing the global cost of emission reduction and the equity goal of not shifting to less industrialized states the burden of

---

Box 5.10   Global Environment Facility

The Global Environment Facility (GEF), managed jointly by the World Bank, the United Nations Development Programme, and the United Nations Environment Programme, was established in 1990 as an experimental three-year pilot program and given the mandate of allocating $1.3 billion in development assistance for projects related to global warming, ozone depletion and other global environmental concerns that would not otherwise be funded as part of traditional development activities. At UNCED, participating governments favored using the GEF as an interim finance mechanism for the incremental costs of implementing the Framework Convention on Climate Change, the Biodiversity Treaty, and Agenda 21. At the same time, they recognized many shortcomings in the GEF that would need to be remedied prior to its adoption.

The resources of the GEF have been criticized as inadequate for the tasks at hand, but are unlikely to be increased in the foreseeable future. Its greatest impact is likely to come from its ability to redirect the focus of traditional development assistance, and to encourage additional international capital transfers, including private investment. Criticisms of the GEF have been manifold and they concern both its structures and functions. Many critics believe that substantial reforms are required to incorporate an equitable system of representation and transparent governance. In addition, critics question the GEF's scientific and technical criteria for funding projects, maintaining that the institution's activities often address symptoms rather than causes of environmental degradation. This, critics feel, is the result of the GEF's secretariat being housed in the World Bank, which has no environmental mandate per se, and which has had a spotty environmental record throughout its history. Despite these criticisms, the GEF was adopted by the First Conference of the Parties, with relatively little debate. It has not, however, been endorsed as the permanent mechanism.

---

practical actions to limit emissions, especially since only Annex I countries have obligations to limit greenhouse gas emissions.

Richards (1996) suggests that Joint Implementation is likely to evolve through three stages, distinguished by the type and distribution of commitments made by the participants from the Annex I and Annex II countries. In the pilot stage, countries have committed themselves to a rather vague goal of mitigation, but the commitments are de facto nonbinding. In subsequent stages, first the Annex I countries and eventually all signatories to the FCCC may agree to limits on their individual energy-related carbon dioxide emissions.

Tradeable quota schemes could be an alternative to, or provide a larger context for, Joint Implementation. Under this mechanism, countries agree to allocate carbon emissions quotas, perhaps based on an overall emission target. "In a practical sense, signatories to the FCCC have implicitly agreed to such a qualitative target" (Fisher et al. 1996: 404), although how rights to carbon emissions should be allocated remains a critical, and thorny, question (see Ch. 4). International tradeable quota schemes carry the benefits of a market-based approach—a least-cost way of reaching targets—but whether benefits are realized in practice depends upon the form of the scheme (Grubb 1989). There are several ways to control emissions through systems of interchangeable permits.

Box 5.11   Joint Implementation

At the core of the Joint Implementation (JI) debate is the question of whether Annex I countries should be allowed to meet part of their emission reduction commitments by undertaking mitigation measures outside their own borders. Industrialized countries, in particular, emphasize the benefits of JI in terms of economic efficiency—pursuing the most substantive, and least-cost options first, regardless of where those options are located. In contrast, less industrialized countries consider JI to be a means for the rich nations to buy their way out of the need to reduce their own emissions and to continue their affluence at the expense of the rest of the world's economic development.

As part of a compromise solution, the First Conference of the Parties (COP) meeting in Berlin (1995) officially established a pilot phase, to be reviewed annually by the COP and conclusively decided on by the year 2000. During this pilot phase, no credits accrue to any Party as a result of greenhouse gas emissions reduced or sequestered through JI. The pilot phase of JI is exploratory; no countries have made binding commitments to limit national carbon dioxide emissions. The form of JI to follow this phase was left for later deliberations.

In the future, a JI program may be formalized within the FCCC, or countries seeing an advantage in JI-type projects may pursue them on an ad hoc basis, possibly through some form of bilateral agreement. Even before the meeting of the First COP, several countries, including the Netherlands, Norway, and the United States, had already begun undertaking JI projects. The Netherlands program is based on government-sponsored projects; the US program has been based largely on the initiative of private parties. The programs have different sets of evaluation criteria and have involved a variety of types of projects. Over time, experience is expected to demonstrate which elements of each of the programs appear most promising and might be incorporated in a multilateral program.

As a result of compromises reached in Berlin, JI is now formally on the international climate change agenda. Including JI reflects a trend in international environmental treaties of increasingly looking at incentive mechanisms and efficiency principles.

All have in common that countries would adopt whatever domestic policies they preferred to meet their quotas.

The economic efficiency gains of Joint Implementation and the international tradeable permit schemes are attractive because they promise to reduce compliance costs and increase compliance levels correspondingly (Victor & Salt 1994). Nonetheless, as Mitchell (1996) pointed out, both of these regulatory strategies pose special political problems. A tradeable permit scheme will require negotiation of specific targets and timetables, measuring each country's annual emissions, and tracking all trades to determine each country's final *adjusted emission limit* based on permits allocated, bought, and sold (Tietenberg & Victor 1994). For either tradeable permits or Joint Implementation projects, independent evaluation will be required, both to certify compliance with particular trades and to support the credibility of the market itself (Tietenberg & Victor 1994). The COP will also need to clarify which party to an emissions trade or Joint Implementation project is responsible for compliance. Eventually, the COP will need to develop some mechanism to evaluate the claims of states that sell allocated emissions rights and then fail to comply with their remaining emissions limits because of inadvertence or an incapacity to comply.

Given the resistance of many less industrialized countries, most notably China, to submitting to any type of emissions limit, Joint Implementation is likely to remain in the pilot stage for the foreseeable future. Furthermore, with high transactions costs and poor incentives for private party participation, the pilot phase is clearly not going to induce substantial emissions reductions.

Richards (1996) proposed that the Joint Implementation Pilot Program seems most likely to serve two functions: the advancement of social learning and the development of institutional solidarities across national boundaries. Although the incentives for Joint Implementation in the Pilot Program are weak and transaction costs high, the possibility of future benefits in a more formalized program may encourage participation now. This exploratory stage provides insight into both technical and institutional aspects of designing an open system of Joint Implementation—building institutions, and creating solidarities and developing consensus among key interest groups, including Annex I nations, non-Annex I nations, and environmental nongovernmental organizations. More importantly, perhaps, it serves as a mechanism for communication across nations and organizations regarding the goals and ultimate design of a more mature system.

Given the open nature of the Joint Implementation Pilot Program, it is not going to contribute to learning about the operation of a closed emissions trading system. However, it has already contributed to technical learning about such issues as constructing reference cases, designing monitoring programs, and the differences between energy-related and land-use projects.

Perhaps more important than the technical or institutional insights gained from the pilot stage are the relationship and common experiences that develop (Richards 1996: 183):

> Every time a successful transaction is completed between two parties, there is an increased sense of trust and interdependence. While these "transaction benefits" have been addressed in both the contracts (Williamson 1985) and social science (Cantor et al. 1992) literatures, they seem to have received little considerations in the traditional economics literature. Building this sense of solidarity, a common understanding of acceptable goals, behavior and relations, may be the most important product of the pilot stage of JI.

Compliance, monitoring, and enforcement

The FCCC, which takes the soft law approach (Box 5.12), requires very little in terms of measurable compliance by signatories. In this respect it is consistent with the apparent preference of states for agreements whose guidelines are not rigidly set, that contain nonbinding objectives, and that have flexible timelines for implementation. It is also consistent with the pattern of successfully negotiated international environmental treaties that do not threaten core state interests. And, as Hurrell & Kingsbury (1992) pointed out, state autonomy is invariably maintained in the reporting, monitoring, and inspection procedures.

The track record of the international community in monitoring and ensuring compliance with environmental agreements reflects its poor performance in policing international agreements and treaties on a wide range of issues, including human rights and intellectual property rights (Chayes & Chayes 1991, 1993). One exception is the International Atomic Energy Agency (IAEA), which has been quite effective in intrusive monitoring and control of nuclear proliferation.

Box 5.12   Hard and soft approaches to international law

In their formal efforts to address global climate change, negotiators have favored a combination of *soft* and *hard* approaches to international law. The soft approach primarily seeks to facilitate and encourage—rather than mandate—state behavior, through international institutions and cooperative arrangements. This involves building scientific and normative consensus incrementally, through joint assessments of scientific knowledge, the creation of regular forums for discussion and negotiation, and the establishment of international organizations, to encourage rather than enforce compliance—for example, by addressing barriers to compliance such as distrust between states and lack of domestic capacity.

The 1972 Stockholm Declaration is an example of soft law instruments: texts that have been adopted by states without being legally binding. This instrument made valuable contributions to international law by addressing emerging social values that have subsequently been formally confirmed in international conventions. Similarly, Agenda 21, the nonbinding action plan opened for signature at UNCED in 1992, has spawned national policies and international cooperation to prevent climate change and promote sustainable development. Nevertheless, "there is obviously a difference between the affirmation of principles by national delegations in the euphoria of international assemblies and practical implementation where perceived national interests are involved" (Caldwell 1984: 106).

For this reason, many environmental NGOs, among others, have advocated a hard approach, a climate change treaty that would carry substantial sanctions for violators. The hard approach views international law as a vehicle for imposing specific obligations on nations, that such obligations should be enforceable through compulsory, binding dispute resolution, and that sanctions should be imposed on those who renege on promises to adhere to these principles.

Elements of both hard and soft law approaches have been employed in international efforts to deal with global environmental concerns. Although the instruments initially adopted by the international community to address climate change are more characteristic of a soft than a hard approach, more-stringent elements are emerging and receiving international acceptance.

Sources of weapons-grade nuclear materials are few, however, and mostly under the direct control of governments themselves. By contrast, sources of greenhouse gas emissions are literally countless and ubiquitously distributed throughout all nations. A centralized approach to compliance with greenhouse gas protocols would seem to be prima facie inappropriate.

In the absence of coercion, states generally comply with an agreement when they perceive it to be in their interests to do so. Nevertheless, achieving compliance may be a problem where states are concerned that other parties may defect or fail to comply. A common source of noncompliance is concern about loss of comparative advantage to other signatories, who delay their own compliance, or about *free riding* by other signatories. For example, the initial 1987 Montreal Protocol contained few incentives to encourage large less industrialized nations such as China and India to participate. This lack of incentives might have led them to abstain from reducing the use of chlorofluoro-carbons and to have left the reduction goals to the main users. The 1990 London Amendments Protocol contained measures designed to rectify this situation, after which both China and India announced their intention to join the regime at a later date.

Compliance is often a matter of degree (Mitchell 1996). Countries may comply with one treaty provision while ignoring another. Once the FCCC adopts clear requirements, some actors will have several reasons to act consistently with the FCCC (see, for example, Mitchell 1994). Required behaviors will coincide with the independent self-interest of those actors who perceive the rules as reflecting their pre-existing interests, who do not need to make behavioral changes, or who view treaty rules as legitimate standards for action (Franck 1990). The incentives and capacities of countries already committed to reducing greenhouse gas emissions and other unilateral compliers will lead them to comply, independently of the treaty's compliance system. Other contingent compliers will base their behavior on whether other actors' behaviors conform to treaty requirements and on how other actors respond to the failure to conform with their obligations.

Despite compliance by some actors, others are likely to fail to comply with regime provisions for a variety of reasons (Koskenniemi 1992, Mitchell 1994, Mitchell & Chayes 1995). Even for actors committed to complying, the breadth and complexity of activities that contribute to global warming mean that compliance will take time. Some actors will fail to comply because they lack the financial, administrative, or technological capacity to comply (Kimball 1992, Chayes & Chayes 1993, Greene 1994). Other actors may inadvertently fail to meet treaty standards, because the policies that they adopt do not achieve intended results. This outcome is particularly likely in cases such as carbon taxes to reduce greenhouse gas emissions (Epstein & Gupta 1990, Victor & Salt

1994). Some actors will view climate change policies as a virtuous goal that is simply less pressing than other needs. For other governments and private actors, the present costs of required behavioral changes will exceed the uncertain and future benefits. Such intentional violators will fail to sign an agreement or will violate it regardless of its supporting compliance systems (Mitchell 1996).

Environmental law and international bodies that support or enforce compliance may help overcome barriers to trust, just as incentives may be added to dissuade potential defectors from an agreement. Legal and environmental institutions established to aid implementation of international agreements can assist in stabilizing expectations and providing frameworks for negotiations and platforms for cooperation for an increasingly wide range of long-term issues. The need for cooperation and negotiation among states to manage these issues is characteristic of high levels of interdependence. To prevent escalations of distrust in such a scenario, transparency and good communication become increasingly important. Precedent shows that these conditions can be satisfied, which tends to undermine the realist notion that anarchy breeds distrust and forces states to act only on worst-case scenarios. There is evidence that states will comply with the guidelines established in international environmental agreements, even if it runs contrary to their short-term interests, because they are more broadly concerned with their reputation as reliable partners and their long-term position in the international system. The reality of recognized interdependence among nations challenges the idea that global environmental bargaining can be compared to a one-off Prisoners' Dilemma game where it is rational to defect. Rather, as game theory suggests, restated games and "lengthening the shadow of the future" increase the chance of cooperative solutions being found (see Vol. 3, Ch. 2; Axelrod 1984, Oye 1986).

The parties of the FCCC have various options to attempt to enforce compliance with future climate protocols, including economic sanctions, legal penalties, and private enforcement (Dudek & Tietenberg 1992, Tietenberg & Victor 1994). However, as Mitchell (1996) argued, adopting centralized sanctioning in response to noncompliance faces several problems. First, in the many cases in which noncompliance arises from factors other than intentional violation, sanctioning seems an inappropriate, and therefore unlikely, response. Second, even when noncompliance can be shown to be intentional, governments rarely have sufficient incentives to offset the costs of sanctioning noncompliance by other states (Axelrod & Keohane 1986). Third, countries that support the FCCC would be unlikely to make their greenhouse gas emissions subject to some form of tit-for-tat strategy, because of both the high domestic political costs and practical obstacles to actually doing so. The climate regime will most likely need to rely on mild forms of collective opprobrium, such as diplomatic shaming and jawboning, which may prove adequate to induce compliance in some cases, and on providing legal authority for decentralized sanctioning by nonstate actors (Chayes & Chayes 1993, Mitchell 1994).

New views on sources of noncompliance have prompted interest in response strategies that address incapacity or inadvertence problems (Chayes & Chayes 1993). Trade incentives, technology transfer, and funding mechanisms have become increasingly popular, although empirical evidence of their effectiveness remains scant, and funding for the GEF and technology transfer projects has fallen short of initial expectations (French 1994, Victor & Salt 1994). The European Union's eco-labeling program suggests that the FCCC could adopt forms of positive incentives other than financial transfers to induce actors to exceed treaty standards (Salzhauer 1991).

Top-down implementation of intergovernmental obligations, however, is not the only way in which political action can be coordinated among citizens of different countries. The process of achieving solidarity across national boundaries does not necessarily require the active engagement of the nation state. For example, scholars have described a *polycentric* decision process by which like-minded groups coordinate policies directly across national boundaries (Gerlach & Rayner 1988, Rayner 1991). In this process (Fig. 5.1) national culture provides only one dimension of affiliation for decisionmakers, who also play particular roles in various, often competing, interest groups.

In our contemporary world of high-speed communications, these groups are able to communicate rapidly and effectively with comparable actors in other countries. In this way, communication across national cultures by common

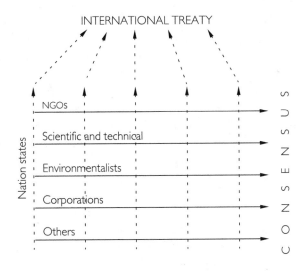

Figure 5.1 A polycentric model of international decisionmaking (Rayner 1991).

institutional cultures can lay the groundwork for internationally shared understandings of issues. In the two years between the Vienna Convention and the Montreal Protocol, many such crossnational linkages were employed to create an international consensus to cut chlorofluorocarbon emissions drastically. In particular, scientific and technical organizations and environmental networks were active in changing the European interpretation of the scientific issues, while the United States moved from supporting an aerosol ban to favoring production cuts. All parties, including industrial producers and users of chlorofluorocarbons, came to agree that international production controls would be a powerful incentive for the development and marketing of substitutes (Morrisette 1989, Benedick 1991).

In addition to laying the grounds for a formal agreement, this process created its own framework for implementation and compliance. For example, on the basis of the new scientific consensus, DuPont (which had 25 percent of the global market) decided unilaterally to phase out chlorofluorocarbons altogether. The polycentric regime model offers the possibility that international constituencies may reach consensus about how to deal with various aspects of a complex large-scale problem, such as climate change, without committing nation states to positions that may be viewed by powerful internal interests as being contrary to national self-interest. Furthermore, such small-scale interventions may have far-reaching consequences, even without requiring nation states to enter into formal comprehensive agreements. Ultimately, the participants in such a process could generate global solutions, even if no central body of global decisionmakers formally decides upon a concerted course of action. Participants in such a multistranded and loosely coupled network are free to innovate in many small ways, without facing the challenge of accepting or rejecting a single large treaty (Gerlach & Rayner 1988).

The process is analogous to that by which the United States established its national policy for nuclear energy throughout the 1970s and 1980s: to continue research while holding a moratorium on installing new capacity. This policy was clearly established for two decades, but no decision point or decisionmaker can be identified. Because the decision process remained implicit, the process itself did not become a focus of conflict between powerful constituencies with incompatible preferences for ways of making policy decisions. Important discussions need not be stymied by interminable wrangles about the shape of the conference table or the presence of ideologically repugnant delegations.

In the polycentric model, treaties may be primarily of symbolic value. This is not to say that they are unimportant (Rayner 1991). The Montreal Protocol actually had a technology forcing effect. It demonstrated the political will of major producing countries to take action to protect the ozone layer. However, the USSR was exempted from the strict reduction requirements of the treaty and allowed to put new factories into production if it became a signatory. Soviet participation in the process was considered more important than immediate adherence to the most restrictive terms of the treaty. There was an implicit understanding that the symbolic statement of intent was more important than the instrumental effects of the immediate production cutbacks that the treaty required. For this reason, and because this kind of treaty is based on prior consensus at the substate level, the problems of enforcement inherent in the realist model may be less threatening to the desired outcome.

Although each component of the international relations theoretical literature discussed earlier in this chapter offers some valuable insights into the nature of the international system, global climate change poses unique challenges to its explanatory power. Its focus has been principally on the nation-state level of analysis and on the linear transactions within the interstate system. The recognition of a need for new theoretical perspectives accounting for a broader set of actors, roles, and dynamics in world politics is now gaining greater currency in the mainstream of the discipline. Acknowledgment and understanding of the linkages among informal local institutions, domestic voluntary associations, and transnational networks of nonstate actors will be as important as government agencies and international organizations in dealing with the challenges of global climate change. It is to these networks that we now turn.

Policy networks and subsystems

We have described how far the international politics of climate change in the late twentieth century are removed from the struggles of power elites that characterized the international system of nation states before the Second World War. Some analysts have suggested that the transborder characteristics of global environmental issues underlie the opening up of international politics to more many and diverse players. However, in turning to climate politics at the state and nonstate levels, we find a similar pattern of the rational self-interested exercise of power by governmental elites being displaced by a complex and turbulent structure of competition and collaboration. Multiple overlapping networks of stakeholders represent diverse patterns of social solidarity, interests, values, and social-choice strategies. This may suggest that the structure and dynamics of climate politics at all levels are driven not so much by the characteristics of the problem itself (about which there is widespread disagreement anyway) as by changes in political systems themselves.

We also find a similar breadth of theoretical frameworks to describe and explain climate politics at the state and substate level. The principal cleavages are between self-interest and cognitive accounts of behavior and between individual and institutional accounts. Wherever a researcher comes down between these four cardinal points, it is increasingly clear that focusing purely on the structure and resource capabilities of individual actors, such as government departments and pressure groups, does not yield satisfactory explanations of climate policy outcomes. Rather, outcomes are determined by the interactions among groups, the underlying rules of the game, common values, and shared assumptions that underpin the procedural values that regulate interaction in the political process. This dynamic pattern of alliances is variously described as a *policy network* (Smith 1993) or *policy subsystem* (Sabatier & Jenkins-Smith 1993; see also, for example, Heclo 1978, Sabatier 1988).

The concept of policy networks (or subsystems) is based on the observation that policymaking tends to be fragmented into specific *issue areas*, and that most issues are dealt with by a few actors within small groups of participants from governmental and nongovernmental agencies (Rhodes 1990). It describes the close and consensual nature of policymaking and the often blurred relationship "between the governors and the governed" (Smith 1993: 56) through channels that are often informal and, almost always, extra-constitutional. According to Richardson & Jordan (1979: 74):

> It is the relationship involved in committees, the policy community of departments and groups . . . that perhaps better accounts for policy outcomes than examinations of party stances, of manifestos or of Parliamentary influence.

Within each specialized issue area, interest groups cluster around one or several government departments in the hope of influencing policy. But the flow of resources is not merely one way; the state also needs the support of certain groups to make, legitimize, and eventually implement policy. Thus, a policy network has been defined as a "cluster or complex of organizations connected to each other by resource dependencies and distinguished from other clusters or complexes by breaks in the structure of dependencies" (Benson 1982: 148).

Rhodes (1986) has elaborated upon this definition by identifying various forms of networks according to the number of participants, the degree of resource exchange among them, the extent to which the other interests can enter or leave the grouping, and the frequency of interaction among members. Marsh & Rhodes (1992) propose a continuum of types of policy network. At one end they identify tightly formed and highly stable *policy communities*, normally formed around one particular government department. Policy communities are stable networks with a limited number of participants. According to Jordan (1990a: 327), "A policy community exists when there are shared community views on the problem. Where there are no such shared attitudes, no policy community exists."

Although the policy community is not formally recognized, its members share an appreciation of what is important in political life. There are shared values and a dominant worldview within the community. Its members interact frequently. There is a constant and two-way flow of resources among actors, who tend to agree upon what specific problems justify a policy response and how, in turn, that response should be structured. In climate politics, the policy communities that appear to matter revolve around science, energy supply and use, regulatory agencies, and bureaucracies of governmental machinery controlling finance, trade, industry, transport, environment, and foreign affairs.

At the other end of the continuum is the much more diffuse *issue network*, characterized by a larger number of participants, a lack of consensus on the problems at issue and the means by which they should be tackled, more open access to different groups, and, consequently, less permanence and stability. Issue networks tend to encompass two or more government departments, and there is plenty of opportunity for other groups to become involved. In general, climate politics occurs in issue networks (or at least the less cohesive policy communities) involving energy, transport, environment, and the foreign ministry.

Which type of policy network actually forms in any particular case seems to be shaped by the characteristics of the issue area concerned. Smith (1993: 234) suggests that policy communities tend to develop in situations where the state needs the assistance of nongovernmental groups to implement policy, whereas issue networks tend to develop in more politicized areas, where resource dependencies are not as pronounced.

Sometimes policy communities and issue networks come into conflict. When this occurs, the stability and cohesion of the policy community probably prevail over the more radical and informal issue networks. This seems to have occurred in the European case studies of climate policymaking reported in O'Riordan & Jäger (1996), where entrenched policy communities established around government departments concerned with economic issues, such as trade and employment, thwarted proposals for carbon taxes that were backed by weaker climate change issue networks emerging around environmental agencies.

The policy network model shows how institutions determine the pattern of interest-group participation in decisionmaking (O'Riordan & Jordan 1996). The extent to which the network is open to new players is determined not only by organizational factors (e.g., there are always important committees to attend, august bodies of which to be members, and advisory panels on which to sit); less perceptible factors such as ideology, worldview, and legitimacy also play a role. Participants in stable communities are bound to abide by certain rules, which dictate standards of reasonableness, legitimacy, and acceptability. To

389

enter the more formalized policy community in particular, pressure groups must show that they will abide by the prevailing ideological consensus. Groups and individuals that do not are routinely excluded from the locus of power and decisionmaking. In some cases, a conscious decision is made to exclude other groups from important meetings, but, in others, groups are excluded not because of the conscious decisions of individuals but by the very process of decisionmaking (Smith 1993). This is because, over time, patterns of solidarity (exclusion and integration) become habituated within the policymaking system. Certain groups hold power because they are trusted by the policy community to observe its norms.

Policy networks are stable, but not immutable. The opening and closing of networks gives them a dynamic quality (Richardson et al. 1992), which is sometimes missing from more deterministic accounts of politics. Smith (1993), for example, shows how policy networks shift according to changes in political party, problem analysis, technology, external relationships, key personalities entering and leaving, and internal restructuring. The concept of policy networks is a useful way to envision and explain continuity and change within political life. Stable policy communities—for example, those that cluster around the transport and electricity generation sectors—become an effective constraint to radical policy change; they tend to change slowly, if at all. The main feature of the British system, for example, is that (Jordan 1990b: 471):

> ongoing problems and constraints force successive governments into very similar policy positions. Problems are handled similarly irrespective of what government is in power. Agreement will be sought within the community of groups involved.

A government faced with a new policy problem, such as climate change, is forced to negotiate with, and gain the support of, relevant and important communities. Where there is no powerful policy community that sees its interests threatened, change is likely to be more rapid and pervasive.

The significance of policy networks lies in their relative freedom of information exchange; their information evaluation function (both within their own networks and among society at large) and their ability to create or block consensus around controversial issues.

Policy formulation can, therefore, be viewed as a process of negotiation among coalitions of institutional actors (e.g., political parties, government department and agencies, private sector firms, social movement organizations, and communities), with the policies themselves reflecting the programs and preferences of a dominant coalition in a particular policy subsystem. Changes in policy are therefore likely to depend very strongly on shifts in dominance within a subsystem and among competing subsystems.

In an insightful article, Sewell (1996: 139) points out that the coalitions dominating the domestic and international policy subsystems of the various parties to the convention may not be the same:

> ... a nation that is a party to the convention is not likely to adopt strong national policies to implement the convention unless: (1) the coalition that has dominated the international climate change subsystem also dominates the national climate change policy subsystem, and (2) no perturbations occur either external to or within the national policy subsystem that causes this coalition to lose its domination.

In the best dichotomizing tradition of the social sciences, Sewell identifies two principal coalitions: the *precautionary coalition* and the *economic growth coalition*, corresponding closely to the *catastrophists* and *cornucopians* described in Chapter 4. The (catastrophist) precautionary coalition consists primarily of environmental groups, environmental ministries, and many in the scientific community, whereas the (cornucopian) economic-growth coalition is represented mainly by business interests, and economic and trade ministries. In terms of the triangular framework proposed in Chapter 4, the precautionary coalition is an alliance of egalitarians with one part of a segmented hierarchy, whereas the economic growth coalition consists of another segment of the hierarchy and the market constituency.

The policy subsystem addressing the international dimensions of climate change has been dominated in most countries by the precautionary coalition (although this has not been the case with China and the major oil producing countries). The formal motivations of environmental agencies require relatively little elaboration. Nurtured through the polycentric linkages of international environmental and scientific conferences and organizations, they have been successful in presenting climate change to foreign ministries as an opportunity to strengthen bonds of international solidarity among nation states worldwide. By exploiting superior familiarity with the science and fortuitous events, this coalition was able to dictate most of the terms of the international policy process and its agenda in its initial stages.

The economic-growth coalition became active only in the later stages of the policy-formulation process, coming too late to substantially influence the shape and terms of the FCCC. Subsequently, this coalition has become more active in determining national policies and, through them, the shape of the actual negotiations.

Sewell's (1996) contrast between the patterns of dominance among these two coalitions in the Netherlands and the United States (Box 5.13) illustrates the difficulty that emerging issue networks, such as the various national precautionary coalitions on climate change, face when their proposals impinge on the agendas of established policy communities, such as those that exist around economic growth.

Without a major policy stimulus, such as a significant carbon tax, and without an incontrovertible signal that climate change represents an imminent and real threat, the inertia within the domestic policy system of any country is likely to delay the kinds of behavioral changes envisaged by the precautionary coalition. These examples also indicate that issues that are perceived by governments to be on the *policy periphery*, like climate change, are not easily factored into consideration of issues at the *policy core* such as national economic policy or corporate manufacturing strategy (even though, when discussed or considered in isolation, such as at international environmental conferences, these issues may be described as pressing or important by government ministers or corporate executives). At the same time, policies such as carbon taxes, explicitly formulated to address issues on the policy periphery, are likely to be carefully scrutinized for potential adverse effects on the policy core by its institutional stewards.

For example, an extensive study of climate change politics in Europe (O'Riordan & Jäger 1996) revealed the relative weakness of issue networks and policy communities around environmental ministries in all of the countries examined (Britain, Germany, Norway, and Italy) as well as within the European Commission. In none of these cases has climate change been perceived within the powerful ministries and their policy communities as sufficiently threatening to their departmental interests to disrupt their existing policy agendas. The findings of Beuermann & Jäger (1966: 223) in Germany are typical:

> Reviewing the policies of other ministries that concern climate change-related issues, such as transport policy or energy policy, we find that climate change has not become one of the bases on which policymakers and administrators found their decisions. Traditional thinking about the policy needs of the economy has not been overcome.

Clearly, climate change either has to be shown to be a compelling threat that overshadows other policy demands or it has to be integrated into the routinized decisionmaking frameworks of government organizations and agencies whose primary policy concerns (such as finance and energy) are widely recognized as compelling.

However, authentic policy integration across government departments is hard to achieve. Merely piggybacking climate change policies onto other goals does not guarantee their success where there are strong countervailing interests. For example, the defeated Clinton energy tax was actually proposed as part of the bill explicitly designed to reduce the federal budget deficit—a concern close to the US policy core in the 1990s.

Although these aspects of national politics are important, they may obscure another fundamental reason why, even when policy is accepted, as in the Netherlands, it nevertheless proves to be remarkably ineffective. Both academic and practitioner analysts continue to focus policy studies at the level of the nation state, whether their focus is on the ability of states to develop solidarity with one another or to create appropriate frameworks of political and economic solidarity to implement their policy goals domestically. However, in most cases, the state is actually very far removed from the sources of emissions. Therefore, the policy levers of the state have to be very long to reach the locus of desired action. All too often, especially (although by no means exclusively) in the less industrialized world, the levers of state power are not connected to anything at all at the local level, where policies must be implemented by ordinary people living face to face in communities.

There is much variation among countries in the relationships of national to provincial and local governments. However, in the day-to-day lives of most people in the world, local government is the more salient political actor. It delivers or withholds essential services, it mediates between the citizen and the nation state through local officials, such as police officers, who may have to monitor vehicle emissions, or building inspectors, responsible for seeing that new construction meets energy efficiency standards. Furthermore, over 50 percent of the world's population now lives in urban areas, contributing a significant portion of global emissions of greenhouse gases. The density, mixture, and physical layout of residential and commercial neighborhoods and so forth, all influence the energy intensity of the community. Yet many of these factors are more directly under the control of community governments than of national ministries.

Already cities around the world are networking with one another at the level of municipal administrations and citizen activists, without the intermediation of national authorities. For example, urban leaders met at the Municipal Leaders Summit for Climate Change in New York in 1993 to establish the Cities For Climate Protection program. This program extended an earlier initiative linking 14 cities in the United States, Canada, Europe, and Turkey, designed to strengthen local commitment to reduce urban greenhouse gas emissions, to research and develop best practices in pilot communities, to share planning tools and experiences, and to enhance ties among municipalities across national boundaries, especially between those in industrialized and less industrialized countries.

The bulk of climate change politics may have to devolve to the local level, if policies are to become effective in the informal institutional dynamics of individuals and households. The rise of informal networks of cooperation is an important development here, spurred on via schools and colleges, various social groupings, and local businesses (e.g., see O'Riordan & Jäger 1996). Whether policy innovation and behavioral change are led locally or nationally, they will be marked by a process of institutional learning that either moves presently peripheral concerns about climate change to the core of people's daily concerns or, at least, palpably and convincingly links climate policies to these everyday concerns.

Institutional learning

In general, institutionalist accounts of politics give a good account of political and organizational continuity but are relatively quiet on the subjects of learning, innovation and change:

> The critical inadequacy of institutional analyses to date has been a tendency towards mechanical, static accounts that largely bracket the issue of change and sometimes lapse inadvertently into institutional determinism (Thelen & Steinmo 1991: 16).

Krasner's model of *punctuated equilibrium* (1984) is helpful in explaining the origins of abrupt institutional shifts and short-run crises, and Hall (1986, 1993) provided an interesting analysis of the medium-term transition from Keynesian to Monetarist worldviews in the 1970s. Other institutionalists have sought to explain crossnational differences in policy outcomes with reference to an individual state's (static) institutional configurations (such as constitutional, legal and judicial factors). As yet, however, there has been a relative paucity of theoretically informed work on the subject of how institutions change (but see also Olsen 1992), especially in the environmental realm. Smith (1993), in a helpful but brief contribution, suggested that institutions at the national level change in response to several stimuli, including changes in external relations, economic and social changes, the emergence of new problems, internal divisions within established policy communities, and new technologies.

O'Riordan & Jordan (1996) suggested at least three factors that might create the opportunity for an issue to shift from the institutional periphery to the core, and hence from the more ephemeral issue networks to the more central policy communities:

- scientific knowledge
- circumstances or events
- the repercussive effects of small but purposeful steps.

As outlined in Chapter 1, the science of global climate change has gathered enough credibility—by networking, by peer review, and by sympathetic media coverage—to play the role of stimulus for change. The credibility of climate change science rests particularly with the IPCC because of its pre-eminent role in influencing the FCCC, and because of its adaptation to include more policy-relevant analysis and social scientists in its second round of operation. Science has also influenced national governments through formal commissions of enquiry into climate change issues—for example, the German Enquete Kommission and the UK Royal Commission on Environmental Pollution. These bodies articulate scientific consensus, create plausible evidence of possible futures, indicate the consequences of doing nothing as opposed to doing something, and convey a sense of urgency that captures public concern. In this process, the credibility of science as an institution and climate change as an issue may both be enhanced. However, cracks in the credibility of the science, or the policy actions that are based on it, may result in a dramatic decline in the credibility of scientific and political institutions (Wynne 1996). For example, scientific reversal of assurances by British public health officials that mad cow disease could not be passed to humans damaged both public confidence and, ultimately, the British economy. One institutional solution to the problem of scientific credibility in the face of high uncertainty may be the introduction of civic science. *Civic science*, a term coined by Lee (1993), has also been referred to as *vernacular science* (O'Riordan & Rayner 1991) or *postnormal science* (Funtowicz & Ravetz 1992). It is an extension of conventional science through which both data and projections are subject to open negotiations among a wide range of stakeholders, including indigenous people, women, youth, business, academia, agriculture, trade unions, local government, and nongovernmental environmental and developmental organizations.

However, such innovation in policy formulation, is hampered by the fact that institutions stabilize around a common procedural culture that governs learning, role playing, sharing, competing, and justifying. The result is a tendency for formal organizations in particular, but also policy communities or issue networks, to build up coherent worldviews or mindsets based on shared norms of behavior that are internally unchallenged. This tendency is one reason why the ideas and concerns at the cores of policy communities are usually very stable and difficult to change. The stability of this routinized mindset partly explains why environmental ministries and departments are making little headway in climate change politics in the face of concerns of the more powerful ministries and departments, such as finance, and their industrial constituencies.

Bureaucratic *roles*, *standard operating procedures*, and *departmentalism* (Box 5.14) all have implications for understanding the progress (or lack of progress) of climate change policies, even in countries, such as Germany, which have been

---

Box 5.13   Contrasting climate policy formulation in the Netherlands and the United States

Sewell (1996) described how the precautionary coalition has dominated both the international and domestic climate change policy subsystems in the Netherlands. Led by the Ministry of Housing, Environment, and Spatial Planning, it consists also of the Ministries of Foreign Affairs and Development Cooperation; Education and Science; and Agriculture, Nature Management, and Fisheries, as well as members of parliament, and environmental groups. He attributes this success to the previously well-established national environmental policy planning process (through which climate policy was to be formulated and implemented), parliamentary support for legislation, and membership of the European Union. The coalition was enhanced by the limited participation of major private interest groups in the national planning process.

However, the precautionary coalition does not enjoy complete control. Certain ministries responsible for policy implementation are controlled by the economic growth coalition, consisting principally of the Ministries of Economic Affairs; Transport; Public Works and Water Management, and various industry interests. It has been successful in forcing significant compromises in the policy formulation process. In particular, it forced the government to abandon the precautionary coalition's plan to introduce a carbon tax, by arguing that such a tax would stimulate energy-intensive industries to relocate.

Despite the political acceptance of the climate change policy measures embodied in the National Environmental Policy Plan, greenhouse gas reduction measures in the Netherlands have been implemented with difficulty and delay, if at all. Although emissions did decline in 1993, this was attributable to a slowdown in economic activity, rather than to the implementation of reduction policies.

Until 1992, the climate change policy process in the United States was dominated by the economic growth coalition, which concentrated on scientific research (on the basis that the uncertainties concerning climate change did not justify aggressive emissions reduction measures). The precautionary coalition at this time consisted of the Environmental Protection Agency, federal scientific agencies concerned with the atmosphere (the National Aeronautics and Space Administration and the National Oceanic and Atmospheric Administration), parts of the State Department, environmental groups and a handful of vociferous members of the Congress. The economic growth coalition consisted of President Bush and his closest advisers, the Office of Management and Budget, the Department of Energy, and various trade associations, largely representing the fossil fuel industry.

The election of President Clinton in 1992 brought the precautionary coalition to ascendancy in the White House, which, in May 1993, committed the United States to reducing its greenhouse gas emissions to 1990 levels by the year 2000. In October the President issued his Climate Change Action Plan, consisting of 47 policy actions designed to meet that emissions reduction goal, including an energy tax and more stringent fuel efficiency standards for cars. But, despite its domination of the executive branch, the precautionary coalition did not gain control over the national policy subsystem. Congressional opposition, especially in the Senate Finance and Energy Committees, replaced the energy tax, which was intended to meet about 20 percent of the emissions reduction goal, with a gasoline tax of 4.3 cents per gallon. After this defeat, promised legislation to increase the corporate average fuel efficiency (CAFE) standard for cars was never introduced. The Republican takeover of both Houses of Congress the following year led to severe cuts in appropriations for measures in the Climate Change Action Plan, which made achievement of the year 2000 target practically impossible.

characterized as exhibiting a precautionary national policy style. These factors affect the substantive outcomes of decisionmaking by regulating the access of participants, and by affecting the patterns of negotiation and consultation, the participants' allocation of attention, their standards of evaluation, priorities and perceptions, identities, and resources. On a day-to-day basis, standard operating procedures have an important influence on who is consulted and in what form that consultation takes place; in other words, what kinds of evidence and information are passed to ministers and what is routinely screened out as being irregular, unfeasible or dysfunctional.

Nonetheless, two innovations in bureaucratic behavior reflect institutional adaptation to climate change in Europe. These appear to have been stimulated, at least in part, by the requirement of the FCCC for signatories to produce reasonably reliable estimates of their greenhouse gas emissions and to generate carbon dioxide emissions reduction plans. One is the formation of a host of interdepartmental committees at both ministerial and official level. The other is the creation of environmental policy units within government departments, bold enough to change viewpoints within established organizations, yet not too obvious to create opposition and dismissal. For example, connections between response to climate change and economic, industrial and employment policy are gradually becoming acceptable and innovative in some parts of Europe (O'Riordan & Jäger 1996).

Corporations, although they participate in markets as institutional actors, are, like government, organized along lines of bureaucratic authority. The learning behavior of firms is particularly critical to the implementation of climate change policies. For example, efforts to reduce greenhouse gas emissions from the electrical, transportation energy, and manufacturing sectors depend upon the readiness of firms in those sectors to invest in the development of new technologies and to adopt those technologies (see Vol. 2, Chs 4 and 5). Where firms are strongly motivated and markets are able to reflect the true environmental and social costs of providing goods or services, then firms may be expected to seek the best performing technologies and to lead government regulation in their development and adoption. On the other hand, firms and industrial sectors may be compliance driven, rather than performance driven. These tend to follow regulation in response to concern about sanctions and adopt only those technologies and practices that are officially required.

There are several approaches to understanding how the institutional structure of the firm shapes its responses to technological opportunities and policies. For example, one study characterized the decisionmaking structure of US electric utilities to evaluate their long-term interest in novel nuclear power technologies 25 years in the future (Braid et al. 1986). This study disaggregated the electric utility decisionmakers according to whether they sought to optimize

---

Box 5.14   The Bureaucratic Politics model

In an influential book entitled *Essence of decision*, Allison (1971) set out to explain how decisionmaking is crucially determined by the organizational context in which it takes place. Although Allison is not without his critics (e.g., Smith 1981), the models he presented have been used by scholars to appreciate the mechanics of decisionmaking in large organizations.

Bureaucratic roles

First, an individual's motivations and perceptions are shaped by his or her organizational role and the situation of the agency in which that role is located. That participants tend to opt for courses of action that reflect their own institutionalized position within an organization is a theme running through many accounts of politics, summed up by the pithy aphorism "where you stand depends upon where you sit."

Individual bureaucratic roles become particularly critical for the *bureaucratic politics* model, discussed by Allison. Policies emerge from a process of bargaining and conflict among key personnel within an organization, or among different parts of an organization. These *bargaining games* are not haphazard, but follow specific *action channels*. In other words, "The individuals whose stands and moves count are the players whose positions hook them on to the action channels. An action channel is a regularized means of taking government action on a specific kind of issue" (Allison 1971: 169). Action channels are longstanding arrangements governing the procedures to be used for tackling an issue. Individual role players act as information gatekeepers within and between institutions, and therefore may exert a powerful influence on what issues are taken up by them as well as how they are resolved.

Standard operating procedures

Allison's *organizational process* model sees policy as the output of organizations. For the most part, however, organizations are not monolithic units with a set of clearly defined goals. They are internally divided into components and subcomponents, each of which follows its own set of *standard operating procedures* (SOPs), defined by Allison (1971: 68) as "the rules by which things are done."

All organizations develop SOPs as a means of dealing with the uncertainty, conflict, and ambiguity in policymaking. Clearly, it is easier for organizations to fit problems to an existing template of solutions than to continually work out new answers to each new problem—in other words, these institutionalized routines and repertoires exist prior to any specific assessment of the problem at issue. All problems tend to be processed in a routinized and regular fashion, despite their individual qualities, and existing practices tend to become important determinants of the way in which new problems are treated. For example, Olsen (1991: 105) described how the Norwegian government responded to the discovery of oil in the late 1960s: "Oil issues were interpreted and dealt with by pre-existing departments in the light of established routines." In general, policymakers seldom considered several choice alternatives or examined their various consequences in any great detail. "Rather, the government followed a few, simple, experience-based rules and standard operating procedures" (Olsen 1991: 105). These findings reinforce a large corpus of social science research on the routinization of behavior in organizations to manage the pervasive influence of uncertainty.

Departmentalism

Allison also described how SOPs become translated into specific ideologies or worldviews within entire departments: a phenomenon sometimes known as *departmentalism*. For example, the Department of Transport in the UK has traditionally favored the building of more roads over the provision of better public transport facilities. Similarly, the departments taking responsibility for energy-related issues have tended to favor nuclear power generation over coal, and increased supply over demand reduction. The fact that departments are physically oriented in a certain way—the allocation of staff, resources, and time, for example—tends to predetermine particular policy responses to emerging policy problems. Evidence of the existence of departmentalism is ubiquitous. Politicians, for example, have been known to display a fundamental ideological conversion when they move departments, and departments tend to be associated with particular forms of policy involvement and not others. This aspect of policymaking is captured by another well-used aphorism: the departmental *view* (such as, "the Treasury view" or "the European Commission's view"). Thus, we might expect an environment ministry to adopt a position on climate change that would, for example, focus on the car as an emitter of pollutants, whereas industry and finance ministries see the car as a manufacturing issue or a catalyst for economic growth.

profitability (maximizers) or stability (satisficers), and whether they relied on single-source internal analyses for information (bounded) or multiple internal and external sources (unbounded). The researchers found that:

- Bounded satisficers were least likely to be first adopters of a new technology.
- Bounded maximizers were likely to exhibit a "not-invented here syndrome" unless they were integrally involved in developing the technology.
- Unbounded satisficers were most likely to respond to technological mandates, but were unlikely to initiate innovation.
- Unbounded maximizers were most likely to experiment with a variety of technologies, but were unlikely to commit to a single fuel or process.

In principle, information of this sort can be used to tailor climate change policies to firms likely to adopt technologies that would lower greenhouse gas emissions. This typology may be generalizable to the variety of strategies and responses in other industries and in other countries. Some key trends indicate that the environment is increasingly being acknowledged as a major strategic issue for national and multinational corporations (Box 5.15).

Climate change is no different from other situations in which certain businesses are so dependent upon processes or products that lie at the root of the problem that they see their very survival as threatened by any acknowledgment its existence. Just as the tobacco industry continues to dispute the health impacts of smoking, certain business interests, in Britain and the United States at least, have promoted scientific interpretations that are contrary to, or critical of, IPCC viewpoints. The American Petroleum Institute, for example, has cooperated

---

Box 5.15   Environmental strategies of firms

- Large international companies (IBM, Shell, Ford) see the environment as a regional and global issue. Accordingly, they are responding nationally and internationally.
- Environmental management is rapidly becoming a routine business function as many companies establish environmental departments.
- Companies in many sectors are investing in pollution control, recycling, and clean technology.
- Companies in sectors, such as banking, investment, and insurance, are explicitly confronting the consequences of their investment for the environment as well as the potential impacts of climate change on their investments.
- Many trade associations (e.g., electric power, chemicals, and paper) have environmental units or committees and are commissioning research and collaborating nationally and internationally.
- A growing number of companies (including chemical manufacturers, supermarkets, and banks) are taking a *cradle-to-grave* or *product lifecycle* approach. Some are conducting supplier audits.

---

with the Coal Association to review and critique general circulation models and to promote the views of scientists who are skeptical about climate change or, in some cases, who believe that its benefits will outweigh damages.

The response of some other industries seems to be strongly time dependent. For instance, the US automobile industry seems quite accepting of the idea that cars in the long-term future may not be powered by gasoline engines. However, the industry is also very sensitive to current consumer demand for sport utility vehicles that are exempt from federal fuel efficiency standards.

There are also broader concerns within the private sector that climate change policies could have a depressing effect on the overall economy, particularly in view of the central role of energy. For example, the Confederation of British Industry actively assisted the British government in blocking European Union attempts to introduce a carbon tax. British trade unions also opposed the tax: in a period of prolonged recession and uncertain recovery, organized labor is not anxious to raise the costs to industry.

European case studies demonstrate the stability of the industrial and finance policy communities to exclude climate politics in a meaningful way in all the countries studied (O'Riordan & Jäger 1996). But they also found that in the transport and fiscal arenas the issue networks offer opportunities to pursue policies beneficial to climate stabilization, notably in various forms of mopping up consumer surplus in the face of falling oil prices and energy prices generally, and in the growing coalitions of local-protest and public-interest groups against further road developments and the experience of chronic traffic congestion.

In contrast with coal and oil interests, the insurance industry has already demonstrated a significant level of concern about the potential impacts of climate change. In particular, the industry has responded to concern that even early stages of climate change may be characterized by extreme weather events such as unseasonal freezes, more frequent hurricanes, and unusually strong storms. Large insurers have the capability to impose their own standards on property and technology as a means of reducing the risks that they bear. The most obvious opportunity for action here is in adaptation to climate change, for example, by requiring and ensuring through inspection that buildings meet certain standards for storm resistance.[3] It may be possible for insurers to incorporate greenhouse gas emissions into the safety standards that they require for insuring boilers and other industrial equipment.

Such rules and regulations, whether emanating from or enforced by the private sector or by national and local governments, are examples of *policy instruments* by which institutional learning is transformed into institutional action to effect behavioral change. To these policy measures we now turn our attention.

Policy instruments

Politicians and government bureaucracies seek to implement the goals that they choose or are assigned through selecting appropriate policy instruments. A wide array of instruments exists for translation of global environmental agreements into action at the national and local levels.

Many policy instruments are aimed at changing the behavior of firms. Others seek to directly influence the behavior and choices of the final consumer of products or services. Sagoff (1988) distinguishes between the individual as consumer and the individual as citizen. As a consumer, the individual seeks to satisfy personal or self-regarding needs and wants, usually in the short term. As a citizen, the individual is concerned with the public interest and the communal good.

An example for climate politics is that of the ambivalent attitude of most individuals in the industrialized world toward the car. Its consumer benefits are large; its citizen dividends are negative. It provides the consumer with mobility, choice and convenience, while depriving the citizen of clean air, quiet neighborhoods, accessible routeways, and, potentially, a climate in tolerable equilibrium. This ambivalence is why it is so difficult for legislators to tackle the motor vehicle, why its emissions remain the fastest growing element in greenhouse gas inventories, why it is such an influence on land-use alteration—itself a key component to climate change—and why any policy measure is likely to be limited in its effectiveness.

---

3. Following Hurricane Andrew in the United States one builder of private homes stood out for resilience of its structures. The charity, Habitat for Humanity, which uses voluntary labor, explained its secret: "We build to code."

Transportation is a major area of opportunity to control greenhouse gas emissions, restrict acid rain, and limit the instances of respiratory ailments for the young, the old, and the medically vulnerable. Vehicle ownership is a widely attainable proposition for the citizen as consumer, who perceives in the car a great measure of personal benefit rather than a tiny addition to global change. Policy communities wax and wane around the car as evil and the car as economic salvation and social lubricant. The car is not only a convenience; it may be a necessity where no other means of transportation exist, or where national cohesion requires face-to-face contact across swathes of empty and inhospitable territory—as in the case of Norway (Sydnes 1996).

The key to unlocking this dilemma lies in the realization that real consumption decisions are almost never made by single individuals, but by families, communities, partnerships, and firms, consisting of individuals with diverse goals, priorities, and preferences that must be negotiated through institutional arrangements (Douglas & Isherwood 1979). For example, automobile purchases are known to reflect competing desires for appearance, performance, carrying capacity, style, and other factors that vary with family size, stage of family lifecycle, and other aspects of the family as an institution. Chapter 3 argues that consumption choices are not made merely to gratify internal desires, but are made for the community of which the consumer is a member. The political challenge of altering consumer behavior is not merely one of education, but of changing institutional relationships within and among communities. Various combinations of policy instruments are available to pursue both of these ends. Such instruments may be grouped broadly under five headings: fiscal incentives; regulation; information; research, development, and demonstration (RD&D) programs; and direct government provision of goods and services (DOE 1989).

Fiscal incentives generally are designed to ensure that consumers and producers face the true costs of their decisions, but allow them a high level of discretion about how to deal with those costs. The definition of a fiscal incentive consists of two parts:

- any tax, fee, loan, subsidy, or rule change that is designed to alter the consumption of a good or activity by changing its price relative to the prices of other items that consumers might choose freely
- direct government expenditures.

The major instruments affecting prices are emission fees, tradeable emission rights, deposit refund systems, and the introduction or removal of subsidies (Hahn & Stavins 1991). Emission fees put a price on pollution and confront the emitter with the full cost of his or her actions. This has considerable political appeal as well as widely recognized properties of economic efficiency. However, uncertainty about costs of damages, emission control costs, and the effectiveness of such a system to influence decisions reduces the attractiveness of emission fees. In addition, the concept of paying to pollute may be unacceptable to an array of environmental advocates, and the sudden rearrangement of property rights may be highly objectionable to manufacturing interests.

Regulation is defined as legislation or rules, supported by sanctions, that are designed to limit the discretion that may be exercised by public and private decisionmakers. Such legal and administrative means of forcing private firms to incorporate some or all of the social costs of their contribution to global warming are exemplified by rigorous effluent emission standards with large effective penalties or command and control requirements that stipulate the use of specific technologies (Hahn & Stavins 1991). The major benefit of regulatory programs is that they tend to help managers and consumers rapidly incorporate the social, as well as private, costs and benefits of their actions. However, the effectiveness of regulatory programs may depend heavily on the quality of information available to the regulator. Furthermore, they may be administratively quite costly and inflexible. For example, certain restrictive standards, particularly those that specify the technological means to achieve environmental ends, may hinder the progress of new technologies.

Information is a commodity that is especially subject to problems of market failure. Once information is produced, the producer faces difficulty in capturing its full value. Consequently, the markets for some types of information can fail to exist or can function poorly. As a result, economic agents often are forced to make decisions with far less information than could be available to them if information markets worked better. Government can influence private sector actors to alter their behavior by improving the information available to them. Four major types of informational programs are advertising, education, moral suasion, and signalling (for example, by announcing an intention to regulate if firms or industries do not change their behavior voluntarily). These programs are more effective when combined with other types of incentives, for example, with fiscal, regulatory, or RD&D programs. They can improve the effectiveness of those other programs by strengthening or creating informational markets that are weak or nonexistent.

Information programs can intervene at several points to various ends. Governments may wish to increase the volume of information available or the rate at which it moves from producers to final users; they may wish to bolster memory capacity or facilitate learning, both altering the effective stock of knowledge; and they also may want to influence evaluative activities by improving information feedback loops.

Research, development and demonstration (RD&D) programs offer another set of instruments for policy implementation. It is difficult, if not impossible, for an individual or firm undertaking basic research to appropriate the full benefits and to exclude others from using the knowledge derived from it. Consequently, private agents will tend to undertake less basic research than is desirable from a society-wide perspective. Applied research, on the other hand, sometimes suffers from a common-property problem associated with the possible capture of a valuable patent by the first party to develop an invention or innovation. In these common-property situations, too much research tends to be undertaken by multiple private parties, with the society-wide benefits from the eventual discovery being dissipated in competitive research to get the patent rights.

Demonstrations can suffer from high risks associated with expensive projects that may or may not be capable of commercialization and from attendant free-rider problems. Once the technology is demonstrated successfully, agents who did not share in the costs and risks of the demonstration usually can use it, often through a license fee that may fail to capture the full social value of the new technology. A major goal of RD&D strategies is to reduce risk and uncertainty, including technological uncertainty, cost uncertainty, demand uncertainty, institutional uncertainty, and uncertainty about external and indirect effects of the technology on, for example, health, safety, and the environment.

Various voluntary programs for greenhouse gas emissions reductions are combinations of informational and RD&D instruments. These include prizes to firms for technological innovation in refrigerator design and manufacture, public recognition for installation of energy-efficient lighting systems in commercial buildings, and labelling programs for so-called green appliances. These voluntary programs tend to be driven by several factors. First, where the government has advantages with respect to gathering certain types of information, such as performance and costs of energy-efficient lighting, communicating that information may induce firms to implement conservation or abatement programs out of direct financial interests. Also, some firms seem motivated to participate in voluntary programs by the prospect or promise of public relations benefits (Arora & Cason 1995). Firms may also participate in voluntary programs as a way to forestall or influence future regulation. Volunteering in the shadow of regulation makes sense where the activity (such as emission of greenhouse gases) is highly likely to be regulated.

Direct government provision of goods and services may be appropriate in the case of public goods, such as air quality, that cannot be provided by the private sector. Generally, when uncertainties regarding the character and level of goods and services needed make it impossible to develop full contracts between the government and private sectors, government production may be the only viable alternative.

Economic considerations in instrument choice

The economics literature on environmental instrument choice reflects three primary areas of inquiry, which in turn reflect the three primary types of costs with which economists and policy analysts have concerned themselves (Richards 1995)—production costs, implementation costs, and public finance costs. Unfortunately, the studies of these three areas have tended to address only one, with a resultant lack of research on the whole bundle of costs.

The first of these areas addresses the issue of production costs: identifying those mechanisms that will induce decisionmakers to adopt the most cost-effective technologies for pollution abatement (see, for example, Baumol & Oates 1975, Hahn & Stavins 1991). The studies conclude are that incentive-based instruments encourage more economizing on pollution abatement costs by taking advantage of the decentralized body of technical knowledge possessed by the private sector and by providing uniform economic incentives to polluters for emissions reduction (Box 5.16).

This incentive-based approach has been discussed for many different applications, including water pollution control (Shaw 1991), hazardous waste reduction (Russell 1988), ocean dumping (Lahey 1984), toxics disposal (Sullivan

---

Box 5.16   Production costs

Under circumstances of complete information regarding the costs and benefits of pollution abatement, either taxes or marketable allowances can induce the socially optimal level of pollution abatement at the lowest cost. However, where there is uncertainty on either the costs or the benefits of protection, the government may have to select targets arbitrarily.

Part of the research on the effect of instrument choice on costs of producing pollution abatement services has been devoted to identifying the limitations of the efficiency properties of incentive-based instruments.

Where local action is being taken to control pollutants of a global nature, there may be substantial problems with *leakage* or secondary effects (Oliveira-Martins et al. 1992, Pezzey 1992). For example, in the case of a carbon tax to reduce energy-related emissions of carbon dioxide, if one country (or a subset of countries) were to act unilaterally, raising a tax on energy and thereby reducing the demand for energy, the world price of energy would drop. The drop in the price of energy would induce other countries to increase their demand for energy, leading to an increase in emissions from the nonabating countries. Thus, the environmental benefits created by the taxing country (countries) would be partially (perhaps wholly) dissipated because of the secondary effects working through the price system.

The efficiency benefits of a marketable allowance system also depend upon the costs of undertaking the trading itself. If the trading process is costly because it is difficult to identify trading partners, because the property right being traded is poorly defined, because there are few parties eligible to trade, or because there are extensive administrative costs associated with government approval of trades, then the volume of trading will be reduced. In a such a situation, opportunities for reducing the aggregate costs of emission reduction would be missed.

1987), reduction of substances that deplete the ozone layer (Barthold 1994), and carbon dioxide emissions reductions (Hoeller & Wallin 1991, Leary & Scheraga 1993, Jorgenson et al. 1992, Manne & Rutherford 1994).

Incentive-based environmental policy instruments have been employed in many countries. For example, various forms of marketable allowances have been used in the United States and Germany, and environmental charges or taxes have been applied in France, Germany, the United States, and the Netherlands (Hahn 1988).

The incentive-based instruments not only provide flexibility and economic rewards for polluters who adopt the most cost-effective technologies available, but they also encourage innovation (Milliman & Prince 1989, Marin 1991). With command and control technology-specifying regulation, polluters receive no immediate rewards for developing low-cost pollution abatement methods. However, with a tax system or a marketable allowance system, those firms that discover means to reduce their emissions benefit in the form of either lower tax liabilities or income from the sale of surplus allowances.

The discussion of production costs concentrates on the costs incurred by the polluter or the party responsible for pollution abatement. But an environmental program can also involve substantial costs to the government that is implementing the program (Box 5.17). These costs can generally be cast in one of three categories: costs of establishing the program, costs of monitoring and enforcing the program, and costs associated with establishing any special mechanisms that facilitate the program. It should be noted that the costs of implementation and the costs of abatement are not independently determined (Sullivan 1987).

Environmental programs, regardless of the instrument chosen, will involve setting environmental goals. That process requires gathering and processing information, such as identifying the marginal costs and benefits of abatement. Command and control regulation is generally considered to require greater initial information input because, not only must initial goals be set, but the government must also identify the technologies that will be employed.

The third category of costs that have been separately examined by the instrument choice literature are the public finance costs (Box 5.18). When governments raise revenue through taxes, they introduce distortions into the price system. The distortions cause producers and consumers to lower their demands for the taxed goods, leading to misallocation of resources and overall loss of social welfare.

If policymakers were concerned only with minimizing the costs of production, and all environmental problems involved situations where private firms have better information about technologies than the government, then a tax would be all that was needed to achieve environmental goals. Even if policymakers were concerned about implementation costs, an environmental tax

---

Box 5.17   Costs of monitoring and enforcement

The monitoring and enforcement costs of a pollution abatement program will vary according to the type of pollutant, available measurement technologies, the number and type of parties involved, the types of penalties available for noncompliance, and the level of compliance required. Generally, a system should be designed to control the activity that most directly contributes to environmental degradation (Barthold 1994). Without being able to measure individual firms' contributions to ambient pollution levels, measurement of their effluent levels may be the best proxy (e.g., continuous emissions monitoring of sulfur dioxide emissions). However, in some cases, even this level of measurement is not practical, and systems must be based on material inputs (e.g., coal input as a proxy for carbon dioxide output) or even technology inputs (e.g., scrubber technology combined with coal assay as a proxy for sulfur dioxide output).

Monitoring and enforcement programs designed to achieve 100 percent compliance are generally costly and probably impractical, primarily because of the increasing marginal costs associated with inducing compliance through monitoring and enforcement (Sullivan 1987). Further, the design of a monitoring and enforcement system should recognize that there are social costs associated with both the government's monitoring and enforcement efforts and the polluters' efforts to avoid enforcement.

The implementation costs associated with monitoring and enforcement will also vary according to which parties are targeted. Where many parties or many points of emissions are involved, the costs of monitoring can be expected to be high. Fewer parties or large stationary sources will lead to lower costs. This suggests that monitoring costs should figure prominently in the design of the instrument. For example, regulators may limit the number of private parties involved in control by focusing on upstream producers and distributors. In contrast, trying to control end users of fossil fuel in the United States would entail a massive undertaking that could probably only be accomplished through the use of command and control regulations. The implementation costs would likely be much higher. Note, however, that in the case of carbon dioxide, controlling a small number of upstream producers rather than tens of millions of end users is possible only because of the nature of the pollutant, the technologies that produce it, and the structure of the fossil fuel industry. Where the inputs are a relatively good proxy for the output of the pollutant and the industry producing the input is relatively concentrated, decreasing the cost of monitoring is possible.

---

would be the only instrument needed, so long as the government had perfect information about the environmental benefits function, firms' pollution control cost functions, and firms' compliance with regulations.

In less than ideal conditions, however, the scope of instruments must be expanded. For example, where there is significant uncertainty about the marginal costs of pollution abatement and the benefit function is relatively steep, quantity-based instruments such as marketable allowances may be preferred (Gruenspecht & Lave 1989). And where the costs of monitoring firms' abatement performance outputs are high, command and control technology-based approaches may be preferable. Both of these factors may be involved simultaneously. A simple example is provided by the case of regulation of firms with water pollution emissions on a river. Each firm has a different damage

---

Box 5.18   Public finance costs

The literature on the public finance impacts of environmental instruments, which is very recent by comparison with the treatment of production and implementation costs, has focused on two separate, although closely related, questions.

The first question is whether, given the distortionary effects of standard revenue-raising taxes, it is possible to reap a double dividend from environmental taxes. The reasoning behind this question is that introduction of a revenue-neutral environmental tax, such as a charge for water pollution where the revenue is recycled by lowering other distortionary taxes, might be able both to increase environmental quality and to displace other taxes, thereby reducing the distorting effect of revenue raising. If this were the case, then it would not be necessary to justify the cost of environmental cleanup on the basis of valuing the environment. Rather, environmental improvements would simply be an added bonus. The real justification for the environmental taxes would be that they expand the tax base and reduce distortions in the price system.

Unfortunately, the world is not so simple. Recent research has demonstrated that, where the revenues from environmental charges are used to lower the taxes on labor, distortions in the public finance system are not likely to be reduced (Goulder 1994, Parry 1995). In simplest terms, this result stems from the fact that the environmental taxes shift the burden to the dirty goods that cause the pollution. Although the direct tax on labor decreases, the buying power of labor's wages also decreases because of higher prices on those dirty goods. Hence, the under-supplied good—labor—is not likely to increase, and may in fact decrease. This does not imply that environmental taxes should not be used, but rather that, in the absence of accounting for the environmental benefits induced by the taxes, there is unlikely to be an improvement in social welfare (Bovenberg & de Mooij 1994). That is, environmental taxes need to be justified by the environmental benefits they provide. This result must be modified if the revenues of the environmental tax are used to displace a tax that is more distortionary that the labor tax, for example, a tax on capital (Bovenberg & Goulder 1995). However, this observation begs the question of why the government is not already shifting tax burden from the more distortionary tax on capital to the relatively less distortionary tax on labor.

The second line of inquiry on the public finance impacts of environmental instruments picks up where the discussion of double dividends stops. Rather than asking whether an environmental tax can be justified even if it provides no environmental benefits, this second area starts with the assumption that some form of environmental improvement is mandated by the political system, and explores the normative question of which instruments have the least negative (most positive) impact on the public finance system. The results are fairly intuitive. Given a non-revenue-raising quota (e.g., command and control regulation or marketable allowances) on environmental discharges, replacing the quota with a revenue raising instrument (such as a tax or auctioned marketable allowance) will improve the public finance system without reducing environmental quality (Terkla 1984, Parry 1995). Conversely, use of subsidies requires that additional revenue be raised by increasing already distortionary taxes (Sullivan 1987, Richards 1995).

The result is a rank ordering of instruments with respect to their impact on the public finance system, in which revenue-raising instruments are preferred to quota-based systems, and quota-based systems are preferred to subsidies or other instruments requiring government payments (Richards 1995).

---

function associated with its emissions (Rose-Ackerman 1973). Assuming that each firm also has a different cost function for abatement, it would be necessary to calculate separate taxes for each firm, and to monitor the pollutant output of each firm. Given the substantial information requirements of a pure tax scheme, it may be cost minimizing to mandate uniform technology-based treatment regulations.

The need for multiple instruments is explained, at least in part, by information constraints on the government's attempt to minimize the sum of production and implementation costs. But what explains the existence of subsidies, government contracts, and direct government production, which arguably reduce neither production costs nor implementation costs relative to the standard environmental instruments, but that do introduce additional public finance costs because of revenue raising requirements? To understand the value of these instruments it is important to understand the legal, political, and cultural constraints that accompany the instrument choice exercise.

Legal, political, and cultural considerations in instrument choice

A common complaint about instrument choice analysis is that analysts tend to compare one set of instruments under ideal conditions to another set of instruments under "as implemented" conditions. Differences in performance among instruments may be better explained by variations in the institutional circumstances under which they are employed than by any inherent difference among the instruments themselves (Majone 1976: 593):

> to use a statistical image, the "within group" effects (the differential results obtained when the same tool operates under different institutional circumstances) dominate the "between groups" effects (the results of different tools used under approximately equal conditions).

These institutional constraints can be broadly characterized as legal, political, and cultural.

Legal constraints may limit the choice of instruments. In the United States, for example, the Constitution limits the extent to which the government can regulate the use of private property. If a regulation is intended to provide a public benefit (as compared to preventing a harm), the government is required to provide compensation to the affected property owners. Faced with this constraint, the government will avoid regulation altogether, using instead subsidies, contracts, or direct government production to achieve its policy goals. Similarly, legal restrictions that limit a legislative body's ability to forbid itself from changing laws in the future, prohibitions that prevent higher levels of government from intervening in the local affairs of lower levels, and provisions regarding bankruptcy, can all restrict the use or effectiveness of various instruments. In the face of these legal restrictions on the use of standard regulatory instruments, the scope of instruments must include those that have less desirable public finance characteristics such as subsidies, contracts and direct government production.

The political constraints on instrument choice are every bit as powerful as the legal constraints. The instruments will vary with respect to their impacts on various income groups and geographic regions (Kopp & DeWitt 1991), businesses (Buchanan & Tullock 1975), and employment categories (Hahn 1987). The differential impact will give rise to pressure groups who favor one instrument over another, not on the basis of efficiency, but on distributional or equity grounds. Hence, substantial resistance to environmental taxes comes from businesses opposed to the transfer of wealth associated with such a shift (Hahn & Stavins 1991). Also, to reduce political resistance, many regulations exempt existing facilities from new regulations or other forms of control (Majone 1976).

Carbon taxes are receiving sympathetic attention among some European governments (O'Riordan & Jäger 1991) because they are increasingly pressurized to cut public spending, privatize former public services, and yet find money to fund job creation and industrial restructuring for an increasingly global competitive age. One way of squaring this circle is to impose taxes on polluting emissions and resource depletion, and to earmark the revenue for environmentally and socially beneficial projects. O'Riordan (1996) has summarized the case for such a switch. One interesting innovation is the creation of charitable trusts to channel that money into specific schemes such as mobility reduction, home insulation, and energy-saving technologies and processes. These trusts would be locally administered for local needs and would fit into the emerging commitment to Local Agenda 21—the local government equivalent of the sustainability transition.

The brief summaries and examples of implementation instruments given above also indicate that each has characteristics that might be more or less attractive to important constituencies that exercise very different levels of political and economic power within different countries (Rayner 1991). Private sector institutions tend to favor implementation policies that maximize the discretion of individual decisionmakers and firms. They prefer carrots to sticks. Positive fiscal incentives, such as subsidies and tax breaks, are favorably received. Government support for RD&D, for example, into biomass energy, also could be popular with this constituency, especially if private firms can enjoy proprietary control over innovations. On the other hand, private sector institutions may be suspicious of informational programs that hint at moral persuasion or jawboning (strongly urging compliance), which could put firms at a competitive disadvantage.

At the other extreme, environmentalists, especially deep ecologists (see Ch. 4), may emphasize sticks rather than carrots. They often favor command and control regulation, uniformly applied without the exercise of discretion by regulators or regulated firms and individuals. Such discretion violates principles of strict equality. Fiscal incentives may be acceptable, especially if linked to regulation. However, systems such as emissions permits are frequently frowned upon as licenses to pollute (see, for example, Mott 1990). Information programs, particularly those designed to expose weaknesses in the compliance records of firms, are also well received here, where information can be used as a stick to beat slow bureaucracies or sly entrepreneurs.

Regulatory agencies, on the other hand, are likely to see themselves caught between a rock and a hard place. Their orderly instincts may incline them toward the predictability and ease of monitoring associated with command and control regulation. However, their need to reconcile their own agendas with those of the firms and individuals they must regulate may lead them to favor a combination of fiscal incentives backed up by regulation. In any case, regulators are often sympathetic to demands from market constituencies for the exercise of discretion in the application of regulatory rules. Regulators' ability to exercise such discretion (e.g., grandfathering activities of firms that were practiced prior to regulatory rule making) is likely to be restrained in proportion to the strength of environmentalist objectors. Information is likely to be favored by regulators to the extent that it facilitates their own regulatory tasks, although they may tend toward skepticism as to the usefulness of public information programs. In summary, we may expect regulators to favor policy instruments that combine carrots and sticks according to pressures from the other two constituencies.

These observations about institutional preferences for implementation measures are summarized in Figure 5.2, which defines a triangular policy space within which any mix of instruments can be located. In turn, the distribution of power and population density within the triangle varies from country to country and over time. For example, in the United States, the Reagan–Bush decade signaled a preference for fiscal instruments for a wide variety of government policies, in contrast to the regulatory approach of the Carter years. The Clinton administration has placed an increasing emphasis on information and RD&D as environmental policy instruments, especially in collaboration with the private sector. However, although environmentalists have begun to explore fiscal incentives to promote their goals, they remain concerned about regulatory capture and bureaucratic inertia. Many environmentalists continue to favor regulations that allow little discretion to either the regulators or the

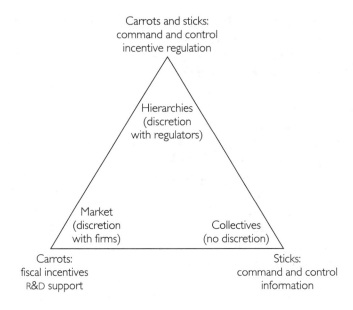

Figure 5.2   A policy space for implementation instruments (Rayner 1991).

regulated industry. Industrial and commercial interests are likely to favor fiscal incentives because of the high degree of discretion that remains with firms. An example of this tension is the recurrent debate over the relative merits of a gasoline tax and the standards for improving vehicle fuel consumption (Green 1990, Rayner 1993a).

Institutional preference alone will not determine which implementation instrument will be selected. Nonetheless, these institutional preferences are as valid and defensible as the homogenizing individual self-interest assumptions of approaches that focus on efficiency alone.

Figure 5.2 indicates that, depending on the institutional culture of intervention, different parts of the policy space could be occupied. The institutional key to climate change is a mixture of all three approaches for all countries, when traditionally one approach or another has held sway. In the United States and Great Britain, for example, the cultural bias has rested on market-based voluntarism, whereas in the Scandinavian countries and the Netherlands, the bias has rested on a hierarchical mix of regulation and carbon taxes. Egalitarian concern for the underprivileged or vulnerable can also be seen. The British government's decision not to impose a second tranche of value added tax to domestic fuel bills, because of the political outcry against the potential adverse impact on the poor and on pensioners, is one example of egalitarian constraints on the use of efficient economic instruments for greenhouse gas emissions reductions.

Most analyses of the implementation of climate change policies focus on the impact of emissions reductions policies on the energy sectors of industrialized countries. The bounding conditions for such analyses bear some reasonable resemblance to the idealized models of the economy that are used to model them. For the most part, fossil energy fuels are highly substitutable for one another, especially for stationary energy uses. They are consumed in reliable and predictable ways. Especially in the industrialized countries, they are widely traded in well-established markets where information is plentiful and prices are responsive to fairly uniform trading opportunities.

It is much more difficult to analyze the effects of policy instruments in circumstances where these close-to-ideal circumstances do not pertain:

- where emissions information is less reliable, such as in forestry
- where market conditions are much less ideal or even nonexistent, as in important segments of the economies of less industrialized countries
- where political conditions give rise to uncertainty over the sustainability of the policy program
- where policies focus on highly uncertain adaptation strategies rather than on emissions.

For example, the first three of these conditions applies in assessing the effects of forestry policy on carbon dioxide emissions and carbon sequestration. Carbon yields in forest plantations vary according to region, species, soil type, precipitation, and management practices. Even in the United States, where land and timber markets are perhaps closer to the economists' ideal market than elsewhere in the world, it is difficult to predict how landowners will respond to various carbon sequestration programs. Finally, because the programmatic and political uncertainties inherent in development of a carbon sequestration program, models that examine only general policy instruments—taxes and subsidies, allowances and offsets—may not capture some important factors that will determine the effects of the program. These three considerations— scientific, behavioral, and programmatic uncertainty—create a very complex analytic problem (Rayner & Richards 1994). In some cases the uncertainty applies even to the direction of expected change in both the costs of carbon sequestration and the potential accomplishments of the policy. These conditions are more properly characterized as indeterminacy, which exacerbates the challenges of designing and implementing appropriate policy options.

Less industrialized countries often have poor infrastructures to begin with, exacerbated by a lack of human, financial, and technological resources. In addition, these countries are likely to be focused on more basic and fundamental considerations of nation building and economic development; environmental issues can be low on their scale of priorities. In principle, the economic conditions of less industrialized countries also present opportunities to achieve emissions reductions at lower absolute cost than in the industrialized nations that have already made capital-intensive commitments to fossil fuel technologies and may lack the land resources available for carbon sequestration programs. This is the basis for the Joint Implementation provisions of the FCCC that permit countries to share credit for emissions reductions achieved by their efforts outside of their own territorial boundaries. However, despite the theoretical attractiveness of such schemes, they have proven to be controversial from the viewpoints of both industrialized and less industrialized countries (see Box 5.11).

Even industrialized countries exhibit significant variation in the presence of those characteristics that could be considered ideal for the successful application of the whole suite of conventional policy instruments listed above. These attributes include:

- a well-developed institutional infrastructure to implement regulation
- an economy that is likely to respond well to fiscal policy instruments because it possesses certain characteristics of economic models of the free market
- a highly developed information industry and mass communications infrastructure, for educating, advertising, and jawboning
- a vast combined private and public annual RD&D budget for reducing uncertainties and establishing pilot programs.

To the extent that these close-to-ideal institutional conditions for conventional policy implementation are missing, policymakers may expect to encounter further obstacles to the effectiveness of policy instruments. This situation is exacerbated in the case of policies addressing land use, key not only to carbon sequestration policies but also to most adaptive strategies such as migration, crop switching, and changes in the design of buildings and human settlements.

For example, many less and newly industrialized countries have excellent legal, even constitutional, provisions for environmental protection including protection of forests. Many of these are clearly modeled on US precedents.

The Brazilian *Codigo Florestal* of 1965 defines permanent areas of conservation along rivers and headwaters, prohibits the use of natural resources in national and other protected parks, and stipulates that no more than 50 percent of landholdings in Amazonia may be cleared. However, monitoring and enforcement of the *Codigo Florestal* is poor to nonexistent. Even where it is enforced, no limits are placed on subdivision of holdings, and the law has often been circumvented by clearing half of a plot and reselling the remaining forested half where once again the 50 percent law applies. The code has been modified and supplemented several times, but funds and credits for reforestation have never been reliable, and most of the fiscal incentives that did appear were applied in subtropical parts of Brazil where pines and eucalyptus could be grown.

The Brazilian Constitutional Convention of 1988 established national obligations for environmental protection. Title VIII explicitly discusses the importance of forest conservation, and Title IX provides for the implementation of large-scale regional management exercises, such as the *Planofloro* zoning program for the state of Rondonia. *Planofloro* has focused on directing economic activities into appropriate areas using economic and ecological criteria elaborated from satellite imagery and ground mapping. Unfortunately, such exercises suffer in implementation from the absence of effective regulatory agencies to enforce zoning rules, as well as from conflict with other powerful government agencies with different development priorities, which receive stronger private sector backing than forest protection (Rayner & Richards 1994).

Although this is by no means a comprehensive review, it is enough to indicate that, although Brazilian environmental law is well developed and, in certain sectors, quite innovative, the implementation of those laws may tend to leave few marks on reality.

Brazil is not the only example. Petrich (1993) describes almost identical conditions in Indonesia. This is a pattern repeated again and again across the less industrialized world. Neither are these observations in any sense an indictment or criticism of such governments. The harsh reality is that they all face a serious problem of scarce resources to carry out the most elementary functions of government. Competition among state agencies for whatever resources are available inevitably leaves environmental protection and natural resource management agencies without the necessary investment to establish effective monitoring and implementation programs. The shortage of program resources is exacerbated by pressures to exploit natural resources to earn foreign income, increasing demands of the population for energy, and pressures to convert forest land to agriculture and human habitation. Under the combined weight of all these factors, the issue of optimizing across regulations, taxes, permits, education, and demonstration projects becomes academic.

Lack of implementation infrastructure may be the largest single obstacle to effective policies under frontier conditions. These are situations where prior claims of indigenous populations are nonexistent or disregarded, and where the ability to monitor behavior, settle disputes, and enforce rules and contracts lie with individuals and groups possessing the power to coerce (Cantor et al. 1992). Unfortunately, conventional development approaches tend to dismiss these characteristics of the society as mere details of implementation, when in fact they represent fundamental structural differences between frontier societies and those where the institutions of civil society, essential to the functioning of regulatory regimes or efficient markets, are either severely curtailed or altogether absent.

Conventional development approaches are equally complacent about other political, economic, and cultural structures that differ fundamentally from those that we take for granted in economies that most closely resemble the economists' ideal model. In particular, as we move away from societies in which production and consumption are distinctly separated by the operation of the free market, we begin to appreciate more clearly that the use of land, including forested land, is intimately tied to the satisfaction of a broad spectrum of basic human needs and wants. The concept of market failure is inadequate to capture the interlocking demands and expectations of the land and the human arrangements for its multiple use. The further we move away from the market concept, the more the land itself becomes a medium of social relations and less a commodity subject to market forces (e.g., Davis 1973, Stevenson 1991).

Other important changes accompany a change of focus from economic to social principles of human organization. Socially constrained exchange systems carry more complex information about the relationships among parties to transactions (Cantor et al. 1992). Exchange does not depend solely on signals about price, quantity, and quality among anonymous traders, but signals status, kinship, ethnicity, time of year, and a host of other factors essential to sustaining society. The homogeneity of *Homo economicus* is replaced by localized adaptation of human society to ecological variation. This transformation is being recognized as an important factor in energy use. Whereas different societies adjusted their attire, construction practices, and work schedules according to climatic, seasonal, and diurnal variation, the tendency toward homogeneity in market-driven systems increases demand for space conditioning, lighting, and transportation. Similarly, homogeneity in forestry and land-use practices may increase stress on local environments, once protected by human adaptation. Examples include the consequences of irrigation, enforced settlement, and changes in land management practices.

In these contexts, the application of tools from the standard toolkit of policy instruments has sometimes provoked spectacularly perverse effects (Box 5.19). Of course, "Development experts have learned to their cost that the impressive arrays of policy levers displayed in the ministries of many of the less developed countries are, all too often, not connected to anything" (Thompson et al. 1986: 92). This is usually interpreted as a symptom of underdevelopment, which can be remedied by nurturing market-style institutions and regulatory regimes typical of the industrialized world. The effectiveness of this approach is debatable, even when dealing with a relatively homogeneous commodity, such as energy. It completely ignores the fact that "Land use patterns are an expression of deep political, economic, and cultural structure; they do not change when an ecologist sounds the alarm that a country is losing its resource base" (Eckholm 1976: 167). If the threat of losing valuable national resources does not motivate structural change, there seems little hope that any conventional policy instrument that ignores these aspects of deep structure will persuade people to alter their behavior to obtain uncertain benefits for the global climate.

Perhaps the challenge for policy implementation is not to force the free-market model on the world, but to design programs for policy implementation that exploit political, economic, and cultural diversity. The first way in which policymakers might approach this goal is to abandon the search for the magic bullet of implementation. Even in the case of highly developed market economies, we have noted that different constituencies may have strong preferences for different kinds of implementation instruments, based on considerations other than economic efficiency. This is not to argue that policymakers should abandon the conventional suite of policy instruments, but that they need to pay more explicit attention to the reasons for these preferences and account for the relative distribution and strength of each constituency among the parties that the policy is designed to affect. This is also a powerful argument for focusing on policy implementation packages rather than individual instruments in the process of policy design and implementation.

A second, complementary, approach is to supplement the conventional suite of policy instruments by examining indigenous traditional mechanisms of social regulation that could be harnessed to the policy goal of reducing greenhouse gas emissions. The traditional institutions of forest guardianship in Nepal and the traditional land tenure systems of West Africa are obvious examples (Box 5.19).

Consideration of the wide variation among countries in the legal, political, and cultural considerations involved in the selection of policy instruments raises the related issue of whether there are distinctive national policy styles.

National policy styles

A substantial body of political theory is geared toward identifying and explaining the existence of specific national policy styles or political cultures (Box 5.20). The underlying assumption of this work is that individual countries tend to process problems in a specific manner, regardless of the distinctiveness or specific features of the problem at issue. Traditional categories of political science, such as *capitalist* or *socialist*, *authoritarian* or *democratic*, *developing* or *developed*, are too large scale and sweeping to capture this kind of variation in characteristic policy style which arises from the complex interaction of historical, cultural, political, economic, and geographical factors.

National policy style has been defined as a routinized institutional method of dealing with issues; a national style or legitimate "way of doing things" (Richardson 1982: ix). A national policy style can be identified when, for

417

Box 5.19   Perverse effects of policy instruments

For 400 years the Sherpas of the Khumbu forests of Nepal maintained a sustainable system of forest management that assured them a plentiful supply of fuelwood (Thompson et al. 1986). This system was based on a rotating village office of *forest guardian*, who monitored villagers' extraction of the resource and whose office was maintained out of the fines he was permitted to levy on those who violated the commons by excessive use. However, in the name of modernity and efficiency, the forests were nationalized during the 1950s and control was removed from local hands to those of distant bureaucrats. Once the gentle controls of community self-management were removed, people began taking too much wood from close by and not enough from farther away, resulting in patchy and partial deforestation, leading to severe erosion, land degradation, and fuelwood shortages in the villages.

The situation was exacerbated when development experts, anxious to provide appropriate technological solutions to a perceived fuelwood crisis, provided kerosene cookers to villagers to relieve pressure on the forests. Unfortunately, villagers perceived the forest as a resource convertible to farmland, rather than as a renewable resource that could now be preserved, and proceeded to cut the remaining stands of forest upon which they no longer depended for cooking and heating.

Examples of the perverse effects of development programs based on conventional economic theory are not confined to any one geographical area. They are ubiquitous. Certain traditional West African land-tenure systems are based on tenure in standing crops. Planting trees provided people with tenure in land for extended periods, which also secured their right to farm annual crops on the understory. This resulted in a sustainable agroforestry system. Furthermore, the trees often provided cash crops for the farmers. Development economists, however, anxious to promote production of these cash crops reasoned that fewer than the optimal number of trees were being planted precisely because people did not have tenure in the land itself and, therefore, lacked security in their investment in trees. Providing tenure in the land, however, actually removed the principal tree-planting incentive. Farmers pursuing shorter term productivity of annual crops actually removed trees, resulting in baked soil and loss of windbreaks, leading to soil erosion, land degradation, and the collapse of sustainable agroforestry.

Perverse effects such as these are not exceptions to the rules of formal economics, but the reality that those rules fail to account for. Economists assume *ceteris paribus* when making instrument choices just as in determining goals. The point is that *ceteris* seldom is *paribus*, and the results, as described above, are frequently disastrous or, at best, irrelevant.

---

example, transport problems are dealt with in the same manner as economic, employment or environmental issues. Richardson et al. (1982: 8) identify national policy style as arising from the interaction of two components "(a) the government's approach to problem solving and (b) the relationship between government and other actors in the policy process."

So far as the second component is concerned, we must bear in mind that there are as many political cultural variations within nations as there are among national public or political cultures. Many different constituencies or social groups each have their particular cultural orientation. There are many ways to define and distinguish these cultural levels. For example, Goodenough (1971) discriminates between *cultural pool, public culture*, and *private culture*. Other

distinctions are made within the modern state between the cultures of territo-
rially based groups, such as nationalities or tribes, and the cultures of groups
based on common institutional interests and involvements, such as government
officials, corporate executives, environmental activists, or scientists.

Although Richardson et al. accept that some problems are dealt with in
different ways by a single national government, "it is equally true that policies

---

Box 5.20   National policy styles in institutional perspective

No matter how much the various constituencies in a process of environmental decisionmaking
are shaped by their particular adaptive strategies and tasks, they also are operating in and from
a larger cultural context. They are products of their larger society and its culture. In the terminology of Chapter 4 of this volume, British corporations may tend to be more hierarchical than
those of the United States, which are strongly influenced by decentralized market and egalitarian
forms of organization. Centralized bureaucracies may be more acceptable to the French than
to the Americans (which may also account for the differences in acceptance of nuclear energy
in these countries). Until recently, the entrepreneurial spirit has not been admired in cultural
hierarchies such as the former Soviet Union. However, the theory is not deterministic. America
has ossified bureaucracies, egalitarian champions trumpet their causes in Europe, and Chinese
and former Soviets attempt, in different ways, to harness entrepreneurial talents to their cause
of economic development. The particular mixture of institutional cultures gives each country
its characteristic cultural flavor, a particular preference for the German, British, French, or US way
of doing things, including domestic implementation of international accords (Gerlach & Rayner
1988).

Existing research on the topic of national differences in institutional arrangements for making
and implementing environment and technology policy is somewhat fragmented. Some comparative studies have been made of national debates over certain technologies. For example,
Nelkin & Pollack (1981) compare French and German controversies over nuclear energy. Sweden and the United States have been compared with regard to air quality (Lindquist 1980) and
occupational safety and health policies (Kelman 1981). An IIASA study of the siting of liquified
natural gas terminals in Europe and the United States (Kunreuther et al. 1982) focuses on different institutional arrangements for managing technology and potential environmental disaster.

Many of these studies tend to emphasize contrasts between the essentially cooperative
approach to environmental protection in Europe and the more confrontational approach that
predominates in the United States. Their emphasis is on the demands of interest groups and
the responsiveness of political and legal institutions to rival claims about nature and technology.

Scientific and technical knowledge about health and the environment also is dominated by
cultural interpretations. Indeed, Jasanoff (1986) illustrates that information about established
technologies, such as formaldehyde use, is interpreted differently by scientific advisory committees in different countries. In particular, Brickman et al. (1985) argue that the decentralization
of decisionmaking in the United States both increases demand for scientific details of technological and environmental hazards, and engenders competition between different explanations.
Hence there is more intensive public debate in the United States about environmental regulation than in France, Britain, or the Federal Republic of Germany. Such differences appear to
have played an important role in determining the different positions of the United States and
the European Community on banning CFC aerosol propellants in 1985.

---

are not so distinctive as to prevent them being accommodated in a basic simple typology of policy styles" (Richardson et al. 1982: 5). Using a basic typology of styles, Richardson et al. subdivide countries according to whether national decisionmaking is anticipatory or reactive and whether the political context is consensus based or impositional. The former characterizes a government's general policy orientation, whereas the latter helps to capture the essence of a government's relationship with, and attitude to, other actors, especially pressure groups. Cultural theorists have applied their typology of bureaucratic, egalitarian, and individualist approaches to national policy styles (Rayner 1991, Grendstad & Selle 1997), as indicated in Chapter 4.

Two examples will illustrate policy styles. The United Kingdom appears to have a predilection for "consultation, avoidance of radical policy change and a strong desire to avoid actions which might challenge well-entrenched interests" (Richardson et al. 1982: 3). The British style allegedly has five overlapping features: clientalism, sectorization, consultation, institutionalization of compromise, and the development of exchange relationships (Jordan & Richardson 1982). Others have described the United Kingdom as executive-dominated, fragmented into policy communities, and consensual rather than conflictual, giving rise to a reactive approach to problem solving (see Greenaway et al. 1992 for a fuller review). By way of contrast with the British, the German style is described as anticipatory, consensus-oriented, and corporatist; characterized by a strong and interventionist state which is more likely to be precautionary and proactive in its decisionmaking (Richardson & Watts 1985: 21).

The whole idea of a national policy style is, of course, at odds with Lowi's celebrated thesis, which holds that the nature of the policy itself (e.g., climate change or ozone depletion) shapes the manner in which a problem is processed, that the type of policy is one of the conditions that cause variations in the procedural characteristics of political systems (Lowi 1964). As Richardson et al. aver, "Lowi would presumably dissent from the notion of national policy style and would instead demand that the policy content would have to be first stipulated" (Richardson et al. 1982: 4). In other words, distinct types of politics flow from different types of policy issues; climate change, for example, would be dealt with in a similar manner by all countries.

With this in mind, two questions seem particularly pertinent to a study of national government responses to climate change. The first is the extent to which the same issue—in this case, climate change—has been processed in the same manner by different states, and whether national responses are consonant with a predetermined national style. According to Lowi, we should expect some convergence in style, whereas Richardson's work suggests a more variegated series of responses, molded and structured by the precise configuration of institutions within each state.

The second question relates to any evidence that the internationalization of environmental policymaking—for example, the intervention of the European Commission in the domestic affairs of member states of the European Union—is eroding (or at least deflecting) extant policy styles. In the case of the European Union, empirical research, such as that reported in O'Riordan & Jäger (1996), indicates an intriguing blend of convergence and divergence, which is not entirely consonant with Lowi's or Richardson's characterizations of policies and politics.

In another insightful and wide-ranging discussion of environmental policy processes in the European Union, Wynne (1993) emphasizes the tension between the formal top-down decisionmaking elites, which emphasize universal rationalities and abstract principles, and bottom-up approaches, which emphasize the role of informal networks of diverse actors. In particular, Wynne describes the curious alliances that form between the staff of the European Commissions responsible for issuing environmental directives and local bodies, such as town councils and the staff of NGOs, to force national governments to implement policy goals. Wynne argues that the shifting balance of authority from formal institutions toward informal networks and associations is a positive force for the development of innovative policy formulation and implementation. This is particularly important in a context of coexisting diverse political cultures that demonstrate distinctive preferences for different policy instruments to implement shared goals, such as reducing greenhouse gas emissions.

In China also, there is tension between the traditional centralized planning of the national government and the decentralizing forces that place real responsibilities on the shoulders of local communities and enterprises. This tension is exemplified by the application of the polluter pays principle and the environmental responsibility system, in which managers publicly negotiate contracts with communities for environmental protection. Perlack et al. (1993) report that the extent to which local communities are responsible for environmental protection may also prove to be a weakness of the Chinese system. Local enforcement officials often report to the same authorities who are responsible for the operation of the polluting enterprise. Local air pollution is an endemic problem in a country that has few realistic alternatives to coal for fuelling its economic development. Although China is jealous of a position of world leadership and recognizes that the global environment is an important plank of any leader's platform, the practical imperatives are to focus on domestic issues.

Hence, evidence can be found to support the hypotheses of both Richardson and Lowi. There is both convergence and divergence in the ways that different countries seek to come to grips with environmental challenges, although it is not clear that the convergence arises from any specific demands or constraints that environmental issues place upon institutions, as has been argued in the political science literature. Convergence may be as well explained by fundamental processes inherent in institutions themselves, such as the ubiquitous tension between independence and interdependence in the construction and maintenance of social solidarities (Gerlach & Palmer 1981). Reviewing case studies from five countries, Rayner (1993b: 10–11) concludes:

> In sum, the overall picture is that there is a dynamic relationship between centralized programmes and local decentralized initiatives through which informal institutions are becoming an increasingly critical factor in shaping and implementing environmental policy . . . wide variations in political culture do seem to exert a significant influence on the choice of policy instruments and how legitimate targets are defined.

The presence of diverse national policy styles may represent a significant obstacle to adopting uniform common measures or policy instruments by all countries (or at least all Annex I signatories to the FCCC) for implementing climate change policy goals such as emissions reductions. Proposals for such common measures have been forthcoming from the European Union, which since the early 1980s has been engaged in a process of *harmonization* of economic and environmental goals, regulations, and practices. The European Union has been pursuing the agenda of greater uniformity (Box 5.21). However, setting goals and targets that allow countries to achieve agreed-upon results, using whatever means are most compatible with their resources and national policy styles, appears to be more compatible with the existence of national policy styles.

National policy styles should not necessarily be viewed as an obstacle to rational policymaking. Indeed, O'Riordan & Jäger (1996) suggest at least one reason why such diversity may be advantageous to measures designed to mitigate climate change or its impacts. Their analysis suggests that climate change, on its own, has only a very weak organizing focus for political mobilization and therefore is likely to lose out in competition for the attention and resources of both public and private institutions faced with other policy imperatives; such as jobs, trade, or social security. They suggest that the effectiveness of climate change policies depends upon their thorough integration with other policy agendas, notably macroeconomic and industrial policy, where shifts in these arenas can help to reduce greenhouse gas emissions. They further indicate that the existence of diverse policy styles presents a variety of potential points of attachment on a global scale that might not be available if all nations shared a single policy style.

Box 5.21   Harmonization of national policies in the European Union

The European Union has been pursuing harmonization of national policies through two policy instruments. First is the *directive*, which sets a goal (such as maximum permitted levels of nitrates in drinking water), but, under the principle of *subsidiarity*, permits member states to determine how they will meet that goal. This course respects and preserves national policy styles. The second category of instruments comprises uniform European *regulations*. For example, standards specify which varieties of fruits and vegetables may be offered for sale. Bans, such as a proposed ban on heavy motorcycles, prohibit the use of certain products within all of the member countries. These uniform regulations often conflict with national policy styles. For example, efforts to introduce community-wide taxes, such as a European carbon tax, have been defeated because of sovereignty concerns on the part of member states such as the United Kingdom.

The signing of the Maastricht Treaty was the occasion of widespread debate on the merits, extent, and pace of closer European unity. The European Commission has been a prime mover in the drive toward federalization, a goal that is less popular in some countries (e.g., the United Kingdom) than others (e.g., Germany), but is contentious in all. In the event, the treaty signed in Maastricht represented something of a retreat for both federalists and anti-federalists. Since that time, the federalist movement and the European Commission in particular have suffered further disappointments. The FCCC may provide an opportunity for the Commission and the supporters of the federalist agenda to revitalize the European harmonization agenda.

The first move in this direction was the attempt by the Commission to introduce a European carbon tax. However, this move was strongly opposed by the United Kingdom and has fallen by the wayside. The common measures proposals appear to be another attempt to move the Commission's agenda forward under the flag of the FCCC and in the broader context of the Annex I countries. The looseness with which commonness is defined in such proposals lends further credibility to this interpretation, since "common" is not necessarily interpreted as including all of the Annex I countries, but could be potentially a subset of the Annex I countries, such as the member states of the European Union.

Conclusion

The growing prominence of global environmental issues as matters of high politics presents the social sciences with the occasion—and the imperative—to transcend disciplinary boundaries. For instance, the nation state retains an important and powerful position. However, the character and the role of the state are changing rapidly in fundamental aspects of its international and domestic activities. Political influence and real power are diffusing to international and domestic policy networks, in which governments and their agencies interact directly with social movements, firms, and communities. The notion of unitary *national interest* is increasingly difficult to sustain. The rising importance of nonstate actors and the emergence of aspects of a global civil society, in the light of global climate change, are phenomena that are now garnering much attention from sociologists and international relations scholars alike, and that may also present new opportunities for and constraints on global solidarity.

This chapter, which has focused on the concept of solidarity to explore the politics of global climate change, is an attempt to begin to address the need for new synthesizing perspectives that account for this broad set of actors, roles, and dynamics. The emphasis on solidarity is, in effect, a decision not to focus on individual states, actors, and interests, or on the collective units of a national or international system. The theme of solidarity guides the observer's gaze to the bonds among the units at all levels in the system, to the connective tissues rather than to the organs exclusively. Analytically, our interdisciplinary focus on axes of solidarity provides a scale-independent perspective on institutions that enables the analyst to understand how they articulate across, as well as within, levels and functional sectors. This represents a significant departure from the constraining functional typologies of traditional approaches.

One advantage that this focus confers is a vantage point from which the balance of structure and agency in political relations may be observed. Most theories of political relations provide a fair representation of the importance of either structure or agency—structural determinism versus free will—and most, likewise, choose sides concerning the primacy of one over the other. The solidarity perspective seeks to show that such arguments are ultimately of passing interest, since the operations of both phenomena are equally real, equally important, and closely related. The "double involvement" of individuals and institutions, as Giddens (1986: 11) proposed, shows that human beings, through their individual decisions, through their membership in kinship groups, associations, movements, and nation states, continually construct and reconstruct the world, collectively determining and constraining the range of behavioral possibility in the future. Although the structure of human society is constrained by the particular configuration of institutions at any given time, individual and group actions within these parameters ensure a dynamic process of social evolution and change over time. A focus on the bonds and transactions among groups emphasizes the dynamic, reflexive nature of human relations. Traditional schools of politics and international relations, concentrating on concepts such as the state, political stability, and institutional structure have often inadvertently produced a view of the world as static and lacking politically meaningful activity below the level of the nation state.

The fact that scholars have devoted much attention to the instrumental dimensions of politics may help to explain this. For instance, one of the common assumptions of many theories of politics and international relations is that nations act purely out of self-interest in pursuit of their desired material ends. Realists, for instance, maintain that this core principle ultimately undermines the development of durable international cooperation and institutions, since, in the words of Lord Palmerston, nations have "no permanent allies, only permanent interests." Institutionalists, for their part, hold that institutions may alter payoff structures in such a way as to make cooperation consistent with self-interested action over the long term. Thus, institutions are not a substitute for interests as motivators of political action, but rather have a strong effect in channeling self-interest.

Where realists and institutionalists, and their counterparts in theories of domestic politics, differ most is not on the primacy of self-interest or the possibility of cooperation at international, national, or local levels, but rather on the position of institutions as actors in the political system. The two schools differ principally regarding the status of institutions as either independent or intervening variables, and on the ability of institutions to persist in altering payoff structures in such a way that cooperation will endure as self-interested means to explicit ends.

The insights of the traditional schools of international relations, notably realism and institutionalism, continue to contribute to the understanding of world politics and global climate change. Scholars persist in seeking to understand, for instance, the conditions for cooperation and conflict in international politics, the design principles for successful international institutions, issue linkages in international political economy, and structural constraints in international politics. The persistent importance of considerations such as these must be recognized, even under current conditions of major change in world politics.

The focus on the nation state, sovereignty, and the centrality of self-interest in the international relations literature is an outgrowth of the historical context of the discipline itself. International relations, as a discrete discipline, took shape in the years following the First World War—a time when world politics was dominated by the governing elites of competing colonial empires, and overshadowed by the rising specter of fascism. In the era following the Second World War, the discipline was to a great extent preoccupied with the strategic challenges of the Cold War, such as the containment of the Soviet Union, alliance politics and the military balance, and the alignment of nations of the Third World. As traditional considerations of high politics, these issues lent themselves to the development of an international relations discipline that, by and large, reified and internalized the Westphalian principle of the territorial sovereignty of states and the rational actor model of human behavior.

Climate change provides a forum to develop significant aspects of the international order after the Cold War; in particular, it provides a framework and an imperative for action on issues of population and development in the less industrial countries and of consumption and dematerialization of industrial production in the industrialized countries. The end of the Cold War and the growing prominence of global environmental problems as political issues have also opened up new avenues for the study of international relations. Recent challenges to core concepts such as sovereignty, self-interest, and the nation state have arisen and include phenomena ranging from the resurgence of nationalism and ethnicity as political forces to problems of transboundary pollution requiring collective action on a global scale. Such changes are prompting the reconstruction of world politics as a process shaped not only by the actions of nation states, but also by the interactions of state and nonstate actors, transnational networks, domestic and international institutions, science, technology, and knowledge, and ecological and value systems. Traditional, core concepts of political science and the study of international relations, although still central, have grown more ambiguous as their contents have become matters of contention.

What some would view as a crisis in international relations theory might also be viewed as a welcome growth stimulus that has reinvigorated debate and is pushing the disciplines to broaden their scope. The new landscape of world politics—and global environmental politics in particular—has given voice to perspectives formerly marginalized or excluded from the dialogue.

For instance, the Marxist and dependency theory schools have been influential in elevating issues of North/South equity in the climate change negotiations, and in emphasizing the interrelationships of environment and development (see Ch. 4 of this volume for a more thorough discussion of equity in global climate change). Marxists argue that the outcomes of climate negotiations, and particularly the funding mechanisms that have been created, reflect the interests of industrialized nations and multinational corporations, while presenting less industrialized nations as the major obstacle to the mitigation of regulating climate change. In the climate change debate, this has been the primary avenue of argument employed by critics of the Global Environment Facility (GEF) and other institutional arrangements such as Joint Implementation. Although Marxists have been criticized for a broad-brush treatment of the interests of OECD nations and of industry, their contribution to the analysis of climate politics has been critical to the representation of equity issues.

Dependency theorists have also argued that international institutional arrangements such as the FCCC and the IPCC are, in effect, the instruments of a new imperialism. Since few less industrialized countries have the resources to devote to the large-scale scientific and technological infrastructures found in industrialized nations, most Annex II nations are dependent upon the scientific information and expertise of the Annex I nations. Their subsequent *de facto* status as consumers rather than producers of science hinders their ability to participate fully in the both the scientific and policy arenas and confers substantial advantages to the wealthier nations at the global climate change negotiating table which, as a result, shape the discourse. Scientific dependencies, real and perceived, compromise international solidarity in the same way that technological and economic dependencies do. Without adequate capacities, developing nations are not only institutionally ill equipped to participate in and comply with international environmental regimes and to reap the full range of related transaction benefits, but also lack the foundation of trust on which effective action must be based in the long run.

Cognitive and cultural approaches also have broadened theoretical debate by attempting to unpack traditional concepts in the face of new classes of problems, such as global climate change. Cognitivist scholars have focused on the nature of power, self-interest, or sovereignty in a world evolving away from dominance and control by a small set of governmental hegemonic elites toward more complex pluralistic decisionmaking. Knowledge and discourse (see Chs 1 and 4) as the primary instruments of political power lie at the heart of cognitive theory. Where military and economic power have traditionally been regarded as the currencies of world politics, cognitivists suggest that the creation of knowledge and its application in framing issues for debate—in effect, the cognitive construction of the political agenda—might more appropriately be regarded as the locus of power. Cognitive approaches have contributed greatly to the study of global climate change especially, since scientific knowledge and expert opinion play particularly important roles in both the policymaking and international negotiation processes.

Cognitive and cultural theories have also helped to illuminate the problems associated with traditional concepts of self-interest. Far from explicit, well-articulated utility functions of governing national elites, self-interest is ambiguous, pluralistic, complex, and constantly evolving, reflecting the development and construction of the climate change problem itself. Self-interest is not self-evident and is constituted in different ways by many groups of actors who interact in a dynamic political space and engage in a creative push/pull process of social learning that defines solidarities and shapes the political agenda. The interactions of national and international NGOs, formal bodies such as IPCC and INC, national governments, industry coalitions, local communities and nation blocs such as AOSIS and OPEC reflect the richness of the solidarities and the dynamism of the climate change discourse.

The FCCC provides an important symbolic framework expressive of worldwide concern about climate and about the persistent issues of global development that are inextricably bound up with it. However, the real business of responding to climate concerns may well be through smaller, often less formal, agreements among states, states and firms, and firms, NGOs, and communities. This is likely to be a messy and contested process. Differential patterns of interest group mobilization and representation help to sustain a bias in favor of activities that lead to increasing greenhouse gas emissions. The status quo is insulated from fundamental change by the influence of routines, established procedures, traditional and close ties between certain groups, and reputations. Policy networks may be closed or open to different parties.

At the international level, governments are keeping a tight grip on their prerogatives to represent their respective national interests in climate negotiations, whereas domestically the interests that are represented as national are shaped by the interaction of policy networks, including bureaucracies, businesses, and citizen groups. At this level, institutionalized patterns of behavior currently tend to give the business sector a privileged position; other interest groups may find they are deflected from the locus of decisionmaking by their inability to penetrate institutionalized patterns of consultation and representation. Still other demands—those made by the radical environmental groups, for example—may simply go unheard because they are not considered legitimate or appropriate by network gatekeepers.

However, although it is undoubtedly true that the institutional structure is biased in favor of some groups (and that others may be effectively prevented from entering the political arena and even prevented from articulating their concerns by acts of conscious and unconscious exclusion), it would be quite wrong to portray institutionalized patterns of domination as being immutable. Institutions enable as well as constrain in a "dialectic of control" (Giddens 1984: 16), which offers even the weakest and most disenfranchised the means to influence the activities of the hegemonic.

Effective actions designed to mitigate or respond opportunistically or adaptively to climate change are likely to be those that are most fully integrated into more general policy strategies for economic and social development. The more that climate change issues are routinized as part of the planning perspective at the appropriate level of implementation (e.g., the firm or the community), the more likely they are to achieve desired goals. Climate policies per se are bound to be hard to implement meaningfully. This conclusion recasts the issue of compliance and implementation in important and challenging ways as we move away from the idea of a rational instrumental framework of evaluation, decision, and implementation to a continuous framework of interactive negotiation in which policy explicitly becomes the formalization of actions being undertaken by participating parties.

However, mere piggybacking of climate change onto an existing political agenda as another stick to wave at political opponents is unlikely to succeed. Likewise, dressing up climate change measures as the means to pursue higher taxation or welfare expenditure is also likely to run into substantial opposition. There are no easy answers, as true win–win solutions continue to prove elusive. So far, it must be said that no country has seriously addressed the reduction of its greenhouse gases as a matter of genuine commitment. Those that have tried to do so (e.g., Denmark, Norway, and the Netherlands) have encountered serious impediments in the economic lobbies of industry and transport—so much so that even these environmentally motivated countries have had to back off. Unless and until climate change is perceived as a real economic threat with major consequences for the stability of future trading partners, and until there is a collective will to map a common trajectory to agreed limits, then climate change will produce plenty of rhetorical hot air, but little concerted action.

This chapter has sought to illuminate the breadth encompassed by the concept of social institutions and the manner in which such diverse entities adhere to one another—solidarities—particularly with regard to global climate change. The social sciences reflect a wide spectrum of theory, research, and opinion on the subject; their division and divergence, as summarized here, might likewise appear to be cause for despair rather than hope for progress in achieving greater understanding of important global problems such as climate change. Yet optimism is perhaps more in order. The richness of debate and contention within the social sciences ultimately preserves a large discussion space and a broad theoretical species diversity that is vital in a physical and political environment characterized by complexity and rapid change. Multiple solidarities, among social scientists as among other climate change constituents, are preferable to consensus, for so long as major uncertainties underlie global climate change.

References

Adorno, T. W. 1950. *The authoritarian personality*. New York: Harper.

Allison, G. 1971. *Essence of decision*. Boston: Little, Brown.

Arora, S. & T. Cason 1995. An experiment in voluntary environmental regulation: participation in EPA's 33/50 program. *Journal of Environmental Economics and Management* 28(3), 271–86.

Ashley, R. K. & R. B. J. Walker 1990. Speaking the language of exile: dissident thought in international studies. *International Studies Quarterly* 34(3), 259–68.

Asimov, I. 1990. *The business implications of globalization*. Ottawa: Government of Canada.

Atkinson, A. 1991. *Principles of political ecology*. London: Pinter (Belhaven).

Axelrod, R. 1984. *The evolution of cooperation*. New York: Basic Books.

Axelrod, R. & R. O. Keohane 1986. Achieving cooperation under anarchy: strategies and institutions. In *Cooperation under anarchy*, K. Oye (ed.). Princeton, New Jersey: Princeton University Press.

Balandier, G. 1967. *Anthropologie politique*. Paris: Presses Universitaires de France. [Translated by A. M. Sheridan-Smith as *Political anthropology*. London: Allen Lane, 1990.]

Banks, M. 1985. The inter-paradigm debate. In *International relations: a handbook of current theory*, M. Light & A. J. R. Groom (eds). London: Pinter.

Barthold, T. 1994. Issues in the design of environmental excise taxes. *Journal of Economic Perspectives* 8(1), 133–51.

Baumol, W. & W. Oates 1975. *The theory of environmental policy: externalities, public outlays, and the quality of life*. Englewood Cliffs, New Jersey: Prentice-Hall.

Baylis, J. & N. J. Rengger (eds) 1992. *Dilemmas of world politics: international issues in a changing world*. New York: Oxford University Press.

Benedick, R. 1991. *Ozone diplomacy: new directions in safeguarding the planet*. Cambridge, Massachusetts: Harvard University Press.

Benson, K. 1982. A framework for policy analysis. In *Interorganizational coordination: theory, research, and implementation*, D. L. Rogers & D. A. Whitten (eds). Ames: Iowa State University Press.

Beuermann, C. & J. Jäger 1996. Climate change politics in Germany: how long will the double dividend last? See T. O'Riordan & J. Jäger (1996).

Biersteker, T. J. 1989. Critical reflections on post-positivism in international relations. *International Studies Quarterly* 33(3), 263–7.

Blackford, L. 1994. Nongovernmental organizations and the United Nations: increasing diversity and coordination. In *Papers on international environmental negotiation* (vol. IV), L. E. Susskind, W. R. Moomaw, A. Najam (eds). Cambridge, Massachusetts: Program on Negotiation Books.

Bodansky, D. 1993. The United Nations Framework Convention on Climate Change: a commentary. *Yale Journal of International Law* 18(2), 451–558.

——— 1994. Prologue to the Climate Change Convention. See Minster & Leonard (1994).

——— 1995. The emerging climate change regime. *Annual Review of Energy and Environment* 20, 425–61.

——— 1996. The history and legal structure of the global climate change regime. See Sprinz & Luterbacher (1996).

Bovenberg, A. & R. de Mooij 1994. Environmental levies and distortionary taxation. *American Economic Review* 94, 1085–1089.

Bovenberg, A. & L. Goulder 1995. Costs of environmentally motivated taxes in the presence of other taxes: general equilibrium analyses. Paper presented at the National Bureau of Economic Research's Summer Institute Workshop on Public Policy and the Environment, Cambridge, Massachusetts.

Braid, R. B., R. A. Cantor, S. Rayner 1986. Market acceptance of new nuclear technologies. In *Nuclear power options viability study* (vol. III), ORNL/TM–9780/3, Oak Ridge National Laboratory, Oak Ridge, Tennessee.

Brickman, R., S. Jasanoff, T. Ilgen 1985. *Controlling chemicals: the politics of regulation in Europe and the United States*. Ithaca, New York: Cornell University Press.

Bryant, R. C. 1994. Global change: increasing economic integration and eroding political sovereignty. *Brookings Review* 12(4), 42–4.

Buchanan, J. & G. Tullock 1975. Polluters' profits and political response: direct controls versus taxes. *American Economic Review* 65(1), 139–47.

Caldwell, L. K. 1984. *International environmental policy: emergence and dimensions*. Durham, North Carolina: Duke University Press.

——— 1990. *Between two worlds*. Cambridge: Cambridge University Press.

Callon, M. 1986. Some elements of sociology of translation: domestication of the scallops and fishermen of St Brieuc Bay. In *Power, action and belief: a new sociology of knowledge?*, J. Law (ed.). London: Routledge.

Callon, M. & J. Law 1982. On interests and their transformation: enrollment and counter-enrollment. *Social Studies* 12, 615.

Cantor, R., S. Henry, S. Rayner 1992. *Making markets: an interdisciplinary perspective on economic exchange*. Westport, Connecticut: Greenwood Press.

Cardoso, F. H. & E. Faletto 1979. *Dependency and development in Latin America*. Berkeley: University of California Press.

Carroll, J. E. (ed.) 1988. *International environmental diplomacy: the management and resolution of transfrontier environmental problems*. Cambridge: Cambridge University Press.

Chayes, A. & A. H. Chayes 1991. Compliance without enforcement: state behavior under regulatory treaties. *Negotiation Journal* 7, 311–30.

——— 1993. On compliance. *International Organization* 47, 175–205.

Conca, K. 1994. Rethinking the ecology–sovereignty debate. *Millennium: Journal of International Studies* 23(3), 701–711.

Dalton, T. 1994. *The green rainbow: environmental groups in western Europe*. New Haven, Connecticut: Yale University Press.

Davis, J. 1973. *Land and family in Pisticci*. London: Athlone Press.

Deutsch, K. W. 1966. *The nerves of government: models of political communication and control*. New York: The Free Press.

Dobson, A. 1990. *Green political thought*. London: HarperCollins.

DOE 1989. *Compendium of options for government policy to encourage private sector responses to potential climate change* [3 volumes]. Washington DC: US Department of Energy.

Douglas, M. 1986. *How institutions think*. Syracuse, New York: Syracuse University Press.

Douglas, M. & B. Isherwood 1979. *The world of goods*. New York: Basic Books.

Douglas, M. & A. Wildavsky 1982. *Risk and culture*. Berkeley: University of California Press.

Dowdeswell, E. & R. J. Kinley 1994. Constructive damage to the status quo. In *Negotiating climate change: the inside story of the Rio Convention*, I. M. Mintzer & J. A. Leonard (eds). Cambridge: Cambridge University Press.

Downs, A. 1957. *An economic theory of democracy*. New York: Harper & Row.

Dryzek, J. 1987. *Rational ecology*. Oxford: Basil Blackwell.

Dudek, D. J. & T. Tietenberg 1992. Monitoring and enforcing greenhouse gas trading. *Climate change: designing a tradeable permit system*. Paris: Organisation for Economic Cooperation and Development.

Durkheim, E. 1895. *Les règles de la méthod sociologique*. Paris: Alcan. [Translated by S. A. Solway & J. H. Mueller as *The rules of sociological method*. Chicago: University of Chicago Press, 1938.]

Dyer, G. 1985. *War*. New York: Crown.

Eckersley, R. 1992. *Environmentalism and political theory: towards an ecocentric approach*. London: UCL Press.

Eckholm, E. P. 1976. *Losing ground: environmental stress and world food prospects*. New York: W. W. Norton.

Eisenstadt, S. N. 1968. Social institutions. In *International encyclopedia of the social sciences*, D. Sills (ed.). London: Macmillan.

Epstein, J. M. & R. Gupta 1990. *Controlling the greenhouse effect: five global regimes compared*. Washington DC: The Brookings Institute.

European Science Forum 1996. *Reassessing climate change*. London: European Science Forum.

Feldman, D. L. 1992. Institutions for managing climate change: compliance, fairness, and universal participation. *Global Environmental Change* 2(1), 43–58.

Fisher, B. S., S. Barrett, P. Bohm, M. Kuroda, J. K. E. Mubazi, A. Shah, R. N. Stavins 1996. An economic assessment of policy instruments for combatting climate change. In *Climate change 1995: economic and social dimensions of climate change*, J. P. Bruce, H. Lee, E. F. Haites (eds). Cambridge: Cambridge University Press.

Franck, T. M. 1990. *The power of legitimacy among nations*. New York: Oxford University Press.

Freeman, J. (ed.) 1983. *Social movements of the sixties and seventies*. New York: Longman.

French, H. F. 1994. Making environmental treaties work. *Scientific American* 271, 94–7.

Funtowicz, S. O. & J. R. Ravetz 1992. Three types of risk assessment and the emergence of post-normal science. In *Social theories of risk*, S. Krimsky & D. Golding (eds). Westport, Connecticut: Praeger.

Gallie, W. B. 1955. Essentially contested concepts. *Proceedings of the Aristotelian Society* 56, 167–98.

George, J. & D. Campbell 1990. Patterns of dissent and the celebration of difference. *International Studies Quarterly* 34(3).

Gerlach, L. P. 1987. Social movements and the construction of risk. In *The social and cultural construction of risk*, B. B. Johnson & V. T. Covello (eds). Dordrecht: Reidel.

—— 1991. Global thinking, local acting: movements to save the planet. *Evaluation Review* 15(1), 120–48.

Gerlach, L. P. & G. Palmer 1981. Adaptation through evolving interdependence. In *Handbook of organizational design*, vol. 1: *Adapting organizations to their environments*, P. C. Nystrom & N. Starbuck (eds). New York: Oxford University Press.

Gerlach, L. P. & S. Rayner 1988. Culture and the common management of global risks. *Practicing Anthropology* 10(3), 15–18.

Giddens, A. 1984. *The constitution of society*. Cambridge: Polity Press.

—— 1986. *Sociology: a brief but critical introduction*. London: Macmillan.

Gilpin, R. G. 1975. *US power and the multinational corporation*. New York: Basic Books.

Goodenough, W. 1971. *Culture, language, and society*. Reading, Massachusetts: Addison–Wesley.

Gould, S. J. 1991. Institution. In *The Blackwell encyclopedia of political science*, V. Bogdanor (ed.). Oxford: Basil Blackwell.

Goulder, L. 1994. *Environmental taxation and the double dividend: a reader's guide*. Working Paper 4896, National Bureau of Economic Research, Cambridge, Massachusetts.

Green, D. L. 1990. CAFE or price: an analysis of the effects of federal fuel economy regulations and gasoline price on new car MPG, 1978–89. *The Energy Journal* 11(3), 37–57.

Greenaway, T., S. Smith, J. Street 1992. *Deciding factors in British politics: a case study approach*. London: Routledge.

Greene, O. 1994. Verification and the Climate Change Convention: some issues for further examination. In *Greenhouse gas verification: why, how and how much?*, W. Katscher, G. Stein, J. Lanchbery, J. Salt (eds). Jülich, Germany: KFA Forschungszentrum Jülich.

Grendstad, G. & P. Selle 1997. Cultural theory, postmaterialism, and environmental attitudes. In *Culture matters*, M. Thompson & R. Ellis (eds). Boulder, Colorado: Westview.

Grieco, J. M. 1990. *Cooperation among nations: Europe, America, and non-tariff barriers to trade*. Ithaca, New York: Cornell University Press.

Grubb, M. 1989. *The greenhouse effect: negotiating targets*. London: The Royal Institute of International Affairs.

Gruenspecht, H. & L. Lave 1989. The economics of health, safety, and environmental regulation. In *Handbook of industrial organization* (vol. II), R. Schmalensee & R. D. Willig (eds). Amsterdam: Elsevier.

Haas, E. B. 1964. *Beyond the nation state*. Palo Alto, California: Stanford University Press.

Haas, P. M. 1990. *Saving the Mediterranean: the politics of international environmental cooperation*. New York: Columbia University Press.

Haas, P. M., M. A. Levy, E. A. Parson 1992. Appraising the Earth Summit: how should we judge UNCED's success? *Environment* 34(8), 7–11, 26–33.

Haas, P. M., R. O. Keohane, M. A. Levy (eds) 1993. *Institutions for the Earth: sources of effective international environmental protection*. Cambridge, Massachusetts: MIT Press.

Hahn, R. 1987. Jobs and environmental quality: some implications for instrument choice. *Policy Sciences* 20, 289–306.

—— 1988. Economic prescriptions for environmental problems: how the patient followed the doctor's orders. *Journal of Economic Perspectives* 2(4), 95–114.

Hahn, R. W. & K. R. Richards 1989. The internationalization of environmental regulation. *Harvard International Law Journal* 30(2), 421–46.

Hahn, R. & R. Stavins 1991. Incentive-based environmental regulation: a new era from an old idea? *Ecology Law Quarterly* 18(1), 1–42.

Hall, P. A. 1986. *Governing the economy*. Oxford: Oxford University Press.

—— 1993. The movement from Keynesianism to monetarism. In *Structuring politics*, S. Steinmo, K. Thelen, F. Longstreth (eds). Cambridge: Cambridge University Press.

Hampson, F. O. 1990. Climate change: building international coalitions of the like-minded. *International Journal* **45**, 36–74.

Heclo, H. 1978. Issue networks and the executive establishment. In *The new American political system*, A. King (ed.). Washington DC: American Enterprise Institute.

Hoeller, P. & M. Wallin 1991. Energy prices, taxes and carbon dioxide emissions. *OECD Economic Studies* **17**, 92–105.

Huntington, S. P. 1993. The clash of civilizations. *Foreign Affairs* **72**(3), 21–49.

Hurrell, A. & B. Kingsbury (eds) 1992. *The international politics of the environment*. Oxford: Oxford University Press.

Ignatieff, M. 1993. *Blood and belonging: journeys into the new nationalism*. New York: The Noonday Press.

Ingram, H. M., H. J. Cortner, M. K. Landy 1990. The political agenda. In *Climate change and US water resources*, P. E. Waggoner (ed.). New York: John Wiley.

International Negotiation: A Journal of Theory and Practice **1**(1).

Jäger, J. 1992. From conference to conference: a guest editorial. *Climatic Change* **20**, iii–vii.

Jasanoff, S. 1986. *Risk management and political culture*. New York: Russell Sage.

——1990. *The fifth branch*. Cambridge, Massachusetts: Harvard University Press.

——1998. Contingent knowledge: implications for implementation and compliance. In *Engaging countries: strengthening compliance with international accords*, E. B. Weiss & H. K. Jacobson (eds). Cambridge, Massachusetts: MIT Press.

Jervis, R. 1976. *Perception and misperception in international politics*. Princeton, New Jersey: Princeton University Press.

——1993. International primacy: is the game worth the candle? *International Security* **17**(4), 52–67.

Jordan, A. G. 1990a. Sub-governments, policy communities, and networks: refilling old bottles. *Journal of Theoretical Politics* **2**(3), 319–38.

——1990b. Policy community realism vs "new" institutionalist ambiguity. *Policy Studies* **38**, 470–84.

Jordan, A. G. & J. Richardson 1982. The British policy style or the logic of negotiation. See Richardson (1982).

Jordan, A. J. 1994. Financing the UNCED agenda. *Environment* **36**(3), 16–30.

Jorgenson, D., D. Slesnick, P. Wilcoxen 1992. Carbon taxes and economic welfare. In *Microeconomics*, C. Winston & P. C. Reiss (eds) [Brookings Papers on Economic Activity]. Washington DC: Brookings Institution.

Kelley, H. H. 1984. Interdependence theory and its future. *Representative Research: Social Psychology* **14**, 2–15.

Kelley, H. H. & J. W. Thibaut 1978. *Interpersonal relations: a theory of interdependence*. New York: John Wiley.

Kelman, S. 1981. *Regulating America, regulating Sweden*. Cambridge, Massachusetts: MIT Press.

Keohane, R. O. 1980. The theory of hegemonic stability and changes in international economic regimes, 1967–1977. In *Change in the international system*, O. R. Holsti, R. M. Siverson, A. L. George (eds). Boulder, Colorado: Westview.

——1984. *After hegemony: cooperation and discord in the world political economy*. Princeton, New Jersey: Princeton University Press.

——(ed.) 1986. *Neorealism and its critics*. New York: Columbia University Press.

——1988. International institutions: two approaches. *International Studies Quarterly* **32**, 379–96. [Reprinted in *International institutions and state power*, R. O. Keohane (ed.). Boulder, Colorado: Westview.]

Keohane, R. O. & J. S. Nye 1977. *Power and interdependence*. Boston: Little, Brown.

Kimball, L. A. 1992. *Forging international agreement: strengthening inter-governmental institutions for environment and development*. Washington DC: World Resources Institute.

Kindleberger, C. 1973. *The world in depression*. Los Angeles: University of California Press.

Kopp, R. & D. DeWitt 1991. Distributional consequences of a carbon tax. *Resources* **105**, 6–8.

Koskenniemi, M. 1992. Breach of treaty or non-compliance? Reflections on the enforcement of the Montreal Protocol. In *Yearbook of international environmental law*, G. Handl (ed.). London: Graham & Trotman.

Knutson, J. N. 1973. *Handbook of political psychology*. San Francisco: Jossey–Bass.

Krasner, S. D. (ed.) 1983. *International regimes*. Ithaca, New York: Cornell University Press.

———1984. Approach to the state: alternative conceptions and historical dynamics. *Comparative Politics* **16**(2), 223–46.

Kunreuther, H., J. Linnerooth, R. Starnes (eds) 1982. *Liquified energy gas facility siting: international comparisons*. Laxenburg, Austria: IIASA.

Lahey, W. 1984. Economic charges for environmental protection: ocean dumping fees. *Ecology Law Quarterly* **11**(3), 305–342.

Lake, D. A. 1993. Leadership, hegemony, and the international economy: naked emperor or tattered monarch with potential? *International Studies Quarterly* **37**(4), 459–89.

Lapid, Y. 1989. The third debate: on the prospects of international theory in a post-positivist era. *International Studies Quarterly* **33**(3), 235–54.

Lasswell, H. D. 1930. *Psychopathology and politics*. Chicago: University of Chicago Press.

Latour, B. 1987. *Science in action: how to follow scientists and engineers through society*. Cambridge, Massachusetts: Harvard University Press.

Layne, C. 1993. The unipolar illusion: why new great powers will rise. *International Security* **17**(4), 5–51.

Leary, N. & J. Scheraga 1993. The costs of different energy taxes for stabilizing US carbon dioxide emissions: an application of the Gemini Model. *World Resource Review* **5**(3), 372–86.

Lee, K. N. 1993. *Compass and gyroscope: integrating science and politics for the environment*. Washington DC: Island Press.

Levy, M. A., O. R. Young, M. Zürn 1994. *The study of international regimes*. Working Paper WP-94-113, International Institute for Applied Systems Analysis, Laxenburg, Austria.

Lindquist, L. 1980. *The hare and the tortoise: clean air policies in the United States and Sweden*. Ann Arbor: University of Michigan Press.

Linklater, A. 1992. The question of the next stage in international relations theory: a critical-theoretical point of view. *Millennium: Journal of International Studies* **21**(1), 77–98.

Lipschutz, R. D. 1992. Reconstructing world politics: the emergence of global civil society. *Millennium: Journal of International Studies* **21**(3), 389–420.

Lipschutz, R. D. & K. Conca 1993. *The state and social power in global environmental politics*. New York: Columbia University Press.

List, M. & V. Rittberger 1992. Regime theory and international environmental management. See Hurrell & Kingsbury (1992).

Litfin, K. 1994. *Ozone discourses: science and politics in environmental cooperation*. New York: Columbia University Press.

Livernash, R. 1992. The growing influence of NGOs in the developing world. *Environment* **34**(5), 14–20, 41–3.

Lowi, T. 1964. American business, public policy, case studies and political theory. *World Politics* **16**(4), 677–715.

Luard, E. 1990. *The globalization of politics: the changed focus of political action in the modern world*. London: Macmillan.

Maddock, R. 1992. The global political economy. In *Dilemmas of world politics: international issues in a changing world*, J. Baylis & N. J. Rengger (eds). New York: Oxford University Press.

Mair, L. 1962. *Primitive government*. London: Allen Lane.

Majone, G. 1976. Choice among policy instruments for pollution control. *Policy Analysis* **2**(4),

589–613.

Manne, A. & T. Rutherford 1994. International trade in oil, gas and carbon emission rights: an intertemporal general equilibrium model. *The Energy Journal* **15**(1), 57–93.

Marin, A. 1991. Firm incentives to promote technological change in pollution control: comment. *Journal of Environmental Economics and Management* **21**, 297–300.

Marsh, D. & R. Rhodes (eds) 1992. *Policy networks in British governments*. Oxford: Oxford University Press.

Merchant, C. 1992. *Radical ecology: the search for a livable world*. New York: Routledge.

Milliman, S. & R. Prince 1989. Firm incentives to promote technological change in pollution control. *Journal of Environmental Economics and Management* **17**, 247–65.

Mintzer, I. & J. A. Leonard 1994. *Negotiating climate change: the inside story of the Rio Convention*. Cambridge: Cambridge University Press.

Mitchell, R. B. 1994. *Intentional oil pollution at sea: environmental policy and treaty compliance*. Cambridge, Massachusetts: MIT Press.

—— 1996. Implementation of the FCCC—compliance, effectiveness, and institutional design. See Sprinz & Luterbacher (1996).

Mitchell, R. B. & A. Chayes. 1995. Improving compliance with the climate change treaty. In *Shaping national responses: a post-Rio guide*, H. Lee (ed.). Washington DC: Island Press.

Morgenthau, H. J. 1948. *Politics among nations*. New York: Knopf.

Morrisette, P. M. 1989. The evolution of policy responses to stratospheric ozone depletion. *Natural Resources Journal* **29**, 793–820.

Mott, R. 1990. Emissions-trading in the greenhouse? A cautionary view. *World Climate Change Report* **2**(2), 23–6.

Nelkin, D. & M. Pollack 1981. *The atom besieged*. Cambridge: MIT Press.

Neufeld, M. 1993. Reflexivity and international relations theory. *Millennium: Journal of International Studies* **22**(1), 53–76.

Nollkaemper, A. 1992. On the effectiveness of international rules. *Acta Politica* **27**(1), 49–70.

Oliveira-Martins, J., J. Burniaux, J. Martin 1992. Trade and the effectiveness of unilateral CO_2 abatement policies. *OECD Economic Studies* **19**, 123–40.

Olsen, J. P. 1991. Political science and organizational theory. In *Political choice: institutions, rules and the limits of rationality*, R. Czada & A. Windhoff-Heritier (eds). Boulder, Colorado: Westview.

—— 1992. *Analyzing institutional dynamics*. Working Paper 92-14, LOS-Senteret, Bergen.

O'Neill, J. 1993. *Ecology, policy and politics: human well-being and the natural world*. London: Routledge.

Ophuls, W. 1977. *Ecology and the politics of scarcity*. San Francisco: W. H. Freeman.

O'Riordan, T. (ed.) 1996. *Ecotaxation*. London: Earthscan.

O'Riordan, T. & S. Rayner 1991. Risk management for global environmental change. *Global Environmental Change* **1**(2), 91–108.

O'Riordan, T. & J. Jäger (eds) 1996. *Politics of climate change: a European perspective*. London: Routledge.

O'Riordan, T. & A. Jordan 1996. Social institutions and climate change. See O'Riordan & Jäger (eds).

Ostrom, E. 1990. *Governing the commons: the evolution of institutions for collective action*. New York: Cambridge University Press.

Oye, A. (ed.) 1986. *Cooperation under anarchy*. Princeton, New Jersey: Princeton University Press.

Packenham, R. A. 1992. *The dependency movement; scholarship and politics in development studies*. Cambridge, Massachusetts: Harvard University Press.

Palma, G. 1978. Dependency: a formal theory of underdevelopment or a methodology for the analysis of concrete situations of underdevelopment. *World Development* **6**(7/8), 881–924.

Parry, I. 1995. The interactions between environmental policy and the tax system. Paper presented at the National Bureau of Economic Research's Summer Institute Workshop on "Public policy and the environment," Cambridge, Massachusetts.

Paterson, M. 1993. The politics of climate change after UNCED. *Environmental Politics* **3**(4), 174–90.

——— 1996. International relations theory: nonrealism, neoinstitutionalism and the climate change convention. See Vogler & Imber (1996).

Pepper, D. 1986. *The roots of modern environmentalism*. London: Routledge.

Perlack, R. D., M. Russell, Z. Shen 1993. Reducing greenhouse gas emissions in China: institutional, legal, and cultural constraints and opportunities. *Global Environmental Change* **3**(1), 78–100.

Peterson, V. S. 1992. Transgressing boundaries: theories of knowledge, gender and international relations. *Millennium: Journal of International Studies* **21**(2), 183–206.

Petrich, C. H. 1993. Indonesia and global climate change negotiations: potential opportunities and constraints for participation, leadership, and commitment. *Global Environmental Change* **3**(1), 53–77.

Pezzey, J. 1992. Analysis of unilateral CO_2 control in the European community and OECD. *The Energy Journal* **13**(3), 159–72.

Porter, G. & J. W. Brown 1991. *Global environmental politics*. Boulder, Colorado: Westview.

Princen, T. & M. Finger 1994. *Environmental NGOs in world politics: linking the local and the global*. New York: Routledge.

Rahman, A. 1996. A view from Bangladesh. See O'Riordan & Jäger (1996).

Raiffa, H. 1982. *The art and science of negotiation*. Cambridge, Massachusetts: Harvard University Press (Belknap).

Raustiala, K. 1996. Non-state actors. See Sprinz & Luterbacher (1996).

Rayner, S. 1984. Disagreeing about risk: the institutional culture of risk management and planning for future generations. In *Risk analysis, institutions, and public policy*, S. Hadden (ed.). Port Washington: Associated Faculty Press.

——— 1991. A cultural perspective on the structure and implementation of global environmental agreements. *Evaluation Review* **15**(1), 75–102.

——— 1993a. Prospects for CO_2 emissions reduction policy in the USA. *Global Environmental Change* **3**(1), 12–13.

——— 1993b. Introduction to special issue: national case studies of institutional capabilities to implement greenhouse gas reductions. *Global Environmental Change* **3**(1), 7–11.

Rayner, S. & K. R. Richards 1994. I think that I shall never see . . . a lovely forestry policy: land use programs for conservation of forests. Proceedings from the Tsukuba Workshop of IPCC WG III.

Redclift, M. & T. Benton (eds) 1994. *Social theory and the global environment*. London: Routledge.

Rengger, N. J. & M. Hoffman (eds) 1991. *Critical theory and international relations*. Hemel Hempstead, England: Harvester.

Rhodes, R. A. W. 1990. Policy networks. *Journal of Theoretical Politics* **2**(3), 293–317.

——— 1986. *Beyond Westminster and Whitehall*. London: Unwin Hyman.

Richards, K. R. 1995. Rethinking environmental instrument choice. Paper presented at Association for Public Policy Analysis and Management Annual Research Conference, Washington DC.

——— 1996. Joint implementation in the Framework Convention on Climate Change: opportunities and pitfalls. In *An economic perspective on climate change policies*, C. E. Walker, M. A. Bloomfield, M. Thorning (eds). Washington DC: American Council for Capital Formation.

Richardson, J. (ed.) 1982. *The concept of policy style*. London: George Allen & Unwin.

Richardson, J. & A. G. Jordan 1979. *Governing under pressure*. Oxford: Martin Robertson.

Richardson, J., G. Gustafsson, A. G. Jordan 1982. The concept of policy style. See Richardson (1982).

Richardson, J. & N. Watts 1985. National policy styles and the environment: Britain and West Germany compared. WZB IIUG DP 85-16, Wissenschaftszentrum, Berlin.

Richardson, J., W. Maloney, W. Rudig 1992. The dynamics of policy change: lobbying and water privatization. *Public Administration* **70**(2), 157–75.

Rose-Ackerman, S. 1973. Effluent charges: a critique. *Canadian Journal of Economics* **6**(4), 512–28.

Rosenau, J. N. 1990. *Turbulence in world politics: a theory of change and continuity*. Princeton, New Jersey: Princeton University Press.

——— 1995. Governance in the twenty-first century. *Global Governance* **1**(1), 13–43.

Rosenau, J. N. & E. O. Czempiel (eds) 1992. *Governance without government: change and order in world politics*. New York: Cambridge University Press.

Rowlands, I. 1996. Theoretical perspectives. See Sprinz & Luterbacher (1996).

Russell, C. 1988. Economic incentives in the management of hazardous wastes. *Columbia Journal of Environmental Law* **13**, 257–74.

Sabatier, P. A. 1988. An advocacy coalition framework of policy change and the role of policy-oriented learning therein. *Policy Studies* **21**, 129–68.

Sabatier, P. A. & H. C. Jenkins-Smith (eds) 1993. *Policy change and learning: an advocacy coalition approach*. Boulder, Colorado: Westview.

Sachs, W. A. (ed.) 1993. *Global ecology: a new arena of political conflict*. London: Zed.

Sagoff, M. 1988. *The economy of the Earth*. Cambridge: Cambridge University Press.

Sagasti, F. R. & M. E. Colby 1993. Eco-development perspectives on global change from developing countries. In *Global accord: environmental challenges and international responses*, N. Choucri (ed.). Cambridge, Massachusetts: MIT Press.

Salter, L. 1988. *Mandated science*. Dordrecht: Kluwer.

Salzhauer, A. L. 1991. Obstacles and opportunities for a consumer ecolabel. *Environment* **33**, 10–21.

Saurin, J. 1996. International relations, social ecology and the globalization of environmental change. See Vogler & Imber (1996).

Schotter, A. 1981. *The economic theory of social institutions*. Cambridge: Cambridge University Press.

Schwartz, M. & M. Thompson 1990. *Divided we stand: redefining politics, technology, and social choice*. New York: Harvester Wheatsheaf.

Sebenius, J. K. 1991. Designing negotiations towards a new regime: the case of global warming. *International Security* **15**(4), 110–48.

Sewell, G. C. 1996. Conflicting beliefs: national implementation of the United Nations Framework Convention on Climate Change. *Environmental Impact Assessment Review* **16**, 137–50.

Shaw, C. 1991. Green taxes, blue taxes. *Natural Resources Forum* **15**(2), 123–31.

Shaw, M. 1994. *Global society and international relations*. Cambridge: Polity Press.

Skea, J. & S. Boehmer-Christiansen 1994. The operations and impacts of the Intergovernmental Panel on Climate Change: results of a survey of users. STEEP Discussion Paper 16, Science Policy Research Unit, University of Sussex.

Sklair, L. 1991. *Sociology of the global system: social change in global perspective*. Hemel Hempstead, England: Harvester Wheatsheaf.

——— 1994. Global sociology and global environmental change. See Redclift & Benton (1994).

Smith, M. J. 1993. *Pressure, power and policy: state autonomy and policy networks in Britain and the United States*. Hemel Hempstead, England: Harvester Wheatsheaf.

Smith, R. M. 1988. Political jurisprudence, the "new institutionalism" and the future of public law. *American Political Science Review* **82**(1), 89–108.

Smith, S. 1981. Allison and the missile crisis. *Millennium: Journal of International Studies* **9**(1), 21–40.

Snidal, D. 1985. The limits of hegemonic stability theory. *International Organization* **39**(4), 579–

614.

Sprinz, D. & U. Luterbacher (eds) 1996. International relations and global climate change. PIK Special Report 21, Potsdam Institute for Climate Impacts Research, Potsdam, Germany.

Steinbruner, J. D. 1974. *The cybernetic theory of decision*. Princeton, New Jersey: Princeton University Press.

Stern, P. C. 1978. When do people act to maintain common resources. *International Journal of Psychology* **13**, 149–57.

Stevenson, G. G. 1991. *Common property economics: a general theory and land-use applications*. New York: Cambridge University Press.

Sullivan, A. 1987. Policy options for toxics disposal: laissez-faire, subsidization, and enforcement. *Journal of Economics and Management* **14**, 58–71.

Susskind, L. & C. Ozawa 1992. Negotiating more effective international environmental agreements. See Hurrell & Kingsbury (1992).

Sydnes, A. K. 1996. Norwegian climate policy: environmental idealism and economic realism. See O'Riordan & Jäger (1996).

Szasz, P. 1991. The role of international law: formulating international legal instruments and creating international institutions. *Evaluation Review* **15**(1), 7–26.

Terkla, D. 1984. The efficiency value of effluent tax revenues. *Journal of Environmental Economics and Management* **11**, 107–123.

Thelen, K. & S. Steinmo 1993. Historical institutionalism in comparative politics. In *Structuring politics*, S. Steinmo, K. Thelen, F. Longstreth (eds). Cambridge: Cambridge University Press.

Thomas, C. 1992. *The environment in international relations*. London: The Royal Institute of International Affairs.

Thompson, M. 1993. Good science for public policy. *Journal of International Development* **5**(6), 669–78.

Thompson, M., M. Warburton, T. Hatley 1986. *Uncertainty on a Himalayan scale*. London: Milton Ash Editions.

Tietenberg, T. & D. G. Victor 1994. Administrative structures and procedures for implementing a tradable entitlement approach to controlling global warming. Paper prepared for the UN Conference on Trade and Development, International Institute for Applied Systems Analysis, Laxenburg, Austria.

Tolba, M. 1989. A step-by-step approach to protection of the atmosphere. *International Environmental Affairs* **1**, 304.

Tolbert, D. 1991. Global climate change and the role of international non-governmental organisations. In *International law and global climate change*, R. Churchill & D. Freestone (eds). London: Graham & Trotman.

Touval, S. 1989. Multilateral negotiations: an analytic approach. *Negotiation Journal* **5**(2), 159–73.

Underdal, A. 1992. The concept of regime effectiveness. *Cooperation and Conflict* **27**(3), 227–40.

Verweij, M. 1995. Cultural theory and the study of international relations. *Millennium: Journal of International Studies* **24**(1), 87–111.

Victor, D. & J. E. Salt 1994. From Rio to Berlin: managing climate change. *Environment* **36**, 6–15, 25–32.

—— 1995. Keeping the climate treaty relevant. *Nature* **373**, 280–82.

Vogler, J. 1995. *The global commons: a regime analysis*. Chichester, England: John Wiley.

Vogler, J. & M. F. Imber (eds) 1996. *The environment and international relations*. London: Routledge.

Waltz, K. N. 1959. *Man, the state, and war: a theoretical analysis*. New York: Columbia University Press.

—— 1979. *Theory of international politics*. Reading, Massachusetts: Addison–Wesley.

Westing, A. H. (ed.) 1986. *Global resources and international conflict*. Oxford: Oxford University Press.

Williamson, O. 1985. *The economic institution of capitalism*. New York: The Free Press.

Wynne, B. (ed.) 1987. *Risk management and hazardous waste: implementation and the dialectics of credibility*. New York: Springer.

—— 1993. Implementation of greenhouse gas reductions in the European Community: institutional and cultural factors. *Global Environmental Change* 3(1), 101–128.

—— 1996. May the sheep safely graze? A reflexive view of the expert–lay knowledge divide. In *Risk, environment and modernity: towards a new ecology*, S. Lash, B. Szerszynski, B. Wynne (eds). London: Sage.

Yearley, S. 1994. Social movements and environmental change. See Redclift & Benton (1994).

Young, O. R. 1989. *International cooperation: building regimes for natural resource management and the environment*. Ithaca, New York: Cornell University Press.

—— 1992. The effectiveness of international institutions: hard cases and critical variables. See Rosenau & Czempiel (1992).

Zacher, M. W. 1992. The decaying pillars of the Westphalian Temple: implications for international order and governance. See Rosenau & Czempiel (1992).

Zaelke, D. & J. Cameron 1990. Global warming and climate change: an overview of the international legal process. *American University Journal of International Law and Policy* 5, 249–90.

Sponsoring organizations, International Advisory Board, and project participants

INSTITUTIONAL SPONSORS AND COLLABORATORS

Pacific Northwest National Laboratory (PNNL), USA

US Department of Energy (DOE), USA

Electric Power Research Institute (EPRI), USA

Economic and Social Research Council (ESRC), UK

International Institute for Applied Systems Analysis (IIASA), Austria

National Institute for Public Health and Environment (RIVM), Netherlands

Korean Energy Economics Institute (KEEI), Korea

National Oceanic and Atmospheric Administration (NOAA), USA

Centre for Social and Economic Research on the Global Environment (CSERGE), UK

LOS-Senteret, Norway

Musgrave Institute, UK

Centre for the Study of Environmental Change (CSEC), UK

Potsdam Institute for Climate Impacts Research (PIK), Germany

Swiss Federal Institute for Environmental Science and Technology (EAWAG), Switzerland

Commonwealth Scientific and Industrial Research Organization (CSIRO), Australia

Research Institute of Innovative Technology for the Earth (RITE), Japan

THE INTERNATIONAL ADVISORY BOARD

Dr Francisco Barnes

The Honorable Richard Benedick

Professor Harvey Brooks

Professor the Lord Desai of St Clement Danes

Professor George Golitsyn

Pragya Dipak Gyawali

The Honorable Thomas Hughes

Dr Jiro Kondo

Dr Hoesung Lee

Professor Tom Malone

The Honorable Robert McNamara

Professor Richard Odingo

Professor Thomas Schelling

PACIFIC NORTHWEST NATIONAL LABORATORY

Steering Committee

Chester L. Cooper

James A. Edmonds

Elizabeth Malone

Steve Rayner

Norman J. Rosenberg

Support staff

Allison Glismann

Laura Green

Suzette Hampton

Jenniffer Leyson

K Storck

AUTHORS, CONTRIBUTORS, AND PEER REVIEWERS

W. Neil Adger, *University of East Anglia, UK*

Ahsan Uddin, Ahmed *Bangladesh Centre for Advanced Studies, Bangladesh*

Mozaharul Alam, *Centre for Advanced Studies, Bangladesh*

W. B. Ashton, *Pacific Northwest National Laboratory, USA*

Marjolein van Asselt, *University of Maastricht, the Netherlands*

Viranda Asthana, *Jawaharlal Nehru University, India*

Tariq Banuri, *Sustainable Development Policy Institute, Pakistan*

Richard Baron, *International Energy Agency, OECD, France*

Igor Bashmakov, *Center for Energy Efficiency, Moscow*

Richard E. Benedick, *World Wildlife Fund, Conservation Foundation, USA*

Wiebe Bijker, *University of Limburg, the Netherlands*

Daniel Bodansky, *University of Washington School of Law, USA*

Larry Boyer, *George Washington University, USA*

Judith Bradbury, *Pacific Northwest National Laboratory, USA*

Harvey Brooks, *Harvard University, USA*

Katrina Brown, *University of East Anglia, UK*

Ian Burton, *Atmospheric Environment Service, Canada*

Frederick H. Buttel, *University of Wisconsin, Madison, USA*

Karl W. Butzer, *University of Texas at Austin, USA*

Robin Cantor, *Law and Economics Consulting Group, USA*

Bayard Catron, *George Washington University, USA*

Florian Charvolin, *Centre National de la Recherche Scientifique, France*

Chipeng Chu, *Stanford University, USA*

Chester L. Cooper, *Pacific Northwest National Laboratory, USA*

Robert Costanza, *University of Maryland, USA*

Edward Crenshaw, *Ohio State University, USA*

Pierre Crosson, *Resources for the Future, USA*

Margaret Davidson, *NOAA Coastal Services Center, USA*

Ogunlade Davidson, *University of Sierra Leone, Sierra Leone*

Robert Deacon, *University of California at Santa Barbara, USA*

Ota de Leonardis, *University of Milan, Italy*

Meghnad Desai, *London School of Economics, UK*

Mary Douglas, *University of London, UK*

Hadi Dowlatabadi, *Carnegie Mellon University, USA*

Thomas E. Downing, *University of Oxford, UK*

Otto Edenhofer, *Technical University of Darmstadt, Germany*

James A. Edmonds, *Pacific Northwest National Laboratory, USA*

Paul N. Edwards, *Stanford University, USA*

Paul Ekins, *Birkbeck College London, UK*

Mohammad El-Raey, *University of Alexandria, Egypt*

Aant Elzinga, *University of Gothenburg, Sweden*

Shirley J. Fiske, *National Oceanic and Atmospheric Administration, USA*

Silvio O. Funtowicz, *Joint Research Center, European Commission, Italy*

Erve Garrison, *University of Georgia, USA*

Des Gasper, *Institute of Social Studies, the Netherlands*

Luther P. Gerlach, *University of Minnesota, USA*

Peter Gleick, *Pacific Institute, USA*

George Golitsyn, *Russian Academy of Science, Russia*

Dean Graetz, *Commonwealth Scientific and Industrial Research Organisation, Australia*

Philip C. R. Gray, *Research Center Julich, Germany*

Wayne Gray, *Clark University, USA*

Michael Grubb, *Royal Institute of International Affairs, UK*

Arnulf Grübler, *International Institute for Applied Systems Analysis, Austria*

Howard Gruenspecht, *US Department of Energy, USA*

Simon Guy, *University of Newcastle upon Tyne, UK*

Dipak Gyawali, *Royal Nepal Academy of Science and Technology, Nepal*

Peter M. Haas, *University of Massachusetts, Amherst, USA*

Bruce Hackett, *University of California, Davis, USA*

Nick Hanley, *University of Stirling, UK*

Russell Hardin, *New York University, USA*

Shaun Hargreaves-Heap, *University of East Anglia, UK*

Susanna B. Hecht, *University of California, Los Angeles, USA*

Gerhart Heilig, *International Institute for Applied Systems Analysis, Austria*

Edward L. Hillsman, *Oak Ridge National Laboratory, USA*

Frank Hole, *Yale University, USA*

Leen Hordijk, *Wageningen Agricultural University, the Netherlands*

John Houghton, *US Department of Energy, USA*

Hiliard Huntington, *Stanford University, USA*

Saleemul Huq, *Bangladesh Centre for Advanced Studies, Bangladesh*

Evert van Imhoff, *Netherlands Interdisciplinary Demographic Institute, the Netherlands*

Helen Ingram, *University of Arizona, USA*

Alan Irwin, *Brunel University, UK*

Saiful Islam, *Global Challenge Network, Germany*

Henry D. Jacoby, *Massachusetts Institute of Technology, USA*

Carlo C. Jaeger, *Swiss Federal Institute for Environmental Science and Technology, Switzerland and Darmstadt University of Technology, Germany*

Dale Jamieson, *Carleton College, USA*

Marco Janssen, *National Institute of Public Health and the Environment, the Netherlands*

Sheila S. Jasanoff, *Cornell University, USA*

Craig Jenkins, *Ohio State University, USA*

Denise Jodelet, *Ecole des Hautes Etudes en Sciences Sociales, France*

N. S. Jodha, *World Bank, USA*

Andrew Jordan, *University of East Anglia, UK*

Tae Yong Jung, *Korean Energy Economics Institute, Korea*

Hélène Karmasin, *Institut für Motivforschung, Austria*

Rick Katz, *ESIG/NCAR, USA*

René Kemp, *University of Limburg, the Netherlands*

Willett Kempton, *University of Delaware, USA*

Richard Klein, *National Institute for Coastal and Marine Management, the Netherlands*

Rob Koudstaal, *Resource Analysis, the Netherlands*

Chunglin Kwa, *University of Amsterdam, the Netherlands*

Denise Lach, *Oregon State University, USA*

W. Henry Lambright, *Syracuse University, USA*

Bruno Latour, *Ecole Nationale Supérieure des Mines, France*

Stephen Leatherman, *University of Maryland, USA*

Harro van Lente, *KPMG Inspire Foundation, the Netherlands*

Ronnie D. Lipschutz, *University of California, Santa Cruz, USA*

Diana Liverman, *University of Arizona, USA*

Ragnar Löfstedt, *University of Surrey, UK*

Janice Longstreth, *Waste Policy Institute, USA*

Michael Lovell, *Wesleyan University, USA*

Sven B. Lundstedt, *Ohio State University, USA*

Urs Luterbacher, *Graduate Institute of International Studies, Geneva, Switzerland*

Wolfgang Lutz, *International Institute for Applied Systems Analysis, Austria*

Loren Lutzenhiser, *Washington State University, USA*

Michael Lynch, *Brunel University, UK*

F. Landis MacKellar, *International Institute for Applied Systems Analysis, Austria*

Antonio Maghalães, *Ministry of Planning, Brazil*

Elizabeth L. Malone, *Pacific Northwest National Laboratory, USA*

Tom Malone, *Sigma Xi, USA*

Gavan McDonnel, *University of New South Wales, Australia*

Jacqueline McGlade, *Warwick University, UK*

Tom McGovern, *City University of New York, USA*

Douglas McLean, *University of Maryland, USA*

A. J. McMichael, *London School of Hygiene and Tropical Medicine, UK*

Judith Mehta, *University of East Anglia, UK*

Robert Mendelsohn, *Yale University, USA*

William B. Meyer, *Clark University, USA*

Rob Misdorp, *International Centre for Coastal Zone Management, the Netherlands*

Elena Milanova, *Russian MAB UNESCO Committee, Russia*

Clark A. Miller, *Cornell University, USA*

Vinod Mishra, *East–West Center, USA*

Ronald B. Mitchell, *University of Oregon, USA*

Emilio Moran, *Indiana University at Bloomington, USA*

Tsuneyuki Morita, *National Institute for Environmental Studies, Japan*

Peter Morrisette, *Institute of Behavioral Science, USA*

Han Mukang, *University of Beijing, China*

Dwijen Mullick, *Centre for Advanced Studies, Bangladesh*

Nebojsa Nakicenovic, *International Institute for Applied Systems Analysis, Austria*

Steven Ney, *Technical University, Vienna, Austria*

Robert J. Nicholls, *University of Middlesex, UK*

David Norse, *University College London, UK*

Richard Odingo, *University of Nairobi, Kenya*

Jackton B. Ojwang, *University of Nairobi, Kenya*

Steve Olson, *University of Rhode Island, USA*

Brian O'Neill, *Environmental Defense Fund, USA*

Hans Opschoor, *Free University of Amsterdam, the Netherlands*

Timothy O'Riordan, *University of East Anglia, UK*

John O. Oucho, *University of Nairobi, Kenya*

Edward A. Parson, *Harvard University, USA*

Matthew Paterson, *University of Keele, UK*

David Pearce, *University College London, UK*

Sanjeev Prakash, *Eco-Tibet, India*

Martin Price, *University of Oxford, UK*

Atiq Rahman, *Bangladesh Centre for Advanced Studies, Bangladesh*

Kal Raustiala, *Harvard Law School, USA*

Jerome R. Ravetz, *Research Methods Consultancy, UK*

Steve Rayner, *Pacific Northwest National Laboratory, USA*

John Reilly, *US Department of Agriculture, USA*

Ortwin Renn, *Academy for Technology Assessment and University of Stuttgart, Germany*

John Richards, *Duke University, USA*

Kenneth R. Richards, *University of Indiana, Bloomington, USA*

Richard Richels, *Electric Power Research Institute, USA*

Arie Rip, *University of Twente, the Netherlands*

James Risbey, *Carnegie Mellon University, USA*

John Robinson, *University of British Columbia, Canada*

Richard Rockwell, *Inter-University Consortium for Political and Social Research, USA*

Eugene A. Rosa, *Washington State University, USA*

Luiz Pinguelli Rosa, *Federal University of Rio de Janeiro*

Adam Rose, *Pennsylvania State University, USA*

Norman J. Rosenberg, *Pacific Northwest National Laboratory, USA*

Jan Rotmans, *University of Maastricht, the Netherlands*

Ian Rowlands, *University of Waterloo, Canada*

Paul Runci, *University of Maryland, USA*

Vernon W. Ruttan, *University of Minnesota, USA*

Robert Sack, *University of Wisconsin, USA*

Colin Sage, *Wye College, UK*

Paul Samson, *International Green Cross, Switzerland*

Gerrit Jan Schaeffer, *Energy Research Centre, the Netherlands*

Thomas Schelling, *University of Maryland, USA*

Jurgen Schmandt, *University of Texas, Austin, USA*

Michiel Schwarz, *Independent Consultant/ Researcher, the Netherlands*

Michael J. Scott, *Pacific Northwest National Laboratory, USA*

Galina Sergen, *University of New South Wales, Australia*

Elizabeth Shove, *University of Lancaster, UK*

P. R. Shukla, *Indian Institute of Management, India*

Udo Simonis, *Science Centre, Berlin*

Jim Skea, *University of Sussex, UK*

Eugene Skolnikoff, *Massachusetts Institute of Technology, USA*

Paul Slovic, *Decision Research, USA*

Youba Sokona, *ENDA–TM, Senegal*

Zofia Sokolewicz, University of Warsaw, Poland

445

Contents of Volumes 1–4

Index of names

Subject index

469